MW01697577

Shadows of the Beast

How the Identity of the Coming Antichrist Will Be Revealed to the Faithful Church

By James Jacob Prasch

Cover Art by Keith Locke
Typesetting and Layout by Daniel Isom

First Edition May, 2011

SHADOWS OF THE BEAST

Moriel Ministries
P.O. Box 100223
Pittsburgh, PA 15233-0223
U.S.A.
(412) 321-6154
www.moriel.org

Library of Congress Control Number 2011926777
Trade Edition ISBN 978-0-9828599-1-9

Table of Contents

Introduction

Same Game, Same Rules - But On A Different Level

Some of the finest players of pocket billiards in the world have been amateur pool hustlers who worked their way up to becoming professionals. I doubt Minnesota Fats, as talented as he was, ever thought much about physics or geometry. He was playing a two-dimensional game on a flat surface. It was, rather, the mathematician G. D. Birkhoff who postulated axioms for Euclidian geometry who demonstrated principles of free particle motion in a two-dimensional convex of the plane. Birkhoff did this not because he was interested in billiards but because he was interested in using geometry to explain dynamics.

I doubt Birkhoff, brilliant as he was, could "run a table" like Minnesota Fats, the same as I doubt Minnesota Fats could understand the Euclidian analysis of Birkhoff. But if we were to escalate the game of pocket billiards from a two-dimensional to a three-dimensional game, we would not only need the pool hall skill of Minnesota Fats, but the mathematical genius of Birkhoff. More and more factors would come into play. We would have to go beyond plain and solid geometry to the kind of elliptical geometry used by Johannes Kepler to explain planetary orbits and we would have to elevate the pool cue ability of Minnesota Fats to the level of the rocket science of Werner Von Braun.

In fact, in fields such as astrophysics and ballistic science this is exactly what happens, but it becomes more complicated. Kepler could not have explained the propositions of Galileo and Copernicus by mathematics alone. He required the observations of Tycho Brahe. To achieve the goal there is the need for ***both*** a Minnesota Fats ***and*** a G. D. Birkhoff; we need a Brahe ***and*** a Kepler; we need ***both*** the observationist ***and*** the technician. Eschatology is no different.

Erasmus of Rotterdam and the leaders of 16th-century Humanism who precipitated the Reformation viewed theology as the queen of the sciences. Yet like the medical sciences and modern computer sciences, it is also an art as much as a science. True doctrinal theology, however, ventures well beyond this into a dimension that cannot be charted by art, science, or metaphysics. It is the realm of the Spirit where the only sure textbook is the Judeo-Christian Scriptures and the only reliable guide is the illumination of the Holy Spirit.

But let us for a brief moment return to the billiard parlor. The same basic principles of physics and geometry governing velocity, trajectory, energy of activation, force of mass, properties of angulations, motion and dynamics that occur two-dimensionally on a billiard table are expanded into three-dimensional applications in ballistics, astronomy, and rocket science. Most efforts aimed at understanding the Antichrist or attempts to definitively identify the two Beasts of Revelation 13 have taken place two-dimensionally instead of three-dimensionally. In a sense, they are trying to perfect an interception system for an intercontinental ballistic missile in a billiards parlor on a street corner of Chicago or Detroit. A Minnesota Fats could not design an antiballistic missile system. By the same token those who have taken the task out of the pool hall and into the theological library forget that G. D. Birkhoff could not sink every ball on the table calling his shots ahead of time in a high stakes gamble. These are different skills.

With Kepler and Brahe the theorist knew he needed the observationist. A scientist knows he needs the engineer. The academic theologian likewise needs the preacher, otherwise we get nowhere fast. But in eschatology believers desperately need the illumination of the Holy Spirit. The human scholarly disciplines consecrated to God's service are essential, but even those skills will not unravel the ultimate interpretation of Revelation 13. We must go from the pool hall to the theological library, but from the theological library to the throne of grace. Until the Lord Jesus by His Spirit identifies these ultimate two Beasts, they ***cannot*** be identified.

Let us, for the final time, return to the billiard parlor. Imagine the task was to sink every ball racked up on the table with the opening breaking shot. No one has ever done this. So, too, to know the *"son of perdition,"* no one has ever done this except Jesus and no one else can. Yet He expects us to chalk up our pool sticks as His partners and get into the game.

The biblical premise to approach this issue is the diabolical tripod. There is the spirit of antichrist, many antichrists, and the two Beasts of Revelation 13, one of whom is the *"man of lawlessness."* Unless we comprehend the spirit of Antichrist, how it ***operates***, how it ***has*** operated, and how it ***is*** operating today, we cannot even sink the first ball let alone the whole table. This is often overlooked. Before we can do the physics we have to do the math. The billiard player thinks in terms of stop shots, follow shots, and draws. He thinks in terms of putting English on the cue. He should be thinking of derivatives, exponential quantification, and velocity increase. He should not think of it as a shot until he thinks of it as a vector. If we want to do the physics, first do the math.

The dynamic of how Christ operates in the present age is through the ministry of the Holy Spirit, convicting the lost of sin, empowering and uniting the true Church, and speaking to us first and foremost through the Scriptures and by charismatic revelation (that must be verified and tested by revealed biblical doctrine to be sure it is the Holy Spirit and not another spirit). This function of the Holy Spirit is mimicked and counterfeited by the spirit of antichrist pointing people away. Multiple scenarios have been proposed to identify the Antichrist. Problematically, this first principle is too frequently overlooked or at best understated. The Antichrist will counterfeit Christ, putting himself in place of Christ when in fact it is the Holy Spirit who rightfully acts in place of Christ. Therefore if there is a counterfeit of Christ, there must be a counterfeit of the Holy Spirit working in the fallen world.

In Revelation 13 this spirit of antichrist (1 Jn. 4:3) will indwell the False Prophet to the point of virtual personification approximating a de facto incarnation or something very close to it. It is futile to understand the biblical Jesus without the Holy Spirit. We cannot understand the Antichrist without first having a biblical comprehension of the spirit of antichrist. The first and foremost means of identifying the counterfeit is to understand the authentic. When we understand the nature and function of the Holy Spirit we will have the primary basis to understand the nature and function of the spirit of antichrist (which is closely associated with the mystery of iniquity) and the False Prophet.

Without this as our launching point, we have positioned the cue ball in the wrong location and the game is lost from the break.

There are fifteen balls in the rack, but only one eight-ball and one nine-ball. One is striped and one is solid. All of the other solid color balls are similar to the eight-ball in appearance, yet the eight-ball is unique. So, too, the other striped balls resemble the nine-ball, but the nine-ball is unique. There are many false prophets, but one ***ultimate*** False Prophet who is Antichrist; there are many antichrists, but one ***ultimate*** Antichrist who is the "*man of lawlessness*." In playing the game Eight Ball, the balls must be sunk in order. So, too, we must understand all of the other false prophets in order to correctly identify the final one. And we must identify, in order, the other antichrists, not in order to be able to identify the "*man of lawlessness,*" (we ***cannot*** identify him) but in order to have Christ identify him to us. Christ our partner takes the final shot. Just as Jesus identified the "*son of perdition*" to his disciples, so He will identify the "*son of perdition*" once again. The balls, however, must be sunk in order. Unless we grasp the many antichrists and types of the Antichrist in biblical history, and secondly in church history, efforts to recognize the "*man of lawlessness*" when Christ fingers him are useless.

Hence in light of these things the focus of this book will largely be concentrated on understanding the spirit of antichrist and an understanding of the many antichrists who provide us a repertoire of types and shadows of the one who is to come in satanic counterfeit of the true one who is to come.

Finally, we must avoid the twin errors of conclusion based on speculation and also of not exploring the panorama of possibilities. God placed Israel at the center of the nations according to Isaiah. Israel is the geographic heart of the Levant in what is to date variously called the Middle East or what was once called the Near East. From there the Jews who accepted their Messiah were geographically facilitated in carrying His message of salvation omni-directionally. By historical tradition Thomas took it eastward to India and Matthew southward into black Africa. Paul and Barnabas carried it northward into Europe while at the same time it spread rapidly in an eastward direction to the sub-Mediterranean Roman Empire in the area today we call Arab North Africa, but in biblical times was Indo-European Berber and Greco-Roman. The convergence of continents at the Levant with Israel at its center demonstrates that geographically and culturally the Judeo-Christian faith is neither Eastern ***nor*** Western, but ***both*** Eastern ***and*** Western. Theologically it is likewise ***both*** Occidental ***and*** Oriental.

Because the Book of Acts records the expansion of the Gospel in a western direction only, and because the Greco-Roman world was at the center of human civilization and of political, economic, and strategic power in the 1st through 3rd centuries, ethnic Europeans impose a Western interpretation of Scripture and eschatology, forgetting that the Armenian Empire was Christianized before the Roman Empire period; they forget that the forefathers of African Coptic Christians and the Eastern church have claims preceding any institutionalized Christianity of the West. Meanwhile,

East, West, North and South all forget that biblical Christianity is theologically and spiritually in its ontogeny a Judaic faith that was later Hellenized by the so-called church fathers.

Biblically those figures who foreshadow the Antichrist are drawn by Scripture from ***both*** the East and West. Those with a Western perspective and orientation have tended to view the Antichrist to come as a Western figure, variously being identified with the cities of Pergamum and Rome and with institutions controlled by the spirit of antichrist such as the Roman papacy and the European Union. Others, with an Eastern perspective, have sought to identify the Antichrist with the Islamic Mahdi, pointing out biblical descriptions of decapitation by the Antichrist that are still decreed by Islamic law long after the guillotine was replaced by other methods of execution in the West. They further argue that the Islamic world today spans not only the Middle East, but extends into areas that were part of the Greco-Roman West in the apostolic age such as Turkey, North Africa, and areas of the Balkans. These arguments are further reinforced by the demographic growth of Muslim populations and of radical Islam not only in Russia but in Western Europe and Britain and, to a lesser extent, in North America and Australasia while reaching to Indonesia, Malaysia, and the Southern Philippines in the Far East.

It is our argument that there are clear elements of truth in ***both*** perspectives, yet both perspectives fail when they attempt to establish themselves as mutually exclusive without having better biblical and historical arguments than they presently base themselves on. The question must be asked, if the faith of Christ was both Eastern and Western, will not the same be true of Antichrist? Since all who dwell on the earth will worship the Beast (Rev. 13:8), can he not be all things to all lost and unbelieving peoples? Buddhists await the Fifth Buddha; New Agers await Maitreya; Jews await the Messiah; Christians await the *Parousia*; and Muslims await the Mahdi.

The Pantheon of pagan Rome was a fusion of all major pagan and false religions and cults of the period under the guide of the emperor in his function as Pontiff. In Pergamum, identified in the Book of Revelation as the location of Satan's throne, the overlooking mount contained the altar of Zeus, the shrine of Mithras (which was adopted by Rome but which originated in Egypt), and the temple of Athena and of Ascleptus. But it was also the shrine for the worship of Caesar, the deified emporer. Pergamum blossomed as a pilgrimage of Pantheism with false gods converging from every direction, both East and West. Yet the probable route of all of these demonic religions was Babylon. However, in the New Testament the Apostle Peter identifies pagan Rome with Babylon. (1 Pe. 5:13). From Dionysus and Zeus to Demeter and Caesar, they were all worshiped in Pergamum.

It was not East ***or*** West, but East ***and*** West. The Body of Christ must centrally address the question, "Are both the Westernists and the Easternists alike correct in what they affirm but mistaken in what they omit?" One thing is for certain: the *"man of sin"* as a political figure will be empowered by a quasi-unifying religious system headed by the False Prophet who functions by mimicking the Holy Spirit and uniting false religions as the Holy Spirit unites members of the true biblical faith. The spirit of antichrist also guides and empowers the apostate church, albeit satanically, as the Holy Spirit empowers the true Church. Problematically, the spirit of antichrist and the Antichrist operate under the Luciferian guise, manifesting as light the most unfathomable darkness. So deceptive will be this trap camouflaged as light that only the greater Light of Jesus and His Word illuminated by the Holy Spirit can expose the deception for what it is. The world, false religions—including unbiblical expressions of Christianity—and even apostate Evangelicalism will bask in the beams of Antichrist's light; the faithful bride ***alone*** will see the truth for what it is.

Additionally, the principle of counterfeit must be applied to every consideration in contemplating the Antichrist. In some way the False Prophet will parody the function of Aaron the high priest as a religious leader, and the *"man of lawlessness"* will parody Moses, counterfeiting miracles of God in the character of Jannes and Jambres (as Paul tells us in 2 Timothy). Moses and Aaron acted on behalf of God; Jannes and Jambres acted on behalf of Pharaoh who was not only a type of Antichrist, but a biblical symbol of Satan as the god of this world in biblical typology.

Moreover, because Jesus was a Jew, an Antichrist must imitate Him. The question of the ethnicity of the Antichrist becomes inescapable. Due investigation must be conducted into whether or not at least one of the two Beasts is of Jewish descent. The Antichrist himself will be the consummate Jew-hater, making a treaty with Israel which he will break and attempting to exterminate them in order to prevent the return of Christ. In a historical sense, figures such as Adolph Hitler and Joseph Stalin foreshadow him. Orthodox Jews will never believe in a Messiah who is not a Jew.

Hence it is again imperative that we do not restrict ourselves to the conventional parameters as well-intentioned Bible expositors of the past have done in addressing Revelation 13. The text must be viewed from a Hebraic perspective more than a Hellenistic one. No less important is the need to shun dogmatic propositions given the fact that these two figures are yet to be revealed by God. Not least of all, we must avoid the "either/or" mindsets of mutual exclusivity. It is not Birkhoff or Minnesota Fats; the task requires ***both***.

Eschatology is not a theological art or a theological science but both. It is not the theorist or the observer; both are required. The biblical perspective is not Eastern ***or*** Western, but Eastern ***and*** Western. As we shall note in the course of this book, neither is it the futurist, historicist, preterist, or poemicist approach to biblical eschatology, but it is all four. (A concept largely alien to the Hellenistic mind, but quite coherent to the Judaic one.) Above all, it is not a sanctified scholarship consecrated to divine service or pure Holy Spirit revelation and illumination through the Scriptures; it is, in fact, ***both***.

At this point in time, the author is convinced that many true Christians have individual pieces of the puzzle. The challenge before us is to put all the pieces together, abandoning the delusion that our piece is all that there is.

Preface

This book is not intended as an instruction manual as to how to identify the ultimate two Beasts of Revelation 13. It is, however, a biblically structured way written from a Judeo-Christian perspective containing core material without which any identification of these two figures will in all likelihood not be possible.

It will be centered on these key aspects:

- A Judeo-Christian treatment of this subject which seeks to understand eschatological (End Time) prophecy in light of the Judaic culture (*Sitz im Leben*) and hermeneutics methodology of biblical interpretation of the 1st-century Jewish believers in Jesus divinely inspired to author the New Testament.

- An understanding that as the character of God is visibly manifested in Christ, the character of Satan will be visibly manifested in the character of Antichrist, and that as the Holy Spirit prepares the faithful Church for the Second Advent of Christ, the spirit of antichrist working through the "*Zeitgeist*" ("spirit of the age") and ultimately through the False Prophet is the way he is preparing the apostate church and the world for the advent of the Antichrist.

- That as the "Word of God" is the *Logos* (the incarnate Christ in published form) there is a *pseudologon*—a false word of God coming in the form of many books advancing doctrines, beliefs, and practices fundamentally contrary to the actual *Logos* (the Judeo-Christian Scriptures). These range from papal encyclicals, the *Quran*, Talmudic edicts, and *The Book of Mormon* to popular Christian books propagating fundamentally contra-biblical content such as *The Shack*, *The Purpose Driven Life*, *The God Chasers*, and a range of books redefining biblical Christianity as a psychologized, consumerist, ecumenical and Inter-Faith, New Age religion, which all misrepresent themselves to be biblical in content. Worse still are the compendium of censored, inclusive, and hyper-paraphrased

Bible translations that severely mutate the original meaning of the original Hebrew, Aramaic, and Greek texts such as *The century Bible*, *The Recovery Bible*, Roman Catholic mistransla-tions, *The Voice*, and above all Eugene Peterson's *The Message* (Rick Warren's translation of choice).

- That the essential key in the final identification of the Antichrist is to understand the meaning of "many antichrists" in John's First Epistle, where they are first of all in Scripture, but also in history—***many*** Antichrists, each one of them typologically foreshadowing the ultimate Beast of Revelation 13 (bearing in mind that Revelation 13 itself does not specifically employ the term "Antichrist").

Prologue

Few things are more futile and time wasting than reinventing the wheel. An avalanche of material on the subject of the Antichrist has been written over many centuries. This has ranged from Neronian speculations from the Patristic Era by the church fathers, to the anti-papal polemics of the Reformation, to academic commentary focused on scholarly perspectives of Greek New Testament passages dealing with the subject of Antichrist from a literary and grammatical-historical perspective in terms of critical scholarship. Attempted Judeo-Christian approaches to the subject have usually concentrated on the possible use of Gematria (the numerical value of Hebrew letters, which some have tried to apply to Greek and Latin) to arrive at the number of a name amounting to "666."

While I shall interact with these kinds of considerations where appropriate, I do not want to review their merits at length or contribute to the endless maze of speculation that has fueled everything from anti-Semitic propaganda to an army of modern conspiracy theorists who pursue their often fanciful, and at times paranoid, speculations under the guise of a supposed "discernment ministry" or biblical eschatology.

This first category brandishing this particular sort of anti-Semitism is propagated by fringe element Jew-haters imagining themselves to be on a Christian crusade who detest the fact that the God of Christians is the God of Israel, that Jesus is a Jew returning as King of the Jews, that the human authors of the New Testament were all Jews (with a partial exception of Luke who had converted to Judaism), and that as a matter of historical ontogeny, spiritually and theologically Christianity is a Judaic faith. They further dislike the fact that New Testament literature, like the "*Tanak*" (Old Testament), points out Israel's sin, yet in fact is a Philo-Semitic composite document, affirming God's unconditional love for His ancient people Israel for the sake of the patriarchal promises to their fathers, and predicts a future prophetic destiny for an Israel and the Jews purged from sin.

In evangelical circles these figures are by and large biblically ignorant and subscribe to the doctrinal errors of Replacement Theology and Supersessionism which without an inductively stated biblical basis falsely teaches that the Church has replaced Israel to the negation of any prophetic destiny for national or ethnic Israel. They further deny any biblical significance to contemporary Middle East events. Not infrequently these errors stem from the Covenant Theology and Reconstructionist camps of Reformed/Calvinistic Protestantism (although many more moderate Calvinists do not subscribe to this matter of error).

Those deceived into the false doctrine of Replacement Theology rejecting the prophetic significance of contemporary Middle East events and who teach this false doctrine to others (e.g. John Piper, Rick Godwin, John Stott, the late D. James Kennedy, and Reconstructionist Calvinists) are too far from the truth to be in any biblical sense prepared for the advent of Antichrist or to prepare the Body of Christ for events to come. Worse still are those with no eschatology (traditional Lutheranism) or those captivated by the Emergent Church and the *Purpose Driven* agenda. The anti-Semites who feed off of their errors are even further away. Nonetheless, it is crucial to understand how Antichrist deceives and will deceive Israel and the Jews in order to understand what he will attempt to do.

In the present climate there are those claiming to be Christian who subscribe to the age-old nonsense of Jewish power and wealth bent on world domination propagated by Ted Pike and Roman Catholic equivalents who find their cheerleaders in Pat Buchanan, Robert Sungenis, and Holocaust-denying Roman Catholic Bishop Richard Williamson (who was restored by Pope Benedict XVI).

In actual fact, the institutionalized anti-Israel biases in the majority of global media from the BBC, much of CNN, UK ITV, UK Channel 4, Al Arabya, Al Jazeera, a host of newspapers from *The Pittsburgh Gazette*, to much of Gannett, to Britain's *Independent*, to *Euronews* dispels the myth of Jewish control of the media. Neither of the world's two biggest news moguls, Ted Turner and his rival Rupert Murdoch, nor America's oldest news dynasty, the Hearst family, is Jewish. Neither are most of America's financial dynasties, be it the Rockefellers, the DuPonts, the Kennedys, the Melons nor America's richest, Bill Gates or Warren Buffet. Jewish power in Europe such as the House of Rothschild was never powerful enough to stop the Third Reich or to force wider European support for Zionism even as Europe itself faces the same radical Islamic intimidation as Israel. The anti-Israel detractors likewise ignore the fact that most neo-conservatives such as Richard Perle, Britain's Michael Howard, and many of the conservative and pro-family voices in the media such as Michael Savage, David Horowitz, Ben

Stein, Michael Medved, Jay Sekulow, Bernie Goldberg, and Melanie Philips are likewise all Jewish. Yet there remains no shortage of anti-Jewish figures parading themselves as a Christian cause seeking to vilify the Jews as "Antichrist" when in fact Scripture reveals plainly that the Jews will be the final intended victims of the coming Antichrist.

The second category is the folly-clad array of "Christian" conspiracy theorists. Such people are immune to the fact there are purely secular conspiracy theorists engaged in the same manner of fanciful speculation where a trace of fact is amplified out of proportion and transformed into wild and almost delusional conjecture resulting in a semi-paranoid mindset where those not in agreement are therefore suspected as party to the conspiracy. Clinically this has not infrequently ended in diagnosed psychosis. When such "connecting the dots" conspiracy speculation is pursued under the auspices of "biblical discernment" and end-times prophecy, we have borderline lunacy masquerading as Christianity. We have witnessed no end to this in the pseudo-gematrial treatments of the names of Henry Kissinger, King Juan Carlos of Spain, and Britain's Prince Charles. Not infrequently the Ted Pike and Alan Morrison branch of so-called "Christian" conspiracy theorists harmoniously dovetail with the anti-Semitic strain.

There has indeed been a panorama of literature of every description, some of it credible, much of it hideous (anti-Semites, conspiracy theorists) addressing this highly serious subject. While there are, no doubt, things that are of prophetic significance in relation to the advent of Antichrist, too many have ventured into the realm of speculation; some of it plausible and some of it devoid of credibility. The Hebrew letter "*vav*" is the alpha-numeric digit for "6" and in transliterated words in modern Hebrew is used for a "w" for which there is no Hebrew equivalent. Thus "World Wide Web" (WWW) in Hebrew is "*vav vav vav*," or "6-6-6." While the Internet, like barcodes and credit and debit cards, point to a Revelation 13 monetary system, it is over-speculative to say "This must be it." More pointedly, advances in biogenetic engineering that will facilitate cloning to the point of approximating a reincarnation by cloning the DNA of a terminally ill person is another example of how such fast-rising technologies could conceivably help facilitate a counterfeit of the resurrection by the Antichrist at some future point.

It is important to be aware of such eventual possibilities, but any dogmatism is again speculative and we must endeavor to avoid speculation even where what it postulates may carry some possible credence. I will again interact with the credible where helpful to do so, and will ignore the hideous. We shall, however, all but ignore the speculative other than taking occasional note of its possibilities in relation to more solid matters being addressed in the text. The focus of the book will be, or mostly be, on Scripture, biblical history, and Judeo-Christian history reviewed and examined in light of Scripture.

More to the point, however, I once more do not wish to reinvent the wheel. I will remain concentrated on saying that which has not been said before and will seek to illuminate and elucidate things largely ignored until now but which need to be highlighted at this time as we approach the revelation of the "man of lawlessness."

This book is in no way intended to be, nor is it, an exhaustive treatment of the subject of the Antichrist. Its purposed intent is to address the manner in which his identity will be revealed through the Scriptures by the Holy Spirit to the faithful Church. There is much material concerning what the Antichrist and False Prophet will engage in, particularly in the books of Daniel and Revelation, that are not directly pertinent to their initial identification. We shall mainly fix our attention on those aspects of their predicted actions required to know who they are before it is too late. Indeed for many it is already too late.

The Great Myth

In that Jesus can come tonight or at any moment for any of us personally, I hold to the doctrine of "immanency." Paul the Apostle wrote of "*the blessed hope*" (Tit. 2:13). This is the *Parousia*, the revelation of the true sons of God set to take place not simply at the Rapture (*Harpazo*) but at the *episunagoge*—"our gathering together to Christ." This gathering is the Rapture and Resurrection of the righteous as a concurrent event meeting the Lord in the sky whether we have died in Christ or are alive at His Second Coming. "*The blessed hope*" is not the Rapture but the return of Christ. Irrespective of whether we are raptured or resurrected we retain "*the blessed hope.*" It is the same event, as if when attending a Bible study in a home it matters not by which door one enters the house. This event is typologically illustrated in the Transfiguration of Jesus on Mt. Hermon (not actually Mt. Tabor). Typology teaches no doctrine. The use of literary symbolism as a basis of doctrine is not a biblical hermeneutic but rather Gnostic mysticism. The properly interpreted typology of a biblical narrative, however, ***illustrates*** and ***illuminates*** doctrine.

The Jews of Jesus' day properly understood from Zechariah 5:12 that the Messianic fulfillment of *Hag Sukkot*—the Feast of Tabernacles or Booths, would be the millennial reign of the Messiah. Hence when Jesus was transfigured (on the same mount where the demonic Nephilim came down in the days of Jarrod according to Jewish history), Peter wanted to build three booths. Moses—a man who died in the Lord, Elijah—a man who was raptured, and the Messiah were all transfigured 10,000 feet in the sky on Mt. Hermon. Peter thought it was the inauguration of the millennial reign fulfilling the Feast of Tabernacles or Booths. Christ, Moses, and Elijah when they were once transfigured all appeared the same. It matters not if we are dead in Christ or are raptured when the Lord returns; we shall meet Him in the air and "be as He is" as He establishes His millennial Kingdom.

The clearest picture of the Rapture and Resurrection is the Transfiguration. Neither our blessed hope nor the doctrine of immanency depends on a belief in a Pre-Tribulational Rapture. This Pre-Tribulational Rapture position as it is usually presented necessitates the erroneous view that truly saved, Bible-believing Christians do not need to be concerned with the identity of the Antichrist because the true Church will be raptured before He is manifested.

The patriarch of Pre-Tribulationism, Dr. John Walvoord of Dallas Theological Seminary admitted there is no stated biblical passage overtly teaching a Pre-Tribulational position. Walvoord states that "the Rapture is between the lines." It is a fact that the proponents of Pre-Tribulationism themselves admit they are unable to produce an inductive exegetical argument for their belief, but must rely on deductive opinion as the foundation for their understanding of an event marking the climax of human history.

Problematically, Dr. Walvoord was a good man as is John MacArthur. Indeed, most Pre-Tribulationists are in many ways excellent preachers and authors. Among these brethren are some of my closest personal friends who seek to uphold biblical truth in an age of apostasy where it is being eroded. Among these are Dave Hunt, Dr. Arnold Fruchtenbaum, Dr. David Hocking, Pastor Chuck Smith, Dr. Thomas Ice, Dr. Randolph Price and a large host of others whom I both personally like and respect and whose ministries I value. At a time when the doctrinal truth of the Rapture is being denounced by Rick Joyner and Gerald Coates, or ignored at the behest of Rick Warren, these brethren and others have staunchly defended the truth of the *Harpazo*. In this they are indeed my allies. Here lies the dilemma. The proponents of Pre-Tribulationism are the "good guys" who are, in my conviction, absolutely correct about the reality of the Rapture (and a range of other things), but who in my firm view simply misunderstand its timing and sequence.

For me this is a matter for prayer, study, and dialogue and not a basis for division. We stand on the same side of the divide concerning the fact that there ***is*** a Rapture, that current Middle Eastern events are of prophetic significance, and that God still has a prophetic and salvific destiny for Israel and the Jews. I would be in further agreement with Pre-Tribulationist brethren that the Mid-Tribulational and Post-Tribulational arguments are flawed and that the Pre-Wrath position misidentifies the restrainer of 2 Thessalonians to be an angelic being when, as Pre-Tribulationists rightly teach, it is the person of the Holy Spirit. It is rather with Rapture deniers, ultra-Preterists, and Replacementists that we all divide, and not with each other. In fairness, none of these aforementioned brethren holding a Pre-Tribulational position have ever allowed it to become a barrier to fellowship or to standing together on the vast common ground that unites us. But with regard to identification of the Antichrist the issue unavoidably remains.

Without a single scriptural passage stating their point of view they must speculate that the meanings of the Greek terms for "tribulation" (*thelipsis*) and the eschatological testing in Revelation 3:10 are precise synonyms despite linguistic evidence to the contrary. Jesus in fact informed Christians that they would have tribulation in the world.

Secondly, they must define the Tribulation as the full 70th week (final 7 lunar years) of Daniel's vision despite both the books of Daniel and Revelation dividing the final seven year period in half (with the second half worse than the first). They must also fail to draw due distinction between the Great Tribulation and "the Day of the Lord" which are distinct time periods.

Not least of all, while lacking a plainly stated biblical passage verifying Pre-Tribulationism, not infrequently they ridicule the literalist interpretation of Revelation 7 placing the Rapture and Resurrection during the interlude between the 6th and 7th seals: "*These are the ones who come* ***out*** *of the great tribulation*," (Rev. 7:14) not prevented from entering it to begin with.

The biblical position of Pre-Wrath fails in that it misunderstands the restrainer of 2 Thessalonians 2 to be an angel or the angel Michael instead of the Holy Spirit, and the Pre-Wrath view was to a degree discredited by the late Bob Van Kampen who postulated a resurrection of Adolph Hitler.

Pre-Tribulationists correctly identify the restrainer as the Holy Spirit, for it is the Holy Spirit who convicts of sin and empowers the church to proclaim the Gospel. Where Pre-Tribulationists flounder is that they equate the removal of the Holy Spirit with the removal of the church. This is a mistaken eschatology resulting from a mistaken pneumatology; they misunderstand the doctrine of the Holy Spirit, which results in a further miscomprehension of 2 Thessalonians.

In John 20:22, upon His resurrection Jesus breathed on His apostles, with them receiving the indwelt Holy Spirit prior to Pentecost, at which time the Holy Spirit was poured out on the Body of Christ corporately, and convicted the unsaved to repent. Prior to Pentecost the Church did not exist except in an embryonic but powerless state (Lk. 24:49). The Lord will never leave nor forsake His people, and the indwelling of the Holy Spirit will always be a reality for the faithful believers. A time will come, however, when the Holy Spirit will no longer convict the world of sin (Jn. 16:8). The Church will not be empowered. This is what Daniel calls, "*Shattering the power of the holy people.*" (Dan. 12:7, 8:24) Scripture typologically represents this period with the metaphor of "the night."

- "*We must work the works of Him who sent Me as long as it is day; night is coming when no one can work.*" (Jn. 9:4)
- *...the day of the Lord will come just like a thief in the night.*" (1 Th. 5:2)
- The bridegroom comes for the bride in the night. (SS 3:1, Mt. 25:6)
- The raptured are taken in the night. (Lk. 17:34)

Again, the symbolism of the night ***illustrates*** the truth but is not the basis of it.

In other words, Pentecost is reversed. The distinction must be drawn between when the Holy Spirit indwells and when the Holy Spirit is outpoured. (Although related, this should not be confused with pro and con arguments about Holy Spirit baptism subsequent to salvation.) As Jesus left and sent the Holy Spirit, the Holy Spirit leaves and Jesus is dispatched. There is once more a short period of waiting akin to the time between the Ascension of Christ and Pentecost. Now conversely the Holy Spirit will depart and the Lord Jesus shall descend.

The Holy Spirit will not be taken from the hearts of true believers but He will be taken from the world (Gen. 6:3, 2 Th. 2:6). God will, as it were, return to an Old Covenant dealing with man. His judgments on Egypt in the Book of Exodus are recapitulated on the whole planet (Rev. 16); as a falsely deified Pharaoh and his sorcerers counterfeited the miracles of Moses and Aaron, the falsely deified Antichrist and False Prophet will likewise perform counterfeit miracles (Rev. 13:12-13). At this time God will once again shift His redemptive purposes back to the salvation of Israel and the Jews. Both Pre-Tribulationists and Pre-Wrath advocates fail to understand this sequence of events (as do both Mid-Tribulationists and Post-Tribulationists), but it is imperative that this sequence be grasped.

This view, however, is not new but predates any other main major position for the timing of the Rapture and Resurrection. There are credible arguments that it was held in the pre-Nicean church by those close in time to the apostles, and it was held by the more learned of the early Dispensationalists such as Dr. Samuel Tregellas in the 19th century with no reference to the inventions of men like Scofield. Indeed, I myself was taught this position in the hippie–days of the Jesus Movement in the 1970s long prior to Marvin Rosenthal, Charles Cooper or other later proponents. While deficient in what it omits due to a partially flawed pneumatology, and wrong in its misidentification of the restrainer of 2 Thessalonians 2, the Pre-Wrath position is otherwise closest to being biblically correct of all of the major Tribulational positions.

There are a number of dangers in the Pre-Tribulation position. One danger is that Christians in the Western World who have enjoyed the historical anomaly of religious freedom and affluence have, in the character of the church of Laodicea, been deluded by forgetting that persecution of Christians in much of the world has increased considerably and will eventually become global. Being told they will not suffer the way Christians in so many countries are now, and have been throughout history, they will not be prepared for reality, as if being a Christian in the USA or Australia or Britain immunizes them from the persecution suffered by Christians in Islamic countries and China. ***Forewarned*** is ***forearmed***. Tragically they are not being forewarned by their pastors, hence they will not be forearmed. The second ramification of Pre-Tribulationism is that those subscribing to it will not concern themselves with identifying the Antichrist because of the mistaken presupposition that it does not apply to them.

If only those who have wisdom will understand how to calculate the number of the beast (Rev. 13:18), and if it requires the true believers (whose wisdom is Christ), then who will be here with the wisdom to do the calculation? These cannot be the Tribulation saints because if they had wisdom they would not be here either. There are no grounds in the text read in context to identify those calculating the number of the Beast as un-raptured Tribulation saints.

Whenever a biblical text centers on believers in the Tribulation, Pre-Tribulationists once again deductively and eisegetically assume it applies to the Tribulation saints. No other eschatological doctrine has been as overstated and amplified out of all proportion as to what Scripture actually teaches than the issue of Tribulation saints. Most of what the New Testament inductively and exegetically states about events on earth after the Rapture and Resurrection indicate that once the faithful Church is removed, God turns His focus and purposes to dealing with His ancient people Israel and the Jews—a fact that many Pre-Tribulationists themselves admit.

Exegesis seeks to draw ***out*** of a text what is contained in it; eisegesis, however, reads things ***into*** a text. Pre-Tribulationism has issued itself a bogus theological license to assign to those calculating the number of the Beast an identity of their own design custom fit to accommodate their own faulty non-exegetical and non-inductive presuppositions. A solid doctrinal position can be predicated only on exegetical induction, not on eisegetical deductive opinion.

Jesus Himself warned us of false Christs and false prophets in the Olivet Discourse, yet just as Preterists falsely teach it no longer applies to Christians because it has all (instead of partially) transpired in the events surrounding A.D. 70, Pre-Tribulationists are left agreeing with them that it does not apply to us because we will have already been raptured before the Antichrist and False Prophet become an issue. This in itself creates an exegetical quagmire in their overall treatment of the Olivet Discourse. Their case depends on an assumption which by their own admission is never plainly taught in Scripture.

Fortunately the Holy Spirit is illuminating more of these deeper biblical truths as we get closer to the Lord's Return (Dan. 12:4), and more pastors and individuals are progressively realizing the erroneous nature of Pre-Tribulationism and the need to understand how to properly identify the final Antichrist and False Prophet—the Beasts of Revelation 13.

The heart of the issue itself is found again in 2 Thessalonians 2. Taken literally and in context, Paul states that the Rapture and Resurrection and the consequent "Day of the Lord" (when God pours out His wrath on the kingdom of Antichrist) will not occur until the "*man of lawlessness*" is revealed.

The argumentation that some Pre-Tribulationists resort to in order to circumvent the clearly stated implications of this text can at times be virtually implausible. Some even venture so far as to identify the apostasy (*apostasia*) as the Rapture, not, as the context dictates, the departure from the truth when a delusional judgment comes upon those rejecting the truth they once professed (2 Th. 2:10-11). To state as some have that the apostasy is not the departure from the truth but the Rapture is an interpretation eluding the context and ignoring the co-texts addressing the apostasy of the Last Days.

Indeed, whole-scale denominations which had biblically Evangelical origins—such as Reformed Anglicanism, Presbyterianism, Methodism, the Reformed Churches, etc.—have ventured so far into theological liberalism, interfaith ecumenism, and even the moral depravity of homosexual and lesbian ordination, that the prophetically foretold apostasy of the church is undeniable. But Pre-Tribulationists must ignore it with reference to the 2 Thessalonians passage foretelling it to support their "opinion" that is essentially void of inductive exegetical foundation.

We are reminded that a very good translation of Laodicea is as a compound Greek term *lao-dikaomai* meaning "people's rights" or "people's opinions." Pre-Tribulationists may have a right to their opinion, but they have no right to expect others to believe it when they themselves admit they cannot prove it with a single verse or passage by any inductive exegetical means.

This again returns us to the dilemma that most Pre-Tribulationists are solidly in the camp of scriptural orthodoxy representing firm biblical dogma in the face of what they themselves quite properly comprehend to be Last Days apostasy. Yet when it comes to this central New Testament passage of 2 Thessalonians elaborating on this End Times apostasy, they scramble—seemingly pseudo-logically and eisegetically—to redefine Paul's use of the very term "apostasy" in this vital passage. Thus they are resorting to *reductio ad absurdum* argumentation in the process. This exercise is of course pursued not in the name of defending a clear inductively stated doctrine such as the Rapture itself, but rather an unstated deductive presuppositional opinion about its timing.

The Rapture and Resurrection cannot and shall not take place until the faithful believers can identify the ultimate two Beasts of Revelation Chapter 13.

The popular myth asserting the contrary as if it were an exegetical fact is a dangerous myth which must be debunked as a deception perpetrated against the Elect. Tragically, many good believers accept this error. And many otherwise good Bible teachers, theologians, and pastors have been wrongly directed (often by their own theological professors) into teaching it, howbeit with good yet misguided intentions.

The faithful Church will know and will need to know the true identity of the Beast before Jesus comes. The great myth that we do not need to concern ourselves with biblical passages alerting and instructing as to the identity of the Antichrist is a myth that must be urgently debunked for the ludicrous and auto-destructive erroneous folly it is.

Exegetically 2 Thessalonians is an Epistle in its literary genre and is designed to be read literally. Epistles are inspired apostolic commentary explaining other Scripture; we read other Scripture (apocalyptic, narrative, Hebrew Poetry, etc.) through the prism of a literalist reading of apostolic commentary. There is no need to read into the text things it does not state or to engage in *reductio ad absurdum* verbal exercises to negate what it does plainly state. Paul's explanation to the Thessalonians says exactly what it means and means exactly what it says: The Rapture and Resurrection cannot happen until the "*man of lawlessness*" is revealed.

> *Let no one in any way deceive you, for it will not come unless the apostasy comes first, and the man of lawlessness is revealed, the son of destruction,* (2 Th. 2:3)

Part One: The Spirit of the Antichrist

To understand the ultimate fulfillment in the final person to come as the Antichrist we must first understand how the spirit of antichrist is, and has been, at work during every age of history. Every act of the spirit of antichrist teaches something about the final Antichrist to come. As we shall attempt to explain, in the same manner in which the Holy Spirit is preparing the faithful Church for the Second Advent of Christ, the spirit of antichrist is preparing the apostate church for the advent of ***the*** Antichrist. This has its complement in the *Zeitgeist* (or "spirit of the age") preparing the fallen world to accept this counterfeit messiah, which is a much easier task as the fallen world is already in the power of the wicked one.

We have repeatedly stated over the years that in God's economy there are three kinds of people: Israel and the Jews, the Gentile nations, and the Church which is composed of both Jews (as the natural branches) and Gentiles (as those grafted in). Satan already has Israel and the Jews deceived apart from the growing faithful remnant of Jewish believers in Jesus (Yeshua) as their Messiah. Likewise Satan already has the nations oblivious to their true state of being ensnared in his web of deception and delusion, much of it achieved by means of false religion and the vain philosophies of men, especially by means of secular Humanism. This leaves the Church as the only remaining target of Satan which he must deceive in preparation for his animation of the person of Antichrist who will approximate a very nearly virtual and de facto incarnation mimicking the incarnation of Christ as fully human and fully divine. Thus the Antichrist will be just slightly shy of fully human and fully Satan, and which may in fact become in essence an enfleshment of Satan once the Antichrist is killed and comes back to life in a further counterfeit of the resurrection of Christ.

To make any headway in contemplating these mysteries our approach must be systematic, scriptural, and Holy Spirit illuminated. The first step in this process is to comprehend the nature not of the Antichrist himself who is still to be revealed, but rather beginning with the spirit of antichrist that is already with us.

Finally, it must be remembered that the spirit of antichrist has ***always*** been active at least since the time of the birth of the Church and is a very close relative of what the New Testament calls "the mystery of iniquity" (2 Th. 2:7). We must also note that as the spirit of antichrist works to delude the apostate church in preparation for the arrival of the Antichrist, Satan's goal is to seduce as many as possible out of the true Church into the false one. In this regard the spirit of antichrist at this very second is hard at work through the Ecumenical Movement, the Purpose Driven agenda, and the Emergent Church, to name but a few.

Chapter 1: Understanding the Hermeneutics of the Apostolic Church

When the New Testament is read as a Jewish book instead of as a Hellenistic book it reads quite differently than the Western, mainly Gentile Church reads it. Every writer of the New Testament, except for Luke, was a Jew, and even Luke was a convert to Judaism. Let us begin by looking at the way the New Testament handles the Old Testament.

How the New Testament Handles the Old

After Jesus is born and King Herod dies, the Gospel of Matthew says:

> *OUT OF EGYPT I CALLED MY SON.* (Mt. 2:15)

He was quoting Hosea 11:1 which says, "*And out of Egypt I called My son.*" In our modern way of interpreting the Bible, by our Western hermeneutics (if you like theological terms), Matthew is taking Hosea 11:1 out of all reasonable context. It is talking about the Exodus. It is talking about the children of Israel coming out of Egypt. But Matthew says it is about the Messiah when Herod died. One of two things are possible: either the New Testament is an absurd document because it is twisting Scripture and taking it out of all context, or else the Church is not interpreting the Bible correctly. There are liberal theologians and Jewish rabbis who say just that, that the New Testament does not handle the Old Testament in an exegetically responsible manner, therefore it should not be believed.

There are many instances like that in the New Testament. This is an example of what is known as "*Midrash.*" While some Jewish rabbis will say the New Testament is taking the Old Testament out of all reasonable context, Jewish academic theologians—the serious rabbinic scholars—do not dismiss it as nonsense. They realize how close the New Testament is to things we read in *The Dead Sea Scrolls* and are very acquainted with Midrash. Jesus was a rabbi, Paul was a rabbi, and they taught the way other rabbis did by utilizing Midrash. Matthew 2:15 is known as a "*Pesher*" interpretation.

Two elements of Midrash are these: the *mashal* and the *nimshal*. A *mashal* is an example of something from nature or everyday life, and the *nimshal* is its spiritual meaning. A parable is nothing more than an elongated *mashal*: here is the story and here is what it means. The Book of Proverbs is a book in Hebrew which we call *The Book of Mashals* or *Mishla*. The first half of a proverb is the *mashal*, and the spiritual explanation in back of it is the *nimshal*. *"As a ring of gold in a swine's snout"* (that is the *mashal*) *"so is a beautiful woman who lacks discretion"* (that is the *nimshal*) (Prov. 11:22).

The basis for Midrash in the times of Jesus was something known as the "Midot of Rabbi Hillel." Of far less (if any) significance to the New Testament is the further expansion at a later point by Rabbi Eliezer to fifteen *midot*, but the original seven *Midoth of Hillel* are essential to New Testament scholarship because in these Paul was schooled and inspired to be employed in the authorship of Scripture. We think of the Pharisees as the "bad guys," but compared to the Sadducees and the other sects in Judaism, they were the "good guys." Jesus agreed with the Pharisees on most things. He was much closer to them than He was to other kinds of Jews. Paul was a Pharisee as was Nicodemus.

There were two major schools of the Pharisees: the School of Hillel and the School of Shamai. Hillel was famous for devising basic methods in approaching the Bible called *midot*. The Apostle Paul was educated in the school of Rabbi Hillel and his tutor was Rabbi Gemaliel who was the grandson of Hillel. Paul had some very famous classmates in Judaism such as Rabbi Johannan Ben Zakkai who founded Rabbinic Judaism. After the Temple was destroyed they decided to make the synagogue a replacement for the Temple, and the rabbis the replacement for the Levites and for the priests, the Kohanim. He had some very famous classmates in a very famous school with a very famous tutor. Paul was educated in the School of Hillel and you see him continually using the *midot* of Rabbi Hillel in his Epistles.

Midrash in John

If a Jewish Christian were to read the Gospel of John in the 1st century, he would have recognized it as a Midrash on *B'reshit*—a Midrash on the Book of Genesis.

In Genesis chapters 1, 2, and 3 we have the narrative on the creation. And in John chapters 1, 2, and 3 we have the narrative on the new creation. A first-century believer would have said God walks the earth in the creation in Genesis—in *B'reshit*—and then God walks the earth in the ***new*** creation in John. They would have said God comes to separate the light from the dark in the creation in Genesis, and God comes to separate the light from dark in the ***new*** creation in John. They would have said the Spirit moves on the water and brings forth the creation in Genesis, and then the Spirit moves on the water and brings forth the ***new*** creation in John. And then they would have said God created the small light and the great light in the creation in Genesis, but then God created *Johannan Hamadvil* (John the Baptist) and Yeshua HaMashiach—the small light and the great light—in the ***new*** creation in John. That is how they would have seen it.

In rabbinics, the fig tree is a metaphor for the Tree of Life. It seems to appear in Ezekiel 47, certainly it reappears in the Book of Revelation, and it is in the Garden at the creation. So rabbinically, in the opening chapters of John, when Rabbi Yeshua Ben David (Jesus son of David [that is His real name, *Rabbi Yeshua Ben David*]) sees Nathanael under the fig tree, He was not just saying to him, "I saw you under a literal fig tree over on Main Street" (Jn. 1:48). In rabbinic metaphor, midrashically, he was saying, "I saw you from the creation; from the foundation of the world I foreknew you." The Church does not know how to read the Bible that way anymore. We have lost sight of our roots. We of course are referring here to ancient rabbinics when it comes to Midrash, not the use of Midrash in Talmudic Judaism which developed later.

Going Back to the Root

In Romans 11, Paul says we do not support the root, the root supports us (Rom. 11:17-18). Think of an olive tree: the root is underground and one cannot see the roots. But we know the root is there because if the root was not there, we would not be there either. And if the root dies, we would die. Do not lose sight of the root even though you cannot see it. Stand and interpret the Word of God.

The apostles taught midrashically. Jesus taught midrashically. But as the Church got further and further from its Jewish roots, people began "Greekifying" (or Hellenizing) Christianity. Even in the beginning Paul was trying to contextualize the Gospel for a Greek world; in other words, to explain it to people with a Greek worldview and a Greek mentality in a Greek way. There was the Greek way of thinking and the Hebrew way of thinking – Paul used ***both***. He said Jews seek a sign, Greeks seek wisdom (1

Co. 1:22). He had no problem explaining the Gospel to people in their own framework.

When the Wycliffe translators went to a certain place in equatorial Africa to translate the Bible, people there did not know what "snow" was. So when they got to Isaiah 1:18, "*Though your sins are as scarlet, they will be white as snow*," they translated it, "Your sins will be white as coconut." That is contextualization. It is one thing to explain the Gospel in the ***context*** of somebody else's culture to enable them to understand it, but it is something else to try to ***redefine*** the Gospel or reframe the Gospel in somebody else's philosophy and worldview. And that is what began to happen as the Church got further and further from its Jewish roots, and more and more paganistic influences entered into it.

As a result, the Hebrew way of allegory and typology became replaced by Greek methods. A pivotal person in this was someone called Philo (a pre-Christian figure), as well as the people who imitated him. They began adopting Greek methods of allegory. Today there are people involved in Restorationism and Kingdom Now who are doing the same thing. The core of this comes from Gnosticism. The New Testament uses typology, allegory, and symbolism to ***illustrate*** and ***illuminate*** doctrine; a doctrine is ***never based*** on these things. For instance, in 1 Corinthians Jesus is our "Passover Lamb" (1 Co. 5:7). In the Gospel of John, John the Baptist announces, "*Behold, the Lamb of God who takes away the sin of the world!*" (Jn. 1:29). And in Peter's Epistle he says, "*...as of a lamb unblemished and spotless*" (1 Pe. 1:19). To God, one man without sin is worth more than all the men with sin; that is how one could die for all. When we see Christ in the Passover demonstration, and we understand the symbolism of the Passover meal at the Last Supper, we will understand the Lord's Supper in a way we never could before. Typology and allegory ***illustrate*** and ***illuminate*** doctrine.

The account of Jesus seeing Nathanael under the fig tree ties in with a verse in the Epistles that says, "*those whom He foreknew, He also predestined*" (Rom. 8:29). I did not base the fact that Jesus pre-knew Nathanael on a type or an allegory, I simply said the ***symbolism***—rabbinically—***illustrates*** it. We can dig deeper into the Word of God through the types and allegories contained within it because that is how the New Testament handles Scripture. It is very dangerous, however, and totally unscriptural, for people to base doctrines on some subjective, mystical insight into the types and allegories, or to invent allegories that the

Bible does not make. ***Never*** base a doctrine on an allegory; the Bible never does.

Things Begin to Go Wrong

In Alexandria, Egypt, things really began to go wrong. That was the place where East met West. Buddhist monks, Zoroastrians, and others from the East came to Alexandria and brought Eastern ideas. These Eastern ideas became more and more apparent in the thinking of the Church in all kinds of issues, not the least of which was the way they interpreted the Bible.

Augustine adopted these ideas and took them West to the Roman Empire—ideas such as this: since God knocked Paul to the ground and used violence to convert Paul, the Church has a justification to use violence to convert people. Augustine attached mystical meanings based on Bible passages such as the Good Samaritan, saying his journey from Jerusalem to Jericho is the plight of fallen man. Well, one can say this, and that the Levites and the priests could not really help this man who had fallen. That makes sense. That is biblical so far, but then he goes on to say that the inn keeper is St. Paul, and he gives definitions to the two coins, and all kinds of crazy things. These ideas came from the Greek world and began defining doctrine.

These Gnostic ideas get worse and worse until the Middle Ages. With the Renaissance the Crusades go to the East and they come back to Europe and bring with them Eastern influences from the Islamic world. Remember, when Western Civilization declined under medieval Roman Catholicism, the Byzantine Empire—the eastern part of what had been the Roman Empire—under domination by the Islamic world, was having a golden age in science, history, literature, medicine, architecture, everything. The Crusades brought these things back and that planted the seeds for the Renaissance.

Thomas Aquinas came along and brought in the ideas of Aristotle, replacing the ideas of Plato. And for over a thousand years, Roman Catholic history is the Aristotelians fighting the Platonists. It is crazy. The whole idea of transubstantiation comes from a concept that nobody believes anymore. It is unfounded. The idea of the "accidents" and the host being transubstantiated is absolutely absurd! But that is where it comes from. Be this as it may, we have this whole Aristotelian thing, and then what was already bad in the way they interpreted the Bible became even worse. When the pope was deposed from Rome to Avignon, France, for 70 years they said this event was the Babylonian Captivity! And it gets worse and worse.

Judaism takes the same path under Rambam (Moses Maimonides). What Aristotle did with Christendom, Rambam did likewise with Judaism—he Aristotelianized Judaism. He wrote *The Guide for the Perplexed* which was the Jewish equivalent of Thomas Aquinas' *Summa Theologica*. Things get really bad, and from Aquinas' influence comes this crazy kind of allegorization called "Medieval Scholasticism." Things became theologically and spiritually terrible.

Things Begin to Change Back Somewhat

But then, after the Renaissance, there is this rediscovery of Greek and Roman learning, and people begin studying the classics of Latin and Greek literature. They begin studying it in the plain meaning in the original languages, reading it as literature and history. Then people begin reading the Bible as literature and history. These people were called "Humanists."

Thomas Moore was a Humanist, John Colet was a Humanist, Luther's mentor Staupitz was a Humanist. In France, Levèvre was a Humanist. But the main one was Erasmus. Forget about Luther, Calvin, and Zwingli. All these people are the result of Erasmus of Rotterdam. He was the real brains behind what happened in the Reformation. The others were dynamic personalities, but he was a dynamic thinker; they were his ideas. He laid the egg, the others just hatched it. He began studying the Bible as literature and history, and rediscovered what the Roman Catholic Church had done, how it had gotten away from the simplicity of faith in Jesus. When he did that, he opened the door for people to rediscover justification by faith—the Gospel—that we are not saved by doing penance (going to confession, which was not made a doctrine until the 13th century). The word *metanoia*, when studied in the original Greek, does not mean "to do penance"; it means "to repent." They began reading Romans and Scripture as Luther did, and they rediscovered the Gospel. Luther learned this from Levèvre.

The problem was the Reformers used Humanist scholarship to react against Scholasticism: "We do not want ***any*** kind of allegory. We do not want ***any*** kind of symbolism or typology if it can be avoided. Only if we are forced to do it should we consider it." So what they did was throw out the baby with the bathwater. "We do not want to know about these things" because of what some people do with them.

There are people doing these erroneous things even today in the Reconstructionist Movement and in certain elements of Kingdom Now theology. "We do not want any typology or allegory." So they just reduce the study of Scripture to an academic study of history and literature.

Hence, in reaction to the Gnostic hermeneutics of Kingdom Now dominionists in the Latter-Rain Movement who spiritualize pivotal chapters such as Joel 2 out of all context (as was the forte of the Kansas City "False" Prophets), people are driven to a stoic literalism. At the same time, they react to the ridiculously spiritualized mishandlings of Scripture by proponents of the Toronto, Pensacola and Lakeland deceptions and by such organizations as Promise Keepers. Those reacting revert to the same brand of stoic literalism.

This proverbial tossing out of the baby with the bath water is not a new phenomenon. The Reformers and Humanist scholars who inspired them reacted against medieval Scholasticism and a Roman Catholic version of Gnosticism called "*Sensus Plenior*." This narrow literalism in effect corrects error with error. In ignoring the uses of typology and midrashic hermeneutics in the canon of Scripture, hermeneutical literalists set the stage for other error. While doctrine is ***never based*** on type, allegory or Midrash, such divinely inspired literary devices employed in Scripture do ***illustrate*** and ***illuminate***.

This problem has ancient origins with the rival Antioch and Alexandria schools of biblical interpretation. In Alexandria the proto-Gnosticism of Philo had incipient negative influences on the hermeneutics of Clement and Origen. The Alexandrian School was correct in what it affirmed, but insufficient in what it omitted. The same is largely true of the hermeneutics that the Protestant Reformers borrowed from 16th-century Humanism. For instance, one need only read Calvin's secular work, his commentary on Seneca De Clementia to observe that Calvin's biblical hermeneutics were identical to how he exegeted the Scriptures' doctrine on a deeper and clearer level. This stands in diametric contrast to Gnosticism where symbolism becomes the flawed basis of doctrine.

If we read John Calvin's secular work, his commentary on the Roman writer Seneca De Clementia, Calvin interpreted the Bible with the same rules of literary criticism with which he interpreted secular literature. Calvin's work in turn bequeathed to much of Protestantism the way it interprets the Bible. Thus mainstream Evangelical Protestantism interprets the Bible based on the rules of 16th-century Humanism, studying it as literature and history. This was good as far as it went, in that it helped people see how ridiculous and unscriptural Roman Catholicism was, and to rediscover the Gospel. (Actually, there were people who never lost the Gospel, such as John Wycliffe in England and his followers, as well as several others in Europe. The Protestants pretended they rediscovered the Gospel, but in fact there were people who were more doctrinally sound than the Protestants and who had never lost it to begin with.) So the Reformers threw out all typology and allegory; today's rules for interpreting the Bible come from the Reformers.

Liberal Protestantism says, "We also study the Bible as literature and history. Only the Reformers believed it was inspired; we just think it is literature and history." Liberal Protestantism (non-believing Protestantism) is the degeneration of original Protestantism, but they both interpret the Bible the same way: critically, in the academic sense of studying it as history and literature. It is not wrong to do that, it is not wrong at all. The problem is that this is as far as they go. In other words, while both are Hellenistic in ontogeny, the secular Humanism that gave rise to Darwinist-influenced Higher Criticism is but the later spiritual and intellectual degeneration of the original 16th-century Christianized Humanism that gave rise to the Protestant Reformation.

They make rules which people will teach you. One of their rules is this: when the plain sense of Scripture makes sense, do not seek any further sense. You ever heard that? So Jesus saw Nathanael under the fig tree—big deal, that is all we need to know. No, that is not all we need to know. Jesus was saying something much deeper and much more important and much more profound than seeing him under a literal fig tree. This is a Protestant rule, not a biblical rule: "There are many applications of the Scripture, but only one interpretation." It is purely a well-intentioned yet misguided and unbiblical invention of Protestantism.

The Approach of Jesus and the Rabbis

Ancient rabbis said there are multiple interpretations of Scripture. Jesus agrees with the rabbis, not the Reformers. For example, Jesus told the Jews that there would be no sign given to their generation except the sign of Jonah. (Mt. 12:39; Lk. 11:29). In one of the Gospels it says the sign of Jonah is "*as Jonah was three days in the belly of the sea monster, so will the Son of Man be*" (Mt. 12:40). But in another place He says Nineveh repented—the Gentiles repented—but the Jews would not (Lk. 11:32). He gives two entirely different, but totally valid, meanings for "*the sign of Jonah.*" Jesus was a rabbi who had a rabbinic perspective; He had a Jewish perspective of a Jewish book and He quoted it that way.

Western Protestantism has its own perspective, and it treats it as if it is sacrosanct, as if theirs is the only way to handle Scripture. Jesus never did that. Now it is not wrong to do that; it is not wrong to study it as literature and history and to do our exegesis verse-by-verse, studying the Book of Romans chapter-by-chapter. It is not wrong as long as it is only the first step. But think about it: Jesus never taught exegetically as such; He often taught topically. He would say "It is written," and He would quote from Isaiah. Then He would say, "For it is also written," and quote from Psalms. He argued topically. That is how the rabbis taught.

It was the devil who tried to pick apart one verse with a pair of tweezers and a magnifying glass with "this is what it says" verse-by-verse exegesis. The church in its hermeneutics is following the method of the devil more than the method of Jesus. We are not maintaining that it is wrong to grammatically dissect a verse piece-by-piece in the original Greek, Hebrew, or Aramaic text. It is not wrong, but only correct in as far as it goes. But it fails to go far enough exegetically. It is where Western hermeneutics too often draw the line, and that is the problem. After we pick that verse apart, we can go to a verse speaking on the same subject even if it is not in the same book.

This is what transpires when we try to base doctrine on one passage out of context. We need to think of exegesis as a tripod requiring all three legs to stand—text, context, and not least of all co-text (other verses and passages addressing the same subject and/or applying the same typology; when the same typology is applied in two texts they are usually theologically related even if the connection is secondary and may not be overt).

In most purely Western (Hellenistic/humanistic) approaches, exegesis becomes their text and everything rests on that one text. Luther did that with Romans. We can find hyper-Charismatics and hyper-Pentecostals who will take one verse in Acts and construct a whole theology about the subject in order to promote an unbiblical view of tongues without looking at other things the Bible says. We often find that the Calvinists will take one verse in Romans 8 and construct a whole theology on it. Jesus did not teach that way, He ***never*** taught that way, therefore we should not either.

With all due respect to the Reformers, I can understand why they did what they did; they were trying to correct something. They were reacting to a wrong situation. To a degree, in fact for their time and circumstances, they did the right thing. They may have been faithful to the light they had; we do not say otherwise. But for us, that is not good enough. John Robinson, a chaplain to the Pilgrim fathers, said there is a deeper light in this Book that we do not see. He believed that if Calvin or Luther came back they would complain and say, "Look, we showed you the way back, we showed you the Gospel, we showed you the authority of Scripture instead of tradition, but why didn't you continue on the road on which we sent you? We put you on the right road, but you did not go any further."

Not Just Exclusively Reformers

I am not condemning the Reformers, because they were trying to correct a wrong situation the best they could in a difficult time in history. The problem is what ***we*** have done with it, and also ***failed*** to do with it. The Christianized Humanist scholarship of 16th-century Europe and Britain which intellectually engendered the Reformation and the consequent deeds of the Reformers, to a limited degree at least helped place the true Church back on the right road soteriologically (doctrines of justification by faith and salvation by grace), ecclesiologically (the priesthood of all believers), and hermeneutically (biblical interpretation). The problem is that the Reformers failed to travel on that road back far enough to pre-Patristic apostolic New Testament Christianity, and too much of Protestantism not only progressed no further, but regressed into theological liberalism, Higher Criticism, and Ecumenism reversing back toward Rome.

The saner elements of Anabaptists (such as the early Mennonites), and more obscure Reformers such as Caspar Schwenenfeld in Silesia, attempted to revert to a purely biblical Christianity (a fact noted by Erasmus himself in his preface to Matthew's Gospel and in a letter to a pope), while the Zwickau false prophets of Muenster, and heretics like Severitus, discredited Anabaptist Christianity. The mainstream Anabaptists were far more scriptural.

Unfortunately, most of the Mennonite and Anabaptist sects surviving today have long departed from biblical Evangelicalism, but their forbearers had it right and were often grossly persecuted and murdered in the name of Christ not only by Rome but by Protestants (particularly, but not only, Zwingli) as the terrible price for being by far the most biblical. Their strength was not only in believers baptism and rejection of Erastianism (the church being an agency of the state or the state an agency of the church), but doctrinally and hermeneutically in their rejection of patristic authority. They read Scripture in light of Scripture, not in light of what Augustine said about Scripture as Calvin, Cranmer, and Luther did. They at least wiped the dirty slate clean.

Plainly the apocalyptic literature of the Bible demands something more than the Protestant hermeneutics borrowed from 16th-century neo-Hellenistic Humanism. The Epistles are inspired commentary on other Scripture. We can read the Epistles as letters verse-by-verse, but look how the Epistles handle other Scripture. Looking at Galatians 4:24-34, the example is the two women Sarah and Hagar. That is how it interprets Genesis—that is Midrash. Look at the Epistle of Jude about backsliders and false believers in the churches. It is all Midrash; all of it is *Pesher* interpretation. Scripture does not handle Scripture the way the Gentile Church does.

Someone's computer cannot properly read and decipher highly complex digitalized information unless it has the correct software program for doing so. Too often, what we have today among even conservative Evangelical expositors interpreting eschatology in general, and End Times teaching of the Antichrist specifically, is akin to being able to read an introductory part of an email transmission but not having the right program to open an attachment. In the world of data science, old computer languages such as COBOL and FORTRAN are largely forgotten by most people; only a handful of experts are still familiar with these computer languages, yet everything else in the cyber-world is still built on something that most people can no longer handle.

So, too, the eschatology of the Scriptures is based on an approach to Scripture that was prevalent among the 1st-century authors of the New Testament which was largely based not on later rabbinic Midrash, but on principles first introduced in the books of Chronicles that may be called "midrashic." This includes a use of typology and allegory that is not the ***basis*** for doctrine as in Gnosticism, but is very much the ***illustration*** and ***illumination*** of doctrine. All other Scripture prophecy to do with the Last Days depends upon it, yet in popular theology few have the expertise. This is not to suggest that illumination by the Holy Spirit is not the ultimate imperative in the proper interpretation of God's Word, nor is it to say that it is all a matter of exegetical technique. It is simply to say that too few of us in the Church today can open the attachment, and this is what needs to happen in order for the Antichrist to be revealed to the faithful.

Apocalyptic Literature

We have different literary genres in the Bible. The Epistles are one kind—they are letters. But we have Gospels, narratives, historical books, wisdom literature, and apocalyptic literature such as Revelation, Daniel, etc. Daniel was told, as was John, "*Seal up the book until the end of time*" (Dan. 12:4; Rev. 10:4). These things are sealed up. The Holy Spirit has to decipher what these mysteries of the end and the Antichrist mean for the faithful. They have to be deciphered for the people of God in the end.

Be careful of people who write a commentary on Daniel or Revelation and say they have got it all figured out. Remember, the Bible itself tells us that these things are going to be revealed by the Holy Spirit to the faithful when the time comes. We are never going to understand these things about the End Times and the Last Days using these Western/Gentile/Protestant methods.

Beginning More Simply

Before we begin looking at more complex genres, let us look at a more simple genre, an Epistle.

> *Do not love the world nor the things in the world. If anyone loves the world, the love of the Father is not in him. For all that is in the world, the lust of the flesh and the lust of the eyes and the boastful pride of life, is not from the Father, but is from the world.* (1 Jn. 2:15-16)

All this goes back to the Garden, the way Satan got to Adam and Eve. Then it goes back to the temptation narrative. The same things that Satan tried on Adam he tried on Jesus but failed. The first Adam failed, the second Adam did not fail; Satan failed. These are the things of the world—the cosmos—the lust of the eyes.

> *The world is passing away, and also its lusts; but the one who does the will of God lives forever.*
>
> *Children, it is the last hour; and just as you heard that antichrist is coming, even now many antichrists have appeared; from this we know that it is the last hour. They went out from us, but they were not really of us; for if they had been of us, they would have remained with us; but they went out, so that it would be shown that they all are not of us. But you have an anointing from the Holy One,*

> *and you all know. I have not written to you because you do not know the truth, but because you do know it, and because no lie is of the truth. Who is the liar but the one who denies that Jesus is the Christ? This is the antichrist, the one who denies the Father and the Son. Whoever denies the Son does not have the Father; the one who confesses the Son has the Father also.* (1 Jn. 2:17-23)

First of all, these verses are alluding to Judas: "He went out from among us." Remember, both Judas and the Antichrist –**THE** Antichrist (it is a definite article) are *"son[s] of perdition"* (Jn. 17:12; 2 Th. 2:3). They are the only two people ever possessed by Satan personally. A lot of people are ***demon***-possessed, but not ***satanically***-possessed. There are many, many parallels between Judas and the Antichrist. A false brother going out from among us is one.

But it is saying three things: **THE** Antichrist, antichrists (there are many of them), and what we might call the spirit of antichrist. He is already in the world; he has always been there. Something that denies the Father-Son relationship is, by definition, "Antichrist." The False Prophet and the second Beast of Revelation 13 are co-equally "Antichrist," and likewise have the same spirit. The Antichrist of Revelation 13 (the two Beasts not specifically called "Antichrist" in this chapter) and Satan (as it were the Antichrist, the False Prophet and Satan) constitute the "Diabolical Trinity"—Satan's counterfeit of the Holy Trinity of Father, Son and Holy Spirit. In this the one Beast counterfeits Christ, the False Prophet is the satanic counterfeit of the Holy Spirit, and Satan attempts to usurp the place of the Father. As God the Father achieves His will through Jesus His Son by His Holy Spirit, Satan seeks to mimic this.

Parallels to Ancient Rome

The Greek prefix for "anti" does not simply mean "against"; it also means "in place of." A "vicar" is one who behaves vicariously. If we were to translate "anti" into English, it would be "vicar," as one who acts vicariously on behalf of another. There is someone who is, in fact, the true Vicar of Christ. This is He whom Jesus in the Gospel of John tells us is the Holy Spirit (Jn. 16:13-14). It is the Holy Spirit alone who acts ***in place of*** Christ and brings the indwelling and leading of Christ to us. It is therefore unbiblical and inappropriate that the Church of England calls its pastors "vicars." This is not a valid or accurate translation of either the Greek word for "pastor" –

episcopo, or the Hebrew term *roa*. (Both the Hebrew and Greek terms in actuality mean "shepherd," not "vicar" or "vicarious.")

But there is also obviously someone else who wears a white *kippah* (and he is not even Jewish) who claims to be the "Vicar of Christ." If we were to take the term "the Vicar of Christ"—"*Vicarious Christus*" (which is the pope's Latin title)—and translate it into Greek, it would be *antichristos*. Yet this is only the beginning.

In the early Church there were two kinds of religions: *religio elicita* and *religio illicita*—"legal religions" and "illegal religions." As long as someone acknowledged the emperor they could have any religion they wanted. The Romans would take their god and put it in the Roman Pantheon, making it part of the Roman religious system, the head of the system being the emperor. The emperor's title was "*Pontificus Maximus*" or, for short, "the Pontiff." He was the head of the Pantheon.

There were two classes of people who had a problem with emperor worship: Jews and Christians. Emperor worship is a major element that teaches about the Antichrist. The Jews made a deal: "Since we cannot sacrifice ***to*** the emperor, we will sacrifice ***for*** the emperor." Initially, Christians were protected because they were seen as a messianic sect within Judaism; they were simply Jews who believed Yeshua was the Messiah, so they were protected. But when the rabbis ostracized Jewish believers and booted them out of the synagogue, they were no longer protected. They became *religio illicita* and they were persecuted because they would not bow their knees to the Pontiff.

The Spirit of Antichrist

The spirit of antichrist denies the Father and Son relationship (1 Jn. 4:3). This can be seen in liberal Protestantism which generally holds that "Jesus was just a uniquely inspired man who, as a result, became the Christ." The theological term for this lie in the ancient church is "Adoptionism." Such heresy is ancient. People believed that Jesus was just a great rabbi or a great moral teacher. That is the spirit of antichrist; it denies the Father and Son relationship. As a unique individual, Jesus became God's Son by adoption, not by eternal nature.

Beyond liberal Protestantism, Islam is another example. On the Dome of the Rock on the Temple Mount is a quotation from a Suraht in the *Quran*, "Allah is not begotten and neither does he beget"—"God has no son"—right on the Temple Mount, an abomination of desolation foreshadowing partial fulfillment of the ultimate one. Islam is an Antichrist religion denying the Father-Son relationship and elevating Mohammed above Jesus.

Let us consider what Jesus says about Rabbinic Judaism in the Book of Revelation. He is speaking to the early Church:

> *... the blasphemy by those who say they are Jews and are not, but are a synagogue of Satan.* (Rev. 2:9)

Rabbinic Judaism, not to be confused with Mosaic Judaism, is not the Judaism of the Old Testament or the *Tanak*, but what the rabbis have invented to replace it after the Temple was destroyed. It is a false religion. It is a demonic device of Satan, archenemy of the Jews, to mislead them from their own Messiah and the true meaning of their own Torah in order to destroy their souls (2 Co. 3:14; 2 Co. 4:3-4). It is as Jesus said, "*a synagogue of Satan*" leading precious souls from among God's own covenant people into eternal perdition, and usually rejecting and often persecuting faithful Jews who do believe in their Messiah. The term "synagogue" is of Greek, not Hebrew, origin, essentially meaning in its New Testament usage, "a religious assembling." It has the same root for the term used for the concurrence of the Rapture and Resurrection in 2 Thessalonians 2—*episunagoge*.

Everything from Buddhist and Hindu temples to Jehovah's Witness Kingdom Halls, to mosques, to Roman Catholic churches, are all co-equally "synagogues of Satan"; they ***all*** mislead souls from the true Christ, the true God, the true Gospel, and into damnation. But Jewish synagogues rejecting their own Messiah are no exception, and are cited specifically by Christ in Scripture because salvation itself is to come from the Jews (Jn. 4:22) and not from any Gentile nation or other religion. The One True God is the God of Israel, and the Jewish Messiah alone, who is Yeshua (Jesus), is the one and only agent of salvation for Jew and non-Jew. But His salvation by virtue of covenant is available to the Jew first (Rom. 1:16), and so are the ramifications of rejecting Him (Rom. 2:9).

We see born-again Christians going to these feasts of various kinds in Jerusalem saying, "Judaism! Isn't it wonderful!" They do not know what they are doing when they are elevating rabbis as some kind of holy men. These rabbis do not merely practice Cabala, they practice witchcraft. Jesus calls it "*a synagogue of Satan*" (Rev. 2:9; 3:9).

Christians need to avoid non-evangelistic versions of Philo-Semitism and Christian Zionism, which is just as bad as anti-Semitism. Love the ***Jews***? Yes, but do not love ***Judaism***. If you love Jews you cannot love Rabbinic Judaism; it is a false religion that is leading those people to hell. There is today only one true Judaism: Messianic Judaism, the Judaism fulfilled in Jesus. There was at one time the now-fulfilled Judaism of Moses which prepared the way for Jesus, but today there is but one valid Judaism: belief in Yeshua as Messiah. And then there is this other "ism" we have today that is not the Judaism of the Old Testament, just as Roman Catholicism is not the Christianity of the New Testament. Rabbinic Judaism is fundamentally unscriptural in its rejection of its Messiah.

Organizations like the International Christian Embassy, Bridges For Peace, and others with published non-evangelistic policies are not scriptural. Jews require the Gospel to be saved, which requires its proclamation (Rom. 9:1-3; Rom. 10:4). And those who withhold the preaching of Christ to the Jews will have the blood of the unsaved generally, and the unsaved Jews whom they refuse to evangelize specifically, required of their hands (Ac. 20:26, Eze. 3:18, Eze. 33:6-8). In direct defiance of plain and unambiguous New Testament teaching, many of these organizations hold to a heretical Dual Covenant Theology. They maintain that Jews can be saved by the Torah, which itself cannot be kept since A.D. 70 when the Second Temple was destroyed in fulfillment of the prophesies of Daniel 9 (that the Messiah would come and die prior to its destruction), and by Jesus in the Olivet Discourse. John Hagee, in rejection of the words of Jesus in John 4:26, goes so far as to claim that Jesus never claimed to be the Messiah.

In circa A.D. 90, rabbinic authorities issued a proclamation, "*Birkhat Ha Minim,*" excommunicating Jewish believers in Jesus from the synagogue. To this day certain ultra-orthodox synagogues incorporate a curse on Jewish believers in Jesus into the list of *bruchot* or "blessings" in the *siddur* (liturgy), praying that the names of "*minim*" (Jewish believers in Jesus among them) will be blotted out of the Book of Life. This is direct literal fulfillment of the prophetic prediction of Jesus (Jn. 16:2). It is not only absurd but a slap to the face of Christ and to Jewish believers in Yeshua for Christian Zionist organizations to refuse to evangelize unsaved Jews while pandering to Rabbinic Judaism. Rabbinic Judaism is a false religion controlled by the spirit of antichrist, just as are the Church of Rome, Eastern Orthodoxy, and, worst of all, liberal Protestantism.

The Antichrist will deceive the Jews into believing him to be a messianic figure (Jn. 5:43), coming in the character of the 2nd-century false messiah Simon Bar-Kochba (literally, "son of a star," also known as "*Bar Kozba*" meaning "son of a lie") who tricked the Jews into thinking he was the Messiah with the backing of Rabbi Akiva who counterfeited John the Baptist as the harbinger, and who foreshadows the False Prophet of Revelation 13. He will then, as is commonly accepted, make a treaty with Israel which he will break (Dan. 9:27). Antichrist is the supreme enemy of Israel and Jewry.

The "spirit of antichrist" (working through the *Zeitgeist* or "spirit of the age") is preparing the world generally, the apostate church, and unbelieving Israel specifically, for the advent of the Antichrist—the same as the Holy Spirit is convicting the world of sin and preparing the faithful remnant Church, including the faithful believing remnant of Israel, for the Second Advent of Christ.

As we have the "spirit of antichrist," we also have many antichrists, and there always have been. There are many types of the Antichrist in modern history—political demagogues who demand to be worshiped: Ceauşescu of Romania, Mao Tse Tung, Joseph Stalin, Adolph Hitler, and Idi Amin. These autocrats effectively demanded to be deified; that is the spirit of antichrist and that is the same spirit in Roman Catholicism.

There is the spirit of antichrist, many antichrists, and then ultimately there is ***the*** Antichrist. It helps to recognize the spirit of antichrist and the many antichrists in order to understand the one. Some of these guys take the cake, but ***the*** Antichrist is going to walk off with the whole bakery. It is going to be unbelievable.

Chapter 2: "In Place Of" and "The Pseudologon"

Technically there are three terms for "Antichrist" found in the New Testament. In addition to *antichristos*, meaning the one who wrongly inserts himself in place of Christ, in Revelation 13 the Antichrist and False Prophet are called "Beasts" (not "Antichrists"). The third and final term, however is "*pseudo logos*" (or "*pseudologon*" with a varied case ending) meaning "a false *logos*" or "false word of God" such as in the Greek text of 1 Ti. 4:2.

> *But the Spirit explicitly says that in later times some will fall away from the faith, paying attention to deceitful spirits and doctrines of demons, by means of the hypocrisy of liars ["**pseudologon**"] seared in their own conscience as with a branding iron, men who forbid marriage and advocate abstaining from foods which God has created to be gratefully shared in by those who believe and know the truth.* (1 Ti 4:1–3)

As Jesus is the true incarnate *Logos* and the Word of God (Greek "*Logos*," "*D'var Adonai*" in Hebrew, and "*Mamre*" in Aramaic), conversely, in effect, Jesus in print is "the Truth." (That is, the publication of God's Word is the printed embodiment of Divine Truth while Jesus is the *Logos*, the Word who became flesh in John 1:14.)

Therefore, in the economy of Antichrist there must be a false *logos* or *pseudologon* attempting to operate in place of the *Logos*; bearing in mind that "*pseudo*" implicitly conveys the concept of it trying to appear authentic while it is in fact not only a bogus facsimile but a doctrinal counterfeit contradicting the doctrine of the true *Logos*. (As we shall see in our next section, Peter's Epistle directly eschatologically connects *pseudologon* with false teachers and false prophets.) Under some degree of demonic influence or manipulation these must propagate a false/counterfeit word of God to propound their deceptions. False prophets generally do this with false prophetic words—both proven false prophets in the supposed church sent to deceive the Elect such as Benny Hinn, Kenneth Copeland, Cindy Jacobs, Mike Bickel, Gerald Coates, Paul Cain, C. Peter Wagner, Rick Joyner, and Rodney Howard-Browne, and false prophets in obvious and overt cults and false religions sent to deceive the unregenerate such as Charles Taze Russell, Judge Rutherford, Joseph Smith, Brigham Young, Mohammed and Lucy of Fatima.

False prophets, whose ranks multiply prior to the return of Christ, helping set the stage for the dawn of the Antichrist, bring a *pseudo logos* in accordance with Deuteronomy 18:21-22.

> *"You may say in your heart, 'How will we know the word which the* LORD *has not spoken?' When a prophet speaks in the name of the* LORD, *if the thing does not come about or come true, that is the thing which the* LORD *has not spoken. The prophet has spoken it presumptuously; you shall not be afraid of him."* (Dt. 18:21-22)

They predict in God's name things that fail to happen, bringing a false word of God. These are often predictions directly contrary to biblical truth. False teachers conversely bring a *pseudo logos* with books containing unbiblical doctrine that in effect replace the teaching of Scripture in the undiscerning minds of the readers.

Applied to False Religions and Cults

Among false religions and cults there will be a false Scripture or body of doctrine that exceeds what is written (1 Co. 4:6). Jehovah's Witnesses have *The Watchtower* and *Russell's Sermons* (which he called "the Bible in an arranged form"). To Mormons it is *The Book of Mormon* and other archaeologically debunked texts. To Roman Catholics it is *imprimatur/nihilat obstat* catechisms, creeds of the church, and papal encyclicals. To Rabbinic Judaism it is the Talmud (originally deriving from "*torah b'al pei*"—the "oral law"), the *Schulchan Aruk* (codification of *Halacha* or rabbinic law), and other rabbinic writings such as Rambam's *Guide for the Perplexed* and *Mishnah Torah*, plus mystical cabbalistic literature such as *Zohar* (held particularly to be canonical by ultra-orthodox Hassidic Jews). To Hindus it is the *Bagavahgita* ("*Gita*" is the Hindu equivalent of the gospels), *The Mahabarat* (the Hindu equivalent of *The Book of Joshua*), the *Kama Sutra* (the Hindu equivalent of *Song of Solomon*), etc. With Muslims, their *pseudologon* is the *Quran* and the *Hadith*.

From *The Tibetan Book of The Dead* to *The Aquarian Bible* to the Gnostic gospels there are countless volumes of *pseudologon* materials from Eastern religious sects such as Sikhs to cults such as Antichrist Sun Myung Moon's Unification Church with its *Divine Principle*. To a frightening degree these are deceiving the Elect as Jesus warned in the Olivet Discourse in Matthew 24. Just as the true *Logos* (the Judeo-Christian Scriptures incarnated in Christ) are the "God-breathed" true Word of God, directly inspired by the Holy Spirit, so false religions and cults will have a demonic counterfeit in the form of a *pseudo logos* inspired by the spirit of antichrist.

Gray Areas

There are also more subtle deceptive gray areas such as the canonization of the apocryphal books such as *Maccabees* and *Enoch* by Roman Catholicism, Eastern Orthodoxy, and Rabbinic Judaism. Such books are not a basis of doctrinal authority but do represent biblically important history and literature of practical importance in properly understanding biblically canonical texts such the books of Daniel and Revelation. Other literature in this category would be:

- *The Book of Jasher* (assisting in our understanding of the Book of Genesis);

- *The Shepherd of Hermes* and *The Didache*, (assisting in our understanding of the New Testament in the Early Church);

- *Antiquities* and *Wars of the Jews* by Flavius Josephus (useful in recording the historic fulfillments of Daniel 9 and the introductory portions of the Olivet Discourse);

- Portions of the early *Haggadic Midrashim* and sections of the *Mishnah* (aptly used by Alfred Edersheim in assisting in our understanding of sections of *Tanak* or the Old Testament and the Gospels);

- Eusebius' *History of the Church from Christ to Constantine* (helping in our understanding of the Book of Acts and the Church history immediately following it).

But such literature is not a divinely inspired canonical basis for doctrine. Such works are simply companion literature helping to historically and/or linguistically illuminate the background of certain portions and areas of Scripture and serving to confirm the historicity of Scripture by way of apologetics, etc. Properly understood, these texts cannot be considered inherently *pseudologon* in and of themselves, even though some false churches may misuse them in this way.

The same is true of "patristic authority." Some of the writings of the church fathers mainly defend and support Scripture (e.g., *Against All Heresies* by Irenaeus). Others, particularly around the time, and after the time, of the Council of Nicea, distort, redefine and Platonize Christianity (particularly many of the writings of Augustine of Hippo, despite his being correct in his refutation of the heretic Pelagius). Treated as fallible commentary, the patristic writings of the church fathers can be scrutinized and dissected as merely sanctified opinion (or as the case may be with each of the church fathers, "pseudo-sanctified" opinion, especially among the post-Nicean fathers from the time of Constantine onward). But their writings should ***never*** be treated as a ***basis*** of doctrine even though Roman Catholics, Eastern Orthodox, and Protestants alike have wrongly done so. This has been and remains particularly true of the writings of Augustine in both Roman Catholicism and in Reformed and Lutheran Protestantism, and also of John Chrysostom in Eastern Orthodoxy.

This was one of the fundamental errors of John Calvin, who in his *Institutes* pontificated strongly, citing patristic authority for the establishment of doctrine. On a number of occasions Calvin made such proclamations "on the authority of Augustine." Hence there is a predisposition to spiritual seduction within Protestantism that is no less than what we recognize in Roman Catholicism and Eastern Orthodoxy. The Antichrist and False Prophet will be able to capitalize on such erroneous traditions. There can be no doctrinal authority beyond Scripture (1 Co. 4:6). Bearing in mind that Christ is the *Logos*, something else comes into place that is "***in place of***" the *Logos*.

Like any other opinion, no matter how well-intentioned, not only can the church fathers be either right or wrong, but more commonly (and therefore more problematically) they contain elements of ***both*** truth and error. This combination of truth and error moreover makes it resemble *pseudologon*, even though strictly speaking theses patristic texts are not necessarily that. The majority of patristic literature, while often mistaken in its opinion, is not by definition *pseudologon*. Indeed, few if any of the church fathers themselves, very rarely if ever, intended their views to be held as canon.

We therefore read Scripture prayerfully, illuminated by the Holy Spirit through the prism of other Scripture, and not through the prism of the church fathers, the Reformers, the Credos, the Church Councils, or the popes. Scripture is always primary and the only grounds for doctrine; Old Testament Apocrypha is secondary (because it is cited in canonical Scripture), while other historical sources and sanctified opinion authored by regenerate believers is tertiary. Nonsense such as Gnostic forgeries, pseudigraphical writings, and above all any *pseudologon*, are to be ignored (except to debunk them in evangelism and apologetics). And the works of Philo, other later rabbinic writings, and even the earliest post-apostolic creeds from church councils researched for purely academic purposes are best treated with ultra caution and ***never*** in order to arrive at any doctrine. It is imperative, however that we nonetheless remember that, inspired by the Holy Spirit, the apostles warned of those coming after them in the patristic era bringing unbiblical doctrines.

> *"I know that after my departure savage wolves will come in among you, not sparing the flock; and from among your own selves men will arise, speaking perverse things, to draw away the disciples after them.* (Ac. 20:29-30)

It is also absolutely critical to realize that as the true Church is united, empowered, and guided by the Holy Spirit on the basis of the *Logos*, heretical churches, pseudo-Christian cults, and false religions are united, empowered, and guided by the "spirit of antichrist" on the basis of a *pseudo logos*. Satan always has a counterfeited equivalent, much as the occult counterfeits charismatic gifts of the Holy Spirit.

In Addition to the Logos

Thirdly, in considering the issue of the *Logos* versus the *pseudo logos*, no pseudo-Christian cult or false church can exist without a *pseudo logos* that is added to the actual *Logos*. Roman Catholicism or Mormonism would not deny the validity of the New Testament because of their respective *pseudo logos* any more than rabbis would deny the validity of Torah because of the *Talmud*. What transpires is that the Scripture (*Logos*) is added ***to*** the *pseudologon* in violation of the commandments of Moses, Jesus and the apostles (Dt. 4:2, Dt. 12:32, Prov. 30:6, 1 Co. 4:6, Rev. 22:18-19).

From the "Talmud contra Torah" to papal decrees contra the New Testament, any such addition of a *pseudo logos* inevitably results in a reduction and consequent contradiction or negation of essential components of what is taught by the *Logos*. The authors of these demonically inspired deceptions are self-deluded into falsely believing that Scripture and their writings are compatible and complimentary. This effect increases eschatologically as we draw nearer to the revelation of the Antichrist which precedes and counterfeits the revelation of the true sons God (the *Parousia*) with the return of Christ.

> *But evil men and impostors will proceed from bad to worse, deceiving and being deceived.* (2 Ti. 3:13)

None of these cultic, heretical, or apostate churches (as they call themselves and as are so sociologically identified) controlled by the spirit of antichrist can again exist without a *pseudo logos*. In short they only exist by doing what Jesus, quoting from Isaiah 29:13, condemned the Sanhedrin for, and by becoming what the Sanhedrin and Pharisees were: those who negate the Word of God by attributing to their own inventions a doctrinal authority.

> *"You hypocrites, rightly did Isaiah prophesy of you: 'THIS PEOPLE HONORS ME WITH THEIR LIPS, BUT THEIR HEART IS FAR AWAY FROM ME.* (Mt. 15:7-8)

Without doing this, Roman Catholicism, Eastern Orthodoxy, Mormonism, or Jehovah's Witnesses could not exist, as neither could Talmudic Judaism. While based on *sola scriptura*, someone could (and many have) become biblically Evangelical Christians. Yet no one has ever, or could ever, simply pick up and read a New Testament and become a Roman Catholic, a Mormon, or a Jehovah's Witness. Too many of their most fundamental doctrinal beliefs are alien from the Word of God.

Having already deceived the world, the Jews and non-biblical expressions of Christianity (perhaps better described as "Christendom"), Satan now turns his efforts to deceiving the Elect with a *pseudo logos* in preparation for the emergence of the Antichrist. This is already underway with such *pseudo logos* literature as *The Shack*, Brian McLaren's *Generous Orthodoxy*, Dan Kimball's *The Emergent Church*, and Rick Warren's *Purpose Driven* agenda. As Rick Joyner, Cindy Jacobs, and Gerald Coates are false prophets with false prophecies as their *pseudo logos*, these authors are false teachers along with heretical books as ***their*** *pseudo logos*. Satan's aim is always to have something "**IN PLACE OF**." It is imperative to grasp this because it constitutes the essence of what and who Antichrist is and what it means.

In Place Of

Talmudic Judaism, although having roots with the earlier Pharisaic Schools of Shamai and Hillel, essentially commenced with Rabbi Johannan Ben Zakkai (like St. Paul, a disciple of Rabbi Gemaliel) at the Council of Yavne after the Temple destruction which was prophetically predicted explicitly by Daniel, Jesus, and implicitly by the Epistle of Hebrews. From this time onward the rabbi functioned ***in place of*** the biblical Levitical priesthood, the synagogue functioned ***in place of*** the Temple, and the *mitzvot* ("prescribed works," many of them invented by the rabbinic "tradition of the elders") functioned ***in place of*** the no longer possible Temple sacrifices. Something is always offered "***in place of***."

In Roman Catholicism the inerrancy of Scripture is counterfeited (since the First Vatican Council of 1874) by a claimed papal *Ex Cathedra* infallibility attributing a divine attribute to a fallen man making his pronouncements function ***in place of*** what Scripture actually states and teaches. Such examples are the contra-biblical *Munifenticimus Deu* pronouncement and assorted claims of the immaculate conception and ascension of Mary the mother of Jesus as *Theotikos*, or "mother of God, a pagan concept borrowed from the Babylonian Semiramus and Babylonian Tammuz worship outlawed by Scripture. In Roman Catholicism likewise purgatorial salvation and ritualistic *Ex Opere Operato* sacramental soteriology (salvation by sacraments without the necessity of a personal believing faith by the recipient; e.g., a baptized infant) is put in place of a regenerative biblical salvation of justification by grace through faith.

In Islam, Allah (the Arabian moon god) replaces the God of Israel, Mohammed is in place of Christ as the greatest of God's messengers, and the *Quran* functions in place of the Old and New Testament. It contradicts it by claiming to be the last testament correcting the corrupted previous two. *The Book of Mormon* makes similar bogus claims to being the "Third Testament," when, like the *Quran*, It contradicts the previous two genuine ones. A *pseudologon* always operates with the same focus, "to act in place of" what is actually true, with the short-term aim of drawing the deceived away from true salvation only available in Christ, and the final aim of pointing them toward the Antichrist to come.

Pseudo Logos in the Emergent & Contemporary Church

With the arrival of Rick Warren, Brian McLaren, Rob Bell, Leonard Sweet and other figures in the Emergent Church (McLaren and Warren jointly wrote forewords for Dan Kimball's book *The Emergent Church*), we witness the spirit of antichrist making *pseudo logos* inroads into Evangelical churches.

The Emergent Church is in essence post-Modernism in pseudo-Christian masquerade, or a redefined "paradigm shift" of Christianity (or Christendom) that is a New Age religion literally looking to the mysticism and Gnosticism of the Dark Ages (instead of to the New Testament) as its model. What can be less illuminating than looking to the Dark Ages? Insanely, these deluded people literally look to the post-Patristic period of the 5th through 9th centuries as their blueprint for "Christian" spirituality.

Gnostic Eastern religion originating in Babylon made incipient infiltration into the Judeo-Christian world with the influences of Philo. It has since staged three major invasions of Western Christendom, the first being in the post-Nicean Church with the Gnostic ideas of Basilides, Valentinus, Clement of Alexandria, and Origen, who began to spiritualize biblical texts out of context in isolation from co-text, thus deriving beliefs ascribing subjective, imagined meanings to biblical passages as a ***basis*** for doctrine. The desert fathers followed this while being influenced by Buddhist monasticism.

The second invasion was when the Crusaders introduced the superstitions and idolatry copied from Byzantine Christendom, Shia and Sufi Islam, and Hinduism when the troubadours reached Bombay in the spice trade. Everything from candles, incense, icons, and flagellation rituals to counting repetitive prayers on beads (pioneered by the Dominicans who brutally tortured and exterminated hordes of people in their inquisitions), prayers to the dead (practices condemned as heathen by the Judeo-Christian Scriptures) were transplanted into the churches, monasteries, and convents of Europe.

The third invasion is the current New Age movement where Hindu mysticism and oriental metaphysics are again invading Western society.

Emergent Church advocates seek a refined version of what they think to be Christian by drawing on ancient mystics, medieval religious philosophies and practices rooted in mysticism such as *Lectio Divina*, contemplative prayer, and visualization in the style of the later post-Reformation brainwashing *Exercises* of Ignatius Loyola (founder of the Jesuits who slaughtered droves of Bible-believing Christians). The predecessors of what would become known as "emergence" was Joyce Hugget who taught Hinduistic breathing exercises adopted from Yoga and Jesuit visualization techniques, and author Richard Foster who penned *The Celebration of Discipline*. The false prophet cum guru of this neo-mystical movement of the post-modernist New Age church, however, was the late Jesuit author Teilhard De Chardin. Most emergence and mysticism is either directly or indirectly influenced by his demonically inspired seminal influence.

The stage was set for this seduction by extremist elements of modern Pentecostalism and hyper-Charismatic Christianity (better termed "charismania"). A biblical understanding of charismatic gifts and the ministry of the Holy Spirit are not to be rejected, and the error of Cessationism (the outlandish belief that biblical charismata ended with the original Apostles) is to be rejected (1 Ti. 4:14, 1 Co. 14:39, Rom. 11:29). Yet the apostasy, experiential theology, and counterfeits of authentic charismata with no testing of these revelations or manifestations with Scripture (1 Co. 14:29) prevails in most of today's charismatic churches, and popular Pentecostalism remains a very dangerous snare of Satan. Those seduced by demonic lies in Toronto, Pensacola, and Lakeland marked by wild, frantic, uncontrolled frenzy on top of unbiblical doctrine failed to grasp that the fruit of the Spirit is self-control (*egkrateia* in Gal. 5:23) and not the lack of it. The pandemonium is a deed of the flesh generated by the spirit of antichrist heralding the coming of the Beast.

The mysticism, emotionalism, often heretical doctrine, counterfeit revivals, ecumenism, Word-Faith money preaching, and, above all, Experiential (instead of biblical) Theology of most of the charismatic movement and much of mainstream Pentecostalism was Satan's means to lure Christians to the wider apostasy represented by the Emergent Church and its varied adjuncts, heresy, post-Modernism lies, and mysticism. (This is not, however, to assail a proper exercise of charismatic gifts of the Spirit or biblical Pentecostalism.)

Going beyond emergence, there is yet another dimension of post-Modern spiritual seduction aimed at the Body of Christ. With an occult interpretation of theoretical elements of particle physics and a new philosophical reinterpretation of the world of physics after Einstein, we also see a philosophical post-relativism that ventures beyond post-relativity. As the astronomy of Galileo and Copernicus went beyond Ptolemais, and as the physics of Einstein went beyond Newton, particle physics and astrophysics alike are once again on the precipice of a new horizon. Unfortunately, not only has this resulted in new emphases in philosophy and worldviews, but a new emphasis in theology that is neither scriptural nor scientific, but pseudo-scientific and mystical.

The popular term is "quantum thinking" involving fractals and other concepts transversing even beyond conventional notions of modern New Age thinking and neo-Gnosticism. These ideas are becoming increasingly incipient in the apostate church and even among the supposed Evangelicals being seduced by it. In short, it is pantheism packaged in new thought, and it has influenced such figures as Eugene Peterson and William Young. It may be described as the neo-theology of chaos theory and has more to do with Marilyn Ferguson and Aldus Huxley than with Matthew, Mark, Luke, or John. More problematic, it accounts for the "God is in everything" New Age orientation and the thinking of Rick Warren. It does not derive from proven science, but from unproven theory, and is not related to particle physics or cosmology itself, but to a subjective interpretation that is largely mystical in origin.

We must remember that the spiritual seduction which commenced in the Garden with the fall of man at the dawn of human civilization found its stratospheric launch in Babylon with its infamous Tower. In the pre-Christian era the seduction of mysticism and false religion originated in the East as the prophet Isaiah warned (Is. 2:6). In this sense we might say the first major type of the Antichrist was Nimrod. But that spirit continues to permeate religious thinking not only in the long-recognized neo-Babylonian character of Roman Catholicism and Eastern Orthodoxy, but also now in the modern New Age Movement that has so aptly infiltrated much of Evangelicalism through the Ecumenical Movement and in the form of the Emergent Church. Nimrod died, but his legacy will endure until Christ destroys the Antichrist.

Also, however, New Age is not actually "new" but ancient. The "as above, so below" proposition was central to the thinking of ancient mystics. Now it has come to church. What we have is metaphysics masquerading as physics and ancient mysticism masquerading as newfound theology. Such things are acutely preparing the way for Antichrist and the distorted thinking that characterizes it is animated by the spirit of antichrist.

Once the Door Was Opened

The main door into the Emergent Church, however, has been *The Purpose Driven* lie with its social gospel, interfaith spiritual pluralism, repentance-free gospel, and psychologized soothsaying that has replaced biblical exposition.

The charismania and hyper-Pentecostalism seen since the Toronto Experience (of John and Carol Arnott, Ken Gott, Colin Dye, Wynne Lewis, Randy Clark, Rodney Howard-Browne, Mark Du Pont, Andrew Evans , Ian Bilby, Philip Hills, Stacy Campbell, Kenneth Copeland, Mike Evans and others), the Brownsville Pensacola deception (of John Kirkpatrick and Michael Brown), or the Lakeland fiasco (of Todd Bentley and the Strader clan, supported by C. Peter Wagner, Bill Johnson, and Rick Joyner) was the climactic aftermath of Pentecostalism gone apostate.

This followed the de facto acceptance of the Manifest Sons/Latter Rain insanity of deranged figures like William Branham which were once rejected by early Pentecostalism, and the Word-Faith "Jesus Died Spiritually" heresy that E. W. Kenyon borrowed from the Christian Science cult of Mary Baker Eddy, becoming the underlying message of hyper-Pentecostal televangelist money preachers. These trends among hyper-Pentecostal and ultra-charismatic churches were the lure toward emergence.

The *Purpose Driven* agenda of Rick Warren is the door into emergence; the Emergent Church itself is the trap. While Brian McLaren has been the guru of emergence, Rick Warren has held the key to enter into it. Based on the marketing psychology of the late Peter Drucker (a non-believer), Warren's unbiblical ideas also have incipient roots in Robert Schuller's Crystal Cathedral in Garden Grove, California, and Bill Hybels' "seeker sensitive" Willow Creek Church near Chicago.

Once again, Antichrist and *pseudologon* are by biblical definition always "in place of" what and who are true. Biblical Christianity depends on the propositional truth of the historicity of the resurrection as a literal, objective, historical, propositional true fact. (Propositional truth is an objective either-true-or-false statement). According to St. Paul, it is the heart of the Christian faith.

> *But if there is no resurrection of the dead, not even Christ has been raised; and if Christ has not been raised, then our preaching is vain, your faith also is vain. Moreover we are even found to be false*

> *witnesses of God, because we testified against God that He raised Christ, whom He did not raise, if in fact the dead are not raised.* (1 Co. 15:13–15)

Christ crucified, Christ arisen, and Christ returning, are the propositional truths upon which biblical Christianity depends. Abandoning this biblical truth, former English teacher Brian McLaren preaches that Christianity is not, and never was, based on propositional truth. McLaren's book *A Generous Orthodoxy* would be better titled "An Apostate Heterodoxy." Moreover, his book on parables states that the key to understanding the parables is found in the use of one's imagination. This is pure Gnosticism; one can imagine or dream up any meaning they wish without any inductive regard to exegetical text or context. In McLaren's emergent world of pseudo-Christian post-Modernism, subjective delusion operates in place of objective truth. What is really happening is that the spirit of antichrist is operating ***in place of*** the Holy Spirit of Jesus.

Further Corruption of the Gospel

The thinly disguised Antichrist nature of the *Purpose Driven* agenda should not be understated. We do not suggest Mr. Warren or his followers are fully cognizant of this; they not only deceive others, but are, in fact, deceived themselves (2 Ti. 3:13). Rick Warren's theological modus operandi is likewise satanic in origin. In Isaiah and Ephesians we see that God's peace plan is enacted as a result of biblical evangelism.

> *How lovely on the mountains*
> *Are the feet of him who brings good news,*
> *Who announces peace*
> *And brings good news of happiness,*
> *Who announces salvation,*
> *And says to Zion, "Your God reigns!"* (Is. 52:7)

> *and having shod YOUR FEET WITH THE PREPARATION OF THE GOSPEL OF PEACE;* (Eph. 6:15)

Jesus taught that His peace was not as the world gives (the Hellenistic concept of *eireen*—an absence of conflict), but the Hebrew concept of "*shalom*" from the infinitive of the Hebrew verb *L'shalem* meaning "to pay, to fill, and fulfill." *Shalom* is the result of believing the biblical Gospel which demands repentance from sin (Acts 2:38). Upon regeneration believers have *shalom* because Jesus came to *L'Shalem*—to ***pay*** the price for our sin, to ***fill*** us with His Spirit, and to ***fulfill*** the Torah (Law of God). In the millennial reign of Jesus, God's peace will certainly include the absence of conflict (Is. 2:4), but that is not per se the divine peace provided in ***this*** life.

Believers can have *shalom* now through means of the Gospel. A truly saved Christian can be in the midst of the biggest crises of his life and yet have *shalom* through the power of the Gospel. He can have peace with God no matter how turbulent the temporary situations of this fallen world (Phil. 4:7, Col. 1:20). Far from bringing *eireen* (until Christ establishes His Messianic Kingdom), Christ will have it removed (Rev. 6:4). Once again, in Rick Warren's *pseudologon* a false *eireen* functions in place of God's true *shalom*.

Rick Warren teaches something different in other crucial areas as well. Confusing justification with sanctification, Warren urges a non-repentant substitute for biblical evangelism, proposing that when someone sees a non-believer involved in substance abuse or living immorally that non-believer should not be told to repent, but rather to ask Jesus into their lives and then He will clean them up. Biblically, in the true Gospel, if there is no *eklenctic* (conviction if sin), and no repentance, Jesus just is not coming into their life until and unless there ***is*** repentance. The *Purpose Driven* lie is, among other things, a false gospel whose preachers are accursed by God (Gal. 1:8), and is a formula for false conversion. There is no real Gospel, hence no Christ. And if there is no Christ there is no peace.

The *Purpose Driven* gospel of Rick Warren functions ***in place of*** the true Gospel of Jesus Christ; his *Purpose Driven Life* is a *pseudologon* functioning ***in place of*** the *Logos*. Instead of the Holy Spirit convicting of sin and drawing sinners to Christ, the spirit of antichrist deceives and leads them away.

Divergent Rather Than Emergent

More diabolical than Rick Warren, however, is Britain's "evangelical" premier youth minister Steve Chalke, who claims he no longer believes that Jesus atoned for his sin because such substitutionary propitiation would make God the quintessential cosmic child abuser. These views are approximated by the son of Tony Campolo, Bart Campolo, who states that if there are biblical passages he disagrees with, such as condemning homosexuality or judgment for homosexuals, etc., he will simply ignore them or interpret them away. His father, Tony Campolo, went so far as to state on BBC radio that the reason God loved King David was because even when David sinned he did so with "gusto." In fact God hated his sin but heard his repentant supplication in Psalm 51.

Mr. Chalke goes down the same "religious pluralism" road as the Vatican and at this point has ventured down that "common ground" road even further than Rick Warren and Britain's Colin Chapman, a former Evangelical from the Church of England who asserts that he cannot say Muslims and Hindus cannot be saved without faith in Jesus. Steve Chalke openly teaches Britain's Christian youth that Muslims and Hindus can even be born-again and saved without a faith in Jesus because of "true things" within those religions.

The Emergent Church depends crucially on a diminution of the Word of God in order for emergence to exist. Again, in the very style imitated from Lucifer by power of the spirit of antichrist coming as an angel of light straight from the text of 2 Corinthians 11, Emergent Church proponent Rob Bell borrows the old Roman Catholic argument against "Evangelical Protestantism," warning against "Bible-olatry" as if it is a form of idolatry. In fact, as Jesus is the Word who became incarnate, and since He is God, how can worshipfully holding scriptural doctrine as Christ Himself or Christ as Scripture incarnate itself (being the very nature of the divine *Logos*) be called "idolatry" either biblically ***or*** logically? Some have tried to claim that "God is greater than His Word." In truth, God claims that He magnifies His Word above His name (the essence of His eternal Triune being) in Psalm 138:2. Mr. Bell's biblically irrational argument can only reflect an unbelievable ignorance, an unbelievable intended wickedness, or both.

What is being witnessed today is a new humanistic religion colored by demonic mysticism and New Age religiosity that is packaged in psychology which has hijacked the "Christian" name. It all is ***in place of*** the *Logos* and comes proclaimed by those in the character of Lucifer appearing as angels of light of whom the true *Logos* commands us to be aware (2 Co. 11:13-15).

Pseudologon Books

In examining the spectrum of most best-selling Christian books of recent years, some of these such as *The Prayer of Jabez* (reducing the biblical prayer from 2 Chronicles into an incantation formula guaranteed to get the desired results) are too silly to warrant serious comment. But others, while ridiculous, are lethal due to the undiscerning biblical ignorance of the majority of modern Christian readership.

The Shack has a pantheistic New Age concept of God in place of the God of the Judeo-Christian Scriptures. *The God Chasers* demeans the Epistles as "dusty old letters" instead of the eternal Word of God; in that book the New Testament is where God was then, but readers are told they must chase to where He is now.

As God's Word is eternal, and His Son is His Word, there is no euphemism for this wicked book other than unmitigated apostasy. It is a kind of current fad functioning ***in place of*** the eternal relevance of biblical truth.

In 1 Timothy 4, the apostle Paul warns of such *pseudo logos* books that come in the Last Days, and that their authors will be demonically inspired, backslidden apostates with dysfunctional consciences espousing teachings that are purely demonic in origin. He then goes on to list the kinds of things they will propagate, such as dietary legalism (extremist elements of the Messianic Movement attempting to nomianistically live under two covenants as do Seventh-day Adventists), and those who leave sound biblical doctrine for a mythologized Christianity (*The Shack*, the Faith-Prosperity gospel or whatever tickling their ears appeals to their carnal nature), and acceptors of mandatory celibacy (ecumenical Evangelicals such as Chuck Colson compromising with the depravity and lies of a false Roman Catholic demonic doctrine).

The False Peace Plan

Far more seriously still, believers are specifically and in no uncertain terms to be aware of those with a different peace plan from God's who will come in the Last Days.

> *While they are saying, "Peace and safety!" then destruction will come upon them suddenly like labor pains upon a woman with child, and they will not escape.* (1 Th. 5:3)

They are warned of those like Rick Warren who will come in the Last Days just as such deceivers came in the days of Jeremiah, saying, "Peace, peace" when there can be no peace without Christ.

> *"They have healed the brokenness of My people superficially, Saying, 'Peace, peace,' But there is no peace.* (Jer. 6:14)

Rick Warren's P.E.A.C.E. plan needs no Christ. In Davos, Switzerland, Warren spoke of a future world of religious pluralism. Rick Warren is correct in that this is what the Book of Revelation calls "*Babylon the Great*," the religious platform for the Antichrist for whom Rick Warren is helping pave the way under the inspiration of the spirit of antichrist. Warren's acronym P.E.A.C.E. plan is:

P = **P**romoting Reconciliation	Biblically this requires the Gospel and a saving faith in Jesus according to Ephesians 2:13-14 which is not included in Rick Warren's idea of promoting reconciliation.
E = **E**quip Servant Leaders	Biblically equipping requires an emphasis on Scripture according to 2 Timothy 3:16-17. Scripture is not Rick Warren's emphasis.
A = **A**ssisting The Poor	While helping the poor is indeed biblical, we are told that Christ came that the biblical Gospel would be preached to them according to Jesus Himself in Luke 4:18 and Matthew 11:5; yet again this is not found in Mr. Warren's plan.
C = **C**aring For The Sick	Again biblically this is necessary but only done as part and parcel of preaching the Gospel. (Mt. 5:11)
E = **E**ducation	Where in Scripture (or indeed in history) has education ever engendered peace? While we agree with education, it is not a key to peace unless the biblical model of education is followed which is predicated upon a saving faith in Christ according to 1 Timothy 4:10-11; Timothy speaks more of educating – *didaskalia* – than any other Book in Scripture.

Given the fact that Rick Warren has two E's in his peace plan, should not at least one of them be "Evangelism," since evangelism is central to God's peace plan? (Over the years Warren continually changes the components of this acronym but the results remain tame.)

What Rick Warren has, however, is not ***God's*** peace plan but his ***own***. As always with a *pseudo logos*, a counterfeit functions ***in place of*** what is in the *Logos*. Rick Warren's P.E.A.C.E. plan is a purely social gospel with no power of salvation. Mr. Warren says he can work for his peace plan with Hindus, Muslims, unbelieving Jews, or any other faith apart from Jesus Christ, the Prince of Peace, through whom only real peace can ever come.

As Scripture warns, a time will come in the Last Days when they will say, "*peace and safety*," then destruction will come. Rick Warren's P.E.A.C.E. plan offers a false peace. Scripture warns that the Antichrist will broker a false peace (Dan. 7:27; 11:31). It is little wonder that Rick Warren, contrary to the instructions of Jesus in the Olivet Discourse in Matthew 24:42, tells his *Purpose Driven* followers to avoid end-times prophecy. Satan does not want the Church ready for what lies ahead, and neither does Rick Warren. Both Rick Warren and the Antichrist have a false peace plan because both are, in fact, driven by the spirit of antichrist.

The Counterfeit Employs the Counterfeit

The present situation, however, ventures even beyond this. The Bible of choice of mainstream Protestant denominationalism is increasing becoming "inclusivist" translations filtering out passages they disagree with, such as portions of Deuteronomy and Romans 1 warning against homosexuality. Rick Warren and his *Purpose Driven* agenda and partners, the Emergent Church pundits, have abandoned not only literalist but even dynamic equivalent translations in favor of a paraphrase often bearing no relation to the original Hebrew, Aramaic, and Greek autographs. In his writing, Rick Warren shifts from translation to translation using a "proof texting" hermeneutic trying to find the version that he can use (or misuse) to fit his own position instead of allowing the text to speak for itself. Ultimately he has no translation of choice, but rather a fanciful ***mis***translation of choice: Eugene Peterson's *The Message*.

This is the very last approach of the ultimate *pseudologon*, a kind of paraphrase that in effect is a counterfeit Bible in and of itself. Here once again is something which textually and functionally is "***in place of***" the Word of God, actually claiming to ***be*** the Word of God and ***accepted*** as being valid Scripture, which it most certainly is not. As the Holy Spirit inspired authorship of Holy Writ, the spirit of antichrist inspires inclusivist and hyper-paraphrased bibles such as *The Message*.

The Word of God is used by the Holy Spirit to prepare the faithful Church for the return of Jesus Christ; these hyper- paraphrases and inclusivist bibles are used by the spirit of antichrist to prepare the apostate church for the dawn of the Antichrist, while its arch-proponent is used by

Satan to tell the Church to not even entertain the subject of the coming return of Christ. As true teachers and true prophets prepare the faithful Bride for the Second Coming of Christ, false teachers and false prophets prepare the apostate church for the Antichrist.

Truth Next to Error

> *But false prophets also arose among the people, just as there will also be false teachers among you, who will secretly introduce destructive heresies, even denying the Master who bought them, bringing swift destruction upon themselves.* (2 Pe. 2:1)

Notice that Peter is inspired by the Holy Spirit to use "false teachers" and "false prophets" interchangeably. The reason he does this is because if somebody's ***doctrine*** is wrong, if their ***teaching*** is wrong, if their "***didaskin***" is wrong, then their ***prophecies*** will be wrong.

Why do people like Rick Joyner, Cindy Jacobs, C. Peter Wagner, Mike Bickel, Bill Johnson, Paul Cain, Kenneth Copeland and Benny Hinn prophetically predict things that do not happen? Why do they get it wrong so often? There are fortune tellers and astrologists using con-artistry and occult means who are more accurate than many people in the Church claiming to be prophets. People who openly practice the occult—witchcraft—have a better track record than people like Benny Hinn and Cindy Jacobs. As fortune tellers sometimes have a demonic power called "familiar spirits" ("*ovot*" in Hebrew), not infrequently so do some false prophets in the Church.

As in Jeremiah 23:13, most commonly these masquerade as God just as the false prophets prophesied by Baal in order to confuse this demon idol with Yahweh. (*Baal* is the Hebrew term for "husband" and "master" where Yahweh is Israel's true Baal in the Book of Hosea, etc., but the Canaanites had a pagan equivalent with backslidden Israel and Judah confusing the two.) More often they simply copy other false prophets (Jer. 23:27) or prophesy from the futility, guessing, and deception of their own carnal imaginations (Jer. 23:16, 26, 32). The themes of Jeremiah such as Babylon, the Temple destruction, but most of all false prophets, provide a backdrop for New Testament eschatology with these themes recycled in *Pesher* interpretations in the Olivet Discourse and in the Book of Revelation.

Why do these false predictors get it wrong? Their prophecies are wrong because their ***doctrine*** is wrong. If somebody's ***teaching*** is wrong their

prophecies will be wrong. God will not give a prophetic revelation, certainly not something with some future prediction, to somebody who is unable to test its weight and evaluate it biblically. It just does not work that way.

But it specifically states...

> *...who will secretly introduce destructive heresies...*

The Greek prefix "para" as in "paramedic," "paralegal," "paramilitary" means "next to." The Greek word used here for "destructive heresies" is "*pareisaxousin*," which means they put truth next to error.

As Scripture warns, God does not like a mixture. The Hebrews could not make a garment of wool and flax (Dt. 22:11). In Laodicea there was the hot water and the cold—"I wish you were either cold or hot." But when there is the mixture—the lukewarm—it is spit out (Rev. 3:16). Forget about the argument there is "some" good in it, that there is "some" truth in it, so "We'll take the 'good' bits." That is man's wisdom not God's. "*A little leaven leavens the whole lump*" (1 Co. 5:6; Gal. 5:9). But it says when they do this they will deny "*the Master who bought them*." Believers will see this and then they will know.

Kenneth Copeland said on television once (and it is on a DVD) that he could have died for our sins instead of Jesus Christ because he is born-again. He denies the Master who bought him. On the cross Jesus said, "*It is finished!*" (Jn. 19:30) and, "*Father, into Your hands I commend My spirit*" (Jn. 19:30; Lk. 23:46).

These false teachers say, "No, Satan got the victory on the cross; Jesus was tortured in hell three days and three nights and had to be born-again in hell after He became one nature with Satan." They deny the Master who bought them.

The believability, the credibility, the plausibility of the Gospel depends on the historicity of the resurrection. If Christ is not risen as an objective, historical fact, the New Testament actually says we should be gambling and getting drunk and fornicating and carrying on with the world (1 Co. 15:32). We are foolish for not living decadent, immoral lives. We are foolish to believe what we believe. We should be out living like the world does, partying with the world. We are foolish for not being like them if Christ is not risen.

Again, we have the Emergent Church demagogue Brian McLaren telling people Christianity is not now, nor has it ever been, based on propositional truth. If Christ has not risen as a propositional truth, then there is no Gospel worth believing! They deny the Master who bought them. And they always play the same game: they put truth next to error.

The Allure of Sensuality

> *Many will follow their sensuality, and because of them the way of the truth will be maligned;* (2 Pe. 2:2)

What draws people to follow such false teachers as Kenneth Copeland, or Benny Hinn, or Cindy Jacobs? These people are sensual and those who are led by sensuality are attracted to them.

Some of the videos of the "Laughing Revival" in Toronto were not only sensual, they were sexual; they were vulgar; they were immoral; they were unspeakable. Something happens when the biblical base is lost: feeling and emotion become confused with spirituality. Once the Bible is thrown out, so goes with it discernment; what follows is a spirit of sensuality taking over, which they imagine to be spiritual.

This is exactly, precisely what takes place in Kundalini Yoga within mystical Buddhism and Hinduism; it is the reproduction of Kundalini Yoga, the serpent's spirit. The soothsayer at Philippi had a python spirit (Ac. 16:16). It goes back to the snake, the serpent in the Garden. People are drawn into it by sensuality. Emotion and physical expression are to be controlled and applied in a biblical and godly way. They are to be the "tools," not the "carpenter"; they are to be the "servants," not the "master." But where there is sensuality, the sensuality usurps what should be the new creation controlling these things. The new creation, in league with and motivated by God's Spirit, is intended to work on the basis of His Word. This gets usurped.

So there is an element of sensuality in this process. Sensuality leads itself to spiritual seduction and even to something called "post-hypnotic suggestion." Psychologically it leaves people open to post-hypnotic suggestion, but theologically it leaves them open to spiritual seduction. A lot of what is seen today is a combination of spiritual seduction and post-hypnotic suggestion.

...the way of the truth will be maligned..."

Jesus is the Way, the Truth, and the Life (Jn. 14:6). He is the ***Way of Truth***—the ***real*** Jesus and His teaching. The way of salvation becomes maligned and what follows?

> *...and in their greed they will exploit you with false words.* (2 Pe. 2:3)

According to Peter, writing under direct apostolic inspiration of the Holy Spirit, those who do this are financially motivated. They have an economic incentive to malign the Word of God and manipulate people with sensuality, calling it "spirituality." But this reveals an important character trait on their part. In order to do this, their greed motivates them to exploit others with their false words.

Imitations of the Real Thing

Jesus is the "*Logos*," the incarnate Word. "*En arche kai ho logos*"—"*In the beginning was the Word*" (Jn. 1:1). The Word is the Bible, the Word is Jesus. (Again, in Hebrew it is "*D'var Adonai*" and in Aramaic "*Mamre.*")

The Greek language has case endings—nominative, accusative, genitive—but "*logon*" is the same word. It simply conveys how the word "*logos*" is used in a sentence (explaining who is the performer and who is the recipient of the action). In Greek the order of words does not matter; words can be placed in any order because the case ending will identify who is the subject, who is the object, and so forth. Word order is irrelevant. But when considering the spirit of truth and the spirit of error in 1 John, we understand "*pseudologon.*" We have a "*logon*" and a "*pseudologon,*" a false word of God which those trapped in error believe. And if they have a spirit of error they are given over in judgment by God to believe it.

As already explained and noted, *The Book of Mormon* is a *pseudologon. The Watchtower* is a *pseudologon*. A papal encyclical is a *pseudologon*. The *Quran* is a *pseudologon*. All these cults and religions have *pseudologons* which attempt to mimic, imitate or counterfeit the Bible in some way. The *Quran* takes biblical passages and twists and changes them. The Mormons put *The Book of Mormon* into King James English to try and make it look like Scripture. They all try to make it ***look*** like the *Logos. Pseudologon* will always try to ***look*** like the *Logos*. They all try to mimic the Word of God in some way; they all ape the Word of God and people get taken in by it. The Mormons have television commercials in America: "It's another testament of Jesus Christ." They try to make it ***look*** the same as the first one. This is a *pseudologon.*

As previously explained, *pseudologon* is the other term for "Antichrist" which most people do not think of. "Antichrist" means "in place of Christ" or "a false Christ." As Jesus is the Word or incarnate *Logos*, a false word of God is something counterfeiting and putting itself in the place of the *Logos*. However, there is a term employed in 2 Peter 2:3 that is just as important, but it is ***not*** a *pseudologon*. When understood in the original Greek language it is really very shocking.

> *Kai en pleonexia* ***<u>plastios logois</u>*** *oupas emporeusontai hois to krima ekpalai ouk argei kai he apoleia auton ou nystazei.*

"***Plastios*** *logon*."

"*Plastios*" is the source of two English words. It is the ancient Greek word for "fabricated," but it is also the root from which the English word "plastic" is derived. Literally translated it means "the plastic Bible."

> *...in their greed they will exploit you...*

They are looking to exploit others, to exploit Christians. Bear in mind that Peter is writing mainly to Jewish believers. That is also important and interesting. They will exploit others with a "plastic Bible"—*plastios logos*. That is quite a thing. In their greed they will exploit others with a plastic Bible.

Cults, false religions, corruptions of Christianity which are obviously non-Evangelical in the biblical sense because they promote a different gospel will normally have a *pseudologon*. They will have a *Book of Mormon*, a *Watchtower*, a papal encyclical—some source of doctrine claiming to carry inspirational authority on par with Scripture which will in some manner always supplant the true teachings of Scripture; they will have a *pseudologon*—another book which they claim is equal in authority to the Scriptures. But now Peter addresses something even more sinister: this is the *plastios logos*. This is a maligning of the ***actual*** Bible. It is not another book like *The Book of Mormon*, it is not another book like the *Quran*; this is an actual hatchet job on the Word of God ***itself***.

Their Own Interpretation in Place of the Biblical

As with Jude's Epistle, the context of Peter's Epistle is undergirded by an eschatological emphasis. Right after this he begins speaking about events to come eschatologically, comparing Sodom and Gomorrah and the rescue of Lot to the coming Rapture and so forth. He puts this into an eschatological context. As with the Olivet Discourse, the Sodom and diluvian themes are typological illustrations of eschatological events to come. But understand the relationship between *pseudo logos* and *plastios logos* in context to the previous chapter. Remember, there is no chapter division in the original Greek.

> *But know this first of all, that no prophecy of Scripture is a matter of one's own interpretation, (1 Pe. 1:20)*

When these individuals engage in this practice, one of the first things—if not ***the*** first thing—they do is make biblical prophecy a matter of their own interpretation, often to the point of being ridiculous.

> *Hear the word of the LORD, you who tremble at His word...* (Is. 66:5)

Some of the advocates of these counterfeit revivals have claimed that Isaiah 66:5 is a prophecy justifying someone behaving irrationally, vibrating and shaking uncontrollably. This of course is an exegetical distortion that appeals only to the sensuality of scripturally ignorant Christians. More seriously, however, in the UK Patrick Dixon has argued that an altered state of consciousness, a phenomenon of Eastern Mysticism, is a manifestation of the Holy Spirit that is characterized by irrational behavior. Such error and false teaching is notoriously dangerous. The lack of self-control and the absence of the power of a sound mind can only lead us to conclude graphically on the basis of God's Word that such madness is just that—a delusional religious madness that has nothing to do with the Holy Spirit. Thus we must keep in front of us the awareness that Antichrist does not merely involve a counterfeit of Christ, but a counterfeit of His surrogate, the Holy Spirit, as well as a *pseudologon*—the counterfeit of His Word.

To anyone having a scripturally grounded doctrinal theology guided by the illumination of the Holy Spirit and the discernment that naturally goes with it, it is frighteningly obvious how the dangerous seduction posed by deceived men such as Patrick Dixon is controlled by the spirit of antichrist. It is predisposing to deception by the coming Antichrist, those who subscribe to such seduction. Such people will easily be deceived by the Antichrist because they are ***already*** deceived by the spirit of antichrist, and are reading *pseudologon* Antichrist books at the expense of rightly dividing the Word of God.

The Original Languages

In Nehemiah 8:8 the historical setting is the time when the people come back from the Captivity in Babylon. At that particular time, Hebrew was merely a liturgical language known, essentially, only by the Levitical priests. The common people had taken on the *lingua franca*, which was Chaldee, the original Aramaic. There was a Hebrew dialect of Aramaic that is the closest thing to it, probably what Jesus would have spoken. Something called a *Peshita Text* is probably the closest example we have of it, but they spoke Aramaic; they did not know Hebrew that well because it had become a liturgical, or ceremonial, language.

> *They read from the book from the law of God...*

Actually it would have been a scroll, a "*megilot torah*"...

> *...translating to give the sense so that they understood the reading.*
> (Neh. 8:8)

Not the ***meaning***, but the ***reading***. God gave His Word in Hebrew, Greek, and in certain sections of Daniel, Aramaic. The priority is always on the original manuscripts in the original languages. These are called "autographs."

Jesus is fully human and fully divine. He's not 50% God, 50% man—that was the Greek concept. Hercules was half man and half god. That was the Greek concept. Jesus is not half-and-half; He is 100% and 100%, fully human and fully divine—He is God ***and*** man. He is the *Logos*, and the *Logos* became "*sarx*"—the Word became flesh. Therefore the *Logos* is fully human and fully divine.

The Gospel of Matthew is 100% the word of Matthew and 100% the Word of God. The Book of Isaiah is 100% the Word of God and 100% the word of Isaiah. It is the Word of God in the word of men. It does not make it any less human or any less divine. Jesus is no less human because He is God and He is no less God because He is human. The Bible is no less divine because it is human and it is no less human because it is divine. That is the Bible—that is the autograph. Whatever language in which the Holy Spirit inspired the initial authors to write is the language in which they wrote. That is the autographs. Nehemiah says this was the priority.

People had to understand what they were reading. The original meaning of the original Hebrew had to be explained to the people because they did not know it anymore. The priority was on the original language. We can therefore surmise that anything seeking to displace the priority of the original languages of the original autographs is spiritual seduction by the spirit of antichrist because it seeks to put something "***in place of***" God's Word as God originally gave it. The extreme cases are intentionally corrupted translations such as inclusive versions and the Jehovah's Witness *New World Translation*. The complication comes when valid translations that are not at all wrong in themselves get lifted up above the authority of the original languages.

This was another error of John Calvin, whose appeal was rarely to the original Greek or Hebrew texts, but rather to Jerome's *Vulgate*— the Latin Bible of the Roman Catholic Church. It is ironic that Calvinism and Roman Catholicism both stem from Augustine and both share a common Bible. Likewise, as the Eucharistic Christ of Roman Catholicism is another Christ, so, too, the Christ of ultra-Calvinism that leads people to hell is no less another Christ. This becomes a problem. On one hand Catholics and ultra-Calvinists alike believe many true things about the true Jesus Christ, but they also believe false things about the true Jesus Christ that in some ways lead them toward another Christ. It is therefore of little coincidence that so much of Calvinistic Protestantism has gone into the Antichrist religion of theological liberalism, from the Church of Scotland to most of the United Reformed churches, to most of the Presbyterian Church in America.

As with Roman Catholicism, there was an incipient Antichrist thread capable of replicating itself sewn into the fabric of their church traditions from the beginning. Satan put a time bomb into these institutions—what we might compare to a cancer cell that Satan knew would eventually become metastatic. We have witnessed Robert Schuller, pastor of the largest Reformed church in the USA, and the moderators of the Church of Scotland alike, abandoning scriptural Christianity. Schuller even taught that Jesus Christ went to the cross to magnify His ego. Schuller hosted the Grand Mufti of Damascus in his Crystal Cathedral, with Schuller stating that he would not object if his grandchildren became Muslims.

This is pure Antichrist. But the genesis of it can be traced back to the original mistakes of Calvin, not the least of which was his functional elevation of the Latin translation over the originals.

Accurate translations are not in any sense "Antichrist" in and of themselves; God has used them consistently in the New Testament itself as under divine inspiration by citing the *Septuagint* instead of the Hebrew originals. What ***is*** Antichrist, however, is replacing the ***priority*** of the originals with the false priority of a translation even if the translation is an otherwise good version.

The Problem of the Ruckmanites

There are many prominent figures today who are doing this. The worst malefactors are Ruckmanites—followers of Peter Ruckman, a man on his third divorce. In a tape of one of his sermons he was trying to defend the fact he was on his third marriage, and he prefaced the tape by saying, "As usual, at no time on this tape will I refer to the original Greek or Hebrew for the simple reason that anyone who goes into error goes into error by deviating from the *King James Version*—the 1611 edition of the King James" (which, for the record, is actually a translation of a translation).

Peter Ruckman takes a post-Elizabethan translation of a translation and affords it priority over the original languages to the point where he posits that additions in the KJV not found in the original take priority over the original autographs. Although they follow the *Textus Receptus* in the New Testament and the *Masoretic* in the Old, he actually says the additions in the KJV are "further revelation." This is open heresy (Dt. 4:2, Prov. 30:6, 1 Co. 4:6, Mt. 15:9, Rev. 22:18). By the very words of Jesus, Peter Ruckman is a heretic and an adulterer (Mt. 5:32). Yet he and his followers somehow ignore this. In their thinking, orthodoxy and sometimes even morality is not defined by what someone believes or the moral codes by which they live, but rather by what translation of the Bible they read. This of course is not only absurd, but lends itself to things more sinister.

By placing a 1611 edition of a translation with additions it holds to be "further revelation" ***in place of*** the authority of the closed canon of the original and divinely inspired autographs, Ruckmanism is animated by the spirit of antichrist. The KJV itself is absolutely in no sense a *pseudologon* in place of the *Logos*. However, men introduced later additions which they may have pronounced as canon. That is certainly *pseudologon,* and therefore an Antichrist doctrine inspired by the spirit of antichrist for the same reasons as the *Quran* and *Book of Mormon.*

There are all manner of sad if not pathetic souls of a delusional persuasion in a characteristically arrogant brand of ignorance believing that they are upholding biblical textual orthodoxy (particularly adherents to the heretical views of Peter Ruckman, British-Israelites, and mystics such as Gail Riplinger), who in effect elevate the 17th-century translation of a translation above the languages of the original autographs, or else idiotically maintain the King James translation to be inerrant. The Anglo-Israelists (some in the USA called "Armstrongists" who subscribed to the cultic beliefs of Ted Armstrong) ridiculously argue that the Anglo-Saxon and Celtic nations are the lost tribes of Israel. Such a position is complete anthropological and biblical nonsense. The "purity" of the English language over the originals? The result is that Replacement Theology becomes a basic tenet of this lunacy.

While it is demonstrable nonsense, its followers love it. Concerning Armstrongism and the cult engendered by it, fortunately the majority membership of this cult under the able guidance of Joseph Tkach have abandoned this lunacy and embraced biblical Evangelicalism. Another such proponent is KJV-Only conspiracy theorist Texe Marrs, whose fanciful conjectures and apparent disapproval of all things Jewish are often viewed as lunacy even by other conspiracy theorists. Marrs is an arch-propagator of Jewish conspiracy myths.

This is not to demean the KJV or its translators and editors themselves; a distinction must be drawn between these heroes of the true faith and the cultic fringe element of KJV exclusivists. We cannot underestimate the significance of the work of Coverdale or the work of Tyndale—godly men whose legacy must indeed be esteemed. But such noble figures of Christian history as these admitted they were faithful to the manuscript evidence they had at that time. God used the King James Bible tremendously, and the sad instances of Peter Ruckman, Gail Riplinger, and Texe Marrs cannot be allowed to tarnish the legacy of mighty saints of God such as Tyndale or Coverdale, or to deny the merits of the KJV. But to say that the KJV is the divinely authorized "standard of orthodoxy" is ridiculous. God did not give His Word in English, nor did He give His Word in the 17th-century. Once Christians behave as if He did, they are falling into a trap in their thinking that will mislead them further. Once the priority is stripped away from the original languages, Holy Spirit inspiration is stripped away with it. And once the Holy Spirit is stripped away it is only a matter of time before the spirit of antichrist steps in to counterfeit the Holy Spirit.

The KJV Specifically

More than this, it can be demonstrated to any reasonable person that there are obvious mistakes in the KJV. It sometimes does not always even follow the *Textus Receptus* or the *Masoretic*. Over fifty translational errors have been cited in the KJV, some of them (such as referring to the Holy Spirit as "it" as the Jehovah's Witness cult maintains) are of key doctrinal importance. This is not to say it is a corrupted Bible, but it is to say that it is most decidedly not perfect.

There are multiple examples of how giving priority to the KJV above the originals misguides the readers into erroneous beliefs. As one example, the KJV employs the term "Easter." "Easter" comes from Ashtoreth worship. According to all four Gospels and the first epistle to the Corinthians, Jesus rose from the dead on the Hebrew Feast of First Fruits the first day of the week of *Hag Mazot*, the Feast of Unleavened Bread. The translators of the KJV had no license to use the word "Easter." Easter was the first Sunday after the spring equinox and a pagan holiday that was adopted by the Church following the Quadradesimian Schism. Yet such marked errors are enshrined in the King James translation which claims to follow the *Masoretic Text*. But even in examining the *Masoretic Text* we discover that the King James contains ***many*** such concrete mistakes.

This is not a condemnation of the KJV or of those who read it; it is simply affirming that Scripture itself maintains the priority in the authority of the original languages, and it is the original autographs whose contents have been faithfully preserved which is inspired—***not*** translations, KJV or otherwise. There are differences in the underlying manuscripts, but in the majority texts it is nothing that affects doctrine or historicity taken comprehensively as a whole.

The extreme "King James-Only" advocates afford priority to a translation over the original autographs as we have noted. The extent to which devotees of the King James Only cause will go to rationalize or present an artificial apologetic for their professed convictions, at times borders on the hideous. One such woman wrote the ridiculous assertion with regard to the KJV that, "There's nothing wrong with our Reformation Bible!" In actual fact, Luther nailed the *95 Theses* to the door of the

Wittenberg Cathedral in 1513, and the first comprehensive edition of the King James Bible was published ***a hundred years later***. The King James Bible had nothing to do with the Reformation! Associating the KJV with the Reformation is a mythologized revision of Church history as nonsensical as counting John Calvin a trigger of the Reformation. John Calvin was in fact a baby when the Reformation occurred. The Reformation was Erasmus, Luther, and Zwingli—***these*** figures were the Reformation, accompanied by William Tyndale in England, later followed by Thomas Cranmer and the Oxford martyrs. During all of this time and beyond it, the King James Bible simply did not yet exist. The definitive edition of the King James did not arrive until 1611.

More than that, when the Pilgrims came to America they would not touch the King James Bible. They used the *Geneva Bible* which was brought back to England from Calvin's Geneva, and translated by people who were forced out of England under persecution by Queen Mary. Why did they dislike the King James Bible? Because its mother was Mary Queen of Scotts, a Catholic, and there was too much Roman Catholic influence in the original King James. The "Feast of the Ascension," the "Feast of the Annunciation" of the Virgin Mary—such things were in the King James Bible. Additionally King James was renowned to be, and to this day historians (including Winston Churchill in his *History of the English Speaking People*) maintain, he was a man of debauchery generally held to be a homosexual. The Pilgrims did not want a Bible authorized by such a wicked and perverse man.

Who "authorized" the Authorized Version? A reported homosexual who had a young male lover? Within today's so-called gay and lesbian agenda contending for ecclesiastical consecration of same-sex marriages and homosexual and lesbian ordinations, they love the King James. Their outspoken claim is, "Gay people gave you your Bible!"

Yet the Mayflower Pilgrims would not touch the KJV because King James persecuted born-again Christians. In fact, he martyred them—he killed Independents and Baptists; he killed saved Christians.

We must note that it is not only homosexuals and lesbians who cite the KJV in support of their positions, it is Darwinists who delight when the KJV mistranslates the Hebrew word "*yom*" as something other than "day." It is the Ecumenical Movement which sees the authorized inclusions of Roman Catholic and feast days of Mary and of apocryphal books as a bridge to Protestant/Roman Catholic reunification. It is also the Mormon cult who holds to a staunch KJV-only position because the prose of their *Book of*

Mormon imitates it and uses this literary device to make the two appear compatible and complimentary.

Again, this is not an objection to the KJV or its many readers, but a dismissal of Ruckmanites as unprincipled religious kooks. One woman in particular is their mystic and a proven charlatan: Gail Riplinger. When she was interviewed by *CRI Journal*, she could not even read the Greek or Hebrew languages! It turned out that her university degree was in home economics.

If we were to read *El Cid* in Spanish, how can those who cannot read literary Spanish tell us which translation of *El Cid* is the closest to what Cervantes actually authored? If one cannot read Norwegian they cannot offer a valued opinion about superior translations of Ibsen. How can one possibly misrepresent themselves as an "expert of accuracy" in a language they themselves cannot even read? Riplinger ultimately resorts to what is provided in Cabala (mystical Judaism). She does not of course call it that, but she begins using cabalistic methods to substantiate her contention that God showed her weird and imagined acrostic patterns in biblical texts.

The KJV largely follows the work of William Tyndale and what is known as "Bishop's Editions," and involves the efforts of Coverdale. The KJV is a valid literal translation, but not an infallible one. It is not without some obvious mistakes, and is deficient in that its translators and editors did not have access to the full plethora of ancient manuscripts and codex resources we have today. The translation itself follows the Erasmus fusion of four earlier Byzantium texts and the primary rabbinic text again known as *Textus Receptus* and *Masoretic* respectively.

We must respect the legacy of William Tyndale and the nobility of those who gave us the Scriptures in vernacular languages—an honorable feat for which many of them were persecuted and even martyred. It would be a notorious folly and a gross injustice to the heritage of such brave souls who gave their lives that others could have access to the Word of God, to even suggest there is an antichrist element in the manuscripts that were redacted into the KJV. Mormonism, however, is indeed an antichrist religion. Darwinism is indeed controlled by the spirit of antichrist, which puts another creator in place of the One through Whom the universe was created, that is Christ as we see in John 1 and Proverbs 8. The so-called Gay Christian Movement, citing the celibacy of Jesus and Paul, has attempted in some cases to present Jesus as a "gay male"; this is a different Christ. Such things are conspicuously antichrist. But from where comes the transition?

The transition commences with a departure from the priority of the original meaning of the original languages in disregard of Nehemiah 8:8.

Making the Legitimate into a Pseudologon

In no sense can the KJV be considered a *pseudologon* itself. It is a valid translation God has used tremendously. But the inclusion and citation of non-canonical apocryphal texts in the 1611 edition elevate non-canon to the level and authority of canon and adds to it the lists of liturgical material for the veneration of Mary, saints, etc. Thus there are ***elements*** of *pseudologon* contained in the original 1611 edition.

More problematic, however, is that too many King James-Only proponents, particularly the followers of Peter Ruckman, in practical terms reduce a valid literal translation to a *pseudologon* by exalting the authority of a 17th-century translation of a translation ***above*** the original languages of the original autographs. Moreover, the radical elements of King James-Only exclusivism (who are largely ignorant of the original languages and manuscript history themselves) determine orthodoxy not on the basis of what someone actually believes, but on the basis of which translation they read. Thus, although Ruckman himself is on his third marriage, and in his recordings refers to Black Africans as "niggers," such a bigot in what is scripturally an adulterous marriage is seen as a faithful leader simply because he holds the authority of the KJV above the priority of the original languages.

British-Israelite groups propounding the anthropologically and scripturally absurd position that the Anglo-Saxon and Celtic nations are the "lost tribes of Israel" likewise must for obvious reasons hold up the KJV above the original languages as "the pure language of the people of God." Advocates of the erroneous teaching of Replacement Theology similarly have a vested interest in subordinating the languages of the original texts to their own.

> *They read from the book, from the law of God, translating to give the sense so that they understood the reading.* (Neh. 8:8)

While the KJV translation itself is certainly not a *pseudologon*, it is a tragic misfortune that King James-Only extremists in essence attempt to turn it into one. The point here is that Nehemiah 8:8 confirms that it is the original meaning of the original languages that establishes authoritative priority. After the Babylonian Captivity, returning Jews who were literate only in Aramaic required exposition of the original meaning of the original texts in the original Hebrew language. This is the only verse in Scripture explicitly addressing the issue of translation. And when we deviate from its principle we step into the shadow of *pseudologon*.

The subject of biblical translation and etymology and the details of manuscript history lie beyond the purpose and scope of this book. We only address the matter insofar as it relates to the subject of Antichrist. Much can be said and has been said elsewhere by ourselves and by others concerning the issues of literalist translations, dynamic equivalents, textual analysis of the *Masoretic* and *Textus Receptus*, and questions of paraphrases and their dangers. These are involved areas of study vital in their own right, but become relevant only through the issue of Antichrist when they become a *pseudologon*, which is what takes place with certain corrupted translations. In print and on our ministry's website (www.moriel.org) we make freely available articles such as *Bible Versions* and *The Plastic Bible* dealing with the aforementioned and other translation-related issues. With regard to the Antichrist,, however, we must focus on such important matters only insofar as they relate to the *pseudologon*, which is the literary key to the person and actions of the Antichrist to come.

The Worst Offender

The Message is one of the most horrific Bible translations imaginable when contrasted to the original meaning of the original texts. When engaging in the Dynamic Equivalence approach to scriptural translation which highlights translating the meaning as opposed to a more literalistic tackling of the text, something subtly begins to happen: gravitation away from translation toward interpretation. But when someone goes from Dynamic Equivalence into paraphrasing, they are really going further away from translation, and mainly into the realm of interpretation. It is a progressive, subtle form of spiritual seduction and not infrequently a demonically inspired deception.

We can examine *The Message* by reading John's Gospel. Right from the first chapter one is clearly struck with the outlandish rewriting of Scripture by Eugene Peterson. His is not "translation" or even "paraphrase," but a redefining redaction. John 1:14 translates that the *Logos* (Divine Word) became *sarx* (incarnate flesh) and *kateskeno* (tabernacled) among us. *Kataskeno* is a Greek translation combined with a transliteration of the

Hebrew *Shekinah*. Thus the original meaning of the verse is that the same Shekinah presence of God in the Holy Ark that led Israel through the wilderness would be physically present in the person of Jesus, the Word made flesh conceived by the Holy Spirit. In the paraphrase, *The Message*, it is mistranslated, "The Word became flesh and blood, and moved into the neighborhood," an assigned meaning by Eugene Peterson bearing no relation to the original inspired meaning!

Yet this bastardization of Holy Writ is the preferred Bible of *The Purpose Driven* agenda. The Word of God does not teach the marketing psychology and New Age tenets of Rick Warren upon which his ecumenical/interfaith *Purpose Driven* agenda is built, so he must find a suitable replacement for the Word of God that pretends to be the Word of God but, in fact, is a fabrication of it (*plastios logos*).

Nehemiah says the original language is the standard, but when people do not know the standard the meaning must be explained; this is the work of an expositor. When people cannot read the originals they can go literalist so it will be readable. Then some go into "dynamic equivalence." This may not indeed be best, but caution must be exercised in vocalizing criticism of it because there is still the issue of the New Testament use of *The Septuagint*. It is not as easy as it is often made out to be. "We shouldn't have paraphrases!" But how will little Henry, who is four, be taught about Jesus?

Adding to the Word of God

Dynamic equivalence does something else which is also done with the literalist: it annotates. When one annotates a Bible it may not be completely bad, but a *Scofield Bible*, for instance, is annotated so it will be read along the lines of dispensational presupposition—so that Scripture will be seen with a Dispensationalist worldview. That is the *Scofield Bible*.

The Catholic *Jerusalem Bible* annotates to explain away how Joseph could have "known" (Greek "*gnosco*") Mary while maintaining her virginity. How can one consummate a marriage if the bride remains a virgin? Somehow they seem to have it figured out in their annotations to explain away the obvious meaning of the biblical text.

When annotation takes place the unavoidable tendency is to read the text through the prism of the annotation. Effectively this results in building commentary into the text. The first ones to do this were not Christians; they were rabbis who produced the Talmudic commentary on the *Haftorah*, but they would read it together. The first ones to employ this practice were of the ancient world, but this discussion concerns today's Evangelicals. Peter says they are going to aim at them (2 Pe. 2:1); they are going to aim a "plastic Bible" at believers.

In his *Purpose Driven* books, Rick Warren most frequently quotes from *The Message*. He engages in a practice called "proof texting." Proof texting is bad exegesis utilizing a form of hermeneutic ("hermeneutic" is the fancy seminary word for "biblical interpretation") that was first invented by liberation theologians; it is also known as "conscientiousization."

Bonino, Sobrino and other Liberation Theology proponents argue along the following lines: "Well, the main need of the people in Latin America is for a political liberation against the hacienda class, so therefore we have to reinterpret the Bible to meet their need. The Exodus of the Jews was a national liberation so therefore the central event in Scripture is not the death, resurrection, and promised return of Christ, but rather the Exodus."

Rather than look at what God's Word states concerning social injustice (a major theme in the Book of Amos), they look at God's Word from their personal position of experiencing injustice, and then assign a meaning of their own to Scripture. Instead of doing what Habakkuk did, getting up on the watchtower to "Look out" (Hab. 2:1)—instead of observing a situation from the perspective of the Word of God—they look at the Word of God from the point of view their own situation. Instead of looking at a situation biblically, they look at the Bible from the point of view of their own situation and assign their own corresponding meaning customized to the situation.

This begins with proof-texting. They come with a presupposition about what they ***want*** to say and then try to find a verse that fits it. This does not begin by doing an exegesis of the text ("this is what ***God*** says about the situation"); they have their own preconceived idea and try to find a text that supports it, which usually means taking a text out of context and making it a pretext. Usually those doing this must take a text ***out*** of context and make it a ***pretext*** to have a supposedly biblical argument for their presupposition. "If you cannot find it in the original Greek and Hebrew, go to a translation. If you cannot find it in a translation, go to a paraphrase." That is exactly what Rick Warren does. He will bounce from version to version, but it is mainly *The Message* which suits him.

The fact that he is not consistently using one translation or appealing to the original meaning of the Greek and Hebrew should be the first warning sign. The first warning sign is that Rick Warren lends no stated priority to the original texts. The second warning sign is that he is bouncing from translation to translation. The third warning sign is that he must resort to a paraphrase.

Rick Warren is not the first to do this, but something else happens: they malign the way of the truth (2 Pe. 2:2). The first ones to do this, and they still exist today, were the ancient Samaritans. They actually changed the text of the Torah to make Mt. Gerizim look like the holy mountain of Moses, and simultaneously dropped all the prophets; they kept only the five books of Moses, which they doctored. This is the whole background of John 4, the argument between Jesus and the woman at the well. They were the first ones to do it and these guys still exist. They still sacrifice sheep and everything, the same ones descended from the times of Ezra, Nehemiah, and John 4. They were the first ones to do this.

Probably the first in the modern world to do this (and these people have been characterized as taking the proverbial "cake") was the Jehovah's Witnesses' *New World Translation*. They butchered the text, such as mistranslating John 1:1 to read, "The word was **A** God." (This is completely absurd as there is no indefinite article in Greek.) And do they properly translate that they "worshiped" Him (Jesus)? "No," argue the Jehovah's Witnesses, "they did obeisance to Him." Yet the Greek word is "*proskuto*"—they "worshiped" Him, not rendered "obeisance." What are they doing? *Pseudologon*? Yes, but a particular and very deadly (spiritually lethal) form of *pseudologon*, a *plastios logon*—a plastic Bible.

Psychology, Marketing & Inclusivism

An adopted form of conscientiousization is prevalent in the realm of those who have sought to combine Christianity with secular psychology. Having origins with the Freemason Norman Vincent Peale of Marble Collegiate Church in New York City, Robert Schuller has psychologized the pastors of America via Bill Hybels and Rick Warren. And James Dobson (an ecumenical Protestant) has sought to psychologize the women of Christian America. Bill Gothard with his "self-esteem" emphasis sought to psychologize Christian youth.

While C. S. Lovett was among the first to blend secular psychology with Christianity, it was Hybels who devised his own approach to biblical hermeneutics where instead of exegesis and induction (taking ***from*** Scripture what it states) he would engage in eisegesis and deduction (reading ***into*** the text ideas of his own to support his own invented presuppositions). Gothard would develop doctrinal theology from his subjective interpretation of narratives (Bible stories). This is the harbinger of modern psychologized Bible translations such as *The Recovery Bible*, where 12-step rehabilitative psychology that refocuses on past sin (instead of on the new creation in Christ reckoning the substance-abusing sinner dead) likewise subjectively interprets Bible narratives as examples of recovery from substance abusive lifestyles, etc.

However, an already ugly situation gets even worse than this! What can be worse than a bad paraphrase like *The Message* or psychologized Bibles? The answer is "inclusivist translations." They have to be inclusive, geared to the agenda of feminists, homosexuals, and non-Christians in general. Passages such as Romans 1 and Leviticus categorically state homosexuality is wrong so those passages have to come out. The Lord's Prayer is rendered, "Our Father **and our Mother** who art in heaven." This is inclusivism.

With an ordinary *pseudologon* such the *Quran* or *Book of Mormon*, the world is presented a false word of God that tries to either correct what it claims are errors in our Bibles (as does the *Quran*), or tries to add or explain what they claim is a more correct understanding based on a "further revelation" that continues the story while actually contradicting the Judeo-Christian Scriptures (as does *The Book of Mormon*).

The *Quran* and *Book of Mormon* both violate the prohibition of Colossians 2 and base their existence on angelic revelations; both claim to be a "Third Testament"; both exalt a supposedly prophetic figure as their focus (Mohammed or Joseph Smith); both contain historically implausible and demonstrably bogus statements that cannot possibly be true; both foster other religions beyond the Judeo-Christian faith of the Bible while falsely claiming to be compatible with it. Ultimately both present a different Jesus than the biblical one and, in actuality, a different God altogether despite claims to the contrary. The fact that both mimic the Judeo-Christian Scriptures is the quintessential attribute of a *pseudologon*. The Muslims say the 5th-century Gnostic forgery of the Gospel of Matthew was the real gospel and the *Quran* is the final testament that sets out to correct the Old and New Testaments. The Messianic prophecies about Jesus, they contend, are actually about Mohammed. But this *pseudologon* is a different codex, as is *The Book of Mormon*.

Plastios Logos in its Most Abominable Form

What happens when we have a *pseudologon* called "*The Holy Bible*"? It has the same number of Books, it has the same order of Books, and above all else it calls itself *The Holy Bible*. Unlike the *Quran* or *Book of Mormon* it is not a different codex but an altered facsimile of the Scriptures. What is being presented? This is not merely a *pseudologon* but a *pseudologon* that has been transformed into a *plastios logos* and *The Holy Bible* itself becomes a false word of God. Peter says this will happen in the Last Days. *The Reader's Digest* published the first major edition of one, but several have since been published.

But it becomes even ***worse***. Something is happening now that is so unbelievable that even a Jehovah's Witness would not have the audacity to do it. Something has taken place that is so outrageous the inclusivists would not have the audacity to do it either. Indeed something so crudely evil is happening now that is so diabolical that no one has ever done it before, and the one who is doing it is the most respected born-again author in this country and most of the world!

> *So when they had come together, they were asking Him, saying, "Lord, is it at this time You are restoring the kingdom to Israel?"* (Ac. 1:6)

As believers in Jesus we now understand "One Messiah, Two Comings": Son of Joseph/Son of David, *HaMashiach Ben Jozef/HaMashiach Ben David*. The Messiah had to restore the throne of David, fulfilling the Messianic promises to David which Jesus did not do in His First Coming literally or historically; that is His purpose in His Second Coming. So what the apostles are actually asking is, "We know You are the Suffering Servant '*Ben Ephraim*', but when are You going to restore the throne of David?" They want to know when Jesus is going to fulfill the role of *HaMashiach Ben David*, the "Conquering King" who establishes God's Kingdom on earth.

The apostles asked Jesus on the Mt. of Olives,

> *...is it at this time You are restoring the kingdom...*

Jesus answers, "When am I going to restore the kingdom to Israel? When am I going to re-establish the throne of David? When am I going to reign from Jerusalem? When am I going to reunite the kingdom and restore it? In other words, when does the Millennium commence? Is it at this time I am going to begin the millennial reign?"

> *He said to them, "It is not for you to know times or epochs which the Father has fixed by His own authority; but you will receive power when the Holy Spirit has come upon you; and you shall be My witnesses both in Jerusalem, and in all Judea and Samaria, and even to the remotest part of the earth."* (Ac. 1:7-8)

"Let ***Me*** deal with that. It is not for you to know when the Father's going to send Me back. You do not know the day or hour of My coming. Oh, it is going to happen; I am going to come back and establish my millennial Kingdom, re-establish the throne of David—it is going to happen but that date is not your concern. ***Your*** concern is evangelism. The timing is not your worry of when I restore the Kingdom to Israel."

In fact after His resurrection the apostles understood Jesus as the Suffering Servant Messiah, also called "*Ben Ephraim*." He is identified as the Suffering Servant of Isaiah 52-53 and in the character of Joseph in the Book of Genesis. What they were asking Him is when He would fulfill the Old Testament prophecies as the Conquering King (known as "*HaMashiach Ben David*"—Messiah Son of David) in the royal character of King David restoring the throne of David. However, in Matthew 24:3 the apostles ask a different question entirely:

> *As He was sitting on the Mount of Olives, the disciples came to Him privately, saying, "Tell us, when will these things happen, and what will be the sign of Your coming, and of the end of the age?"*

Both episodes take place on the Mount of Olives and deal with eschatology. However, both the questions and the answers are completely different. The question of Matthew 24:3 is, "What is the sign of Your coming at the end of the age?" While the question in Acts 1:6 is, "When are You going to restore the Kingdom to Israel?" They are related, but they are not one and the same. And when asked the question about His coming the first words out of His mouth are,

> *"See to it that no one misleads you.* (Mt. 24:4)

He follows this with a long list of signs to look out for. And in verse 42, after giving this very long list along with *The Parable of the Fig Tree* to illustrate the need to be ready, He says...

> *Therefore...*

...because of all of these signs to look for and because of the parable of the fig tree...

> *... be on the alert, for you do not know which day your Lord is coming.*

"Be on the alert! Watch these signs!" Satan does not want us to be ready for the return of Christ. Jesus says, "Preach the Gospel of the Kingdom" (Mt. 24:14) and use eschatology evangelistically to see people saved. "No," says Rick Warren, "***we*** are going to restore the Kingdom."

As observed earlier, Rick Warren's interfaith global P.E.A.C.E. Plan contradicts Scripture. Jesus, Daniel, Paul, and the Apostle John tell us of increased wars preceding the return of Christ. Warren's plan has at its core, "We are going to save the world." Such beliefs are rooted in Post-millennialism and Triumphalist Kingdom Now Theology combined with a biblically Christ-less social gospel. Jesus said three times that the Jews must be back in Jerusalem for Him to return. It says it in Zechariah; it says it in Luke 21; it says it in Matthew 23, plus in the Book of Revelation.

This is Warren's teaching in his book and on his web site about the Last Days. This is *Purpose Driven* eschatology, the Saddleback theology of the Second Coming of Christ: just forget about it, align with other religions not accepting Christ, and have a man-made "peace plan" without Christ that is designed by Rick Warren himself. It is another example of something "***in place of***" Christ. Rick Warren is by biblical definition an Antichrist controlled by the spirit of antichrist, armed with an Antichrist Bible—a *pseudologon*. But now Rick Warren goes ***further still***.

Cut-and-Paste Textual Trans-Location

Re-examining the bible text as offered by Rick Warren:

> "When they asked Jesus about the time of His coming and the end of the age He said, 'It's not for you to know the times and seasons the Father has fixed by His own authority, but you shall receive power when the Holy Spirit comes and be My witnesses."

Is that what it says? They did not ask Jesus about the sign of His coming at the end of the age, they asked Him about the restoration of the Kingdom to Israel. What did Rick Warren do here? ***Highlight and delete, cut-and-paste***.

What Rick Warren has performed is "trans-location," a re-arranging of biblical verses from chapter-to-chapter, text-to-text, and-book-to-book in order to make the text state whatever he wishes it to in order to promote his own unbiblical and contra-biblical agenda. All this with no regard for what God has actually stated in His Word! Rick Warren trans-locates verses from one passage, chapter, and book to another in order to make it ***appear*** that Jesus said and taught the diametric ***opposite*** of what Jesus actually said!

Imagine the New Testament on your computer screen. Take your mouse, go to Acts 1:6, highlight it and delete it; take it out of the Bible. Then go to Matthew 24:3, highlight that and do a cut-and-paste. Insert verse 3 of Matthew 24 into Acts 1 where verse 6 used to be. This in essence is what Rick Warren does. He gives a ***different*** answer to a ***different*** question! He literally shifts verses around! This is not just simply taking something out of context; this is actually moving verses around to ***change*** the context! This is not simply a case of cut-and-paste exegesis (that would be contemptible enough); but actual textual trans- location. Warren actually does this, and there are God-knows- how-many thousands and tens of thousands of pastors pushing his antichrist agenda.

Warren actually replaces Scripture with another Scripture ripped from its context and inserted into another passage out of context. The only one who has ever done anything remotely like this before is Satan himself in Matthew 4! A Jehovah's Witness has never done this. The Roman Catholic Church has never done this. Warren actually shifted verses. He is telling people to believe one thing with an answer to a different question. This is unbelievable! This is a plastic Bible and no longer merely a "bad" translation. He teaches people to do the ***opposite*** of what Jesus said to do by inserting one verse from one book in the place of another, and most Christians do not see it while most pastors simply will not see it.

From his denunciation of Christians recognizing the signs of Christ's return eschatologically, his opposition to Christian recognition of God's prophetic purposes for Israel and the Jews, and his ecumenism which has now become a quest for common ground with Islam having the same God as Christians and Jews, Warren's supreme, demonically inspired achievement is his deranged version of the Word of God, transforming even the original text into a ***plastios logos***. Once more, Satan attempted this very same thing with Jesus Himself in Matthew 4.

Possibly the Most Damaging Plastios Logos of All

Yet there is the other heretical figure respected among many professing Evangelicals who is more dangerous in his demonically inspired maligning of the Word of God.

In John's Gospel Jesus told the apostles that the Holy Spirit would remind them of all He had taught them. In the Great Commission Jesus told the apostles that they were to teach us ***all*** (not some) of what He taught them. Thus the Holy Spirit inspired the apostles to author the epistles to explain to us the teachings of Jesus and what He meant. The Gospels and other Scriptures are properly interpreted through the prism of the apostolic letters. The epistles can be thought of as canonical or divinely inspired commentary. The epistles are a biblical literary genre devoted to explaining other Scripture with particular reference to the teaching of Jesus. What Jesus taught and did is understood on the basis of the apostolic writings.

This fundamental truth is denied by none other than Tony Campolo who argues for a "Red Letter/Black Letter" approach to understanding God's Word. He subordinates other Scripture to the words of Jesus (shown in many translations by red letters). In truth, ***all*** Scripture is Jesus who is the *Logos*, and Jesus taught that the apostles would explain what He taught.

Instead Campolo argues that since Jesus never taught against abortion, neither should the church! The fact that John the Baptist recognized Jesus from his mother's womb is relegated to the status of mere "black letters." This convoluted deconstruct-tion of God's Word by Tony Campolo is nothing less than satanic. If the hand of Lucifer is on anyone more firmly than it is on Rick Warren and Brian McLaren it must be on Tony Campolo. In times past he was a Bible twister; now Tony Campolo has become the Bible butcher.

> *... because of them the way of the truth will be maligned...*

The Gospel will be maligned. And if anyone maligns the Gospel, it is Tony Campolo.

> *...in their greed they will exploit you with false words...* (2 Pe. 2:2b-3)

Rick Warren's books have sold millions of copies. We do know this: The *Purpose Driven* crowd is doing something with the Bible that Peter says was going to happen in the Last Days in verse 3—"false words" or "*plastios logos*"—a plastic Bible.

The list of *pseudologon* Bibles is endless. There are the censored versions generally referred to as "inclusive." There are annotated Bibles where people are to read the text through the prism of the redactor's notes. This stems not only from non-canonical editions to the 1611 *King James Version* and the Roman Catholic *Jerusalem Bible* (designed to explain away contradictions between the Word of God and Roman Catholic dogma), but also psychologized Bibles such as "counseling" Bibles transforming Scripture into a psycho-therapy textbook. After both literal and dynamically equivalent translations, popular selling copies of Scripture became paraphrases amounting to highly subjective interpretations rather than objective translations.

Yet today it has degenerated well beyond this and by all accounts it is becoming worse still. It is likely only a matter of time before Satan will arrange by the spirit of antichrist for the publication of comprehensive translations that will combine inclusivist mistranslations of Scripture with texts from the *Quran*, *The Book of Mormon*, and other overt *pseudologons*, marketing and presenting them as a "Bible." There is no doubt that the end product of this process will be an antichrist Bible.

Synthetics began with Formica. They could make Formica look like mahogany. They could make Formica look like rosewood or pine. Whatever anyone liked, the manufacturers could make Formica look like it. And it was good quality. Then they found a cheaper way to do it called Masonite. But then through the miracles of polymer chemistry they found out they can do it with plastics. They can make plastics look like metal. They can make plastics as strong as wood. They can even sometimes industrially use plastics as replacements for alloys in the manufacture of components for airplanes and automobiles.

But the Word of God is not a consumer durable or an industrial commodity. Today, exactly as Peter and the apostles warned under the direct inspiration of the Holy Spirit we have a "Plastic Bible."

Because the Bible prepares Christians for the coming of Christ, Satan ***wants*** a plastic Bible in their hands. If Christ is coming soon, so is the Antichrist.

Chapter 3: False Prophets, False Teachers & the Antichrist

> *For we did not follow cleverly devised tales when we made known to you the power and coming of our Lord Jesus Christ but we were eyewitnesses of His majesty. For when He received honor and glory from God the Father, such an utterance as this was made to Him by the Majestic Glory, "This is My beloved Son with whom I am well-pleased"—and we ourselves heard this utterance made from heaven when we were with Him on the holy mountain. So we have the prophetic word made more sure, to which you do well to pay attention as to a lamp shining in a dark place, until the day dawns and the morning star arises in your hearts.* (2 Pe. 1:16-19)

We have three specific events being referred to or alluded to in this passage: the term "coming" of our Lord Jesus Christ is inherently indicative of His First Coming, but is also eschatological because it alludes to His Second. We also have a final reference, the Transfiguration of Jesus on Mt. Hermon.

The idea of the morning star arising alludes to the Resurrection, but notice that "*the prophetic word is made sure*" and it is associated with a lamp. The lamp in the Bible is generally figurative of the Word of God.

> *"Your Word is a lamp to my feet*
> *And a light to my path."* (Ps. 119:105)

A "*prophetic utterance made more sure*" is always a prophetic utterance which is biblically based. If a prophetic word is not biblically based, it is not going to provide any real light. But then Peter continues:

> *But know this first of all, that no prophecy of Scripture is a matter of one's own interpretation, for no prophecy was ever made by an act of human will, but men moved by the Holy Spirit spoke from God.* (2 Pe. 1:20-21)

"*Know this **first of all**, that no prophecy of Scripture is a matter of one's own interpretation.*" Making prophetic passages of Scripture matters of one's own subjective interpretation or based on one's presuppositions is an error which is formulaic for further error. The capacity of Satan to distort Scripture has been true from the temptation of Eve in Genesis 3 and the temptation narrative of Jesus in Matthew 4. In the Last Days the spirit of antichrist is already at active work making prophetic Scriptures of eschatological consequence matters of subjective interpretation and personal opinion. This concept of people's opinions is inherent in the meaning of the Greek term "Laodicea," a church in which people actually believe they have a right to their own opinion, where subjective meaning supplants objective meaning.

We see this increasing today with people discussing passages of Scripture in certain home Bible groups saying, "This is what it means to me." We have additionally witnessed demonstrable false prophets from the Mike Bickel/Paul Cain/Kansas City category engaging in Gnostic methods of exegesis and mystical and hyper-allegorical methods of scriptural interpretation in order to assign eschatological passages of Scripture false meanings of their own choosing. This brand of misinterpretation based on a subjectivism that discounts and often contradicts objective meaning, and mystical revelation that attempts to counterfeit the revelation of the Holy Spirit, is an unnatural deviation that has become perilously normative. When one can make a passage of Scripture, particularly a prophetic Scripture, say anything one wishes, one can believe anything, including that which is of Antichrist is of Christ, and that which is false is believed to be true.

In the American Midwest an article was published by Francis Frangipane entitled *Beware of True Doctrine* in which he postulates the proposition that true doctrine is dangerous because it can lead someone into spiritual pride. Scripturally, however, the diametric opposite is true. Frangipane's colleague, Reuben Doron, preached that the suffering of his infant daughter was propitious, in effect putting his infant daughter's suffering in the place of the suffering of Christ who was the only propitiation for our sin. Tragically his innocent infant daughter died almost immediately. Whether her tragic death was in some way a consequence of the theological insanity of her father, we cannot say. But Doron placed his infant daughter into that position and calling which belongs to the Messiah alone. The convoluted thinking that produces this kind of distorted reasoning in flagrant contradiction to the teaching of Scripture carries an implicit antichrist nature.

Yet professing Evangelicals are openly and widely seduced by it. Such false teachers would be wise to heed the warning of James 3:1 that teachers of God's Word will be judged more strictly than the rest. Yet false doctrine breeds a blinding spiritual pride as its byproduct, preventing them from realizing either the error of what they are propagating, the adverse consequences of it, or the spiritual pride that it engenders. To openly write and teach to beware of true doctrine is the Church gone mad, and the spiritual pride that lubricates the engine driving this theological and spiritual insanity is that same pride found in the heart of Satan reported in Isaiah 14 that will become incarnated in the ultimate person of the Antichrist.

Where Doctrine is Wrong, Prophecies are Wrong

> *But false prophets also arose among the people, just as there will also be false teachers among you, who will secretly introduce destructive heresies, even denying the Master who bought them, bringing swift destruction upon themselves. Many will follow their sensuality, and because of them the way of the truth will be maligned; and in their greed they will exploit you with false words; their judgment from long ago is not idle, and their destruction is not asleep.* (2 Pe. 2:13)

We can easily document false teachings of an eschatological nature made on the basis of a subjective mystical reinterpretation of a prophetic text using Gnostic hermeneutics. We see that in the Joel's Army/Manchild/Manifest Sons heresy arrived at by a Gnostic butchering of the Book of Joel as propagated by the Kansas City (false) Prophets and defended by theologian Jack Deere. Many tens of thousands, if not hundreds of thousands, of naïve and undiscerning Evangelicals fundamentally ignorant of basic exegetical principles of text, context, and co-text were seduced into accepting it as if it were a biblical fact, when in truth it is a contra-biblical compendium of seductive nonsense that can in no way be justified by what the pertinent texts actually say or mean. It all becomes a matter of their own interpretation.

This bears more resemblance to the beatnik poetry of Allan Ginsburg or the pop lyrics of Bob Dylan, Leonard Cohen, and John Lennon, all of whom acknowledged that any personal meaning in their intent when authoring or composing their compositions was purely personal for them and does not invalidate any other personal subjective meaning anyone else wishes to ascribe to it. The attitude of the beat culture and the psychedelic culture of the Hippies who followed them lent itself to a predisposition to such thought where meaning was a matter of self-discovery through means broadly described as "cosmic" or "inner-self," facilitated by the assistance of everything from Eastern religious mysticism to psychedelic mysticism.

It is as if Christians of this generation took the influences of the non-Christian subculture of the 1950s and 60s and transported it into the Church, much the same as the Christians in Corinth were taking into the Church the mystical philosophies and dualism of pagan Greek culture that Paul combated in his first Epistle to the Corinthians. The charismania and spiritual counterfeits of the gifts of the Spirit and a combination of carnality and emotionally charged mysticism that masqueraded as spirituality in Corinth have resurfaced in the Western Church culture of the late 20th and early 21st centuries. From a sociological perspective it is easy to understand this because the last major revival in Western Civilization was in the mid-to late-1960s with the Jesus revival among the Hippies that was followed by the Charismatic Renewal. Too much of their old baggage that should have been left at the door of the Church was instead brought inside and rechristened as "Christian." This despite the fact that the born-again Hippies at the same time revitalized a faltering Church that would be teetering on the brink of self-extermination had there not been a move of God (even though what succeeded evangelistically was less successful in the area of discipleship).

This, however, is a mere sociological appraisal. The spiritual appraisal is no less simple. When the Word of God was compromised and discernment was demeaned as being "judgmental" and "unloving," the spirit of antichrist easily and readily counterfeited the Holy Spirit of Christ just as experiential theology displaced scriptural theology, emotionalism and mysticism displaced authentic spirituality, and pop-psychology using Christian jargon displaced discipleship and pastoral ministry.

While elements evaded these chaps, as always throughout the history of the Church such elements at the end constituted a remnant. The mainstream constituted a religious con that endures to this day and that is worsening as Satan prepares the way to literally indwell the coming Beast of Revelation 13.

Just as wrong doctrine results in wrong praxis, so, too, wrong doctrine inevitably results in false prophecy. As discussed previously, people often inquire as to why the likes of Benny Hinn or Rick Joyner predict things that do not happen. The scriptural reason is that their prophecies are wrong simply because their doctrine is wrong. Peter explained, "*They will secretly introduce destructive heresies*"—"*pareisaxousin*"—which could be translated as, "*they put truth next to error.*" The way false prophets work is they put truth next to error.

When a Jehovah's Witness knocks on the door, respondents will agree with at least 50% of what they are saying. When a Mormon knocks on the door, respondents agree with 50% of what they are saying. They put truth next to error. "*A little leaven leavens the whole lump*" (1 Co. 5:6). People will tell you, "Well there is ***some*** truth in what the televangelists, the money preachers say." Of course there is ***some*** truth; there is always real cheese in the rat trap! That is how they work.

As noted previously, the Hebrews could not make a garment of wool and flax because God hates a mixture (Dt. 22:11). In Revelation 3 Jesus made it clear that lukewarm water—mixing cold and hot—would be spit from His mouth. One cannot say they will swallow the cold and spit out the hot or swallow the hot and spit out the cold; the solution is homogeneous. So, too, one cannot ingest a body of doctrine mixing truth and fundamental error and reject some but accept other aspects. If something contains fundamentally false doctrine of a heretical or apostate nature it must ***all*** be rejected. The compromised failing to do so is opening the doors of the Church to the spirit of antichrist who will open them for the "*man of lawlessness*" himself.

What Jesus Warned About

Turning again to the Olivet Discourse, they asked Jesus about the Last Days and the sign of His coming, and He says:

> *..."See to it that no one misleads you. For many will come in My name, saying, 'I am the Christ,' and will mislead many.* (Mt. 24:45)

When they asked Jesus what would be the sign of the end of the age He does not initially talk about wars, rumors of wars, earthquakes, famines, pestilence, or the Jews returning to Israel; He first talks about deception aimed at the Elect. He continues this repeatedly.

> *At that time many will fall away...*

...into apostasy...

> *... and will betray one another and hate one another. Many false prophets will arise and will mislead many.* (Mt. 24:10-11)

Jesus warns of wars increasing one time, rumors of war increasing one time, famines increasing one time, pestilence increasing one time, seismic activity increasing one time, the Jews returning to Jerusalem one time (and then only in Luke's version in Lk. 21:5-36). But He warns of deception perpetrated against believers ***four*** times. He warned about deception ***four times more*** than anything else.

If asked why, when I first became a saved Christian in the Jesus Movement in the early 1970s, I believed it was the Last Days, my response would have pointed to a well-known constellation of events including the rebirth of the nation of Israel, the trend toward globalization of the world economy, and the re-confederation of the Roman Empire toward what is increasingly becoming a non-democratic Europe. I would have pointed toward environmental pollution, an unprecedented increase in wars, pestilences and famines, as well as increasing meteorological changes and the documented increase in seismic activity. While I would still remain persuaded of the prophetic significance of these events and trends, if anything, more than I did 30+ years ago, with a partial exception of events in the Middle East, none of these things any longer constitute the reason for my conviction that we have entered the Last Days. By far, again, with only the partial exception of prophetically crucial events in the Middle East, the clearest sign that we are approaching an End Time scenario is the magnitude of the deception and heresy in the Body of Christ and the momentum this apostasy has so rapidly achieved, particularly the proliferation and acceptance of false teachers and false prophets.

While such deceivers have existed since the dawn of the Church as they did in Old Testament Israel, the magnitude of what is happening now, concurrent with what is happening in the Middle East, sets an historical precedent. The closest we have come to anything like what we are experiencing today is the events of the 1st and 2nd centuries. After the apostles, the avalanche of wolves in sheep's clothing proliferated to shocking proportions to the point when Irenaeus penned *Against All Heresies,* stating that scriptural Christianity was just another thread of many belief systems broadly called "Christian." At that time, however, the

Jews were not being restored to the land as prophesied by Jesus in Luke 21 and Zechariah 12, but were driven out of it.

The post-Nicean Church, the Roman Catholicism of the Dark Ages, the medieval papacy, all witnessed exponential explosions in the numbers of false prophets and false teachers, many of them popes. The birth of Higher Criticism and 19th-century German Rationalism associated with Bultmann, Counzelmann, and Perrins, and the Protestant theological liberalism that came out of Tubingen University in Germany, were in many respects more doctrinally debauched than the most far-fetched apostate exploits of the church of Rome. Indeed, during the Crusades, with the attempted Islamic invasions of Europe and at one point or another Napoleonic wars, the Middle East also again became the focus of the strategic, political, and economic concerns of the world.

Never before, however, has what has happened with Israel and the Jews simultaneously converged with what is happening in the Christian Church. Both, broadly speaking, are covenant people of God, and the agenda of the Antichrist is centrally fixed on attempting to seduce both. This has ***not*** happened before ***ever***, but it is of course what is taking place at the present time.

This is historically unique and precisely fits what Jesus, the apostles, and the Hebrew prophets foretold. Those denying the prophetic importance of Israel (John Stott, John Piper, Rick Godwin, etc.) are doing the work of the wicked one, however inadvertently. Instead of picking up the trumpet and sounding the alarm, they are playing taps. Likewise those pastors who turn a deaf ear and a blind eye from the seduction in the Church are not shepherds but are the very hirelings Jesus warned of, fully prepared to allow the wolves to devour the sheep (Jn. 10:24).

The darkness we already see is but a shadow of the darkness that is to come, and the deception we have already witnessed via the Ecumenical Movement, the Interfaith Movement, the money preaching televangelists, the hyper-charismatic extremism, the *Purpose Driven* agenda, and the Emergent Church hint at what is to come. But such an erosion of scriptural truth that we have already witnessed will one day be remembered as nothing more than a prelude. It is a prelude to the dawn of the Antichrist.

It Multiplies in the Last Days

"*Kal v'homer*" is the first principle of Jewish exegesis used by St. Paul in what is called "*Midrash*." It literally means "light to heavy." St. Paul used it continually. *Kal v'homer* is used most frequently by Paul in passages and contexts addressing eschatology and the Last Days. One instance would be...

> *not forsaking our own assembling together, as is the habit of some, but encouraging one another; and all the more as you see the day drawing near.* (Heb. 10:25)

What Paul is instructing is that while fellowship is always important as a ***general*** truth, as we approach the return of Jesus in the Last Days it becomes absolutely ***vital***. If true Christians cannot stand together, they will never stand alone. The general truth (that which is "light") becomes a more urgent truth eschatologically (the "heavy"). Likewise, there have always been false prophets, but in the Last Days they proliferate exponentially.

It is more than tragic that today, Christian leaders who 25-30 years ago would have been virtual role models have since abandoned any scriptural map or compass for where they are travelling, and have been swallowed in a storm of apostasy. That apostasy's storm-tossed winds now determine where they drift to and what they do. This has now engulfed much of the Church at large, much like what happened to the ship on which Paul travelled in Acts 27. There is no shortage of leading pastors, theologians, Christian authors, and denominational leaders ranging from scholars to popular evangelists today compromising with things they never would have when they began their ministries years or decades earlier. Yet when pressed privately we discover that so many of them now fit into one of two categories: 1) there are those who understand these trends are dangerously wrong but they do not love the Lord, the truth, the lost, or the Church enough to take a stand against it, placing their self-interest before the interests of the things God values most, and 2) there are others who have abandoned the scriptural orthodoxy they once held sacrosanct and have now become proponents of these deceptions themselves. To understand this let us remember 2 Timothy 3:1-8...

> *But realize this, that in the last days difficult times will come. For men will be lovers of self, lovers of money, boastful, arrogant, revilers, disobedient to parents, ungrateful, unholy, unloving, irreconcilable, malicious gossips, without self-control...*

It did not take much scrutiny of the phenomena coming out of places like Pensacola, Florida and Toronto, Canada, to substantiate they were marked by participants lacking self-control. Yet Paul states in Galatians that the fruit of the Spirit is self-control (Gal. 5:22-23). If such fads now proven by history to have been false or failed revivals were truly of the Holy Spirit, God's people would have been in control of themselves. By virtue of the fact such people were ***out*** of control, by scriptural standards it proves categorically it could not possibly have been the Holy Spirit.

If an alcoholic went into a drinking establishment after he had been saved and as a Christian returned to alcohol abuse, he or she would not be in control of themselves for the simple reason that the Holy Spirit is not in control of them. The fruit of the Spirit is self-control, a principle which also applies to the practice of the gifts of the Spirit. If they are genuine, and exercised in a scriptural fashion, then the fruit of the Spirit is self-control.

The spirit of the prophets is subject to the prophets (1 Co. 14:32). When people are observed babbling, supposedly in tongues where there is no order or interpretation, this is ***not*** a biblical manifestation of tongues and may not be the Holy Spirit at all, or in some cases may be another spirit. Someone is only in control of themselves scripturally when the Holy Spirit is in control of them. If someone is not in control of themselves, the Holy Spirit is not in control. In the Last Days such deceptions discrediting the Church and leaving people disillusioned and confused such as we have witnessed in Pensacola, Toronto, and Lakeland have proliferated steadily in their frequency and insanity. The combination of carnality and demonic deception speaks for itself, for as Paul also says, in these difficult times, men will be...

> *... malicious gossips, without self-control, brutal, haters of good, treacherous, reckless, conceited, lovers of pleasure rather than lovers of God...*

The "fruit of the Spirit" is also "gentleness." Yet in Lakeland, Florida we witnessed Wendy Alec of *The God Channel*, Bill Johnson, C. Peter Wagner, and Rick Joyner singing the praises of convicted homosexual pedophile Todd Bentley who kicked elderly women in the face on *YouTube* as God's instrument of revival. A few days later Bentley abandoned his wife and children, filed pre-divorce proceedings and took off with another woman.

> *...holding to a form of godliness, although they have denied its power; Avoid such men as these. For among them are those who enter into households and captivate weak women weighed down*

> *with sins, led on by various impulses, always learning and never able to come to the knowledge of the truth. Just as Jannes and Jambres opposed Moses, so these men also oppose the truth, men of depraved mind, rejected in regard to the faith.* (2 Ti. 3:5-8)

Outrageously, Rick Joyner brought Bentley back into ministry together with the woman he ran off with when he left his wife and children. In practice, dangerous false teachers and false prophets such as Rick Joyner effectively place a benediction on what Christ calls "immorality."

We have seen similar expressions of such debauchery in the guidebook for the Promise Keepers movement, *The Masculine Journey*, by Robert Hicks, and in its accompanying workbook. Before being withdrawn under pressure, Promise Keepers first issued an 8-1/2 page defense of the book, placing the Promise Keepers logo on the cover. James Ryle of the Promise Keepers movement had labeled the Beatles as "God's prophets" when in fact this author, having attempted to evangelize two of the Beatles (both of whom are now deceased) can testify that far from being God's prophets, they were essentially New Age in their beliefs. *The Masculine Journey*, however, drew Promise Keepers into a further level of moral debauchery and blasphemy of Christ.

The Masculine Journey urged Christian fathers to respond to their children losing their virginity out of holy matrimony or having their first experience with substance abuse as a rite of passage in which they should shake their hand and congratulate the next generation for being human. The workbook also instructed Christian men to give other men the right to question them about sexual matters of marital intimacy with their wives. Not content with urging Christian husbands and fathers to drown themselves in a quagmire of moral perversion, Hicks' book then celebrated open blasphemy, portraying Jesus Christ as a phallic male who was tempted to have sex with other men. The New Testament clearly documents the areas where Christ was tempted, but this was not one of them. Although He was tempted in all matters as we were, this is plainly a broad statement meaning that Satan attempted to induce Him toward sin in the same areas others are so induced. While all men are indeed tempted sexually, not all men are tempted homosexually, except possibly in the perverse mind of the blasphemous organization Promise Keepers.

Spiritual leadership does not commence in the church but in the home. The spirit of antichrist indeed is manipulating pastors and leaders to prepare the Church for the coming Antichrist deception. But on a more fundamental level the spirit of antichrist is likewise seducing Christian families and marriages by so corrupting the values of Christian husbands and fathers as spiritual leaders of their families and marriages. With a "phallic Christ" in place of the biblical one, we see the true antichrist nature of the ecumenical Promise Keepers movement. Not only are churches being set up, but so are families and marriages. Just as the Holy Spirit of Jesus is to permeate our congregations and our households, Satan is infiltrating the spirit of antichrist into the same on every level possible. We must understand there is always a bigger picture.

It may be easy for the discerning and doctrinally literate to identify what is wrong with money preaching televangelism, or the Ecumenical Movement, or Promise Keepers, or the Vineyard Movement of the late John Wimber, and of demonstrable false prophets such as Mike Bickel, Rick Joyner, and the homosexual drunkard Paul Cain. Now, it is important for the discerning and doctrinally knowledgeable to understand how these individual deceptive trends, fads, and religious con games are but facets of Satan's greater strategy that will ultimately culminate with the advent of the "*man of lawlessness*" who is the Antichrist, and his counterpart, the False Prophet.

Counterfeit Miracles

> *Just as Jannes and Jambres opposed Moses, so these men also oppose the truth, men of depraved mind, rejected in regard to the faith.* (2 Ti. 3:8)

They are like Jannes and Jambres. Who were Jannes and Jambres? Pharaoh's magicians. What did they do? Counterfeit signs and wonders. They were miraculous, they were supernatural, but they were not of God. The way that Pharaoh's magicians counterfeited the miracles of Moses and Aaron is the way the Antichrist and False Prophet will counterfeit the miracles of Jesus and His Witnesses. Be careful of the signs and wonders movement. "*An evil and adulterous generation seeks after a sign*" (Mt. 16:4). When people flock to stadiums for this stuff—blowing people down or falling to the ground out of control—it is a wicked and adulterous generation seeking a sign. Jesus warned against it. Keep away from it.

It is no secret that Pastor Chuck Smith had the good sense to throw the late John Wimber out of the Calvary Chapel Movement when he ventured into his unbiblical experiential dogma and praxis, just as Chuck Smith at that time displayed the wisdom to recognize the serious problems with the late evangelist Lonnie Frisbee. This is, again, not to demean signs and wonders when practiced scripturally, but when signs and wonders (in Hebrew *nissim v'niflaot*) become the epicenter of the message, the entire focus has become distorted. Jesus refused to put on a show. All He had to do was put on a show for Herod and they would not have crucified Him. He would not put on a show; He would do only what He saw His Father doing. There are no "miracle crusades" in the Bible. There are miracles, but no miracle crusades. Jesus never allowed signs, wonders, miracles, healings and such things to be the focus of His message and His ministry; they were ***repentance*** crusades in the Bible. "These signs follow" (Mk. 16:20). Once those signs become the aim, Jesus is no longer in it, if He ever was to begin with. Once more, eschatologically this trend multiplies exponentially. In the Last Days such problems become ***extraordinarily*** predominant.

They Cannot Endure Sound Doctrine

Spiritual fragmentation becomes endemic and inescapable when the person of Christ and the teachings of His Word (beginning with the message of salvation) are supplanted with other considerations. Yet the name "Christian" or "Evangelical" is still applied to things which by scriptural definition are neither. In the Bible Belt of the American South we have a cultural evangelicism. In sub-Sahel Africa we have widespread tribal evangelicism. In Northern Ireland we find political evangelicism. And in the Dutch Reformed Church among the Calvinists of apartheid South Africa we at one time witnessed racial evangelicism. None of these things, however, are scriptural evangelism. Such definitions of evangelism are sociological, not theological. In a church environment, doctrine—particularly true doctrine—is no longer important because the raison d'être of such churches and denominations is no longer scriptural. Paul writes the following:

> *For the time will come when they will not endure sound doctrine...*

(Many people calling themselves "Christians" will not even tolerate the truth.)

> *...but wanting to have their ears tickled, they will accumulate for themselves teachers in accordance to their own desires, and will*

> *turn away their ears from the truth and will turn aside to myths.* (2 Ti. 4:3-4)

So much of what is heard on popular Christian television are of course myths.

Paul Crouch was on the front page of the *L.A. Times* three days in a row, charged with allegations of homosexual activity, which he has attempted to deny, following a wrongful dismissal of civil litigation. The out of court settlement included a hush clause about these allegations. The automatic question becomes why, if he was not guilty, did he pay $435,000 in hush money? This is the way non-believers—to whom we should be maintaining a testimony for Christ in order to reach them with the Gospel—view TBN and Paul Crouch. On TBN Paul Crouch once called doctrine "excrement." (Although he did not use the word "excrement.") The Greek word for "doctrine" is "*didaskin*"; it is the teaching of Jesus. He actually called the teaching of Jesus "excrement" and people clapped. Crouch shouted on his broadcast, "Don't talk to me about doctrine!" What he appeared to be saying in other words was, "Don't confront me with what the Word of God actually teaches, I am going to instead teach you myths of my own invention for which I want you to send in large amounts of money to propagate." Again, his television audience applauded. One day such people will also applaud for the Antichrist.

As we are warmed, they accumulate teachers in accordance with their own desires. As always, these things worsen in the Last Days. Paul Cain, an alcoholic, and Ted Haggard, formerly of the National Association of Evangelicals who was a sex pervert and an abuser of dangerous illegal substances, were both publicly disclosed as homosexuals. Yet both remain in the ministry.

In the next verse we are not exhorted to "be drunk" but to "*be sober.*"

> *But you, be sober in all things, endure hardship, do the work of an evangelist, fulfill your ministry.* (2 Ti. 4:5)

The Scriptures in Joel and in the Olivet Discourse, the good and faithful servant, were not an admonition to get drunk and beat one's fellow servants. "Beating" the sheep of course, is a clear picture of heavy shepherding. In this crazed lunacy, Rodney Howard-Browne was advocating singing *At Joel's Place* as if they were inebriated. It is easy to conclude what unsaved people think when they observe such hideous carnality that, of course, never delivers the promised revival. In fact in Joel 1:5, in the text of Joel, sobriety, not lunacy, is directed: "Awake ye drunkards and weep!" not collapse in drunken hysterics. Yet even such conspicuous maligning of what is plainly stated in God's Word, cited as saying the opposite, does not so much as raise an eyebrow among those swallowed by such lies and deception. By the time the Antichrist arrives, there will be nothing for such people to do except believe in them.

An enhanced understanding of this is provided by Jeremiah 23 where the people ingest a diet of straw instead of grain. The straw of Galilee at a distance resembles wheat, but has in effect nothing of nutritional value. It is composed of a high proportion of cellulose that is not digestible by humans who do not have the digestive enzymes to metabolize it. Yet the brain is tricked through an artificial raising of monosodium glutamate levels in the blood into thinking the body has been nourished when in fact it is not only being malnourished but slowly starving. In the long-term effectiveness, mothers cannot lactate and nurse newborn babies. So such churches cannot give milk to the lambs.

Another effect physiologically is that the immune system goes into systemic failure, predisposing an organism to easy infection. Thus, once the Body of Christ is progressively malnourished, it can no longer provide any new believers the nutrients needed to survive spiritually, nor can it defend itself from infections detrimental or lethal to it.

Discernment is to one spirit what immunoglobulin is to one's metabolism. Systematic malnutrition will leave the body helplessly vulnerable. Satan has thus taken great pains, working through the spirit of antichrist, to feed the Church and Israel straw as an indirect means of killing its young and opening it up to the Antichrist whose spirit is already osmosing into its very being at the behest of its own depraved leaders.

The Babylon Motif

> *And another angel, a second one, followed, saying, "Fallen, fallen is Babylon the great, she who has made all the nations drink of the wine of the passion of her immorality."* (Rev. 14:8)

> *The woman was clothed in purple and scarlet, and adorned with gold and precious stones and pearls, having in her hand a gold cup full of abominations and of the unclean things of her immorality, and on her forehead a name was written, a mystery, "BABYLON*

THE GREAT, THE MOTHER OF HARLOTS AND OF THE ABOMINATIONS OF THE EARTH." (Rev. 17:4-5)

The recurrent features surrounding the persona of Antichrist and his mystique are without doubt false religion and its consequences—spiritual confusion. In Revelation 14 and 17 we see Babylon the Great, which is generally agreed to be some ultimate form of the confederation of the world's corrupt political and economic system with its united false religious system. Its purpose is to bring about an artificial unity that will mimic the unity of the Holy Spirit which Jesus prayed for in John 17:21. In Revelation we see the Antichrist making use of the harlot for his political ends, then disposing of her (Rev. 17:16). The harlot, of course, is the counterfeit of the true Bride of Christ, and the title of what Babylon represents in contrast with what Jerusalem in its ideal form represents.

To understand this motif relative to the Antichrist we must take the proverbial shovel and dig down to the root, discovering the source of Babylon. Prior to Revelation, the previous reference to Babylon is in the salutation of 1 Peter 5:13. Geographical Babylon was not a functional city in the 1st century, nor is it today. But the false religious systems born there journeyed further afield in multiple directions including to Pergamum. It was eventually adopted by the Greco-Roman world. Early historical traditions and archeological inscriptions in the Roman catacombs lead us to conclude that Peter was writing from Rome. The capitol of the false religious systems of the world having Babylonian origins, were by the 1st century firmly enshrined in the pontifical religions of pagan Rome.

With good reason this has led to attempts to apply gematrial principles to Greek, and even Latin. And given the antichrist nature of the papacy, with the pope as heir to the pontifical position enjoyed by the Roman emperors, efforts to ascribe "666" to the pope resulted. We again solidly affirm that the papacy is an antichrist institution, and speculative attempts to identify the False Prophet with a final pope also warrant serious and prayerful consideration. We must, however, avoid falling into the trap of being prematurely definitive as have traditional conservative Protestants keen to resist the already existing antichrist spirit that abused Roman Catholicism, lest we become prematurely conclusive. Clearly such people see part of the truth, but we should not resign ourselves to a position that states they have all of it.

By assuming such a narrow focus, those fixed on attribution of the Antichrist identity to the papacy have gravitated into doctrinal error in their quest. That error includes extreme forms of eschatological Historicism that go so far as to say the pagan emperors who persecuted the Church and the Jews were the restraining power in 2 Thessalonians 2:6-7 that prevented the Antichrist in the form of the pope from coming into play. This must be dismissed as a nonsensical proposition serving more to discredit their accurate association of the Antichrist with the papacy than to illuminate the Antichrist's ultimate identity.

What carries more weight, however, is to note that the Greek word "*onoma*," translated as "name" in Revelation 13, is used to mean "title" (when applied to Christ in Revelation 19:16). Thus speculation is raised of the number of his name possibly being the number of his title. Indeed, in addition to *Vicarious Christus* or "the one who is in place of Christ," the companion title of the pope is "*Vicarious Felii Dei*," meaning "in place of God," whose alphanumeric value in Latin is "666." (We also note in Hebrew that the term "*romiti*" meaning an adjectival description of Roman translated into Hebrew would be: "*resh*" = 200, "*vav*" = 6, "*mem*" = 40, "*yod*" = 10, "*tav*" = 400, and "*yod*" = 10, totaling "666.") Although we would not say this constitutes anything remotely approaching conclusive proof, it is not unlikely that it is to some degree a component of the truth and not coincidental.

Efforts to associate "666" with both pontifical emperors and pontifical popes have never been in short supply. We again consider Nero. A varied spelling of Nero as "Caesar Neron," translated into Hebrew and Aramaic, has been proposed as amounting to an alphanumeric value of "666." The problems with this are multiple. First of all it requires a varied spelling, secondly it requires a translation from one language to another, and finally the Hebrew letter "*nun*" when occurring at the end of a word is known as a "*nun sofit*" which has an alphanumeric value of 700. Nonetheless, there is without doubt a New Testament Babylon motif which we can identify with Rome and a New Testament Antichrist motif which we can identify with Rome. We shall find elsewhere further gematrial evidence in support of this.

Considering Luther's epic *The Babylonian Captivity of the Church* which identified papal Rome with Babylon, with the view of the Reformers that the pope was Antichrist, we may say there were assertions that were correct in what they said but flawed in what they failed to say. While the issues surrounding Rome are indispensable pieces of the final puzzle, they are not the final pieces of the puzzle. There is more to the False Prophet than the pope, and more to the Antichrist than the papacy.

Digging Further Back

Previous to this, of course, is the Old Testament Babylonian Empire prophesied of and railed against by the Hebrew prophets Joel, Isaiah, Jeremiah, Ezekiel, and Daniel. The Babylonian Empire is not merely a shadow, but in many respects a reflection, of what Babylon the Great will be. This is not necessarily in the geographic sense, but certainly in the political, economic, strategic, and religious sense. What becomes important here in understanding the mark of the Beast in Revelation is that the contrast between the mark of the Beast and the seal of the Lamb is first of all found in Ezekiel 9:4-6 where the faithful servants of the Lord in Jerusalem were sealed with a mark that was the Hebrew letter "*tav.*" In the ancient Hebrew script *"tav"* would have graphically resembled a cross, unlike the modified character in later Hebrew scripts. Those having this mark of divine salvation and favor would be spared from the onslaught of Babylon with its antichrist type, Nebuchadnezzar, much as those in Revelation 7 would be spared from the onslaught of Babylon the Great with its ultimate Antichrist.

It is interesting to note that in Babylonian priestcraft we have archeological evidence of the symbolic importance of "666" deriving from an astrological table. The number is featured on a Babylonian amulet with the number of the Beast inscribed at its base where 36 characters corresponding to stars representative of spiritual beings were placed in a construct totaling "666," and present a "god of the sun" standing on a lion.

Going back further, however, we find the original Babylon in the Postdiluvian period in the construction of the Tower of Babel with Nimrod and his wife Semiramus. Ham, the son of Noah, was the father of Cush, who settled in the area of Ethiopia and begat Nimrod. Nimrod, in turn, invaded the Near East with a naval flotilla in alliance with the inhabitants of Sheba and Dedan in modern Arabia. They sailed through the Straits of Hormuz into the Persian Gulf, and north to Mesopotamia in what is modern Sha'at al Arab in the region the ancient Hebrews came to call "*Shinar.*" There they established the first Postdiluvian empire. The crux of this account is found in the narratives of the Book of Genesis. The background accounts are found in Josephus' *Antiquities*, portions of the book of *Jasher*, and the *Epic of*

Gilgamesh where the historical material must be sifted out from the embellished myth.

Here Nimrod marries Semiramus, and from this comes the infant god Tammuz, the demon nemesis with which the Hebrew prophets would later contend. Tammuz was worshiped as an infant, held by a Madonna, and who eventually came to be imitated by the Roman Catholic Church in a later expression of Babylon.

Back to the Tower Again

The Tower of Babel was built for purposes of the deification of man and the glorification of Nimrod based on the concept that architectural technology could make man immune to a further flood brought by the God of Noah, the great-grandfather of Nimrod. It is likely that Nimrod was in fact Gilgamesh. In Genesis 3 the serpent was at least a biped and probably a quadruped, a walking lizard that was cursed to crawl on his belly as a manifestation of Satan the seducer. In Revelation the dragon personifies the persecution of the Church with particular reference to the Herodian antichrist in Revelation 12. In the Gilgamesh myth, however, the dragon becomes the rightful lord in opposition to the God of Noah, much as we see later in Revelation. Nimrod in the myth had a counterpart in Enuk, which was a hybrid of human and animal. This was related to the acute interest of Nimrod's empire not only in engineering technologies and metallurgy, but biological technology in the form of animal husbandry which in the Last Days becomes biogenetic engineering misused for devious ends.

The concept of the Gilgamesh religion of Nimrod was that the dragon could prevail against the God of Noah, and that with his technology and control of biology, man could challenge the power of the God of Noah. Nimrod had come to destroy the God of Noah, even claiming to have done so in an ancient form of the "God is dead" philosophy of 19th-century German Rationalism with Hegelian philosophers such as Frederick Nietzsche and liberal higher critical theologians such as Rudolf Bultmann.

Thus through an allied constellation of strategic, economic, technological, political, and religious unity, which was geographically centered in the Middle East, the God of Scripture could be displaced by mankind with Nimrod as its leader and Enuk as his deputy, Nimrod claiming to be part human and part divine in the character of the promised Savior from Genesis 3.

Christ, of course, was fully human and fully divine, but through Noah, Antediluvian monotheism and the promise of salvation were known concepts against which Nimrod and Semiramus rallied, promising fallen man that since God is dead, man can do as he wished and have Nimrod as both spiritual and temporal ruler. Thus we see that the later features of Babylon and Babylon the Great had their origins with Nimrod, the first type of the Antichrist in Scripture whose birth is recorded in Genesis 10 and the table of nations. Nimrod assumed this power with the help of Semiramus who facilitated his rise with the use of a false religious system that distorted and mythologized the antediluvian faith of Noah, astrology, and other occult practices in a false religious system that among other things became defined by immorality.

Hence the later institution of the papacy, seeking to embody both temporal and spiritual power in a man other than Christ, in New Testament Babylon, began with Nimrod. The "God is dead" philosophy of modern secular Humanism and the bastardized Protestantism of liberal theology seeking by demonic influence to pseudo-Christianize such philosophy, likewise have their roots with the first type of Antichrist, that is, Nimrod. So, too, the attempt to use technology and biotechnology to deify man to the negation of his Creator likewise has its birth not with the Enlightenment or the misuse of modern science, but once again is a concept that was born on the plains of ancient Shinar in the days of Nimrod.

Not least of all, however, we find the ontogeny of referring to wicked men as "beasts," or in the case of Nimrod, a beast that came out of the sea (as he literally sailed from the Horn of Africa). These are not fanciful New Testament inventions but have their origins with the first figure that typified the Antichrist. It all goes back to Nimrod's drive to depose the God of Noah and to prevent God from again being able to destroy the biosphere.

It is interesting to note that the decomposition of elements ("*stoicheia*" in Greek) found in 2 Peter 3, causing dissolution by explosive fire, was not even understood as a possibility until the 20th century when critical mass and nuclear fission were first proposed by Einstein, Oppenheimer, and others. Yet just as the key *stoicheia* in water that destroyed the earth the first time was hydrogen, so, too, it can be the key element in destroying it again in the form of hydrogen through cobalt, uranium, and plutonium bombs. The concept of the Tower was to immunize the human race from the possibility of another deluge sent as a divine judgment. But Peter tells us this will not work in the Last Day any more than it worked in the days of Nimrod.

Finally, we must understand the role of Semiramus who became a harlot queen. We again note the harlot in Revelation 17 identified with Babylon as a personification and metaphor for a false religious system and a spiritual seductress that demonically parodies the Bride of Christ and Israel as the wife of Yahweh. It involves yet transcends the harlot church, and is scripturally and historically represented primarily by Queen Jezebel, but also to a lesser degree in biblical imagery and typology by Queen Athaliah and by the seductress of Proverbs 5-6.

The beginning and forerunner of the spiritual harlot, however, is personified by Semiramus. Following a dispute over the legitimacy of the son born to her, a schism occurred between Semiramus and Nimrod who, having used her to gain power and to achieve the position he coveted, turned against her. So, too, we see in the Book of Revelation that once the Antichrist no longer has need of the woman, he moves to rid himself of her (Rev. 17:16). All of this is a replay of the first Babylon in the days of the Tower, the first harlot religion of Semiramus and the first antichrist Nimrod.

Parallels to the Babylonian Captivity

When Jeremiah wrote what became his 23rd chapter, it was during the commencement of the Babylonian invasions predicted earlier by Isaiah and Joel. With this in view, we address the central role of false prophets in the Last Days that must take place for the Antichrist to assume his prophesied position from which Christ will depose him. As we often point out, to understand the Last Days, one must understand the events which led up to the Babylonian Captivity. New Testament eschatology takes what happens before the Captivity primarily from the Book of Jeremiah, but also from Isaiah, Joel, and Ezekiel—the pre-Captivity prophets and the Captivity prophets—and recycles their message for the Last Days.

For instance, Jeremiah speaks of the coming destruction of the Temple. And in the Olivet Discourse Jesus prefaces His explanation of what to expect in the Last Days while predicting the events of A.D. 70 which foreshadow it. Jeremiah talks about the destruction of the Temple as does Jesus. Both Jeremiah and Isaiah contain the theme, "*Fallen, fallen is Babylon*" (Is. 21:9; Jer. 51:8), God's judgment to come on Babylon. The New Testament takes it right from the Septuagint, the Greek Old Testament.

> *And another angel, a second one, followed, saying, "Fallen, fallen is Babylon the great, she who has made all the nations drink of the wine of the passion of her immorality."* (Rev. 14:8)

Jeremiah's recurrent theme is the false prophets who mislead the people. Judgment was looming but the false prophets were telling them, "Prepare for blessing, prepare for victory, prepare for prosperity!" Jesus says the same thing. He warns about false prophets/false teachers more than He does anything else. Wars one time, rumors of wars one time, famines one time, earthquakes one time, pestilence one time, the Jews going back to Israel one time, but false prophets coming to deceive you and me four times. Jesus warned about deception four times more than He warned about anything else. It is imperative to understand why Jesus recycles the themes from Jeremiah as to what the Last Days are going to be like.

It Begins with the Word

> *The words of Jeremiah the son of Hilkiah, of the priests who were in Anathoth in the land of Benjamin, to whom the word of the LORD came in the days of Josiah the son of Amon, king of Judah, in the thirteenth year of his reign.* (Jer. 1:1-2)

Notice "*the word of the LORD*" came to Jeremiah (in Hebrew, "word of the Lord" is *D'var Adonai*). To really prophesy by the Holy Spirit an encounter with Christ is needed. In the Old Testament the Holy Spirit was only for certain people at certain times. High priests, kings, prophets, judges, patriarchs—that was about it. To really speak God's Word one needs an encounter with the *Logos*—with the *D'var*. "*The word of the LORD*" came to Jeremiah.

True prophets will always give you ***the*** Word; false prophets will give you ***a*** word. So often we hear of what is misrepresented to be prophetic ministry characterized by someone claiming to have a prophetic gift (however, ostensibly, that may often be) performing with clichés and catch-phrases. These usually include making claims such as, "The Lord gave me a word!" or "I have a word for you!" This is generally not prophecy; it is more often mere attempted clairvoyance. Prophecy will always be ***scripturally*** based. False prophets will give you ***a*** word; true prophets will give you ***the*** Word.

They have lied about the LORD
And said, "Not He;
Misfortune will not come on us,
And we will not see sword or famine.
The prophets are as wind,
And the word is not in them.
Thus it will be done to them!" (Jer. 5:12-13)

Whenever the Lord reveals something of a predictive nature via prophetic utterance, it will be firmly based on scriptural doctrines and principles. And if predictive and time-specific, the prophesied event will come to pass. Additionally, biblical prophets rarely had such predictive prophecies, although when they did, the prophecies were scriptural and accurate; but they were only occasional, sometimes no more than a few times in the prophet's life or ministry. Most of the ministry of scriptural prophets was calling people back to the Word of God, warning them to repent, and issuing a caveat of what would transpire if they did not. Prophets were generally raised up not when things were good, but rather when conditions were difficult or in danger of becoming difficult.

There appears to be little if any correspondence with the biblical ministry of a prophet amid most of what is misrepresented as prophetic ministry today, although there are individual exceptions who do meet the scriptural criteria. There is additionally no correspondence whatsoever between the false prophetic movements of the so-called "New Apostolic Reformation" associated with figures such as proven false prophets C. Peter Wagner and Cindy Jacobs—the former of whose false predictions at Lakeland and the latter of whose false predictions in Zimbabwe say all that needs to be said to any thinking person standing on the Word of God.

And similarly we read in Jeremiah,

"Behold, he goes up like clouds,
And his chariots like the whirlwind;
His horses are swifter than eagles.
Woe to us, for we are ruined!"
Wash your heart from evil, O Jerusalem,
That you may be saved.
How long will your wicked thoughts
Lodge within you? (Jer. 4:13-14)

The true prophets were telling the people to repent; the false prophets were saying judgment is not going to come, but instead people were going to prosper. False prophets will tell people what they ***want*** to hear; true prophets will tell people what they ***need*** to hear.

No one in their right mind would wish to be a prophet in the biblical sense. Who would want to be rejected, probably persecuted, and possibly killed? There are, however, many people who wish to be false prophets; their motives are easy to understand. First of all, there is plenty of money in prophesying lies and deception. And secondly, it feeds the spiritual pride of the most self-righteous of religious hypocrites, including those who brandish a false humility—who subcutaneously are usually the most arrogant of all. As long as they are backslidden or a false believer and have no fear of God, to be a false prophet is an advantageous position with its financial aggrandizement and notoriety. All such deluded hustlers must do is tickle the ears of carnally minded Christians, telling them what they want to hear. Indeed, a ***false*** prophet will always tell people what they ***want*** to hear; only a ***true*** prophet will tell them what they ***need*** to hear.

Backsliders Love Lies

> *"An appalling and horrible thing*
> *Has happened in the land:*
> *The prophets prophesy falsely,*
> *And the priests...*

...that is the clergy...

> *...rule on their own authority;*
> *And My people love it so!*
> *But what will you do at the end of it?* (Jer. 5:30-31)

The reason false prophets have a market for their product is because there **IS** a market for their product! *"The prophets prophesy falsely...and My people love it so!"* Once they make a false prediction and it does not happen, they just make the next one. *"My people love it so!"* People ***want*** it! If God's people were not in a backslidden state, the false prophets would not predominate; there would be no market for their product. *"My people love it so."*

That is what happened in the last days of Jeremiah, that is what happened in the last days of Samaria and Judah, and it is what will happen in the Last Days "full-stop" as we say in England. Backslidden people love lies.

Greed and Immorality

> *"Therefore I will give their wives to others,*
> *Their fields to new owners;*
> *Because from the least even to the greatest*
> *Everyone is greedy for gain;*
> *From the prophet even to the priest*
> *Everyone practices deceit.*
> *They heal the brokenness of the daughter of My people*
> *superficially,*
> *Saying, 'Peace, peace,'*
> *But there is no peace.* (Jer. 8:10-11)

What often drives these people is greed, spiritual pride, and sexually predatory opportunity. Where one finds false prophets, one will usually find the fast buck and/or personal immorality. One will always, however, find an all-consuming sense of spiritual pride if the false prophet actually believes himself to be a prophet; the rest, of course, are contrived con-artists.

It is no secret that the followers of Paul Cain, the great Kansas City false prophet, admitted he is a homosexual and an alcoholic, and always has been. He was the one they were all going to in order for him to prophesy over them in the so-called apostles and prophets movement. For the whole of Peter Wagner's crowd and John Wimber's crowd, Cain was their great guru. Now they are finally admitting he was a drunk and a homosexual, and always has been.

The world sees this deception and its false blessings. Jeremiah says, "They do not profit My people anything." They predicted Toronto would bring a revival, then Pensacola, then Lakeland, but no revival came. The Church was discredited, the Church was divided, but nobody experienced biblical revival. Where is the touted revival? Anyone who would have been with us in Kenya would have seen a revival—people saved at every meeting. Impoverished and in places persecuted, they have nothing ***but*** a lot of Jesus. The missionary Church in the Third World, at least much of the Third World, is functioning like the church of Philadelphia (Rev. 3:7-13), whereas the Church in suburban America is the church of Laodicea (Rev. 3:14-22).

In the Third World they do not provide people with earthly prosperity, but with an abundance of spiritual wealth in Christ. Unfortunately, in the age of the Internet and satellite TV, the false doctrines of the developed world have made easy inroads into the Third World. And although evangelism is not a problem, discipleship and leadership certainly are. We must be aware that the aims of the Antichrist will not simply be on the Church of the developed world, but on the Church as a whole. And the spirit of antichrist is actively at work in the tribal cultures of Asia, Africa, and to a degree Latin America. Some pastors of large churches have degenerated into virtual cult leaders, teaching all manner of false doctrines usually copied from the televangelists of the first world.

Another problem in the developing world is that the attributes of shamans, witch doctors, and other such figures in animism and tribal religion provide a model too commonly adopted and practiced by supposedly Evangelical pastors. Everything from the sale of charms to an acceptance of the pastor becoming wealthy at the expense of the poor are features copied from the pagan religions from which so many of these people were saved. This is compounded by widespread doctrinal ignorance disposing Christian beliefs to be combined with pagan ones, resulting in a mystical hybrid Christianity that still calls itself "Evangelical." The reverential submission to a tribal chief, a witch doctor, or a shaman as a "head honcho" is very much akin to the deference of papal authority by convinced Catholics, and is of the same spirit—the spirit of antichrist. It is not difficult to see how droves of Christians in the Third World can so easily be taken in. Without doubt, when Antichrist arrives, many indeed shall be easily taken in.

Rejection of True Prophets

> *"And I set watchmen over you, saying,*
> *'Listen to the sound of the trumpet!'*
> *But they said, 'We will not listen.'* (Jer. 6:17)

> *"How can you say, 'We are wise,*
> *And the law of the LORD is with us'?*
> *But behold, the lying pen of the scribes*
> *Has made it into a lie.* (Jer. 8:8)

"The lying pen of the scribes." These were the theologians. False theology, false doctrine, false teaching, and false prophecy go hand-in-hand. They are natural counterparts for each other. True prophets are popularly ***rejected***; false prophets are popularly ***accepted***.

Today there is no shortage of "lying pens" from would-be scribes:

- Rick Warren is but one Christian leader whose pen lies pathologically.

- Emergent Church guru Brian McLaren denies that the Christian message is propositional truth, meaning it is not predicated on being factually true or false. While the New Testament emphatically stresses that if the historicity of the death and resurrection of Christ is not propositionally true, saved Christians are the most foolish among all men for not living a lascivious, hedonistic, and morally reprobate life. (1 Co. 15:32)

- In his book, *The God Chasers*, Tommy Tenney denounces the writings of Paul as "dusty old letters," when, in fact, Scripture claims that the Word of the Lord endures forever (1 Pe. 1:25). Tenney's argument is that Scripture is where God "used to be" and we must go to where He is now.

- *The Prayer of Jabez* reduced a valid prayer in the Book of Chronicles to a formulaic incantation somehow guaranteed to produce a desired result, but does not mention the Gospel of salvation, despite it having been widely read by a secular as well as Christian readership.

- Author of *The Shack*, William B. Young, teaches that any God who requires His Son to die for sin does not exist, while British author Steve Chalke writes that if Jesus atoned for our sin on the cross it would make God the Father the quintessential child abuser.

- Statements demeaning sufficiency of Scripture have been made in Britain by Gerald Coates, who likewise has an established reputation of false prophetic predictions made in the Lord's name.

The Word of God centrally affirms the sufficiency of Scripture (2 Ti. 3:16-17), stating that it equips faithful Christians for *"every good work."* But the repertoire of apostate books and articles has mushroomed progressively. They seem to go into vogue successfully one after another, each one introducing a new gimmick built on some heretical denial of essential scriptural truth. Globally there are now countless Christians using such books in Bible study groups, or at best using them as a prism through which to read and understand the Word of God.

The contents of such books have already proved spiritually detrimental, but the fact that so many Christians are serially reading them at all will ultimately prove to be nothing short of lethal. It is on one hand another example of Antichrist activity in the form of *pseudologon*; on the other hand it obliterates the capacity of the readers of such books to identify the workings of Antichrist at all. In short, those who become engrossed with reading the products of the poison pens of these latter-day scribes are identical to those in the days of Jeremiah. In Jeremiah they went to Babylon where the image of Nebuchadnezzar was set up. In these Last Days they will go to Babylon the Great and at some point will realize that what they are left with is the image of the Beast.

The Ecumenical Road To Self-Inflicted Doom

> *Behold, listen! The cry of the daughter of my people from a distant land:*
> *"Is the LORD not in Zion? Is her King not within her?"*
> *"Why have they provoked Me with their graven images, with foreign idols?"* (Jer. 8:19)

The false prophets will point others to the ecumenical vortex that will ultimately swallow up all who venture into it—into a centrifugal maelstrom, sucking them toward the pit of hell.

Here, however, we must exercise caution and must not be angry with anyone except Satan and the false teachers he uses to deceive God's people. My own family is a mixture of Roman Catholic and Jewish. I of course love Jewish people. One cannot believe in the God of the Jews, the Scripture of the Jews, and the Messiah of the Jews and be an anti-Semite. Such can only be a false Christian. But because we love them we want them to know the truth. The fact is the rabbis have not told them the truth because the rabbis do not know the truth. The truth is that Jesus is the Messiah.

Similarly, we must love Catholic people. But every time a Roman Catholic kneels down to a statue, lights a candle, and prays to the dead they are committing the sin of necromancy. They are calling on the spirits of the dead for the living God. There is one Intercessor between God and man, Jesus the Righteous—not Mary. The pope is not the heir of Peter; Peter was not the first pope. Does the blood of Christ cleanse from all sin, or do we atone in Purgatory for our own? Is salvation by an *Ex Opere Operato* ritual called "the sacrament," or is it obtained by the new birth? Are we saved by grace, justified by faith, or is it a sacramental soteriology (if you like theological terms)? Paul tells us to flee if an angel of God comes with another gospel (Gal. 1:8). Anyone who truly wants to know what the Roman Catholic Church is like should not ask Chuck Colson or Pat Robertson; they should ask an ex-Catholic. They will testify what the Roman Catholic Church is—the whore of Babylon in Christian masquerade (Rev. 17:5). That is what it is. But because we love Catholic people we want them to know the truth.

False prophets will point others to the ecumenical. They go into the worship of false religion and false gods.

> *"If a prophet or a dreamer of dreams arises among you and gives you a sign or a wonder, and the sign or the wonder comes true, concerning which he spoke to you, saying, 'Let us go after other gods (whom you have not known) and let us serve them,' you shall not listen to the words of that prophet or that dreamer of dreams; for the LORD your God is testing you to find out if you love the LORD your God with all your heart and with all your soul.* (Dt. 13:1-3)

It is important to note that signs and wonders are a means for false prophets to deceive people. We know people today who claim they saw a miracle or healing, viewing that as some kind of vindication of a movement or a leader. Scripturally, however, this is not necessarily the case (Mt. 7:22).

The Ecumenical Movement championed by such figures as Chuck Colson is not merely a sell-out, but a betrayal of the true Gospel itself. It puts those for whom Christ dies on the road to Babylon. Such false unity and the emotionally tempered appeal with which it is presented is the very trap that Ezra saw through in Ezra 4:1.

Those with a different doctrine of salvation, be it sacramental, works-based, or otherwise, are not our brethren in Christ. It is rather our prayer that they become our brethren in Christ. And if those in such false churches as Rome do indeed become regenerate believers, they may not remain in such idolatry, necromancy, Eucharistic cannibalism, and papal corruption and remain in the will of Christ. This is no less true of any true believers counted among the ranks of Eastern Orthodoxy or, worse still, the liberal Protestantism of the World Council of Churches and other such strongholds of Satan that will form the pillars, foundations, and cornerstones of the coming kingdom of Antichrist that the true Christ will destroy with the breath of His coming. (2 Th. 2:8)

There is only one way to salvation, and it is not sacraments. We do not pray to the dead; we do not bow down to graven images. The Hebrew word "*hishtava'ot*," indicating someone who bows down to something, is an act of worship. False prophets will always point others to the ecumenical road. That is exactly what they did in the book of Jeremiah, and they are doing it today. They did it in those days, and they do it in the Last Days.

> *We applied healing to Babylon, but she was not healed;*
> *Forsake her and let us each go to his own country,*
> *For her judgment has reached to heaven*
> *And towers up to the very skies.* (Jer. 61:9)

Babylon cannot be healed. Many people tried to change the Roman Catholic Church from within and failed. ***Many*** people. John of the Cross tried it, Madame Guyon tried it, Francis of Assisi tried it, Vincent DePaul tried it. ***Many*** people tried to change the Roman Church from within and they all failed. And not just the Roman Church. Liberal Protestantism is further away from the Gospel than Rome ever was. At least Roman Catholics believe in the virgin birth or the resurrection; there are many liberal Protestants who do not.

Blessings Measured by the World's Standard

> *Righteous are You, O LORD, that I would plead my case with You;*
> *Indeed I would discuss matters of justice with You:*
> *Why has the way of the wicked prospered?*
> *Why are all those who deal in treachery at ease?* (Jer. 12:1)

They are at ease and they have money. False prophets will measure blessing the way the world does—money. The televangelists who are into money think because they have received money it proves God is blessing them. This is the "Laodicea Syndrome." They are at ease. "*Woe to those who are at ease in Zion*" (Am. 6:1). There are over fifty verses in the Old Testament that are clearly direct references to the message of Revelation 3:15 concerning Laodicea.

> *Woe to those who are at ease in Zion*
> *And to those who feel secure in the mountain of Samaria,*
> *The distinguished men of the foremost of nations,*
> *To whom the house of Israel comes.* (Am. 6:1)

False prophets again proliferate in the age of Laodicea. Money becomes the barometer of gauging blessing, and people are at ease. This is the very definition of a lukewarm church.

The Lie of Hyper-Calvinism

Just as the many false Christs prepare the way for the ultimate Antichrist, so, too, the many false prophets prepare the way for the ultimate False Prophet, the former being harbingers of the latter. In contemporary Evangelicalism we have generally associated the marked increase in false prophets with hyper-charismatics and ultra-Pentecostals, but this is a narrow-sightedness. In order to deceive the Church, the Antichrist must be able to seduce as much of the Church at large as possible. This includes those churches and denominations that we would normally define as cessationist and non-charismatic, or even anti-Pentecostal.

We must remember that the agenda of the Antichrist will concern Israel and the Jews as much as it concerns the Church. He has ***both*** in his crosshairs, and his designs on both are already to some degree underway, and to a lesser degree always have been underway.

Replacement Theology, denying the prophetic purposes of God for Israel and the Jews, and rejecting the prophetic importance of contemporary Middle East events, is as widespread among non-charismatics such as John Piper and John Stott as it is among charismatics entrapped in Dominion Theology and the over-realized eschatology of Kingdom Now. In a curious meeting of the strangest of bedfellows, Restorationists and Dominion Theology hyper-Pentecostals and charismatics have borrowed their farcical eschatology from extreme Calvinists of the Reconstructionist camp, both living and dead, among them Rousas J. Rushdoony, David Chilton, Gary North, and D. James Kennedy.

Those who propound these Reconstructionist views believe that the Kingdom will be restored to the Church when, in truth, the only reference to restoration of the Kingdom in the NT is in Acts 1 where it is mentioned as something to be restored to Israel (Ac. 1:6). Just as the Kingdom Now hyper-charismatics borrow their Dominionist eschatology and preterist view that the Olivet Discourse and the Book of Revelation were totally fulfilled in the 1st century, Replacementist Calvinists borrow their hermeneutics from ultra-charismatics—in short, Gnosticism. They must spiritualize the text out of context in isolation from co-text in order to artificially create the proverbial pretext. "Israel" becomes spiritualized out of all reasonable context to mean "the Church."

Additionally, Jesus made it clear that the events of the Great Tribulation would be so awful that nothing as terrible would have transpired earlier nor occur afterward, but far worse events than the traumatic ordeal of A.D. 70 (which Dominionists and Reconstructionists like to identify as the Great Tribulation) have historically happened both to the Church and to the Jews. While being ***an*** antichrist, and a type of the Antichrist to come, the emperor Nero was certainly not ***the*** Antichrist. Moreover, it was Titus, not Nero, who set up the ensigns on the Temple Mount. Similarly, the historical background in the Book of Revelation (introduced by the letters to the seven churches in chapters 2-3) adequately demonstrate that the Book of Revelation could not have been written prior to A.D. 70 as the Dominionists and Reconstructionists claim. Among other inconsistencies, there was no Christian church in Smyrna until after A.D. 70, and the absence of any prophecy of a destruction of the Temple in the Book of Revelation plainly shows the Temple was already gone. The notion that Christ in some spiritual sense returned in A.D. 70 to separate the sheep from the goats, more closely resembles the bogus babbling of the Jehovah's Witness cult that Christ in some abstract way returned in 1914 than it does any manner of scriptural truth or historical fact. Such hideous conclusions found in the preterist eschatology of the Reconstructionists and academic preterists are Gnostic spiritualizing devoid of exegetical substance.

So we have a situation where hyper-charismatic false prophets and false teachers obtain there eschatology from hyper-Calvinistic cessationists, while at the same time the hyper-Calvinistic cessationists obtain their Gnostic hermeneutics by which they arrive at their ludicrous eschatology from extreme Charismatics. As I have sardonically asked the rhetorical question, "Where does a kook get their doctrinal beliefs?" They obviously get them from another kook. Ultra-Calvinists advancing the tenets of Replacement Theology, extreme preterism, and cessationism are as doctrinally absurd and spiritually deluded on one extreme as hyper-Pentecostals and hyper-charismatics are on the opposite extreme. The spirit of antichrist is at work in both extremes.

It is imperative for the Antichrist to take the eyes of the Church away from end-time prophecy. Thus Satan, working through the spirit of antichrist, is presently engaging in multiple strategies in order to achieve this. The first and most obvious is the Rick Warren false teaching to simply avoid the issue altogether in flagrant rejection of the direct commandment of Jesus for us to be watchful and alert.

The second strategy of Satan involves conspiracy theories reframed as end-time prophecy, where naïve Christians become obsessed with conjecture and embellished scenarios about secret societies such as Freemasonry, the Illuminati, and the conspiratorial allegations of the Ruckmanites. Although it is fine for Christians to be aware of the dangers of being involved in cultic lodges, and Christians should be aware of the serious dangers of corrupted translations as *pseudologon* products of the spirit of antichrist, such issues are not where Scripture places the emphasis eschatologically.

Indeed, there are secular conspiracy theorists saying many of the same things minus the Christian jargon in attempts to repackage it as end-times prophecy or discernment ministry. Hence when Satan is unable to persuade Christians who follow Rick Warren and ignore end-times prophecy altogether, his alternative strategy is to channel them into becoming absorbed by that which they falsely think to be the study of end-times prophecy but for the most part is not.

The third strategy of Satan is to try to induce Christians to believe that God no longer has a prophetic plan for national Israel and ethnic Jewry. Satan uses false teachers such as John Piper, John Stott, Stephen Sizer and others to either ignore the prophetic importance of Israel, or to oppose it in sympathy with Islamic nationalism in disregard of the biblical and historical reality of territorial Israel being the land God has designated to the Jews. Thus when the Antichrist launches his quest to enter what Daniel calls "the Beautiful Land" (Dan. 8:9; 11:4) and to set up an abomination of desolation in what appears to be the Tribulational Temple of Revelation 11, Christians in these churches will have no clue as to what is actually happening until it is too late.

Replacement Theology and Christian anti-Zionism are not merely devices of Satan to enlist support of the Church in his campaign to obliterate national Israel in order to prevent the return of Christ, but are also devices of Satan to render the Church itself unprepared to meet the Antichrist challenge of the future. We do not say that the John Stotts and John Pipers of this world are cognizantly on Satan's payroll, but they may as well be. Such misguided leaders who misguide others and their churches are best avoided by all who love the Lord and believe the Scriptures. What is important to remember is that the root of their deception is found in the covenant theology of Calvinistic thought from which the Protestant version of Replacement Theology largely derives—although it has the same incipient influences of Augustine that is found in the Roman Catholic version of Replacement Theology or supersession.

A quarter of a century ago it could be categorically stated that most doctrinal lunacy was found among my fellow charismatics and Pentecostals, albeit within the extreme axes of those movements. This is no longer the case. The false teaching, including the false prophetic teaching, in Reformed churches and among hyper-Calvinists, are little better and in some aspects worse. They will again play a role in deceiving Christians to be unprepared to identify the Antichrist.

Their Own Agenda

Once again, we recall that false prophets are motivated by the same spirit of antichrist that will animate the ultimate False Prophet, although to a much lesser degree. We do not suggest that there is necessarily a direct demonic source for all of their messages which they falsely claim to be prophetic utterance. Such things can rather emanate from their own mind and imagination even though the blossoming of the numbers of such false prophets and the general thrust of what they say is satanically orchestrated.

> *Thus says the LORD of hosts,*
> *"Do not listen to the words of the prophets who are prophesying to you.*
> *They are leading you into futility;*
> *They speak a vision of their own imagination,*
> *Not from the mouth of the LORD.*
> *They keep saying to those who despise Me*
> *'The LORD has said, "You will have peace" ';*

And as for everyone who walks in the stubbornness of his own
heart,
They say, 'Calamity will not come upon you.' (Jer. 23:16-17)

They are always going to tell people what they want to hear. Do not listen to them. Look what Scripture says: futility, deception, visions of their own imagination. God did not show them what they claim and teach. Sometimes it can be demonic, but usually it is simply the deception and futility of their own minds.

"I did not send these prophets,
But they ran.
I did not speak to them,
But they prophesied.

(If God spoke to them the stuff they predicted would have happened.)

But if they had stood in My council,
Then they would have announced My words to My people,
And would have turned them back from their evil way
And from the evil of their deeds. (Jer. 23:21-22)

Straw Instead of Grain

Once again, we remember the straw vs. grain analogy used by the prophet Jeremiah. This is how the Church is being set up by the spirit of antichrist even as we speak. Instead of telling people to repent of mammon worship, they are encouraging it. They actually call the sin of covetousness "faith." They give the people, Jeremiah says, "*straw*" not "*grain*" (Jer. 23:28). If ever visiting Israel and afforded the opportunity to visit the Sea of Galilee, visitors can see where they grow wheat, but there is also wild tares; they look almost the same. It is only by getting up close that anyone in the Middle East can tell the difference between the weeds and the indigenous strains of wheat because they look the same. They make it ***look*** like the Word of God, but it is ***not***.

saying,
"When will the new moon be over,
So that we may sell grain,
And the sabbath, that we may open the wheat market,
To make the bushel smaller and the shekel bigger,

And to cheat with dishonest scales,
So as to buy the helpless for money
And the needy for a pair of sandals,
And that we may sell the refuse of the wheat?" (Am. 8:5-6)

They sell the junk and when the shekel gets bigger, the bushel gets smaller. The more they talk about money, the less they provide the Word of God. The more junk they serve, the higher they charge for it. They give people a Big Mac® and tell them it is filet mignon and charge $35. The shekel gets bigger, the bushel gets smaller. It is a con game. And the inevitable consequence? The world sees it, the politicians see it, and as these guys get caught and nailed it is going to provoke new laws that are going to be used against honest ministries and honest churches. Satan is using these money preachers to provoke new legislation to be used against honest churches and honest ministries.

They Prophecy Things Failing to Come True

> *"For thus says the LORD of hosts, the God of Israel, 'Do not let your prophets who are in your midst and your diviners deceive you, and do not listen to the dreams which they dream.* (Jer. 29:8-9)

And in the same chapter...

> *"Because you have said, 'The LORD has raised up prophets for us in Babylon'— for thus says the LORD concerning the king who sits on the throne of David, and concerning all the people who dwell in this city, your brothers who did not go with you into exile— thus says the LORD of hosts, 'Behold, I am sending upon them the sword, famine and pestilence, and I will make them like split-open figs that cannot be eaten due to rottenness.* (Jer. 29:15-17)

The situation in Jeremiah 28 is that Jeremiah prophesies a true prophecy, but Hananiah a false one.

> *Then Jeremiah the prophet said to Hananiah the prophet, "Listen now, Hananiah, the LORD has not sent you, and you have made this people trust in a lie. Therefore thus says the LORD, 'Behold, I am about to remove you from the face of the earth. This year you are going to die, because you have counseled rebellion against the*

> *LORD.'" So Hananiah the prophet died in the same year in the seventh month.* (Jer. 28:15-17)

False prophets will prophesy time-specific things that do not happen. Deuteronomy 18:20-22 warns that if a prophet prophesies something in God's name and it does not happen, he is a false prophet. By the standards of the Word of God, Charles Taze Russell, Judge Rutherford, Joseph Smith, Brigham Young—the founders of the Jehovah's Witnesses and Mormonism—are all false prophets. By the standards of the same Word of God, Benny Hinn, Rodney Howard-Browne, Rick Joyner and many others are also false prophets. *"A false balance is an abomination to the LORD"* (Prov. 11:1). If it makes the JW's and Mormons false prophets, it makes Kenny and Benny false ones too. Jacob Prasch did not say that; God did. They predict in God's name things that do not happen.

"How can you name them?" Because Jeremiah was told by God to name Hananiah. Because the apostle John said, "Look out for Diotrophes!" (3 Jn. 1:9). Because Paul said, "Look out for Philetus! Look out for Alexander the coppersmith! Look out for Hymaneus!" (2 Ti. 2:17; 4:14). When people deceived and misled the church, the apostles and Hebrew Prophets warned against them by name.

False Eschatologies

False prophets have a false eschatology. The predominant false eschatology today is Post-millennialism. Another is Replacement Theology.

> *"Behold, days are coming," declares the LORD, "when I will make a new covenant with the house of Israel and with the house of Judah, not like the covenant which I made with their fathers in the day I took them by the hand to bring them out of the land of Egypt, My covenant which they broke, although I was a husband to them," declares the LORD.* (Jer. 31:31-32)

With who is the New Covenant made? With the Baptists? With the church of Rome? With the World Council of Churches? The New Covenant is made with Israel and the Jews. If God is finished with the Jews He is automatically finished with the Church because He never made a covenant with the Church to begin with. Non-Jews who accept Jesus by the new birth are grafted in, but they do not replace it. Replacement Theology is not just a false doctrine; it is a symptom of something much more sinister.

Latter Rain, The Manchild, The Manifest Sons—these are all movements claiming they are going to conquer the whole world and set up Christ's Kingdom before He comes. (This is a core teaching of Rick Godwin.) Look out for this. It comes from hyper-Reformed people called "Reconstructionists."

Hyper-charismatics who are caught up in the Latter Rain/ Manifest Sons movements are people who do not hold to doctrine. Instead they embrace experiential theology. They are kooks. So where does a kook get their doctrine? They get it from ***another*** kook! They go to the ultra-Calvinists. Kook meets kook. In retrospect one can explore Calvin's police state in Geneva and compare it to a Vineyard church. By placing them together the result is the Manifest Sons. John Wimber admitted his theology was experiential so they have to go get it from somebody else. Where does a kook get there doctrine? They get it from another kook.

The Apostolic Church was, again, premillennial. All this other a-millennial/postmillennial conjecture was invented under the unfortunate influence of Augustine, incipient to Roman Catholicism, in order to accommodate Constantine's pseudo- Christianizing of the Roman Empire—a political move. Do not believe it.

The Harbingers Of Massive Spiritual Seduction

It is prudent that we again recount part of the history of the modern so-called prophetic movement and understand the workings of the spirit of antichrist in it and through it. The predecessor to the failed revivals and demonic deceptions of Toronto, Pensacola, and Lakeland was the London fiasco of Mike Bickel of the so called "International House of Prayer" in Kansas City, and his so-called "Kansas City Prophets" inspired by the publicly revealed homosexual alcoholic Paul Cain and the publicly revealed sexual predator Bob Jones. These were introduced to Great Britain by the late John Wimber in October of 1990 and championed by Sandy Miller of Holy Trinity Brompton, proven false prophet Gerald Coates, Restorationist Terry Virgo and Bishop David Pytches who authored a book promoting them, titled, *Some Said It Thundered*.

In an outlandish display of public folly at London's Docklands Arena in August, 1990, Bickel, Cain, and Jones falsely predicted a massive revival for Britain spreading into Europe for October of 1990. Since that time, of course, more mosques have been built in Britain than churches, and Britain and Europe have swooped further and further into moral decay, New Age, blossoming cults, expanding radical Islam, and a fast-declining Christianity. Europe is descending into a post-Christian/neo-pagan continent that is utterly postmodern, non-Christian, and increasingly anti-Semitic. This was the promised "revival" of Mike Bickel whose prophets meanwhile were found in very serious immorality and drunken perversion.

Bickel denounced the doctrine of a faithful remnant as "raggedy," taught that the rapture of Elijah was a judgment on that prophet for lacking grace, and prophetically predicted the coming "latter rain." More recently, in 2009 this same Mike Bickel claimed a divine revelation admitting his spiritual immaturity to understand Scripture, but he again issued alleged prophetic predictions about coming world events, alluding to the Antichrist.

The notion that God would give such revelations to a man self-confessed as deficient in "spiritual maturity," lacking biblical discernment—a demonstrable false prophet with a failed track record of false prophecy—must border on a spiritual derangement. God will never give prophetic revelation to an established false prophet who, according to His Word, He commands to be ignored (Dt. 28). And even less likely is God going to speak through someone who admits he lacks the biblical means to test the supposed prophecy. Yet some people will still pay heed to such a dangerous deceiver.

The actual text of the Book of Joel identifies the four swarms of locusts that devour, as the four invasions by the Babylonians culminating in final destruction of Jerusalem and the onset of the Babylonian Captivity in 585 B.C. Revelation 9 further states that these locust swarms reappear eschatologically as the demon cohorts of hell foreshadowed by the ancient Babylonians. Yet supported by Mike Bickel and John Wimber, Paul Cain taught that these locusts were the triumphant Church. This kind of fanciful distortion and spiritualization of texts out of context is hermeneutically pure Gnosticism. Once more, as Peter's Epistle warns us, false prophets must have false doctrine.

What is more perverse still is the contra-biblical and illogical arguments these deceivers resort to in order to justify their proven failed prophetic predictions and debunked bogus exegesis. Rick Joyner wrote that it is a mistake to believe true prophets cannot prophesy falsely and still be prophets, even though this is precisely what God states in His Word. Joyner does not provide a single Scripture to support his position. He simply states it as if it is factual and requiring no authority from God's Word—in effect behaving as if his own word supersedes the plain Word of God!

While this maelstrom of spiritual subterfuge exhibits the capacity to wreak short-term havoc, we must understand also the greater strategy of Satan. These false prophets and false teachers redefine scriptural prophecy into something not only unscriptural but contra-scriptural. We are presented with a version of prophetic ministry that is not biblically based and which is often directly contradictory to the doctrines, principles, and standards of God's Word. By accepting a wrong and unscriptural definition of prophets, Christians who pay attention to such deceivers are being set up for a false prophet like no other, and they will not have the spiritual or scriptural capacity to even know it until after the fact.

Three Times Deceived

In the present divine economy we may identify three kinds of people: Israel and the Jews, the Gentile nations, and the true Church composed of both Jews and Gentiles. Satan will certainly deceive unbelieving Jews. The Antichrist may initially count on assistance from the rabbinic establishment, most Israeli politicians, and popular opinion.

As he already has the apostate church deceived, he is now targeting born-again Christians, apparently with some success. Here he may count on Reconstructionists, ecumenists, extreme charismatics, and hyper-Pentecostals, particularly those in the Word-Faith Movement, the Kingdom Now Movement, the Emergent Church Movement (post-Modernism disguising itself with Christian jargon), and the *Purpose Driven* agenda (marketing-psychology misrepresenting itself as the Gospel).

By far the most vulnerable to spiritual seduction will be the unsaved, primarily because they are deceived already. The moral breakdown of Western society—everything from divorce, abortion, and euthanasia, to New Age pseudo-spirituality and an avalanche of the occult—has already placed the minds and souls of the majority of the world's people in the hands of the one whom Jesus warned is the wicked one with the world in his power.

In Summary

False prophets are not interested in a biblical position. False prophets climb out of the woodwork; there are more than we can count. The real problem is, again, pastors who will not protect their sheep from those false prophets. They will give people ***a*** word instead of ***the*** Word. They will go down the ecumenical road, they will chase money, they will tickle ears, they will tell people what they ***want*** to hear instead of what they ***need*** to hear, they will put on a show, and they will say anything and everything except God's honest truth. As true prophets are led by the Holy Spirit (grounded in the *Logos*) and prepare the way for the coming of Christ, false prophets are led by the spirit of antichrist, and are largely *pseudologon*-grounded. Even if their ignorance and own delusion prevent them from realizing it, they prepare the way for the coming of the Antichrist.

In short, we may say that true prophets and true teachers led by the Holy Spirit to prepare the way for the coming of Christ are diabolically paralleled by false teachers and false prophets inspired by the spirit of antichrist to prepare the way for the coming of the two Beasts of Revelation 13. It is a cardinal tenet of Judeo-Christian eschatology to grasp this point firmly. It is equally vital that faithful believers comprehend that just as the Holy Spirit inspired the authorship of Scripture, the spirit of antichrist inspires the authorship of the various *pseudologons* which additionally are crucial elements in Satan's plan to establish a domain of the Antichrist.

Of this all may rest certain: to correctly and finally identify the "*man of lawlessness*" (the Antichrist) who is the first Beast of Revelation 13, one absolutely must identify the False Prophet, that is, the second Beast of Revelation 13. If people professing to be Christians—even saved regenerate Christians—cannot, due to their ignorance of biblical doctrine and lack of discernment, identify obvious false prophets such as Mike Bickel, Benny Hinn, Gerald Coates, Cindy Jacobs, Rick Joyner, Rodney Howard- Browne, Paul Cain, Bob Jones, and Kenneth Copeland—what will happen when ***real*** deception comes upon the world and the church? What hope can they possibly have of identifying the ultimate False Prophet?

Considering these things, it is therefore of the utmost consequence that we recognize and define the relationship between false prophets and the spirit of antichrist. It is not simply a matter that the two work in harmony, but rather that one empowers the other. As true prophets on the basis of right scriptural doctrine prophesy by the Holy Spirit, false prophets on the basis of false doctrine prophesy by the spirit of antichrist. We must remember that as Scripture tells us, "*the testimony of Jesus is the spirit of prophecy*" (Rev. 19:10); therefore there is the diabolical equivalent.

Moreover, as those who speak truly prophetically on the basis of God's Word herald the approach of the return of Christ as we see in Joel 2 and recited in Acts 2, so, too, false prophets rooted in a corruption of God's Word are heralding the dawn of Antichrist. This phenomenon will become progressively more acute as we draw both closer to the return of Christ and the coming of the counterfeit Christ. The spirit of antichrist has by definition always been an active ingredient and it has been theologically and spiritually associated with not only the *zeitgeist*, but what Scripture calls "the mystery of iniquity" (2 Th. 2:7). While this has always been a general truth, in the Last Days this ugly truth becomes eschatologically amplified. In other words, we may say that just as the verse, "*the testimony of Jesus is the spirit of prophecy*," is presented to us in an eschatological context in the Book of Revelation, the satanic counterpart is also true. The false testimony of the Antichrist is likewise the spirit of false prophecy when understood in an eschatological context.

Part Two: The Many Antichrists - Biblical

Deuteronomy 18 informs us that the Messiah would be a prophet like Moses. Moses gave a covenant; God spoke ***through*** him but audibly ***to*** him from the heavens. When he first came to save his people he was rejected, only to be accepted by Gentiles as a shepherd of Midian. It was only the second time he came to save his people that he was accepted.

Joseph in the Book of Genesis is also a type of Christ, as is King David. The foreshadowing of the Messiah by Joseph and David is recognized not only in Christian typology but also by the rabbis. Jeremiah likewise is compared to a lamb struck for slaughter (Jer. 11:19), and Ezekiel is addressed as "*son of man*" (Eze. 2:1, etc.). Similarly, Isaac was given over by his father for sacrifice as a shadow of Christ. These truths have been recognized by Bible-believing Christians for centuries, and to a large degree even by unbelieving rabbis.

Indeed a key way in which the Messiah was to be recognized was by coming in the character of those who foreshadowed Him with Himself as antitype. The same truth applies to the Antichrist. Much the same as we have noted, the spirit of error or the spirit of the age—the *zeitgeist*—and the spirit of antichrist parody and counterfeit the Holy Spirit. There is likewise a diverse range of figures in Scripture typifying the Antichrist. The Holy Spirit has included these for the same reason He included details in the lives of the patriarchs and Hebrew prophets who prefigure Christ. The reason of course is to be able to identify the individual who was foreshadowed.

Just as for Israel and the Jews the Messiah was to come in the character of Moses or Messiah Son of David (*HaMashiach Ben David*) and in the character of Joseph (*HaMashiach Ben Jozef*), so, too, the Antichrist will come in the character of key figures included in Scripture by divine providence and inspiration in order to equip the faithful Elect to know who he is. Unless this is understood, efforts to identify him based on any conspicuous fulfillment of passages such as Revelation 13 will prove fruitless.

First of all, there are simply too many of them. As the apostles teach there are ***many*** antichrists, and as Jesus warned in the Olivet Discourse, they are numerous. By the time his identity becomes as obvious as most popular approaches to identify him have made out, it will be too late. His identity must be known before it is too late, and this includes distinguishing the ultimate two Beasts of Revelation 13 (one of them being the "*man of lawlessness*") from the many other false prophets and false christs who will be of the same antichrist spirit. The task is formidable, requiring ***both*** the guidance of the Holy Spirit and scriptural understanding of the challenge.

Just as it is impossible to identify the Antichrist without first identifying the spirit of antichrist, so, too, it is impossible to identify the ultimate Antichrist without correctly identifying his types and shadows and the details surrounding him. In this second section, by the grace of God, we shall endeavor to embark on that task. The list of figures we shall present and the observations we make concerning them should not necessarily be considered exhaustive. It is the prayer of the author, however, that it will at least point the people of God to the correct road of understanding this troubling yet crucial truth.

Chapter 4: From Among Us, Come Among Us

In the Olivet discourse Jesus warned that false christs and false prophets will appear (Mt. 24:24; Lk. 21:8). Most born-again Christians make the mistake of thinking, "False prophets? That is the Jehovah's Witnesses. That is the Mormons. That is the Hare Krishnas. That is the Christian Scientists. False prophets? False christs? That is Sun Myung Moon." This is not to question for one second that the proliferation of these evil cults and these false messiahs are themselves a sign of the end of the world—this is without question. But a Sun Myung Moon, or a David Koresh, or a Joseph Smith, or a Mohammed, or a Menachem Schneerson are not the false messiahs Jesus is mainly warning believers against. Neither are Jehovah's Witnesses or Mormons mainly the false prophets Jesus is warning against. The ones Jesus primarily speaks of are those who infiltrate the Church ***as well as*** deceive the Jews and con the non-Judeo-Christian world, *"so as to mislead, if possible, even the elect"* (Mt. 24:24; Mk. 13:22).

Satan already has the unsaved world deceived. If somebody with credibility came along and said he could bring economic stability to the world and really bring in a New World Order where there would be lasting peace, what unsaved person would not follow him, particularly if he could counterfeit miracles? He already has them deceived! People in Roman Catholicism, the cults, nominal Christianity, and Islam are already following the Antichrist. Who is he trying to reach? Two kinds of people: the Jews and the Church.

There are two kind of people the New Testament calls "God's chosen": Jews and born-again believers (Rom. 11:7; 2 Th. 2:13). Who were the two kinds of people most persecuted by the old Communists? Jews and born-again Christians. Who were the two kinds of people most persecuted by the Roman Catholic Church for centuries with their inquisitions and crusades? Jews and born-again Christians. Who do the Muslims hate the most? Jews and born-again Christians. Both come from Genesis 3:15, *"I will put enmity both between you and the woman, and between your seed and her seed"* God's woman—that is who Satan is out to get, because those are the two vehicles God has ordained to establish His kingdom and His righteousness.

Today, unfortunately, Israel remains in spiritual darkness. But the Bible promises in Romans 9-11 that in the Last Days not only will the Jews begin returning to their land, but they will begin returning to their Messiah. And it says, "*For if their rejection is the reconciliation of the world, what will their acceptance be but life from the dead?*" (Rom. 11:15).

When Jews become Christians—believers in Yeshua—they say, "How could I have been so blind? How could I have not seen the truth that He is the Messiah? The prophecies in the Tanak speak so clearly of Him, as does the Talmud." (It can be argued from the Talmud that He was the Messiah.) But then something happens to Jewish Christians a little while later: they begin meeting nominal Gentile Christians.

Wisdom and Faithfulness

> *Some of the people therefore, when they heard these words, were saying, "This certainly is the Prophet." Others were saying, "This is the Christ." Still others were saying, "Surely the Christ is not going to come from Galilee, is He? Has not the Scripture said that the Christ comes from the descendants of David, and from Bethlehem, the village where David was?"* (Jn. 7:40-42)

The Jews were expecting the Messiah to come, but only a small remnant was ready. The Church should be expecting the Messiah to come, but once again only a small remnant is ready. There is a lot of speculation about what is going to happen and where it is going to happen; the answers to those questions are in the Bible. But when people do not know their Bible, all kinds of theories begin floating around and silly arguments begin taking place. That is what happened among the Jews when He came the first time, and the same thing happens when He comes again among both Christians and Jews. It requires wisdom to understand the Word of God in order to be ready for the Messiah to come. That is what Israel needed when He came the first time, and that is what is needed by the present generation when He comes again. In the end, wisdom and faithfulness become very closely associated, and faithfulness and evangelism become closely associated.

As we go into much further detail later, all this deception of the Antichrist happens, replaying the events that surrounded Antiochus

Epiphanes in the story of Hanukkah, similar to the ways of the Maccabees in those days. Daniel the Prophet says...

> *"Those who have insight among the people will give understanding to the many; yet they will fall by sword and by flame, by captivity and by plunder for many days. Now when they fall they will be granted a little help, and many will join with them in hypocrisy. Some of those who have insight will fall, in order to refine, purge and make them pure until the end time; because it is still to come at the appointed time.* (Dan. 11:33-35)

Only the people who had wisdom in the days of Antiochus Epiphanes knew what to do, the Maccabees and those who listened to them, instead of going the popular way which was the way of compromise. Daniel describes these things, which provide a shift in the time frame. Some of these things were about Antiochus, but then it shifts and there are things Antiochus never did historically, at which point it is talking about the Antichrist. In the last chapter of Daniel it says...

> *"Many will be purged, purified and refined, but the wicked will act wickedly; and none of the wicked will understand, but those who have insight will understand* (Dan. 12:10)

Daniel describes those who have wisdom. Not only will they understand, but where he talks about the Resurrection he says they will turn many to righteousness. The people in the Last Days who are going to be ready for Jesus to come back are going to have wisdom through the Scriptures to understand what is happening. Not only that, their understanding and their wisdom will propel them to a radical sense of evangelism.

Types of the Antichrist: Figures Who Teach About Him

In addition to the major types of the Antichrist in Scripture there are a number of other figures in Scripture who typify him to a definite but less extensive degree. We will deal with the latter group not in the repertoire of major types, but we will bring them and their significance into play in others sections and chapters where appropriate.

We must also draw a distinction between scriptural and historical types of the Antichrist. Purely historical types (such as a Hitler or Napoleon) must be subordinated to those types found in the pages of Scripture. The exception to this would be those whose history is not explicitly recorded in Scripture but are, however, predicted in Scripture—such as Antiochus Epiphanes, the highly important Simon Bar Kochba, and of course the ultimate two Beasts of Revelation 13.

The amount of detail from Scripture highlighting traits and actions to be re-performed by the Antichrist are too voluminous to be addressed in a mere "list format." This is particularly true of figures such as Antiochus Epiphanes, Solomon, and above all Herod the Great, all of whom will require more extensive explanation further along in this book. We also must note that we cannot establish any definitive doctrinal conclusions based on figures who are purely historical even though they add an important area of depth to our understanding, and their patterns of behavior are in tune with what Scripture teaches about both ***the*** Antichrist and the ***many*** antichrists.

Finally, we again note that the basis of doctrine can never derive from typology, allegory, or Midrash. Attempts to do so will summon the specter of Gnosticism. An equal caveat, however, and highly erroneous, is the failure to use typology and midrashic exegesis to illuminate and illustrate what is plainly concluded from Scripture by inductive grammatical-historical means.

The difference may be compared to a microscopic examination of tissue. There are multiple organs and structures in a human or animal organism that will be histologically composed of the same kind of epithelium. As an example, one form of epithelium is called "ciliated," having hair-like follicles protruding from the cells, that assist the motion of liquids along the tissue base. Ciliated epithelium is normally associated with mucosa tissues—that is, mucous membranes. But just looking at the epithelium through a microscope will not tell us which mucous membrane comes from which organism. Diagnostically a physician would look at the oral buccal cavity of a sick person with a nose and throat inflammation and high fever before sending a tissue swab to a lab to find out what kind of bacteria or virus is causing the epithelial lining to be inflamed with infection. Just taking a swab of any mucosa tissue will tell a physician nothing; he must look at the macro before the micro. So, too, we must look at the macro before the micro.

In contemplating these types, as we prayerfully seek the guidance of the Holy Spirit in the process, we must first comprehend what we are looking at. It is not only futile but silly to exegetically apply midrashic, typological, or allegorical hermeneutics without first knowing what we are looking at. If someone cannot handle an inductive grammatical-historical interpretative method (*Peshet*), they will never begin to understand the underlying meaning (*Pesher*). There is no point in looking at tissue through a microscope if we do not know where the tissue came from and if we do not know why we are looking at it in the first place.

It is impossible not to perceive a danger as perilous on one extreme that will arise from failing to understand the typology and the need for midrashic exegesis. That can result in Gnostic mysticism if not properly handled, just as there is a perilous blindness in ignoring the need for the typological and midrashic approach and sticking only with a Stoic grammatical-historical perspective. Both approaches if attempted in isolation from each other are certain formulas for error and failure. As we have explained, we begin with the *Peshet* then move on to the *Pesher*. The failure to do anything else will produce only failure. When it comes to the final identification of the two Beasts in Revelation 13, however, as with the epic of Apollo 13, "Failure is not an option."

Whenever we witness in Scripture or in history a human other than the Lord Jesus accepting divine worship, it is a type of the Antichrist. These include deified figures such as Pharaoh, Herod (Ac. 12:22), and the Roman emperors who were known as Pontiffs (for "*Pontificus Maximus*," the imperial title assigned to the head of the poly-religious Pantheon). The ritualistic tenets of emperor worship have, of course, been transferred to papal veneration of the pope. Forms of emperor worship also traditionally exist in Japanese Shintoism and in the monarch as "son of god" motifs in multiple ancient Near Eastern cultures.

As we shall review more closely, the first example to begin with is Pharaoh. He was worshiped as a god. They gave him credit for all kinds of things. The Nile overflowing was attributed to him and the other Egyptian gods—Osiris, all of them—whose worship today is perpetuated in Freemasonry. Pharaoh is the god of Egypt. Egypt in the Bible is a symbol, or a metaphor, of the world. Moses leading the children of Israel out of Egypt through the Red Sea and into the Promised Land is a symbol of how Jesus leads believers, as it were, through baptism into Heaven. Moses goes to a mount and makes a covenant and sprinkles the people with the blood. That is a type of Jesus. And Pharaoh and his army pursue the children of Israel to destroy them, and God's people are rescued. That is how Satan comes after believers in general.

Numbers 11:4 states that the rabble who were among them wanted to go back to Egypt and backslide. Isaiah 30 and 31 proclaims woe to those who go down to Egypt, who want to go to Egypt for help. That is a type of trusting in the things of the world and trusting in Pharaoh, the god of this world.

The treasures of Egypt were given to the children of Israel to take with them to the Promised Land. So, too, *"But seek first His kingdom and His righteousness, and all these things will be added to you"* (Mt. 6:33) in God's way and God's time. But God's way is the way of the blood of the Lamb that was slain at the Passover and applied to the doorways. It is Jesus. At the Lord's Supper, Jesus said to proclaim the Lord's death until He comes (1 Co. 11:23-26). It is looking back to the blood of the Lamb when believers take the Lord's Supper, but it is also an appetizer—a foretaste—of the marriage supper of the Lamb. They are looking forward ***as well as*** back.

Pharaoh is a very major type of the Antichrist. This whole idea of the flesh and spirit goes back to the Patriarchs: Ishmael's relationship with his brother, Esau's relationship with his brother, the flesh persecuting the spirit. The son of the flesh persecuting the son of the promise typifies the Antichrist.

The Titles of the Antichrist

The use of the definite article in the Greek text which we translate as "the" makes the titles ascribed to the Antichrist not simply titles or descriptions, but connotes a uniqueness. There are many "***men*** of sin," but because of the nature of Satan who literally indwells him, the Antichrist is called "***the*** *man of sin.*" There are likewise many "***lawless*** men," but again, because the satanic nature will so animate the Antichrist, he is "***the*** *man of lawlessness.*"

Concerning these two titles of Antichrist we must again contrast him to Christ whom he attempts to imitate. True believers, for instance, are indeed "kings," but Jesus is ***the*** "King of kings." True believers similarly are "sons of God," but the Lord Jesus is ***the*** Son of God. Our sonship and our kingship derive from our connection and subordination to Him. We acquire these titles and positions because of our relationship to Him. So, too, the Antichrist acquires these unique titles because of his relationship to Satan.

The third title, the "*son of perdition*", however, ventures beyond this still, remembering that the scriptural concept of sonship entails "being in the character of" and denotes an acquired destiny foreknown by God. It is as if he was born for this purpose much the same as Christ as the Son of Righteousness was born for a redemptive purpose. We may understand "*son of perdition*" as a diametric contrast to Christ as the Son of Righteousness with the inherent implication that just as Christ was on earth for a purpose, so is Antichrist. This does not, however, negate the human element of either. Just as Jesus was fully human and fully divine, the Antichrist as the "*son of perdition*" will be fully human and fully satanic. Also, as Christ prayed, "Father, Thy will, not Mine be done" (Mt. 26:42), Jesus of His own volition accepted and affirmed that task for which He was ordained from birth (as was appointed in eternity). The Antichrist will in every sense be the satanic equivalent, choosing that which was satanically ordained for him, howbeit with the foreknowledge of God.

The clearest way for us to comprehend this is by contrasting him with Jesus; Antichrist always mimics Christ. Additionally, however, we have in the Gospel narratives describing Judas Iscariot a specific illumination of how this will play out in the person of the Antichrist. "*The Son of Man is to go, just as it is written of Him; but woe to that man by whom the Son of man is betrayed! It would have been good for that man if he had not been born*" (Mt. 26:24). By offering Judas the sop at the Last Supper (Jn. 13:26), Jesus was showing him favor above the other disciples and extending him a final chance to repent. But then Jesus urges him, "*What you do, do quickly*" (Jn. 13:27). The Antichrist, the "*son of perdition*," will operate according to the same pattern.

The varying passages describing the Antichrist employ these different titles according to the context of the pericope just as the varying titles for Christ such as "*the Son of Man*," or "*the Savior*," or "*the Son of God*" are employed in different scriptural passages referring to Jesus. Which aspect of Christ's nature is being highlighted by each title suits the context of the passage and the surrounding circumstances as well as the doctrinal theme being conveyed in each passage. The precise same thing is true of the Antichrist. In some passages he is called "*the man of sin*," in others "*the man of lawlessness*," and in still others, "*the son of perdition*." Once more we need to keep in mind that where the Antichrist is concerned we always have a distorted copying of Christ. A key example, 2 Thessalonians 2, addresses apostasy and the Great Falling Away, and those who do not love a knowledge of the truth. They depart from God's law. Hence in this context he is called "*the man of lawlessness*" or the "*anthropon anomon*."

In the contemporary Church, when unbiblical practices are questioned or challenged on the basis of Scripture such as what we witnessed in the counterfeit revivals of Toronto, Pensacola, and Lakeland, proponents of such deceptions attack even Pentecostal and charismatic moderates who warn against these counterfeits. They are accused of being "legalistic" because they insist upon a biblical basis to justify phenomena that is without scriptural foundation. In 1 Corinthians 9 Paul draws a distinction between being under the Law of Moses and under the law of Christ, making it clear that believers were neither under the Law of Moses nor were they without any law, but rather under the law of the New Covenant. There are in fact "do's" and "don'ts" in the New Testament the same as there were in the Old, yet the extremes of the modern Charismatic Movement and most of Pentecostalism have abandoned a scriptural premise for much of what they believe and do, denigrating as "legalists" those who uphold a scriptural standard. Indeed, earlier generations of Pentecostals cleaned their own house from the errors of Azusa Street and the heretical teachings of William Branham and E. W. Kenyon. Most of contemporary Pentecostalism, however, has embraced what the earlier generation of Pentecostals rejected, and have gone into what the New Testament defines as "*lawlessness*."

As the Antichrist is a counterfeit of Christ, there is therefore a counterfeit of the Holy Spirit (whom as we shall see will be ultimately personified in the person of the False Prophet). The counterfeit of the Holy Spirit we witnessed in Toronto, Pensacola, Lakeland, and in churches such as Holy Trinity Brompton and Kensington Temple in London, England, were moves of the spirit of lawlessness pretending to be a move of the Holy Spirit. Such are false revivals in spite of the churches and false shepherds and televangelists who promote them; they function under the seducing influence of the spirit of antichrist. This is evident in the lawlessness of the contra-scriptural doctrines, practices, and effects of such spiritual fraud.

Additionally, the Antichrist, like Judas, is closely tied to the love of wealth. So, too, the televangelists and others propounding these deceptions are to a large degree financially motivated. It is all the spirit of antichrist. There is, however, a further dimension that we are instructed about in 2 Thessalonians 2, where those who reject His Word reject Him and in their lawlessness are drawn by the spirit of antichrist to the "*man of lawlessness*" which God gives them over to. The contrast here parallels what we read in John's Epistle (a letter which also delves heavily into the Antichrist). In this

Epistle we read of a contrast between the spirit of truth and the spirit of error. Those who are swept away by the spirit of antichrist into the domain of the *"man of lawlessness"* reject God's Word and, consequently, God Himself, causing God to allow the delusion as judgment. Having abandoned the love of the knowledge of the truth as 2 Thessalonians 2:12 informs us, they inevitably are handed over to a spirit of error to believe false signs and wonders (2 Th. 2:9) that will eventually reach its climax with the full activity of Satan in the *"man of lawlessness."* We already see this at work. For as this passage tells us in 2 Thessalonians 2:7, *"the mystery of lawlessness is already at work."*

Once the Holy Spirit is taken, however, there will be no restraining of the power of Satan who will seek to incarnate himself in the Antichrist, a venture in which he will succeed. We can be sure that those following the present avalanche of spiritual seduction contradicting God's law—which seduction is already underway in everything from ecumenism, interfaith worship, emergence, false peace, *Purpose Driven* agendas, and the wide range of other deceptions—are already being manipulated by Satan in preparation for the advent of the Antichrist. This is described as a *"mystery"* in 2 Thessalonians. Those who are caught up in it and refuse to repent do not, will not, and ultimately shall not, be able to understand the *"mystery."* The faithful Church will. This is the crux of the meaning of the *"man of lawlessness"* just as Judas provides us the crux of the meaning of the *"son of perdition."* Likewise, the embodiment of Satan as the author of sin in the person of Antichrist is the crux of our understanding of the *"man of sin."*

We should note, however, that although Revelation 13 is indeed speaking of the Antichrist and the False Prophet, neither of them are called "the Antichrist" in that passage—the reason being in part that both the first Beast and the second are ***equally*** antichrist. Just as the Holy Spirit is the Spirit of Jesus and communicates Christ to us, the False Prophet, by religious subterfuge, will communicate Antichrist to the fallen world.

A second and more focal reason, however, is again the theme and context of the passage. Revelation 13 operates within the paradigm established in the Book of Daniel both typologically and prophetically. Hence the term "***the***" Beast comes into play as the fourth major titular description of the Antichrist in addition to the *"man of sin,"* the *"man of lawlessness,"* and the *"son of perdition."* Once more the theme, the context, and the doctrinal emphasis of the passage determine by which descriptive title he is called. Along this line, the same process holds true. Just as there are many men of sin but only one called **THE** *"man of sin,"* or many lawless ***men*** but only one called **THE** *"man of lawlessness,"* so, too, in Daniel and in Revelation we see many ***beasts***, but only the Antichrist and False Prophet are called **THE** Beast. That is, the first and second—one from the earth (in some way referring to Israel and/or the Church), and the other from the sea (that is, the nations with particular emphasis on the nations around the Mediterranean).

Judas

Judas Iscariot is without dispute the single most important type or shadow of the Antichrist in the New Testament, although in a number of key aspects Herod the Great would be a very close second, even typifying Antichrist in areas Judas does not, particularly with regard to ethnicity. In the person of Judas we see at least three cardinal aspects of what the Antichrist will be and do.

- Foremost he is the *"son of perdition"* (Jn. 17:12; 2 Th. 2:3);

- Secondly, he will "go out from among us" (Ac. 1:17; 1 Jn. 2:18-19) after deceiving the Elect that he is one of us. Like Judas, this is something the Antichrist will be able to do up to a certain point when Christ reveals him;

- Thirdly is his coveting of material and financial wealth and use of a social gospel to pull the wool over the eyes of otherwise sincere people about who he actually is and concerning the nature of his actual agenda.

His love of money should strike an alarm bell in the mind of every Christ-loving Christian with reference to money-preaching televangelists who in effect worship mammon while calling Jesus "Christ." It should also sound a loud alarm about the social gospels that have rebranded so many ministries that began scripturally, ranging from organizations such as World Vision to Barnardo's and many others. The capacity of Judas to deceive the apostles is probably the clearest picture we have in the New Testament of the capacity of the Antichrist to deceive the Elect.

The Gospel of John gives this account:

> *Mary then took a pound of very costly perfume of pure nard, and anointed the feet of Jesus and wiped His feet with her hair; and the house was filled with the fragrance of the perfume. But Judas Iscariot, one of His disciples, who was intending to betray Him, said, "Why was this perfume not sold for three hundred denarii and given to poor people?" Now he said this, not because he was concerned about the poor, but because he was a thief, and as he had the money box, he used to pilfer what was put into it* (Jn. 12:3-6).

Judas loved money; so will the person he represents or typifies. In Matthew's parallel account it is recorded…

> *But the disciples were indignant when they saw this, and said, "Why this waste? For this perfume might have been sold for a high price and the money given to the poor."* (Mt. 26:8-9)

So now it is the disciples. In one place it is "*Judas*," in another place it is "*the disciples*." But then again in the Gospel of Mark a slightly different, third perspective, is given. Mark says "*now some of the disciples*." John says it is Judas, Matthew says it is the disciples, and in Mark is portrayed the connection between the two.

> *But some were indignantly remarking to one another, "Why has this perfume been wasted?"* (Mk. 14:4)

Remember, John teaches that where the Antichrist and his many precursors are concerned, "they went out from among us" (1 Jn. 2:18-19). Judas exemplifies this qualification. Additionally, Judas and the Antichrist both love money, they are both called the "*son of perdition*" (Jn. 17:12; 6:70), and they are the only two people who are demon-possessed by Satan personally. The Bible even speaks mysteriously about Judas and says he went to his own place (Ac. 1:25), that he is going to be in some way not reincarnated, but will come back in the way that the spirit of Elijah comes back. That spirit of betrayal comes back.

Every biblical account of Judas is God trying to teach something about the Antichrist. In John he pretends to care about the poor. He does not really care about poor people, but he uses a feigned concern for the poor and the disenfranchised to gain support for himself. When the synoptic accounts are read together, some of the disciples agree with him in Mark.

But then Matthew takes it a step further, saying, "*the disciples.*" In other words, he instigates this thing by being someone who pretends to care for the poor people, which first inflames a few disciples and then ultimately enrages all of them. He did not care about poor people; he cared about himself and how to get power and influence for himself. We will examine how the Antichrist will use false philanthropy in the pursuit of his agenda.

A Reincarnational or an Incarnational Antichrist & the Question of the Nephilim?

When the Scriptures speak about Antichrist, there is a quasi-mysterious confusion. For instance, as we shall see, King Saul, who foreshadows the Antichrist in certain aspects, was stabbed and hung, and Judas was hung and stabbed. The sons of Adonikam in Ezra and in Nehemiah vary by one. In one account they number "666" but in another "667." (I do not believe this to be a mere textual error. Neither do I believe that at present I fully understand the reasons for such variations.)

The Scriptures also state that Judas "*turned aside to go to his own place*" (Ac. 1:25). The automatic question is, "Why does it phrase his journey into the afterlife in these terms?" It is as if he is coming back in some way.

We of course must reject reincarnation as Hinduism's counterfeit of second birth, although at the Resurrection the dead in Christ will be reincarnated, as it were, into their same bodies. This brings us to the proposition of a reincarnational Antichrist that was posed by the late Robert Van Kampen. Whatever the merits, no matter how substantial Mr. Van Kampen's position for the sequence of End Times events and the timing of the Rapture, we fundamentally reject his reincarnational view of the Antichrist which he moreover applied not to Judas but to Hitler. In the reincarnational view, if one of the Two Witnesses in Revelation 11 is either Moses or Elijah as many (if not most) postulate, it will of necessity need to involve some form of reincarnation.

On the basis of God's Word of course, we must fundamentally reject pre-resurrectional reincarnation as a norm, and the Resurrection itself will ***not*** be reincarnation in the Hindu sense of coming back as another person or being, but as rather the physiological reconstitution of resurrected believers in a renewed body—although this does leave the question of how the two olive trees seen in Zechariah become incarnated in Revelation 11. This, however, does not directly relate to the subject of the identification of the Antichrist. In theory, this may be part of the explanation for both

Revelation 11 and Judas, at least among those holding to this view. A more straightforward explanation, however, may in large part be the ***spirit*** of Judas coming upon another person in terms of the ***character*** of Judas, much the same as John the Baptist had the spirit of Elijah. This issue, once more, represents something deeply mysterious. Scripture only contains resurrectional narratives, not any reincarnational ones.

When Jesus died, Old Testament saints were seen walking about in Jerusalem, and there is no indication in the text that their apparition was that of a ghost as in the case of Samuel's posthumous apparition to backslidden Saul or the transfigured Moses on the Mount of Transfiguration in Matthew 16. The exact means or nature of how Satan will achieve this fete is not as yet thoroughly clear, although we emphatically reject the Hindu doctrine of reincarnation. We caution against any speculation beyond the Scriptures concerning a pre-resurrection physical reappearance of any biblical figure which we note with all due regard both to Revelation 11 and to Matthew 27:52-53. Despite our own objections and reservations, however, on this note we are further compelled to lend due credence to the fact that Antichrist will counterfeit Christ, and that Jesus came back from the dead and lived for a short while on the earth, literally and biologically, and continued in ministry. Even if there were any scripturally defensible support for a reincarnational Antichrist, however (a proposition with which we are prone to strongly question), it would be a case involving Judas and not Hitler.

We also cannot ignore the stated fact that as Christ had 3-1/2 years, the Antichrist will have equal time to counterfeit the miracles of Jesus. Among others, Jesus raised Lazarus, the widow's son at Nain, and a little girl. The question then becomes, "On what scriptural basis can we absolutely determine that Satan will not be able to raise Judas from the dead?" The reason we are prone to reject such a proposition is that it would mean the Antichrist would not be biologically born of a woman in imitation of Christ. This is again a complicated question, and even if it were true it would, among other things, raise further questions about the ethnicity of the Antichrist. Into which nation will he have to be born? Nonetheless there is too much fundamental impediment to readily justify the concept of a reincarnational Antichrist and too many of the arguments that can be set forward are mainly deductive in nature, even if the Antichrist were to somehow be utterly unique in this regard.

It is simply not possible on the basis of any ***scriptural*** evidence thus far presented to solidly affirm the Antichrist as a reincarnation of Judas with any categorical certainty, to say nothing of the myriad of arguments both scriptural and practical against it. If the possibility exists it is not to be found in the spurious case made by Robert Van Kampen despite the fact we cannot dismiss the reality of the unanswered question surrounding what does God's Word mean when it states he "*turned aside to go to his own place*"? (Ac. 1:25). As with "666" and "667," there must be some significance. The issue of the Antichrist, like Judas being the "*son of perdition*," may, in the view of some, leave us with questions concerning proposed possibilities of some form of reincarnation. The inductive content of Scripture, however, speaks of resurrection and incarnation only, and not of reincarnation.

The unexplored possibility, however, concerns the highbred incarnation of demonoids facilitated by a return of the Nephilim, noting that black necromancy, Satan worship, and some forms of witchcraft all involve initiation rituals involving surrogate sex with the devil or with demonic beings. In some cases this is practiced by acclaimed proxy through sexual union with a satanic high priest. However, there is yet another proposed possibility that has come into vogue among those obsessed with extraterrestrial life. Those claiming some form of UFO abduction, even under hypnotic drugs administered psychiatrically, commonly ascribe an interest or fascination with reproductive organs by the extraterrestrial abductors. Again, we are aware from the warning of Jesus that His return will emphatically be just as the days of Noah in Genesis 6 when the Nephilim appeared. At this point we cannot be dogmatic about the manner in which this wicked phenomenon will transpire. However, it would appear from the Olivet Discourse that it ***shall*** transpire. And along this line we cannot ignore a potential significance of either satanic worship or UFO activity in this regard.

> *The Nephilim were on the earth in those days, and also afterward, when the sons of God came in to the daughters of men, and they bore children to them. Those were the mighty men who were of old, men of renown.* (Genesis 6:4)

Scripture informs us that the Nephilim procreated with human women before the Flood, but also states, "*and also afterward*." The Nephilim were on the earth both before ***and*** after the Diluvian Age—certainly in the

Antediluvian Era at least. This was probably a satanic effort to genetically corrupt and mutate the human race in order to prevent the birth of the Messiah from a female human agency (although Eve additionally typifies Israel, and to a lesser degree by typological implication, also the Church). The Postdiluvian descendants of the Nephilim included the Anakim, the Rephaim, and what Ezekiel 32:27 calls the *Giborim Nephilim* ("fallen giants" or "great ones").

We additionally have an historical record of the leader of the Nephilim as Sem Jaza in reference to the watchers, who in Greek are called "*egregoroi*." Enoch 10:3-8 states that there were two hundred such angels called "watchers." This Postdiluvian activity would account for the giants of Numbers 13:32-33 who are descendants of Anak. This is supported by *The Dead Sea Scrolls*— by apocryphal *Enoch*, by the Geez Ethiopian translation of *Enoch*, by the book of *Jubilees*, by the Aramaic Targum pseudo-Jonaton, and by the rabbinic tractate Yoma 67. We therefore reject as not likely that these were descendants of Seth in the Book of Genesis, a concept having its origins possibly in the Essene community from the Qumran record in the 4Q-4:17 instruction. The weight of evidence—biblical, apocryphal, and historical—supports a Postdiluvian attempt at procreation with demonoids.

While it is in theory possible that the offspring of these fallen angelic beings could have maternally been descended from Seth's female descendants, it is not probable that the "sons of God" were male progeny from other human lineages (instead of being fallen angels), nor therefore that the offspring from the union were paternally descended from Seth. For any purposes of examining implications of this text the focus remains a hybrid of the supernatural and natural. What these demons perpetrated resembles the supernatural conception of Christ as a divine man and may hint that Satan in the Antichrist will in some manner attempt the same mixture of natural and supernatural. It will of course not be possible because Christ was 100% human and 100% divine, while the demonoid hybrids were but 50% - 50%; yet the attempt to counterfeit and resemble is always present in the antichrist spirit.

We must note that in Genesis 6:4 we are told that the fallen angels (also mentioned in Jude 6) perpetuated their heinous copulation not only in those days of the Flood, but afterward as well. This would explain how past Postdiluvian incarnations of the Anakim, etc., took place and can do so again. An obvious avenue for this to occur would be black necromancy, even without exploring the prospects of artificial biogenetic engineering combined with occult practices.

In the first attempt Satan's plan was eradicated by the Flood; in the second attempt it was eradicated by God's people Israel during faithful periods of their service to Him in the days of Joshua and later David. We note that some of David's wars were fought in the Valley of Rephaim, and this explanation would give a straightforward account of Goliath and the villainous giant of whom we shall consider further on. (2 Sam. 21:20; 1 Chr. 20:6)

Again, we cannot say that the Antichrist will be a procreated demonoid, although it would strongly appear from both the warnings of Jesus about the days of Noah returning and apparent implications in the Book of Revelation that there will be such demonoids during the time the Antichrist is perpetrating his onslaught. We are told in Peter's epistle that God will not destroy the earth again with water as with Noah, but rather with fire (2 Pe. 3:5-7). The first divine extermination of the descendants of the Nephilim was achieved by water, the second by divinely empowered warfare, and the final will be with thermal obliteration. The second relates to the divine instruction given to Adam to subdue the earth when the serpent was already in the Garden seeking control but did not have it. Joshua and David are types of Christ, both of whom did manage to subdue the satanic presence on the earth in a physical sense, prefiguring and foreshadowing the final elimination of the forces of Satan by Jesus.

Our only point is twofold: during the reign of Antichrist there will be a likely reappearance of demonoids as in the days of Noah. Without doubt the spirit of antichrist is currently at work preparing the way for this in black necromancy and Satanism, extraterrestrial deception, and quite possibly unnatural genetic manipulation of the human species, potentially combined with bio-interactive microchip technology. The second aspect is that if there is some incarnational explanation for the origin of the Antichrist, it will not be reincarnational but procreational involving the Nephilim.

If we were to take this approach, it is not unfathomable that the Antichrist, already a demon hybrid, would then become wholly satanized when he counterfeits the resurrection. The point here is that Jesus had a human mother but a divine Father. So, too, Satan would want to counterfeit the incarnation of Christ with a human mother and a demonic/satanic father. If this were indeed to be the case, and if the non-canonical historical tradition is correct, Sem Jaza (leader of the Nephilim) would of necessity likewise typify the Antichrist. As a caveat, however, we are once again emphatic that at the present point in time we cannot categorically affirm this possibility. Nor can we categorically dismiss it even though a more conventional approach would be to merely look for a demon-possessed man who would become Satan-possessed after counterfeiting the resurrection of Christ.

The Ethnicity of Judas

Another question that arises, however, is the issue of Judas and the ethnicity of the Antichrist. Although few in number, based on what is allegedly known of the local demography of the home of Judas "Iscariot" (derived from "Kerioth," a town in the country of Judah), it has been suggested that Judas was a Jew by religion and not by ethnicity. However, it is not possible to positively either affirm or deny this possibility with any categorical certainty. Regarding the Antichrist,, however, we note the Apostle John's description of not really being of us as well as of going out from us (1 Jn. 2:18-19). Judas was a non-Galilean, and if he were the descendant of proselytes it would further match the description where John characterizes Antichrist in the mold of Judas.

We must note that in both Judaism and Christianity there were in the 1st and 2nd centuries ethnic non-Jews who by virtue of religion and culture were fully accepted as being Jews. Such would be the Apostle Paul's probable classmate Onkilos, Rabbi Akiva (whom we shall see was a type of the False Prophet), and Herod the Great. The term "proselyte," as in the prodigal case of Luke the evangelist, is generally applied in the New Testament to non-Jews who themselves converted to Judaism; it would not apply to non-ethnic Jews whose forbears converted to Judaism. At this point we can neither determine conclusively nor dismiss absolutely that Judas cannot fit into this category. How the "*son of perdition*" reappears in the character of Judas can be more readily explained in terms of the Judaic concept of sonship as related in Scripture, which we will note in our section regarding Pharaoh.

However these matters unfold, of one thing we may rest assured: in some way we have not yet heard the last of the "*son of perdition*." What we have seen of him so far in the person of Judas is the mere shadow of some kind of satanically animated reappearance. Because of the problems of so closely resembling pagan reincarnation beliefs, and because of the lack of hard evidence and, above all, the present lack of focal clarity of what the

Scriptures reveal, we must be extremely cautious in considering this issue. Yet whether it will be someone in the mere character of Judas or something more sinister, the *"son of perdition"* is reappearing on the present horizon.

The ethnicity of Judas, however, is not necessarily the same as the ethnicity of the Antichrist. We shall address that subject in greater scope when we deal with his other major New Testament shadow, Herod the Great.

It Leads to Deception

Satan is going to use philanthropy to get people to follow the Antichrist. He is going to pretend, like Judas, the *"son of perdition,"* to care about the poor as a way to manipulate God's people. If possible, even the Elect will be deceived, and that is one of the ways he is going to do it. And after doing so, all of a sudden he goes out, and it is night (Jn. 13:30), a metaphor for the Tribulation.

> *and with all the deception of wickedness for those who perish, because they did not receive the love of the truth so as to be saved.* (2 Th. 2:10)

They do not receive the love of the truth, but receive a social gospel. Here we understand the social-political emphasis of the dying Protestant denominations. They have died a self-inflicted spiritual death by negating the authority of Scripture, a self-inflicted moral death with lenient decrees on moral issues ranging from divorce to homosexuality and lesbianism, and an intellectual death with Higher Criticism. They need a new raison d'être.

Often, as with the Presbyterian Church of America, the Church of England, and the World Council of Churches, this includes turning a deaf ear to the persecuted Church in Islamic countries and ganging up in league with Islam. It also involves embracing ecumenical harmony with Roman Catholic and Eastern Orthodox voices to condemn Israel. Ironically, Israel has the best human rights record in the Middle East and is the one nation protective of the religious freedom of Arab-Christians. The antichrist spirit is supremely anti-Semitic, as the Antichrist will muster the nations against Israel.

Another example of the social gospel is, again, Rick Warren's "Global P.E.A.C.E. Plan" and the spiritual and doctrinal erosion of organizations such as World Vision which began as biblically Christian, but has degenerated into adopting a mere "social and political" salvation message also biased against the nation of Israel.

> *For this reason God will send upon them a deluding influence so that they will believe what is false, in order that they all may be judged who did not believe the truth, but took pleasure in wickedness.* (2 Th. 2:11-12)

The deluding influence is sent by God! Satan as the king of Babylon (where Nebuchadnezzar is a type of the Antichrist) is called "a servant of God" in Jeremiah (Jer. 25:9). The Antichrist works as God's agent in Zechariah (Zech. 11:16). All these wicked kings, like the king of Babylon, were God's agents to judge His people. Because His people wanted to believe a lie, God sent them a ***real*** lie. If someone ***wants*** to believe a lie, if they ***want*** to be religious, if they ***do not*** want to believe the truth of God's revealed Word, God says, "Go ahead. Here is a ***real*** lie for you to believe!" That is what is going to happen. That is beginning to happen already. It is a very, very serious business. The night is very near.

> *Now as the times and epochs...*

(The seasons of prophetic history.)

> *...brethren, you have no need of anything to be written to you. For you yourselves know full well that the day of the Lord will come just like a thief in the night. While they are saying, "Peace and safety!" then destruction will come upon them suddenly...*

(How?)

> *...like labor pains upon a woman with child, and they will not escape.*

Birth pangs! In Revelation it is the same as in Jeremiah and the rest.

> *But you, brethren, are not in darkness, that the day would overtake you like a thief;* (1 Th. 5:14)

Have wisdom; do not love this world; do not be in darkness; believe the truth; do not be deceived. That is what it is saying; no one has to be deceived. And for anyone whose heart is right, who trusts Jesus and obeys His Word, and who is led by His Spirit, they are not going to be deceived.

"While they are saying, 'Peace and safety!'" The Berlin Wall came down, "Hallelujah! The Cold War is over! It is a new world order!" A couple of weeks later the Americans and British are rushing tens of thousands of troops to the Persian Gulf for the biggest war since Korea. Incidents like Yugoslavia or Somalia—that is the New World Order. The Antichrist is going to come and try to bring peace.

Look at what is happening in Yugoslavia now. When the Roman Empire divided between the East and West, Yugoslavia was the cutting edge between the Greek-speaking East and the Latin- and Romance-speaking West; it was the center of conflict between the Roman Catholic world and the Eastern Orthodox world. Just like Thebes and Nineveh, two demonic cities, there was friction between Constantinople and Rome.

In the 1940s, the Ustashi (the Croatians) and the Roman Catholic hierarchy under the papacy of Pope Pius XII made an alliance with Hitler and they murdered 750,000 Serbs. That is why they are so angry about what happened; they had a holocaust against the Serbs. They are both anti-Semitic—neither of them have any place for born-again Christians—but it was also the cutting edge between the South and the North. The Islamic world and the Christianized world met in the Balkans. The Saracens were always fighting Yugoslavia in the Balkans. That place was always the "crunch," where the rubber meets the road, as Americans would put it.

Daniel sees the divide between the kings of the North and the kings of the South (Dan. 11). The time would come when geopolitical conflict would be between the North and the South. This is what is happening now, conflict between the developed world and the developing world.

He Will Be Revealed

> *Now we request you, brethren, with regard to the coming of our Lord Jesus Christ and our gathering together to Him, that you not be quickly shaken from your composure or be disturbed either by a spirit or a message or a letter as if from us, to the effect that the day of the Lord has come. Let no one in any way deceive you, for it will not come unless the...*

...("*apostasia*" in Greek)...

...the apostasy...

...(the "falling away")...

...comes first, and the man of lawlessness is revealed, the son of destruction, (2 Th. 2:1-3)

The Rapture of the Church will not happen until the identity of the Antichrist is revealed to the faithful Elect. "*Let him who has understanding calculate the number of the beast*" (Rev. 13:18). No one knows who this guy is until God reveals him, and we cannot be taken up until we know who he is. But remember, up to the last minute he has the Gentile woman totally flabbergasted, and then all of a sudden, 666.

Everybody thought Judas was a great humanitarian, and then all of a sudden it was night and Jesus was betrayed. Believers are really up against somebody here. His wisdom is greater than Daniel's.

who opposes and exalts himself above every so-called god or object of worship, so that he takes his seat in the temple of God, displaying himself as being God. Do you not remember that while I was still with you, I was telling you these things? And you know what restrains him now, so that in his time he will be revealed. For the mystery of lawlessness is already at work; only he who now restrains will do so until he is taken out of the way. Then that lawless one will be revealed whom the Lord will slay...

...(as has been seen in the Old Testament)...

...with the breath of His mouth and bring to an end by the appearance of His coming;

(This manifestation of Satan has come to be called the Antichrist.)

...that is, the one whose coming is in accord with the activity of Satan, with all power and signs and false wonders,

Just as Jesus' activity was in accord with the power and activity of God, Satan has his equivalent. At some point, just as Jesus came into an awareness of who He was, the Antichrist comes into awareness of who he is before anyone else knows it.

> *...and with all the deception of wickedness for those who perish, because they did not receive the love of the truth so as to be saved. For this reason God will send upon them a deluding influence so that they will believe what is false,* (2 Th. 2:4-11)

There are two primary ways the Antichrist will deceive: the first is a social gospel aimed at global peace apart from a saving faith in Christ. Here we must understand the Antichrist nature of Rick Warren's Global P.E.A.C.E Plan, Satan's device for sucking naïve and undiscerning Evangelicals into this Christless lie.

> *While they are saying, "Peace and safety!" then destruction will come upon them suddenly...* (1 Th. 5:3)

The other is counterfeit signs and wonders which may be supernaturally achieved by satanic power as with Pharaoh's magicians. Con-artist televangelists with bogus claims and medically undocumented healings are likewise setting the stage to lure supposed Evangelicals into this deception. If Christians cannot discern an obvious heretic like Benny Hinn or Todd Bentley, what will take place when ***real*** deception comes? While no one should negate a biblical understanding of the miraculous, believers are commanded to test all things spiritually (1 Jn. 4:1). As always, "*An evil and adulterous generation craves for a sign*" (Mt. 12:39).

Believers must ignore the folly of belief that the Rapture and Resurrection can transpire prior to the revelation of Antichrist. The monkey tricks done with the Greek text of 2 Thessalonians 2 are a "*reductio ad absurdum.*" The Lord would not give the faithful so much instruction on how to identify the Antichrist if there were no ***need*** to identify him.

The full implication of his being "revealed" in 2 Thessalonians 2:3 is in part based on his desire to be God (which reflects Satan's desire in Ezekiel 28 and Isaiah 14) made manifest in human form. The concept revealed here is "*apokalypto*" (the same Greek word as "apocalypse") conveying a scenario where the Antichrist is already on the scene and possibly, if not probably to some degree, already operational before his identity is revealed. This again precisely matches both the modus operandi and the revelation by Christ of Judas as the "*son of perdition.*" He was already a known figure, active in his surreptitious designs, but his identity was initially, and for some time at least, known only to Christ until He revealed him at the Last Supper. In a kind of final feeding of the Church before a humungous betrayal and falling away, Christ will once again reveal the identity of the *"son of perdition"* through His Word and by His Spirit. This His true disciples in the faithful Church will know at the appropriate time, but not ***until*** the appropriate time.

Chapter 5: The Other Major Biblical Types

Pharaoh

As we have recurrently emphasized, deified political and religious rulers who are worshiped as divine incarnations always prefigure the Antichrist. Few approach the importance of Pharaoh in the Book of Exodus in understanding this.

There are multiple theories as to which pharaoh and even from which specific dynasty the pharaoh of Exodus was. This in itself is not important in that, with one monotheistic exception in Arkhenaten, all of the pharaohs were seen as divine. Because of the influence of Joseph, Pharaoh Montu-Hotep I may have declined acceptance of divinity for himself. It is most likely that Pharaoh Amenemhat III drove Moses out and that Pharaoh Amenemhat IV was the Pharaoh of the Exodus. These identities, however, cannot be definitely proven. It is also likely that after the death of Joseph the Pharaohs Yotef I, II, and III in dynastic succession progress toward compounded idolatry and a departure of the legacy of Joseph, ending in the Jew hatred evident in the Book of Exodus.

This is very much akin to what would later be seen in the Roman emperors, although certain of them (particularly Caesar Augustus and Nero) are more prominent types of Antichrist than the others even though they all foreshadow him. Much the same is true in the historical succession of pontifical Imperial Rome found in the Roman Catholic papacy. All popes are antichrists but certain individual ones more acutely typify Antichrist than others.

The deification of the pharaohs, Imperial Roman emperors, and the kings of Babylon all share a common feature as the means of explaining deification, and that is sonship. Emperors, pharaohs, and the kings of Babylon where uniformly seen as incarnated sons of a chief deity in each demonic culture. It is of course Christ alone who holds deity by virtue of a Sonship that is not really incarnational, but eternal and pre-existent.

As we elsewhere note, the judgments on Egypt in the Book of Exodus that are recounted in the Paschal Seder liturgy even today foreshadow the judgments on the kingdom of Antichrist in the Book of Revelation.

Darkness, blood, etc., are all recapitulated. And as we will note in addressing Jannes and Jambres, Pharaoh's magicians counterfeited the miracles of Moses and Aaron to a high degree in the manner in which the False Prophet will likewise counterfeit the miracles of Jesus and His Witnesses.

The Exodus judgments on Egypt parallel Pharaoh's persecution of the people of God before they are rescued. The destruction of Pharaoh and his armies following the rescue of God's people foreshadows the wrath of God; that is, the "Day of the Lord" when God will not simply pour out His multiplied judgment, but destruction upon Antichrist and his forces. Thus in the Book of Revelation the saints of God once more sing the song of Moses, celebrating the defeat of the Antichrist (Rev. 15:3-4).

The continual lying, backtracking, breaking of promises, and false assurances of Pharaoh are indicative of the character and behavior of the Antichrist to come. So is his hatred of ethnic Israel and the Jews.

Joseph's bones being taken out of Egypt at the time of the Exodus is a picture of the dead in Christ coming out of the world with the resurrected, the Exodus depicting not only the Rapture and Resurrection, but the judgment on the enemies of God and His people set to follow it.

Everything from the fanatical building programs of Pharaoh, to his arrogance, to his paranoid hatred of the Jews, to his reliance upon sorcery, reveals the person of the Beast during the Great Tribulation more than any other figure. The gods of Egypt, moreover, have a broad correspondence to where the judgments of the God of Israel fell. These deities are thought by some scholars to have included Aker who helped the dead, Atum the sun god, Bes the protector at birth and the god of sexual virility, Heket the primordial goddess (represented by a frog), Isis the goddess of life, Khepri the god of the rising sun (represented by the beetle), Khnum the god of the Nile and creator of man, Mut the eye of the sun (represented by a vulture), Nut the sky goddess, Osiris the ruler of the dead, life, and vegetation, Rah the sun god and god of the nation, Selket the guardian of life (represented by a scorpion), Seth the god of chaos, Sosthis the god of floods, and Thermuthis the goddess of fertility (represented by a serpent). Biblical typology employs the serpent, scorpion, and the vulture as representations of the demonic in scriptural symbolism.

What is important for Pharaoh, however, was Bes, the god who protected at birth and who is symbolized in hieroglyphics by a cluster of demons. As the angelic hosts of heaven who appeared to the shepherds afforded divine protection of Jesus at birth, and as Christ was supernaturally protected in his infancy by angelic visitation and intervention, so, too, Antichrist will from his birth be demonically protected or guided in some way.

This further assists us in understanding how Antichrist can reappear without reincarnation. The issue becomes a matter of sonship. As the divine nature of God was by Sonship manifested in Christ, the nature of Satan will be manifested in the person of Antichrist, although like Pharaoh he will affirm and elect his assumed position through his own choice.

As recorded in Exodus 5:2, God did not harden Pharaoh's heart as He told Moses He would, until Pharaoh already withstood God on Pharaoh's own terms. In this episode we see that what Pharaoh would do was prophetically ordained. Yet in what is sometimes theologically called an "antimony," he first chose his own position against God, without doubt under strong demonic influence. The same will be true for Antichrist as it was for Judas. The fact that who they were and what they will do is foreknown by God and foretold to His people before ordination, however, does not negate his own choice in the matter. As a result of that choice God causes him to be the enemy God will judge.

The Hebrew concept of sonship does not always entail pedigree. Yet even where it does it carries a further meaning, and that meaning is "in the character of." This conveys an easier understanding of "*son of perdition*" in much the same way as Pharaoh was a son of Rah, Caesar a son of Jupiter, and the kings of Egypt sons of Bel, all of which are in some way appellations for Satan. Moreover, in the Hebrew text of Scripture there is a wordplay between the name of the supreme Egyptian sun-god Rah and the Hebrew word "*rah*" which means "evil."

Nimrod

Nimrod as an historical figure is a metaphor for Babylon where false religions began. The conflict between Jesus and false religions is foreshadowed in Genesis with Nimrod in Assyria. Nimrod is a complicated figure to consider because although the historical background of the origins of Babylon and the Tower of Babel depend upon him, the historical record we have of him and Semiramus is found in the book of *Jasher*. This historical material should not be negated, but of more important concern is what Scripture says of "*the Assyrian*."

And He will deliver us from the Assyrian
When he attacks our land
And when he tramples our territory.
Then the remnant of Jacob
Will be among many peoples
The Jews will be scattered.
Like dew from the LORD,
Like showers on vegetation
Which do not wait for man
Or delay for the sons of men.
The remnant of Jacob
Will be among the nations,

(...in the Diaspora...)

Among many peoples... (Mic. 5:6-8a)

And it goes on describing what would happen. But it is Jesus who comes from Bethlehem who would make war against the king of Assyria and rescue them. Chapter 4 of Micah speaks of Babylon. And right in the middle of the story about its king comes Jesus to rescue those who are His people. This is not speaking about a great king from Babylon or Assyria, but a baby born in a manger. That is God's way.

There is actually a verse in Micah in Hebrew that says, "Do not follow the '*aluf*'" (Mic. 7:5). It is usually mistranslated as "neighbor" or "guide," and it is the modern Hebrew word for "general." In biblical Hebrew it is the lead steer of a herd. It says not to follow him. In other words, the leaders are going to lead people into destruction at the end. Satan will get hold of the leaders among God's people to misdirect them. That is what Zechariah 11 is warning about. They are trafficking in their sheep, becoming personally rich at the expense of the people Jesus entrusted them to care for.

That is what is going to happen, but that is what is happening already. The Book of Micah in chapter 5 prophetically deals with both the First and Second Coming of Jesus. The earlier verses foretell His First Coming to Bethlehem. In verse 5 there is an allusion to the Antichrist as "*the Assyrian*." The Assyrian invasion of Israel had come into the southern towns of Judah in Micah's own time and Israel was saved by direct divine intervention, but not by a messianic figure (Is. 36-37). What transpired then foreshadows what will happen at the end of the age concerning not primarily the Church, but national and ethnic Israel with regard to the Antichrist and the intervention of Christ to save them.

The land of Assyria is geographically, theologically, spiritually, and typologically almost synonymous with the land of Nimrod (Mic. 5:6). It seems from verses 7 and 8 that the faithful remnant of Jewish believers will still be not only in Israel but in the Diaspora. (This may be due to discriminatory immigration practices against Jewish believers by the religious political parties in Israel such as "Shaas," "Aguvat Israel," and the National Religious Party.) There will also be in Israel at the time an upsurge of idolatry, graven image veneration, and occult activity including fortune telling and sorcery (Mic. 5:12-14). These verses appear to make some reference to the idolatry and icon veneration of the Roman Catholic and Eastern Orthodox churches that pollute Israel and many of its holy sites on behalf of the apostate church. But for the Jews themselves (to whom the passage primarily refers), the practices of Cabala which stem directly from the occult and have origins in the land of Nimrod are a pseudo-Judaized Babylonian mysticism much as the Eastern Orthodox and Roman Catholic churches are a pseudo-Christianized Babylonian mysticism which likewise have their origins in the land of Nimrod. God again uses the Antichrist as His servant to purify His own people in His own land much the same as He used Nebuchadnezzar, another type of the Antichrist, as His instrument of judgment.

This culminates, however, with God judging these nations who come against Israel at the behest of, and with, the Antichrist, once more alluded to as "*the Assyrian*" in verse 5. Just as Sennacherib, the Assyrian invader in the days of Micah, foreshadows the Antichrist, so, too, the Antichrist will come from Babylon the Great. The lands of the Assyrians and the Babylonians were both in the land of Nimrod after the Flood. Centuries later the Babylonians defeated and swallowed up the Assyrians strategically, politically, economically, and to a degree culturally, incorporating it within the Babylonian Empire, thus once again uniting the two lands of Nimrod into one. This has its parallel in Israel of the north and Judah of the south again being reunited as one nation. The surviving Jews of the Assyrian Captivity either came south to Judah before 721 B.C., or were integrated into Judah and returned from Babylon and Persia with them following the Babylonian Captivity. Thus, as God's Kingdom became one geographically, so does Satan's.

Daniel makes it clear that the Antichrist is one of the ten horns who puts down three others from Europe in the West having to do with Babylon the Great in a spiritual sense (Dan. 7:7-8). Yet there is still the Eastern dimension trumpeted by such authors as Walid Shoebat and others who say that it is Islam. Meanwhile, the Western view looks at the Antichrist coming from Europe via the conservative Protestant tradition which came out of Roman Catholicism. In the identification of the Antichrist there must be a solid, scripturally based explanation reconciling the two. Will he be the Assyrian or the Roman? Will he be the Arab or European? Will he come from the Eastern Islamic world or a Western Christendom? This is a pivotal issue which we shall address later in this book.

As with Pharaoh, while Pharaoh's own actions accept and determine his role, so it will be with the Antichrist as viewed in Zechariah 11. God raises up Antichrist as an agent of judgment in Zechariah 11 just as God raises up the "*son of perdition*" as an agent of judgment in 2 Thessalonians 2. Although he is in the character and working of Satan, and comes at the initiation of Satan, as with anything else God allows Satan to do, it integrates into the greater purposes of God. The Antichrist will not simply be the ultimate deception and weapon of Satan; the Antichrist will be an instrument of God.

We understand this irony not as enigma or antimony, but as plot and counterplot. It was God who put lying spirits into the mouths of the false prophets of Ahab in an act of divine judgment (1 Ki. 22:22), and it was God who used Satan to put into David's mind to number the people. This was not an act of divine judgment, but of divine correction (1 Chr. 21:1). In both cases, however, God allows the wicked intent of Satan to thrive up to a limited point in order to cause it to backfire on him. This, just as God allowed the crucifixion of Christ when satanically-motivated forces of the Roman government and the Sanhedrin crucified the King of Glory, only for Him to be resurrected.

Goliath

Along with Nebuchadnezzar and Solomon, Goliath is one of the chief types of the Antichrist, revealing not merely hints but facets of the number of the Beast, "666." Like Goliath, the Antichrist will worship a god of fortresses (Dan. 11:38). He will look to military strength as a source of power, although other passages confirm he will also look to finance and wealth. David who slew him is a type of Christ as King, the direct descendant of David. The five stones David selected from the brook in the Valley of Elah correspond to the five Books of the Hebrew Torah; as Paul writes in Corinthians, the Torah is engraved in stone (2 Co. 3:3). Christ will speak His Word to Antichrist and destroy him with the "*breath of His mouth*" (2 Th. 2:8). The Greek word for "breath," "*pneuma*," has its parallel in the Hebrew "*ruach*," meaning "spirit." Christ will destroy Antichrist; the Holy Spirit of Christ will destroy the spirit of antichrist; the Word of God will destroy the *pseudologon*.

As Daniel tells us, the Antichrist will speak blasphemous things against the Most High (Dan. 7:25), so we read of Goliath doing the precise, same thing. Joshua destroyed the Anakim except in the area around Gath (Josh. 11:22), today an absorption village of mainly Russian Jews not far from the Gaza strip. It was from here that Goliath and another demonoid giant emerged. It may be significant that Gath lies between Jerusalem and the Mediterranean Sea, where Daniel tells us Antichrist will likewise pitch his tent (Dan. 11:4). This, however, we only mention in passing as a possible factor not to be overlooked.

In 1 Samuel 17:4 we see that Goliath was six cubits and a span. This in itself is not significant unless we realize that repeated combinations of sixes associated with an individual are always important. In verse 4 we see the weight of his armor was 5,000 shekels, and in verse 7 we have 600 shekels of iron. If we read this in the original Hebrew text we see the characteristic combination of sixes. In Hebrew, as in English, the "six" stands as a separate word from "thousand." In verse 4 there is a simple "six," in verse 5 there is a "five" that stands as a separate word from "thousand," plus a "one" that does not in the original text stand separate, but is connected ("*vzaret*"—meaning, "and one span," but all as a single digit term). Add to these verse 7 in which we have a "six" that stands apart from the term "hundred," and it leaves us "666."

Goliath's armor bearer went ahead of him. It is not uncommon, when we see a type of the Antichrist, to see a type of the False Prophet accompanying or preceding him. There is also a kind of reappearance of Goliath in a kinsman Philistine giant plainly sharing the same DNA program (2 Sam. 21:20). We again see this combination of sixes associated with him. And yet again we see in 1 Chronicles 20:6 that a combination of sixes are present, but they do not add up to exactly "666" as they do with Goliath, even though they shared most of the characteristics of Goliath in their ethnicity, vocation, pedigree, and humungous size. The point being, there are ***many*** antichrists and ***many*** false prophets. It was the "666" that set Goliath apart. The same will be true of the coming Antichrist.

While we may correctly point to religious figures such as Sun Myung Moon and the pope being antichrists, and although we may point to political figures such as Henry Kissinger, Xavier Solano, and Barack Obama as having the spirit of antichrist, there are ***many*** antichrists. The others teach about the ultimate one much the same as the other Philistine giants teach about Goliath. On one hand we must learn what each of the many antichrists teach us about the ultimate final Antichrist, while at the same time not wrongly believing that any of these others are he.

There have been Christian websites carrying slide presentations trying to argue for Barack Obama being the Antichrist (or at least strongly suggesting it). Indeed he is, again, of that spirit. He came from out of nowhere; he promised one thing, but after assuming power he made it clear that he did not tell the truth; he forces his will on the populace against the will of the democratic majority of those whom he conned into supporting him. He is causing them to turn against him after it was too late and after he had done immeasurable harm. The fact that he practiced an aberrational version of Christianity that preaches a hatred of Israel and invites as a preacher Louis Farrakhan, an anti-Semitic Muslim who claims to travel in flying saucers, are obvious elements of Antichrist activity indicative of the spirit of antichrist at work. The fact that Obama is able to simultaneously represent himself as a Muslim (even having a Muslim name) while claiming to be a Christian, is again a hint of how the ultimate Antichrist will operate.

But the game becomes much more complex in its intrigue and deception. The Elect must be deceived if possible, and few truly saved Christians are deceived by an overtly pro-abortion politician like Obama. However, at the same time, many saved Christians are misled by Obama's nemesis, Glenn Beck, who speaks of Judeo-Christian values, of biblical heritage, and a need to return to the God of our forefathers, ignoring the fact that Mr. Beck is a Mormon who does not worship the same God as Christians or Jews. The Jesus of Mormonism is the spirit brother of Satan and the God of Mormonism is someone who was once a man but is now a god on a different planet, a religious proposition every bit as theologically ludicrous as Louis Farrakhan's flying saucers. Both the Jeremiah Wright Christianity with its connections to Islam, and the perverse beliefs of Mormonism with another God and another Jesus, are ***equally*** demonic in origin.

Again, the proliferation of such deception reflects the spirit of antichrist. The world is in the power of the wicked one, and Satan's reins can easily cover both ends of the political spectrum. But while some saved Christians have the small amount of wisdom required to distrust a Barack Obama, a smaller remnant of saved Christians have the wisdom and wherewithal to discern the problems associated with Glenn Beck even though they might agree with his politics and, in principle, with his rhetoric about returning to a faith in God. The Antichrist will be much more shrewd than Barack Obama and Glenn Beck combined. Such men (Christians should pray for the salvation of both of them) are indeed controlled by an antichrist spirit. If true believers in Jesus are unable to discern the obvious antichrist nature of a Barack Obama who avoids the Christian National Day of Prayer but celebrates Ramadan at the White House, or discern the less obvious Glenn Beck who knows how to sound scripturally Christian, they will never be able to fathom the depths of deception that will be encompassed in the ultimate Antichrist.

In the tactics of the enemy, decoys are invaluable. He raises up many antichrists in part to make it more difficult to pinpoint the main one. It was David, the Old Testament shadow of Christ as Shepherd and King, who slew Goliath. And so it will be Jesus the Son of David who will destroy the Antichrist with the breath of His coming.

The Nameless Shadow - The Man of Sixes

In 1 Chronicles 20 and in 2 Samuel 21 we read of a trio of the descendants of the giants once again. In 2 Samuel 21:2 we see Ishbi-benob who was slain by one of David's commanders who feared for David's life lest "the lamp of Israel would be extinguished" (2 Sam. 21:17). Afterward another of David's commanders struck down Saph, another descendant of the giants, and another of David's generals killed the second Goliath known as "Goliath the Gittite" (2 Sam. 21:18-19), who by parallel account is actually a brother of the original Goliath. Finally, however, once again at Gath there was a final giant associated with a combination of sixes, with six digits on each hand and foot.

> *There was war at Gath again, where there was a man of great stature who had six fingers on each hand and six toes on each foot, twenty-four in number; and he also had been born to the giant.*

When he defied Israel, Jonathan the son of Shimei, David's brother, struck him down. (2 Sam. 21:20-21)

We are told that all four of these were born to the giant in Gath, though perhaps not Goliath, but certainly Rephaim (2 Sam. 21:22). The point here is that there are a number of antichrists before the final, ultimate one comes in the character of his father the devil. This last one, however, is unnamed, carrying the typological implication that the name of the Antichrist is as yet to be revealed. This fourth giant is rather identified by the combination of sixes that was peculiar to his anatomy. The first three were simply called "descendants" of the giant; the final, however, was one who resembled the original Goliath even though he did not have the same name as did Goliath the Gittite.

The parade of antichrists who will precede the Antichrist once again complicates and confuses the scene and camouflages the final exploits of the man of sixes. Indeed his predecessor is even called "Goliath." With the Antichrist, all of the other antichrists will complicate the playing field. In one text he is called "Goliath," and in another, "brother of Goliath," as we shall attempt to explain. We see a progression where in succession each of this trio becomes progressively more like the original Goliath. The first Ishbi-benob carried a new sword and intended to kill David who is a type of Christ as King. We understand the sword as a type of the Word of God, that is the "*Logos*," but the sword of the Antichrist is a picture of the *pseudologon*. The fact that a new sword is highlighted indicates that as the advent of the Antichrist approaches there will be a spiral of claimed new religious and spiritual revelation that is in opposition to Christ as the sword of Ishbi-benob was in opposition to David. The weariness of David in this text probably relates to the efforts of Antichrist as described in Daniel of wearing out the saints of the Most High (Dan. 7:21), suggesting a focused pressure on the faithful leadership among God's people. The defeat of the second member of the trio again indicates that there will be intermediate periods of respite and victory which are little more than deceptions setting the stage for the next opponent operating in the spirit of antichrist.

The third one, however, becomes highly problematic. In the account in 2 Samuel 21 the third is named as "Goliath the Gittite"; the account in 1 Chronicles, however, tells us the third was his brother "Lahmi." Once more, we have the element of confusion as observed in other texts dealing with the Antichrist where there are apparent discrepancies that cannot be simply written off as textual error alone. One possibility is that "Elhanan the Bethlehemite" (also carrying the messianic connotation of the one from Bethlehem who would kill the Antichrist) in fact killed two villains: Goliath the Gittite and his brother Lahmi. We cannot, however, be certain that Elhanan the son of Jair and Elhanan the Bethlehemite are the same. To explain this apparent discrepancy we must delve into literary and textual criticism; not the Higher Criticism of liberal theologians, but simply an investigation into the original text.

Again, the size of the spear being compared to a weaver's beam indicates the javelin to be a very heavy weapon indeed. There may be an implication that the trio consisting of Sippai (seemingly called "Saph" in the 2 Samuel account, although some may postulate him to be yet a fifth figure), Lahmi, and Goliath the Gittite because they are referred to as mere "descendants" of the giants, may have looked like ordinary Philistines while only the man of the sixes appeared differently.

We always interpret Scripture in light of Scripture. This is not only a truth for arriving at a doctrinal unity but for arriving at a unified view of historicity and textual compatibility. The Scriptures tell us that, "*The sum of Your Word is truth*" (Ps. 119:160). Thus one passage illuminates another.

Just as Jesus was fully human and fully divine—the incarnate "*Logos*"—the written "*Logos*" is likewise fully human and fully divine. The Bible is 100% of divine authorship and 100% of human authorship just as Jesus was fully God and fully man. Its human element does not detract from its divinity, nor does its divinity detract from its humanity. As Jesus was God in a man, the Scriptures are the Word of God in the word of man. The complication is that people, in this case later copyists, make mistakes, but God does not.

The original autographs are indeed infallible; later manuscripts can vary. The fact that the variation was not textually corrected by later redactors testifies to the authenticity of the text and demonstrates that the structure of the Scripture is not contrived. Otherwise the later redactors would have obviously smoothed over apparent contradictions, although none of these apparent contradictions affect essential historicity or doctrine. While the original autographs were without error, there are copyist errors in later scrolls and codices. What we are left with is the unified compendium of divinely inspired texts that are doctrinally infallible and true in their historicity, but containing minor yet sometimes significant deviations in parallel to synoptic accounts even though doctrine and fundamental historicity are not affected.

In this case we must on the whole see the 1 Chronicles account in chapter 20, probably authored by Ezra, as the one that is accurately preserved, while the account in Samuel contains materials not in Chronicles that simply further elucidate the account. The weaver's beam in verse 19 in Samuel may have been inserted in the wrong line according to some scholars. The *Katav*, or scribal tradition, that began in the time of Ezra in the aftermath of the Babylonian Captivity, saw a perfection of transmission using Gematria as a mathematical method to assure accurate reproduction of the text. This was also the period when Midrash is first introduced into Scripture in 2 Chronicles 13:22 (where the Hebrew term "*midrash*" is usually mistranslated as "*treatise*" and is not to be confused with the later writings of the rabbis called "Midrash" well after the time of Christ). We additionally see the inclusion of Midrash in 2 Chronicles 24:27. Samuel's account is an older one preserved or retrieved from the national catastrophe of 585 B.C. when so many of the older canons were burned or destroyed in the Babylonian invasions. Ezra, who was a scribe as well as a prophet, was raised up by God to rectify the situation.

We can account for the two contradictory records of the killing of Goliath by understanding either the copyist error or manuscript damage of 2 Samuel 21:19 where the term translated into English as "Bethlehemite" in the original manuscript is "*eth lahammi.*" The Hebrew letter "*beht*" is missing in the oldest existing manuscripts, indicating that it may have not been there to begin with. Thus the "eth" could simply be an accusative particle while "*lahammi*" is more correctly preserved in the Chronicles accounts as "*Lahmi*" with its root being "*ah,*" the Hebrew term for "brother." Although we cannot absolutely conclude that there were not two figures named Goliath, this is a far more likely explanation—that Elhanan killed the brother of Goliath. This conclusion is supported by the fact that 1 Samuel 17 attributes the killing of Goliath to David. In this text it is unambiguous and without any mitigation in manuscript records. When we understand the nature of the textual deviation, we are left with a perfectly rational and probable reconciliation. There is no real contradiction between the accounts in Samuel and Chronicles despite the deviation we can attribute to copyists which in any event affects neither historicity nor doctrinal theology and has no bearing on the infallibility of the original autographs.

There is, however, another very possible explanation that does not attribute a deviation to any copyist error but would explain it as being intentional. Although beyond the purpose and scope of this book, we must return to some of the Jewish methods of exegesis employed in the New Testament that were common among rabbis in the time of Jesus which we also see evidence of in *The Dead Sea Scrolls*. These are principles of Midrash and, as always, we must staunchly issue the caveat that Midrash is never a basis for doctrine, nor should scriptural examples of Midrash be confused with the rabbinic traditions written some centuries later. In this situation and others concerning the Antichrist (including the apparent discrepancy between the numbers "666" and "667" for the sons of Adonikam, meaning "my Lord has risen" in Ezra and Nehemiah) we have a quite possible use of the phenomena known as "*Remes*."

Remes comes from the Hebrew acronym "*Pardas*" (PRDS), a word meaning "orchard" consisting of four approaches to interpretation midrashically.

- The "P" represents "*Peshat*" – "the simple, straightforward meaning."
- The "R" represents "*Remes*" – meaning "clue or hint."
- The "D" represents "*Drash*" – meaning "homiletic application."
- The "S" represents "*Sod*" – meaning "a secret meaning" that in certain contexts relates to a possible *Pesher* interpretation.

Again, we must tread extremely cautiously and ***never*** make the *Pardas* the basis of doctrinal determination. It can, however, help explain the text.

If we fail to adhere to these guidelines and first seek the *Peshat* (that is the *Pesher* interpretation) based on conventional grammatical-historical exegesis, we can easily fall into the trap of Gnosticism as the later rabbis did with Cabala and cabalistic approaches to scriptural texts. Such Gnostic mysticism is at best erroneous, but more often demonic and occultic. Nonetheless we cannot ignore elements that may be scriptural for fear of gravitating into paths that are not scriptural. We must stick closely to the rules and keep the caveats in mind.

Of particular concern in contemplating the issue of Antichrist's identity, our emphasis in this instance and in other such passages related to Antichrist is *Remes* and *Sod*. The discrepancy surrounding the number of the Beast provides a *Remes* that hints at a *Sod* or an underlying meaning that is the reserve of those enlightened by the Holy Spirit. We must understand that the demonic teachings of Illuminism counterfeit this with demonic practices such as special enlightenment for the initiated, revelation via ascended masters, and the demonic animation that takes place through channeling. Such practices which counterfeit the illumination of the Holy Spirit inevitably involve Gnosticism and the basing of doctrine on subjective mystical interpretations of scriptural texts.

Observed midrashically from a scriptural standpoint, the *Remes* of the numerical discrepancy is analogous to a landmark on a map for a treasure hunt informing the pilgrim where to dig. When we act on the *Remes* of "666"/"667" we see in the name of Adoniakam an allusion to the Antichrist being called "the Lord who raises from the dead" in counterfeit of the resurrection of Jesus. In other words, when pondered midrashically the discrepancy between "666" and "667" may not be attributed to a scribal error (particularly in view of the *Katav* traditions and uses of Gematria to mathematically assure accuracy in transmission), but may be intentional road marks planted to inform us that there is a *Sod* or hidden meaning in the text. This is an example of how midrashic hermeneutics, when properly understood and not confused with later rabbinic distortions, is such an effective weapon against liberal Higher Criticism in defending the orthodoxy, historicity, and accuracy of the preserved scriptural record in the original languages.

There is possibly a New Testament instance of something quite similar concerning apparent discrepancies in the number which may variously be attributed to either rectified copyist error or an at least remotely possible occurrence of *Remes*. Some early manuscripts and manuscript fragments of Revelation 13 similarly do not record the number of the Beast as "666," but rather as "616." Again, this almost characteristic element of confusion surrounding deeper biblical texts dealing with the identity of Antichrist once more appears. Yet because "666" occurs so abundantly in other Scripture, and because the majority of manuscripts have "666," it is safe to conclude that "616" is not the number of the Beast. But as with Ezra and Nehemiah, we cannot dismiss the possibility of *Remes* as an explanation for the variance in the manuscript record. (In the 2nd century A.D. Irenaeus posititvely assured from apostolic sources (probably via Polycarp) that the "sure number" of the Revelation 13 text reads as: "*hexakósioi hexēkonta héx*", which is "six hundred and sixty-six".)

When we apply the *Remes* principle to the synoptic discrepancy of whether the man of sixes was Goliath or his brother, we may also be looking at a *Remes*. It is a clue to dig for something deeper and may not be a mere copyist error at all.

There are two diverse features of these accounts that are of significance in the identification of the Antichrist. One is that although they are Rephaim of demonic origin or descent, they are identified with a specific race—in this case the Philistines. The modern Philistines are Palestinian Arabs (the word "Palestinian" merely means "Philistine"). The ancient Philistines, however, were an Indo-Grecian people. Thus we see a figure who can claim both Eastern and Western ethnic identities, yet be of a satanic ontogeny. The other feature again is that there is a host of antichrists, each resembling the ultimate Antichrist in some way. This will make people prone to finger ***an*** antichrist as **THE** Antichrist much as the Protestant Reformers did with the popes who were and are antichrists, but not **THE** Antichrist.

The final facet of this incredible account in Scripture inclusive of its Antichrist typology, however, is again in fact that the man of sixes resembles the original Goliath more than the others. Each of the others contains some aspect of the original one who prefigured the final one. So, too, we see the same pattern when dealing with other types of the Antichrist. The final Antichrist will in some way highly resemble Caesar Augustus even though the successive emperors and the popes encompass some of those attributes of the original Caesar Augustus and the final one, that is the person of Antichrist, whom they will foreshadow. So, too, the Antichrist will again be the *"son of perdition"* as was Judas. We see this concept of an attempted reappearance of someone evil who already existed, with the attempted reappearance approximating the original by supernatural demonic and even satanic power.

The King of Assyria

> *So the God of Israel stirred up the spirit of Pul, king of Assyria, even the spirit of Tilgath-pilneser king of Assyria, and he carried them away into exile, namely the Reubenites, the Gadites and the half-*

tribe of Manasseh, and brought them to Halah, Habor, Hara and to the river of Gozan, to this day. (1 Chr. 5:26)

Another frequently overlooked type of the Antichrist is the king of Assyria. His importance is that he embodies the nature and character of Satan displayed in a human form. As with the "*son of perdition*," 1 Chronicles 5:26 shows us that he will likewise be an instrument of God's judgment—which is once more consistent with the end-times prophecy of Zechariah 11 regarding the "*son of perdition*." We again know it refers to Antichrist because Zechariah 11 refers to Judas in a prophetic context.

Isaiah, however, exhibits the mindset of Satan and shows how this mindset is displayed in a human:

> *So it will be that when the LORD has completed all His work on Mount Zion and on Jerusalem, He will say, "I will punish the fruit of the arrogant heart of the king of Assyria and the pomp of his haughtiness." For he has said,*
>
> *"By the power of my hand and by my wisdom I did this,*
> *For I have understanding;*
> *And I removed the boundaries of the peoples*
> *And plundered their treasures,*
> *And like a mighty man I brought down their inhabitants,* (Is. 10:12-13)

Here the king of Assyria is the one with the arrogant heart and the pomp of his haughtiness. In verse 13 he ascribes to himself divine attributes, attempting to convince himself that he, too, is a creator-god having the divine properties of understanding and wisdom, and draws the map of the earth and its ethnic nations. He gathers all the earth to himself, accumulating its wealth for his own control. This, however, is preliminary. The manner in which the Antichrist will play this out on the stage of history is witnessed in Isaiah 36-37, where the king of Assyria has conquered most of the known world and now demands Jerusalem in the days of Hezekiah and Isaiah.

In these chapters we see that he blasphemes the Most High in a manner identical to how Daniel describes the behavior of the Antichrist speaking blasphemies against the Most High. In this narrative Sennacherib the king of Assyria is a picture of the Antichrist, while Rabshakeh his messenger is a picture of the False Prophet. The manner in which Rabshakeh's speech parodies the words of Sennacherib demonstrates the way in which the pronouncements of the False Prophet will echo the exact blasphemies of the Antichrist.

Following his conquest of most of the known world and of Israel and Judah, his final designs on Jerusalem are magnificently and supernaturally thwarted. This is precisely what the Antichrist will do. As Rabshakeh lied, demanded, cajoled, and did all he could to press the Jews to make a covenant with the king of Assyria, so, too, the False Prophet will in some way play a role in pressuring the Jews to enter into a covenant with death prophesied by Daniel (Dan. 9:27). Jerusalem will once again be saved by divine intervention, this time in the person of the returning Christ prophesied by Isaiah.

Even at the present moment the Vatican, the World Council of Churches, the World Congress of Religions, and the religious agencies of the United Nations are all pressuring Israel to make a covenant with Islam which Islam will never keep. Isaiah 36-37 is one of the Antichrist-inspired events due to happen once again. Rabshakeh tried in desperation to convince the surviving Jews that their salvation was not in their own God, but in the king of Assyria. The Antichrist will present the same kind of scenario. Contemporary with Isaiah was the prophet Micah who likewise prophesied both the First and Second Coming of Christ and the destruction of the Assyrian. Let us consider the following.

Micah 5 speaks prophetically about how Jesus, who will be born in Bethlehem, will redeem His people from the king of Assyria. Most Christians think of Micah 5:2 as a major Messianic prophecy when it talks about the Son of David who will be born in Bethlehem.

> *"But as for you, Bethlehem Ephrathah,*
> *Too little to be among the clans of Judah...*

(It actually says that Jesus was pre-existent from eternity.)

> *From you One will go forth for Me to be ruler in Israel.*
> *His goings forth are from long ago,*
> *From the days of eternity."* (Mic. 5:2)

Let us look at what this one from Bethlehem does.

> *And He will arise and shepherd His flock*

In the strength of the LORD,
In the majesty of the name of the LORD His God.
And they will remain,
Because at that time He will be great
To the ends of the earth.
This One will be our peace.
When the Assyrian invades our land,
When he tramples on our citadels,
Then we will raise against him
Seven shepherds and eight leaders of men.
They will shepherd the land of Assyria with the sword,
The land of Nimrod at its entrances; (Mic. 5:4-6)

The King of Tyre

A typological half-brother of the king of Babylon and a typological first cousin to the king of Assyria is the king of Tyre in his foreshadowing of the Antichrist. Like the others, his biblical description unveils how the nature, character, and personality of Satan are to be manifested in human flesh, thus typifying the Antichrist. While the theological content of Ezekiel 27 applies primarily to the nature of Satan as an historical figure, the king of Tyre as described in Ezekiel 28 foreshadows the Antichrist. Much as the fullness of the Father is incarnated in Christ, the fullness of Satan will be incarnated ultimately and finally in the Antichrist. From differing aspects the king of Tyre, the king of Babylon, and the king of Assyria all highlight this.

In Ezekiel 28, the wicked cities and their kings are types of the devil. Just as the full character, personality, and nature of God are demonstrated spiritually in Jesus, the character, personality, and nature of Satan are demonstrated in the Antichrist. The same holds true with the Old Testament prophets. The faithful ones, like David, Joseph, Isaac, and Jeremiah, teach about Jesus—especially the prophets where there is the "S-H" sound: Isaiah ("*Ishael*"), Hosea ("*Hoshea*"), Joshua ("*Yehoshua*") Jesus ("*Yeshua*"). They all have the same Hebrew root "*shoresh,*" meaning "salvation." They all teach about Jesus just as all these wicked people teach something about the Antichrist.

There is an ultimate conflict coming between Christ and Antichrist, between Jerusalem and Babylon, by those who go the way of Nimrod—man trying to reach God through his own way—and those who go with the baby from Bethlehem. Ezekiel 27:36 alludes to Revelation 15:18-19:

"The merchants among the peoples hiss at you;
You have become terrified
And you will cease to be forever."

That is the same language as the judgment against the king of Tyre beginning in Ezekiel 27, and a description of him in chapter 28:

Again the word of the LORD came to me saying, "Son of man, take up a lamentation over the king of Tyre and say to him, 'Thus says the Lord GOD,

"You had the seal of perfection,
Full of wisdom and perfect in beauty.
You were in Eden, the garden of God." (Eze. 28:11-13a)

The serpent was already in the wilderness before Adam and Eve fell. God was going to subdue the enemy even before the creation fell through man. It was through the woman that God said He was going to destroy the beast. That is why it was through Esther that God destroyed Haman, who is a type of the Antichrist in the Book of Esther. Bruise his heel; bruise his head (Gen. 3:15).

In the Book of Judges, Jael driving a stake through Sisera's temple prefigures the judgment of Satan (Judg. 4:21). He is going to do it through this woman.

You were in Eden, the garden of God;
Every precious stone was your covering: (Eze. 28:1-3a)

(These are the same stories that appear in Revelation.)

You were the anointed cherub who covers,
And I placed you there. (Eze. 28:14)

The Ark of the Covenant was a type of Jesus. It was wood and it was gold because Jesus was God and man. Inside the Ark was the Law, the stones of the Covenant. And the lid of the Ark was called "the mercy seat." The mercy seat corresponds to the throne of grace—the grace of Jesus covering the Law that condemns everyone.

There are two Greek words for "throne of judgment": *bema* and *thronos*. *Thronos* is "*throne*" which is where unsaved people will appear, but believers appear before the *bema*. That is the name given by the Greek kings to the place where they gave a reward to those who competed successfully in the Olympics. That is what Paul was referring to when he said, "I have run the good race" (1 Co. 9:24). The mercy seat is the *bema*, the throne of grace covering the Law. And there is an angel on either side—the angels closest to Jesus such as the ones seen on the Mt. of Olives at His Ascension, or the ones who were guarding the grave of the tomb at the resurrection. Lucifer was an angel very close to Jesus.

You were the anointed cherub who covers,

(It is alluding to the same angels on the *Aron Qodesh*, the holy ark.)

"You were blameless in your ways
From the day you were created
Until unrighteousness was found in you.
By the abundance of your trade
You were internally filled with violence,
And you sinned;
Therefore I have cast you as profane
From the mountain of God.

(Remember, the Jerusalem on earth is a reflection of the Jerusalem in Heaven in Revelation.)

And I have destroyed you, O covering cherub,
From the midst of the stones of fire.
Your heart was lifted up because of your beauty;
You corrupted your wisdom by reason of your splendor.
I cast you to the ground;
I put you before kings,
That they may see you.

(This deals with the subject of why God allows evil to exist.)

By the multitude of your iniquities,
In the unrighteousness of your trade
You profaned your sanctuaries.
Therefore I have brought fire from the midst of you;
It has consumed you,
And I have turned you to ashes on the earth

In the eyes of all who see you.

(Satan's judgment will be seen by all.)

All who know you among the peoples
Are appalled at you; (Eze. 28:14-19a)

What happens to Lucifer is played out in the Antichrist. In his vanity he believes he is going to succeed.

Nebuchadnezzar

Once more in the person of Nebuchadnezzar the Book of Joel reveals him as an instrument of God to judge His own people in order to drive them to repentance. He is foretold in detail in the Book of Joel where the day of the Lord draws near (Joel 1:15), and his army—represented by locusts invading Israel in four incursions—is called the "*great army*" of the Lord (Joel 2:25) whom God later destroys when His own people repent.

There are two aspects of Nebuchadnezzar that are vital in understanding the Antichrist. The first is the historical and prophetic aspect conveyed in the Book of Joel, and the second is the satanic nature of him as the king of Babylon of which we read in Isaiah 14. The judgments of Judah represented by four invasions of locusts (Joel 1:4) suggest that the effort by Antichrist to conquer Israel will happen in stages, and only in final desperation do the surviving people of God repent and believe.

We again find a *Pesher* interpretation of this prophetically in Revelation 9:7 where the locusts return as the demon cohorts of hell with their king "*Abaddon*"—who in Greek is called "*Apollyon*" meaning "Destroyer." We see this in Revelation 9:3-11 between the first and second recorded woes. The events of 585 B.C., as with the fall of Samaria in 721 B.C. and the destruction of Jerusalem and the Temple in A.D. 70, all prefigure the Great Tribulation from the viewpoint of the Time of Jacob's Trouble; that is primarily as it applies to Israel and the Jews.

The king of Babylon aspect of Nebuchadnezzar is of equal importance as we see in Isaiah 14. To understand this, however, we must first consider his relationship to the coming Antichrist from the Book of Daniel. In Daniel 2 we see the statue of which Nebuchadnezzar dreamed. In verse 28 we are told it was for "*latter days*," which could not simply mean the latter days of Nebuchadnezzar's own life because its prophetic fulfillment extended well beyond his longevity. Its ***construction*** represents the building of the kingdom of Antichrist from the dawn of time; its ***destruction*** represents the return of Jesus to demolish the kingdom of this world which will be replaced by the Kingdom of God and His Messiah.

In Daniel 3, Nebuchadnezzar is said to build an image of himself made of gold. This is a major picture of the image of the Beast in Revelation 13, complete with the theme of musical instrumentation summoning people to worship him, paralleling what we see in Isaiah 14:11 concerning Satan. As we shall again return to in the final person of the Antichrist, in the Aramaic text the wordplay of the dimensions of the statue in Daniel 3:1 come to "666" with the plural of the Hebrew and Aramaic for "sixty" meaning "two or more sixes." (Hebrew = "*Sheshim*"; Aramaic = "*Shephim.*") Three times in the text, the importance of musical instrumentation in the worship of the image is emphasized.

The spirit of antichrist is once again subtlety putting in place the mechanisms for this to happen in a time where Christian worship has become the worship of "worship" itself. Today, Christian music ministry has become an industry often owned by secular conglomerates and where biblical worship has been supplanted by unbiblical worship that is little more than entertainment. Instead of learning doctrine from exposition of Scripture, more and more Christians are absorbing false doctrine by mindlessly and repetitively singing choruses in the style of a mantra. Again, this is the spirit of antichrist preparing the way for the coming of ***the*** Antichrist. Contemporary Christian worship has been subverted and corrupted much like the sons of Aaron burning strange fire and not realizing the implications of what they were doing (Lev. 10:1; Num. 3:4). In the Hebrew Scriptures unbiblical worship and idolatry are called by one and the same term: "*avodah zerah.*" Unbiblical worship inevitably results in idolatry, but the origins of this run much deeper.

As Daniel wrote,

> *Nebuchadnezzar the king to all the peoples, nations, and men of every language that live in all the earth: "May your peace abound!* (Dan. 4:1)

Nebuchadnezzar is a ruler of the world, but something very telling is revealed about him…

> *"The king reflected and said, 'Is this not Babylon the great…*

(Take note of this term, as it is the same one found in Revelation.)

> *...which I myself have built as a royal residence by the might of my power and for the glory of my majesty?' While the word was in the king's mouth, a voice came from heaven, saying, 'King Nebuchadnezzar, to you it is declared: sovereignty has been removed from you,* (Dan. 4:30-31)

(This teaches about the judgment of the Babylon that's coming.)

> *but you have exalted yourself against the LORD of heaven...* (Dan. 5:23)

He exalts himself against the Lord of Heaven. Isaiah speaks about a time when the Lord will again choose Jacob—choose the Jews—and have compassion on them.

There is a difference between "Israel" and "Jacob." After God broke him, Jacob's name was changed; he was now called "Israel." After that, whenever Jacob behaved according to his old nature as a carnal man, Genesis still refers to him by his old name, "Jacob." But when he behaves spiritually he is called "Israel." That is true with every believer. Jesus says they receive a new name in their new birth (Rev. 2:17). When they behave like the new creation, they are called by their new name in Heaven, but when they behave in their old, fleshly ways He sees their old creation. But the Israel of God is made up of both Jew and Gentile. "Jacob" always has a specific meaning exclusive to the Jews. Jacob wrestled with the angel until the end of the night. Unsaved Jews go through the entire Tribulation.

From here, however, our focus shifts to the parallel passage in Isaiah 14 where the character of Satan is again visible in the king of Babylon.

> *that you will take up this taunt against the king of Babylon...* (Is. 14:4)

And it pronounces all of these judgments against him:

> *"They will all respond and say to you*
> *'Even you have been made weak as we,*
> *You have become like us.*
> *Your pomp and the music of your harps*
> *Have been brought down to Sheol;*
> *Maggots are spread out as your bed beneath you*

And worms are your covering.'

(This was historically fulfilled, but it is alluding to the devil.)

"How you have fallen from heaven,
O star of the morning, son of the dawn!
You have been cut down to the earth,
You who have weakened the nations!

(That word "Gentiles" in Hebrew is "*goyim*" – "nations.")

"But you said in your heart,
'I will ascend to heaven;
I will raise my throne above the stars of God,
And I will sit on the mount of assembly In the recesses of the north.
I will ascend above the heights of the clouds;
I will make myself like the Most High.'" (Is. 14:10-14)

The devil wants to be God. References to the "*recesses of the north*" allude to the Temple Mount, and "*the stars of God*" can be spirits (angels) but they can also be believers. In Genesis, God told Abraham that his descendants would be as the stars of heaven (Gen. 26:4). Even Gentile Christians are descendants of Abraham by faith in the Messiah; that was the promise to Abraham (Gal. 3:29). But the devil wants to be above the stars in heaven. Remember, the dragon in Revelation sweeps one-third of the stars from heaven—a massive backsliding happens (Rev. 12:4).

O star of the morning, son of the dawn! (Is. 14:12)

Satan is a counterfeiter. Jesus is called the bright and morning star (Rev. 22:16). Even Satan's title is almost the same as the title of Jesus with a subtle twist. The most difficult types of the Antichrist in the Bible are the ones who also typify Jesus, such as Nebuchadnezzar or Solomon. When Solomon takes the Shulamite woman in the Song of Solomon, he is a type of Jesus and the Church; but when he backslides he becomes a type of the Beast. He very closely looks like Jesus. "If possible, even the elect will be deceived" (Mt. 24:24).

Haman

Haman, the villain in the story of Esther, is another type of the Antichrist. Like Satan, he goes before the king's throne and accuses the Jews. The king gives a decree, which is like Torah (the Law), and the king's decree could not be revoked, just as the Torah cannot be broken. But there is an intercessor before the throne: Queen Esther. Haman is important because he teaches about anti-Semitism. The Antichrist will ultimately turn against the Jews. Like the Roman emperors, first they turned against the Church, then they turned against the Jews. That is what will happen at the end.

What is crucial about Haman is not only his devious character, but how he manipulates himself into a position in order to hatch his agenda. The Antichrist will likewise already have his plan and know his objectives step by step as he seeks to position himself politically and in concert with the False Prophet in the religious sphere.

He is an Agagite, a descendant of Amalek, and as such an ancient Middle Eastern enemy of the Jews. This hints strongly at the possible ethnicity of the Antichrist. Most but not all of the types of the Antichrist are ethnically non-Jewish, although the exceptions cannot be ignored, particularly Judas. (Unless we subscribe to the minority scholarly opinion that Judas may have been born of ethnic non-Jewish converts to Judaism.)

As a typological counterfeit of Christ, Haman, like Absalom, also dies accursed by God by hanging on a tree. (The Hebrew word for anything made from wood is the same as the Hebrew word for "tree.") Likewise Judas also died accursed by God by hanging on a tree.

Haman also thought he achieved his victory and was about to execute his "final solution" to the problem of the Jews much like Adolph Hitler after the Battle of Dunkirk and the initial onslaught of Operation Barbarossa. From the point of view of an anti-Semite with a pre-planned agenda to exterminate the Jews, no type of the Antichrist foreshadows him more from this aspect than Haman.

Caesar Worship

In the ruins of modern Ephesus we can walk on the ancient stones of the promenade leading into the ancient agora, or market area, where the inhabitants, visitors, and traders bought and sold. Along either side of the promenade were posts to which the early Christians were tied and set alight to illuminate the thoroughfare at night. The gateway to the promenade had an inscription on an overhead sign under which those approaching the market area had to walk to buy and sell. It read, "Caesar, son of god." Walking to the market required an acknowledgment of the divinity of Caesar. Those not complying faced the cruelest of repercussions, an example being the early Christians who were turned into human street lamps for their faith in Jesus and refusal to acknowledge the emperor as the son of god. This is a major foreshadowing of Revelation 13.

Certain emperors had been deified by the Roman Senate posthumously. But when Jesus came the first time, something else transpired. Caesar Augustus, formerly known as Octavius and renowned for the Battle of Actium, was deified in his lifetime. It was this emperor, Caesar Augustus, who reigned when Christ was born according to the Nativity narrative in the Gospel of Luke.

Caesar Augustus had the population of most of the known world—that is the Roman Empire—counted and assigned a number. He actually did this twice, once being the recorded census when Jesus was born. His motive was to exercise economic control of what was then the lion's share of the global economy. Just as this numbering of people by a deified emperor took place at the first coming of Christ, so it shall happen again.

Most of these emperors were bisexual and undoubtedly many, if not most, were demon-possessed. In dispensational eschatology the "*ten days*" of persecution of the church of Smyrna (Rev. 2:10) prophetically corresponds to ten periods of persecution under ten key emperors who were anti-Christian. The most notorious of these were Marcus Aurelius, Diocletian, Caligula, Decius, and Septimus Severitus. Others, like Claudius, while less ferocious, were by no means benign to the early Church. Christians became the scapegoats for problems social, economic, and strategically catastrophic, much as the Jews under medieval Christendom.

In the *religio illicita* system of pagan Rome's Pantheon, the emperor took the title of *Pontificus Maximus* as "the great bridge builder" among faiths. As long as one worshiped the emperor, one could have any religion one wished. The Jews obtained a license for worship by sacrificing ***for*** the emperor instead of ***to*** him. Once Christianity was excommunicated from the synagogue, however, the Church was no longer protected. After certain emperors such as Vespasian, his general, Titus—later to become emperor—and Hadrian presided over the persecution of Christians, they shortly thereafter took aim at Israel and the Jews. This, too, is a pivotal foreshadowing of how the Antichrist will operate—first going after the body of Christ and then refocusing on the eradication of Israel and the Jews.

Outside of Caesar Augustus, the two emperors who most acutely foreshadow the Antichrist are Nero and Domitian. Domitian is important by mere virtue of the fact he was the emperor at the end of the 1st century when the apostle John was exiled to Patmos and Jesus appeared to him, giving him the apocalyptic prophecies recorded as the Book of Revelation. Centuries later some erroneously attempted, by changing the spelling of Nero's name and translating it to Hebrew, to make the numerical value of Nero's name a gematrial value of 666. Although Gematria does figure in the identification of Antichrist, its application to Nero is of dubious if not abject merit. However, Nero's importance as a shadow of Antichrist stems from the kind of spiritual seduction that Queen Jezebel and Queen Athaliah had on their sons in the books of Kings and Chronicles. It was under Nero, according to extra-biblical historical records, that the apostles Peter and Paul were cruelly executed.

The Worshiped Emperors in Daniel 7:3-6

> *"And four great beasts were coming up from the sea, different from one another. The first was like a lion and had the wings of an eagle. I kept looking until its wings were plucked, and it was lifted up from the ground and made to stand on two feet like a man; a human mind also was given to it. And behold, another beast, a second one, resembling a bear. And it was raised up on one side, and three ribs were in its mouth between its teeth; and thus they said to it, 'Arise, devour much meat!' After this I kept looking, and behold, another one, like a leopard, which had on its back four wings of a bird; the beast also had four heads, and dominion was given to it."* (Dan. 7:3-6)

Daniel 7:3-6 indicates some kind of reconstituted Roman Empire. We must be aware that when empires revive they do not attain former superpower status. The Egyptian, Assyrian, or Babylonian empires are not coming back, and modern Iran will never revive the ancient Media-Persian Empire anymore than Saddam Hussein could resurrect the Babylonian Empire. 25 years ago the Western world was speaking of the meteoric economic rise of Japan, much as they speak of China today. But Japan has declined demographically and economically, and long-range thinkers believe that 25 years from now (should the world exist) India, as an English-speaking democracy, will be eclipsing China demographically and economically. India is projected to boast the world's largest population. It already has the world's largest Middle Class and more engineers and scientists per capita than any other nation, to say nothing of a film and media industry second only to Hollywood. In other words, despite China's growth, the Ming Dynasty will not reappear.

Neither the Holy Roman Empire nor the Byzantine Empire ever achieved the prowess of the original Roman Empire. Neither Charlemagne, Napoleon, nor Mussolini were able to restore the Roman Empire to what it was. So, too, Daniel tells us that iron does not adhere to clay and the prospects of the former European empires such as the French and British uniting in a Federal Europe is not working well either. Just as Daniel prophesied, they will look for stronger and stronger forces and leaders to make something stick together which by nature cannot. Despite the ambitions of fundamentalist nationalists in Turkey, the Ottoman Empire is not coming back any more than the Roman Empire, the British Empire, or China's Ming Dynasty. Once a superpower collapses it does not become a superpower again. But the Antichrist will create the illusion that he is able to make that happen.

His counterfeit physical resurrection will be paralleled by a counterfeit imperial resurrection, yet ultimately this will be thwarted by the return of Christ (Dan. 2:35). This great stone that comes from heaven that fills the whole earth is something that the Antichrist will attempt to preempt and mimic in advance.

The prophetic future is always foreshadowed by the historic past. The Antichrist's conquest of three kings carries ambiguous possible meanings and to this day is disputed by theological commentators both Christian and Jewish. In the Middle Ages Rashi, one of the most formative saviors in Jewish thought, related the horns of Daniel 7 to Roman emperors. Others emphasize that Rome replaced Babylon, Media-Persia, and Greece. Both perspectives must be taken into account, except that the Greco-Roman world fought only Persia; it did not fight Babylon.

Daniel 10 makes it clear that the demonic powers Daniel foresaw would gain ascendancy in Iran and turn a nation traditionally friendly toward Israel into its most hostile enemy. And as there was a conflict in the days of Alexander the Great and the Persian kings, so there will arise another conflict with the Western world. This was replayed again during the reign of the 1st-century Caesars who strove against the Persians, at that time called Parthians. As with the Celts of Scotland and Wales, these were the other people Rome was not able to conquer but only contain. The importance of Iran—an actual Aryan nation anthropologically (an Indo-Germanic people)—in End Time prophetic conflict with Israel and the West cannot be overstated.

The Triumvirates

Going back to the 1st century and the period immediately preceding it, we saw the First Triumvirate of Julius Caesar, Pompeii, and Marcus Licinius Crassus take Rome from being a republic into a dictatorial empire, with the power of the senate diminished (to the lament of figures such as Cicero). As was expressed in Seneca's *De Clementia*, now people could no longer look to representative government, but could simply appeal to a hoped-for virtue to be found in an autocrat. So, too, the modern European Union which began as a mere common market, and with little and sometimes no democratic mandate from the population, has transformed itself into an increasingly non-democratic political union attempting to bring about economic union by political means, and political means by economic means such as a common currency. As the economic glue becomes unstuck per Daniel's prophecy, and as Europe faces strategic threats from the Islamic world, more power is given to the Brussels bureaucracy. The European Parliament functions like the Roman Senate, a rubber stamping institution creating a hollow façade of representative government.

In the ancient world this led to the assassination of Julius Caesar at the end of the tenure of the First Triumvirate that lasted from 59-53 B.C. The opponents and assassins of Caesar such as Cassius and Brutus, who both committed suicide, were pursued relentlessly by the Second Triumvirate led by Octavius who became the deified emperor Caesar Augustus. Octavius was related to Julius Caesar, and Julius Caesar's violent death paved the way for Octavius' ascension to power. His deification by the senate and the changing of his name to Caesar Augustus reflected a public image of him as a resurrected Julius Caesar, not in a reincarnational sense, but in the sense that he embodied the perceived ideal personified by Julius Caesar whose legacy became mythical. What is important here is that, in a turbulent time, people acquiesced, and many even desired dictatorial rule. Even those who did not celebrate it as an optimum form of government saw it in their interest and in the collective interest to support it much the same as most

Germans and most Italians in the 1930s were neither doctrinaire Fascists nor doctrinaire Nazis.

In Germany, for instance, there was a desire to reverse the injustices of the Versailles Treaty and to find a scapegoat for their plight during the Weimar. In the Western world this same kind of trend had its inception in the Roman triumvirates. Bearing in mind that Caesar Augustus cum Octavius, the deified emperor who ruled the empire at the First Coming of Christ, is such a vital type of the Antichrist, we must understand the events and series of exploits for which he gained that kind of power.

Octavius joined Marc Antony and Marcus Aemilius Lepidus to form the Second Triumvirate which, unlike the first, was *Imperium Maius*, an actual governing tribunal. In order to consolidate power, Octavius would ultimately put down three kings. The first was Sextus Pompeius, son of Pompeii Magnus from the First Triumvirate. He controlled Sicily, Corsica, Sardinia, and at other times the Peloponnesian parts of Greece, and was the last vestige of power from his father Pompeii from the last Triumvirate. This was achieved with the help of his partners Marc Antony and Lepidus and with the able assistance of Agrippa I, his naval commander who would also play the central role in the Battle of Actium. Octavius would then dispose of his partner Lepidus, and then, at Actium, Marc Antony who had married Cleopatra. This saga is likewise prophesied in the Book of Daniel with the kings of the North and South, and will be replayed in the history of the Antichrist (Dan. 11). Thus Caesar Augustus put down three kings, was worshiped as god, numbered the people for economic control, and reigned at the First Coming of Christ as dictator perpetuus from 31 B.C. to A.D. 14, to be succeeded by his son Tiberius. From a political aspect there is no other figure in biblical history more important to understand as a type of the Antichrist than Caesar Augustus, although Judas Iscariot, backslidden Solomon, and Antiochus Epiphanes are more important from other aspects.

It was also during the time of the First Triumvirate that prepared the way for the Second that Pompeii (Pompeius Magnus) deceived the Jews into an alliance and entered the Holy of Holies. From both the perspective of the prophetic events in Europe and prophetic events in the Middle East, it is crucial to understand the history of this period with reference to Daniel's prophesies. In some way these things will happen again and are already happening again. What ***will*** transpire is in the pattern and character of what ***has*** transpired.

The Roman historian Suetonius authored his account of *The Twelve Caesars*, looking at the twelve post-republic emperors of the 1st century until the time of Domitian, circa A.D. 81-96 when John was exiled to Patmos and the Book of Revelation was written. The eleventh of these emperors during the age of the apostles (but counting from Julius Caesar the first Imperial dictator) was Vespasian who reigned from A.D. 67-79. As the eleventh he followed the previous ten, and although he did not subdue previous rulers as Caesar Augustus did, he did put down at least three important generals. His haughty character resembled the haughtiness of Antichrist described by Daniel (Dan. 7:8). What is important in Vespasian is that the general, Titus, who would succeed him as emperor, conquered Jerusalem in A.D. 70 in accordance with the prophecies of Jesus and Daniel. Although a lesser type of the Antichrist, there are aspects of the Antichrist to be found in Vespasian as there are in other emperors. All, however, are overshadowed by Caesar Augustus.

In Rome's transition from a republic to an imperial dictatorship the mechanism for this transformation in government was war. Even under the terms of the Republic, in times of war the senate would elect a dictator much the same as a declaration of martial law and a suspension of certain civil liberties were temporarily implemented during, for instance, the Second World War. By perpetuating a continual security crisis threatening the safety of the Empire and its population, imperial interests could create the impetus to gain public support for autocratic and non-representative government.

As we again witness the nations at the center of world events in biblical times functioning in that role, we see in the modern world how the "war on terror" and terrorist threats are politically exploited to manipulate people into parting with their constitutional rights. Such an undefined war, even though the radical Islamic world is the enemy, furnishes the precise climate required to achieve the same thing. Such a war with terror is open-ended and ongoing. Therefore government control over commerce becomes a perceived necessity to stop the funding of terror. Personal searches without warrants and intrusion by governments into private database information all become ostensibly justified as select interests capitalize on a perpetuating threat to clamor for more and more power and the suspension of more and more rights. What we witness today is with little doubt preparing the way for the Antichrist. Its origins, however, are not September 11, 2001, but rather the Ides of March, 44 B.C.

The Continuing Line of Emperors

The last of these emperors when Revelation was written and the New Testament canon completed was Domitian.

> *"The beast that you saw was, and is not, and is about to come up out of the abyss and go to destruction. And those who dwell on the earth, whose name has not been written in the book of life from the foundation of the world, will wonder when they see the beast, that he was and is not and will come. Here is the mind which has wisdom. The seven heads are seven mountains on which the woman sits, and they are seven kings; five have fallen, one is, the other has not yet come; and when he comes, he must remain a little while. The beast which was and is not, is himself also an eighth and is one of the seven, and he goes to destruction. The ten horns which you saw are ten kings who have not yet received a kingdom, but they receive authority as kings with the beast for one hour. These have one purpose, and they give their power and authority to the beast."* (Rev. 17:8-13)

In looking at the seven heads and ten horns, we are told that the ten horns are still to come as future kings although they will be in the character of ancient emperors who prefigure them. The final emperor of the 1st century was Domitian during John's exile on Patmos when he authored the Book of Revelation. While the ten horns according to Revelation 17:12 were future figures still to arise when the Book was written, this was not true of the seven heads corresponding to seven mountains but also to seven kings (Rev. 17:9-10) where we are told five have fallen already, one is, and the other is yet to come. We are also told in verse 11 that the Beast which was and is not is himself also an eighth, and one of the seven, and goes to destruction. This is a direct satanic counterfeit (by Antichrist) of Christ as the one who was, who is (although not visibly), and is visibly to come (Rev. 1:4).

At the time of John's exile and authorship, Domitian was the emperor. If we were to count from Tiberius who was emperor at the time of Jesus' death and resurrection to the time of the authorship of Revelation, we would have throughout the Apostolic Period ten emperors (Tiberius, Caligula, Claudius, Nero, Galba, Otho, Vitellius, Vespasian, Titus, and Domitian). As with the ten periods of persecution prophesied to the church in Smyrna by Jesus in Revelation 2 , there were ten emperors who conducted major persecutions of the Church, ranging from Nero who martyred Peter and Paul through Domitian, Trajan, Marcus Aurelius, Septimus Severitus, Decius, and Diocletian. The future meaning of the ten is prefigured in these lists in both the Apostolic and Post-Apostolic/Early Patristic periods. The complication becomes the seven heads. At this time we shy away from any dogmatically definitive explanation in any comprehensive or conclusive sense, but what we do reiterate strongly is that the one who was, is, but is not, but is to come, is the Antichrist functioning in his usual counterfeit mode mimicking the Lord Jesus.

The Aim is Jerusalem, Not Rome

Most commentators have recognized some correlation between the seven heads as mountains corresponding to the seven major hills of Rome, such as the Palatine, the Capitoline, the Vaticanus, etc. Construction, landfill, and erosion make most of these hills less distinctively visible than they were in the 1st century, apart from the Capitoline and Palatine around the Forum, and the Vatican. There are, however, other interpretations offered by different schools of thought apart from the Pre-millennial dispensational approach.

We must remember that the aim of Antichrist is Jerusalem and not Rome. In the Book of Revelation, in its desecrated state, Jerusalem is metaphorically referred to as "*Sodom and Egypt, where also their Lord was also crucified*" (Rev. 11:8). And of course 2 Thessalonians 2 examined in light of the Tribulational Temple in Revelation 11 lends strong credence to the paramount of Antichrist activity being on the Temple Mount. Although it is contested by some biblical geologists, it has been argued that Jerusalem is the city with seven hills. Although there is some dispute about the identity of Mt. Zion being confused with Mt. Moriah, it has been argued that in the Second Temple Period the walled city of Jerusalem was constructed on seven mountains including Goath, Acra, Bezetha, Moriah, Zion, Ophel and Gared. This does not take into account the surrounding mountains such as the Mt. of Evil Counsel, the Mt. of Offense, the Mt. of Olives, and Mt. Scopus. What we may conclude, however, is that in some way as both Rome and Jerusalem feature prominently in their importance in the 1st-century Church, both will feature prominently in the last-century Church, and both will involve Antichrist.

If we were to examine the Jerusalem explanation (for which there are substantial biblical grounds), it gives us a very plausible explanation to the seven heads. We must, however, bear in mind Revelation 17 which describes the harlot on the seven heads and ten horns. Without doubt this harlot personifies the false religious system of the world with its origins in Babylon and a history in Pergamum, Rome, Mecca, and even Salt Lake City. The harlot church, via Roman Catholicism and the modern ecumenical movement, has with good reason often been—at least since the Reformation and arguably in the early Church— identified with Rome. The Antichrist, however, will attempt to imitate the Triumphal Entry of Jesus into Jerusalem. And while Jesus declined political dominion, the Antichrist will both accept and demand it.

Jerusalem today is an epicenter of three false religions claiming to worship the same God:

- The paganistic and idolatrous Christendom of Roman Catholicism and Eastern Orthodoxy as well as a liberal Protestant presence;

- Islam with the Dome of the Rock and the Mosque of Aqsa;

- Talmudic Judaism with the rejection of its Messiah.

We do not discount the merit of arguments for identifying the harlot being present in the city of Rome. Neither, however, can Jerusalem be ignored as a viable possibility. Moreover, in the absolute sense the two are not necessarily mutually exclusive.

It can be argued (although perhaps not conclusively) that with the apocalyptic metaphore of the city on 7 hills likened to a wicked woman, the text of Revelation compares late first-century Rome to Babylon from one aspect, and late first-century Jerusalem to Babylon from another aspect. These two aspects reflect the two cardinal aspects of what Babylon represents—the false religious system of the world and the corrupt political system of the world in a united league under the Antichrist and the False Prophet. In such a proposed interpretation, Rome, as the seat of the Beast from the Sea, corresponds to the corrupt political nature of Babylon, while Jerusalem, in a spiritually desecrated state, and as the seat of the Beast from the earth, corresponds to the corrupt religious nature of Babylon.

Various scriptural, historical and modern realities can very well render plausibility to such an interpretation. Herod the Great as a very major type of the antichrist redesigned and expanded the Second Temple, not to please the Jews, but to please Rome. And

Rome placed the Imperial Fortress Antonio adjacent to the Temple, thus overshadowing it as a symbol of Roman dominion over the Temple as a religious institution.

It was the aspiration of the emperor, moreover, to be seen as the divine pontiff by Jews as well as Gentiles. Such aspirations were perpetrated in the Middle Ages by the papacy during the long era of the Holy Roman Empire established by the crusades. Today the papacy clearly acts to become a pivitol force in brokering an internationalization of Jerusalem based on religious pluralism. The Vatican has persistently sought in its diplomatic agenda to reapproach both the Islamic world (among whom the ageless legacy of the crusades endures) and the Jewish world (among whom the unforgotten legacy of inquisitional anti-Semitism endures). To this end the Vatican has lobbied the UN and pressured the EU, promoting everything from papal visits to the Holy Land to the persistent politicking in Jerusalem by its Latin Patriarchate and Papal Institute. The ultimate consummation of this ultimate diabolical political and religious union will be facilitated by the False Prophet in Jerusalem with the Abomination of Desolations.

Rome has to do with Babylon the Great as a false religious system in league with the world's corrupt political and economic system. Babylon lies more within the sphere of Rome from the political aspect while it lies more within the sphere of Jerusalem from a religious aspect, especially prophecies concerning the image of the Beast and the Abomination of Desolations in the Temple.

Both a Gentile and Jewish Aspect

A straightforward explanation would be found in understanding why both horns and heads represent kings. If the ten horns correspond to the ten 1st-century emperors from the time of Jesus' death and resurrection, beginning with Tiberius through to the time of the closing of the New Testament cannon during the reign of Domitian, we have the perfect ten focusing on the ***Gentile aspect*** of the phenomenon of Antichrist. However, when we recall that the seven heads are not simply hills but also kings, we have what appears to be a neatly fitting picture of the ***Jewish aspect*** of the Antichrist—that is, the House of Herod extending from Herod Antipater to Herod the Great, Archelaus, Antipas, Herod Philip, Herod Aristobulus, and finally Herod Agrippa—a perfect seven.

The weakness of this argument may be that the sixth one of these would still have to be reigning at the time of the authorship of the Book of Revelation. This, however, is easily resolved. Herod Agrippa I was held by some Jews to be a divine being because he united Galilee and Judea under a Jewish surrogate king who enjoyed a great deal of autonomy from Imperial Rome due to his friendship with the mad emperor Caligula. And he was one figure before Simon Bar Kochba who was perceived as an antichrist by Jewish believers because of the messianic fervor ascribed to him, and because, like Herod the Great, he renovated the Jerusalem Temple. Again, with these features in mind, he stands as a minor type of the Antichrist, but his reign was over by the time John was exiled to Patmos and Revelation was written, unless we accept an earlier pre-A.D. 70 date for the authorship of Revelation, which most of the internal textual evidence and historical evidence prohibits.

The explanation is found in that Jesus was born during the reign of Herod the Great, not Herod Antipater, and Herod Agrippa I was not the last of the Herodian kings, but Herod Agrippa II was. Herod Agrippa II would have been a child in Galilee during the earthly lifetime of Jesus, having been born in approximately A.D. 28. However, he lived until the dawn of the 2nd century, dying during the reign of Trajan. He was nonetheless the last of the Herodians. Thus if we commence our tabulation of Herodians with the birth of Jesus from Herod the Great, we would have no problem explaining the seven heads as the Herodians with the one who is to come being among those who already had been.

Yet the realm of Herod Agrippa II's domain as king was not in Israel proper, but in what is today Lebanon, although there were some Jews under his domain. It is on this basis that some voices have tried to dismiss the possibility of any prophetic significance of the last of the Herodian kings fitting into any design in the Book of Revelation. However, while ethnic Jews were a small minority in the area over which he presided as Rome's surrogate king, there were also Syro-Phoenician proselytes to Judaism, as well as Christians and some Jewish Christians, notably Luke the Evangelist who was the Gospel author and physician to the apostle Paul.

This is also an area where Jesus Himself ministered on His journey to Tyre and Sidon as recorded in the Gospels which make it clear there were significant enough numbers of Jews living there through the 1st century to warrant a journey to the region by the Messiah. This is confirmed on the basis of the internal evidence of the New Testament where Jesus made reference to not giving the bread of the children of Israel to the dogs (Mk. 7:24-30), meaning there was a mixture of Jews and converts to Judaism living in an integrated community with the Syro-Phoenician pagans.

The record of Josephus also indicates that Jesus also had many followers among the Gentiles in regions such as Lebanon, Galilee of the Gentiles, and the Decapolis. Thus the region over which the last of the Herodian kings reigned was part of the scriptural Holy Land and an area with a Jewish-Christian and Judeo-Christian demography.

To regard the last of the Herodians as a nominally Jewish king of a non-Jewish area is not a highly sustainable argument as most of the evidence shows that this was not by any replete measure wholly the case. The last of the Herodians did reign over some Jews as well as converts to Judaism, but also over what was probably significant numbers of Christians. From the earliest era of Middle Eastern Christian history there were large Christian communities stemming from southern Lebanon as far north as the Syrian city of Aleppo.

Bearing in mind that the Book of Revelation was written to Christians, the importance of a Herodian king from the same dynasty that was responsible for the death of Jesus and John the Baptist as well as the persecution of the apostle Paul would have figured strongly in the minds of the Christian readers of John's apocalypse.

Thus, just as Caesar Augustus was emperor when Jesus came the first time and prefigures the Antichrist, so, too, Herod the Great was emperor when Jesus physically arrived on the scene the first time in His advent. So he, too, prefigures one who is to come in that same Antichrist character.

It is again important to note that most of the key Herodians, including Herod the Great, Agrippa I, and Agrippa II, were politically and culturally 100% Roman in their own eyes and in the eyes of the Romans. Agrippa left Israel in his youth and was educated in Rome where he befriended Caligula and spent much of his life. Thus we have an easy harmony between the seven heads and ten horns. We state, however, that at this time we do not wish to be absolutely dogmatic about anything other than the fact that both Cesar Augustus and Herod foreshadow the one who is to come, although the above explanation is more than credible and entirely plausible in its historical and theological detail.

Nero & Other Emperors

The categorization of Nero is difficult in terms of whether he should be pigeonholed as a scriptural type of the Antichrist or an historical one of scriptural significance. For centuries numerous commentators have identified either rightly or wrongly Nero as "the one who is, but yet is to come" (Rev. 17:10-11). Without doubt, Paul, in his epistles writes of the end of his life drawing near as he was incarcerated (most likely in Rome's maritime prison). It was certainly under Nero that both he and Peter were executed according to the earliest sources cited by Eusebius and from supported bits of data gleaned archeologically from the catacombs and Roman history. Thus there is a case to be made to classify Nero as a biblical type of the Antichrist.

Without any dispute, however, is the description of the Antichrist in Revelation 17:10-11 as the Beast which was, is, and is again to come. This is a satanic counterfeit of the description of the Lord Jesus as the One "*who was, and who is, and who is to come*" (Rev. 4:8). In the beginning of John's Revelation a "Holy, holy, holy" chorus carries implications of the worship of God in His triune nature as the One who was, and is, and is to come. When we move from Revelation 4 to 17, however, we see Satan, the Antichrist, and the False Prophet in counterfeit of the Trinity, likewise claiming a supernatural past, present, and future existence.

Thus if we agree with traditional views identifying Nero with Revelation 17:10-11, he would indeed be a scriptural type of Antichrist, although the other emperors with the notable exception of Caesar Augustus are all historical shadows.

What is important in the character of Nero is that he initially began as a benevolent emperor, showing his true colors only after gaining full political, economic, and strategic power in a process through which he became increasingly deranged both spiritually and mentally. In this, Nero paints a dim yet definite picture of the "*man of lawlessness.*" Nero indeed sought to change the times and the laws as Daniel prophesied of Antichrist (Dan. 7:25). The burning of Rome, for which Christians were blamed, transpired as the stage was being set for the First Jewish Revolt that would lead to the destruction of the Temple in A.D. 70 as prophesied by Daniel and Jesus (Dan. 11:31; Mt. 24:15). In the minds of the first readers of the Book of Revelation, the literary imagery of "*Fallen is Babylon*" (Rev. 14:8) is not only borrowed from the prophecies of Isaiah and Jeremiah, and recycled from the Persian destruction of Babylon prophesied by Daniel, but also invoked images of the burning of Rome in Nero's reign.

There is also a peculiar parallel between Nero and his relationship with his mother, and the relationship of Queen Athaliah of the Old Testament and her son. We have already addressed the typological expressions of false religious systems as wicked women seeking to advance their aims by seduction and manipulation of a political establishment while also being used by a political establishment to advance the interests of corrupt rulers. This played an important role in the reign of Nero and held dire ramifications for the Church. Nero was also keen to import and promote the violent entertainment of Corinth from Greece into Rome which gave sharp rise to the popularity of gladiatorial entertainment that would eventually likewise victimize Christians and speak to a level of human debauchery that is in every sense diabolical. (The Old Testament Scriptures honored noble warriors but never glorified war itself.) The Antichrist will raise bloodcurdling violence as entertainment to the level of a pretended divine attribute, but like Nero he will not do this at first. In the early stages of his ascent to power he will falsely pass himself off as benevolent.

Additional Aspects of the Roman Emperors

There are, however, at least three other aspects of the Roman emperors that we must weigh in our efforts to understand how the Antichrist will be identified.

Rome was to be ruled by a Senate that would elect a dictator in times of war. The emperors often perpetuated conditions of strategic threat to the realm in order to sustain a dictatorial permanence of power. Arguably, for instance, the United States in the modern world has been on a wartime economy since 1938. Even in the strongest democracies such as Britain and America, civil rights are being abrogated and woefully forfeited in face of the Islamic terror threat by governments and politicians more willing to deprive their own citizens of civil and constitutional rights than they are willing to face up to the real threat of Islam for what it truly is. Because this threat emanates from the Middle East it must bear some degree of prophetic significance. Imperial Rome saw senatorial democracy subordinated to emperors' decrees. There have been identifiable trends toward this in the modern world in everything from presidential wars to the governing policies of politicians such as Tony Blair in the UK and Barack Obama in the USA.

Secondly, the emperors were able to reinforce strategic threat by the threat of impending economic collapse with unchallenged imperial rule reaching an apex after a period of hyperinflation. Hence, strategic and economic forces united in the de-democratization process.

Thirdly was *Pax Romana* where a relative political stability and economic prosperity prevailed through the extension of imperial power in a multiethnic, multireligious empire. This again dovetailed with the Pantheon worship of pagan Rome which included the gods of all of the nations in the empire apart from the God of Christians and Jews, against whom the emperors would eventually turn.

Once more in today's world we witness a Barack Obama stating, "America is not a Christian nation," and a George Bush placing a Quran in the White House to honor Islam after 9/11. At the same time, interfaith and multi-faith worship, as well as ecumenical union within Christendom, are phenomena to be promulgated continually for the same politically motivated reasons. Such practices were present in pagan Rome. They are falsely seen as being able to deliver a social stability and prevent religious conflict. Again, false peace is a hallmark of the Antichrist.

In addition to these three features, it is historically established that nearly all of these emperors were either bisexual or homosexual. Such sexual deviance was not only commonplace and popularly accepted, but was usually the orientation of the emperors themselves. As we approach the dawn of Antichrist there will be a quest by radical homosexual and lesbian communities for more and more political and legal power in everything from public office to appointments in the judiciary, the aim being the arrest and prosecution of those not bowing the knee to the perversion. What was in the court of Imperial Rome under the emperors is already once more rapidly taking shape. There are those who have suggested that the verse in Daniel stating that the Antichrist will have no regard for the love of women (Dan. 11:37) may be more than a satanic imitation of the celibacy of Christ, but a suggestion of homosexuality. Although it cannot be proven at this point, they may be correct. The typology of certain emperors such as Claudius and Nero would tend to support their contention as at least credible.

Finally, as the Roman Empire faced disintegration under the weight of its own moral, economic, and political corruption, progressive emperors became more and more frantic in their hatred of Christians and Christianity. What began with Nero, Septimus Severitus, Marcus Aurelius, Domitian,

Caligula, Decius and others, became madness under the reign of Diocletian. As he feels more and more pressure, the Antichrist will become more and more incensed along the same lines. Moreover, as in A.D. 70 in the aftermath of Nero's reign with Titus, and in A.D. 120 in the reign of Hadrian, after waging persecution against the Christian Church, the Antichrist in the same way will viciously turn against the Jews.

From Roman Emperors to the Roman Papacy

The Roman Empire had its last hurrah under Constantine the Great who pseudo-Christianized the Empire and, with the help of the post-Nicean church fathers, transformed what was Christianity into Christendom. Just as beginning with the Emperor Justin, what had been the Roman Empire would be progressively transformed into the Holy Roman Empire (that would become neither holy nor Roman). The later fragmentation of the Roman Empire between Ravenna and Constantinople would continue the two legs of the statue in Daniel into the Latin West and the Greek-speaking East.

Another overlooked foreshadowing of the designs of the Antichrist on biblical Israel would later be found in the efforts to reunite the two halves of the Roman Empire by force with the sword of the Crusades. When the kings and emperors of the Holy Roman Empire operated at the behest of the papacy, the Crusades for two hundred years established the holy Latin kingdom with Jerusalem as its capitol until their defeat by the Muslim Saladin. What transpired with the holy Latin kingdom laid the foundations for the Vatican's interest in the Holy Land which endures to the present day with the growing political ambitions of the pope to be party to any negotiated Middle East peace.

Likewise, a conflict between Europe and the Muslim world at that time led by the Turks once again foreshadows a coming conflict between the Western world and Islam for political, strategic, and economic dominance of both Europe and the Middle East. The roots of all of this must be traced back to Imperial Rome and the deified emperors. From modern history back to the Middle Ages, and back further to the early Church, it all stemmed from Imperial Rome. And somehow in the paradigm of Imperial Rome the geopolitical conflicts of the Middle East and Europe will again be focused in some kind of a Roman Empire with an agenda in the Middle East.

It is not difficult to imagine a Europe willing in its desperation to bow the knee to a leader in the character of the emperors who is capable of defending Western Civilization from the satanic scourge of Islam, not realizing that the one to whom it turns is likewise satanic. It was on behalf of Imperial Rome that Pompeii made his treaty with the Jews that would leave the Jews double-crossed by their Faustian endeavor. Of all of these emperors, without doubt the two most important in lending understanding of the Antichrist would be Nero and Caesar Augustus.

It Continued in the Papacy

The imperial title of "Pontiff" was bequeathed to the pope after Constantine pseudo-Christianized the Roman Empire and relocated his capitol to Constantinople, instituting the papacy as the primary political-religious force. The office of pope in its ultimate form commenced with later emperors such as Justin, and later popes such as Gregory the Great, Leo the Great, Siricius, and Symmachus.

Beginning with Constantine, the papacy developed in stages through something that would be unrecognizable both to the apostles and the first elders in Rome. The Second Ecumenical Council of Lyon in 1274, the Council of Trent, the aftermath of the Reformation, and the First Vatican Council of 1870 (which approved the doctrine of papal infallibility) crystallized the papacy into what it became. Its spiritual origins, however, are found neither in the New Testament nor, for that matter, in Christian history, but rather in the emperor worship of pagan Rome. That worship comes complete with Pontiff veneration, from kissing the feet to genuflecting and kissing the ring, and with various other traditions adopted directly from emperor worship. The first pope was not Peter, but the first pontiffs were the pagan emperors. The papal office was required to preserve and promulgate the Holy Roman Empire much the same as the patriarchate of Constantinople was vital to the Byzantine Empire, and the regal papacy of Henry VIII would become vital to the British Empire.

Unless we understand the cult of emperor worship biblically and historically as the early Church confronted it, and the institution of the papacy as the persecuted true Church was presented from the Waldenseans to Savonarola to the Reformers, we will not be able to come to terms with the issue of the Antichrist and False Prophet. Roman emperor worship and the antichrist institution of the Roman Catholic papacy that derives from it are antichrist with a small "a," yet are only one type of what and who is to come.

As in every case, the type illustrates and illuminates doctrine but does not define it. The shadow prefigures the substance, but is not the substance. Pagan emperors and popes were and are indeed antichrists who teach about ***the*** Antichrist, but they themselves are not he.

The House of Herod & the Herodians

Herod Archelaus ruled Galilee as the Roman designated ruler during the boyhood time of Jesus (Mt. 2:22). And he, too, presented a threat, as did his father, to the life of Jesus. Yet another Herod was Herod Philip II (Lk. 3:1), who was tetrarch of the regions of Ituraea and Trachonitis. Herod Philip II ruled as the Roman tetrarch the same time his brother was tetrarch of Galilee, Lysanias was tetrarch of Abilene, and when Pontius Pilate was originally appointed imperial governor of Judea. This was during the high priesthood of Annas and Caiaphas. Later, in Acts 12:1, we see Herod Agrippa I, and afterward his son Herod Agrippa II in Acts 25:13. The patriarch, however, was Herod the Great of ethnic Idumean origin, yet who was equally accepted both as a Jewish ruler and as a Roman and surrogate of Caesar. We must take into careful account that what was true of Herod the Great became true of his sons and grandsons. The House of Herod was an antichrist dynasty. Just like Herod the Great, most of the Herodian kings foreshadow the Antichrist in some pronounced way.

Herod Archelaus, having assumed part of his father's mantle, would have been threatened by another king of the Jews and shared his father's incentive to eliminate Jesus. The House of Herod stands in contrast to the House of David from which Jesus would come. Although he was a direct descendant of Saul and a potential rival to the throne, David not only spared the life of Jonathan's son, but blessed him in tribute to his father's loyalty. This stands in diametric contrast to the subterfuge and suspicion that defined the Herodians. Herod the Great, in paranoid delusion, demonstrated a capacity to kill some of his own sons in order to preserve his position.

Thus, at the birth of Christ the House of David was in spiritual conflict with the House of Herod because the true King of the Jews would present a challenge to restore the rightful throne of David at the expense of the false one. This relates to the prophecy of Jacob in Genesis 49 that the scepter would not depart from Judah until "Shiloh," a metaphor for the Messiah, would come from the tribe of Judah (Gen. 49:10). And later, not only would He come through the lineage of David (Is. 11:1), but He would be born in Bethlehem, the birthplace of David (Mic. 5:2). This conflict that raged in the

1st century was continued not simply between Jesus and His Herodian adversaries, but at first between Jesus' cousin, John the Baptist, and the House of Herod, and later the apostles and the House of Herod. The final Antichrist will indeed be Herodian in character as we shall examine.

Herod Agrippa I, in the Herodian spirit, persecuted the early Church (Acts 12:2-23). What becomes important here concerning Agrippa I is that the Jews fully accepted him as a Jew (Acts 12:11) just as the Romans fully accepted him as a Roman (Acts 12:21) despite the fact that his primary ethnic origin was ***neither*** Jewish nor Roman.

The final Herod listed in Scripture conducted the trial of Paul in Acts 25:23-27. This was Herod Agrippa II. We notice in this chapter that Festus the Roman speaks to Herod Agrippa II once more as if he were a Roman (Acts 25:19-20). Acts 26, however, presents to us a curious comparison between the presiding Roman official Herod Agrippa II who was by religion a Jew, and Paul the apostle cum Rabbi Shaul of Tarsus. Paul was likewise a Roman citizen in the eyes of the Romans such as Festus, a Roman, yet in the eyes of the Jews he was a Jew. The text of Acts 26 amplifies that Paul as a Roman citizen highlights the fact that Herod Agrippa II is also a Roman who is similarly expert in Jewish religious customs (Acts 26:3) and sharing in the common religion of the Jews (Acts 26:5). In appealing to Herod Agrippa II, Paul refers to his fellow Jews who accuse him as "the Jews," while addressing Herod Agrippa II as a Roman (Acts 26:7).

> *"So, having obtained help from God, I stand to this day testifying both to small and great, stating nothing but what the Prophets and Moses said was going to take place; that the Christ was to suffer, and that by reason of His resurrection from the dead He would be the first to proclaim light both to the Jewish people and to the Gentiles." While Paul was saying this in his defense, Festus said in a loud voice, "Paul, you are out of your mind! Your great learning is driving you mad." But Paul said, "I am not out of my mind, most excellent Festus, but I utter words of sober truth. For the king knows about these matters, and I speak to him also with confidence, since I am persuaded that none of these things escape his notice; for this has not been done in a corner. King Agrippa, do you believe the Prophets? I know that you do." Agrippa replied to Paul, "In a short time you will persuade me to become a Christian." And Paul said, "I would wish to God, that whether in a short or long time, not only you, but also all who hear me this day, might become such as I am, except for these chains."* (Acts 26:22-29)

This oscillating gravitation of speaking first as a Roman then as a Jew in the judicial dialogue takes place among Herod Agrippa II, Festus, and Paul where the perspective of the identity —be it religious, ethnic, or civil— begins to shift from sentence to sentence in Acts 26 from verses 23 to 29. In verse 27 Paul appeals expressly to Herod Agrippa II's Jewishness. Yet in the same dialogue he appeals to him as a Roman official, Paul being a Roman himself. As a result of Paul's legal testimony, it appears that Herod Agrippa II came under some kind of conviction, even being persuaded to consider the claims of Christ (Acts 26:28). Shortly after this, however, as Caesar's legal surrogate, Herod Agrippa II, speaking as a Roman, issues a judicial instruction to Festus for Paul to be able to exercise his right as a Roman to appeal directly to Caesar.

This integrated mixture of identities meant that just as a believer Paul could be a Jew, a Roman, and a Christian without any thought of contradiction as a result of the combination of identities which defined him, the same was equally true of the House of Herod. The Herodians would simultaneously be seen as Jewish, European, or ethnically Arab Idumean without any thought of these identities being contradictory. Festus was speaking to a Roman when he addressed Paul and Herod Agrippa II. Paul and Herod Agrippa II could address each other as either Roman or Jewish. This will be an important ingredient in the identification of the Antichrist. Various peoples will not only equally claim him as their own, but authentically accept him as their own.

It is well known that when Frank Sinatra visited Italy he was fully accepted as an Italian despite also being fully accepted as an American. When JFK visited Ireland he was fully accepted as being Irish while at the same time accepted as fully American. When Steven Spielberg or Barbara Streisand visit Israel the same thing happens, just as when Afro-American athletes or entertainers such as George Foreman, Mohammed Ali, and Wilson Pickett visit Africa. These are simultaneous identities which in other circumstances would be mutually exclusive.

Indeed the pre-incarnate Christ walked in incarnate form in the Garden with Adam before Jewish identity existed, yet with His conception that same Christ appeared incarnated as a Jew. He is the Savior of both Jew and Gentile, which is the reason for the inclusion of Gentile matriarchs such as Ruth and Rahab in His genealogy. At the same time, He is both God and man. No believer has a problem relating to Jesus as a Jew or as someone who appeared on the earth before Abraham was and therefore as a non-Jew, or as God, or as man. The combination of these identities is equally valid and not mutually exclusive. So, too, the Antichrist will attempt to counterfeit this. He will be both natural and supernatural (howbeit in a satanic sense); he will be both human and a pretended divine; his background will make him acceptable to and accepted by both Jew and non-Jew. We see this among the Herodians.

Herod the Great, functioning as a Roman, executed countless Jews, in one instance alone having hundreds of them thrown to their death off a high cliff above the Sea of Galilee in the same region where the ministry of Jesus took place. His credentials as an ironfisted Roman who could kill his fellow Jews were impeccable. The Romans would not question his Roman identity or his loyalty. Neither did Jesus or the apostles question the Jewish identity of the Herodian kings. Yet at the same time, everyone knew they were Arabs. This must be carefully understood when we consider the coming Antichrist.

Continuous with the importance of the Herodian kings, however, was the Herodian political party. As a party it was both political and religious, yet was both Jewish and Roman. The Herodians were those who stood in contrast to the Zealots and supported the Roman colonization even though it was technically packaged as a protectorate status, having Jewish kings and a Jewish national identity prior to Pontius Pilate and afterward. The Herodians entered into political and religious deals and were able by Roman collaboration to exercise functional control over the Levitical priesthood that had become so badly corrupted in the late Hasmonean Period. Hence we see the relationship between corrupt high priests named in Luke 3:1-2 who are linked to the Imperial Romans via the House of Herod. This similar kind of corrupt political religious union in the Last Days will affect both backslidden Judaism and backslidden Christendom. It will play a decisive role in how the Antichrist will operate in the character of the Herodians and Imperial Romans, and how the False Prophet will operate in the character of the politically and doctrinally corrupted high priesthood.

Herod the Tetrarch

Herod the tetrarch, like Herod Archelaus, was a son of Herod the Great and was the Roman ruler of Galilee at the time of Jesus. He was also responsible for the execution of John the Baptist. His actual name was Herod Antipas, son of Herod the Great, and the brother of Herod Philip I, whose wife he took (Mk. 6:17).

Herod the tetrarch is the same Herod who gave consent to the illegal execution of Christ by Pilate in which Herod and Pilate who had been rivals became reconciled. Under the Antichrist, unbelieving Jew and unbelieving Gentile will for a brief season be reconciled based on their hatred of Christ and the true people of God, both Jew and Gentile, and Israel will be betrayed by its pagan Roman partners just as it happened in the 1st century.

Herodias was a harlot wife who had a harlot daughter. So, too, a harlot Talmudic Judaism has a harlot apostate Christendom for her daughter, although we state this chiefly as a matter of analogy and not necessarily as a hermeneutical interpretation. We do this on the basis of the Song of Solomon where faithful Israel, having the milk of the Word, had a little sister with no breasts (SS 8:2). The predominantly Gentile Church was unable to dispense the milk of the Word (as it is described in Corinthians and Hebrews) because Israel was the custodian of the Word (Rom. 3:2). Just as there is a sibling relationship between faithful Israel and the faithful Church, there is a kindred relationship between unfaithful Israel with its Talmudic Judaism and the apostate ecumenical church.

What is important to realize in this regard is that the Sanhedrin cooperated with Herod the tetrarch and with Pilate. Although having the credentials of the Levitical establishment, John the Baptist chose to go outside into the wilderness where all Israel was going to hear him preach. Likewise, in the Last Days the people of God will need to be fed and prepared for the return of Christ outside of the mainstream churches and denominations. As the Sanhedrin were in league with Herod the tetrarch and Pilate, so, too, the World Council of Churches, the ecumenical church of Rome, and the backslidden elements of what had been Evangelicalism will be in league with the corrupt political interests, both Jew and Gentile, of the fallen world. And Israel will once again find herself betrayed as a consequence of her own actions and unbelief.

Like Herod the Great, Herod the tetrarch is from an Idumean pedigree with a Jewish faith by political convenience, yet culturally and politically Roman. In addition to a social gospel, political intrigue, economic manipulation affecting food supply, and knowing the words of the wise and their riddles, a key to the Antichrist's popularity and deception will be satanic counterfeits of the miraculous. Thus we see Herod the tetrarch interested in miracles during the Herodian trial of Jesus. Jesus referred to him as a "fox" (possibly a local species of jackal), meaning "a sneak" (Lk. 13:2). Although all of the Herods named in the New Testament typify the

Antichrist, these specific features combine to render Herod the tetrarch a peculiar type of the Antichrist.

Herod the Great failed to kill Christ in his infancy. Herod the tetrarch did not fail, and according to Peter's testimony in the Book of Acts Herod was a key component in the illegal, wrongful execution of Jesus. The devious character and nature of Herod the Great, the original enemy of Jesus in the New Testament, was embodied in Herod the tetrarch. Analogous to this, the character and nature of Satan, the original enemy of Christ in the Garden of Eden, will be embodied in the Antichrist.

Grasping this is essential to identifying the Antichrist. Since Jesus' birth, Satan working through the first Herod—Herod the Great—tried to kill Him. But divine intervention and providential protection prevailed until the second Herod, the tetrarch. Jesus was then for a season forfeited to the control of Satan to kill Him under this type of the Antichrist. In a divinely orchestrated gambit this backfired on Satan because of Jesus' resurrection. So, too, the Body of Christ will be forfeited to the destructive control of Satan—what Daniel termed "*the shattering of the power of the holy people*" (Dan. 12:7) when the lordship of history will for a season be given to Satan through the Antichrist. Once more, this will backfire because of the Resurrection of the faithful believers and the Rapture.

Summary

The examination of this brief list of types of Antichrist, while more than a prelude, is still introductory. Because of his importance we will need to return once more to looking even more closely at Judas when we peer into the final person of the Antichrist. As we have mentioned, the other more colossal types of the Antichrist, including Herod the Great, Antiochus Epiphanes, and backslider Solomon, will require separate in-depth treatments in their own right.

- Nebuchadnezzar as king of Babylon shows us Satan's nature manifested in human flesh, desiring to be worshiped, desiring the conquest of Israel in order to prevent the coming of the Messiah, and erecting an image of himself made of gold (a non-corrosive metal in biblical typology representing something eternal) that is to be the demanded object of worship;

- The king of Assyria likewise shows us the objectives Antichrist will have with the conquest of Israel and the Jews and the desire to be worshipped by the people of God. The relationship between Sennacherib the king of Assyria and his messenger Rabshakeh furnish a dim illustration of the coming relationship between the Antichrist and the False Prophet;

- The king of Tyre reveals how the Antichrist will be an incarnation of the same Satan who was in the Garden of Eden (Eze. 28:11-13), having the same designs he had when he first tempted and corrupted man;

- Goliath and the man of sixes, in addition to relating Antichrist to a combination of sixes, shows how he will worship military strength and, although being a human, will also be of some kind of highly demonic origin;

- Nimrod typologically connects Antichrist with the workings of Satan through means of false religion and fallen man willing to deify himself dating back to the Tower of Babel;

- Pharaoh shows us in figure how God has destined Antichrist to eternal perdition again in the character of Judas as well as once more highlighting the anti-Jewish ethos the Antichrist will exhibit. More importantly, the Exodus judgments on Pharaoh's kingdom foreshadow God's judgments on the kingdom of Antichrist;

- Judas shows us the capacity the Antichrist will have to deceive even the Elect, bearing in mind that Judas feigned his care for the poor as a false humanitarian image and reputation.

It is imperative that we understand that, in addition to a corrupted wisdom where he will to a degree be able to understand "*the words of the wise and their riddles*" (Prov. 1:6) in the character of Solomon (and as we shall elaborate on when we examine the Antichrist typology of backslidden Solomon with reference to "666"), the Antichrist will also use counterfeit signs and wonders in a recapitulation of Jannes and Jambres.

The third leg of the Antichrist tripod of deception will be a social gospel where a pretended compassion for the poor will simply be a masterfully constructed disguise and a modality to exploit. The clearest picture we have of this third leg of the tripod that will be the Antichrist's methodology is presented to us through the person and character of Judas Iscariot.

The preceding panorama of types serve as an orientation to the nature of the typology required in determining from these types and shadows the elements we need to be looking for when we consider the more major types, particularly Solomon, Herod, Antiochus, and Judas Iscariot. Unless we first comprehend the nature of attributes, characteristics, idiosyncrasies, and behavioral nuances of these types of the Antichrist generally, we will not be able to properly digest the more acute and pronounced details of the "*man of sin*" inherent in the major types. The same is to a lesser degree true of the False Prophet who in essence will be the personification of the spirit of antichrist much as the Antichrist will in essence at some point become the virtual incarnation of Satan.

Part Three: The Many Antichrists – Historical

Scriptural eschatology contains a literary and historical dilemma that is not easy to understand or to explain.

The events surrounding the Maccabean Revolt are prophetically predicted in inspired detail in the Book of Daniel but have no recorded biblical fulfillment. There is rather a post-facto recorded fulfillment in the historical narrative of the Intertestamental apocryphal literature, specifically 1 and 2 Maccabees. Yet Jesus acknowledged the validity of the historical accounts when He observed the Jewish feast of Hanukkah according to John 10 where it is called "*the Feast of Dedication*" (Jn. 10:22). He did this in spite of the fact that the Intertestamental apocryphal books are only biblically important history and literature and not directly inspired canon.

In the Olivet Discourse Jesus Himself gave a prophetic depiction of the events surrounding A.D. 70 and the destruction of the Temple. The only recorded fulfillment of this we have, however, is in Josephus' *War of the Jews* and various mishnaic and other rabbinic references, and references to 1st-century Christian oral sources compiled by Eusebius in the 4th century. While the historical material validates strongly the accuracy of the prophetic predictions of Christ regarding these events, there is no recorded scriptural recounting of their fulfillment as we would have for instance in prophecies regarding the First Coming of Christ or of the Assyrian and Babylonian captivities, all of which were likewise prophetically predicted.

It is providential that the events leading up to the Maccabean Revolt and the events of A.D. 70 are both predicted in Scripture, but having no recorded scriptural fulfillment (but only recorded fulfillments in extra-biblical historical sources) are events prefiguring what is to transpire at the end of the age. The events of the Seleucid defilement of the Temple and of Titus' destruction of the Temple in A.D. 70 will be recapitulated by the Antichrist, yet will likewise have no biblical recording once they transpire. As the believers in A.D. 70 had to know from the current events and contemporary history to flee Jerusalem to Pella under Simeon the cousin of Jesus, and as the Maccabees had to know from the historical events of the time how to react to Antiochus IV, so, too, the final prophecies of the Antichrist foreshadowed by these events will have to be understood in "live time" history. Indeed, the events of A.D. 70 and the Maccabean Revolt do not simply foreshadow and prefigure what is to come, but what is to come will, to a very high degree, actually recapitulate these events.

We may say then that Scripture and the teaching and example of Jesus teach us the need to understand ***past*** history in order to understand ***future*** history. And to understand ***both*** past and future history we must understand them in the light of Scripture. Thus in this section we will look at historical figures not primarily covered to this point—some of them directly related to biblical history, others not so, who teach about the Antichrist. We must take care, however, ***not*** to give ourselves license to do this recklessly or speculatively. We require an overtly biblically-stated mandate to do so. We find that mandate in the instructions of Jesus to be alert to the fact that many antichrists will come in the future, and many of these are coming in His name.

The meaning of this "coming in His name" may be described as trifold, or having three aspects: the first aspect is the more obvious of those claiming to actually be Him. We are warned of ***any*** who pose as a physical return of Christ, and we are commanded to avoid them (Mt. 24:23-26). This warning of Jesus is compounded by the fact that He warned that the aim of Satan is to attempt to deceive even the very Elect (Mt. 24:24). Thus we already witness the supposedly Elect being taken in. The condemnation of the vampiristic consumption of blood in Acts 15, and the cannibalism of the Roman Catholic mass, have done nothing to prevent so-called Evangelicals led by individuals such as Chuck Colson from embracing the legitimacy of Roman Catholicism. This, even though the transubstantiated Eucharistic Christ of Rome is a pretended incarnation and a physical return of Jesus that, in defiance of His own words, is to be worshiped as Him.

Another example is when the late Jerry Falwell physically embraced South Korean cult leader Sun Myung Moon, calling Moon "an unsung hero" after Moon made a major cash donation to Falwell's Christian institution of higher learning. The fact that Moon claims the biblical Jesus failed in His mission and that Moon is the "Lord of the Second Advent" himself—that is, the return of Christ—was no problem for Falwell once $3 million was put on the table up front. Indeed a member of the Elect was deceived.

The second aspect of "coming in His name" is that false Christs would pretend to be Him simply on the basis of having the same name but exuding a very different history and character. These would include the "Jesus" or "Issa" of Islam which downgrades Jesus to a mere mortal, not divine and not God's Son, who was inferior to Mohammed. Another example is the Jesus Christ of the Latter-day Saints. While the biblical Jesus is the *monogenes*—the "only begotten" of the Father—the Mormon "Jesus" is, according to Mormon literature, the spirit brother of Satan. The final aspect of "coming in His name" would include those who do not imitate Him by imitating His name but who imitate Him by an attempted imitation of His deeds and character.

In each of these cases it is imperative that we continually recall that the meaning of the Greek term "antichrist" is once again not simply "against," but "in place of." The Eucharist christ, the Mormon christ, and the Islamic christ all seek to ***displace*** the scripturally authentic Christ.

Lastly, we must recall that ***both*** Beasts in Revelation 13 are co-equally "Antichrist," and together with Satan form the diabolical attempt at mimicking the tri-unity of the Judeo-Christian Godhead—as it were a satanic trinity.

As there are many antichrists per se, there are and shall be many false prophets. Just as we must identify the singularly unique Man of Sin from the many other antichrists, we cannot do so unless we also identify the ultimate False Prophet from among the many false prophets of Satan. The ultimate False Prophet will be the quintessential counterfeit of the Holy Spirit. As we note, what sets the ultimate Antichrist apart from the many antichrists is that the other antichrists are demonically possessed but the final "*man of lawlessness*" is literally satanically possessed.

Chapter 6: Historical Types

The Many Popes

Although we reject the Historicist approach to prophecy promulgated by the Reformers on the basis of what if ***fails*** to say, we do accept and extol what it ***does*** say. In properly comprehending the antichrist nature of the Roman papacy from whose ranks they departed, the Protestant Reformers correctly identified the popes as "antichrist."

According to Jesus in John 14 and 17, the Holy Spirit—and the Holy Spirit alone—is the infallible "Vicar of Christ." By claiming to be "Vicar of Christ"—that is, the "one who acts vicariously in place of Christ"—the pope in Rome in actuality is a counterfeit of the Holy Spirit. And since 1854 the papacy even ascribes to itself infallibility when the pontiff speaks *Ex Cathedra* as head of the Magesterium of the papal system. This is the same entity that pseudo-Christianized the pagan religions of Imperial Rome, resulting in a paganized, distorted reinterpretation of Christianity into a Christendom the apostles would not recognize.

To understand this we must turn to the teaching of Jesus in His polemic against religious hypocrisy.

> *"But do not be called Rabbi; for One is your Teacher, and you are all brothers. Do not call anyone on earth your father; for One is your Father, He who is in heaven. Do not be called leaders; for One is your Leader, that is, Christ.* (Mt. 23:8-10)

In verse 8 Jesus condemns the use of "rabbi" as a religious title because it derives etymologically from the personal possessive Hebrew word "*rav,*" meaning "my great one," as one's teacher. Our teacher, of course, is the Holy Spirit according to Jesus in John 16:13-14. Yet the pope of Rome usurps this position for himself.

In verse 9 Jesus condemns the non-generic/non-pedigree use of the term "father" as a religious title, yet the pope calls himself not only "father" but moreover "**THE** Holy Father" with a definite article. Thus he places himself in the place not only of the Holy Spirit but God the Father.

In the following verse 10 Jesus issues a third prohibition of calling any man our "leader" as a religious title, for this position is the reserve of Christ Himself. In the Roman papacy, and, therefore, in the pope himself, we have the personification of the satanic counterfeit of the Trinity; a man who puts himself "in the place of" the Holy Spirit, the Father, and the Son.

It is not our intention to advocate the Reformation line that the pope is ***the*** Antichrist and so we need look no further, but rather that the pope is a devastatingly accurate personification of the Antichrist, the False Prophet, and the spirit of antichrist which helps us to look further. Although the final Antichrist will encompass much more than Roman Catholicism and backslidden Western Christendom, his domain will pivotally include and yet extend well beyond it into the full gamut of false religion in the character of the Roman emperors as the pontifical heads of the Pantheon.

Although there are many antichrists, no historical type of the Antichrist and no other of the many antichrists are more significant than the pope of Rome. Yet we must bear in mind that there are a host of others. In this section we will attempt as best we are able with the help of the Lord to likewise identify and understand them.

Concerning the popes, however, there are two primary ways in which the Pontiff of Rome foreshadows the Antichrist (beyond the fact that neither has a regard for the love of women). The first is that as Pontiff he is heir to the deified pontifical emperors of pagan Rome. Secondly, he is head of a false religious system and so also typifies the False Prophet who is also of the antichrist spirit from Satan.

The Many Antichrists

A much repeated theme of this book will be the ambiguous nature of Antichrist uniting the religious and political in a situation where by Greek definition there is always someone "in place of" Christ. Among the Jews there is the painful history of false messiahs often hailed by rabbis as the Anointed One. From Yehuda of Galilee cited by Rabbi Gemaliel in Acts 5, to Simon Bar Kochba championed by his false prophet Rabbi Akiva, to Shabbatai Zvi, to Jacob Frank, to Menachem Schneerson, we have many Jewish antichrists who in some way foreshadow something and someone yet to come.

Among Abraham's other children, the Arabs, we have Mohammed and his false prophet Abu Bakir. For the Mormons it is Joseph Smith and his false prophet Brigham Young. For the nation of Islam it is Wallace Farad (whom American black Muslims called "The Divine Being") and his prophet Elijah B. Mohammed. The Rastafarians have their false prophet in Marcus Garbey, although Haili Salasi himself refused to be their messiah. (They made him one anyway.) To the Baha'i's it is B'halua. It seems that every false religion and cult has one, but it also seems their frequency is increasing even more with maniacal figures such as Charles Manson, David Koresh, and Jim Jones springing up at more regular intervals.

It is no coincidence that history has seen in the last hundred years more and more megalomaniac dictators wishing to have themselves, in essence, deified. When Napoleon invaded the Middle East defeating the Mamluks and sought to restore the balance of power in Asia Minor that was lost by the Crusades to Saladin, Evangelical Christians in Great Britain took special note. Promising to liberate Europe, the son of the revolution crowned himself as emperor, had tentative ambitions of bringing the Jews to Israel as part of an imposed peace plan, and ascended Mt. Tabor where the story of Deborah took place in the Book of Judges. And glancing at the Valley of Jezreel below with the plain of Armageddon before him, he proclaimed it the perfect place for the ultimate military campaign. Many Bible-believing Christians not without some reason suspected Napoleon of being ***the*** Antichrist, but like Mohammed he was merely ***an*** antichrist whose legacy discloses something about the Beast to come.

Since the mid-20th century the world has seen a string of self-proclaimed god-men responsible for some of the most unimaginable cruelty ever directed against the human race. Among the more minor ones rank Nicolae Ceauşescu, Kim Il Sung with a colossus of himself erected in Pyong Yang, and his deranged son Kim Jong Il. Iran's Ahmadinejad wishes to see himself as a prophet of the Mahdi, expediting the coming of the Islamic messiah by attacking Israel and the West. Pol Pot exterminated over 2-1/2 million of his own people in Cambodia while Idi Amin, inspired by his combination of Islam and African witchcraft, conducted a tyranny almost unfathomable in its sheer insanity.

These self-deified demagogues are mere pipsqueaks of modern history. When Benito Mussolini concluded the Latin Treaty with the pope, and Hitler signed his Concordat with the Roman Catholic bishops of Bavaria, coming to power in coalition with the Zentrum—the German Catholic party—the spirit of antichrist was again embodied in an individual in league with religious false prophets. The overwhelming majority of Lutheran bishops supported the Third Reich, as did the Roman Catholic prelates of Germany and Austria. Not least of these antichrists was Joseph Stalin who had already seen Lenin turn the Communism of Marx into a humanistic religion that worshiped man to the deification of the party by the Bolsheviks.

The fact that religious charlatans from cult leaders to con-artist televangelists successfully display a religious lure with increasing prominence, while the political realm sees one narcissistic and self-absorbed dictator after another trying to turn themselves into a god, indicates that the spirit of antichrist is at work on a global scale never before experienced in human history. There have always been antichrists and false prophets. Indeed there was a splurge of them before the First Coming of Christ as there will be a splurge of them before His return, but we have never witnessed anything on the level we are seeing now. What we see now, however, is only the shadow; the substance causing the shadow will be the two figures of Revelation 13.

What is no less staggering is the fact that social and economic forces create a market for the product. Fallen man is looking for a savior, but instead they get one madman after another who turns against them and brings them to ruin in the character of the Antichrist who is to come. The reason they so desperately seek for one of these saviors is because fallen man has rejected the true One. As always the microcosm of the tragic human condition is Israel and the Jews. Having by and large rejected the true Messiah, they will be nearly swallowed up by the false one, narrowly saved only by the fact that the true One will return (Zech. 12:1-10).

The Christian Who Cried Wolf

In the modern world, as we focus upon elsewhere, the fact that we have seen in the last 75 years an increase of despotic political leaders who misrepresent themselves as national redemptive figures before disclosing their true intent is of prophetic significance; not just the figures themselves, but the proliferation of them including Mussolini, Hitler, Stalin, Kim Jong Il, Idi Amin, Barack Obama, etc. Likewise, the fact that we have seen an increase in the de facto deification of cultic religious leaders such as Joseph Smith, Sun Myung Moon, Mother Teresa, Maharishi Mahesh Yogi, Menachem Schneerson and others is not without prophetic weight eschatologically. These are historical foreshadowings, not of the Beast who came out of the sea, but the Beast of Revelation 13 who comes out of the earth; that is, the False Prophet who is co-equally Antichrist.

Indeed, fallen man has always deified people who themselves never claimed to be a deity, including Guatama (Buddha) and Confucius. Even in the Book of Acts, pagans attempted to deify the apostles (Ac. 14:11). When fallen man rejects the true God he will always find a false one who will inevitably be anthropomorphic—that is, in man's own image and likeness. The increase in this phenomenon on the present stage in history again exposes the activity of the spirit of antichrist.

Where appropriate, in other sections and chapters we will review prophetically important features of most of these figures. The red light on our dashboard should indicate that such figures are turning up with increasing frequency. In the strategy of the enemy, this again complicates the visibility of what is on the horizon. There are so many antichrists and so many false prophets it will not be initially simple to identify the ultimate Antichrist and False Prophet from the others, and at an early stage they will not look like an Antichrist or False Prophet at all. When the final Antichrist shows up, and the faithful people in the Church who have insight begin to take action, they will battle a lethargy which will just see the Antichrist and False Prophet as two more on a long list of many others. Their uniqueness will not be readily perceived except by those who are truly faithful to Jesus.

Antichrist's Kingdom - The Global Village

What has made the global economy a "global village" more than any other single factor is communication, particularly the mass media. Online trading, international cash transfers, and the instantaneous flow of information themselves propel the planet toward a one-world government. It is not profitable to become overly obsessed with conspiracy theories about Freemasons or the Illuminati. Even without such organizations, technology itself would press human development into a one-world economic and political system. The media are key.

Without doubt Satan has worked through Hollywood, making films such as *The Omen*, causing people to get their eschatology and understanding of the Antichrist from Hollywood's screen scripts instead of from the pages of God's Word. Thus when the Antichrist shows up, there will be an initial impulse that he is just one of the many figures operating under the influence of the antichrist spirit. It is a kind of "boy who cried wolf" strategy of the enemy. More sad still is how popular film culture has so mythologized eschatology and the Antichrist that many people believe they understand about him because they saw some movie.

The capacity of the media to mislead and deceive in this way is by no means limited to non-believers. Foolishly, many saved Christians were taken in by Mel Gibson's film version of the mystical Roman Catholic work, *The Passion of the Christ*. The scriptural and historical inaccuracies of the film were abundant, but its thrust was to support the false spirituality of Roman Catholicism. The film, for instance, had spikes being driven through the metacarpals—that is, the palm—of Christ, instead of what archeology and forensic pathology says is the reality, that the spikes were driven through the radius at the wrist. The reason for this is to support the Roman Catholic superstition and deceptive phenomenon of stigmata.

Everything surrounding the film, including Gibson's personal character and his motives for making it came to public light as a scandal of the racism and anti-Semitism of a troubled man driven only by a desire to make money. Yet he was lorded and extolled as a Christian, and his film was praised as the greatest evangelistic tool of the century. This fiasco showed how Christians, pastors, and Evangelical leaders can be easily deceived *en masse* by the power of the media.

It is without any doubt that with Satan as the prince of the power of the air, the Antichrist who will control the world's economy and politics will likewise control its media and manipulate its religious systems to his own ends. If saved Christians and their undiscerning leaders are unable to see through an obvious deception such as Mel Gibson's *Passion* film, the prospects for what the Antichrist will be able to achieve are staggering. No avenue of communication facilitates the operation of the *zeitgeist* through which the spirit of antichrist operates more than the media in a world driven by Internet, broadcasts, and not least of all the incredible power of Hollywood in the Western world and Bollywood in the Eastern world. The media are subverted by the spirit of antichrist to set the trap in captivating not only the minds but the hearts of the undiscerning, and not only undiscerning non-Christians, but even saved Christians who lack discernment.

We see four of the essential ingredients of Antichrist at work:

- A love of money as a primary motivator;
- Hatred of the Jews that is not at first apparent;
- A false theology of Jesus;
- A capacity to deceive even the Elect.

Islamic Types of the Antichrist in History

The long litany of Roman emperors in the 2nd and 3rd centuries were post-apostolic historical types of the Antichrist, as were their papal successors. With specific reference to the Jerusalem Temple, however, the most typologically important of these was Hadrian the Great (who built the wall across the north of England). Hadrian leveled what was left of the Temple Mount nearly down to the bedrock, constructing the pagan city of "Aeolina Capitolina." The city featured the temple of Jupiter, the Roman version of the Greek god Zeus, worshiped on the same site by Antiochus IV in the Seleucid era. As we have noted, Simon Bar Kochba was the first named Judaic type of the Antichrist in the post-apostolic era, prophetically alluded to by Christ in John 5:43. Moving our concentration to Jerusalem again, however, following Bar Kochba the first major type of the Antichrist was Constantine's nephew Julian the Apostate with his failed endeavor to nullify the Olivet Discourse predictions of Jesus concerning the Jewish Temple.

As we move into the era of Islam and the Crusades we begin to see important Islamic figures who typify aspects of the Antichrist. Just as the Jews await a Messiah, the Muslim world, and specifically the Arab world, await a "Mahdi" who can unify adherence to Islam and bring about the unity of all Muslims. This unity as taught in the Quran, called "*umma,*" connotes a unified community or single nation of Islam, which has never existed. Immediately after the death of Mohammed, Islam divided between Sunni and Shia in fulfillment of prophecies in the Book of Genesis that Esau's sword will always be against his brother and Ishmael's seed will always be divided (Gen. 27:39-40). Not until accepting Jesus Christ can Abraham's other descendants, the Arab peoples, truly acquire that aspired unity.

When we understand this, we see a reason why Islam must have a common enemy in the Christian or in the Jew or in anyone else they can call an "infidel." Without a common enemy Muslims will inevitably kill each other. Islamic history testifies to the reality that most jihads have been holy wars of Muslims slaughtering other Muslims. The great Islamic hope is that the Mahdi will put an end to this division by uniting all the Arab and Islamic peoples against the infidel, particularly against the Christian and the Jew. To this day fundamentalist Islam still identifies all Christians irrespective of denomination or persuasion as "Crusaders."

In the 1870s there was the Mahdist Uprising against the British in Sudan led by Mohammed Ahmad, known as the Mahdi of Sudan. In the

1960s there was a political mania to turn Gamal Nassir into a latter-day Mahdi figure. This quest features supremely in the mentality of fundamentalist Shia Iran.

Following Julian the Apostate,, however, with the onset of the Islamic presence first by Arabs then by Turks and interrupted for two centuries by the Crusades, two under-recognized historical types of the Antichrist emerged. We must be careful not to neglect the fact that the Antichrist to come will likely inspire Islamic sentiments to believe he will fulfill the Mahdist destiny. Even though he will fight on the side of Europe and the West, we recognize even at present that part of the Islamic world is aligned with the West against the radical fundamentalists and their jihadist terror.

The first of these types was Saladin, who delivered the final defeat of the Crusades and who replaced the cross on top of the original Dome of the Rock cum Mosque of Omar with the Islamic crescent. This harkened back to the events of A.D. 70 when the Romans placed pagan ensigns for worship on the site of the Holy of Holies when the Temple was destroyed on or near the same location as the Dome of the Rock. It was Saladin's descendants, moreover, who built the present Mosque of Omar on the same site, inscribing the Suraht quotation from the Quran that God has no son, which is a signature of Antichrist according to the First Epistle of John (1 Jn. 2:2). These events transpired in A.D. 1187-1193.

330 years later, not realizing he was partially fulfilling the prophecies of Ezekiel, Suleiman the Magnificent blocked up the Golden Gate—the East Gate of Jerusalem directly in front of where the Temple had stood—in order to prevent the coming of the Jewish Messiah. He even placed a cemetery immediately in front of it as an added security precaution because contact with the bones of the deceased by Jewish law would render any Messiah as ritually unclean. This is a major foreshadowing of Antichrist who will likewise ascend the Temple Mount and perpetrate actions designed to preempt and prevent the coming of the Jewish Messiah, who is Jesus Christ.

Summary

As we note elsewhere, identification of the Antichrist requires a solid familiarity with both Eastern and Western messianic expectations which the Antichrist will try to apply to himself, at least to a considerable degree in his initial reign. This also requires an understanding not only of a Judeo-Christian picture of prophetic expectation surrounding the Antichrist, but also an Islamic one. It is unthinkable that at the same time the Jewish nation of Israel is historically reborn in accordance with biblical prophecy, the Arab nations also found in ancient biblical history would not be of acute prophetic importance.

Thus, beginning in the post-apostolic era, and in the post-patristic era, as well as through the Dark Ages and into the Middle Ages in both the Eastern world and the Western world, we have had an index of types of the Antichrist and the False Prophet that do provide small yet important pieces of the final puzzle that will tell the faithful Church what it needs to know at the appropriate time.

Much the same as a firm knowledge of biblical doctrine does not require an academic knowledge of biblical languages or literary criticism (although we do require some Christians who have a scholarly background), so, too, understanding Church history and Jewish history as well as Islamic history, all of which are of important value in being able to develop a clear picture of the final Antichrist, does not require an expertise in European, Jewish, and Middle Eastern history. But faithful Christians should know and understand the main historically important facts such as those detailed above.

Part Four: The Milieu of the Antichrist

Each type of the Antichrist, both scriptural and historical, emerged from a plethora of changing social, political, cultural, religious, economic, and strategic circumstances. We cannot properly understand any of these types of the Beast until we properly frame them within the context of the prevailing historical conditions of their respective times. This will be ***particularly*** true of the ultimate Antichrist. The framework of events facilitating his rise will be geographically centered on Europe and the Middle East. The full compendium of these conditions spans both Testaments, but the core understanding is related to us primarily in the Book of Daniel.

While we must exercise caution in not reading contemporary world events either in the Middle East or in Europe ***into*** Daniel's prophecies, we must evaluate such events ***in light*** of Daniel's prophecies. No shadow of the Antichrist ever came out of a vacuum; neither will the Antichrist himself. The constellation of global circumstances with particular emphasis on the Middle East and Europe are an imperative component in working out how these prophecies will be fulfilled.

More importantly, knowing for certain the ultimate identity of the "*man of lawlessness*" is an impossibility without handling specific prophecies concerning him in tandem with those prophecies of events surrounding him. Going back to the statue in Daniel 2, we must understand that the manifestation of the Antichrist will be part and parcel of geopolitical history, religious history, and economic and cultural evolution reaching their apex in a fallen world which "*lies in the power of the evil one*" (1 Jn. 5:19). Thus there must be a cognizance of this historical development from times ancient to the contemporary before any real progress can be made on the identification of this individual who will surface from, and in some way be a by-product of, this complicated milieu.

Chapter 7: The Iron and the Clay

The Statue of Daniel 2

The statue Nebuchadnezzar saw in his dream represents the four empires that correspond to the four beasts found later on in Daniel.

The head, of course, is Babylon: the mind of the world is the mind of Babylon. The way the world thinks is derived from Babylon, going back first to the Tower of Babel in Genesis 11, and more recently to the Babylonian Empire. It looks ahead to Babylon the Great in the Book of Revelation when the false religious system of the world will be in confederation with its political system. The torso represents the Persian Empire, while the groin—the area in which reproductive organs are located—is the Greek Empire, the cradle of Hellenism. We will consider this further when we examine the image of the Beast. The Old Testament shadow of the image of the Beast is not only the statue of Zeus bearing the facial features of Antiochus Epiphanes, which was placed in the Temple, but as we shall see, also the statue of Nebuchadnezzar.

Hellenism: The Origin of Western Civilization

The seminal influence on Western Civilization is Hellenism; the Western world runs on it. Because of this, it is wise to try to understand Hellenism.

The Hebrew worldview was theocentric, or centered on God. To the Hebrews there is one God who is omniscient, omnipotent, and omnipresent; no one can lie to Him, cheat Him, or deceive Him. If they could, He would not be God. There is this one God, and no other. By contrast, the Greeks were polytheistic. Their gods were anthropomorphic, created in man's image, and therefore man could lie to them, cheat them, try to placate them, and so on. In the Hebrew worldview, humans are theopomorphic men and women; in other words, they are created in the image and likeness of God.

The natural result of Greek theology was that man became the center of their universe. So instead of the theocentric Hebrew worldview, the Greeks had an anthropocentric worldview. This ultimately led to secular humanism. Western Civilization, therefore, is a combination of two things: Judeo-Christian faith and Hellenism. In its broadest sense, Hellenization—

or rather anthropocentricity—reached its apex in the Western Enlightenment. The Jews had a separate "Enlightenment" which they called *Haskala*. Therefore Western culture is this combination of Hellenism and Judeo-Christian faith which is further colored by the Enlightenment.

Then there are the two legs, which most people would define as Greco-Roman; others define them as a combination of the Hebraic and the Judaic.

The Ten Toes

Finally we come to the ten toes.

> *"But as for me, this mystery has not been revealed to me for any wisdom residing in me more than in any other living man, but for the purpose of making the interpretation known to the king, and that you may understand the thoughts of your mind.*
>
> *"You, O king, were looking and behold, there was a single great statue; that statue, which was large and of extraordinary splendor, was standing in front of you, and its appearance was awesome. The head of that statue was made of fine gold, its breast and its arms of silver, its belly and its thighs of bronze, its legs of iron, its feet partly of iron and partly of clay. You continued looking until a stone was cut out without hands, and it struck the statue on its feet of iron and clay and crushed them. Then the iron, the clay, the bronze, the silver and the gold were crushed all at the same time and became like chaff from the summer threshing floors; and the wind carried them away so that not a trace of them was found. But the stone that struck the statue became a great mountain and filled the whole earth.*
>
> *"This was the dream; now we will tell its interpretation before the king. You, O king, are the king of kings, to whom the God of heaven has given the kingdom, the power, the strength and the glory; and wherever the sons of men dwell, or the beasts of the field, or the birds of the sky, He has given them into your hand and has caused you to rule over them all. You are the head of gold.*
>
> *"After you there will arise another kingdom inferior to you, then another third kingdom of bronze, which will rule over all the earth.*
>
> *"Then there will be a fourth kingdom as strong as iron; inasmuch as iron crushes and shatters all things, so, like iron that breaks in*

pieces, it will crush and break all these in pieces. In that you saw the feet and toes, partly of potter's clay and partly of iron, it will be a divided kingdom; but it will have in it the toughness of iron, inasmuch as you saw the iron mixed with common clay. As the toes of the feet were partly of iron and partly of pottery, so some of the kingdom will be strong and part of it will be brittle. And in that you saw the iron mixed with common clay, they will combine with one another in the seed of men; but they will not adhere to one another, even as iron does not combine with pottery.

"In the days of those kings the God of heaven will set up a kingdom which will never be destroyed, and that kingdom will not be left for another people; it will crush and put an end to all these kingdoms, but it will itself endure forever. (Dan. 2:30-44)

There has been much speculation about the identity of the ten toes coming from the two legs. Most of these interpretations had elements of merit but also weaknesses. As is commonly known, most Pre-millennial Dispensationalists at one time misinterpreted it to mean that once ten nations were in the European Union the prophecy would be fulfilled. Plainly this was wrong as there are now twenty-five nations with more still applying. Additionally, not all of these nations were part of the Roman Empire. In more recent years others have speculated that the ten toes could well be ten politically united global trade blocs such as the African Union, the European Union, the North American Free Trade Agreement (NAFTA), and similar such blocs in the Caribbean and Southeast Asia. This argument may appear to have merit, but the problem is the toes are attached to the legs, corresponding to the Latin West and Greek East in the Roman Empire, and global trade blocs further afield do not fit the anatomy of the statue. There is, however, another explanation that does appear to fit more comfortably.

The Ten Nations

Europe has two alignments of nations – one economic called the European Union and one strategic called NATO connecting Europe with North America in a joint defense policy. Both alignments of nations are political as well as economic or strategic. There are precisely ten nations, all of them in part or in entirety that were part of the Roman and Holy Roman Empires which today are both members of the European Union and members of NATO. These represent the ten European countries most important in the European Union, with other nations simply having a strategic association and political affiliation with them. The ten nations who are members of both NATO and the European Union and who are the dominant economies of Europe are called the Western European Union. They include Great Britain, France, Holland, Germany, Italy, Spain, Portugal, Belgium, Greece and Luxembourg.

The Western European Union should not be negated as a viable possibility, but it is generally overlooked. There are precisely ten nations, all of which were in the Roman Empire, are both NATO and EU members, and represent the strongest and most influential countries in Europe. The possible weakness in this argument is that only Greece was from the Eastern Roman Empire and the statue did not have one toe on one foot and nine on the other.

A further suggestion has been that the ten toes rather correspond to the ten horns in Revelation 12:3 and in Daniel 7:7. The obvious complication with this proposition is that there is no passage of Scripture identifying toes with either horns or kings, so the conclusion is speculative.

We must be cautious, however, not to confuse the image of which Nebuchadnezzar dreamed in Daniel 2 with the golden image he made of himself in Daniel 3. It is the image he made of himself of pure gold that prefigures the image of the Beast of which we read in Revelation 13. While we shall look at this further in terms of the combinations of sixes that surround it, two features must be noted:

(1) It is solidly of gold, a non-corrosive metal which does not oxidize and speaks of that which is eternal in Temple typology. Everything in the Holy of Holies had to be of pure, unbeaten gold, and the gold of this image represents Satan's attempt at an eternal auto-deification;

(2) The name of Nebuchadnezzar itself carries the Chaldee meaning "may the God Nabu protect the ruler." This must be contrasted to the name Belshazzar, meaning "may Ba'al protect the king," the connotation of the king being the ruling son of Baal. Thus Nebuchadnezzar had two names as king of Babylon, the second name associating him with Baal worship.

The Two Baal's

It is again urgent to note in examining the abomination of desolations, that the Aramaic term for abomination was usually applied in Scripture to the worship of Baal, which is both the Hebrew and Chaldee name for "husband, master, and owner." As Israel's true Baal (or husband) was to be Yahweh, from Babylon comes a counterfeit Baal, a metaphor for Satan trying to usurp God's woman Israel and the Bride of Christ as is discussed in the section of this book addressing the abomination of desolations.

There were Egyptian and Canaanite adoptions and modifications of Baal worship. In the primary Baal myth, Baal raises from the dead every spring. The pagan religions of the ancient Near East associated this with the seasonal fertility ritual and the beginning of a new agricultural cycle. In a demonic parody of what would be written in the Song of Solomon, which is allegorical of Christ's relationship with the Church and of God's relationship with Israel, this is demonstrated through Solomon's romance with Shulamite. Thus we may understand the resurrection of Jesus in the spring in part as a polemic against Baal worship and in refutation of the pagan spring narratives. The Song of Solomon likewise represents a polemic against the pagan spring fertility myths associated with the worship of Baal.

Thus three factors come into play, all important for understanding the Antichrist:

- The first is the "Baal factor" of a false husband. The Antichrist will be a false husband to an apostate church that is supposed to be wed to Christ and a rejectionist Israel that is supposed to be the wife of Yahweh;

- Secondly, the statue of Daniel 3 in addition to the combination of sixes (which we discuss elsewhere) is unlike the vision of the statue in Daniel 2, as there is neither silver, nor iron, nor bronze but only gold indicating the satanic endeavor toward eternal deification;

- Thirdly, the attempt by Antichrist to counterfeit the resurrection of Jesus, just as in the pagan myth Baal arose from the dead every spring.

It is also important to note that, as with the kings of Assyria and Tyre, the king of Babylon is again a metaphor for Satan as we note in Isaiah 14. In Daniel 3 the worshipers needed to bow down and worship at the sound of the musical instruments, which is what we read of the king of Babylon in Isaiah 14:11. In Isaiah 14:12 we see the full personhood of Satan being manifested in the king of Babylon with the description as "star of the morning"/"son of the dawn" in a plain attempt to counterfeit Christ as the "bright and morning star" (Rev. 22:16) and the Son of God who rose at dawn (Mt. 28:12).

Satan's Masquerade

We must note the following concerning the person of Antichrist: Satan is the most superior being God ever created without replicating Himself. Jesus, of course, is the exact replication of the Father but was not created, but is Himself Creator and co-Creator with the Father as pre-existent God eternal. Only the physical body of Jesus was created, as He, being divine, was eternally pre-existent.

In Revelation 2:28 we see *"the morning star"* (*"Ton astera ton proinion"*—which can be translated "the star, the morning one"). In Revelation 22:16 Christ is the *"bright morning star."* In 2 Peter 1:19 we are told, *"Until...the morning star arises in your hearts."* If we examine the Septuagint version of Isaiah 14:12 we see that Satan by nature approximates God to the point he actually thought he could be God. *The King James Version* translates this as "Lucifer," which is doctrinally correct but linguistically erroneous. It is only by looking to the New Testament that we see the difference where as *"bright morning star"* Jesus is also called *"the root and the descendant of David"* (which Satan is not), and Jesus is set apart from other morning stars with the adjective that He is the *"bright"* one in Revelation 22:16. This is crucial to understand because Job 38:4-7 tells us that all of the angels are *"morning stars."* It is Christ being the *"bright"* one that distinguishes Him. Satan, however, is the second brightest to the point he is actually capable of counterfeiting Christ Himself as we see in 2 Corinthians 11:14.

Without a comprehensive examination of all of the Scriptures involved, and without a careful exegesis of Revelation 22:16, it is easy for Satan to masquerade as Christ. There are Luciferians (and by some allegations higher degrees of Freemasonry) who precisely identify the two as one. In Luciferian theosophy, because both Jesus and Satan are on the basis of its flawed exegesis the "*bright morning star*," and because *imago dei* man is made in God's image and likeness where there is both good and evil in mankind, so, too, there is the false assertion that there is both good and evil in God. For light to be light it must exist in contrast to darkness, and for good to be good it can only be good in contrast to evil. Thus they assert that God must be the author of sin in order for there to be righteousness.

Indeed the reaction by Jacob Arminius to John Calvin was spurred by the conclusion that dogmatic Calvinism makes God the author of sin, necessitated by predestining people from eternity to hell. The same perversions are found in the Karma teaching of Hinduism which mandates the perpetuation of evil and sin, as one must suffer the Karma in the next reincarnation for what one has done in the present life. Thus a perpetrator of sin must be the victim of it in the next reincarnated life. This demands a continuation of sin and evil. These infusions of Calvinistic thought into Christian dogma likewise resemble the *inja allah* doctrines of Islam where everything that occurs, be it good or evil, righteousness or sin, is fatalistically the perfect will of Allah.

The invasion of Hindu belief into the Western psyche that began in the 1960s, the ongoing problem of Calvinism requiring sin to exist to facilitate predestination, the issues of such a disproportionate amount of highly influential people in the spheres of politics, business, law, and religion being involved in Freemasonry, and the growth of radical Islam, all contribute to the preparation for the advent of the Antichrist as all have a common ingredient—the necessity of sin and evil which the scriptural Gospel claims that Jesus came to destroy. These things are all encompassed in the person of the king of Babylon as "*star of the morning*," "*son of the dawn*" (Is. 14:12), and an imitator of Christ.

Hindu reincarnation is a demonic imitation of second birth and Karma an imitation of judgment in the afterlife for sins in the present one. Islam is a fatalistic, demonically inspired imitation of the Judeo-Christian faith, and the *Quran* distorts and mimics the Judeo-Christian Scriptures. Calvinism is more philosophically Islamic than it is Judeo-Christian, and is likewise an imitation of what the Scripture actually teaches about the nature of sin. All three—Hinduism, Calvinism, and Islam—relegate God to the status of sin's author, while the Gospel teaches that in and through the person of Christ God is sin's eraser.

The king of Babylon mimics the King of kings. The "*star of the morning*" resembles the "*bright morning star*." The Antichrist will resemble, counterfeit, and mimic Christ. Those who do not properly understand Isaiah 14 and Daniel 3 will not be at the appropriate observation point to be able to see the Antichrist approaching.

> *"But you said in your heart,*
> *'I will ascend to heaven;*
> *I will raise my throne above the stars of God,*
> *And I will sit on the mount of assembly*
> *In the recesses of the north.*
> *I will ascend above the heights of the clouds;*
> *I will make myself like the Most High.'* (Is. 14:13-14)

In Isaiah 14:13 we note that Satan will want to be deified in eternity, and this is connected with the Temple Mount and the recesses of the North when Antichrist sets up an image in the Temple. In verse 14 we see his proclamation of himself as God in exact parallel to 2 Thessalonians 2:4. Thus the key in understanding the image of the Beast in Revelation 13 must be preceded by understanding the image of Nebuchadnezzar in Daniel 3 and the king of Babylon in Isaiah 14.

Mingling in the Seed of Men

> *"As the toes of the feet were partly of iron and partly of pottery, so some of the kingdom will be strong and part of it will be brittle. And in that you saw the iron mixed with common clay, they will combine with one another in the seed of men; but they will not adhere to one another, even as iron does not combine with pottery."* (Dan. 2:42-43)

This clay is potter's clay. It is not raw clay, but rather clay that someone has attempted to fashion into something. Someone has tried to make the clay adhere to something to which it chemically cannot adhere. There is no covalency on an atomic level between clay and iron, no magnetic attraction, ionic bonding, or anything like that. This iron and this clay do not adhere, though people attempt to make it do so.

In this process of attempting to force potter's clay to adhere to iron, this happens: it will "mingle with the seed of men" (Ps. 106:35). In other words, there will be an attempt to achieve this political unity by somehow causing the people to mix and interbreed. Daniel explains what happens: some of this unity is strong, some weak; they will combine with one another in the seed of men, but the unity is superficial and weak so that they cannot adhere to one another. Remember that the head is Babylon trying to build the brotherhood of man in order to achieve divinity through the notion, "Man is God"; this is their Gnosticism.

Iron and clay do not adhere to one another. However, Daniel explains that they will combine with one another *"in the seed of men"* (Dan. 2:43).

Ancient Rivalries Re-emerge

In a rugby game between Scotland and Wales, or between Ireland and Scotland, where Celts are playing against Celts, that is a friendly game. The dynamic changes, however, when England is playing against Scotland. Suddenly the ancient rivalry re-emerges and insults are heaped on the opposing team's nationality. The old Celtic vs. Anglo-Saxon nationalism comes out.

The only way there can be a true union of people from diverse backgrounds is through Christ. Ephesians explains that the wall of partition is broken down, even between Jew and Gentile (Eph. 2:14). This is sung in Hebrew: *Hu Shloneinu Nitachad*—"He is our Peace, we shall be one."

Celts and Anglo-Saxons have never gotten along. However, in the aftermath of the Reformation, there was a common belief in a more biblical form of Protestantism than the one present today. With that came a common fear of the papacy and of the political ambitions of Rome which remain to this day. Why is Scotland part of the United Kingdom? Bonnie Prince Charles was born in Rome, sent with the backing of Rome and the support of Catholic France to attempt to re-Catholicize the British Isles. The one reason that the Duke of Marlborough was able to defeat the Scottish highlanders up in Culloden was because the lowland Presbyterian Scots fought with the English against the Highland Scots. Why did Scots fight against Scots, aligning themselves with their ancient enemy, the English, against their fellow countrymen? Because they had in common Protestantism and a fear of Rome. Otherwise, things would have gone differently. Bonnie Prince Charles reached as far south as the British Midlands; he attained Macclesfield, south of Manchester.

Rome's Role in Uniting Britain

Rome has tried many times to re-Catholicize Britain. She tried it with the Spanish Armada, with Napoleon, and yes, with the Third Reich. The Vatican backed the Third Reich; let no one claim differently. There was the

Lateran Treaty with Mussolini and the Treaty of Munich where the Catholic cardinals made an alliance with Hitler and the Zentrum, the Catholic party of Bavaria led by Hans von Papen who was a terrorist in WWI. Von Papen was sentenced at Nuremberg and was responsible for the second biggest terrorist attack on U. S. soil after 9/11, the Black Tom attack in New York Harbor. They combined in an effort to bring Hitler to power. The Vatican initially had a very pro-Hitler position under Pius XII.

The only reason there is a union, as in the United Kingdom, is because of Protestantism. The only place in which any vestige of this remains today is in Northern Ireland. In a post-Christian, neo-pagan Britain, Wales has its own parliament, as does Scotland, as does Northern Ireland, and then there is Westminster. The United Kingdom is re-fragmenting because the glue is gone; they no longer believe the Gospel.

Culturally and politically Scottish Celts and English Anglo-Saxons never truly fit together to begin with: the Scottish Presbyterian Calvinists and the English Puritan Calvinists massacred each other. Yet in the face of the common threat of Rome, they united. The only way that Jew and Gentile, Celt and Anglo-Saxon, black and white, can ever be one is through a common faith in Jesus. The mentality of the world is to build the Tower of Babel and bring about a man-made unity; but iron and clay do not adhere. So they try to force it to adhere by mixing it with the seed of men.

Interracial Unions?

> *"And in that you saw the iron mixed with common clay, they will combine with one another in the seed of men; but they will not adhere to one another, even as iron does not combine with pottery.* (Dan. 2:43)

There is no biblical prohibition against interracial marriage. There is nothing wrong with a white Christian marrying a black one, a Hispanic Christian marrying an Asian one, a Jewish Christian marrying a Gentile believer. If they are true Christians, they can have true unity in Christ. However, there is no lasting cross-cultural union outside of Christ; they will never adhere.

What has happened in the former Yugoslavia—that is where the Greek-speaking East and the Latin-speaking West of the Roman Empire fragmented—is also where the Saracens (the Muslims) twice tried to invade Europe. This is where World War I began—Sarajevo, Bosnia, when Giovello

Principe assassinated the Archduke Ferdinand, and a lot of big countries got dragged into it. This goes back to the Crusades, to ancient times before the Middle Ages. A Tito may reign awhile through Communism and they can sequester it for a short term, but sooner or later the ancient rivalries always come out.

As long as Great Britain was Christian, Celts and Anglo-Saxons could be united. As soon as they took Christ out, it began to re-fragment. People can try using potter's clay to make things artificially united; but it will not last.

Socialistic Globalism & the Emergence of the Antichrist

In comprehending the emergence of the Antichrist it must be understood that the Book of Revelation reveals a governmental control of global economy where trade and commerce will ultimately not be possible without accepting the mark of the Beast. Political globalism will be perceived as necessitated by a combination of factors. These will include the mere globalization of the world economy in a post-industrialized economic climate. In a manufacturing-based economy, goods and commodities can be taxed by traditional mechanisms of customs and excise. In an information-based economy with massive multi-billion dollar daily electronic transfers of capital and information, such mechanisms can no longer work.

Third world debt default, a subprime lending fiasco in the USA, undervalued or overvalued currencies in Asia, national insolvencies in member states of the European Union—all have global ramifications for all markets in an increasingly integrated equation of world trade and finance. Neither do David Rockefeller's Tri-Lateralism, the elitist International Round Table, groups like the Bilderbergers, the old General Agreement On Tariffs and Trade (GATT), the World Trade Organization (WTO), or The International Monetary Fund (IMF) in their present existing forms have the ability to prevent increasingly unpredictable global economic phenomena from spiraling out of control.

Empires—be they European, American, or Asian—can no longer be the singular dynamos driving the global economic engine. The USA is the last of these and a fundamentally flawed federal Europe is failing to rival it. The next attempt will be to find global solutions to global economic problems in a global economy. Because of Euro-socialism and America imitating it, however, nations will not actually seek economic solutions to economic problems, but rather they will seek political ones.

The second factor is pollution and the environment, even without reference to debates on global warming or global cooling. Industrial toxin emissions in Europe affect tree and shrub health in the Smokey Mountains of the Eastern USA. The Danube flows through so many European nations that pollution controls are impossible unless coordinated internationally. China is an ecological time bomb. When it finally explodes its ramifications will not only be felt in China.

The third factor will be religious terror in multi-ethnic/multi-religious societies such as Russia, tribal Africa, Europe, increasingly North America and Australia, and not least dangerously in India which has three strains of internal religious violence and terror. While Islam is certainly the most dangerous weapon in Satan's arsenal in this regard, it is not the only one. Although prophetically the Middle East will be the epicenter of this conflict, it is not the only one, and Central Asia potentially rivals it as a flash point. India, not China, will be the world's most populace nation, overtaking China and demographically eclipsing the rest of the developing world and, incredibly, nearly matching the populations of the Western first-world democracies of North America, Europe, Australasia, Israel and Japan combined.

East-West Distinctions

As former Islamic terrorist, turned born-again Christian, Walid Shoebat rightly points out, to understand the Antichrist, the Western Church must not only think in terms of the Western World. From the Bosporus Straits, to the Isthmus of Suez, to the Persian Gulf, to the Holy Land itself, it has been the Middle East geographically and historically that has bridged East and West. Although the growth of the Far East and the American Far West has shifted much of the world's economic centrality from the Mediterranean and Atlantic to the Pacific and Indian Ocean with Japan, Hong Kong, Hawaii, Korea, and Singapore culturally being "where East meets West," strategically the Middle East remains the key region, and oil as a vital commodity to both East and West has kept it so.

Yet the Book of Revelation speaks of "*kings from the east*" (Rev. 16:12). It would appear the nations in the first Gog and Magog battle apart from Libya are Central Asian Islamic nations (Arab nations are otherwise missing). The second and third largest economies in the world are in Asia (Japan and China) as are the two largest national populations (India and China).

India will gain economic and strategic ground on China—just as China has gained on Japan—because of its internal market size alone, and because unlike China it is democratic and has a huge English-speaking population with ties to Britain and the West. With the largest educated Middle Class on the planet (the size of the population of the USA) and incredible numbers of scientists and engineers, it also boasts a massive film and media industry in an age of communications.

When looking at the East, one must not underestimate India. As in the epoch of the troubadours during the Crusades, once more it is India exerting the most religious influence on the Western World. While some westerners have embraced Islam via the New Age movement, a disguised Hinduism has taken over a lion's share of Western spirituality since the 1960s, courtesy of hyper-charismatic and hyper-Pentecostal extremism which has infiltrated the Western church on a grand scale. These are subverting entire Pentecostal denominations such as the Assemblies of God in America (under Thomas Trask), Canada, Britain (under Paul Weaver), Australia and New Zealand (under Andrew Evans, Kevin Connor, Phil Pringle and Wayne Hughes) and the Elim Movement (under Wynne Lewis, Colin Dye, and Ian Bilby). By far, however, the movement virtually born out of a Hindu-charismatic Christian hybrid is the late John Wimber's neo-Gnostic Vineyard Movement that grew so far out of hand in the "Toronto Experience" that even Wimber distanced himself from it just prior to his death. This is a case where Dr. Frankenstein blamed his created monster.

Toronto was led by John and Carol Arnott. It had its precursors in Kenneth Copeland and Rodney Howard-Browne. It was parodied by Morris Cerullo, Randy Clark, Benny Hinn, and Stacy Campbell. It was imitated in England by Ken Gott, Sandy Miller, Gerald Coates, and Nicky Gumbel. It was cloned in Pensacola, Florida, by John Kilpatrick, and resurrected in Lakeland, Florida, by Todd Bentley and the Strader family (at least the unindicted co-conspirator members of the family not in prison under RICO laws for professional racketeering). This watershed super-deception that has spawned and inspired so much derivative heretical deception and scandal (often with resulting immorality as with Todd Bentley and Elim's Bilby) did not originate in its antics, tenets, or manifestations imitating Kundalini Yoga spiritually (in the demonic sense); it originated in India.

Indeed, in England Patrick Dixon authored a book arguing that "altered states of consciousness" (the goal of Yoga) and frantic irrational behavior are manifestations of the Holy Spirit. They are indeed manifestations, but not of the Holy Spirit (whose fruit is "*self-control*," not the lack of it) but of the spirit of antichrist. It is Hinduism come to church. Again, India is the religious source.

In India, Sikh terror has seen the assassination of Indira Gandhi and her son Rajif. Muslim terror is responsible for a tirade of mass murder terror attacks with 160 million Muslims (larger than the population of Russia) in a Hindu country. Hindu religious violence (perpetrated by extremists within the BHP) is reactionary to the Islamic threat and to other faiths, including Christianity, due to the large numbers of Dalit outcasts abandoning Hinduism because they are condemned to their fate by Hindu doctrines of Karma and the caste system.

India with Islamic neighbors on either side, an unstable nuclear Pakistan at its door, and Tamil terror to the South, is a social and economic quagmire. Christianity teaches a unique monotheistic theopomorphic incarnation of a deity in the person of Jesus Christ. But because Hinduism also accepts incarnation of deities (albeit unlike Christianity, theirs are anthropomorphic polytheistic deities) Hinduism lends itself closely to the acceptance of the Antichrist. With Hindu ideas being imported into the Western World via Gurus, Yoga, and New Age, and into the church by the Emergent Church and Kundalini manifestations of the false revivals of Toronto and Pensacola defended by figures such as Guy Chevreau and Michael Brown, the antichrist notion not only comes West but ***into*** the Western Church.

Following David Spangler and Benjamin Crème, many Western New Agers await the advent of their Maitreya. While Jesus warned against those saying He would appear in physical form prior to the *Parousia*, the fiasco in Lakeland, Florida, staged by the Strader Family with Todd Bentley as its MC, taught that Bentley receives personal visits from Jesus Christ as well as from an angel named "Emma"—even though female angels are a non-biblical concept (Col. 2:16-19).

In a quest for peace in an atmosphere charged with the prospect of nuclear terror where Islam teaches *shahadi* (death in jihad is the assurance of eternal salvation and award of 72 virgins) and Hinduism teaches reincarnation to a higher caste, nations will become frantic for interfaith coexistence. When as a matter of belief there are religious fundamentalists loving death as much as others desire life, the situation becomes unfathomable. In the New World Order (a term partially coined by

Tri-Lateralist president George H.W. Bush, a bedfellow with dangerous and intolerant Saudi Wahhabists) "political correctness" will increasingly demand "religious correctness." Opposition to the interfaith and ecumenical agenda (championed in Evangelical circles by Chuck Colson and Rick Warren) will increasingly be legally viewed as a hate crime. This is all being controlled by the spirit of antichrist setting the stage for the arrival of the ultimate Antichrist.

Everyone Has One

As Christians await the return of Jesus, Orthodox Jews await the first coming of the Messiah, Shia Muslims particularly await the Mahdi, Buddhists await the Fifth Buddha, New Age devotees await Maitreya. Multiple tribal and folk religions hold to similar traditions.

It is not unlikely that the Antichrist, assisted by the False Prophet, will attempt to cover all of these bases at once in a simultaneous quintessential "all things to all men" brand of incarnated Pantheism embodied in a single individual posing himself as apt to save the world from the brink of self-destruction. Indeed, the Baha'i cult, based on Mt. Carmel in Israel but having a sizeable following in both its birth place in Iran and in the Western World, is based on this very kind of multi-religious philosophy in its beliefs.

This has been witnessed in harbingers of the political realm with Barack Obama, but yet to be witnessed in a globalist religio-political figure. There may or may not be several, but Antichrist will be the final and ultimate one. Neither the Beatlemania of the mid 20th century as cultural icons, or the Obamamania of the early 21st century as a political icon, or frenzied obsessions with Pope John Paul II, the Dalai Lama, or the late Rabbi Menachem Schneerson, will amount to even a dress rehearsal in comparison to the Beast. The mass mesmerizing by Hitler and his focused hatred of Jews (and of the groups he could not politically and socially control such as Gypsies) will also wax him shallow in comparison to the Antichrist.

Hence we have three legs of the tripod upon which the Antichrist will stand: The economic and environmental, the religious, and the political. As Dr. Roger Oakland and certain others have perceptively recognized and discerned, this reflects precisely the "Three Legged Stool" peace plan theology of Rick Warren.

God in Scripture divides the world into three camps: Israel and the Jews, the Gentile nations, and the true Body of Christ composed of both believing Jews and Gentiles. Satan has the first two conned and blinded. That leaves the Church as the remaining target of his spiritual seduction. As Jesus warned in the Olivet Discourse, "If possible the elect will be deceived" (Mt. 24:24). With the assistance, perhaps unwittingly, of Chuck Colson, Rick Warren, Brian McLaren, Robert Schuller, and the money-preaching televangelists, Satan is to a very fair degree already succeeding. Word-Faith theology, ecumenism, Christian psychology, emergence, and *The Purpose Driven* (Lie) are all of Satan. It is Rick Warren's Global P.E.A.C.E. Plan that is doing the most to draw Christians into this trap.

The antichrist agenda as described in Revelation 13 requires an economic globalism which in turn requires a political globalism with government control of the economy (socialism). To achieve this socio-economic and political agenda it further requires a pan-religious globalism that can even, if possible, deceive saved Christians: a three pronged tripod. So enters Rick Warren and his ilk.

The Past Failures of Socialism

Eastern Europe was governed by an unelected socialist bureaucracy where there were federal states—multi-national, multi-ethnic states like Czechoslovakia, Yugoslavia, and the Soviet Union. Federalism broke up and failed in Eastern Europe and it is failing in Britain as well. Socialism caved in on itself in Eastern Europe. The British welfare system caved in on itself in the 1970s. Sir William Beverage began the welfare state after World War II in order to try to rebuild the infrastructure of Britain. At that time, a single-parent family probably consisted of a widow raising her children alone because her husband had been killed in the war against the Nazis or the Japanese. Today a single-parent family is much more likely to be a woman in a Council flat with five children by three different fathers supported by taxpayers. The welfare state became something it was never designed to be and resulted in a socialist Britain. The government taxed industries that were productive in order to subsidize unproductive ones.

This caved in with the Winter of Discontent, when Britain became the biggest borrower in the developed world. Everyone from miners to firefighters to garbage collectors went on strike. Then, of course, Mrs. Thatcher came to power and it has never been the same since. So now the New Labor is fighting the Old Labor and what is happening between Iran and Iraq is just that. What is New Labor? New Labor is Old Tory. As Mrs. Thatcher stood up to the coal miners, Tony Blair stood up to the firefighters.

Maggie Thatcher would always back the Americans in issues of foreign policy, so Tony Blair did likewise.

Britain rejected socialism as unworkable; it caved in; the same for Eastern Europe. Federalism is self-destructing in Britain just as it did in Czechoslovakia, Yugoslavia, and the Soviet Union. Yet now, continental Europe is going into the two things that Britain and Eastern Europe rejected: government by an unelected socialist bureaucracy and federalism—trying to make the iron stick to the clay.

The ultimate failure of socialism was communism, its apex being the Sovietism which with its persecution of the Church, its entrenched anti-Semitism and anti-Zionism, and its demagoguery, had its own antichrist in the person of Josef Stalin, another historical figure foreshadowing the coming Antichrist. The demise of Sovietism was largely self-inflicted. Ronald Reagan and Margaret Thatcher, with some assistance from the Vatican, Soviet Jewry, and China, merely opportunistically capitalized on what Sovietism did to itself. Yet it is this oppressive Sovietism whose demise Vladimir Putin mourns, which propels him and Russia once more in a self-destructive hatred of America and the West.

The re-nationalization of industry (socialism), anti-Western rearmament, curtailment of democracy, and arming the Islamic enemies of Israel—all riding on the back of an imperialistic Russian nationalism—are the pursuits of Putin and his associates. They are oblivious to the fact that these very pursuits are what triggered the dissolution of the Soviet Union to begin with. But this driven irrationality is not even the primary road to national suicide in a Russia with a collapsing economy, unreliable oil and gas commodity prices, and an aging population in an economy looted by now faltering oligarchs and gangsters (many of them like Putin are former KGB agents). The true madness of Putin can only be understood in light of Ezekiel 38-39.

The only sector of Russia's population that is growing is the Islamic community. By some estimates 50% of Russia's army will be Muslim by 2016. Having a major Islamic terror threat witnessed in unspeakable acts of terror by Chechnyan Islamic separatists, and driven by his hatred of America and the West, Putin arms and technologically assists Iran as if Iran's mullahs liked him. In fact, central Asian Islamic fundamentalism presents a bigger threat to Russia than it does to the West. Only Israel is more vulnerable to the threat of central Asian radical Islam.

While Putin's actions and those of his puppet successor make no strategic or political sense, they make perfect sense in preparation for Gog and Magog. Whether or not this Gog and Magog battle of Ezekiel 38-39 is the Battle of Armageddon is a question outside the scope of this book. What is clear, however, is that these nations have hooks in their jaws to be pulled into Israel for their obliteration.

The Pattern of Pagan Rome

This idea of trying to hold an unnatural union together is not new. Pagan Rome, the fourth beast of Daniel, or the fourth section of the statue in Daniel 2, also tried to hold things together. This is the way they attempted to achieve lasting unity:

- First they made Greek rather than Latin the *lingua franca* so that they had an official language;
- Second, they had an integrated legion;
- Third, the emperor was the "Bridge Builder," or the *Pontificus Maximus*;
- Fourth, they had a common currency;
- Fifth, they had an eclectic infrastructure.

What does that mean? From the Phoenicians the Romans got trade routes, from the Egyptians the Romans learned agriculture, and from the Greeks they got culture and science. They built roads linking the whole Roman Empire and established a postal system. They took something from everyone in order to achieve an artificial union that was held together by these five things. Therefore, if a nation pulled out of the Roman Empire, that nation would lose its postal system and its economy would be overturned because it would be unable to trade due to the common currency.

And where the *Pontificus Maximus* was concerned, it did not matter what religion someone had, as long as they also acknowledged him as the pontiff. Pagan Rome turned against two groups: the Jews and the true Christians. In comparison, Pope John Paul II also does not care what anyone believes; he calls the Dalai Lama a "great spiritual leader" and has interfaith gatherings in Assisi, Italy. There is a photo of that deceiver kissing the

Quran. And yet on four occasions he has denounced born-again Christians as "rapacious wolves" just as his predecessors, the pontiffs of the pagan Roman Empire, did long ago. It did not matter to the emperor what religion someone observed so long as they allowed him to be the pontiff.

They also had an integrated legion. The Roman soldiers in the Roman Legion were for the most part Italian and dominated by its Italian contingents. Yet they also had Greek contingents, Bulgarian contingents, and German mercenaries. Ultimately the Germans became the largest part of the Roman army.

They attempted to make iron adhere to clay, but eventually the Roman Empire split. What is it that is happening now? There is a *lingua franca*. English is the computer language in the new economy (much to France's anger). Second, they want a European army; this would mean that Britain could no longer act in the way it did in the Falklands. It would be a situation in which Britain could act only in concert with other countries, either America or Europe.

Rome's Pattern Reemerges

So today there is an English *lingua franca*, a European army, and an increasingly political papacy, combined with ecumenism and interfaith movements. The common currency? The Euro. Mayer Amil Rothschild said, "Once you have control of a nation's money supply, it doesn't matter who writes its laws."

The Jews faced such universal hatred and prejudice, which they did not know how to stop, that they had to find a way to gain influence. Obviously they were unable to gain political control, so they saw instead that they should gain economic influence. This was seen as the way to stop anti-Semitism, so they founded international banking.

Finally, there is an eclectic infrastructure. Why are small and medium-sized businesses in Britain strangled by European regulation? Why is the British farmer and the British taxpayer penalized for being the most productive in Europe? Because they have to fall into line with the unproductive ones. They have to get rid of Imperial British standards, replacing them with Europe's standards.

What is this designed to do? It is designed to make iron and clay adhere, but that is only the beginning.

> *"And in that you saw the iron mixed with clay, they will combine with one another in the seed of men"* (Dan. 2:43a).

Recently the British government said, "We cannot allow these Muslim refugees to come illegally through the Chunnel and then go on the dole, expecting the British taxpayers to support them." But the European Charter of Human Rights says they must do so.

The goal is in part the destruction of national identity so that Britain is no longer British, but multiethnic. Now if everyone were true Christians that would work. During the Millennium, in some way, it may well work, but it will not work now. Iron will never adhere to clay. They can try to force it, but it will not work. As Jesus told us, "Nation will rise against nation." That word "nation" in Greek is *ethnon* from which comes the word "ethnic." In Hebrew, that word is *goy*.

Racial tension exists throughout the world. It can be seen in Asia, Africa, Central Europe, and everywhere else. These racial tensions will increase; iron will not adhere to clay. An African Christian, an Asian Christian, a Hispanic Christian, and a European Christian can all be one in Christ; that will work. But the world is attempting to do this with the mind of Babylon when it will work only with the mind of Christ. They have rejected Christ.

In front of the European Union headquarters in Brussels stands a statue of a woman riding on a beast (Rev. 17:3). This image is also minted on some of the European coins. But in a post-Christian Europe, no one thinks about it and no one cares. Their goal is to build the Tower of Babel, but it will not work. Just like in Yugoslavia, they will turn against each other.

People will be able to take their driving test in Punjabi; they will be able to take that test in England in the Arabic language. This is already being done. The street signs also will be reposted in two languages. If the people in these countries were all born-again, this would not be a problem. But they are not doing this under Christ; they are doing it under Antichrist.

The End of Fallen Human Government

The Book of Daniel centrally deals with the prophetic intentions of God to judge the human government of the fallen world which will find its ultimate expression in the kingdom of Antichrist. This has to do with the fourth beast of Daniel and the legs and feet of the image in Daniel 2 which is a prophetic shadow of the image of the Beast as well as a prophetic and historical object lesson. Ultimately judgment by the real Christ will come.

He is the Rock that smashes the system represented by this statue (Dan. 2:35). But notice this says that some of it is iron, some clay; some of it is strong, and some weak. It will always be like that. Some of the countries of Europe will be strong, while others are weaker.

Why are Catholic and Protestant people in Ireland worried about each other? Why the Protestants in Northern Ireland are afraid of being governed by Dublin is hard to know. And why the Catholics in Northern Ireland are afraid of being governed by London is equally difficult. While all this nonsense is going on, they will both be governed by people in Brussels for whom they did not vote and who they cannot remove. They are ***both*** missing the main point.

The Irish have the Celtic economy into which Europe puts a lot of money—the "Celtic Tiger." "Give Paddy a pint and he will be happy"; that is their mentality. Nobody other than Jesus Christ gives something for nothing. Ireland has lost its fishing rights. What they can and will get for free is a con job. They are actually taking VAT money that is paid to Europe and giving political contributions to pro-European parties that promote European unity. In other words, they are using taxpayers' money to fund elections. This is totally anti-democratic, but no one can say anything about it. They are going to seek to make the clay and the iron adhere.

Quick Succession of World Powers: Ancient and Modern

But some will be stronger than others. What happens in Daniel is what happens in the Last Days: a very rapid succession of the rise and fall of world empires. In Daniel's day everyone was afraid of Assyria; yet one day they woke up to find something far worse than Assyria on the horizon: Babylon. Assyria was erased practically overnight, giving way to the Babylonians.

Many grew up in the fear of the Cold War against the Soviet Union; one day they woke up and it was gone and in its place they face the much greater danger of Islam. Why is Islam a greater danger? Because the Soviets would not use nuclear missiles except in response to an attack; the Muslims would because they are promised heaven if they die in jihad, a holy war. In fact, that is their only assurance of salvation. Because of that mindset they will kill civilians and use their own civilians as shields without compunction.

In Daniel's day, Assyria gave way to Babylon; then Babylon seemingly overnight gave way to Media-Persia. Following the same pattern, the

Persians gave way to the Greeks. Once Alexander the Great died his empire fragmented and out of that chaos came Rome. There was a very rapid series of world empires rising and falling which the Jews were caught in the middle of while returning to their own land. In the Last Days it is the same.

If someone had told our grandparents that today the sun would set on the British Empire every 24 hours, it would have seemed ridiculous to them. Nevertheless, that is true today. Most people today do not realize how big the French Empire was. It included all of Southeast Asia and it split Africa and the Caribbean with England. The French Empire was once enormous but now it is gone. If someone from the Baby Boomer generation had been told that the Soviet Empire would collapse overnight it would have sounded ridiculous; nonetheless, that is precisely what happened.

Economies Rise and Fall

So the new economies became Japan and Germany. Japan is not the same place it was even five years ago; it is in an economic melee, experiencing a downturn from which it cannot recover. Even before the catastrophic earthquake and tsunami that devastated Japan they had zero interest rates, meaning money could be borrowed for free in Japan, yet they cannot stimulate their economy. Now Germany has gone the same way.

Germany was the dynamo of Europe; it had a political victory bought for it by America and Britain (by NATO). The reunification of Germany was a success courtesy of the United States and, to a degree, the United Kingdom. However, though they owe their reunification to America and Britain, it has been an economic disaster. They are in serious trouble, going the same way as Japan; they cannot seem to get out of the hole they are in economically. So France comes along and sees an opportunity for them instead of Germany to dominate Europe. It is all a game on a grand scale. The French never wanted Britain included in the European Union; it was America that forced the issue.

Ever since Otto the Great, Germany has believed that it has some kind of divine mandate to rule over a Christianized Europe. Once the Roman Empire collapsed it became the Holy Roman Empire, which was neither "holy" nor "Roman." It was ecclesiastically dominated by Rome, but politically, economically, and militarily dominated by Germany. What they want to do now is put that back. Many have tried—namely the French and the Germans. That was the goal of Hitler, Charlemagne, Napoleon, etc.; there have been many attempts, but none have succeeded. Why? Because iron does not adhere to clay.

Satanic Strategy

So what is happening in Iraq? Daniel provides details about the principalities over these nations. Satan's ultimate strategic quest is to destroy Jerusalem in order to prevent the return of Christ. He knows that the Jews must be back in Jerusalem because the Book of Zechariah (whose contents Satan is familiar with) stipulates that they will not see the Messiah until they recognize the rejected Christ as Messiah (Zech. 12:10; Rev. 1:7). Therefore, according to his way of thinking, Satan must obliterate that nation.

There was no real reason for Iraq to shoot Scud missiles at Israel; Israel has no love for Kuwait, and vice-versa. There is more to this than meets the eye; it is not about Iraq. In fact, it is not even about oil. If there was not a drop of oil in Iraq, the same problem would still exist, though oil will always be a factor in Middle East politics. The fear was that this psychopathic megalomaniac, Saddam Hussein, would give chemical and biological weapons to terrorists. So America thinks it cannot take the risk of leaving those weapons in the hands of a nut like that because in ten years he might go nuclear. They feel they must stop him now, or they will have an even bigger problem.

He Will Seek to Change the Times & Laws

> *'He will speak out against the Most High and wear down the saints of the Highest One, and he will intend to make alterations in times and in law; and they will be given into his hand for a time, times, and half a time.* (Dan. 7:25)

> *Out of one of them came forth a rather small horn which grew exceedingly great toward the south, toward the east, and toward the Beautiful Land. It grew up to the host of heaven and caused some of the host and some of the stars to fall to the earth, and it trampled them down. It even magnified itself to be equal with the Commander of the host; and it removed the regular sacrifice from Him, and the place of His sanctuary was thrown down. And on account of transgression the host will be given over to the horn along with the regular sacrifice; and it will fling truth to the ground and perform its will and prosper. Then I heard a holy one*

> *speaking, and another holy one said to that particular one who was speaking, "How long will the vision about the regular sacrifice apply, while the transgression causes horror, so as to allow both the holy place and the host to be trampled?" He said to me, "For 2,300 evenings and mornings; then the holy place will be properly restored."* (Dan. 8:9-14)

> *"In the latter period of their rule, When the transgressors have run their course, A king will arise, Insolent and skilled in intrigue. His power will be mighty, but not by his own power, And he will destroy to an extraordinary degree And prosper and perform his will; He will destroy mighty men and the holy people. And through his shrewdness He will cause deceit to succeed by his influence; And he will magnify himself in his heart, And he will destroy many while they are at ease. He will even oppose the Prince of princes, But he will be broken without human agency.* (Dan. 8:23-25)

In Daniel 7:25, we are told that the Antichrist will seek to make changes in times and in law. Daniel's description of Antichrist resumes in 8:9-14. In 8:10 we have a direct reference to Revelation 12:4 where the dragon sweeps a third of the stars to earth and tramples them. This replays the fall of one-third of the angels following Satan. The stars here, however, are the descendants of Abraham in a great falling away.

In speaking about Greece portrayed as a goat in the same chapter, Daniel again begins to speak of the Antichrist. We are told he will be skilled in intrigue; he will have tremendous powers to both destroy and yet cause others to prosper providing they perform his will. What becomes most important, however, is where through shrewdness and deception he will be able to oppose the Prince of Princes and will destroy many while they are "*at ease*." The Hebrew prophets warned of those who are "*at ease in Zion*" (Am. 6:1). While having a meaning for Israel and the Jews, this has a direct application to the final age of the church of Laodicea, a lukewarm materialistic church that is blind to its own spiritual state and is at ease.

The warning must again be resounded that the declining act of interest in the return of Christ and end-times prophecy that is propagated by such things as Rick Warren's *Purpose Driven* agenda are extremely dangerous and directly contradict the very specific instructions of Jesus in Matthew 24:42-43. Daniel's elongated vision and its explanation are punctuated by and interspersed with a series of prophetic events focused on both the

Eastern world of Israel and the Middle East, and the Western world of Europe. Thus we must note the following:

1. Satan acting through the person of Antichrist will seek to change times;
2. He will seek to change laws;
3. He will do this by political and economic as well as religious means;
4. He will achieve it by deceptions perpetrated against both the Jews and a largely unprepared Church.

Our purpose is not to identify either the cause of Christ or the purpose of this book with any political ideology, but rather to show that the deception will be absolutely pervasive in the realm of politics, economics, and religion because the Antichrist will have inimical designs targeting both the Church and the Jews. He will have agents among both the Church and the Jews irrespective of whether or not they initially recognize that they are doing his bidding.

How Changes to Times Take Place

It is our thesis that while it is urgent that Christians be aware of political and economic trends from the viewpoint of prophecy, they do not fall into the trap of aligning the Church or its mission with any political movement or party. Even though being salt and light may require Christians to be active voices on specific moral and prophetic issues, the Lord has not called us to rule in this world system.

There have been multiple proposals concerning what Antichrist seeking to "change the times" may mean. There have been calendric arguments and Sabbatarian legalism claiming that changes of the Sabbath day (as argued for instance by Seventh-day Adventists and certain hyper-messianic Jewish extremists) is antichrist. There have been propositions that moving the resurrection of Jesus from Passover to the pagan holiday of Easter likewise represents an antichrist act. Some have ventured so far as to contend that changes to the Julian and Gregorian calendars likewise represent the workings of Antichrist as do more modern claims that oil-rich Islam is demanding the Islamic calendar and a meridian of Mecca replace the Greenwich Prime Meridian on which global time is calculated. This would follow the Islamic belief that their *Quran* is a "third" testament or covenant; thus we have a seeking to change the times and the law. Without doubt this is a manifestation of the antichrist spirit. However, it is interpreted prophetically in light of the Book of Daniel.

There indeed may be some elements of merit in particular aspects of certain of these claims in the Messianic typology of the Hebrew feasts of Leviticus 23-24 which fulfill, and will be fulfilled in, the First and Second Coming of Jesus. These should be properly understood by all Christians. We are directly admonished, however, to neither judge others, nor allow others to judge us on the basis of our observance of Sabbaths, holy days, etc., as directed in both Colossians 2:16-19 and Romans 14:4-5. Thus we cannot assign a major meaning of "times" to calendric arguments even though specific facets of such should be taken into limited account.

It is more probable that the Antichrist will seek to change times rather than in the spectrum of religion, economy, and politics as we see today with "The New Age" and the over-bantered phrase, "The New World Order." We must exercise extreme caution, however, not to degenerate into conspiracy theory, conjecture, and obsessions with the speculative with regard to these changes in the times, but rather assess them from the viewpoint of God's Word.

In the religious, spiritual, and mystical specter, the New Age and the Age of Aquarius have never dawned as realities except culturally. So, too, the only real force pushing the world into a new order is not the post-Cold War rhetoric voiced for instance by George H. W. Bush, but rather the specter of impending economic and strategic calamities that propel the world for a solution. The New Age has come only to the imagination of New Agers. A harmonious New World Order is non-existent with a New World disorder plaguing global economies in lieu of what was promised. None of this is new. The First World War did not make the world safe for democracy as Woodrow Wilson promised, nor was it the "war to end all wars." So, too, Barack Obama's promise of change has neither changed anything but for the worse. The Antichrist will at his inception appear to be able to deliver the things that politicians and gurus promised but failed to materialize.

With the influx of New Age influence into the Church via the mysticism and experiential theology of the extremes of the Charismatic Movement and of hyper-Pentecostalism, even Christians have been seduced into swallowing the New Age bait in a camouflaged form. This has been accomplished by identifying the Gospel and scriptural values with certain political candidacies of politicians so that many professing Evangelicals have also fallen into the trap of a morally redeemed society. they have often done so at the behest of political cheerleading from the pulpit.

Chuck Colson and J. I. Packer both endorsed Peter Kreeft's book *Ecumenical Jihad*, calling for ecumenical union with Islam to morally save society. When supposed Evangelicals ignoring the false gospel and aberrational theology of Roman Catholicism jumped into bed with the pope, they were oblivious to the fact that the pope was in bed with the Dalai Lama. The antichrist deception which will culminate with Babylon the Great will remain as always in the character of Nimrod and Semiramus at the Tower of Babel and of the Babylonian Empire during which Daniel prophesied. It will in short be a political and religious fusion with an agenda that is largely economic even though this is masqueraded with quests for humanitarian endeavors and for world peace. In fact the Antichrist, we are told, will "*honor a god of fortresses*" (Dan. 11:38) and will be a man of false peace ***both*** for the world and for the Church, but ultimately for Israel and the Jews.

Seeking to Change the Laws

There are two probable aspects of Antichrist seeking to change the laws. One we have dealt with already in our treatment of the *pseudologon* where paraphrased and censored bad translations of Scripture such as inclusive versions and wholesale bastardizations of what is supposed to be God's Word such as *The Message* seek to in effect change God's Law. This has nothing to do with the abject position of Seventh-day Adventists and the legalistic aspect of the Messianic Movement trying to live under two covenants. We are, however, told in 1 Corinthians 9 that there is the Law of Moses (that is, Torah) and the law of Christ. It is these which Antichrist will seek to change. He will endeavor, and through the spirit of antichrist is already succeeding, in achieving this aim by attempting to remove the body of civil, constitutional, and criminal law away from the biblical principles that were their foundation.

This relates to the warning of Jesus in Luke's version of the Olivet Discourse about saved Christians appearing before magistrates for upholding the convictions of their faith (Lk. 21:12-15). Already Christians have been criminally prosecuted as far afield as Canada and Sweden for simply reading the teachings of Romans 1 and the Jewish Torah concerning homosexuality which have been ruled "hate speech." In complete defiance of constitutional principle there have been shameful prosecutions of

Christians in both Great Britain and in Michigan for offending Islam by preaching the Gospel in areas where Muslims or homosexuals could hear it.

Concerning these matters, truly saved Christians will find themselves in a position where they will acquiesce to man's laws at the expense of God's or they will compromise. Those who compromise will do so because they love their lives in this present world more than they love Christ. Hence in his warnings about the Antichrist, the apostle John prefaces his remarks by stating, "*Do not love the world nor the things of the world*" (1 Jn. 2:15-18).

Political Seduction

The other device of Satan will be that the Antichrist is not only "*skilled in intrigue*" (Dan. 8:23), but a satanically empowered master of the art of deception with the Church and the Jews as the intended objects of the deception. Just as Satan has set a religious trap with the Ecumenical Movement, the Interfaith Movement, the infiltration of secular psychology and the counterfeit spirituality of New Age mysticism into the Church, so, too, he will set a trap for Christians and Jews in the domain of temporal politics. It is vital we be aware of this. We deal with the nature of how this seduction will work in our discussion concerning Antiochus Epiphanes and Hanukkah where reprobate Jews were recruited in the service of their enemies. In the Last Days the same will be true for both the Jews and the Church.

The importance of how corrupt government is setting, and will continue to set, the stage for Antichrist cannot be overstated. Scripture tells us not what is simply transpiring in the religious field, but the political, economic, and strategic fields relative to religion. Moreover, for too long too many Christians have underestimated the significance of the fact that Job, Zechariah, Daniel, and the Book of Revelation all directly connect the conflicts taking place on the earth in time and space with conflicts transpiring in the heavens—the former as an extension and reflection of the latter.

We have multiple examples of how this kind of seduction is happening already. Good Christians with good motives have been identifying political ideologies with the Gospel since Cromwell and the Puritans. Jesus' kingdom, however, is not of this world (Jn. 18:36). We are simply called to be salt and light within any system (Mt. 5:13-16). Whenever the Church has institutionally ventured into the political world, and whenever Christians have sought to identify the cause of Christ with a political agenda, it has always brought spiritual and social disaster and required egregious distortions of New Testament doctrine. It has also ultimately backfired to the detriment of the faithful Church. This has consistently been the case from Constantine to Calvin's Geneva, to the political Protestantism of Northern Ireland, and to the modern scenario of Christians in the Western world, particularly the United States, seeking again (with noble intentions) to identify the cause of Christ with the political agendas of men. At no time in the history of the Church has any real good come from such well-intended but spurious and unscriptural pursuits.

In Britain, with the Reformed theologian John Owen as advisor, Cromwell's English Puritan Calvinists and the Scottish Presbyterian Calvinists engaged in genocidal massacre of each other in the name of Jesus Christ after they laid the Catholic people of Ireland to cruel waste. In Colonial America the legacy of pulpit politics remains the Salem Witch Hunts. It has always in the end hurt the Church, and it is hurting the Church now. As in Salem and in Britain, Christians going down this road have obtained more than they have bargained for.

In the Last Days religious seduction will be likewise paralleled with political seduction, and the Church will get double-crossed and betrayed. This is exactly what happened in Israel for placing trust in Pompeii and Alexander the Great. In the end they get an Antiochus Epiphanes, a Pontius Pilate, and a King Herod—all of whom typify and foreshadow the Antichrist. But the worst is yet to come for both Israel and, sadly, for much of the Church. The politicians whom Christians trust will betray them, and the clergy who urge and guide them in this direction will become capable of the most despicable acts imaginable

Modern Day Examples

Examples of this can be plainly seen already. Again, with good intentions, many Christians adhered to the political preaching of Pat Robertson. But Pat Robertson went on to make a series of false prophetic predictions in the Lord's name concerning the outcome of elections and political events. And after building a Christian broadcasting empire on the donations of well-intended Christians, he ended up selling it to Rupert Murdoch and retaining the profits via legal and financial manipulation.

Jesus warned that false prophets would arise at the same time as false Christs (Mt. 24:5, 11). No figure pointed saved Christians into the political arena more than the late Dr. Jerry Falwell of Liberty University. But as we shall see, his deeds became almost unbelievable. This is not to wage polemics against politically active Christians or discourage their personal actions if as a matter of conscious they believe it to be right, but it is to say that the politicians in whom Evangelicals have trusted because they claim to be "born-again," from Jimmy Carter to the present day, have repeatedly and consistently acted against scriptural values. After their election they have quickly abandoned the commitments they made to the Christians who supported them.

These unpleasant realities hint at what Antichrist will do. On the basis of religion he will appeal for political support, if possible, even from Christians, and to a fair degree he will get it. What we have seen happening until now gives us a glimpse of what is likely to happen in the future when the Antichrist carefully plays his cards but then, to the shock of many naïve and undiscerning Christians, shows his hand, reveals his true motives, and discloses his true identity.

The Axis of Evil is not North Korea, Iran, and Iraq—a list to which Libya and Syria have been added. The Axis of Evil includes Saudi Arabia along with all these other countries. The Wahhabis of Saudi Arabia are the ideological dynamos of terrorism. Fifteen of the nineteen hijackers on September 11th were Saudis groomed by Wahhabism and financed by the Saudi government, which persecutes Christians.

I prayed for George W. Bush every day. Let me tell you something: George W. Bush was a political prostitute from a dynasty of political prostitutes owned by international oil. He would never defend America from her number one enemy, which is Saudi Arabia, because he sold his soul in political terms to get elected. His father called the Saudis our friends. No nation that hangs a fifteen-year old boy for accepting Jesus Christ is my friend. They may be the friends of the political whoremasters of Texas oil, but they are not mine. Do I consider George W. Bush trustworthy? No, I do not. I would not trust him as far as I can spit, and I would not trust his father any further. But I prayed for them every single day. I did not like him, did not trust him, did not respect him, nor did I like, trust, or respect Mr. Blair, but I prayed for them every day. Neither do I trust or respect Mr. Obama or Mr. Cameron. Like Mr. Bush and Mr. Clinton and Mr. Blair, they have consistently proven themselves to be men devoid of biblical principles.

In order to honor Islam after the 9/11 attacks, George Bush began celebrating Ramadan in the White House. He placed in the White House what John's epistle defines as an Antichrist book that rejects the divine

Sonship of Christ. Yet Bush claimed to be a Christian. His successor Barack Hussein Obama refused to attend the National Day of Prayer or the National Judeo-Christian Prayer Breakfast but warmly celebrated Ramadan in the White House. These are indeed evil men. In Britain David Cameron did not oppose the aggressive homosexual and lesbian agenda of Tony Blair and Gordon Brown. But if they are not influenced by our prayers, they will be influenced by something far worse. If they turn against Israel, God will turn against Britain and America.

I prayed that God would remove Bush and Blair before they brought the wrath and judgment of God against us. Mr. Blair had four homosexuals in his cabinet and he wanted to lower the age of consent to enable a middle-aged man to seduce vulnerable young boys. I think he is a disgrace; I detest everything about Mr. Blair and his successors. Indeed, on the basis of God's Word, these two are evil men, to some degree controlled by Satan and bent on the moral disintegration of godly standards and biblical principles, even lending credence to sexually perverse agendas. As in the books of Kings and Chronicles, however, nations get the leaders they deserve—and so do churches.

Judgment begins not in the political realm but in the House of God. The late fundamentalist preacher Jerry Falwell embraced a literal antichrist, Korean cult leader Sun Myung Moon who claims that he is Lord of the Second Advent and his wife the Holy Spirit. Yet in accepting a large financial contribution from Moon, Falwell lauded him as an unsung hero. Hence we witness the sick and shameful spectacle of a so-called Evangelical preacher espousing public praise to a literal antichrist. The wickedness in the corridors of power is but ramification of the wickedness in the pulpit. If the churches have leaders who publicly laud open antichrists, how can we bemoan the fact that a supposedly Christian president places an antichrist *Quran* in the White House?

Satan's real battle, however, is being waged in the court system where judicial fascism is replacing representative parliamentary and congressional democracy with agenda-prone judges legislating against the Constitution from the bench, the Supreme Court judges treating themselves as supreme beings. It is for good reason that Jesus warns that we will be brought before magistrates ***and*** kings, placing judges before national leaders as the first opponents of His message (Mk. 13:9). We live in an age of judicial fascism. No one reading the foundational documents of either British parliamentary democracy or American presidential and congressional democracy can reasonably deny that such models of government were foundationally established on the conviction and basis of Judeo-Christian scriptural principles. Yet that is precisely what unelected, politically appointed judges have consistently done.

The Fruit of Political Affiliations

Partnered with this, however, is the fact that Satan seeks to deceive the Elect. In America, naïve and undiscerning Christians have for decades been manipulated into believing it is somehow more Christian to support the Republican Party than the Democratic Party, while other Christians interested in issues of social injustice, the environment, etc., are foolishly prepared to ignore the fact that liberal politicians favor the continued genocidal slaughter of the unborn with tens of millions of aborted babies. Both are deluded to the point of an inexplicable naiveté that at times borders on apparent insanity.

In 2010 it was a homosexual Republican judge nominated by Ronald Reagan and appointed by George W. Bush who, with a stroke of a pen, nullified the democratic will of the citizens in striking down the anti-homosexual and lesbian Proposition 8. It was a Bush-appointed Republican judge in Pennsylvania who outlawed the teaching of Intelligent Design despite the fact that a clear statistical majority of the citizens believe in creation through some Intelligent Design and not an atheistic form of Darwinism. As societies deviate from their scriptural roots, the freedom those scriptural principles engendered progressively disappeared. Politicians meanwhile, afraid of losing votes on controversial issues, are happy to stand by and allow the courts to legislate because they do not wish to lose either the anti-abortion or pro-abortion vote, or the anti-homosexual-marriage or pro-homosexual vote, or indeed the vote on any other controversial issue no matter how important. The hypocrisy of such elected people is eclipsed only by their cowardice. But again, nations get the leaders they deserve, just as churches do.

The scriptural pastor as shepherd of a flock has fast given way to the cheap theocratic pulpit politician. Scriptural leaders are a rare commodity, but hirelings, televangelist con-artists, de facto heretics, and demonstrably false prophets are a dime a dozen. They will even celebrate someone like Sun Myung Moon, claiming to be the return of Jesus Christ, instead of warning the flock against them just as Jerry Falwell did before his death. It is no longer about Jesus, truth, righteousness, reaching the lost, or the flock; it is about money, power, and politics.

It was Eisenhower's Earl Warren Supreme Court that ordered God out of the classroom. It was Nixon's Republican Warren Berger Supreme Court that ordered God out of the maternity ward with Roe v. Wade. And it was Ronald Reagan's pro-abortion Supreme Court appointee Sandra Day O'Connor who ordered God out of the courtroom when O'Connor wrote the decision banning the Ten Commandments from Alabama's judicial building. It was also Ronald Reagan's appointee Sandra Day O'Connor, who penned the ruling outlawing Texas anti-sodomy laws, that opened the way for same-sex marriage—decisions she made in large part on the basis not of the Constitution but of "foreign judicial precedence." Reagan appointed this notorious woman to the Supreme Court despite her pro-abortion orientation after lying to Christian America that he was pro-life. Reagan, even with Republican majorities in Congress, did nothing to reverse non-therapeutic abortion, but only acted by appointing magistrates committed to its continuation.

This is not to make a political statement; it is to understand that the Antichrist will seek to change the times and the law and that magistrates will be at the forefront of persecuting the true Church. And Christians seeking political solutions to spiritual problems are among the Elect who are being deceived. But if my prayers are not influencing these politicians, something else will, as both Timothy and Daniel tell us.

That is what is transpiring today: it is Old Labor versus New; it is a quest to rebuild the Holy Roman Empire. They will do it in the same way in which they always do it: *lingua franca*, common currency, integrated army, ecumenical religion, and an eclectic infrastructure into which they will mingle the seed of men. There is no longer an English England, or a Scottish Scotland. The population of Scotland will decrease by another 4.5 % in the next ten years, what with the combination of a mass immigration out of Scotland and a declining birth rate. Many of the people who remain are older. As the indigenous Scottish population decreases, there is one element of Scotland's demography that is increasing, and that is, again, the Muslims.

This creates an economic reliance on Islamic immigration by pursuing this course. Muslims arrive and receive the same rights which they deny others in their own countries. It is an agenda; it is called social engineering. The powers behind this social engineering will force people to accept same-sex marriages and homosexual adoptions and teach it in schools to children. They will force people to teach your children that there is a co-validity to Islam and Hinduism. All this because they must find a way to make the clay and the iron adhere.

Efforts All in Vain

Nonetheless, despite all efforts they cannot and will not adhere. What will happen? Ultimately, the iron and the clay—the bronze, the silver and the gold—are all crushed.

But for now, some will be stronger than others. There is no way this will result in "The United States of Europe," though that is their thinking. America has a common language in a common market with a common currency. Since America has done it, Europe thinks it can, too. But iron adheres to iron; it does not adhere to clay. The predominant culture in America is Judeo-Christian. Even Italian-Americans or Chinese-Americans look to Britain as the mother country—something that does not work in Europe.

In the face of these things it is important to keep in mind that there is more going on than meets the eye. This war is about oil, but it is also about much more. What the Americans and the British want to do now is develop an alternative source of oil to Saudi Arabia. However, the countries of Soviet Central Asia adjoining Afghanistan are unstable. If a puppet regime is installed in Iraq, it will accomplish two things: 1) create that alternative to Saudi Arabia (Iraq has nine per cent of the proven reserves); 2) outflank Iran in the west as Afghanistan outflanks it in the east.

The Central Issue

The Americans and the British know that in the long-term, Saudi Arabia is unstable. There are always politics going on, but there is more to it than that. The issue is not Baghdad, it is not Europe—the issue is Jerusalem. That is where Jesus Christ will return.

That is the name of the game, the real jewel, the real treasure of the Middle East—not the oil fields of the Arabian Peninsula. Not Baghdad, Mecca or Medina; Satan already has those places. What he wants is Jerusalem and he will get it—"*Sodom and Egypt, where also their Lord was crucified*" (Rev. 11:8). But that is not how it ends.

"You continued looking until a stone was cut out without hands, and it struck the statue on its feet of iron and clay and crushed them. (Dan. 2:34)

Though it will stand temporarily, the United States of Europe will not stand in the long run; iron will not adhere to clay. When they try to make it stick under the rule of Antichrist, Christ Himself will bring it all to ruin. That is what is really going on.

Islam and the Antichrist

As Christians await the return of Christ, Islam awaits its Mahdi. Yet there is also an antichrist figure predicted to come in Islam. Our understanding of the role of Islam in the appearance of the Antichrist must be prefaced by our reiterated affirmation that because of the *pseudologon* of the *Quran*, the magnification of Mohammed above Christ, and the denial of the divine Sonship of Christ, Islam is by every biblical definition an utterly and totally antichrist religion. It is likewise an utterly and totally anti-Jewish religion that carries out the rivalry that began in Rebekah's womb between Esau and Jacob, and that substitutes Ishmael for Isaac as the chosen son. The struggle in the Middle East will be pivotal to understanding the role of Antichrist, but the position of the Arab nations and the Islamic world in that struggle must be understood as the conflict between brothers dating back to the patriarchal narratives in the Book of Genesis.

In contemporary vogue, there is the idea that the Antichrist will be a Muslim. Proponents of this view include Joel Rosenberg and Walid Shoebat. In contemplating the position of such brethren, we must understand that they are right in much of ***what*** they say but are only partially right because of things they ***fail*** to say.

They do well in pointing out that so many of the descriptions of what the Antichrist will do is in tune with Islam which already does many things including decapitations, seeking to change the times and laws, and that such figures foreshadow the Antichrist as "*the Assyrian*," the Kings of Babylon, Tyre and Assyria, and historical foreshadowings of the Beast such as Saladin (which they unfortunately fail to highlight) all emanate from the Islamic world. Additionally, both geographical Babylon and other cities that have become the later homes of demonic religions originating in Babylon, such as Mecca and more importantly Pergamum, are found within the main of Islam. Pergamum, where Jesus said, "*Satan's throne is*" (Rev. 2:13) (or at least was at that time) is at least as viable a candidate for a capitol of false religion as arguments about Rome ever were, given the clear and specific description by Jesus Himself.

It must also be noted that the thinking of Western Christendom is in large part framed by Hellenism and the Patristic reinterpretations of Christianity by the church fathers. This has remained true not only in the history of the Roman Catholic and Eastern Orthodox traditions, but also in the tradition of the Protestant Reformers. There is indeed something to be said to having an Eastern as well as Western interpretation of the Christian faith.

Just as Islam has a theology for an Islamic Messiah, Islam also has a theology of its own for an antichrist. In Islamic theology of the Antichrist there is what is called "*Dajjaal*." It is here more than anywhere else where the Western Church needs to pay attention to what is being explained by Walid Shoebat. What the Judeo-Christian Scriptures teach about the Antichrist, the Muslim world attributes and will attribute to their counterfeit savior the Mahdi. Conversely what those Scriptures teach about the Antichrist, the world of Islam attributes to Christ because of the help He will give to the Jews. Hence the Antichrist of Christians and Jews will in at least some part appear as the Islamic Mahdi. Not only must the Antichrist make a false treaty by deceiving the Jews, he must also deceive the Muslims and other nations. So, too, the one whom the Judeo-Christian Scriptures reveal to be Christ is, and will be to Islam, the "*Dajjaal*," that is, their antichrist.

Once more, while it is clear that Antichrist must come from a reincorporated version of the Roman Empire and be one of the ten horns (Dan. 7:7; Rev. 13:1), this is not necessarily to the negation of what he will be to the non-Western and Islamic world.

This is Not a New Theory

We also must note that many Islamic nations today, including the whole of North Africa as well as Turkey, Lebanon, and Syria, and even a few outposts in Western Jordan, were as much a part of the Roman Empire as Europe. In bringing these solid facts to our attention, Walid Shoebat and Joel Rosenberg have done the body of Christ a service. It was in the early 1970s, however, that Christian apologetics researcher William Brehm (noted as an Evangelical figure within the Mensa high IQ society) had made similar assertions pre-dating what is being written and said at present. Yet dating back to the Islamic invasions of Europe and the times of the Crusades, the concept of an Islamic Antichrist has never ***not*** in some way existed in Western Christian thought.

Weight is lent to arguments for an Islamic Antichrist by the fact that most of the nations in confederation against Israel in the first battle of Gog and Magog in Ezekiel 38-39 are Islamic (though conspicuously not Arab, with the partial exception of Libya). And the surrounding nations coming against Jerusalem to pre-empt the return of Christ in Zechariah 12 are likewise today Arab-Islamic nations against whom Christ will fight in both defense of Israel and in avenging the blood of Arab Christians persecuted and killed in those countries. Traditional views of a Western and Roman Antichrist are forced to confront many of the arguments presented for the Antichrist to emerge from the Muslim world.

Again, varying arguments for an Islamic Antichrist have been with us for some time and have been held over many centuries. Even in Protestantism John Calvin, Martin Luther, and Jonathan Edwards assigned an antichrist identity to Islam. But even then this was hardly new. Cyril of Jerusalem (A.D. 315-386), Sophronius of Jerusalem (A.D. 560-638), and John of Damascus (A.D. 676-749) all recognized the fundamentally antichrist nature of Islam, whose adherents the Vatican now calls “the first among the brethren,” and whose antichrist beliefs have been honored in the White House by George W. Bush and Barack Obama. Perhaps most noteworthy of all is the declaration of Maximus the Confessor (596-662 B.C.) who was witness to the rise of Islam.

There is again no doubt that Islam is an antichrist religion and that most of the nations of the Middle East in biblical history who resurface on the prophetic scene in the Last Days are likewise Islamic. We are reminded that the Roman Empire had two legs, one Eastern and one Western. And apart from Greece and Israel, those nations of the Eastern leg in addition to those of North Africa, supplemented by the burgeoning Islamic demography in Europe, are today Muslim countries. From this point of view the position of Joel Rosenberg and Walid Shoebat cannot be totally dismissed, nor the validity of their observations negated. They are in some measure at least correct in much of what they say, albeit deficient in what they neglect.

It is moreover without doubt that modern Iran, which is biblical Persia, is at the forefront of efforts to establish a Shia caliphate just as Sunni Saudi Arabia with its fanatical Wahhabist government financially partnered with Western oil and financial interests desires a Sunni caliphate. It is Iran, however, that Daniel 10 assures us will emerge as the most serious strategic obstacle to Israel and to the West. And it is the ethos and *raison d'être* of the Mullah government of Iran to usher in the arrival of the Twelfth Imam—that is, the Mahdi who is to rule from Babylon and force the non-Islamic world and, the Judeo-Christian world particularly, to submit to Islam, and is willing to use genocidal barbarism and terror to achieve its intended aim. This explains the involvement of Iran in wishing a Shia uprising against the West and against the Shia government in modern Iraq in order to rescue geographical Babylon as the city for the Mahdi. It also explains Iran's surrogate warfare against Israel through Hamas and Hezbollah because Israel represents the only strategic obstacle that is indigenous to the region.

We must understand that the game plan of the Antichrist is the game plan of Satan that has been with us since the Garden of Eden. In God's promise that the seed of the woman (Gen. 3:15), meaning Jesus who would come from Israel, would crush Satan's head, Satan also would bruise the heel of that seed. The word "heel" in the original Hebrew is "*akov*" which is translated into the name "*Yakov*" or "Jacob." Satan will try to stop the seed of the woman—Christ—by trying to stop Jacob. In biblical typology when Israel is referred to as "Jacob" it is an ethnocentric term having to do with ethnic Israel.

Before the birth of Christ Satan attempted to preempt the arrival of the seed of the woman by destroying Jacob through Pharaoh, Haman, and Amalek—all of them types of the Antichrist. After the earthly ministry of Christ the enemies of the faithful Church have always been the enemies of the Jews, be it pagan Rome, papal Rome, or Sovietism. The penultimate enemy, however, of both the Church and the Jews is Islam. Thus we see the battle chants of radical Muslims in Gaza, "First we murder the Saturday people; then we murder the Sunday people." Islam identifies all Christians irrespective of their theology as "Crusaders," and in the same breath denounces both the Jews and the Crusaders. In the Last Days this quest of Satan that began in the Garden will reach its apex under Antichrist.

There is also something to be said for the possibility of a rapprochement between apostate Christendom and Sunni Islam. Again, if the Antichrist is to come from a Roman Empire the argument could be made he can arise from the mainly Islamic Eastern as well as the mainly Christianized Western legs of what had been the Roman Empire. If this is true, we would refer to the figure of Herod the Great as discussed in the chapter dealing with him.

The Other Side of This Coin

On the other hand, the case set forward by Joel Richardson, Walid Shoebat and some others is not without formidable problems that they do not seem to be easily able to explain concerning a revived Holy Roman Empire versus a revived Caliphate, and historical Babylon versus metaphorical Babylon.

Archeological inscriptions on the catacombs, and historical traditions dating back at least to Eusebius, place Peter in Rome. And it is overwhelmingly most likely that Peter used Babylon as a metaphor for Rome in closing his first epistle (1 Pe. 5:13). Likewise, the description of the woman on seven hills (Rev. 17:9) is much more likely to be a cryptic portrayal of Rome in the *Sitz im Leben* of the Book of Revelation if a late 1st-century Johannine authorship of Revelation is to be accepted as having been written during the persecution by Emperor Domitian. It was Rome who was engaged in the persecution of the Church at the time the text was written, and it was papal Rome throughout the history of the Holy Roman Empire that remained the persecutor of the true Church, from the slaughter of the Lollards, Waldenseans, Bohemian Brethren, and other biblically Christian sects for centuries long prior to the Reformation and afterward. From Priscillian to Wycliffe to Tyndale, the enemy of the Gospel was chiefly Rome. And the pontifical office of the emperor was bequeathed to and remains with the pope to this day.

The European Union moreover was originally established by the Treaty of Rome and we cannot convincingly maintain that both legs of the image of Daniel 2 are the Islamic world except by engaging in a wild brand of fanciful speculation.

We must also accept that the Book of Acts and the Epistles in the New Testament do not trace the expansion of Christianity and the saving message of Christ to the East or to the South, but only to the North and West into Europe. God placed the Jews at the geographic center of the known world so that by tradition Matthew would indeed take the Gospel south to Black Africa, and Thomas east to India. In the East the Armenian Empire embraced it much prior to the Roman Empire. The New Testament therefore gives only a detailed historical account of the Gospel's migration into the Greco-Roman world which was probably the most resistant civilization at that time, and the predominant political, economic, cultural, and strategic power of the day.

In light of this focus of the New Testament on the Western world and the expansion of the Gospel into European civilization, it is not reasonable to impose an interpretation of eschatological events of the Last Days and the Antichrist which focuses on the East when that is not where the New Testament places the primary emphasis.

What About Daniel 9?

Daniel 9 is so vital to multiple aspects of the issue of Antichrist's identification that each aspect will require exploration in its own individual right. One facet of Antichrist's identification where Daniel 9 must be considered, however, is the question of an Islamic messiah as the Antichrist, bearing in mind as we have elsewhere outlined that Mohammed was an antichrist, the *Quran* is a *pseudologon*, and Islam is an antichrist religion. While we are in less than full agreement with them on the basis of what they fail to say, we are in broad agreement with what Christian authors such as Walid Shoebat and Joel Richardson do say. Although not in complete accord with their position, we are indebted to them and to the Lord for them in that they have factored into the equation important variables that others have omitted, ignored, or were simply ignorant of because of an innate Western myopia in their eschatology specifically, and theology generally.

Daniel 9 is a lynchpin that can help reconcile the true and valid considerations surrounding the Antichrist which they highlight with those other elements they downplay or mistakenly dismiss.

> *"And he will make a firm covenant with the many for one week, but in the middle of the week he will put a stop to sacrifice and grain offering; and on the wing of abominations will come one who makes desolate, even until a complete destruction, one that is decreed, is poured out on the one who makes desolate."* (Dan. 9:27)

Cardinal to arguments for an Islamic messiah, moreover, is an exegesis of Daniel 9:27. Here the proponents of an Islamic messiah must, and do, contend that the people of the prince who is to come were soldiers recruited into the Roman legions from the Eastern Roman Empire. This is a very poor argument exegetically and historically apart from the fact that the obvious implication from the original language text is that they share in the same ethnicity as Titus.

To begin with, although there were large contingents of recruits in the 10th Roman Legion and other Roman legions from the Eastern half of the Roman Empire, these were largely of ethnic Greek descent and not primarily ***Arab*** descent. To this day there are Middle Eastern Christians who are an ethnic mixture of Greek and Arab who have never embraced or forcibly converted to Islam. Such a misinterpretation of Daniel 9:27 lacks credible anthropological substance. It is true that these legionnaires spoke mainly Greek while their commanders spoke Greek and Latin, but there is little basis to conjecture that there is a future meaning that their descendants would be Arab Muslims. It is simply a shallow if not hollow case.

We must also note, however, that just as the court magicians and sorcerers practicing occult arts could not rightly interpret the visions in the Book of Daniel, but only Daniel could do so directly inspired by the Spirit of the Lord, so, too, persons of false religious beliefs—New Agers, and occult practitioners—will never be able to properly understand the Book of Daniel as they do not have the Holy Spirit and, as in Daniel's day, do not have the true God. There will in the end be a sure consensus among the true people of God, both Jew and Gentile, as to what these things mean. Meanwhile, it is of solid merit for Christians to exercise humility and recognize that even Daniel could only partially understand the things he saw until he was progressively given divine illumination. The same will be true for us.

There are things in the books of Daniel and Revelation which we can document Evangelical preachers and theologians having predicted on the basis of Holy Writ, which would have happened going back as far as the 17th century. This includes the regathering of the Jews and the rebirth of Israel. But as world events (and Middle Eastern events particularly) unfold and evolve, our understanding becomes progressively more and more defined. Pre-millennial Dispensationalists have since the time of Sir Robert Anderson had a piece of the pie. Messianic Jewish scholars from the saner axis of the modern Messianic Movement also have a piece of the pie. Those taking an oriental perspective such as Joel Richardson and Walid Shoebat have a further piece of the pie. But the final piece of the pie is as yet to be served by the Lord.

North-South and East-West

We also understand from the Book of Daniel that the Antichrist is featured centrally in a conflict between the kings of the North and the kings of the South in the recapitulated character of Antiochus Epiphanes (Dan. 11). A North-South line of confrontation has largely replaced the East-West confrontation of the Cold War. Russia fears the Chechnyan Muslims; Europe is overrun by an Islamic invasion from Africa, Asia, and the Middle East. It has also reached as far afield as Australia (although in the Southern Hemisphere it is part of the family of nations of the Northern Hemisphere) which is in fear of Islamic threat from Indonesia. The Islamic threat has also reached the USA and Canada, while the USA also faces its own North-South line of conflict with illegal immigration from Latin America and the Caribbean, and narcotics wars on the US/Mexican border. This is compounded by the threat of infiltration by Muslim terrorists.

The configuration of conflict has very much become a North-South divide where the industrially rich and capital rich countries of the Northern Hemisphere are at odds increasingly with the less developed nations of the Southern Hemisphere. Within this conflict is particular emphasis on the Islamic "time bomb" that is demographic, cultural, and religious as well as economic due to the corrupting power of the oil lobbies. Indeed, demands by even Western Muslims that Western democracies become compliant with Sharia law lend further credence to the arguments for an Islamic Antichrist as, again, it seeks to "change the laws and the times" with an Islamic calendar and with Sharia.

The hole in the view, however, is that the thrust of Daniel rather supports the idea that the Antichrist will muster the Western powers—that is the kings of the North—against the South. This, again, in the character of both the Seleucid Greeks and the Roman Empire that will somehow replay the escapades of Marc Antony and Cleopatra and the outcome of the historic Battle of Actium where the Roman General Octavius as victor would become Caesar Augustus the emperor. As we have already addressed, at the time of the First Coming of Jesus it was Caesar Augustus who assigned numbers to the people in order to sustain economic control. And he was the first emperor legally deified by the Roman Senate in his lifetime.

The North-South events and the conflicts coming from them so much parallel and revert back to what transpired with both Antiochus Epiphanes and Caesar Augustus as pivotal types of the Antichrist, that a purely Islamic messiah does not seem to be possible. The question becomes how do we account for the fact that so many Middle Eastern figures found in Scripture from what is today the Islamic world rival those types of the Antichrist who come from the Western world? How can these be reconciled?

I have come to believe that an indispensable key in understanding this is found in another type of the Antichrist who is neither Eastern nor Western, but is ***both*** Eastern and Western. Even more importantly, this same figure goes a very long way in explaining how to reconcile those Scriptures which support the idea of the Antichrist being a Jew with those supporting his being a non-Jew. That figure is Herod the Great.

Before we can properly define our understanding of Herod the Great as an optimum type of the Antichrist based on our understanding of Revelation 12, we must again note that historical events emanate from theological and spiritual events, and that theological events emanate from historical ones. Antichrist does not come from a vacuum. Hyper-inflation preceded the rise of Napoleon, Mussolini and Hitler—all historical shadows of the Beast—much the same as transpired in ancient Rome where the emperor became an imperial dictator out of character with "Cicero's Republic," etc. So, too, economic and resulting political chaos will create an opportunity that the Antichrist will exploit to gain power. This, however, is only one factor in what will be the ascent of Antichrist to a level of political, economic, and religious power that will be so unprecedented it will counterfeit the kind of authority that will be wielded by Jesus Christ in the Millennium.

We must understand how events political, strategic, cultural, and economic that are modern have ancient equivalents both in the era of Daniel and the Hebrew prophets, and in the 1st and 2nd-century Church. We must understand the parallel between such events in their modern expression and their ancient occurrences evaluated in light of scriptural prophecy. The Antichrist will surface from a milieu.

Chapter 8: The Seventy Weeks of Daniel

Central to understanding the milieu in which the Antichrist arrives is the time frame. The time frame God gives us in His Word revolves around the 70 weeks of Daniel. If we hold to the view of Dispensationalists that has the age of the Gentile Church occurring between the 69th and 70th week of Daniel (a view I am convinced is correct irrespective of whatever other shortfalls Dispensationalism may have), the *Parousia* of Christ and the identification of the Antichrist which precedes it both apex in that 70th lunar week which both Daniel and Revelation divide into two halves, although the return of Christ is definitely not at the midpoint.

The ultimate false peace treaty (which is already being preceded by minor peace treaties) is made at the commencement and violated at the midpoint of this last 7 years. We must also understand how this relates back to Daniel 9. Just as there were at least three decrees with the Persians and Medes for reestablishing Jerusalem and/or the Temple, there have already been multiple peace treaties made between Israel and Arab nations such as Egypt, Jordan, and both the first and second Oslo Accords. Just as many antichrists will complicate the scene in order to make the ultimate Antichrist initially less obvious, so too, there will be multiple false peace treaties that will render the final one less than conspicuous or unique at its inception. The faithful Church, however, must and will be able to discern the unique one. In our quest to establish how the Antichrist will be identified we cannot overestimate the importance of the 70th week of Daniel and the events surrounding it and leading up to it.

The Hebrew word for "seven" is *sheva*. It is where the word for "week" comes from. Daniel predicts that the Messiah would have to come and die before the Second Temple would be destroyed. The *Talmud* proves it is talking about the Messiah and how He would die before the Temple would be destroyed. Jesus reiterates the prophecies of Daniel in Matthew 24, that there will not be left one stone upon another (Mt. 24:2). Somehow the Temple is destroyed again at the end of the world. This is not necessarily the physical Temple, but the spiritual Temple. Daniel prophesies how this enemy will desecrate the House of God.

But he who comes against him will do as he pleases, and no one will be able to withstand him; he will also stay for a time in the Beautiful Land with destruction in his hand. He will set his face to come with the power of his whole kingdom, bringing with him a proposal of peace which he will put into effect; he will also give him the daughter of women to ruin it. But she will not take a stand for him...

(Some of this happened with Antiochus, some of it did not.)

So he will turn his face toward the fortresses of his own land, but he will stumble and fall and be found no more. (Dan. 11:15-19)

That is what happened to Antiochus, and it will happen to the Antichrist. Only divine intervention gets rid of him because there is nothing that man is going to be able to do. Some people think the Antichrist is going to be assassinated and come back to life; certainly he will counterfeit the resurrection. It is God who will get rid of him the same as Antiochus fell. His forces were defeated by the Maccabees, but his judgment came at the hand of none other than God Himself.

He will also enter the Beautiful Land... (Dan. 11:41)

(He wants Israel, he wants the Church.)

"He will pitch the tents of his royal pavilion between the seas and the beautiful Holy Mountain... (Dan. 11:45)

...yet he will come to his end, and no one will help him. (Dan. 11:42)

We are informed that, somehow, some Arab nations (and certain African nations) will be delivered. It is hard to say if it means literally, figuratively, or both, although it must entail some actual geographical preservation. It is one of the questions in the Bible I have been asking for years and do not understand yet. But I believe if I am faithful to Jesus and I am here, I will understand it when God decides to reveal it.

Remember, whenever a man is seen wanting to be worshiped as God, especially if he is a political ruler, it teaches about the Antichrist. Look what happened in the Book of Acts with Herod Agrippa when the people called out "*The voice of a god and not of a man!*" (Acts 12:22). God's judgment fell. When that happens, it is God teaching something about the Antichrist.

The Image of the King

During the 70th week the image of the Beast will be placed in the Temple. Another key biblical phenomenon, therefore, is the image of the king in Daniel 3, which is the primary Old Testament type of the Beast the Word of God gives us. As always, the shadow guides into recognizing what causes the shadow. The number of the Beast—"666"—occurs in several places in the Bible very directly. But there are two places where it occurs a bit cryptically.

This section of Daniel was written in Aramaic, not Hebrew. Daniel is the only Book of the Bible written in three languages. It has some Greek words for musical instruments, but some parts are written in Hebrew and some parts are in Aramaic. This part is Aramaic which is similar to Hebrew.

> *Nebuchadnezzar the king made an image of gold, the height of which was sixty cubits and its width six cubits;* (Dan. 3:1)

Those who know Hebrew understand that the plural of "nine" is "nines"—"*tesha*"/"*teshim*." The plural of "eight" is "eighty"—"*shamonim*." The singular of seven is "*sheva*" and the plural, "sevens"—"*shevim*." To say "three" is "*shalosh*"; to say "thirty" it is literally said as "threes"—"*shaloshim*." To say "four," one says "*arba*," but to say "forty," one says "fours"—"*arbah'im*." To say "fifty" they say "fives"—"*chameshim*." To say "six" is to say "*shesh*." If they wish to say "sixty," they say "sixes"—"*sheshim*." Aramaic is very similar, only instead of "*sheshim*" it is "*shetim*"—"sixes" and "six." This cannot be arrived at in English or in any other language; it must be read in Aramaic. "Sixes" and "six" are the dimensions of this image when translated literally.

> *Then Nebuchadnezzar the king sent word to assemble the satraps, the prefects and the governors...*

(He rules the whole known world like the Roman emperors.)

> *...the counselors, the treasurers, the judges, the magistrates and all the rulers of the provinces to come to the dedication of the image that Nebuchadnezzar the king had set up. Then the satraps, the prefects and the governors, the counselors, the treasurers, the judges, the magistrates and all the rulers of the provinces were assembled for the dedication of the image that Nebuchadnezzar the king had set up; and they stood before the image that*

Nebuchadnezzar had set up. Then the herald loudly proclaimed: "To you the command is given, O peoples, nations and men of every language, that at the moment you hear the sound of the horn, flute, lyre, trigon, psaltery, bagpipe and all kinds of music...

(And some of these instruments are called by Greek names.)

...you are to fall down and worship the golden image that Nebuchadnezzar the king has set up. But whoever does not fall down and worship shall immediately be cast into the midst of a furnace of blazing fire."

This is what Jesus is talking about. Do not be afraid of him who can destroy your body, but Him who can cast both body and soul into hell (Mt. 10:28; Lk. 12:4). This guy can cast only the body into the fire.

Therefore at that time, when all the peoples heard the sound of the horn, flute, lyre, trigon, psaltery, bagpipe and all kinds of music, all the peoples, nations and men of every language fell down and worshiped the golden image that Nebuchadnezzar the king had set up. (Dan. 3:2-7)

Psalm 92:3 explains something that assists in understanding this from one aspect:

With the ten-stringed lute and with the harp,
With resounding music upon the lyre.

It is about praising the Lord. The same way God is worshiped in His Temple and in Heaven, Satan wants to be worshiped in the Temple.

It became a political crime not to bow the knee to Nebuchadnezzar, just as it became a political crime not to bow the knee to the Roman emperor. It was also a political crime not to bow the knee to the pope and kiss his feet and kiss his ring. For centuries believers were killed for not complying. The Hebrew word for "to bow down" and "to worship" is the same word. The word for "prostrate," "genuflect," "bow down," "bend the knee" is what the word "*hishtava'ot*" means: "worship." And *ta'hishtava'ot* is the infinitive "to worship."

When a Roman Catholic is observed genuflecting before a graven image, lighting a candle before it, that is an act of idolatry according to the original Hebrew language of the Bible. It is making a graven image and genuflecting to it. In the Book of Esther, Mordecai would not bow the knee to Haman; it was an act of worship. No one can be in the will of the Lord and practice sin. Praying to the dead is a sacrilegious abomination. Idolatry, eating food sacrificed to idols, bowing down to images are abominations to God.

The Holy Spirit is *"the Spirit of holiness"* (Rom. 1:4). Holiness is the opposite of sinfulness. The Holy Spirit sanctifies believers and makes them holy. When someone claiming to be a regenerate, biblically-based Christian says, "The Lord told me to stay in the Roman Catholic church" (or a Greek Orthodox church and now the pseudo-Evangelical Emergent church), that is like saying the Holy Spirit, the Spirit of holiness, whose function is to sanctify them and make them holy, has told them to sin. It is impossible. The Holy Spirit will never tell someone to sin. No one can practice Roman Catholicism (according to its doctrines at least) or pray to the dead without sinning. If one does not take the transubstantiated host once a year at Easter time, it is considered a mortal sin, but that is participating in food sacrificed to idols. No one can practice Roman Catholicism without sinning. There are people doing it in ignorance, but no one can say there are people doing it in God's will. The Holy Spirit is the Spirit of holiness; He does not lead people to commit idolatry.

The point is that corrupted Christianity is much like corrupted Judaism in the Old Testament. When Israel went into idolatry it always resulted in the worshipful veneration of icons and statues in violation of the first of the Ten Commandments. Today, be it the Eastern Orthodox tradition, the Roman Catholic tradition, or the Emergent Church, the same is happening.

Just as we understand the Antichrist through his types and shadows and as we also understand the False Prophet through his types and shadows, we must understand the image of the Beast through its types and shadows both biblical and historical. Antichrist is always "in place of" Christ. The Ashtoreth veneration in ancient Israel and the sacrificing of cakes to the queen of heaven in Jeremiah (Jer. 44:19) find their corrupted recapitulation in the veneration of Mary.

What was Tammuz worship with the veneration of the pagan Madonna holding the infant is now absorbed into harlot Christianity. The turning point for this was the Council of Ephesus in the 5th century where what had been the worship of Diana of Ephesus was simply Mary-ized. The female cult deity (not to be confused with Miriam the biblical mother of Jesus) eclipses the prominence that belongs to Christ. This is inherently Antichrist and involves graven images. The claimed apparitions of Mary that we presently hear of increasing in places such as Lourdes, Fatima, Knock, Medjugorje, etc. are demonic deceptions through which the spirit of antichrist works in preparation for the coming of Antichrist.

It is not without coincidence that the bogus statements attributed to Mary at Fatima (which have proved untrue) contained eschatological prophecies regarding the papacy and the Roman Catholic Church. Because Mary is highly venerated in Islam, in interfaith dialog Mary veneration has become a bridge between Roman Catholicism, Eastern Orthodoxy, Islam, and, increasingly, with elements of Protestantism. But as with the idolatry condemned in the Old Testament it always revolves around an image. This female image, however, readily lends itself to the Hindu concepts of mother earth, providing another bridge in interfaith union that will be a key religious mechanism in the ascent of Antichrist to power.

All of this image veneration, however, provides us with a shadow of the image that is to come where the world's false religions will be united in worship of the image of the Antichrist. It begins in Daniel 3. It takes on an androgynous character, but ultimately ends with the Antichrist and the False Prophet.

Precious Metals

In both the statue in Daniel 2 prophetically illustrating the succession of world empires from which the Antichrist will ultimately come, and the statue of Daniel 3 which foreshadows the image of the Beast, Scripture places an emphasis on the typology of the metallic substances involved. An understanding of identifying the Antichrist can again not be limited to understanding one man, but rather two. This has been a recurrent weakness among believers concerned with this subject since the Protestant Reformation. A further blind spot, however, is that failure to recognize the Antichrist identification also demands the third factor, which is understanding the image of the Beast. This requires an understanding of dimensional and metallurgical typology.

Just as the queen of Sheba was enamored with Solomon, the Antichrist is going to sell the church a bill of goods.

> *All King Solomon's drinking vessels were of gold, and all the vessels of the house of the forest of Lebanon were of pure gold; silver was not considered valuable in the days of Solomon.* (2 Chr. 9:20)

Understand the typology: Jesus said, *"We must work the works of Him who sent Me as long as it is day; night is coming when no one can work"* (Jn. 9:4). *"Now is the day of salvation; now is the appointed time"* (Lk. 4:18-19).

A time will come when God will turn His grace back towards Israel during the Great Tribulation. Grace as it is currently known will come to an end.

In the Temple, as someone approached, and went into, the Holy of Holies the metals became more precious. Outside was the brazen altar and the bronze laver; they were covered with something called in Hebrew "*nachosheth*"—"bronze." As someone went into the Holy Place it was more silver, and when they got to the Holy of Holies everything was gold. Gold is a non-corrosive metal; it speaks of that which is eternal. It does not oxidize as silver does. Silver is of temporary value. Silver always has to do with the ***price*** of salvation; bronze has to do with the ***means*** of salvation; and gold with the ***result*** of salvation. According to the Book of Revelation, when all things are restored, things are described with precious stones and metal, but silver is not there anymore because silver is only of temporary value. In other words, believers were created to be God's children, not merely to be saved. Although they will be eternally grateful for their salvation, the fall of man and their salvation is parenthetical. They will always be grateful for it, but the "silver" will not have any value once they have the "gold."

In the days of Antichrist the Gospel will not be preached in the sense it is now. It will be preached, but in a completely different way. Silver is always the price of salvation. Remember the half-shekel for the firstborn (Ex. 30:12-13)? Jesus was the firstborn of the Father. That was the half-shekel. That is why He was betrayed with silver. Silver is the ***price*** of salvation. The brazen altar is a type of the cross where sacrifice was made. The altar was a type of the cross, and all the objects—bronze—represent the ***means*** of salvation. Silver is the price; gold is the result. For iron He will give silver, He will give redemption. For brass—sacrifice—He will give gold.

The Antichrist will try to counterfeit the Millennium imagery. Things are not going to be all that bad initially because he is going to try to counterfeit the millennial reign of Jesus when there will be no need for any silver. In the meanwhile, however, there will be an image of the Beast and it will be set up during the 70th week.

What The 70 Weeks of Daniel Is Not - Christ is not Antichrist

We know we are in the Last Days because prophetic events are happening. And where prophetic events begin to happen, confusion automatically results. People need to understand biblically what they see on television in the news and so forth. If they just watch the news they can get really confused as to what is going on, but when these things are viewed in light of Scripture, things become very clear.

The situation today is the same. As prophecy begins to be fulfilled (and it is being fulfilled faster and faster) confusion emerges. We are in the Last Days. God put these things in His Word for a reason, and the reason is He wants believers to understand these things.

> *"Seventy weeks have been decreed for your people and your holy city...*

(That is, Jerusalem.)

> *...to finish the transgression, to make an end of sin, to make atonement for iniquity, to bring in everlasting righteousness, to seal up vision and prophecy and to anoint the most holy place. So you are to know and discern that from the issuing of a decree to restore and rebuild Jerusalem until Messiah the Prince there will be seven weeks and sixty-two weeks; it will be built again, with plaza and moat, even in times of distress. Then after the sixty-two weeks the Messiah will be cut off and have nothing, and the people of the prince who is to come will destroy the city and the sanctuary. And its end will come with a flood; even to the end there will be war; desolations are determined. And he will make a firm covenant with the many for one week, but in the middle of the week he will put a stop to sacrifice and grain offering; and on the wing of abominations will come one who makes desolate, even until a complete destruction, one that is decreed, is poured out on the one who makes desolate."* (Dan. 9:24-27)

There are two princes in this passage. In verse 26 it is, obviously, the Messiah, Jesus. But there are people—usually extreme Calvinists—who teach that Jesus is also the second prince. The second prince is Antichrist. They are confusing Christ with the Antichrist.

Understanding Eschatology

The two most important events in scriptural eschatology are the crowning events, which are the return of Jesus, and the advent of Antichrist which precedes it, both of which again take place during the 70th week. It is dangerous and unfortunate today that many well-intentioned Christians are misled by the kind of religious rhetoric that is trumpeted by well-meaning but misguided Pre-Tribulational preachers and authors who put forth the derogatory cliché that people who do not share their false presuppositions are "looking for the coming of the Antichrist instead of Christ." This argument makes about as much sense as saying a midwife or obstetrician is looking for maternal labor contractions instead of for the baby. However well-meaning, it is a ridiculous argument.

To a substantial degree this and other misconceptions concerning the return of Jesus, and the events which must precede it, including the dawn of the Antichrist, stem from the post-Reformation view of hermeneutics. It rightly makes use of grammatical-historical exegesis in such a way as to get on the right road, but it fails to travel further on toward the final destination. One cannot eat soup with a fork. There may be large pieces of meat or vegetable in a stew which should be eaten with a fork, but not the saucy soup in which the meat and vegetables are cooked. In order to eat a stew, one requires both a fork and a spoon. Conservative Evangelical adherence to a defined grammatical-historical exegesis have the fork but not the spoon. We need both. The result is a failure to properly understand the typology beyond a limited point, and an inability to digest enough of the substance.

The hermeneutical approach of the Jewish authors of the New Testament and of Jesus Himself was midrashic (again not to be confused with the later writings of the rabbis called *Midrash*). One cannot open a pictographic attachment sent by email without the appropriate software. Neither can one open the attachment contained in the text of the Word of God. We can read the email message but not open the attachment. So, too, those limited to the Western Hellenistic grammatical-historical approach to Scripture can read the transmitted text but cannot open the picture contained within it. On the other extreme there are those who use the wrong kind of software to open the attachment and wind up only with a cacophony of indecipherable alpha-numeric scribbling that makes no rational sense. These are those attempting to base doctrine on type or figure to the negation of the preliminary grammatical-historical process. These people are essentially latter day Gnostics.

Again, we return to the road. Those who ignore the Hebraic hermeneutics required to understand apocalyptic literature in the Scriptures and stick solely to grammatical-historical exegesis do not travel far enough along the road. The Gnostics get on a wrong road completely. The scriptural and logical solution is, under the guidance of the Holy Spirit, to handle and interpret Scripture the way that Scripture does. Without this, end-times prophecy cannot be correctly understood, the Church cannot be properly prepared for the return of Christ, and the Antichrist will not be able to be identified. Thus in order to understand the sequence of events concerning the Antichrist, particularly as they are related to us in the Book of Daniel, we must understand the hermeneutical implications of right and wrong approaches to the eschatology of Daniel. There is no shortcut if we are intent on knowing how the Antichrist will be identified to the faithful.

In examining Daniel's prophetic predictions, we again review the four essential approaches to understanding eschatology. The four primary ways to understand Last Days prophecy in Western theological thought:

- Preterism
- Historicism
- Poemicism
- Futurism

Adherents to Preterism hold that these things are purported to have already happened in the Early Church and therefore have no future meaning. To such people, the Book of Revelation has no future meaning because in their misdirected view it has all happened already. This is the eschatology of the Kingdom Now people who say there will be no Antichrist, no falling away, no Rapture, that the Church will go from strength to strength and Satan is bound. And they teach that the Church is going to conquer the whole world for Christ before He comes. It is not logical to believe such nonsense, but there is not much logic in the people who preach it to begin with. This is the usual expression of Preterist error.

There are two kinds of Preterists. First are the liberals, the unsaved so-called theologians. What they say is, "Well, Isaiah could not have known a king named Cyrus would come along 200 years later and send the Jews back to Israel from the Captivity in Isaiah 44-45, so therefore Isaiah could not have written the Book of Isaiah. It had to be somebody we call 'Deutero-Isaiah'; he came along after the fact and he took something that already happened and made it look like a prediction called an *ex vaticina* interpolation." Their presupposition is, "We cannot be sure there is a God, and if there is, He does not know the future, and even if He did He would not tell Isaiah." So therefore Isaiah and Daniel could not have been so accurate in what they predicted in their view and somebody had to come along hundreds of years later and make believe. That is what the liberals say. But then there are people who say they are born-again. They are Evangelicals who will believe in a form of Preterism and say that Matthew 24 and the Book of Revelation were fulfilled in A.D. 70.

Then there is Historicism. Historicism is what some of the Reformers believed. They would say, "Well, there are many antichrists, so we should not look for these two people in the Book of Revelation; that is simply literary illustration. The papacy is an ongoing institution—it is an antichrist institution; so ***every*** pope is the Antichrist." In Northern Ireland the Presbyterians believe this. They go so far as to say that "*the restrainer*" in 2 Thessalonians 2:7 who restrains Antichrist from coming is pagan Rome, and when the Visigoths conquered pagan Rome in the 5th century, then the papacy came to power. That is how far they take it. The restrainer is the Holy Spirit, but they actually say it was imperial pagan Rome. This is Historicism.

Then there is Poemicism which claims, "The Book of Revelation is only poetry. It is given only to encourage the Church that Jesus will come back one day. It is given to encourage the Church during times of persecution. It is not intended to be construed as having any specific meaning because it is like poetry; it is just to encourage people when things are very difficult." Lutherans go with this. Luther basically rejected the Book of Revelation and so Lutherans are stuck with the fact that the founder of their church did not like it. So what are they going to do with it? They diminish it to being mere poetry.

Finally there is Futurism. Futurists are people like the late Barry Smith and Tim LaHaye and others who say that there will be an Antichrist and there will be a mark of the Beast. There will also be a terrible and great falling away, which to a degree is already incipiently well underway.

True Eschatology - Multiple Fulfillments

It is futile to attempt to understand how the Antichrist is identified without understanding the 70th week and what will happen during it. It is not, however, possible to achieve this understanding without comprehending it in light of the prophetic worldview related in Scripture. There, both messianic and eschatological prophecy cannot be reduced to mere prediction and fulfillment; double references and multiple fulfillments in a discernible pattern which, when properly understood with the illumination of the Holy Spirit and on the basis of Scripture, reveal the ultimate fulfillment and meaning.

Concerning the Antichrist and the return of Jesus, there is precious little that is more vital in this process than grasping the Book of Daniel generally, and the 70th week particularly. Without this we approach the New Testament revelation of these subjects in the Olivet Discourse, the epistles to the Thessalonians, and the Book of Revelation with a badly weakened if not flawed approach.

These are the four ways people look at it in the Western world. As pointed out before, that is not the way Jesus and the apostles looked at it. This passage talks about the "*shiqutz ha meshomem*"—the "abomination of desolation"—in Daniel 9, the abomination to come and the one who makes desolate. Jesus spoke of the abomination of desolation.

> *"Therefore when you see the ABOMINATION OF DESOLATION which was spoken of through Daniel the prophet, standing in the holy place (let the reader understand), then those who are in Judea must flee to the mountains.* (Mt. 24:15-16)

The Western world posits that one of these four approaches are true. The Judeo-Christians of the 1st century, the apostles, and those taught by the apostles, did not subscribe to that; they said ***all four*** were true.

The abomination of desolation spoken by Daniel already happened by the time Jesus spoke of it in Matthew 24. By the time the abomination of desolation was spoken of by Jesus in the Olivet Discourse in Matthew 24, it had occurred about 160 years earlier in the days of the Maccabees. (This is the Jewish feast of Hanukkah which Jesus Himself celebrated in John 10, as previously discussed. In English translations of the Bible it is often referred to as "The Feast of Dedication.") So Jesus knew it already happened. He took something that already happened and made it a prophecy. In other words, Jesus used Preterism. But unlike Preterists, He said it is going to happen ***again***. There are ***multiple*** fulfillments.

He used Historicism. He took something that happened and said it is going to happen again, and so it did, because it happened in A.D. 70. According to Josephus, when the prophecies of Jesus and Daniel were fulfilled for destroying the Temple, the Romans set up pagan ensigns on the Temple Mount and began to worship them where the Holy of Holies had been located. That was ***also*** an abomination of desolation. The Emperor Hadrian came along and built a temple to Jupiter, the Roman version of the Greek god Zeus. ***That*** was an abomination of desolation. Today on the Temple Mount resides the Mosque of Omar with an inscription in Arabic from the Quran which says, "God has no son." In 1 John it is clearly stated, that which denies the Father-Son relationship is Antichrist (1 Jn. 2:22). This is yet another abomination of desolation. Jesus used Historicism.

Then there is Poemicism. Jesus appears to John on Patmos during the persecution by the Emperor Domitian. John is the last apostle left; the others had all been martyred, and people were wondering, "When is He coming?" They expected Him, by and large, to come in their lifetime. The Church had to be encouraged that He was coming, that He was going to keep His Word, that it did indeed have an eternal future. And so Jesus used Poemicism.

Yet going back to the abomination, He said it will happen again and again and again. Each time there was an abomination on the Temple Mount (it happened with Julian the Apostate, Constantine's nephew, and there have been many other abominations since) each one of them was a foreshadowing of the ***final*** one. In other words, the Western Church stipulates everyone must choose only one of the four approaches to prophecy; however, Jesus and the apostles employed all four. It is not one of the four, it is ***all*** four. Contrary to the way the Western mind thinks—that one must be chosen over the others—the Eastern mind is able to keep them all in equal tension.

Some of these people are right in what they say but wrong in what they omit. What they are saying is not always completely wrong, but it is what they are ***not*** saying that makes it wrong in part.

Those people with the Preterist–only view say, "Well, it all happened in A.D. 70." In the Olivet Discourse Jesus spoke of the Last Days on the Mt. of

Olives in Matthew 24-25. It is not just chapter 24; it is chapter 24 ***and*** 25. Yes, it had a ***partial*** fulfillment in A.D. 70. The believers fled from Jerusalem under Simeon thinking this was the Rapture. That absolutely happened. However, did Jesus separate the sheep from goats in A.D. 70 (Mt. 25:31-46)? They would say, "Yeah, the Jews who believed were separated from the ones who did not." But then did He give people their eternal reward based on what they did with their talents in A.D. 70? That is Matthew 25. When in A.D. 70 did Jesus give people their eternal rewards based on what they did with their gifts? It never happened in A.D. 70. Referring to the wise and foolish virgins in Matthew 25, did Jesus come back for His bride in A.D. 70? No, He did not. It is complete nonsense. They take the ***partial*** fulfillment and try to make it the ***total*** fulfillment. They take the Preterism but they forget what it means for the future. That is not how Jesus handled Daniel 9. Jesus said, "Yes, it already happened, but it is going to happen again." He did not say it was one fulfillment; it is ***multiple*** fulfillments, with a final one when He comes back for the Bride.

Putting This in Context

The first thing in regard to the context is to realize Daniel was told that this message applied not primarily to the Church but to the Jews.

> *"Seventy weeks have been decreed for your people and your holy city...* (Dan. 9:24)

This is not to say it does not in any way apply to the Church, but it first of all applies to the Jews. To properly understand its application to the Church, its meaning for Israel and the Jews must be understood first.

The people who go into this error are usually—not always, but usually—proponents of Replacement Theology. They say the Church is now "Israel," and God has no future purpose for the Jews. This is absurd. If God does not have to keep His promise to the Jews, He does not have to keep His promise to the Church. The New Covenant was not made with the Church; the New Covenant was made with the Jews.

> *"Behold, days are coming," declares the LORD, "when I will make a new covenant with the house of Israel and with the house of Judah,* (Jer. 31:31)

Jesus never made a covenant with the Church; He made it with the Jews. Non-Jews who accept Jesus are grafted into Israel, and Jews who reject Him are cut off from their own olive tree. But Jesus never made a covenant with the Church. ***Never***.

The second factor needing to be understood about the context in addition to the fact it is for the Jews, is that there is one Messiah, two comings. Daniel 9 specifies that the Messiah would come and die before the Second Temple would be destroyed.

> *"Then after the sixty-two weeks the Messiah will be cut off and have nothing, and the people of the prince who is to come will destroy the city and the sanctuary. And its end will come with a flood; even to the end there will be war; desolations are determined.* (Dan. 9:26)

The Messiah would come and "*be cut off*."

The Talmudic literature refers to this and confirms the Christian interpretation in *Yalkut, Volume 2*, page 79d of the Nazir edition 32B, also the *Midrash Breshit*. (This comes from page 243 of the Warsaw Edition.) The Messiah was to exit in A.D. 33. The Sanhedrin said the same thing. The Messiah was to come and die before the Second Temple was destroyed.

The Jews expected Him to bring in the everlasting kingdom. That was not His purpose in His First Coming; that is His purpose in His Second Coming. His First Coming was to be an atonement for sin. But as previously stated, the Jews wanted somebody to get rid of the Romans the way the Maccabees got rid of the Greeks. That is His purpose when He comes back, to bring in political dominion. But it was not His purpose the first time; it was to be an atonement for sin. The Messiah was to come and die.

What happened with Jesus in his native town Nazareth in the synagogue?

> *And the book of the prophet Isaiah was handed to Him. And He opened the book and found the place where it was written,*
>
> *"THE SPIRIT OF THE LORD IS UPON ME,*
> *BECAUSE HE ANOINTED ME TO PREACH THE GOSPEL TO THE POOR.*
> *HE HAS SENT ME TO PROCLAIM RELEASE TO THE CAPTIVES,*
> *AND RECOVERY OF SIGHT TO THE BLIND,*
> *TO SET FREE THOSE WHO ARE OPPRESSED,*

TO PROCLAIM THE FAVORABLE YEAR OF THE LORD."

And He closed the book, gave it back to the attendant... (Lk. 4:17-20a)

He was reading from what is called the "*Paroch HaShavua*," the Synagogue Liturgical Lection. And He was reading from the Book of Isaiah 61. Only take note of something in Isaiah 61, beginning in verse 1...

The Spirit of the Lord GOD is upon me,
Because the LORD has anointed me
To bring good news to the afflicted;
He has sent me to bind up the brokenhearted,
To proclaim liberty to captives
And freedom to prisoners;
To proclaim the favorable year of the LORD
And the day of vengeance of our God;
To comfort all who mourn,
To grant those who mourn in Zion,
Giving them a garland instead of ashes,
The oil of gladness instead of mourning,
The mantle of praise instead of a spirit of fainting.
So they will be called oaks of righteousness,
The planting of the LORD, that He may be glorified. (Is. 61:1-3)

Jesus stops half-way through verse 2. He reads only the first half of verse 2 then closes the book. He not only stops half-way through the passage, He stops half-way through the verse and closes the book. Why? The rest He will fulfill in His ***Second*** Coming. He only reads about those things that He will fulfill in His First Coming. This is "one Messiah, two comings." He is reading the *Paroch HaShavua*, the synagogue liturgical reading for that week from the *Haftorah*, and He stops right in the middle of the verse, closes the book, and hands it to the synagogue attendant. He reads only up to the point He was going to fulfill. It is one Messiah, two comings.

Some people are trying to say, in effect, that it ***all*** happened back then. No, it did ***not*** all happen back then; He fulfills the ***rest*** when He returns. Of course there will be a millennial reign of Jesus! This was the original plan God had for this planet. What would have happened if Adam and Eve had not sinned is what is going to take place. The plans of God cannot be thwarted; sin has only interrupted it. The Messiah will restore what sin interrupted after He atones for sin. First He comes to atone for sin, then He restores what mankind made a mess of in the Garden of Eden. God had a plan, and neither the devices of Satan nor the sin of man is going to thwart the original plan He had for them and for this planet. Then comes eternity. Nothing can thwart the plan of God. So the second thing needing to be understood is one Christ/one Messiah, but two comings.

The Timing of His First Coming

We shall again make mention of Jesus handling Scripture as He did for eschatological purposes, as we see in the synagogue in Nazareth (Lk. 4:16-21). The 70th week, however, crucial to the identification of the Antichrist, which is found in this pivotal chapter of Daniel, has so frightened Talmudic Judaism that there are rabbinic prohibitions against even reading it. That the Messiah had to come and die before the Second Temple was destroyed is inescapable. yet some later rabbis resorted to rather desperate attempts to apply the prophecy as referring not to the Messiah but to an obscure figure called "Jotham" or "Jotom" (not to be confused with the hero of Judges 8-9 who is also important in understanding how the Antichrist will be identified). Such rabbinic efforts, however, rapidly fail because of both the context of the chapter and mishnaic renderings and commentaries by other rabbis supporting, if not preceding, the Christian interpretation.

There have been multiple academic symposiums with disputing scholars attempting to establish which of the possible three decrees to rebuild fulfill Daniel's prophecy. Perhaps the most common of these, however, is the decree of Artaxerxes I Longimanus of March 14, 445 B.C. (when deciphered from the lunar Judaic and Chaldee calendars). This is based on a straightforward calculation of 173,880 days by the lunar calendar (derived simply from 69 x 7 x 360). What is important, however, is that in prophesying of the calamity of A.D. 70, Jesus specified it was because they had not known *"the time of your visitation"* (Lk. 19:44); in other words, they ignored the prophecy and interpretation of Daniel 9 and were not ready for the coming of the Messiah, but they soon found themselves with a foreshadow of the abomination of desolations in the form of the Roman ensigns on the Temple Mount. The same will happen once again. Those not reckoning the prophecies of Daniel 9 and the 70 weeks will not be prepared for the return of Jesus, but will instead be left with an abomination of desolation in its place.

Once more, the paramount urgency of Daniel 9 and the 70 weeks is absolutely vital to our eschatology, including our capacity to properly identify the Antichrist.

Remembering Jesus' explanation of Daniel 9, following the martyrdom of James in Jerusalem in A.D. 70 the believers in Jerusalem under the senior leadership of Simeon fled to the mountains and into Pella when there was a temporary interruption in the siege. The non-believers in Jerusalem were deluded by false omens and false prophets. We also see in the epistle to the Hebrews that believers were being seduced into considering going back under the Law and rejecting Christ in order to avoid persecution. The same will happen in the Last Days among those who do not understand the 70 weeks. Concerning Antichrist, however, those who have the insight (Dan. 11:33) will give it to the others. This is in the character of the Sons of Issachar in 1 Chronicles 12:32, and more so of Esther and Mordecai in dealing with Haman, a major type of the Antichrist (Est. 1:13). They will know what to do and will alert others. As Daniel tells us, those who truly know their God will take the appropriate action (Dan. 11:32).

Once more, as the Maccabees and their followers reacted to Antiochus (a type of the Antichrist), and as Mordecai and Esther reacted to Haman (a type of the Antichrist), when the ultimate identity of the Antichrist—of whom Antiochus IV and Haman are mere shadows—takes place, the faithful servants of the Lord will know what to do; the others will not.

The Division of Years

There is a third factor, and again it dovetails back to that 70th week which we should never allow to elude our frame of thinking in considering Antichrist's identification.

> *In the first year of Darius the son of Ahasuerus, of Median descent, who was made king over the kingdom of the Chaldeans— in the first year of his reign, I, Daniel, observed in the books the number of the years which was revealed as the word of the LORD to Jeremiah the prophet for the completion of the desolations of Jerusalem, namely, seventy years.* (Dan. 9:12)

Jeremiah prophesied that it would be a 70 year captivity.

This year is known from archeology and from history as the first year of the reign of Darius the Mede, being 539 B.C. It was 539 B.C. when Daniel wrote this. Daniel had this explained to him by the Lord through angelic medium and so forth. He was reading the Scriptures and he saw and understood the Captivity would be 70 years. But then he gets the message it would not be simply 70 years; that is only the Babylonian Captivity. It would be seventy ***sevens***. It is like saying, "I am going to the shop to buy a dozen." A dozen what? Flashlight batteries? Cartons of milk? "I am going to buy a dozen." The word is "*shavua*." "*Shavua*" comes from the Hebrew word "seven"—"*sheba*." There will be seventy sevens. Sevens of what? The beginning of the chapter divulges that it is "weeks of years," sets of 7 years. It is necessary to go back to what Daniel was studying in Jeremiah. It is not only going to be 70 ***years***, it is going to be 70 ***sevens***. That is what it says literally. It does not say "490 years," it says "70 sets of 7 years" or "7 sets of 70 years"—a 490 year period.

Look at how it breaks it down. It says there will be a period of 7 weeks (49 years), and three-score and two weeks (434 years). So there is a period of 7 weeks, which is, of course, 49 years, and then another period of 62 weeks—434 years, before the Messiah would come and be cut off. And ***then*** at the end it says there is ***one more*** week; one final week of 7 years.

The text does not specifically indicate why it breaks the 69 weeks into 7 and 62. However, it is known that there were three decrees. The first was the decree of Artaxerxes in the Book of Nehemiah to rebuild Jerusalem, which Daniel refers back to (Neh. 2). Then followed the decree to rebuild the Temple (Ezra 1). Finally there was the re-issuing of the first decree in the Book of Ezra, issued by a later king who searched the records of the archives of the kings (Ezra 7). It is likely when the people came back, as can be read in Haggai, Ezra, and Nehemiah, that they were lackadaisical or reluctant. Many were reluctant even to rebuild Jerusalem, and most of them were reluctant to rebuild the Temple. The 49 years relates to how long it actually took to get things reestablished as a city and as a place of worship. They did not just come back and do it right away. Haggai and Ezra were fighting with them to get them to do it. That is the main reason, as far as it can be deduced, why it breaks it down into the 7 and the 62. There was a period of time before things really got organized the way it was supposed to because the people were too consumed with themselves to be consumed with the things of God.

Then the final week comes at the end after the Messiah is cut off. Now there are those who would have everyone believe this happened way back when. This decree to rebuild Jerusalem occurred in 451 B.C., but there are two things that complicate it:

(1) The calendar is based on lunar years of 360 days, not solar years of 365 days;

(2) because of the year "0," one must remember to subtract 1 year.

So to make these adjustments renders it to about 450 B.C. When adding the 69 weeks of years, it arrives at the fact that the Messiah would have had to die in approximately A.D. 32.

The 70th Week - A Serious Modern Error

And yet some people maintain that this 70th week also already happened. But many of us believe there is a break between the 69th and 70th week. Why? For the same reason Jesus read half the verse in the synagogue. It equates to "*the times of the Gentiles*" (Lk. 21:24).

When in the synagogue at Nazareth Jesus read the *Haftorah* portion of the week from Isaiah 61:1-2, He stopped short after saying, "*To proclaim the favorable year of the LORD.*" He rolled up the scroll and did not complete reading the second half of the verse, "*And the day of vengeance of our God*" in Luke 4:18-19. The reason He only read the first half of the verse, of course, was because the second half of the verse where the vengeance of God is poured out is to be fulfilled in His Second Coming, not His First. Likewise, upon the death of Jesus on the cross in John 19:37, only the first half of Zechariah 12:10 is cited by John, "*They shall look on Him whom they pierced.*" The second half is omitted. ("*...and they will mourn for Him, as one mourns for an only son, and they will weep over Him like the bitter weeping over a firstborn.*") Once again, as we read in Revelation 1:7, the second half of the verse will be fulfilled with His return. ("*Behold, He is coming with the clouds.*") He did not fulfill all the Old Testament prophecies in their totality; they must still be fulfilled eschatologically. The same remains no less true for the prophecies of Daniel's 70 weeks. It is neither biblically nor historically possible to claim that these prophecies have ever had a ***total*** fulfillment.

Such a misunderstanding is today being propagated by those caught up in the errors of Dominion Theology and Kingdom Now Theology, which is generally a curious hybrid of hyper-Calvinistic Reconstructionism and extreme charismatic pseudo-spirituality that is essentially mysticism (which is not to negate the genuinely biblical understanding of charismatic gifts which still operate within the Church). This over-realized eschatology partially came from the mistaken views of George Eldon Ladd, but have gone well beyond even Ladd's mistaken conclusions. This same mindset attempts to argue that the Book of Revelation and the Olivet Discourse were likewise fulfilled in A.D. 70 with no future meaning. Such a preposterous view must be rejected out of hand by virtue of the fact that Jesus warned that nothing as bad as the Great Tribulation would ever happen again. Yet as tumultuous as those events were as described by Josephus in his *Wars of the Jews*, the fact remains that worse things have happened since then to both the Church and the Jews. The 70th week in Daniel and Revelation categorically must have an as-yet-unfulfilled future meaning.

To understand this further, let us take the illustration of a rugby game. The game is due to be over at 6 o'clock; there are five minutes left in the game, but a player is injured so they stop the clock and freeze the game. There are still five minutes left in the game. If the paramedics get a doctor, get an ambulance, get him medically evacuated off of the field, they begin the clock again, but all the while time freezes. That is what John means when he says, "*Children, it is the last hour*" (1 Jn. 2:18). Time freezes. It is ***always*** one minute to midnight, there are ***always*** five minutes left in the game. As soon as the injured player is removed the clock begins again. Likewise, as soon as "*the time of the Gentiles*" ends, God goes back to dealing with the Jews. On what basis can this be stated?

On the basis of what Jesus said. "*Lord is it at this time that You are restoring the kingdom to Israel?*" (Ac. 1:6-8). "Oh, the kingdom will be restored to Israel; the Father has fixed that by His own authority. But you worry about evangelism. "*Be My witnesses both in Jerusalem, and in all Judea and Samaria, and even to the remotest part of the earth.*" Then He turns His grace back to the Jews and restores the kingdom.

These things could not possibly have been fulfilled in the early Church in the time of Jesus. The 70th week could not have possibly happened.

Why Some Get It Wrong

The first reason this nonsense of Dominion Theology makes no sense is that Daniel relates the same thing as the Book of Revelation:

> *"And he will make a firm covenant with the many for one week, but in the middle of the week he will put a stop to sacrifice...* (Dan. 9:27a)

Antiochus Epiphanes stopped Temple sacrifice, but it could not be Antiochus because the years do not add up. That was 160 B.C. Therefore, that leaves two possibilities: it is either the Antichrist who is prefigured by Antiochus, or it is Christ Himself as others try to assert.

When did Christ ever stop the sacrifice in the Temple? They would say, "When He became the sacrifice we no longer needed a Temple." That is true; however, the Temple was not destroyed until A.D. 70. He gave the Jews 40 years to repent and accept Him as the Messiah before He put an end to Temple worship. It just does not add up.

Additionally, look at the wording.

> *"And he will make a firm covenant with the many for one week, but in the middle of the week he will put a stop to sacrifice...*

Where does the ministry of Jesus break up into two halves of a week? Where is "7 years" seen anywhere in the Gospels, or anywhere in the Bible, of Jesus? The Bible only speaks of Jesus' ministry as 3-1/2 years. There is no "7-year" ministry of Christ. ***No place*** is the ministry of Jesus expressed as 7 years broken into two halves.

Secondly, while it is not about Christ, in Revelation it is certainly about Antichrist. Jesus had 3-1/2 years of public ministry. Satan, in the person of Antichrist, will demand equal time. They are taking verse 27, which is talking about Antichrist, and saying that it is applied to Jesus? When did Jesus ever break a covenant? He is God; God cannot break a covenant. Paul says if God breaks a covenant He would deny Himself, and He cannot do that (2 Ti. 2:13). ***People*** can break covenants, but Jesus never abrogated a covenant. It is complete nonsense to say Jesus would abrogate a covenant.

The Bible never breaks His ministry into two halves of 7 years, He never abrogated a covenant, and He never stopped the sacrifices.

The Lengths Some Will Go To

In order to do what they do, they have to do two things: they have to engage, at least to a degree, in the error of Replacement Theology. "God is finished with the Jews." At least to a degree, they have to engage in Replacementism. Some of them are radically replaced, some of them partially. But more seriously, what they do is engage in the ancient heresy of Gnosticism: spiritualize a text out of context to mean something other than what it plainly states.

There is typology where one thing is a symbol of another thing. It is true that Antiochus Epiphanes is a type of the Antichrist—that is typology. But that does not negate the fact that there was a ***literal***, historical Antiochus. There is Midrash providing a *Pesher* interpretation, but as noted, the *Pesher* interpretation, or deeper meaning, never negates the plain meaning or the "*Peshet.*" ***Never***. When someone begins spiritualizing texts in that manner, it is Gnosticism.

Calvinistic people will claim to be grammatical-historical exegesis experts. They take the Bible literally, going back to the Reformation. They are superbly guilty of the very thing they claim to be most against. What do they do every time they see "Israel" in Scripture? Spiritualize it, claiming that it is the "Church." Not all Calvinists are Replacementists, but the ones who are classic Calvinists are Replacementists. When they see the millennial reign of Jesus, to them that is only a symbol—they spiritualize it. Where do they get a license to spiritualize something? That is what both the Catholic Church and the Gnostics did. "It cannot literally be 1,000 years." But do they believe it is literally 3-1/2 years? "Yes." Then why is time literal in one place in Revelation but only a symbol in another? It is a case of "pick-and-choose."

There used to be aptitude tests back in the 1940s and 50s, before the dawn of computer tests, where they would get pegs and try to place them into holes. There were square ones and round ones and triangular ones. Put this one in and if it fits. If it doesn't fit, get the pen knife out. "Well that fits, and that fits, but we do not like that one. Wait a minute! We should not have cut that one. We should have left that one intact because it would have fit perfectly in here." Now they are stuck with this one that does not go anywhere. Get the pen knife out. That is what it amounts to. It just does not add up.

The math simply does not add up, the historical record does not add up, and the biblical texts do not add up. Verse 26 is Christ, verse 27 is plainly Antichrist. The ministry of Jesus is never divided into two halves of a seven-year period. This is not simply a distortion of Daniel's 70th week, but an outrageously nonsensical rewriting of it. It is akin to replacing the Nativity narrative in the Gospels with the fairy tale of Santa Clause and Rudolph the Red Nosed Reindeer, yet calling both the story of Christmas. Unfortunately, Rudolph trumps Jesus, and, so with the distortion, Antichrist trumps Christ. It is as inherently false as it is dangerous. Jesus did not give people their eternal rewards in A.D. 70 based on what they did with their talents. Time cannot be literal in one passage and then figurative in another. It is either all figurative or all literal. It is a big nonsense, and it is a nonsense that essentially emerges from people's desires to accommodate their own presuppositions, one of which is Replacement Theology.

In its totality the prophecy of Daniel's 70 weeks in its 9th chapter exceeds the parameters of the intention of this book. It strongly addresses predictive prophecy concerning the time of Christ's First Coming, as well as having eschatological content. As our designed intent is to examine how the Antichrist will be identified to the faithful believers, we explore Daniel 9 only to the limited degree that it affects this subject of the identity of the Antichrist.

It is of crucial importance that faithful believers avoid the various preteristic, ultra-reformed and Dominionist misinterpretations of verses 26 and 27 which ascribe to Christ the actions of Antichrist. The ministry of Jesus encompassed 3-1/2 lunar years. This will be imitated by the Antichrist who will then go on for a further 3/1-2 lunar years. With the removal of the Church by Rapture and Resurrection, as is seen in Revelation 7, and occurring between the 6th and 7th seals (Rev. 7:9-17), the Day of the Lord commences with God pouring out His wrath on the kingdom of Antichrist. Any attempt to call Christ the nefarious figure of verse 27 is a dangerous fallacy, yet the deformed eschatology of preterist ultra-Calvinists does precisely this. It is vitally important that faithful Christians not only avoid this error, but avoid the general panorama of hyper-Calvinistic presuppositions that lead to, and result in, such grave error.

Chapter 9: If One Cannot See the Obvious, They Cannot See the Hidden

The Spirit of the Age

As the spirit of antichrist works through the *zeitgeist,* setting the stage for the coming of the Antichrist in the apostate church, among Israel and the Jews, and in the world, we must understand what that spirit of the age is. We have a political correctness gone mad in order to maintain social and political stability in a multiethnic and multireligious world obsessed with a drive to achieve the impossible task of making the iron adhere to clay—as we have noted, a pursuit doomed to failure.

We have witnessed the feminism of the secular world infiltrate the Church with the ordination of women. We have seen the pansexuality of the world infiltrate the Church with homosexual and lesbian ordination. We have seen the multifaith theosophy of the world infiltrate the Church via the ecumenical agenda. We have seen the materialism of the world infiltrate the Church with the consumerist Christendom of the Word-Faith money preachers and televangelists. We have seen the media-driven obsession with entertainment and the culture of celebrity infiltrate the Church. We have also seen the political correctness of the fallen world infiltrate the Church to the point where the discernment and judgment according to God's Word that will be essential to identify the Antichrist have been demeaned as "unloving," while in truth the New Testament teaches the diametric opposite (Phil. 1:9).

Not only has the apostate church outlawed discernment and being critical of things flagrantly contradicting the moral and doctrinal teaching of God's Word, we have also seen a Neo-Universalism denying the substitutionary atonement of Jesus being promoted by supposed Evangelicals such as Steve Chalke and author of *The Shack,* William B. Young. We have witnessed a placation of the indefensible by figures such as Tony Campolo, and an apologetic for the contra-scriptural by Chuck Colson and J. I. Packer in their promulgation of ecumenism.

On top of all of this, in direct and unmitigated contradiction to the plain instructions of Jesus to be watchful and alert for the signs of His return (Mt.

24:42), we have the defiant rejection of this command of Jesus by Rick Warren who urges Christians to avoid end-times prophecy. He achieves this through an unbelievable hermeneutic involving the translocation and deletion of verses.

At the same time, we witness unabashed mammon worship and prostitution of the Word of God by the prosperity preachers to the public discrediting of the Church and the undermining of its witness to the lost.

Yet in the age of political correctness and the spirit that controls it we have a tragically resultant swallowing up of much of the Church, and an obfuscation of the central truths, thus leaving most Christians blind to reality. This is an essential ingredient in the strategy of the spirit of the antichrist for satanically seducing the Church to be both unprepared for the return of Jesus, but also being unable to identify the Antichrist until it is too late to know what to do about it.

The Antichrist Deception - Jews, Gentiles & the Church

I have, over the years, found those such as Calvary Chapel Pastor Chuck Smith who, completely independent of myself, arrived at the same conclusion that in John 5:43 Jesus was making a prophecy of the Antichrist: "*If another comes in his own name, you will receive him*." As we always note, in the divine economy there are three fundamental categories of people: Jews, Gentiles, and the true Church that is composed of both regenerate Jews and regenerate Gentiles.

Satan has plainly deceived the nations (that is, the Gentiles, from the Greek word "*ethnon*") and there is little to stop it. The general public is oblivious to the matter in which the constellation of world events is unfolding along the lines of what is prophesied in Holy Writ. Satan's penultimate feat has been to deceive Israel and most of the Jewish people to reject their own Messiah, much as they rejected their ancient prophets. We are told, in Romans 11, however, that in the Last Days this blindness will be removed and the natural branches—that is the Jews—will again be grafted into their own olive tree. The Book of Revelation makes it clear in chapters 7 and 14, as does Zechariah 12, that just as the first Christians were Jews, the last Christians will be Jews.

We also take note that God has a love and a purpose for Abraham's other children, the Arab nations descended from Abraham through Ishmael and Esau. Yet it will be through a cataclysmic ordeal commonly referred to as "apocalyptic" that final salvation will come to the anthropological descendants of Abraham, both Jew and Arab. The Antichrist will cause two-thirds of the Jews to be slaughtered in their own land. The events of the fall of Samaria in 721 B.C., of Jerusalem in 586 B.C., and again in A.D. 70, as well as the defeat of Bar Kochba's Rebellion in the 2nd century, are but harbingers of what is to come.

Judgment has always come upon the Jews in thirds in fulfillment of Ezekiel's prophecy in Ezekiel 5 where a third of the hair was chopped with the sword, a third burned, and a third scattered to the breeze. In the Holocaust of the 1930s and 40s it was, for instance, one-third of world Jewry and two-thirds of European Jewry who were murdered by the Nazis. In the Holocaust to come it will be two-thirds of the Jews in geographical Israel, eclipsing the worst nightmares the Jews have ever experienced. When the Antichrist tries to destroy them, only in desperation will they look upon their rejected, returning Messiah, as we see again in Zechariah 12, at the close of Matthew 23, and in Revelation 1.

So, too, an unprecedented maelstrom of divine judgment will come against the Muslim world in general, and of the surrounding Arab nations specifically. Apart from the possible exception of Libya, it is conspicuous that no Arab nations are included in the confederation of countries which come against Israel in the first Gog and Magog battle prophesied in Ezekiel 38-39 that will involve Iran and Turkey with the support of Russia. Specific judgments, however, are also declared for the utter obliteration of Islamic Arab capitals, such as Damascus, in Isaiah 17:1. And it is not unlikely that Psalm 83 will have a future prophetic meaning for the Arab world. We note, however, that the prophet Daniel does specify that what is today southern Jordan will evade control by the Antichrist, which may very well relate to predictions of an escape route to the area around Petra for refugees from Israel.

While a broad configuration of these events is evident, we must exercise caution in speculating on how they will specifically be fulfilled, or if they are being fulfilled. Long before the Iranian Revolution of 1979, and long prior to the ascension of an Islamic government in Turkey, many scriptural prophecy expositors forewarned that Iran and Turkey, both nations once friends of Israel and the West, would turn into enemies of both mainly based on prophesies of both Ezekiel and Daniel. They were right, and are being proved to be right, even at this very moment of time. It is just as conservative evangelical preachers dating back to the 17th century flatly stated, that the Jews would one day return to Israel and Jerusalem and the

Jewish nation would be reborn. Once more they, and more importantly the Scriptures they on which they expounded, have been vindicated in irrefutably accurate detail.

The Doomsday Accusation

Yet both the world and the apostate church elect to ignore these realities. So sad has the situation become that those who do not ignore end-times prophecy are not being simply ridiculed, but they are attacked as fatalists who want these tumultuous catastrophes to take place even if it means turning them into self-fulfilling prophecies. By refusing to subscribe to things such as Dominion Theology, the New Apostolic Reformation of C. Peter Wagner, the false prophecies of Mike Bickel, Rick Joyner, and the Kansas City (False) Prophets, and the Reconstructionism of ultra-Calvinists, as well as refusing to buy into Rick Warren's Christless global P.E.A.C.E. plan and Chuck Colson's ecumenical sell-out, those adhering to what the Word of God teaches face an insidious accusation. If a given Christian does not go with the flow even though the tide is unscriptural, they are branded as "longing for doomsday."

In actual fact, the diametric opposite is true; the true catalysts of doomsday are rather the deceivers in the Church. Those who sound the trumpet are the only ones with a prayer of delaying the inevitable. Moreover, what they long for is not the Great Tribulation but the rescue from it; that is the *Parousia*, the return of Christ. Yet even the Rapture is being mocked and denied by figures posing to be supposedly evangelical.

Satan has deceived the Gentile nations, and apart from the faithful remnant he has also deceived Israel and the Jews. Now he has managed to deceive the apostate church, including many who claim to be scripturally evangelical and regenerate. We may rest assured, however, that God will have a faithful remnant of Jews and non-Jews in a faithful Church even though it will in the final analysis not likely amount to much more than a subset of what is popularly defined as "Christianity." Before examining the nature of Satan's final deception of Israel, let us first take a sweeping view of his deception of the popular culture and a view of the failure of most of the Church to either have enough salt and light to delay these events, or even the common sense to sound an alarm.

The Obvious That They Cannot See or the Obvious They Will Not See?

A security company in Cincinnati, Ohio, became the first industry to subcutaneously implant an identifying microchip under the skin in the arms of its employees to simply be waved in front of a scanner to gain access to secure areas. Meanwhile, medical alert services have already implanted prototypes of microchips to replace tags and cards carrying important medical information for patients at serious risk. These technologies were first developed for implantation into livestock for purposes of herd management and veterinary considerations, but they are progressively being introduced into humans even as we speak.

Man is fallen, and anything fallen man can use for evil he will use for evil. Biomedical research to discover cures for diseases inevitably led to the development of biological weapons. Radio isotopes employed in nuclear medicine and clinical oncology to retard metastatic cancers are by-products of the same fissionable materials used to manufacture atomic weapons. No matter how benign or even beneficial a given technology may initially appear, in a fallen world under the power of the wicked one it will inevitably be used for some evil.

Even protagonist nations with democratic governments are compelled to accumulate weapons of mass destruction in order to maintain a mutually assured destruction capability in self-defense against despotic nations having the same weapons systems. Everything goes out of control unless it is under the dominion of Christ. If He does not intervene, and indeed had He not already intervened in His grace and undeserved mercy, it is not unlikely that fallen man would have already destroyed the biosphere and committed a self-inflicted total genocide of our own species. It is, in short, the hand of God alone that stops us from wiping out the human race.

With the corruption of the Evangelical Church into levels of heresy and immorality every bit as reprobate as what was traditionally associated with the harlot church, false religions, and cults, the capacity of such a Church to bring a godly influence that stays our demise has evaporated. Although there may or may not be interim periods of revival, the general trend is such that this evaporation of scriptural standards of truth and morality will continue to degenerate into heterodoxy and moral and ethical dilapidation. Hence those churches and Christians attempting to warn about the prophetic implications of the misuse of technology will be increasingly dismissed as religious "kooks." They will not simply be relegated to the status of alarmist idiots by the secular world, governments, academics, and media, but also by the apostate church.

The boom in credit card fraud, the decline of the U.S. dollar and of the euro, and manipulation of import/export ratios in global trade with the intentional undervaluing of national currencies (most notably by China) are clearly pressing the demand for a global currency. If there were a simple exchange mechanism between the American Federal Reserve and the European Central Bank with a one-for-one exchange rate, the British pound, the Japanese yen, the Swiss franc, the Australian dollar and all other global currencies would need to fall into line as a euro/dollar exchange rate mechanism (ERM) would establish a de facto global currency.

At the same time, electronic currency transfers and purchases are rapidly replacing cash, and the market value of precious metals is much more precarious than the popular markets would have consumers believe. (If gold bullion is as secure as those selling it claim, why are they selling it for cash?) Hence, with the convergence of electronic currency, the astronomical boom in digital fraud, and the drive for international monetary stabilization, it does not take a tremendous amount of imagination to see how the infamous mark of the Beast could become a reality.

Again, the implantation of microchips has gone from animals to humans already, and in the early phases is justified on the basis of humanitarian and medical concerns. This has already incipiently graduated to security concerns. Governments, most notably Great Britain, followed by the USA, are exploiting the terrorist threat to persuade the public to suspend democratic freedoms and rights to personal privacy in exchange for a security from terror they cannot guarantee. Indeed these same corrupt governments will readily misuse the terror threat to justify curtailing of civil liberties and constitutional freedoms, but at the same time refuse to embark on common sense policies such as protecting national borders, restricting Islamic immigration, or profiling Islamic air passengers. It becomes politically incorrect and offensive to an inherently jihadist religion believing itself to have a divine mandate to oppose non-Muslims as infidels, but it is not politically incorrect to rob the electorate citizens whom they are supposedly trying to protect of their constitutionally mandated rights.

No one in their right mind can any longer deny the emergence of a Big Brother society concerned not only with maintaining public safety and order, but with acting as a thought police. In the character of the old Soviet

Union and Saudi Arabia, the emerging Big Brother seeks to criminalize personal, political, and religious opinion. This dissipation of democratic freedom is directly proportional to the fact that the Protestant democracies and their backslidden churches and denominations have abandoned the scriptural principles of their forefathers upon which their constitutional and representative government, democratic freedom, and personal liberty were initially predicated. It is imperative to understand how these trends are preparing the way for the advent of the Antichrist.

This has nothing to do with conspiracy theories about Freemasonry or the Illuminati; it goes well beyond all of that half-truth and the endless spiral of speculation and conjecture that evolve from it. It is more related to the decline of personal liberty through everything from the increased role of government in the corporate environment, the regulation of private enterprise, and personal economic freedom, but also through the abject quest for a social harmony that cannot exist outside of faith in Christ.

Infused in the Culture

This is already having implications in multiple spheres, but none more so than in education where an outmoded school system designed to groom human automatons to function in an assembly line factory culture, performing repetitive tasks in labor intensive industries without thinking, has become a dinosaur that must be fed. The dinosaur does not exist for the benefit of the economy; more and more work is done in cottage industries, and three out of four new jobs are created in small to medium upstart businesses. It is a school system which should be junked, and replaced by small, private, community-based schools combined with home schooling where more and more work is actually done. Yet we have an obsolete education system that is working to the long-term detriment of the economy, and that fails both our children and future generations, and even fails teachers. The only beneficiaries are teachers unions with biased agendas, sporting political action funds that contribute to the campaigns of leftist politicians who keep the dinosaur well fed.

Public education is no longer about education; it is about social engineering where a pansexual, multifaith ideology is implanted into the minds of children at an impressionable age for purposes of maintaining social, political, and religious control. This debauched concept was initially the brain child of the Roman Catholic Jesuits who designed the Roman Catholic school system to prevent the expansion of any form of

Protestantism, particularly Evangelicalism, among Catholics. It was based on the philosophy of education that said, "Give us a child until the age of seven and they are ours for life." This same philosophy of education is now adopted by progressives and other purveyors of the politically-correct agenda. Indeed, with the assistance of the media the outdated school system has managed to popularly redefine "tolerance" as not simply a willingness to tolerate those with different religious identities or sexual orientations, but as an ***endorsement*** of those beliefs and orientations. It is not about education, but ***indoctrination***; it is not about preparing future generations for the workplace, but about ***controlling*** them.

So, too, the war on terror is not about security. If it were, Western governments would stop lying to the public and to themselves about the true nature of fundamentalist Islam. Their reaction to 9/11 and other Islamic assaults on the West would have been the same as Western reaction to Japanese imperialism after Pearl Harbor. Islamo-fascism would be addressed in the same manner that the fascism of Mussolini and the Nazis was—each confronted for what they were. The war on terror has become, once more, about control. Corrupt governments in league with Muslim oil interests demand that Islam be viewed, not as a threat, but as a religion of peace and tolerance, even though they cannot show a single example of an Islamic society that gives Christians and Jews the same rights demanded for Muslims in the West—rights that presidents from Clinton, Bush, and Obama, and prime ministers from Blair, Cameron, and whoever follows, are foolishly according fundamentalist Muslims to the detriment of their nations' futures.

Important to understanding this is how it is creating the sociological, political, and cultural environment for the Antichrist to quickly gain momentum once he appears on the global stage. Again, most of society—its academics and media—remain not simply oblivious to, but ***willfully blind*** to, these realities. How can they not do so, however, when churches professing to be Evangelical are no less blind and, again, ***willfully*** so?

If the Church Cannot See, How Can the World See?

We again note Rick Warren's false doctrine directly contradicting the command of Jesus in Matthew 24:42-43. Warren asserts that we should reject Jesus' instructions to be alert and rather avoid end-times prophecy. We note the false teachings of Rick Warren's associates such as John Piper who mislead the churches with their false doctrines of Replacement

Theology, teaching Christians the lie of Satan that the restoration of national Israel is devoid of eschatologically prophetic importance. Much worse is the anti-Israel rhetoric of noted false teachers such as John Stott (who advocates the false doctrine of Annihilationism), Colin Chapman (who claims the Church cannot say that Hindus and Buddhists cannot be saved without faith in Jesus), Bill Hybels (who invites a Muslim imam into his Willow Creek Church to explain Islam, although no evangelist is invited into a mosque to proclaim the Gospel), and Stephen Sizer (who openly shares platforms with apologists for terror and who broadcasted his anti-Israel polemics from terrorist Iran at the same time Iran was murdering Iranian evangelical pastors).

It is Satan who wishes Christians to be oblivious to the fulfillment of events prophesied in Scripture; he does not want the Bride to be prepared for the coming of the Groom. While this message is authored in hell, it is Rick Warren, Colin Chapman, John Stott, Stephen Sizer, and others, who are the messenger boys who deliver it, no matter how witting or unwitting they may be.

In this regard, few are more dangerous than those who combine hyper-charismatic Dominion Theology with the Reconstructionist eschatology of hyper-Calvinism. Reconstructionist Calvinists, both living and dead, such as Gary North, Rousas J. Rushdoony, David Chilton, and D. James Kennedy, are indeed strange doctrinal bed fellows for hyper-charismatic lunatics who mistake experience for doctrine, mysticism for spirituality, and Gnosticism for exegesis. Their common ground is their over-realized eschatology, stretching the ideas of George Eldon Ladd and Austin Sparks beyond anything those two actually ever said or wrote. Add to this, Replacement Theology that has the Church superseding the Jews, negating a future national purpose, as well as salvific purpose for ethnic Israel.

With the vastly decreased interest in eschatology and end-times prophecy (with the exception of the fictionalized works of Tim LaHaye) and the clear and unambiguous caveats of Jesus and Scripture being ignored and even defied by false teachers within the Church, it is little wonder the world had no idea of what is really happening—although the unsaved world knows that ***something*** is happening. Even as microchips are being implanted in human arms, and we are rushing toward a global currency, most people—and even most Christians—have little if any idea what it means. Once more, in the early stages the implantation is embarked upon for reasons that are benign or medically beneficial, but progressively it is transformed into a mechanism for economic, political, social, and ultimately religious control.

Crowning the Priest - Christian Beware

Justifiably and correctly, most eschatological study has focused on the prophetic and literary relationship between Daniel and Revelation. Unfortunately the obvious necessity of interpreting these two books in light of each other has eclipsed the fact that to only a slightly less degree the same is true in their prophetic and literary relationship between the Book of Zechariah and the Book of Revelation. An absolutely fundamental maxim on which we must always keep our eyes is that Satan wants to be God; Antichrist wants to be Christ. This is a general truth but has a specific meaning for both the apostate church who will be taken in by the Antichrist and unbelieving Israel whom Jesus predictively warned in John's Gospel, "*If another comes in his own name, you will receive him*" (Jn. 5:43).

The Antichrist will want to be seen as a messianic savior preempting the final redemption that will be delivered by Jesus in His return. Moreover, as Satan has already blinded the eyes and heart of most of Israel to the identity of the true Messiah, he intends to show them a false one whom he himself will indwell. Those outside of the faithful Church will crown the wrong king and they will crown the wrong priest. In order to understand this correctly, let us consider the first appellation of the Antichrist in Revelation 6 and what follows it. We will then see how this has a parallel complement in the Book of Zechariah. Taken together in light of each other, what had been a low quality picture of the Antichrist and his endeavors begins to gain definition and increased clarity.

The four horsemen of the apocalypse are dispatched with the opening of the first seal (Rev. 6:1). The four living creatures, however, are before the throne of God (Rev. 5:6). It may be that when the seal is broken each of the four creatures plays a role in dispatching their evil counterparts. This familiar pattern is seen elsewhere in the Book of Revelation and throughout Scripture. For instance, while the angel of God blows the sixth trumpet in Revelation 9:13-21, the massive army from the east comes forth. This army is utterly demonic and in the character of the locusts in the Book of Joel corresponding to the armies of Babylon circa 585 B.C. (Joel 1:4). It is a *Pesher* interpretation. In this context of the Antichrist specifically, however, we must recall that 2 Thessalonians 2 and Zechariah 11 both confirm to us that the Antichrist will be a villain whom God dispatches in judgment, and in order to bring him into a conflict in which the Lord, will destroy him. God has always used the wicked as instruments of judgment on the other wicked, and as instruments for correction of His own people (which can apply in principle to the Church as well as to Israel and the Jews). All of these considerations come into play when we examine Revelation 6 and its relationship to Zechariah, and what it will ultimately mean for crowning the wrong figure and identifying the Antichrist.

The Counterfeit on a White Horse

> *I looked, and behold, a white horse, and he who sat on it had a bow; and a crown was given to him, and he went out conquering and to conquer.* (Rev. 6:2)

> *"And he will make a firm covenant with the many for one week, but in the middle of the week he will put a stop to sacrifice and grain offering; and on the wing of abominations will come one who makes desolate, even until a complete destruction, one that is decreed, is poured out on the one who makes desolate."* (Dan. 9:27)

The first mention of the Antichrist in the Book of Revelation is in 6:2 where he likewise arrives on a horse in imitation of Christ, but brings only a false peace which carries substantial reference to Daniel 9:27 where the treaty will be broken. In both cases we see Satan trying to look like Christ and, once succeeding in misrepresenting himself, discloses his true ambitions which are the diametric opposite of peace. When Jesus appears on a white horse in Revelation 19:11, He dooms the Beast and False Prophet and inaugurates the millennial reign of peace for a thousand years. Hence Antichrist will attempt to disguise himself as Christ bringing millennial peace, but instead will bring horrific war.

We must remember that as New Agers await the Age of Aquarius, as Muslims await a global Caliphate, and as Orthodox Jews following the rabbis instead of the Scriptures await a messianic age along the lines wrongly described by Rambam, all false religions and religious philosophies are seeking a messiah figure to deliver their expectations. The Antichrist will so misrepresent himself as a Christ-like figure that he will know how to manipulate those ignorant of the Word of God and blinded by these demonically inspired false belief systems into rallying to him.

The four horsemen are a representation of what the Antichrist will bring. Initially he brings a false peace, as always trying to be a high-grade counterfeit of Christ. He will then bring the destruction of war followed by the devastation of famine and finally the utter *"Apollyon"* (Rev. 19:11)—destruction of such magnitude that if Christ did not intervene he would bring utter obliteration to the Church, and then to Israel and the Jews. The black horse representing famine (Rev. 6:5-6) will likely take place by the Antichrist's control of commerce where no one can buy or sell without political loyalty and religious homage to him (Rev. 13:16-17).

Throughout history there have been figures both political (Adolph Hitler, Benito Mussolini, Barack Obama, Gamal Nasser) and religious (Menachem Schneerson, Pope Sylvester, Jim Jones) who created cults of personality, promising to deliver the new world and great hope that their followers all long for, only to be very quickly disappointed. All of the deceiving and despotic political leaders of history, and all of the religious frauds of history combined, will not come near to perpetrating the seduction of the Antichrist as presented on the white horse in Revelation 6 even though such cult leaders, politicians, etc., do provide for us a dim hint of what is going to happen.

We have explained that the return of Christ in Revelation 19 ushering in a global peace is the opposite of the white horseman in Revelation 6 ushering in global war, famine, and chaos. Hence Revelation 6:2 cannot possibly be Christ. Yet, as always, the Antichrist makes a well-polished effort to look like Christ. In Revelation 6, moreover, the martyrs dressed in white robes are seeking divine justice against their persecutors, and more are to be killed. But in Revelation 19:11-16, with the second white horseman who is called *"Faithful and True,"* they also return in these white robes with Him. Then the Antichrist and False Prophet are destroyed, together with the binding of Satan and the establishment of the messianic kingdom.

Those commentators seeking to identify the white horseman of Revelation 6 as Christ are making an error very much akin to those who teach that Christ is the one who puts a stop to sacrifices in Daniel 9:27. In both cases they confuse Christ with the Antichrist. This in itself testifies to the capacity Satan will give to the Antichrist to try to pass himself off as the saving Messiah. Indeed to some measure he is already misleading some Christians into this confusion even ***before*** the Antichrist formally arrives on the scene.

The Counterpart to the Four Horsemen

> *'Now listen, Joshua the high priest, you and your friends who are sitting in front of you—indeed they are men who are a symbol, for behold, I am going to bring in My servant the Branch. For behold, the stone that I have set before Joshua; on one stone are seven eyes. Behold, I will engrave an inscription on it,' declares the* Lord *of hosts, 'and I will remove the iniquity of that land in one day. In that day,' declares the* Lord *of hosts, 'every one of you will invite his neighbor to sit under his vine and under his fig tree.' "* (Zech. 3:8-10)

In Zechariah's prophecy the Branch typifying Jesus is first introduced in Zechariah 3 where again we see a High Priest who is called "*the Branch*" (with the definite article, thus foreshadowing the Messiah) who will remove the iniquity from the land in a single day (Zech. 3:9) and then inaugurate a millennial reign alluded to in Zechariah 3:10. In the following chapter, however, we see the two lampstands and olive trees (Zech. 4:2-3) corresponding to the two witnesses of Revelation 11:3-13. In Zechariah 6, after the prophecy of the wicked woman but prior to the coronation of the High Priest (again foreshadowing Jesus), we see the divine counterpart to the four horses of the apocalypse in Revelation 6.

> *With the first chariot were red horses, with the second chariot black horses, with the third chariot white horses, and with the fourth chariot strong dappled horses.* (Zech. 6:2-3)

These horses outnumber the horses of Antichrist and the three following him by a ratio of two to one (or so it would appear) and they are pulling chariots. And as with Revelation 6 they are identified by their color; only their order of appearance is different: the red horses come first, the black horses second, the white horses third, and the dappled horses last. God's response and counterattack to the Antichrist in Revelation 6 will have the reverse order.

The Antichrist tries to show himself as a man of peace on a white horse (Rev. 6:1-2), but instead brings war represented by the red horse (Rev. 6:3-4), then famine and destruction represented by a black horse (Rev. 6:5-6), and finally the pale horse bringing utter pandemonium (Rev. 6:7-8). In Zechariah 6 with Christ, the wars and rumors of war represented by the red horses precede Him followed by the famines, earthquakes, and pestilences represented by the black horses; then come the white horses representing the eternal Christ Himself, with the last dappled horse creating total pandemonium on the kingdom of Antichrist before the High Priest is crowned King and the millennial reign is established. Hence, although the horses are of the same color, the color sequence differs.

> *"Pay her back even as she has paid, and give back to her double according to her deeds; in the cup which she has mixed, mix twice as much for her.* (Rev. 18:6)

The fact that the number of horses in God's counterattack is double the number of those associated with Antichrist in Revelation 6 demonstrates the fulfillment of the prophetic command to repay the wicked woman double.

With the exception of Daniel, no other book in the Old Testament is more crucial to the proper understanding and interpretation of the Book of Revelation than Zechariah, although to varying degrees all of the books of the Old Testament either directly or indirectly come into play in their texts, themes, and motifs in the Book of Revelation, some greater and some lesser. In the greater context of the Book of Zechariah it again replays the events surrounding the fall of Babylon and the return of the Jews to Jerusalem which is as always a prophetic picture of the judgment of Babylon the Great and the return of Christ to establish His kingdom reign from Jerusalem.

> *"Ho, Zion! Escape, you who are living with the daughter of Babylon." For thus says the LORD of hosts, "After glory He has sent Me against the nations which plunder you, for he who touches you, touches the apple of His eye.* (Zech. 2:7-8)

We again see the horses patrolling the earth at the end of the Babylonian Captivity and a warning to God's people to flee from Babylon. Once more, those nations who come against Israel will be like those who have persecuted the faithful Church throughout the centuries and will have touched the apple of God's eye.

> *Then the LORD showed me four craftsmen. I said, "What are these coming to do?" And he said, "These are the horns which have scattered Judah so that no man lifts up his head; but these craftsmen have come to terrify them, to throw down the horns of*

> *the nations who have lifted up their horns against the land of Judah in order to scatter it."* (Zech. 1:20-21)

We also see the judgment of these nations as horns to be thrown down (Zech. 1:18-21). As prophesied by Daniel and seen in the Book of Revelation, the horns will again be thrown down in the judgment of the kingdom of Antichrist (Dan. 8:8). Thus the initial appearance of Antichrist in Revelation 6:2 can only be interpreted in light of Zechariah. What is important in Zechariah is that God's people are commanded to flee from Babylon, as we read in Zechariah 2:7 and again in Revelation 18:4.

The centerpiece of understanding Zechariah relative to Revelation is the crowning of the High Priest which will happen to Jesus, but which Antichrist will first attempt to do for himself in league with the False Prophet. It is important in understanding the convoluted theological argumentation that will facilitate this deception. It is what the New Testament calls "the leaven of Herod" and it relates directly to the Antichrist.

The Leaven of Herod

In a Paschal context, 1 Corinthians 5 explains to us the typological significance of leaven or "*chometz*." It is first of all figurative of sin, but most especially the seminal sin of pride which begets other sin. Indeed, according to Isaiah 14, Satan's first sin was pride, as was man's first sin. Other sin such as greed, lust, and unrighteous anger all stem from the primordial sin of pride either directly or indirectly.

Jesus develops this concept further and applies it to heretical teaching and false doctrine with His famous caveat "*Beware of the leaven of the Pharisees and the leaven of Herod*" (Mk. 8:15). As the Jews ate an unleavened meal in preparation for the Exodus, which is a type of the Rapture, where rescue from Pharaoh prefigures rescue from the Antichrist, the faithful Church will eat an unleavened meal of spiritual food preparing it for the Rapture. Prophecy will be explained by a good and faithful servant who will give proper food at the proper time (Mt. 24:45-51). This once again corresponds to the Passover meal where Christ reveals the "*son of perdition*" in the person of Judas. Jesus further warns, however, that there is a danger for the one who should be a good and faithful servant getting drunk and beating his fellow servants.

We have already seen, courtesy of John Arnott, Rodney Howard-Browne, Colin Dye, Gerald Coates, Randy Clark, and other such figures, the promotion of spiritual inebriation within the Church of the very kind we are warned against in the Last Days (Joel 1:5; 1 Th. 5:6-7) where we are urged to have sobriety and self-control, not drunkenness. We have also seen the beating of fellow servants by leaders in what Ezekiel referred to as shepherds abusing the sheep (Eze. 34:1-10) and in Jesus' mention of the deeds of the Nicolaitans (Rev. 2:6, 15), which carries the Greek meaning of "suppression of the laity" or people.

The people in such backslidden churches who follow the drunken hysterics phenomena falsely called "revival," and those sitting under the ministry and leadership of practitioners of heavy shepherding are in peril. Unless they get out of those places they will not have the proper food at the proper time and will not be prepared to either identify the Antichrist or be rescued from him. Indeed, churches practicing such diabolical things are actually apostate cults masquerading as scripturally based congregations. They are not part of the faithful Church and it is usually little more than a matter of time when financial exploitation and/or sexual immorality are found among their leadership.

The Paschal meal must always be without leaven. There can be no false doctrine in it. Those serving the food cannot be driven by spiritual pride; they must feed the sheep true doctrine and not abuse or exploit the flock of Christ. The faithful Church will, by the Holy Spirit and on the basis of Scripture, be able to recognize faithful servants in the way sheep know a good shepherd. Christians who listen to Christ will know when Christ is speaking through a man and when He is not. The key is never to listen to a man, but to the voice of Christ. The Lord may indeed have many mouths through whom by His grace He sovereignly elects to speak, but He will have only one voice; that is the voice of Jesus communicating by the Holy Spirit even though it may be through some leader whom God desires to use. The responsibility of such a leader is nowhere more acutely presented to us than in James 3:1: "Let few of you be teachers; teachers will be judged more strictly than the rest." There can be no leaven in the grain.

The leaven of the Pharisees is obvious in its meaning. It is the false doctrine of religious hypocrites and false teachers who are in the character of the Pharisees. They are about money and power, and they teach traditions of men as doctrines of God, just as Jesus specified regarding them in Matthew 15. These are they who populate the corridors of ecclesiastical power and have forfeited the God-given calling to be shepherds and teachers in order to be theocrats and theocratic politicians. This, however, has gone on since time memorial, and even existed in the corruption of the Levitical priesthood in pre-Christian times. What is often forgotten is that Jesus gave equal weight of warning to the leaven of Herod.

Again, as we are repeatedly reminded, all of the Herods are antichrists and the ones described in the pages of the New Testament are types of the Antichrist. Although this is supremely true of Herod the Great, it is not simply true of all of them, but Herod the Great himself personifies the entirety of his dynasty. Aspects of all of his descendants who reigned as surrogates of Rome carry not only elements of his DNA, but elements of his inherent devious wickedness and style of manipulating persons, institutions, and circumstances to his own mal-contrived ends.

While the Herodian character and style is incarnated in Herod the Great, it is reincarnated in his son Herod the tetrarch (we do not use the term "reincarnation" in any Hindu or literal biological sense.) Herod the tetrarch, as the son of his ethnically Nabataean father, and like his father a Jew by religion, yet totally Roman by his culture, politics, and personal identity, is the Herod who presided when Jesus warned to beware of his leaven. It was this Herod who decapitated John the Baptist, the typological significance of which we have discussed elsewhere. The mother of Herod the tetrarch, however, was interestingly a Samaritan, bearing in mind that Samaritanism has been a nemesis to the Jews and an instrument of Satan to attempt to seduce the Jews from the time of Ezra and Nehemiah (Ezra 4:1).

While Jesus assumed a benevolent disposition toward Samaritan people as we see in John 4, regarding their perversion of Judaism He told the woman at the well she knows not what she speaks. What is important in understanding why Jesus said this was not simply the wrong location of the holy mountain of sacrifice, the false priesthood, or the pagan influences inherited from the Assyrians, but the quintessential *pseudologon* of the time of Jesus, *The Samaritan Bible* which removed the Prophets and writings and made changes to the five books of the Pentateuch which it retained. It was a masterpiece counterfeit of the Torah because with a few well-placed exceptions it copied the Torah God gave to Moses almost word for word. Yet it contained enough change to mislead the Samaritan nation. Samaritan influences within the House of Herod at the time of Herod the tetrarch would not be merely coincidental.

What is curiously odd concerning Herod the tetrarch is that he expected John the Baptist to return to earth, even suspecting that Jesus could have been he. So, too, the Antichrist will be aware that Elijah the prophet, whose spirit was upon John the Baptist, will return. The specter of John coming again made Herod the tetrarch nervous; so, too, the specter of Elijah—whom John more than typifies and foreshadows—returning will taunt the Antichrist.

Religious and Political Cross-Pollination

We know that the leaven of Herod differed from the leaven of the Pharisees in that the former was theocratic and the latter political. Herod the tetrarch (and the other Herods) misused political power to attain religious power, just as there was a misuse of religious power to attain political power by the Sanhedrin. The False Prophet (the Beast from the earth) coming from a religious establishment will likewise use religion to obtain a political objective, while the Antichrist (the Beast from the sea) will use politics to get religious power, forming a mutually complementary diabolical ascendancy to power. As has been traditionally recognized, the sea suggests the nations around the Mediterranean, while the earth by traditional estimation represents Israel.

In Revelation 13 we read that the False Prophet will exercise the same authority as the Antichrist (Rev. 13:12). His resemblance to a lamb in Revelation 13:11 places him in imitation of Christ but his words place him in the nature of Satan manifested in the character of the dragon in the previous chapter (Rev. 12:3) which in turn relates to the typology of Herod the Great.

This will, again, involve false religion which is typified by a wicked woman. We see her personified not simply in the harlot of Proverbs or in Jezebel, Queen Athaliah, and in the great whore of Revelation, but in Zechariah 5 where in the character of Semiramus, a temple is again built for her in the land of Shinar (Zech. 5:6). This woman is carried by two other women, typologically suggesting an alliance of false religious systems that will build a false house to God in Babylon (Zech. 5:9-11). In the second half of the following chapter in Zechariah 6, we see Joshua the son of the High Priest Johozadak as a type of Christ called "*Branch*" as Christ is called "Righteous Branch" in Old Testament prophecy (Zech. 6:11-12). We also see the Temple of the Lord being built in contrast to the temple of the whore. A crown is placed on his head because a priest will be on the throne (Zech. 6:13).

Here we see a motif that is reserved for Christ and for Melchizedek (a possible Christophony) where a crown is placed on the head of a priest as king. In Revelation 1 we see Jesus in the mixed décor and colors of both the King and Priest. Only the Messiah could be both King and Priest. Kings were required to be descendants of David, while priests descendants of Aaron. While from the two different tribes of Judah and Levi respectively, the Messiah, being from a different order, had the right to be from both. When Jesus hung on the cross as the sacrificial atonement for our sin He was indeed our High Priest making an atoning sacrifice on the altar represented by the cross, while at the same time affixed to the cross was "*This is Jesus the King of the Jews*"(Mt. 27:37). As with John Hyricanus in the Hasmonean Period, the Antichrist will attempt to unite a supreme political office and a supreme religious office which will be achieved with the help of the False Prophet.

We must again keep in mind that this was exactly what transpired in the time of Jesus with the deified emperors who called themselves "pontiff" as a political figure assuming both an imperial title and a religious one—a practice transferred to the popes in the Middle Ages during the period of the papal states. So, too, the Antichrist in his last ditch effort to usurp what is the unique reserve of Jesus will move to fuse together religious and political power.

Examples in the Distant Past

Satan's effort to unite religion and political, economic, and strategic power will be thwarted with the return of Christ destroying Antichrist. Satan's attempt, however, will be very formidable, and the way has always been prepared for it. After the rejection of their Messiah, Rabbi Akiva (a historical type of the False Prophet) uses religion to ascribe power and dominion to an antichrist in the person of Bar Kochba. During the time of the Holy Roman Empire the pope had a similar relationship with German emperors before the Reformation. After the Reformation the spirit of antichrist continued in this vein to unite temporal spiritual and political power.

During the reigns of Louis XIII and XVI, Cardinal Richelieu became the French Secretary of State and the first prime minister in the modern sense of the word, as well as the figure who controlled foreign affairs on behalf of the king. By using religion he centralized political power and restricted the freedom of the Huguenots, many of whom were born-again believers (howbeit of the Calvinistic persuasion). In his political aims he would stop at nothing to contain the Hapsburg Dynasty. But Richelieu, also on the basis of political expediency, fostered a Catholic-Protestant unity in a forerunner of the modern Ecumenical Movement. Again, his aims were political much the same as the Catholicism of countries in the modern European Union is the only uniting factor among them when they are so divided by culture, language, and history. Once more, power in Europe is become centralized, and religion and ecumenical unity are being used to foster the political agenda which in some way is preparing the way for Antichrist.

We again see the spirit of antichrist operating in this character in the history of England. Cardinal Woolsey was to Henry VIII what Richelieu was to Louis XIII. Henry VIII initially opposed Protestantism and any Evangelical interpretation of the Gospel, even encouraging Erasmus of Rotterdam to academically challenge Luther, and being honored by the pope with the title, "Defender of the Faith," meaning the papal faith.

Almost hideously this title has been preserved by the British monarchy and the current Prince Charles has announced that he does not want to be the defender of ***the*** faith, but rather of "faith," meaning ***all*** religions including Roman Catholicism, Hinduism, Rabbinic Judaism, Sikhism, and Islam. When he was Archbishop of Canterbury, George Carey, a former Evangelical, called the pope "the Holy Father." He also appeared in the British media denouncing the presenting of the Gospel to Jews.

His successor Rowan Williams holds to the ordination of homosexuals and lesbians and is a member of a Druid sect, actually ritually identifying himself as the son of an ancient pagan Celtic god, despite the fact Scripture tells us plainly that all other gods are demons according to both Moses (using the Hebrew word "*shedim*") and St. Paul (using the Greek term "*demonoi*"). The oldest opponents of the Gospel of Jesus in England and Wales were the Druids; now the Archbishop of Canterbury is one, publicly labeling himself by a title that is the son of a demon god and sanctioning sexual practices which according to God's Word the Lord finds abhorrent and unnatural. Today we see the spirit of antichrist working strongly through Prince Charles and the Archbishops of Canterbury.

We must, however, understand that the Holy Spirit has been working for many centuries to achieve the prophetic purposes of God, but so has the spirit of antichrist which is closely aligned with the "*mystery of iniquity*" (2

Th. 2:7). Like Richelieu, Woolsey was a complete political animal with religions simply being his vehicle. When Henry VIII could not get a papal dispensation to divorce his wife Catherine, it was due to the political interests of the papacy. Popes would routinely award such dispensations and annulments when it was in their political, financial, or strategic interests, but the pope could not alienate Catherine of Argon. Thomas Moore, who was active in abetting the persecution of Bible-believing Christians in England in the time of William Tyndale, remained loyal to the pope as Woolsey would always remain loyal to the king as the senior clergymen of the country and also the senior minister of government.

Henry VIII made himself head of the church instead of the pope, who in turn had made himself head of the church when God's Word teaches that Christ alone is the Head of the Church (Eph. 5:23). As the papacy is an antichrist doctrine, so is the British monarchy. It replaces a Roman pope with a royal one. Henry VIII who killed approximately 74,000 of his own subjects is an historical type of the Antichrist, and Woolsey was his false prophet. In fairness, however, we should point out that Reformers who were persecuted by Queen Mary arose after the time of Henry, and to a degree reformed the Church of England along more scriptural lines. Today, however, this Evangelical heritage of the Anglicans, exists only among Anglicans still adhering to their *Thirty-Nine Articles* in places such as Africa. It basically no longer exists in England itself. The Church of England has no place to go except back to Rome from which it never totally broke with. It will be part of the Antichrist system.

This is the leaven of Herod, and an unscriptural practice based on contra-scriptural doctrines seeking to unite that which never should be united except in Christ whose kingdom is not of this world (Jn. 18:36). In understanding the Antichrist, however, this worsening situation is becoming more sinister with a monarch of England as the official head of Christianity in the British Commonwealth wanting to unite all religions with a counterpart in a neo-paganized Archbishop of Canterbury. On one occasion Carey consecrated holy sites in a multireligious ritual with Hindus, Muslims, etc., saying, "We consecrate these sites as gifts according to whichever god you serve." Yet again, Carey, while paying homage to demon gods, was accepted by supposed Evangelicals as a brother in Christ. What we see presently happening in the religious climate in Great Britain is in every sense not the Holy Spirit working through the Word of God, but the spirit of antichrist working through the leaven of the Pharisees and Herod. The unfaithful church scarcely has a clue.

More Recent Examples

Whenever the leaven of Herod has been allowed to be propagated in the Church, be it in the papacy or in Calvin's Geneva, or Puritan Salem, Massachusetts, it has always wreaked spiritual havoc and violent cruelty. It is no coincidence that the modern promulgators of such error such as Calvinistic Reconstructionists, following the false teachings of Rousas J. Rushdoony, Gary North, David Chilton, etc., are also preterist in their eschatology, denying there will be an End Time Antichrist. Herod did not want people to know who he was or understand what he was doing. The same is no less true today.

The hyper-charismatic proponents of Dominion Theology advocating such perversions of Bible texts such as Latter Rain/Manchild doctrines and Kingdom Now Theology do the same, completely oblivious to the fact they are being manipulated by the spirit of antichrist to prepare the Church for ***the*** Antichrist. Followers of the Kansas City (False) Prophets have espoused the false belief that Christ will return ***to*** the Church in the Latter Rain before He returns ***for*** it. As ignorant as they may be, however, it is not the genuine Christ who will come before Jesus comes for His Bride. Again, such doctrines are the leaven of Herod.

What we must understand is that Herod the tetrarch, in pursuit of political objectives, attempted to harmonize the faith of the Jews based on the Word of God with the pagan pantheism and emperor worship of Imperial Rome. Antichrist will, of course, do the same as Antiochus IV attempted. But as with the Romans and with the Seleucids, unbelieving Israel will come to realize they have been betrayed and find themselves in a quagmire from which no one but their true Messiah can rescue them. This was, again, what Jesus meant by "the leaven of Herod."

His warnings, however, were not only or primarily to the Jews, but to Jewish believers in Himself, and therefore by incorporation, to the Church. His message remains the same: Beware of the leaven of Herod. Underneath it the subtlety of the spiritual seduction of the leaven of Herod is remarkable. We have witnessed it on the political right by those attempting to identify the Christian cause with politicians such as Billy Graham's endorsement of Richard Nixon, Jerry Falwell's endorsement of Ronald Reagan, and Pat Robertson's endorsement of George Bush. Once elected, all of these politicians engaged in policies that left Evangelicals feeling betrayed.

Equally notorious are those such as Jeremiah Wright and Jesse Jackson who have attempted to identify Christianity with the political left. Wright, the former pastor of Barack Obama, and who was financially supported by Obama, openly prayed, "God damn America!" Jesse Jackson, betraying his wife, diverted large sums of cash donations given to help the urban poor, to pay lavish hush money for a baby he fathered outside of wedlock. Yet contrary to the instructions of the apostle Paul, he was allowed to retain his credentials as a Christian minister. There are similar versions of pulpit politics in Northern Ireland particularly, but it always amounts to the same thing: the leaven of Herod.

Christians are commanded to pray for those in political leadership, but they have no biblical mandate to use the Christian ministry or the cause of Christ to endorse or campaign for any politician. They are entitled to their own views and opinions, but they are not entitled to equate those views and opinions with Christian dogma. The union of secular and spiritual leadership is the reserve of Christ alone. The Church should influence government with its moral principles, but should never engage in the Erastian practice of uniting church and state. The British House of Lords, having members who are bishops known as "lords spiritual" as opposed to "lords temporal," is, again, the leaven of Herod.

In the English-speaking world the history of this is something the founding fathers in America wished to avoid; that is, the establishment of a state church. Nonetheless there are those who have always tried to do so, sometimes with good intention. When the Antichrist arrives, however, the False Prophet will view them as useful idiots and make use of their good intentions by feeding them the leaven of Herod. The politicization of the Church is a satanic deception.

Chapter 10: The Antichrist & the Jews

For the Antichrist to be the Antichrist, he must deceive the Gentile nations, Israel, and the unfaithful church, or what we might call "Christendom." All of the above are to significant degrees already in the grasp of his deception, but we must again revert to John 5:43, *"If another comes in his own name, you will receive him."* He will in some way embody the other false messiahs that have sprung up in Jewish history beginning with Judas of Galilee mentioned in Acts 5.

Isaiah 8 predicts an avalanche of occult activity and false religious leaders of various descriptions that would come before the arrival of the Messiah. Both Acts 5 and Jewish history verify this is what took place before the First Coming of Christ. So, too, it will take place prior to His return. That is, there will be ***many*** antichrists and false teachers and false prophets who will lend credibility to these antichrists. It will be just the same as Rabbi Akiva was the harbinger of Bar Kochba in a demonic counterfeit and parody of the manner in which John the Baptist (*Yochannon HaMatbil*) was the harbinger of Christ coming in the spirit and power of Elijah. It is imperative to understand Rabbi Akiva in order to understand the False Prophet of Revelation 13—a religious leader who by demonic power will point people to a political leader, promising them life but giving them death. The False Prophet will therefore seek to mimic John the Baptist, Elijah, and possibly Elisha (who had the same spirit).

Following Bar Kochba there were multiple other false messiahs in the history of Judaism, all of which gained substantial levels of rabbinic support for their lies that some false messiah was the true one. Chief among these has been Shabbatai Zvi, Jacob Frank, and Menachem Schneerson, the late Lubavitch rabbi guru of the Chabad Movement. Shabbatai Zvi and Jacob Frank converted to Roman Catholicism and Islam. What was curious about Frank, however, was that he allowed his followers and devotees to believe he was the reincarnation of Shabbatai Zvi, returned to fulfill the things Shabbatai Zvi promised. We must understand that, as an imitation of Hindu ideas acquired by Babylonian rabbis and developed through Cabala and its chief work *The Zohar*, mystical Judaism teaches a kind of reincarnation. This of course is a demonic attempt to mimic the manner in which the spirit and character of Elijah was put onto Elisha and onto John the Baptist—but not in a reincarnational sense.

One of the counter-polemics by which the rabbis deal with the fact that even the Talmudic literature admits that all timing as to the Messiah's coming has already passed—and one way they seek to circumvent the clear teaching of Daniel 9—is to say that the Messiah comes in every generation. If that generation of Jews is not worthy, He will not bring the redemption; so indeed He may have come, and will come again. This is a satanically inspired attempt to mimic the reality that the Messiah in fact did come in the person of Jesus (Yeshua), and because of each mainly unworthy generation He must return again.

After the time of Jesus, many rabbis in the 1st-4th centuries A.D. began to actually parody the teachings of Jesus, particularly from the Beatitudes, wanting Judaism to become a sort of Christless Christianity. These mystical ideas adopted from Eastern religion, particularly Babylonian Gnosticism, were adopted by the Hassidic Movement. Following the failures of Shabbatai Zvi and Jacob Frank, Rabbinic Judaism became a very stoic religion based on Talmudic study in the Yeshiva where only the sons of affluent Jews could afford the luxury. The poor ordinary Jews dwelling in the Shtetls and ghettos of Eastern and central Europe were alienated from their religion by the hardships of trying to survive both economic adversity and endless pogroms, most of which were perpetrated by Roman Catholicism, Eastern Orthodoxy, and in some cases Lutheran Protestantism.

They Go Progressively Further Afield

This alienation of the disenfranchised led to the natural emergence of a figure known in Judaism as Bal Shem Tov, a charismatic mystic who adopted the cabalistic ideas borrowed from Babylonian Gnosticism that found their eventual home in Itsfat (also known as Safed) in the more remote mountains of upper Galilee. The Gnostic concept of demiurges was renovated in Jewish imagery where God became the "*En Soph*"—the one having no essence, only attributes or emanations (usually nine basic ones). Hence the theopomorphic man that God created in Genesis is displaced by an anthropomorphic god who has lost his identity which it is the task of mystical Jews through the practice of Cabala to help him regain. They do this by the capture of "holy sparks" (known as "*zum zums*")—bits of flames of fire of the divine presence. This more resembles post-Zarathustran fire veneration of the later Zoroastrians than the Shekinah pillar of fire found in the Torah, known as the "*Shalhevit Wah*" that first surfaces when passing through the bisected carcass of Abraham's covenant sacrifice in Genesis 15:17.

The Hassidic movement incorporated occult influences specifically forbidden by Torah, such as astrology and necromancy with prayers to dead rabbis as intercessors just as in the Roman Catholic prayers to the dead. What had been Gematria was now colored by numerology and embellished by folklore and anecdotes attributed to sages of old. More than this, it was outwardly celebratory, characterized by occult manifestations counterfeiting things truly spiritual. This was much the same as was evident in medieval Roman Catholicism or in the influx of New Age practices, including Kundalini Yoga, into the modern Charismatic Movement as witnessed in such deceptions as the Toronto Blessing and the counterfeit revivals of Pensacola and Lakeland, Florida.

It is important for the believer to recognize that the same deceptions which took place in a Rabbinic Judaism which rejected the true Messiah and then a Roman Catholicism that rejects the true Christ in favor of a Eucharistic one also now permeates most of the modern evangelical Charismatic Movement and much of Pentecostalism. This is not to deny or reject scriptural charismata—authentic manifestations of God's power, or a scripturally based practice of gifts of the Holy Spirit—but it is to say that through means of the occult Satan counterfeits these things not only outside of the Church but also inside just as he does with Hassidic Judaism.

The *zeitgeist* of the present age is very much New Age theosophy sharing the same origins in Eastern Gnostic Mysticism that exists in Hassidic Judaism. The spirit of antichrist always comes dressed as the *zeitgeist* or spirit of the age. Hence we visibly see not only the influx of New Age pseudo-spirituality into the Church, but a fascination by the secular world with the same things. Thus it is not a coincidence we see the popularity of a deluded form of Cabala in pop culture so much in vogue in Hollywood and with pop singers such as Madonna. It is all of the same antichrist spirit, preparing the way for the coming of Antichrist the same as the Holy Spirit is preparing for the coming of Jesus.

The Rise of the Rebbe

At this point enters Rabbi Menachem Schneerson the last rabbi of the Lubavitch sect of Hassidic Jews. The mystical theology of the Hassidic movement has the essence of its comprehensive origins with the teachings of a rabbi called Isaac Luria. But after the death of Bal Shem Tov, rival Hassidic sects began to claim that ***their*** rabbi—or rebbe—had the spirit of Bal Shem Tov known as the "*becht*." Hence there has been hatred and even violence between and among the various Hassidic sects which include Bobov, Setmar, Vishnitz, and Chabad.

In this mystical Judaism that was widely rejected by mainstream Orthodox Jewry at its inception, the rebbe is known as a "*Tsadik*" or "righteous one" who is able to go to God directly through the Torah while others must go to God through him in a system that oddly parodies the Roman papacy. Rebbes are selected through a form of dynasty where, if there is no son, the son-in-law receives the spirit of the *becht* and becomes the new rebbe.

The late Menachem Schneerson rarely left Brooklyn, never went to Israel, and had neither a son nor a son-in-law. Hence his followers have no means to communicate with God in the Hassidic sense because there is no heir, and the dynasty died with Schneerson. Schneerson was by biblical definition a false prophet who made predictions that never happened, such as the advent of the Messiah that was to take place by the time of the high Jewish holy days in 1991. Other antagonistic Hassidic sects denounced Schneerson as "crazy" and his followers as "fools." Confronted with the dilemma of no heir, his followers now claim he will rise from the dead, and they maintain a constant vigil at his grave. As Jacob Frank allowed his followers to believe he was the reincarnation of Shabbatai Zvi and the Messiah, so Schneerson allowed his followers to believe that he was the Messiah. Thus, with no one to follow him, he must arise from the dead.

The notion of a Jewish Messiah that will come and die, then rise from the dead, greatly aggravates other Orthodox Jews because of its obvious resemblance of the claims that the Father was in Jesus. This is central to understanding how the Antichrist will seek to deceive Israel. He will counterfeit the resurrection of Christ. Schneerson was but a shadow, and like all false messiahs a stooge of Satan, the arch-enemy of the Jewish people, of the human race, and of God Himself.

As the Hassidic Movement redefined Judaism with the claims of Bal Shem Tov, Judaism was also redefined as Aristotelian by Moses Maimonides (known as "Rambam"), whose works, *Mishnah Torah* and *Guide for the Perplexed*, Aritistotelianized Judaism—just as Islam had already been Aristotelianized and as Thomas Aquinas would Aristotelianize Roman

Catholicism. Yet like Bal Shem Tov, Rambam was at first popularly rejected by the rabbinic establishment.

Again, this is a satanic counterfeit of the rejection of Jesus by the Sanhedrin. It is Rambam more than any other who has most framed Jewish thought concerning messianic expectation. He strongly argued that the miraculous could be rationally explained on the basis of material science (much like Thomas Aquinas' claims about transubstantiation). He also posited that the Messiah would bring about a series of political changes that would benefit Israel and the Jews and, finally, that the Messiah would rebuild the Temple.

The Location of the Temple

For nearly twenty years I have been pointing to the dispute between two schools of archeological thought in modern Israel regarding the exact location of the First and Second Temples. If the school of thought following Dr. Dan Bahat is correct, the Temple stood nearly precisely on the present location of the Dome of the Rock, or Mosque of Omar, encrusted with the quotation from the Quran that "God has no son" and that Allah is neither begotten nor does he beget. The demonic image of a satanic face naturally embossed on the marble façade of the Mosque of Omar is an ugly and disturbing sight. The quotation from the Quran, however, denying the Father-Son relationship is the hallmark of Antichrist in John's Epistle (1 Jn. 2:22).

The rival position among archeologists is that of Dr. Asher Koffman which would place the Temple more than 300 feet north of the Dome on the present location of the Dome of the Spirits (more importantly known as "The Dome of the Tablets") in a direct line from the present East Gate of Jerusalem, which is constructed upon the Herodian stones of its probable predecessor. If Koffman is correct, or is believed to be correct, it is easily possible to reconstruct a Jewish temple next to the Mosque of Omar with a dividing barrier between the two. This will exactly match the prophecies of Ezekiel 42:20 and would explain the Tribulational Temple of Revelation 11 and the implied Temple of 2 Thessalonians 2.

A possible but not yet definite scenario may be that after attempting to counterfeit the millennial reign of Christ by temporarily improving global stability economically and strategically, the Antichrist will attempt to broker a peace in the Middle East by allowing the Temple to be rebuilt by constructing a barrier between the Jewish and Islamic areas, once more fitting the Ezekiel prophecy like a virtual glove.

We note also in Zechariah 11 that the prophecy of Judas has a double fulfillment in the *"man of sin"* (Zech. 11:17). There will be in Zechariah 11:17 an assassination of the Antichrist whose real god will be one of military power (Dan. 11:38). Revelation 13:12 foretells his counterfeit of the resurrection of Jesus. We are told in Daniel 9 once more that the Antichrist will make a seven year treaty with Israel before replaying the abominable deeds of Antiochus Epiphanes, placing an image of himself in the Temple.

There have already been abrogated peace treaties in the Middle East broken by Islam, most notably the Oslo Accords, The Camp David agreement has barely survived, and that only out of the economic and strategic necessities of Egypt and not by any virtue of goodwill. There may be other peace treaties in the Middle East, and Christians should not be consumed with rambunctious conclusions as to which treaty is the ultimate one. Just as Satan clouds the horizon by raising up many antichrists, so, too, he will cloud the horizon with many false peace deals in the Middle East. The sticking point of each will be the final status of Jerusalem necessitated by the prophecies of Jesus in Luke 21:24 and in Matthew 23:38-39. Jerusalem is where Satan received his biggest defeat and it is where he will receive his final one. He must try to displace the Jews from it. His final attempt will be a false treaty that will be broken.

Jewish Messianic Expectation

Meanwhile, from New York to Los Angeles, to Sydney and Melbourne, to London, Paris, Manchester, Antwerp, and to Jerusalem, the banners, billboards, and bumper stickers on the cars of observant Jews are more and more prevalent: "**We want Mashiach now!**" Be it Bar Kochba or Jacob Frank, be it Menachem Schneerson or Shabbatai Zvi, they will accept ***any*** Messiah except the true one. Yet for Israel the worst of all of them by far is still yet to come. For the remnant to survive, however, so, too, the ***best*** is yet to come—the return of the risen Messiah Yeshua who will no longer be rejected by His own.

For our purposes therefore in understanding how the Antichrist will be identified, it is imperative that we relate the ultra-Orthodox rabbinic promulgation of messianic expectation to efforts by nationalistic Israeli Orthodox Jews to rebuild the Temple. There are two yeshivas in Jerusalem dedicated to the study they deem necessary to re-inaugurate a Levitical priesthood with sacrifices, and for more than 10 years sponsored mitochondrial DNA testing has been pursued among Jews with Levitical names such as "Cohen," "Segal," "Levi," and "Levinson" in an actual attempt at reestablishing Aaronic pedigree for the purpose of the reintroduction of Temple sacrifices.

The link between moves to rebuild the Temple and reestablish a Levitical high priesthood, and the level of propagated hype to see the coming of the Messiah with a fervor not seen since Shabbatai Zvi and Jacob Frank, is to be found in the teaching of "The Rambam," by Moses Maimonides who redefined Judaism as an Aristotelian religion. He taught staunchly that the Messiah's appearance would need to be concurrent with the messianic reestablishment of temple worship requiring a reconstruction of the Temple. Thus for Satan to engineer the rise of Antichrist he must manage a contrived scenario meeting Orthodox Jewish and rabbinic expectations.

It was Maimonides who packaged Orthodox Judaism in its present form. Liberal and reformed Jews would not ascribe high degrees of authority to the "*Shulchan Aruch*" of Joseph Caro, the rabbi who constitutionally organized rabbinic law known as "*Halacha*," nor would non-Hassidic Ultra-Orthodox Jews place authoritative emphasis on mystical rabbis such as Baal Shem Tov, Isaac Luria, or Menachem Schneerson. But virtually all rabbis of every persuasion would give high accord to the teachings of Rambam. Thus Rambam's teaching on the Messiah and the Temple are factors the Antichrist will need to accommodate if he is indeed the Antichrist.

The climax of these things will not be the primary concern only of the Church, but will have a specific national implication for Israel and the Jews, and be almost focally concerned with Israel and the Jews after the faithful Church is raptured. These events will climax and transpire having their ultimate prophetic fulfillment with the Antichrist during the 70th week of Daniel's vision.

"The Broken Treaty"

> *"I will fix your boundary from the Red Sea to the sea of the Philistines, and from the wilderness to the River Euphrates; for I will deliver the inhabitants of the land into your hand, and you will*

> *drive them out before you. You shall make no covenant with them or with their gods.* (Ex. 23:31-32)

From times ancient God warned the Hebrews through their prophets against making alliances with Gentile nations. There were exceptions to this such as the friendship Israel had with the Phoenician King Hiram who assisted with the construction of the Temple, and the benevolence shown the Jews by the Medes and Persians (which is why the Hebrews were reluctant in the later Hasmonean Period to actively side with Alexander the Great against the Persians). Abraham was the father of ***many*** nations and God has used Gentile nations with a scripturally Christian ethos to bless national Israel, such as with the Balfour Declaration of the 19th century and the USA in the 20th and 21st centuries (although politicians aligned with international oil concerns with vested interests in placating oil-producing Muslim states are attempting to uncouple the USA from Israel).

In any event, such alliances, although having strategic implications, concern nations who worshiped the Hebrew God. Israel was repeatedly warned to avoid alliances with other Gentile nations. We must remember that Protestant Britain and Europe, and Catholic Europe, are not scripturally Christian, but neo-pagan and post-Judeo-Christian apart from the faithful remnant of the true Church.

In the modern age of apostasy, even what had formally been considered to be Evangelical is no longer scripturally Evangelical. In the American Bible Belt there is a cultural Evangelicalism. In Northern Ireland there is a political Evangelicalism. And in post-Colonial Africa there is a tribal Evangelicalism. Within the Anglican community of Great Britain, "Evangelical" simply means not Anglo-Catholic and not liberal; it does not necessarily mean "born-again." In Germanic Europe "Evangelical" simply means some form of Lutheran as opposed to some form of a Calvinistic Reformed tradition. There are even curious movements of people claiming to be Evangelical Catholics simultaneously believing two different gospels, one based on regeneration and justification by faith and repentance, and the other *Ex Opere Operato* sacramentalism. There has also been the increasingly vocal emergence of anti-Zionist Evangelicals such as Rick Godwin in the USA and John Stott in Great Britain. Such men teach a plethora of other doctrinal errors, but one of the false doctrines taught by false teachers such as John Stott is Replacement Theology and Christian anti-Zionism.

Thus Israel's capacity to find friends among Gentile nations and peoples is limited and has dissipated with the exception of the true Church who remains faithful to Christ on the basis of Scripture. Indeed the anti-Zionist preachers such as Rick Godwin and John Stott teach a host of other serious doctrinal errors. Stott even denies that the Church can teach eternal conscious damnation of those rejecting Christ, to say nothing of his antichrist beliefs as an Anglican, making a British monarch the "head of the church." (This is a pure replacement of a papal antichrist with a royal one and is indeed a height of danger as is noted in the section of this book addressing the leaven of Herod.)

In the days of King Hezekiah the king was being pressed in very difficult strategic and political circumstances to turn to pagan Egypt for help from the west against a strategic threat from Assyria to the east. Assyria was already invading Israel to the north and was going to take the ten northern tribes into captivity. Isaiah denounced those who were proceeding to Egypt, seeking shelter from Pharaoh without a divine green light to do so (Is. 30:1-3; 31:1-3). Pharaoh is a strongly recognized type of antichrist being a deified human and claiming divine sonship.

Fortunately Isaiah was able to persuade Hezekiah not to enter into an alliance with the antichrist figure of Pharaoh. Later, however, this would not be the case as we shall see when the Jews entered into an agreement with Pompeii and with Imperial Rome, again looking for a protection and a prosperity that only amounted to a false peace when they were double-crossed. The prophet Daniel tells us that when Israel is again placed in what will eventually become the most precarious position in its history, ancient or modern, they will make an ungodly alliance. Daniel 11:23, as we shall later see, explains that this will be in the character not simply of Pompeii, but even more in the character of Antiochus Epiphanes.

The initial interest of Antiochus IV had more to do with plundering the Temple for its wealth. (Like the Antichrist and like Judas, he is consumed by the love of money.) It was at the behest of some of the Jews themselves, however, that Antiochus became involved in their internal affairs when his assistance was sought in the Tobiad Conflict during the tenure of Onias III as high priest, who had royal and political ambitions despite being a Levite. We again see a figure attempting to unite theocratic power and political power by crossing the divide between the line of David and the line of Aaron, and between the tribe of Levi and the tribe of Judah. It would be John Hyricanus in the later Hasmonean Period who would most achieve this. But with Onias III we see another example of there being more than one Antichrist at the same time as there will be in the Last Days; ***many*** false Christs will arise. The issue then was of which of these was Daniel prophesying? So, too, in these Last Days the issue will be which of the many antichrists is the little horn?

We again point to the conflict with the Tobiads and the venture into Egypt where Cleopatra was married to Ptolemy in a north-south conflict. Thus we reiterate our encouragement to the readers to obtain copies of 1 & 2 Maccabees as non-canonical but scripturally important historical material that will relate to the identification of the Antichrist. Ultimately, however, it was two figures to whom the Lord was pointing us through Daniel. The second is the ultimate Antichrist as the antitype and the first was Antiochus Epiphanes, his type.

> *"Then after the sixty-two weeks the Messiah will be cut off and have nothing, and the people of the prince who is to come will destroy the city and the sanctuary. And its end will come with a flood; even to the end there will be war; desolations are determined. "And he will make a firm covenant with the many for one week, but in the middle of the week he will put a stop to sacrifice and grain offering; and on the wing of abominations will come one who makes desolate, even until a complete destruction, one that is decreed, is poured out on the one who makes desolate."* (Dan. 9:26-27)

We see that the Antichrist will make a firm covenant for seven years and then he will break it. What transpired with Rome (whom this chapter identifies with "*the people of the prince who is to come*") will take place again on a grander scale than anything that occurred with ancient Rome or Pompeii. This will be the Antichrist.

It is clear from both Daniel and Revelation that the last seven years of history by the lunar calendar are divided into two halves, and much has been argued if the entire seven years is the Great Tribulation or only the second half. It is clear, however, that the second half is far worse than the first when the Antichrist feigns a pretended effort to introduce his substitute for the millennial reign of Christ in the form of a false peace. (For the purposes of this book we address the subject of the Tribulation only relative to the goal of understanding how the ultimate Antichrist will be identified.) What is important to remember, however, is that the mid-Tribulational Rapture position in the classical sense is not possible in that we cannot know the day of Christ's return, but we would be able to do so by commencing from the counting of the treaty being inaugurated or signed. This again, however, approaches the limits of the purpose of this book, although it is certainly a vital subject warranting serious and prayerful consideration elsewhere.

Secondly, we must remember that deception increases at this time. As with Antiochus in Daniel 11:23, deception defines and characterizes the entire modus operandi of the Antichrist. Just as there will be many antichrists and many false prophets preceding and surrounding the emergence of the final, ultimate Two Beasts, so also there will be multiple treaties in the Middle East supposedly designed to initiate peace which will prove false. We have seen a foreshadowing example of this already in the Oslo Accords brokered by the USA and proposed by Norway supposedly ending conflict between Israel and Palestinian Muslims. With the rise of Hamas and the fact that the Palestinian Authority with its Al Aqsa Brigade never kept the treaty to begin with, it proved to be a false peace.

The "Many" Treaties

With the precarious state of Egypt and Jordan, the Camp David Accords and Israel's treaty with Jordan likewise tread on the thinnest of ice. There may additionally be other treaties the Islamic world will not keep. Again, we must understand that Islam is inherently an antichrist religion, and as with anything to do with Antichrist, it operates by the rules of deception. Islam has a doctrine of "*taqwid*" or "permissible lying" which is not viewed as a lie in the Muslim religion but rather as military disinformation in the Jihad. We already see this visibly today despite the fact that Western politicians lie to us, propagating to us the myth that Islam is a religion of peace and tolerance and that most Muslims are not extreme. Even in an Islamic country supposedly friendly to the West such as Egypt, more than 80% of Muslims believe in the stoning of people for adultery and more than 70% believe Muslims who convert to another religion should be executed. Polls showed that two-thirds of Muslims believed the September 11th attacks against the United States to be justified.

When Islamic propagandists speak to the West they use the English word "peace," but when speaking Arabic they use the term "*hudna*," which means a temporary cease fire until they can get the strategic advantage to attack the infidel. Since their religion teaches permissible lying as military disinformation in the Jihad, there is no reasonable way in which reasonable people can believe anything fundamentalist Muslims say. And the proportion of Muslims subscribing to fundamentalist interpretations of their religion is demonstrably much higher than the false reports churned out by the propaganda mills of the BBC, CNN, network news, liberal academics, and Western governments in bed with oil companies and the House of Saud, or politicians such as former American Presidents Carter, Clinton, and Bush, whose projects, libraries, etc., are funded with Muslim oil money .

The willingness of the media and governments knowing the truth about fundamentalist Islam to lie to their own citizens and to continue to put their own citizens and countries at risk stinks of the very kind of betrayal that the Antichrist will eventually perpetrate against a desperate Israel. The spirit driving this propaganda sympathetic to Islam today is in every sense the spirit of antichrist. Once more, the way is being prepared.

We are reminded that a hundred years before the Reformation, when the Catholic church invited the evangelical preacher John Huss from Prague to Lake Constance for a theological disputation, the Catholic church promised him safe passage only to burn him alive, proudly proclaiming that Holy Mother the Church is not obligated to keep her word to those whom she declares heretics.

The role of the Vatican in the rise to power of modern antichrists such as Adolph Hitler and Benito Mussolini are again indicative of the work of the spirit of antichrist. This includes both the concordat made by the Bavarian Roman Catholic bishops with the Nazis guided by the pro-Nazi Primate Michael Schmauss whom Pope John XXIII would reward by promoting him to cardinal, and the Lateran Treaty and concordats made between Mussolini and the pope. Indeed, at the behest of Pope Pius XXII, Mussolini arrested Italian Evangelicals and, after invading Ethiopia, drove out Evangelical missionaries. Now the same Vatican that saw Pope John Paul II kiss the *Quran* in an act of religious reverence is seeking common ground with Islam based on a common theology of Fatima (which is also the name of Mohammed's daughter), the veneration of Mary. Absurdly Islam identifies Mary the mother of Jesus with Mary the sister of Moses born 1,300 years before Mary. But such ludicrous dogma matters neither to Islam nor the Vatican. Indeed, the pope kisses a book that says "God has no son" just as an American President placed it in the White House to honor Islam.

Now, however, the Vatican has published its agenda, wanting to play a central role in brokering a Middle East peace deal between the Israelis and the Muslims. The spirit of antichrist is well at work in both the political and religious realms. It was the Vatican that first called for the internationalization of Jerusalem. And it was George W. Bush who first called for a second Palestinian Arab state in addition to the one already demographically and geographically, howbeit not politically, in Jordan. Again, from both a political and religious perspective, Israel is in the crosshairs. Yet the unfaithful church and the naïve and undiscerning strangely regarded both Pope John Paul II and George W. Bush to be Bible-believing Christians. By their actions, however, both have already embraced the *pseudologon* of the *Quran* which by New Testament definition is, like *The Book of Mormon* or the papal encyclicals, the word of Antichrist, not the Word of God.

As Israel was misled by her own political and religious leaders in the ancient world into making such a treaty producing a false peace, modern Israeli politicians and the Talmudically deceived rabbis will mislead Israel again. The question becomes which of these multiple false treaties bringing only a false peace will be the one of which Daniel 9:27 speaks. Given the fact that there will be ***multiple*** treaties, ***many*** Christs, and ***many*** false prophets obscuring the identity of the final ones, we understand Satan's strategy of deception. It is not a case of will the real Antichrist please stand up; they are ***all*** real antichrists. It is more a question of the Holy Spirit showing the faithful Church which one is unique. And that one who is unique will, up to a certain point, be the least obvious.

Although there will be earlier indications, the act of breaking the covenant with Israel and entering the Holy of Holies, while not synonymous actions, will be counterpart actions. When this takes place, it will be apparent to others outside of the faithful Church who the Antichrist is as it will become apparent to the Jews, but it will be too late. The faithful Church, however, will already be so enlightened by the Holy Spirit through the Scripture that it alone will be prepared.

Chapter 11: The Recapitulation of Hanukkah & the Nativity

Introduction

In popular religious culture the Nativity and Hanukkah are largely related because they occur the same time of year. Hanukkah as celebrated by Jesus in John 10 commences on the 25th of the lunar month of Kislev from the Jewish calendar. This basically corresponds to Christmas, the 25th of December, which in the Western world is when the Nativity is observed. In Eastern Christendom the Nativity is celebrated on either the 6th or 7th of January. This is the day that Western Christendom calls "The Epiphany." These Christian observances are, in part, of pagan origin revolving around the Roman feast of Saturnalia and have nothing to do with the actual birth date of Jesus historically. Hanukkah, of course, is well-established in the New Testament, visible in the observance by Christ Himself in John's Gospel—what many Bible translations call "The Feast of Dedication."

Biblically and theologically, however, Hanukkah and the Nativity (not to be confused with Christmas) are two historical events that are not linked by the coincidence of calendric observance but by theological doctrine. Both events were foretold by the prophet Daniel in some detail. Both events involved angelic revelation given specifically by the angel Gabriel. Both events were important to the divine plan of redemption generally, and for the salvation of Israel particularly, and both events are paramount in understanding how to identify the Antichrist. The fact that in popular culture the Nativity is commemorated in proximity to Hanukkah is insignificant in and of itself. That the Book of Daniel links the two events, however, is highly significant.

Because of the arch significance of Antiochus Epiphanes as a type of the Antichrist to the point where the Antichrist will recapitulate his actions with an image of the Beast as prophesied by Daniel and Jesus, it is problematically important that we first develop the historical background from the Book of Daniel and the apocryphal history leading up to and including the saga of Antiochus IV.

Beginning in Daniel 11 up until verse 36 we have a partial historical fulfillment in Antiochus including the epoch of the Maccabees. What the Antichrist will do is replay the actions of Antiochus up to verse 36 but then go beyond it and fulfill the rest that, to date, has not had ***any*** historical fulfillment. This situation is historically and theologically unique because the events are prophesied within the canon of Scripture in Daniel, but the recorded fulfillment is found in non-canonical apocryphal history. Yet Jesus lends credence to that extra-biblical history by celebrating Hanukkah Himself in John 10. Old Testament apocryphal books such as 1 & 2 Maccabees and 1 & 2 Enoch are scripturally important history and literature although they are not Scripture and, hence, not a basis for doctrine in and of themselves. Something is foretold in Scripture in the Old Testament and its historical fulfillment is acknowledged by Christ Himself no less in the New Testament. But we must look to what is technically a non-canonical source to understand the fulfillment.

This is not, however, unique in the study of eschatology. The events of A.D. 70 prophesied by Jesus and Daniel and alluded to in the epistle to the Hebrews, as well as having doubly referenced Old Testament prophecies of the destruction of the First Temple (which transpired on the same day of the year by the Hebrew calendar), likewise have the record of their fulfillment ***outside*** the canon of Scripture. To see the events foretold by Jesus in the Olivet Discourse that were fulfilled in A.D. 70 in the destruction of the Second Temple by Titus, we must look to historical accounts found in Josephus and later citations by Eusebius. It is a case where the prophecies are canonical but the record of their fulfillment is not; so, too, with the advent of the Antichrist. The prophecies of the Antichrist and False Prophet are indeed contained in the pages of Scripture, but their fulfillment obviously will not be found there.

While we cannot base doctrine on the apocryphal literature, it is plain that the events prophesied in Scripture in the Book of Daniel and affirmed by Jesus in John 10 render Antiochus as a singularly special type of the Antichrist. He is unlike the others in that he is a canonical figure by virtue of Daniel's prophecies of him, Jesus' reference to him, and his actions in Matthew 24:15. But he is a canonical figure not found in canon except predictively and by post-facto reference. Jesus and Paul in 2 Thessalonians also, without naming Antiochus, leave no doubt that the Antichrist will operate in his character.

Again, in order to properly understand how this diabolical and complex figure prefigures the Antichrist, we must devote ample space to the circumstances that produced him, for these too foreshadow the circumstances that will produce the final Antichrist who will likewise place an abomination of desolation in the Temple.

Hanukkah

"Hanukkah" derives from the Hebrew term "*chanukkat*" meaning "dedication" or "rededication." There are four aspects of Hanukkah: The first is the "traditional" one which is what most people are familiar with. However, the most important are the "historical," the "messianic," and the "eschatological" meanings.

- The "***historical***" aspect of Hanukkah concerns what happened in the time of the Maccabees, about 160 years before Jesus;
- The "***messianic***" implication of Hanukkah is revealed in John 10 when Jesus celebrated the feast;
- The "***eschatological***" view observes how these things will be recapitulated or replayed in the Last Days, heralding the return of Christ.

The main focus is on the historical—"what happened"; the messianic—"how it was fulfilled in Jesus"; and the eschatological —"what it will mean for His return."

The Traditional Aspect

Most of the traditions associated with Hanukkah originated not in the ancient world, but in the Middle Ages. Even the words of the songs associated with the feast, such as the most famous song, "*Ma'oz tzur y'shuati*," derive from the Hebrew of the Middle Ages, not biblical Hebrew or modern Hebrew.

Hanukkah tradition says that the oil burned for eight days. There was enough oil in the lamp in the menorah in the Temple for only one day, but it burned for eight. Again, there is no historical record of this in the book of 1 Maccabees or 2 Maccabees and certainly nothing in Scripture; it was developed later. That is not to say it is not true; it may have happened, but it is never recorded in history. It was not significantly mentioned by Josephus in *Antiquities.* Much of what is focused on today was not the focus or emphasis of *Antiquities*—what is universally accepted as a confirming extra-biblical historical source.

Hanukkah is the Jewish Feast of Light and the Jewish Feast of Miracles. The miracle was seen not in that the lamp burned eight days, but in that God gave them this incredible victory over an all-powerful enemy. And the light, of course, was when they rededicated the Temple and were able to again light the menorah within it. In the *Sitz im Leben* background and setting of John 10, these themes of festal light and the miraculous both come into play in the teaching of Jesus about Hanukkah. In John 10 the miracles are referred to as "*the works*" that did not prevent the opponents of Jesus from wanting to kill Him (Jn. 10:25, 37-38). Likewise, from the 1st chapter of John's Gospel, Jesus is portrayed as "*the true Light*" (Jn. 1:9), and the personification of the light in Jesus reached its climax at Hanukkah in John 10. We see here that although Jesus condemned a legalistic observance of extra-biblical tradition, He incorporated the nuances of the religious culture of His day (such as of Hanukkah) into His message and ministry.

> *Your word is a lamp to my feet light*
> *And a light to my path.* (Ps. 119:105)

The menorah burning in the Temple represented the Word of God to the Hebrews. But the windows of the Temple were unique. Normally, windows were built wide on the outside and shaped going narrow into the inside in order to focus light inside the building. But the shape of the Temple where the menorah stood would be wide on the outside and then, to capture as much light as possible from the menorah, focused narrowly so it would shine out over what today is called the "Millo" and extend from the Temple Mount onto the City of David below. Hence the idea built into the architecture of the Temple was that the light of Yahweh—the light of His Word—would come from the Temple. The architecture of the Temple illustrated that the Law would go forth from Zion and it would shine out. When the Temple was rededicated this was the idea, that now they could re-illuminate the menorah.

Hanukkah is commemorated by Jewish children with a spinning top called the "*dreidel*"—a Yiddish word based on the Hebrew word "*tsvivon*"—"to spin," and there is an acronym on it, "*Nes, Gadol, Hya, Po*"—"A Great Miracle happened here."

Daniel is the only Book of the Bible containing all three original languages: Aramaic (or Chaldee), Hebrew, and Greek. It has Greek words for certain things like musical instruments and so forth that would have most likely been brought there by Macedonian mercenaries. The portions of Daniel that focus on the prophetic purposes of God specifically for the Jews are in Hebrew. The portions of Daniel focused on the prophetic purposes of God for Israel relative to the nations, are in the *lingua franca* of the time, which was Chaldee (Aramaic). It is in Daniel that the rise of Antiochus IV and his demise are foretold, but it is fulfilled and recorded only in history and not in Scripture itself apart from the affirmation of it from Christ in John 10.

The same will be true concerning the Antichrist. He is prophesied and described in the Book of Daniel and in other Scripture including the Olivet Discourse and the Book of Revelation referring back to Daniel, but the fulfillment of the prophecies concerning the Antichrist who was foreshadowed by Antiochus IV will likewise take place in history and not in a scriptural record. The faithful Hebrews who followed the Maccabees and rejected the traitors in their own ranks understood what was to come, who was to come, and what to do about it from something foretold. But we know that it happened from Hasmonean history only after the fact, and by the New Testament affirmation of Jesus. So, too, faithful believers are told in Scripture what is to come, who is to come, and what to do about it. We will need to recognize these events and the Antichrist from what Daniel and other Scripture based on Daniel tell us. Daniel 11 compares those who will do this to the Maccabees and their followers (Dan. 11:33-35).

The Jewish Expectation

It is important to understand that the Jews believed that the Messiah would reveal Himself as Messiah at Hanukkah and they expected a messianic redeemer who would come in the character of the Maccabees, driving out the Romans as the Maccabees had the Greeks. The defiled yet consecrated stones of the original altar were disassembled and stacked in Solomon's Portico. Because they were sanctified they could not be disposed of, but because they were rendered impure with swine blood by the pagan sacrifice of Antiochus, they could not be used, the belief being the Messiah would tell them what to do with the stones. It may have been these stones that were picked up to cast out Jesus in an effort to kill Him when He pronounced Himself divine (Jn. 10:31-33).

In understanding the Antichrist from the point of view of the messianic expectations of the Jews, we must understand what was transpiring in John 10. It was not in Jerusalem where people witnessed the miracles of Jesus at the Feast of Miracles that people believed in Him, but rather in the wilderness to where He fled when His opponents tried to kill Him. The text tells us He went to where John the Baptist had preached, and although John did no miracle, many believed in Jesus there (Jn. 10:40-42). *"So faith comes from hearing, and hearing by the word of Christ"* (Rom. 10:17). With signs and wonders relegated to the status of the confirmatory, "these signs follow" (Mk. 16:20).

While Jesus lamented the fact that people did not believe Him after seeing the works, the Hanukkah narrative of John 10 shows the folly of the modern Vineyard Movement and others to postulate falsely that signs and wonders are the key to people believing and to spiritual awakening. The miracles of Jesus did not prevent His rejection. While we affirm the validity of signs and wonders understood and practiced biblically, today the spirit of antichrist is at work suggesting, contrary to the New Testament teaching, that faith comes not by hearing but by seeing. At His trial, Jesus in fact refused to put on a show for Herod, even though to do so would have likely caused Herod to spare His life (Lk. 23:8-9). The Antichrist and False Prophet, however, will indeed embark on a "give the people what they want" performance and produce acts which may be supernatural, but as with Pharaoh's magicians will actually be achieved by demonic power.

The Antichrist will also come as the political redeemer who most Jews expected Jesus to be, not realizing His purpose in His First Coming; that purpose will be achieved in His Second Coming. The Antichrist will be the kind of messiah figure that the Jews wanted Jesus to be at Hanukkah.

Unlike Jesus standing before Herod (as with all the Herodians, a type of the Antichrist), the Antichrist and False Prophet will among other things understand that Jews seek a sign (1 Co. 1:22), and they will see to it that they get it even though their teaching will not be consistent with the meaning or the spirit of the Torah. A talmudically corrupted Judaism will believe them anyway, and will continue believing them until they realize they have been double-crossed and betrayed.

Another figure in the Hanukkah narrative is the Jewish collaborator with the pagan Syro-Phoenicians named Menelaus. Menelaus was an agent of Antiochus and attempted to marshal Jews into supporting and accepting Antiochus. Epiphanes IV had progressively corrupted the Jews with religious syncretism, political connivance, and progressive legal restrictions on Torah and the worship of Yahweh as prescribed in Torah, as well as by the propagation of a decadent Hellenistic culture. As is common elsewhere (such as the relationship between Bar Kochba and Rabbi Akiva), we see a type of the False Prophet pointing people to the beastly monarch who will set up an image of himself in the Temple.

While not canonical, faithful believers should be encouraged to read the two books of Maccabees in preparation for events to come. Unless we understand the past, we have little prospect of understanding the future. Many Jews were taken in by Antiochus with the help of Menelaus and others and only realized their betrayal when the situation was too far gone to do anything. This will happen again both to Israel and the Jews, but also in much of the Church when the Antichrist arises.

The Rise and Fall of Empires

When reading the Book of Daniel, it is important that we remember in what way the Last Days are like the days of Daniel. The Jews had been terrified of Assyria as the wicked empire who took the ten northern tribes into Captivity and were the cruelest and most powerful of pagan entities. No one imagined that Assyria would one day implode. Once it did, however, there was a false sense of peace lasting a very short time. Israel and the known world were now confronted with the meteoric rise of Babylon, which proved far worse than Assyria, having ancient roots spiritually and culturally dating back to the Tower of Babel.

As the Hebrew Prophets foretold, however, Babylon also collapsed almost overnight in the crushing conflict with Media-Persia. And as Daniel prophesied, Media-Persia rose in its place. The Persians aligned with the Medes and, later known as the Parthians, continued a generally friendly relationship with the Jews. This stretched from the days of Ezra, Nehemiah, Daniel, Queen Esther, and Mordecai virtually until the 20th century and the fall of the Shah of Iran in 1979 when the demonic principality seen by Daniel in the vision of chapter 10 assumed control of modern Iran as Daniel prophesied. The Shah claimed to be a descendant of the Peacock Throne of Cyrus the Great ("*Kowresh*"), whom Isaiah prophesied about twice (Is. 44:28; 45:13), even predicting his name 200 years prior to his birth. The culture and language of the Persians was different from that of the Arabs, the Persians being Aryans and monotheistic Zoroastrian Indo-Europeans who had a long history of being influenced positively by the Jews.

The Magi, who came to find Jesus after His birth, were Mede chaplains to the kings of Persia. That was the origin of the Magi. And because of the monotheistic influences they received from Zoroaster and from the Jews in the Captivity (who influenced Nebuchadnezzar), they journeyed to see Jesus. This link always existed with the Persians and the Jews and lasts until the Last Days.

The Socratic Greeks in the West had the most light where monotheism was concerned, but in the East it was the Zoroastrians who had the most light when it came to monotheism. The Socratic Greeks were in the West much later, but the Persians—Zoroastrian Persians—had the most light. As Zoroastrianism has evolved over the centuries with fire veneration and so forth it has since developed into a system of beliefs quite removed from its origins. However, the destruction of Babylon by the Persian King Cyrus foreshadows the destruction of Babylon the Great and the kingdom of Antichrist by Jesus with Cyrus arguably being the most important Gentile type of Christ in the Old Testament.

We read of this parallel in Isaiah 44:28-45:4 where Cyrus is called "the shepherd of Yahweh" with the definite possessive article as is Christ in Psalm 23, and in the Hanukkah chapter of John 10 in the New Testament. Like Christ, it is prophesied by Isaiah that Cyrus will do the will of Yahweh, not his own, and will restore Jerusalem as Israel's messiah. Strikingly, Cyrus is called "the Messiah of Yahweh" with the definite possessive article, "His anointed one, who rules by the right hand of Yahweh" (Is. 45:1) and is given all dominion and power over the nations, and opens and no one closes, and who ultimately becomes the agent of blessing and salvation to Israel and the Jews.

Just as Cyrus toppled Babylon and re-established Israel with Jerusalem as its capitol following the destruction of the First Temple and desecration by Babylon, so Christ will do likewise for Israel with the destruction of Babylon the Great in the Book of Revelation. In the Last Days, however, Satan manages to turn Persia, the traditional friend of the Jews, into Islamic Iran, Israel's most dangerous enemy. Yet the Hanukkah comparisons of Jesus as the Good Shepherd in John 10 to the description of Cyrus as the good shepherd of Yahweh in Isaiah are astounding. In His return, Christ will demolish Babylon but establish the millennial Kingdom with Jerusalem as its capitol being the substance of what Cyrus foreshadowed.

The Rise and Fall of Greece

The Persian Empire, however, did not last long due to military conflict with Greece, in which the conqueror Alexander the Great ultimately prevailed. Yet Alexander the Great himself did not survive for long. After reaching the desert of Balochistan and conquering most of the known world, he suddenly died at the age of 36. His empire fragmented exactly along the lines of what Daniel prophesied and was divided among four of his generals. The two most important of these were Seleuces—who obtained domain of Syria, Lebanon, Galilee, and central Israel, and Ptolemais—who received the domain of Egypt and southern Israel. These two are the most biblically and historically important.

The Seleucids were Syro-Phoenician Greeks who lived in that area of Phoenicia in modern Lebanon up to the area of Aleppo in Syria and down to the port cities of Tyre and Sidon in southern Lebanon bordering on Galilee. Luke was a Syro-Phoenician who converted to Judaism, and it is in this area where the last of the Herodian kings would reign as Jewish rulers acting as Roman surrogates. Antiochus Epiphanes is one of the most important types of the Antichrist. Coming from the line of Seleuces called the dynasty of Antiochus, he was Antiochus IV known as Antiochus Epiphanes. His Greek-speaking Jewish opponents would ridicule him by referring to him as "*Epimanus*," meaning "the mad one."

This historical situation existed comprising the kings of the North and the kings of the South. Assyria tumbles, followed by Babylon, and Babylon's demise is followed by the ascent of Media-Persia. Once Persia declined, a united Greece became the superpower until the rise of Rome. By New Testament times the Persians, as a regional power, had a partial resurrection known as the Parthians. They successfully resisted the Romans for 300 years, a fete only achieved by the Celts in Scotland, Cornwall, and Wales.

With the death of Alexander a chaotic power vacuum prevailed in most of the known world out of which arose Rome first as a republic and then as an imperial dictatorship. But in the middle of all of this the Jews returned to their land from the Persian Empire after the fall of Babylon, yet maintained a large Diaspora from Rome to Asia Minor to Parthia and as far south as Egypt. This same scenario reoccurs eschatologically with a rapid series of the rise and fall of world empires in which Israel is reborn as a nation and a re-confederated Roman Empire once more takes shape.

The European Union (beginning as the Common Market) and the re-establishment of the state of Israel were concurrent in the chaos following two world wars requiring a redrawing of maps both in Europe and the Middle East. Within a short period of time the collapse of the British, French, and Soviet empires took place as the Jews once more returned to their ancient scriptural homeland.

From the and 2nd century B.C. through the 1st century A.D. a list of antichrist figures surfaces, teaching about the one who is to come. The most important of these, however, was by far Antiochus Epiphanes.

Antiochus IV as a Type of Antichrist

The Hasmonean Period occurred between the time of the Maccabees and Pompeii, the Hasmoneans being the descendants of the Maccabees. It was a prosperous period, a strategic expansion with the rising nationalist expectation of a messianic restoration of the throne of David. Although in many respects a period of theological decline, despite the conversion of the Nabataeans to Judaism, much of the stage was set for the coming of Jesus during this Hasmonean Period. Morally and doctrinally the Hasmoneans began well as the heirs of the Maccabees, but degenerated theologically and politically, ending quite badly, ultimately leading to a betrayal and takeover by the Roman Empire.

From the Seleucid period, Antiochus IV had an agenda to utilize culture and religion as the means to gaining political control. As we are aware, the Antichrist will in effect do the same thing. In accordance with the iron and clay prophecies of Daniel he will attempt to engineer a multi-cultural, multi-faith society and political apparatus in the character of Antiochus. Other figures had with some success pursued similar paths prior to Antiochus, but concerning the Jews none had remotely approached his level of success as is recorded in Daniel 11 up until verse 36. The Antichrist will again parody the deeds of Antiochus, and exceed him, venturing beyond verse 36 into a territory that is the reserve of Satan alone. Just as Old Testament shadows of Christ typify the Messiah only up to a limited point, so, too, shadows of Antichrist typify him only up to a certain point. No type corresponds to its antitype in every detail.

We note, however, the remarkable mention that Jordan will somehow be spared from Antichrist's domain, specifically Moab, Edom, and Amman which Israel may invade at a previous point.

> *"He will also enter the Beautiful Land, and many countries will fall; but these will be rescued out of his hand: Edom, Moab and the foremost of the sons of Ammon.* (Dan. 11:41)

This curious prophecy is usually explained by the belief that a remnant of Jews will escape to the Petra region in Ezekiel 16 (just as the Jewish believers escaped to Pella, now called "Jaresh," in A.D. 70). Invasions of Israel traditionally come from the north, not from the east. This mitigates against the notion of a purely Muslim Antichrist as Jordan is an Islamic-Arab land.

Antiochus Hellenized the Jewish culture. He took the popular culture of the world and imposed it on God's people who compromised with it. They acquiesced to the designs of Antiochus progressively until reaching a point when his agenda became unstoppable. The Antichrist will operate in the same character just as the spirit of antichrist has always operated in this character.

The End Result of Compromise

The legacy of events occurring in the history of the Church reflect what transpired during this period about which Daniel prophesies; this is the Intertestamental Period.

In the Greek world (as in the modern Western world) homosexuality and bisexuality were culturally endemic. Such practices and lifestyles were routinely accepted as sexually and socially normative behavior. In some cases the sexual use of children was acceptable and various expressions of sexual perversion were widespread and conventional, much of it coming from the Isle of Lesbos.

In Greek popular entertainment there was a mixture of pagan religious philosophy incorporated into the presentations. The moral issues to Jews was not of necessity the sports themselves, but the Greek view of the sports activities as even in the primordial Olympics it was lewd and not infrequently violent. Contests took place with athletes competing publicly naked not in a mere biological sense, but with the connotation of sexual exhibitionism that dovetailed with temple prostitution and orgiastic worship in pagan Greek religions. Later adopted by the Romans, violent gladiatorial performances originating in Corinth became popular entertainment for the enthused patrons.

These were the cultural elements of the Greek world which Antiochus wanted everyone in his domain to accept, wishing to Hellenize all culture and season all moral thought with Greek philosophy and paganism, which was often hedonistic. His aims for doing this were in large part political. It would be easier to preserve his domain as a Greek king if all of his subjects were culturally Greek. Unfortunately, many Jews were drawn of their own volition into the schemes of Antiochus IV, resulting in negative ramifications for Jewish society. Others, however, passively accepted it with the end result that laws were surreptitiously passed step by step outlawing Jewish beliefs and practices. Eventually circumcision, "*Kashrut*" (dietary law), and the reading of Torah were outlawed, leading to the development of *Haftorah* where the Jews attempted to find something in the prophets corresponding in theme to what otherwise would have been the Torah portion of the week in the annual *Lection*.

This trend gained such momentum thanks to both Jews who willingly bought into the plans of Antiochus and those who simply compromised with it until the Levitical theocracy was itself banned. These priests had been the Zadokites, the righteous hero clergy in the Book of Ezekiel (Eze. 44:1, 48:1). But after the Hasmonean Period the Zadokites became known as the Sadducees, the theological liberals of the day who denied the angelic, the supernatural, and the Resurrection.

In order to understand this in modern terms we might recall the reflection of a British Prime Minister who said, "In order for wicked men to triumph, good men must merely remain silent." If we were to revisit the 1930s, the equivalent of the nuclear disarmament movement were the Chamberlainists who balked at the warnings of Churchill and his colleagues who attempted to warn the British establishment about the true intentions of Adolph Hitler. Churchill's followers were denounced as war-mongers, and 10 million British citizens signed petitions against war with Hitler. This allowed Hitler to acquire the Sudetenland, given to him for appeasement. Indeed, good men remain silent so wicked ones triumph. But if they remain silent, how good can they really be to begin with?

This painful lesson of modern history is no less a painful lesson of biblical history where the same manner of scenario was played out by Antiochus Epiphanes. His campaign was complete with Jewish collaborators who were culturally and spiritually seduced, and who succumbed to the prevailing trends because of neglect of God's Word and the pursuit of self-interest. As the gates for the coming of the Antichrist are opened, a demonized popular culture will again be the key along the same kind of lines that took place in the Hellenistic world of the time. There will likewise be those claiming to be among the people of God who will be instrumental in ushering as many of the people of God whom they can seduce and persuade in the direction of what is truly a thinly veiled satanic kingdom.

At the onset of the Maccabean Revolt the most conspicuous figure among the Jews who compromised and ultimately betrayed his faith, his nation, and people was once more Menelaus. The modern spectacle of religious and political leaders in the Judeo-Christian world embracing a global inter-faith culture is not a new phenomenon; neither is the moral compromise we see among both national and church leaders concerning morality, including matters related to homosexuality and lesbianism which were commonplace in Hellenistic culture at the time of the Maccabean Revolt. In short, what happened among the Jews then will happen among both Christians and Jews at the end of days. We have no shortage of latter day versions of Menelaus and the end result of this trend was Antiochus Epiphanes—that is, Antiochus IV who set up an abomination of desolation in the House of God. In the modern world with the same trends reoccurring, the end event will be the same, only far worse when the person of Antichrist, of whom Antiochus IV is just a mere yet vital shadow, will make his appearance.

The Maccabees

As we have established, the apocryphal books of 1 and 2 Maccabees are not included in the biblical Canon. However, they are reliable sources of historical fulfillment of specific prophecies found in the inspiration of Scripture even though the books themselves are not considered as inspired Scripture (although since the Middle Ages they have been considered canon by Roman Catholicism and also by Rabbinic Judaism). But because these books record and confirm direct prophecies from God's Word, and because the Apocrypha is twice quoted in the New Testament, they are a special caliber of extra-biblical literature, as is witnessed to by the Lord Jesus in His celebration of Hanukkah in John 10. This apocryphal literature relates the story of Israel and the Jewish people during the Intertestamental Period, and it is again highly recommended that readers be familiar with these books in their entirety in order to understand our own comments, but more importantly, the background of what Jesus was doing in John 10 and the devastating accuracy of Daniel's prophecies, all of which play an important role in the Antichrist's final identification. Knowledge of the history of this period is indispensable.

The Maccabees were a priestly family that lived in a village called Modein outside of Jerusalem in an area known as the "*Shfela*" lying between the Coastal Plain of Sharon and the hills of Judea. It was among other things the area associated with the Prophet Micah and the failed invasion of Judah attempted by Sennacherib, the king of Assyria in the days of Isaiah and Hezekiah (2 Ki. 18-19; 2 Chr. 32; Is. 36-37). A leading Jewish figure and Seleucid collaborator was Menelaus who became the nemesis of observant Jews resisting Hellenization in the Shfela region. The Maccabean Revolt was triggered when the Maccabees assassinated Menelaus and an officer of Antiochus Epiphanes. The Maccabees fled to the nearby hills of Judah to the east and began waging a guerilla war. It is noteworthy that this area between Jerusalem and the Mediterranean is the place where Antichrist will pitch his tent (Dan. 11:4). These Maccabees began small but gained followers and momentum. Some of their followers were compatriots, honestly motivated by a fear of God and a belief in His Word, while others were opportunists with an agenda of their own, jumping onto the Maccabees' bandwagon in order to blow their own horns and advance their own interests.

We must again remember that the historical actions of the Maccabees in Daniel 11 against Antiochus will, up to verse 36, in some way take place again with the person of the Antichrist at the end of the age.

The struggle began with the father and his five priestly sons: Eleazar, Jonathan, Simon, Yehuda, and Mathias. Two of these sons were betrayed from within their ranks by mal-motivated followers with pretended loyalties. This painful aspect of the Hanukkah must be carefully borne in mind because the same is going to happen among both the Jews and within the Church in the Last Days. There are, and will be, persons within discernment circles claiming to be defenders of the Word of God, and not only opponents of the forces of Antichrist, but of the traitors within the Church. Some of these will be manipulated by the antichrist spirit and will behave in the same way in pursuit of their secret self-aggrandizing ambitions. As we are warned by Jesus in the Last Days, many will fall away and betray one another (Mt. 24:10).

Already in the Church we have, in the last 20 years, experienced an ex-flux of leaders and congregants, who we always reckoned to be brethren committed to Christ, who proved to be committed only to themselves. Many we would never have expected, have apostatized into all manner of false doctrine under the deluding influence of the spirit of antichrist, and have even turned against their former comrades in the faith who struggle to uphold the Word of God. What happened with the Maccabees who opposed Antiochus Epiphanes and the Jews who supported the Hellenists is happening again in the Last Days in much the same way.

In the early stages, out of pure self-interest they compromise with what they know to be wrong. Then before long they begin to adopt beliefs and practices they previously would have objected to and then become inimical to those still standing fast on the Word of God and opposing such departures from the truth. As in the days of the Maccabees, it will rapidly become impossible to remain on a fence. Those attempting to do so will inevitably fall off on the wrong side. The pressures will simply be too great. Moreover, by yielding to compromise they also open themselves to being deceived.

And as in the days of the Maccabees we likewise see today that there are those claiming to be watchmen engaged in discernment who merely have an unscriptural and pseudo-spiritual program of their own. Their self-serving and self-righteous endeavors propel them to become something cultic and divisively heretical. As we have stated elsewhere, among these would be Ruckmanites and so-called Christian conspiracy theorists. A number of such people have already attacked mainstream discernment ministries while falsely claiming to be discernment oriented themselves. They are, in fact, agenda oriented and self-oriented. The Maccabees were no strangers to the challenges both internal and external of which the faithful remnant of Christians are up against today as we await the dawn of the Antichrist.

In their revolt against the Seleucids the first to be assassinated by the Maccabees was not a Seleucid, but Menelaus the collaborator. The Antichrist, we are told in Daniel, will attempt to wear out the saints of the Most High. The Maccabees are the Intertestamental picture of those whom the forces of Antichrist will not be able to wear out, although they will desperately try, and the resisters will face hardship and betrayal as the price for their loyalty to God and His Word. As with the Maccabees, however, in the end they will prevail.

We need to consider that in the Last Days there will likewise be two categories of traitors for both Israel and the Jews and for the Body of Christ. The first are the Menelaus sort who openly collaborate with the enemies of

God's people. We see elements of this today in both the Church and among the Jews. Ecumenical and interfaith proponents join forces with opponents of the true Gospel and of those who believe it, be it with Islam, Mormonism, the church of Rome or otherwise. Among these we find Peter Kreeft, Chuck Colson, Tony Campolo, and the signatories to such sellouts to the Antichrist as the *Evangelicals and Catholics Together* accord. So, too, in the Jewish community, left-wing Jews are often latter-day versions of a Menelaus. They are seen in the popular media, government, and academic institutions. These are Noam Chomsky and Norman Finklestein, as well as left-center Jewish politicians such as Jerry Nadler and Michael Bloomberg who sided with radical Islamic elements in the Ground Zero Mosque controversy. In both the Diaspora and Israel itself we find such elements today just as were found in the days of the Maccabees.

The second category of traitors join with those who function in the character of the Maccabees, opposing the seduction and corruption, but who do so motivated not with altruistic intent, but with self-serving goals; these will betray the faithful remnant when it suits their cause.

The Defiling of the Temple

In 1 Maccabees 1 it is reported that the Temple gets defiled. The stones of the altar underwent something horrific: a swine was sacrificed on them by Antiochus. And he built a statue of Zeus, giving Zeus his own features. "Zeus" was a corruption of "*Theos*" in Greek meaning "god." But Antiochus gave it his features so it was an example of a man trying to identify himself as the great God, but basing things on Mt. Olympus as opposed to Mt. Zion.

Against the background of John 10 we again need to recount and elaborate on the dilemma that faced the Maccabees once Jerusalem was liberated and the Temple rededicated: "What can we do with the stones of the Temple? Well, we cannot throw them away because they are "*mei qodesh*"—they are sanctified. But we can no longer sacrifice on them because a pig was sacrificed on them." So they disassembled the altar (which is called a "*misabeach*") into its individual stones and, according to the *Mishnah,* they were stockpiled outside the Temple proper in Solomon's Portico. They came to believe that at Hanukkah, at the time of dedication, either the Messiah, or possibly Elijah the prophet, was going to come and tell them what to do with the stones. "When the Messiah comes, He will know what to do with them. We cannot throw them away."

So they built another altar. Antiochus was empowered by spiritual seduction and by Hellenizing God's people—that is, using the popular culture. Riding on the back of the popular culture was a compromised morality. Thus the climate changed to the point that things would have been abhorrent to any observant Jew in God's own House; even the reading of His Word was outlawed.

There is no denying that there are those afoot who want to rebuild a Temple in Jerusalem, and this is not saying that it will not happen. Nor is it beyond reason that an image will again be set up in it once rebuilt. But there is a greater principle needing to be recognized: the ***physical*** reflects the ***spiritual***.

When Jesus died on the cross, the "*velon*" (the veil) was torn from the ceiling to the ground. An actual, literal, physical event happened in a literal, physical temple; a supernatural event occurred. But that is not what was most important. The most important thing is what it meant: sinful man was no longer separated from a holy God, and now has access to the Father though the blood of the High Priest.

If the Temple is rebuilt—and there is no reason to believe it will not be—and an image is set up; it will only be a reflection of Antichrist being worshiped in Christendom. And it will come about the way it is coming about now—Hellenization: God's people being swallowed up by popular culture.

Keeping the World Out of the Gospel

An overriding principle in understanding how the Antichrist will be identified is the need to keep referring back to the fact that just as the Holy Spirit is preparing the faithful Church for the coming of Christ, the spirit of antichrist is preparing the harlot church for the coming of the Antichrist and False Prophet. This diabolical strategy includes an across-the-board erosion of scriptural standards of ascertaining and defending truth, and the erosion of godly moral standards once the importance of truth has been diminished. Among other things, we note the castigation of doctrine in the Christian media by Paul Crouch of TBN, who denounced doctrine as "excrement" using a vulgar expletive in a broadcast. Doctrine is in fact "*didaskin*," that is, the teaching of Jesus. In substance, what Crouch did was to relegate the teaching of Jesus to the status of mere dung in the minds of his deceived followers. This is truly the spirit of antichrist at work in a visibly prominent expression of the plans of Satan to corrupt the Church from within in preparation for the advent of the "*man of lawlessness*." First, doctrine is attacked, and then morality crumbles almost automatically as a result.

As the Bride of Christ is becoming adorned for her Husband, the harlot church is also getting dressed for hers. Reverting to our "good-girl/bad-girl" motif from Proverbs and Revelation, it is with obvious reason that female televangelists are so characteristically adorned with a gaudy and whorish appearance that even the secular world mocks. We also see the serial practice of unscriptural divorce and remarriage and the de facto worship of money with such women from the late Tammy Bakker to Jan Crouch to Paula White, who after being divorced from her husband, was found walking hand-in-hand with Benny Hinn after his wife divorced him.

This combination of a love of money, departure from biblical standards of marital permanency, and excessive cosmetic appearance expressly denounced in Peter's epistle (1 Pe. 3:5-6) is the calling card and uniform of the harlot church; that is, the bride of Antichrist whom these women personify and represent. That such gaudiness, marital immorality, and mammon worship are a shame and disgrace to the name and cause of Christ serving only to undermine the testimony of the Church to the world is only the visible affectation of what these women do. The invisible is the spirit in back of what they represent, which is the spirit of antichrist. They are microcosms of the harlot church awaiting their true lover, the "*man of sin*."

What transpired with the Hellenization of the Jews in the days of the Maccabees when Antiochus made his power play is what is happening in the modern state of Israel and in the backslidden Church today. The homosexuality and bisexuality that were culturally endemic back then have made inroads into both the Church, which places benedictions on same-sex marriage and homosexual ordination, and among Israel and the Jews who hold large gay pride marches in Jerusalem. It is of little surprise that both the prophet Isaiah, and the apostle John in the Book of Revelation, call Jerusalem "*Sodom*" in an eschatological context (Is. 3:9, 13:19; Rev. 11:8).

The Word Outlawed

The Seleucids outlawed the public reading of Torah, and already in both Sweden and Canada there are moves afoot to call the public reading of Scriptures that denounce sexual sin and homosexuality, such as Romans 1 or the Book of Leviticus, "hate literature." Everyone can read the *Quran*, of course, but the Word of God becomes outlawed. This is exactly the kind of thing that transpired in the days of the Maccabees, when Greek mythology, complete with the sexual adventures of their pagan deities, were encouraged, but the Torah forbidding such things was prevented by law. During the Seleucid period the priests of Pan openly practiced surrogate sex with pagan idols by proxy copulation with goats. Such abominable practices were condemned as unnatural in the Torah, thus the Torah had to be banned.

The Scriptures contain narratives describing everything from decapitations to gang rapes, but never is violence celebrated or sexual immorality glorified. In the Greek culture, however, such practices were prolifically admired as they are today. What began as a campaign for co-existence of Greek and Hebraic beliefs quickly turned to a prohibition of biblical beliefs. So, too, today if one were to pray at a public forum in the name of Jesus Christ, they would not unlikely be the defendants in a private prosecution by the American Civil Liberties Union (ACLU), but if someone used the name of God or Jesus Christ as a curse or swear word in a public venue, the ACLU would defend them on the grounds of the right to free speech.

In the days of the Maccabees, courts followed a politically dictated agenda that was inherently biased against the Word of God and the monotheistic truths and moral standards contained therein. Today it is little different. There is no shortage of theological liberal clergy more than anxious to lend credence to such apostate debauchery. Thus, it becomes impossible for the Church to be a preserving element or moral light in a declining civilization with an increasingly depraved culture when so much of the Church itself at best compromises with, but soon afterward, is swallowed up by that same culture. What we have is a demonically deceived, pseudo-Christian mainstream pretending to be the Church in a post-Judeo-Christian/neo-pagan culture that still pretends to be Judeo-Christian.

This is what the Maccabees faced in Daniel 11, and the result was Antiochus Epiphanes. And this is precisely what we face today, and the result will be the Antichrist with the single exception of the fact that Antiochus IV only fulfilled the predictions of that chapter up until verse 36; the Antichrist will go up to verse 36 and well beyond until the Lord Jesus destroys Him with the breath of His coming (2 Th. 2:8). The state of Judaism in the days of the Maccabees had become absolutely pathetic. The state of what is called "Christianity" today, including much if not most of Evangelical Christianity, is little different and no better.

A Christian magazine published an article asking various Christian leaders about their devotional reading for Lent in Great Britain. Nicky Gumbel, who directs the Alpha Course, said in the article that his Lenten reading was the works of Rowan Williams, the Archbishop of Canterbury, a member of a Druid sect who ordains homosexuals into a supposedly Christian ministry. Yet Gumbel, who tells Alpha Course converts who are Roman Catholic to remain in the Roman Catholic Church with the Eucharistic cannibalism, auto-atonement in Purgatory, and a host of other doctrines condemned by the Evangelical Reformers of Anglicanism, is the figure from Holy Trinity Brompton in London who so many look to to revive British Evangelicalism. This ignores the fact that Gumbel looks for spiritual guidance from a Druid who ordains homosexuals. From Matthew 15 we glean the colloquialism, "the blind leading the blind" (Mt. 15:14). In the case of Nicky Gumbel and the Alpha Course, the sorry spectacle of the blind leading the blind would be an actual improvement. The scriptural standards are gone, and, consequently, so too are the moral standards. There is no stopping it. Therefore there is no stopping the Antichrist. There will be a church waiting for him, and that church will include many professing Evangelicals.

When this happened in Intertestamental Israel, the Maccabees exclaimed, "Enough is enough!" And they took a stand against Menelaus just as faithful Christians must take a stand against figures such as Rowan Williams and Nicky Gumbel today. Once they did, others began to join the Maccabees. This is the faithful remnant of Israel that remained when Antiochus came, and this will be the faithful Church when the Antichrist comes. Indeed, his advance team is already here and at work.

Differences and Similarities

What the faithful Church will have in common with the Maccabees is that many will join with them in hypocrisy. There will be a series of dangerous, internal betrayals. The lesson is that just because someone is against what you are against does not automatically mean they are for what you are for. Just as in the days of the Maccabees, there will be sinister characters playing both sides—unfaithful people who will align themselves with the faithful remnant as a vehicle for advancing their own interests.

At a time when Israel was highly deluded, deceived from within, and ignorant of the Word of God, the Maccabees, who had understanding of the times in which they lived, like the sons of Issachar (1 Chr. 12:32), took action and gave understanding to the many. There will, of course, be no literal rededication of the Temple by the faithful Church apart from the return of Jesus. However, we must understand the typological illustration which demonstrates what is going to happen.

In the Olivet Discourse, Jesus spoke of fleeing to the mountains when seeing the abomination of desolation. Under His cousin Simeon, the Jewish believers in Jerusalem did this in A.D. 70. So, too, the Maccabees, seeing the abomination of desolation, fled to the mountains of Judah. After fleeing to the mountains, they later returned victorious and the Temple was rededicated. In A.D. 70 the flight to the mountains commanded and prophesied by Jesus was a type of the Rapture of the Church. It is not improbable that believers at that point in time expected the literal return of Jesus. So, too, the faithful Church will be removed and then return with Christ who will consecrate the millennial Temple and re-establish the Davidic kingdom, which the Maccabees could not do because they were Levitical and not from the Davidic tribe of Judah.

There is a further aspect in these events foreshadowing what will transpire with Israel and the Jews. It has long been believed that once the betrayal by the Antichrist is recognized by the Jews, and the forces of Antichrist assemble at Armageddon in the Valley of Jehoshaphat for the final battle for Jerusalem, there will be likewise a flight via the hills of Judea toward the east, not to Pella where Simeon fled in A.D. 70, but to Petra in accordance with certain prophecies found in Isaiah 16. This, however, will only concern the unsaved Jews; the faithful Church will already have been removed by this point. As with the Maccabees, the faithful Church will face betrayal, but those with understanding will alert the many and witness the Antichrist taking his place in the Temple from the point of view of both the Church and Israel. Shortly thereafter the Church will be removed.

The Antichrist, meanwhile, having reenacted the deeds of Antiochus IV up to Daniel 11:36, will continue to fulfill the rest of the prophecy. In the amazing sovereignty of God, even the actions as a counterfeit of the Trinity that Satan, the Antichrist, and the False Prophet will be able to perform are already scripted.

The Maccabees are in every sense a type, but as we have been careful to restate, not every type equals its antitype in every aspect. Without doubt, however, up to a significant point (that point being the Rapture corresponding in figure to the flight to the mountains), both in the ecclesiastical sense and in the national sense of Israel, the deeds of the Maccabees and their followers foretell the deeds of the faithful Church when Antichrist arrives on the scene taking his seat in the Temple of God.

Working in Small Groups

In dark times of backsliding and confusion, God has always raised up people who had understanding, who began teaching the truth in small groups and, in turn, began to proclaim the truth to larger amounts of people. Jesus used this strategy with the Twelve and the Seventy, Elijah used this strategy with the sons of the prophets, and of course the Maccabees used this strategy. This will be the strategy that the Holy Spirit ordains for the Last Days. When the Antichrist is manifested in a vortex of biblical ignorance and confusion, the faithful remnant of the Church will largely be smaller groups of people who are going deeper into the Word of God at a time when most Christians in most churches are venturing further and further from it. It is here the understanding will be found, but these groups will be infiltrated.

It is important for the faithful Church to remember the warning from the Hebrew text of Micah 7:5, "Do not trust in an '*aluf*'"—usually translated as "friend" in English. It is rather the modern Hebrew term for a military general, but it is the ancient term for a herd's the lead steer whom the others follow. We must remember the connection with the prophecy about Judas betraying Jesus:

> *Even my close friend in whom I trusted,*
> *Who ate my bread,*
> *Has lifted up his heel against me.* (Ps. 41:9)

This prophecy concerning Judas, as with all scriptural texts concerning Judas, carries some implications for the Antichrist as the "*son of perdition*" whom Judas foreshadows. Just as there was a Judas among Jesus' small group of the Twelve Apostles, there will be Judases among us within our small groups as the faithful Church.

While this is a general truth in that there are people who may join themselves to such small groups because we oppose things they oppose, one cannot base fellowship on what we are ***against***, but only on who and what we are ***for***. Such people will eventually find undue fault in any fellowship once it no longer suits their own ends. This is a *kal v'homer* situation, however, and in the Last Days the problem increases.

The True Shepherds Know What To Do

Reverting again to the Book of Micah, the contemporary of Isaiah, who predicts so much about the First and Second Coming of Christ, we know that the Lord will have shepherds to rise up against the Antichrist and oppose Babylon. And the Lord will deliver them just as God delivered the faithful remnant of the Assyrian Captivity, bearing in mind once again that the king of Assyria typifies the Antichrist and the prophecies of Micah are doubly referenced, having a dual meaning both for his own day and the Last Days.

> *And He will arise and shepherd His flock*
> *In the strength of the LORD,*
> *In the majesty of the name of the LORD His God.*
> *And they will remain,*
> *Because at that time He will be great*
> *To the ends of the earth.*
> *This One will be our peace.*
> *When the Assyrian invades our land,*
> *When he tramples on our citadels,*
> *Then we will raise against him*
> *Seven shepherds and eight leaders of men.*
> *They will shepherd the land of Assyria with the sword,*
> *The land of Nimrod at its entrances;*
> *And He will deliver us from the Assyrian*
> *When he attacks our land*
> *And when he tramples our territory.*
> *Then the remnant of Jacob*
> *Will be among many peoples*
> *Like dew from the LORD,*
> *Like showers on vegetation*
> *Which do not wait for man*
> *Or delay for the sons of men.* (Mic. 5:4-7)

The Maccabees opposing Antiochus would later behave in the same character as the shepherds in Micah. What is important to observe is that those opposing the Assyrian will be the seven shepherds and eight leaders of men (Mic. 5:5). These stand in opposed contrast to the seven and the eighth evil leaders in the rise of Antichrist from Daniel and Revelation (Rev. 17:11). The Antichrist's eighth, of course, will be one of the seven. But our eighth is not Antichrist, but Christ, who will deliver us when our territory is attacked (Mic. 5:6). Beginning with Micah 5:7, Micah uses the ethno-centric term "Jacob," specifically designating ethnic Israel. Once we are delivered by Rapture, the focus comes on the Jews. The Hebrew term in verse 6 for being delivered is "*natsal*," meaning "to be saved or rescued by being drawn out or torn away as a means of escape." It is the Hebrew equivalent of the Greek word for Rapture, "*Harpazo*"—"to be snatched away by force," which, in the Septuagint translation of Micah 5:6, is the ***exact same word*—** "*Harpazo*" (with a varied case ending).

Thus Micah 5:4-7 tells us that before the Rapture there will be those who know what to do about the invader represented by the king of Assyria who embodies the character of Satan and foreshadows the Antichrist. And when this happens the faithful Church will be Raptured, at which point God will turn His focus back toward national ethnic Israel. As Satan has his seven kings and an eighth who is the Antichrist (who is one of the seven in some way), God will have his seven and an eighth, with the Lord's eighth being Christ, who will rescue us by Rapture before the divine plan reverts totally to unbelieving Israel and the Jews.

The pattern of the rescue from the Assyrian in Micah 5 is the same pattern followed by the Maccabees, and will once more be the same pattern of the faithful Church who was able to identify the "*man of sin*," prefigured by king of Assyria and Antiochus IV.

Euro-Federalism: Ancient and Modern

What is also important in understanding the eschatological implications of the story of the Maccabees as prophesied in Daniel, and as celebrated by Jesus in John 10, is how Antiochus as the most important type of the Antichrist outside of the New Testament came into being. Much emphasis has been placed on the European Union as a reconfederation of the Roman Empire through which the Antichrist will come. Such efforts are not without obvious merit. Problematically, however, just as this focus on a revived Roman Empire has diverted attention away from what the Scriptures reveal about the Antichrist relationship to the Middle East and what is today mainly the Islamic world, so, too, it has eclipsed the equally fundamental importance of Greece. Indeed, the principality concerning

Greece in conflict with Iran figures in Daniel 10 for the future in a prophetic reoccurrence of a conflict between the West and Iran.

In the days in which Daniel wrote, Greece was widely encompassing the entirety of the eastern Mediterranean and surrounding regions from Sicily in the west, Northern Egypt in the south, the Balkans in the north, and the Levant in the east. Greece represented European Civilization and Western Civilization. Rome had been Etruscan, and the rest of Europe, including the Germanic, Nordic, Celtic, and Slavic peoples were barbarian. The civilized world consisted of the Greeks, the Phoenicians, the Medes, and a rival Indo-European nation, the Aryans (who became known as the Persians), and lastly the Jews. The Western world was the Greek world to later become Greco-Roman civilization. All of the Roman emperors beginning with Caesar Augustus tried and succeeded to make Rome the new Athens as a cultural and a religious power and to make Rome the new Sparta as a military power. The basis, however, was always Greece. As has been often noted, Rome conquered Greece strategically, but Greece conquered Rome culturally and intellectually.

As Daniel prophesied, Alexander would die and his empire would become fragmented among his four senior generals, which we have already considered. Alexander's conquests were simply the proto-Euro-Federalism of his father Philip who united the city states of Greece to fight Persia, and was then taken to its natural conclusion. Euro-Federalism produced the circumstances in conjunction with the fate of Alexander prophesied by Daniel to bring about the rise of Antiochus IV—who in certain respects is the closest thing to the Antichrist that history has ever witnessed.

This same Euro-Federalism that produced Antiochus as a type of the Antichrist was the mechanism by which the spirit of antichrist has raised up so many historical types of the Antichrist and which will in considerable measure raise up the final Antichrist, that is the Beast of Revelation 13 and the little horn of Daniel (Dan. 7:8).

From Charlemagne onward there were many figures who attempted to reconfederate the Roman Empire in some way. None, however, was more pointed for our understanding the Antichrist from a historical perspective than Napoleon Bonaparte.

Napoleon the Historial Type

Napoleon began as a son of the French Revolution. He came to power out of the chaos that the secular humanism and unbridled libertarianism of late 18th-century France had become. Unlike the American Revolution or the English Civil War under Cromwell, there was no biblical compass for the direction in which the nation was to go. Not only did Marie Antoinette lose her head, but so did Robespierre, the former champion of the proletariat. Fallen man can rave about equality, liberty, and fraternity all he may wish, but without God his Father, God's Word as a moral parameter, God's laws as a template, and a knowledge of God's Son as Savior, man's attempts at liberty, equality, and brotherhood will result in a chaos that will produce a dictator in the spirit of the French Revolution and the later Russian Bolsheviks.

From the ensuing chaos will always come a Stalin, just as Hitler emerged from the social, political, and economic anarchy of Weimar Germany. Both Stalin and Hitler were demon-possessed, but the Antichrist to come will be satanically-possessed, and his evil will overshadow the unspeakable treachery and havoc the Nazis and Stalinists reeked on humanity.

The best prototype of this, however, probably remains Napoleon. Like dictators from King Saul in biblical times to Shaka Zulu in the military history of Black Africa, and like several of the Roman emperors, he is someone who seemed to begin well and benevolent, but quickly showed his truer colors when corrupted by power and pride. Napoleon's aim of reuniting Continental Europe, however, has diverted too much attention from his greater ambitions which were to re-establish European power in the Middle East, and in the Holy Land in particular, which had been lost by the Crusades to Saladin and the Muslims.

Napoleon defeated the Mamluks near the pyramids in Egypt, and like the apostle Paul, he arrived at the biblical port of Ptolemy (today called "Acco") on the coast of Galilee. Ascending to Mt. Tabor where the epic biblical account of Deborah took place in the Book of Judges, Napoleon observed the Valley of Megiddo below, with Mt. Armageddon opposite him on the southern perimeter of the biblical Valley of Jezreel where the forces of Antichrist will accumulate. Here they will seemingly defeat Israel, and march south on Jerusalem into the Valley of Jehoshaphat, only to be destroyed by the returning Christ who comes up from Mt. Seir in Jordan, and whose feet stand on the Mt. of Olives in Jerusalem to establish His Millennial Kingdom. Gazing across the valley Napoleon stated that it was the perfect place for the ultimate military campaign. He had plans for the repatriation of the Jews to the land of Israel. Upon returning to Europe he placed the emperor's crown on his own head. To conservative Protestants in England this looked very much like the Antichrist, and with good reason.

There must be, and will be, a conflict between a Federal Europe and the Western world with Islam for control of the Middle East. From Benjamin Disraeli to the Crusades, to Hitler and his General Rommel, to Napoleon and the modern USA, any global super-power has always realized it could only remain a super-power if it exercises strategic control over the Middle East where three continents come together and where biblical Israel is at the geographical center as the heart of the Middle East. During the Crusades the prize was spices; in the Age of Empire the prize was the Suez Canal connecting the East and West; today it is oil. But no matter what the prize in the history of geo-politics, the location has always been the same. The French, British, Arab, Ottoman, Holy Roman, Soviet, and American empires have ***all*** sought to have the strategic upper hand in the Middle East. So will the Antichrist.

The Roots of Euro-Federalism

To understand this we must go back to the heart of Euro-Federalism. Again, it was the pelvis of Nebuchadnezzar's vision that corresponds to Greece, the pelvic region being the location of reproductive organs. The seminal influence of Western Civilization is Hellenism. From the time of the church fathers in the Patristic Era onward, Christendom has been Hellenistic—be it Roman Catholic, Reformed Protestant, or Eastern Orthodox. From the Byzantium culture of Czarist Russia to the neo-classic architecture of Washington, D.C., we all come from Greece in our science, culture, and polity. Although Rome conquered Greece strategically, Greece conquered Rome culturally. Even Far East nations such as Japan and Singapore are a hybrid of oriental and occidental culture. Korea is likewise westernized in its models of economy and government. During the Golden Age of Islam, while Europe was sweltering in the Dark Ages, Islam experienced a Golden Age only because it Hellenized. And Europe came out of the Dark Ages in the Renaissance only because it re-Hellenized. Scripturally and historically European civilization, be it in Australia, California, Latin America, or Europe itself, all find their ontogeny in Greece.

In the days of the prophet Daniel who prophesied more about Greece and about Antichrist than any other Book in the Old Testament, as we have noted, Greece in the ancient times of Scripture meant something more and different than it does today.

Daniel described Alexander's rival Persia as a shaggy goat with a huge horn butting toward the north, west, and south. In Daniel 8, Greece is represented by the goat that defeated him. The two horns of the ram represented the Medes and the Persians as we have noted. Alexander ceased his march to the east due to the shortage of water in the desert of Balochistan, and he died suddenly at the age of 36, and, as Daniel foretold, his four generals divided his empire.

In his march to the south, however, Alexander was at first not assisted by the Jews in his designs on capturing Tyre because of the traditional Jewish friendship with the Persians from whom they had benefited since the time of Cyrus the Great, as prophesied by the prophet Isaiah. While there was no hostility toward the Greeks, there was an anxiety not to betray the friendship of the Persians. As Alexander proceeded north again after attacking Egypt, he re-entered Israel, striking utter fear into the hearts and minds of the Jews who refused to be his allies. They expected him to destroy Jerusalem. Instead, however, the Jews paid wild homage to him, greeting him as a figure of messianic proportions. He took their salute and acquiescence to his imperial designs; he spared the people, the land, and the rebuilt Temple. We must understand how Alexander the Great foreshadows the deeds of the Antichrist with a federal Europe having designs on the Middle East and a character similar to what Napoleon would attempt centuries later.

It Happens Again

The Antichrist, backed by a federal Europe, will invade the Middle East in some way. This may involve the conflict with Iran prophesied in Daniel 10. By force of might Napoleon, and Alexander to a degree, achieved the same three things: they obtained leadership of a federal Europe, they gained a military dominance in the Middle East, and they initially spared the Jews. The Antichrist will do likewise.

Under Antiochus IV the acquiescence to the Greeks backfired. It will backfire on the Jews once again. When Napoleon came to power, Islam had been largely driven out of most of Europe apart from a small corner of the Balkans. Over a period of centuries the Saracens have been defeated in Italy, Charles Montel defeated Islam in Western Europe, and Ferdinand and Isabella drove the Muslims out of Spain into Morocco. And at an earlier point the Hazer Empire whose king and many of his followers converted to

Judaism (and would later intermarry with the Jewish communities in Eastern Europe) halted Islamic invasions into Europe through the Urals.

The Polish King Jan Sobieski crushed the Turkish Muslims in Austria and a second defeat of the Muslims took place again on the outskirts of Vienna in the 16th century at the time the Protestant Reformation was beginning to get underway. Napoleon, however, went one better and achieved military successes against the Muslims in the Middle East. The Antichrist will come in this character carrying this mandate.

While Alexander the Great is of more importance from a scriptural perspective of these events, Napoleon is important from an historical perspective. Islam has a long memory. It remembers the Crusades and the adventures of Napoleon, the British, and others as recent events. But it remembers the conflict between Jacob and Esau, Ishmael and Isaac even more so. We cannot understand the military adventurism of the Antichrist to come unless we understand the mindset of Islam, the mindset of the Jews, and the past military history of the Middle East, both scriptural and extra-scriptural.

Once again, the Antichrist will enter the Beautiful Land be it Napoleon, Alexander the Great, Caesar Augustus, Pompeii, Antiochus Epiphanes, Herod the Great, Saladin (who finally Islamized Israel), or others. Each unveils one aspect of the Antichrist who is to come. Each one who is ***an*** antichrist furnishes us with a piece of the puzzle providing us a portrait of ***the*** Antichrist.

We have already established that the pattern is a very rapid series of world empires rising and falling very quickly, and in the middle of it all the Jews come back to their land—just like what happened in the Book of Daniel. To understand the Last Days it is critical to understand what happened according to Daniel.

It is very important to pay attention whenever conflict arises between the kings of the north and the kings of the south. Biblically the final conflict will not be East-West; it has to be North-South. It has to be a North-South conflict just like in the days of Daniel and that is what will be seen. There is going to be a North-South conflict creating the same kind of chaos that existed in the days that saw the rise of the Roman Empire. This will rise again out of the chaos.

Pompeii as a Type of Antichrist

The figure recorded earlier in Daniel 11 also enters the "Beautiful Land" in verse 16, and he also makes a false covenant. One of the problems that will be experienced in the Last Days is that there are ***many*** antichrists. So every time somebody tries to sign a peace treaty in the Middle East, people are going to say, "That is it!"

This ultimate Antichrist is going to be different. He will be in the character—insofar as this text is teaching—of two people. One is Antiochus IV—Epiphanes—and the other is General Pompeii. Whenever somebody other than the high priest on the Day of Atonement (or other than Lord Jesus Himself in the Book of Hebrews) enters the Holy of Holies, it is a type of the Antichrist. And the Roman General Pompeii did that. He represented the triumvirate of Rome, made a treaty with the Jews, and then the Jews were double-crossed when he entered the Holy of Holies. He is a major, major type of the Antichrist which people overlook.

We have explored the importance of Pompeii as a member of the Triumvirate and the prophetic significance of this in relation to the coming Antichrist. While important, however, this wanes shallow in comparison to the importance of his type of the Antichrist in that he made a treaty with Israel, persuading them to trust him, and then entered the Holy of Holies as will the Antichrist. The epistle to the Hebrews makes it clear that the Aaronic high priest alone, on the Day of Atonement, was to enter the *sanctum sanctorum* (which the Jews called the *Qodesh Qodashim*), with the high priest being a type of Christ—our High Priest (Heb. 5). When any other person enters, it is always a picture of the Antichrist. Had the Holy Ark been present in the Second Temple, Pompeii quite possibly would have been struck dead.

King Herod

There is of course no significance whatsoever to the fact that Hanukkah and Christmas are celebrated at the same time of year. Hanukkah in the Jewish tradition is celebrated on the 25th of Kislev and Christmas in the Western tradition on the 25th of December, which was a pre-Christian Roman feast called "Saturnalia." There are, however, a number of strong doctrinal and theological connections. Both Daniel and the Nativity speak of the First and Second Coming of Christ, and both feature the angel Gabriel as an angelic messenger to clarify forthcoming events. Both, moreover, speak of the place and position of Israel relative to the Roman Empire in both the First and Second Coming of Christ.

As we have already mentioned, popular Jewish thought in the Second Temple Period expected the Messiah to be revealed at Hanukkah, while in the Gospels the Messiah was also revealed. He was revealed, however, to a select group of Jews and Gentiles, ranging from shepherds to senior citizens to faithful clergy. But as we see, the unfaithful did not know until ***after*** the fact.

Herod and his scribal scholars, the liberal theologians of the day, as well as the Levitical priests, knew from the prophet Micah the prophecies as to where the Messiah would be born. But when He was born, not only where they troubled, but all Jerusalem with them (Mt. 2:3). Only the faithful remnant understood, as was the case with the Maccabees. The others could not properly discern the signs of the times beyond a very limited point. The same will, of course, be true with the return of Jesus. Likewise an Antichrist figure in Caesar Augustus appears in the Nativity just as the Antichrist figure of Antiochus IV appears in Daniel.

Micah 5 instructs the faithful remnant of Israel that the Redeemer from Bethlehem would save—that is, rescue—faithful Israel from the king of Assyria and the king of Babylon, both of whom are appellations of Satan and shadows of the Beast. So, too, the Redeemer from Israel would save God's people from their sin. Micah makes clear that the invasion and subjugation by the kings of Assyria and Babylon were the consequence of the Israel's unrepentant sin; so, too, the Roman occupation in the 1st century was likewise a consequence of national sin. The coming of the Antichrist will be the same. Both Zechariah 11 and 2 Thessalonians 2 reveal that the Beast will be an instrument of God's judgment as were the kings of Assyria and Babylon, and the Caesars, all of whom foreshadow the Beast.

When Jesus was born, Herod obviously felt threatened. The king who was already there wanted to stay in power and get rid of the King who was coming to take his place because his dominion would be lost to the new King. This again harkens back to Daniel 7:20-22 where Christ returns as the Ancient of Days taking back the dominion of Satan from the hand of Antichrist and giving it to those He has sanctified. This is immediately followed in Daniel 7 with prophecies of the four beasts being Rome and the ten horns recurring in a *Pesher* reinterpretation of the Nativity in Revelation 12. Again, we see not only the relationship between Daniel and Revelation, but the relationship between Daniel and the Nativity narratives.

Jesus was of course a proper Davidic king of the correct lineage both by the Levirate line through Joseph in Matthew and the maternal line in Luke through Mary. Because of the curse of Jeconiah (Jer. 22:24-30), Jesus could not be a direct biological descendant of Jeconiah paternally to qualify as king, thus this is one reason Joseph had to be the step-father of Jesus (the other being He could not inherit the fallen nature of man). The ancient rabbis agreed that the genealogy of Luke was Christ's ancestry traced through Mary (Sanhedrin 25g or 25c) where we read, "Miriam bat Heli."

The Davidic authenticity of Christ's lineage both legally and biologically compounded the threat to Herod's position because he was an ethnic Arab—Nabataean, meaning a Moabite whose parents or grandparents converted to Judaism and immigrated westward during the Hasmonean Period. The lineage of David, however, likewise began with a Moabite convert to Judaism in the person of Ruth who bore a baby, named Obed, who, prefiguring Christ, was also called a redeemer and was born in Bethlehem (Ruth 4:14). Obed was the father of Jesse, the father of David through whom Christ would come.

Hence we see the efforts of Satan to as closely as possible counterfeit Christ in the person of the Antichrist. Jesus the rightful King had an ancestor who was the son of a Moabite mother who converted to Judaism; Herod likewise was of ethnic Moabite stock who converted to Judaism. The false king tried to look like the true one. This has a definite future prophetic meaning concerning the manner in which the Antichrist will attempt to replicate Christ in appearance, but in the eyes of the faithful will be unable to do so.

This "good-king"/"bad-king" motif with the bad king desperate to prevent the good king from becoming his successor was inherent in the Davidic line from its inception when King Saul attempted to prevent David (a type of Christ as King) from succeeding him as the monarch. We have already noted the additional similarities between Saul and Judas. However, we must also register similarities between Saul and Herod.

Persecution in the Character of Herod

At the First Coming of Christ, Herod wanted to remain king, so he tried to kill the baby coming out of the woman. When he failed to kill the baby coming out of the woman, he took action in the slaughter of the innocents in Bethlehem, killing all the male babies. In Revelation 12, we find the same event recurring with God's woman giving birth to the man-child who will gain dominion.

> *A great sign appeared in heaven, a woman...* (Rev. 12:1)

(The woman in birth pangs is alluding to the end in some way.)

> *Then another sign appeared in heaven: and behold, a great red dragon having seven heads and ten horns...* (Rev. 12:3)

(Reminiscent of the vision of Daniel.)

> *And his tail swept away a third of the stars of heaven...* (Rev. 12:4a)

This is a picture of tremendous backsliding before the man-child is given up. And this is followed by the 1,260 days (3-1/2 years) by the lunar calendar of the 70th week of Daniel.

> *And she gave birth to a son, a male child, who is to rule all the nations with a rod of iron; and her child was caught up to God and to His throne. Then the woman fled into the wilderness where she had a place prepared by God, so that there she would be nourished for one thousand two hundred and sixty days.*

(There is a war in heaven with Michael and his angels.)

> *And there was war in heaven, Michael and his angels waging war with the dragon. The dragon and his angels waged war, and they were not strong enough, and there was no longer a place found for them in heaven.*

(Again, just like the Book of Daniel, Michael fights the prince of Persia. And what happens? The appearance of the serpent and the dragon.)

> *And the great dragon was thrown down, the serpent of old who is called the devil and Satan, who deceives the whole world; he was thrown down to the earth, and his angels were thrown down with him.* (Rev. 12:5-9)

Satan attacks two ways: the serpent and the dragon. The dragon is outward persecution but the serpent is the seducer. The serpent beguiled—deceived, tricked—the woman. In the Last Days, believers face outward persecution and inward seduction, both happening simultaneously. Satan comes as both the serpent and the dragon.

He is trying to kill the baby coming out of the woman.

> *And she gave birth to a son a male child, who is to rule all the nations with a rod of iron...*

(...just like Jesus...)

> *...and her child was caught up to God and to His throne. Then the woman fled...* (Rev. 12:5-6a)

The same as Jesus' parents fled, she flees for this half of the Tribulation. And then at the end...

> *So the dragon was enraged with the woman, and went off to make war with the rest of her children, who keep the commandments of God and hold to the testimony of Jesus.* (Rev. 12:17)

We would also share the view that there is a probable corresponding between a third of the stars falling from heaven (as the descendants of Abraham as father of many nations are called "stars" in Genesis 22:17) and the traditional view that a third of the angels followed Satan.

When Herod failed to kill Jesus he slaughtered the rest of the babies in a desperate last ditch effort. This is again the type of which Revelation 12 is the antitype when the dragon makes war with the rest of her offspring. We have, once more, not seen the last Herod. In Revelation 12, someone in his character and controlled by the same demonic spirit is coming again before the return of Christ.

Christmas is Coming

As with many believers, I personally do not care for Christmas as such; my concern is rather with the Nativity irrespective of when it happened. There has been a resume of educated guesses for both the year and day of Christ's birth, ranging from 6 B.C. to A.D. 3, and Jewish feasts and holidays ranging from the Feast of Booths to Hanukkah to the modern Israeli Independence Day. While the New Testament does tell us the day of Jesus' death and resurrection being *Pesach* (Passover), it does not tell us the day of His birth. Indeed, if the day of His birth were theologically or doctrinally important God would have included it in the Gospel canon. The emphasis of the New Testament is always on the second (spiritual) birth, not physical birth.

From an eschatological viewpoint, however, there is a further reason beyond the fact that God has called us to remember the death and resurrection of Jesus with a specific day (which the Church abandoned in favor of Easter) instead of remembering His birth. That is, His First Coming teaches about His Second Coming. And as we are not to know the day or hour of His Second Coming, neither can we know the day or hour of His First Coming.

We must recall that there are many antichrists both scriptural and historical, but also mythical. The primary mythical antichrist that has infected Christendom is, of course, Santa Clause cum Father Christmas who has become the focus of what is supposed to be the birth of Christ, instead of Christ Himself. While in certain countries Santa Clause and St. Nicholas are distinct, separate figures, such as in Holland, in the English-speaking world they are one and the same. This of course is not to malign the actual legacy of the historical St. Nicholas who was the senior pastor of the church in Ephesus and who was persecuted for his faith during the last major pagan persecution of Christians in Asia Minor. The noble figure St. Nicholas, however, should not be confused with his impersonator. It is to say that the spirit of antichrist will always place another "in place of" Christ even if it means mythologizing otherwise godly figures, be it Mary the mother of Jesus or in this case St. Nicholas of Ephesus.

While many believers are not observers of Christmas as a holiday, we must have a highly fixated concentration on the reality of the Nativity without reference to either the year or day when Christ was born. Indeed, if we did know that time it would lead to an increase in the unscriptural practice of date-setting concerning His return. The Nativity itself, however, has a future meaning. And those who do not share in a proper understanding of the Nativity will be neither properly prepared for the Second Coming of Jesus or of the revelation of the identity of the Antichrist that must precede it.

As we have already noted, the deified emperor Caesar Augustus, ruling over the Roman Empire, for economic purposes numbered in his census the people when Jesus came the first time. And this directly foreshadows what will happen in the events leading up to His return. It is important to note that the coming of the Messiah coincided with the census. Thus from this we may derive a likelihood that one of the events to transpire in the very final days before the return of Jesus is the numbering of the people by another leader of a Roman Empire with an economic agenda.

The faithful believers will be able to identify the Antichrist by understanding the number of his name (Rev. 13:18). We must dispel the misunderstanding that he will be identified by taking his seat in the Temple of God according to 2 Thessalonians 2. In this epistle Paul simply tells us our gathering together to be with the Lord will not happen until this "*man of lawlessness*" fulfills this, again in the character of Antiochus Epiphanes and in accordance with the direct instruction of Jesus in Matthew 24:15. To understand Revelation 13, we must understand the Nativity.

Secondly, just as the Olivet Discourse and Revelation 6 (as well as Acts 2 and Joel 2) tell us the coming of Christ will be preceded by a sign in the heavenlies, so, too, the wise men recognized the sign in the heavenlies at His First Coming and were prepared for His arrival.

It is further true that Israel and Jerusalem entered into what was supposed to be a treaty with Rome, but soon found itself a subordinated colony. It is not mere coincidence that some European leaders such as Silvio Berlesconi have suggested Israel be invited into the European Union. Rome kept a false and precarious peace, but did so at a high price with the pagan eagles and ensigns of Imperial Rome and its religion towering over the House of God (the Second Temple) from the adjacent Fortress Antonio.

The Role of Herod the Great

All of these events must transpire again, yet the dragon in Revelation 12:4 is personified in the person of Herod the Great as a type. Herod introduced Greco-Roman architecture into the Jewish Temple in his renovation of it, in part using Ezekiel's vision of the millennial Temple as a blueprint. In other words, the Antichrist acting in the character of Herod the Great will also redesign the Temple, bring pagan elements into it, and, as it were, establish a pretended millennial Kingdom which after 3-1/2 years at most will quickly sour. The seven heads and ten horns of Daniel's vision appear in Revelation 4:12 in parody to the deeds of Herod attempting to intercept and devour the man-child. Few things will prove as important in identifying the Antichrist as an understanding of why Daniel's vision reappears in Revelation 12:4 in a replica of Herod and his actions.

Herod was by ethnicity an Idumean—that is, from an Arab nation of Moabite and Edomite origins. According to Genesis 36, Arab nations are the descendants of Ishmael who interbred with the descendants of Esau and lived in a land to the east and southeast of Israel. In the Hasmonean Period some of them migrated toward the Negev in Southern Israel after the Hasmoneans conquered the eastern shores of the Dead Sea and the border region between Moab and Edom. The Idumeans have a Greek name deriving from the Semitic "Edom." They converted to Judaism as their religion but were also influenced by Greek culture. Thus Herod was an Arab by race, a Jew by religion, and a Roman by culture and political allegiance.

His adherence to Judaism, however, was a religion of political convenience. Moreover, he was not a Davidic king, in fulfillment of Jacob's prophecy of Genesis 49:10 that the scepter could not depart from Judah until Shiloh came. Ancient Jewish thought identified this as a metaphor for the Messiah. Thus a non-Davidic king was used to fill the empty throne as the Jews awaited the Messiah who would be of the pedigree of David.

To the Romans Herod was a Roman; his culture was Western and his political loyalties and allegiances were to Imperial Rome. To the Jews he was a Jewish king (although not a Davidic one). And to the Arabian nations he was an ethnic Arab. Herod could be all things to all people. He could bridge the East and West ethnically, culturally, legally, politically, and, above all, religiously.

As the figure who will seek to broker a false peace in the Middle East between Jew and Arab, keeping Israel in the Western sphere of control yet placating Arab demands, the world is awaiting another Herod. There is no other explanation as to why Revelation 12:4 is taken directly from the Book of Daniel, with seven heads and ten horns in the character of Herod the Great, who was also power mad and driven to do all he could to prevent the coming of Christ as King. This will in some way happen again.

What is perhaps most important in understanding the saga of Herod and the Nativity is not simply that the First Coming of Christ prefigures His Second Coming, but also that only a faithful remnant of Jews were ready for His First Coming despite having the Scriptures and the signs. The mainstream religious establishment was not ready, their leaders were not ready, and most people professing faith in Judaism were not ready. There was, however, a faithful remnant that was ready. The same will be no less true for the Second Coming of Jesus in regard to both Israel and the Church.

With specific respect to the Antichrist, we must note that Herod was a devious man and a clever liar, skilled in intrigue. He falsely claimed good intentions for wishing to know where the Messiah—the King of Israel—was to be born. The wise men, however, were divinely guided not only in understanding the signs, but by means of angelic agency were directed away from being duped by Herod. (Precisely the same as Jotham was not duped by Abimelech as we shall see, and recorded in Judges 9.) So, too, those led of the Lord operating in His wisdom will not be duped by the Antichrist. Christmas is indeed coming.

Summary

Just as Christmas is coming again, metaphorically speaking, so is Hanukkah. The events surrounding the Nativity concerning the relationship between Israel and the Roman Empire experience a dramatic replay in everything from emperor worship of Caesar Augustus who numbers people for financial purposes, to a Pompeii who makes a treaty and breaks it and enters the Holy of Holies, to a Herod the Great. Each of these figures provides us a composite and detailed portrait of what the Antichrist will do just prior to the return of Jesus. Likewise, the Euro-Federalism, conflict with Iran (scripturally conveyed as a conflict with Persia in Daniel 10), fragmentation, and the arrival of Antiochus Epiphanes (Antiochus IV from the Seleucid Dynasty) which will likewise culminate with an abomination in the Temple in some manner, all must reoccur with the Antichrist.

The festal typology of Hanukkah and the events surrounding the Nativity, as well as the evolution of historical events leading up to these two points in history, must be understood as foreshadows of what is to come. Just as in the epistle to the Hebrews, if we cannot properly identify, comprehend, and understand the shadow, we will not be prepared to recognize the substance when it arrives. This constitutes the essence of the milieu of future events prefigured by past events that account for how and why the Antichrist will emerge.

Part Five: The False Prophet

As we have noted, Revelation 13 does not identify either Beast as "Antichrist", but merely as beasts. These two characters, however, will be the epitome of all that is Antichrist in the diabolical trinity which includes Satan, the political Antichrist, and the religious Antichrist which we call the False Prophet.

As there are types and shadows of the political Antichrist that establish a pattern which will be a crucial element in identifying him, the quest for identification of the Antichrist likewise applies to the False Prophet. It is not likely that the former will be recognized unless we also identify the latter. We have conveyed that there are foreshadowings of the False Prophet seen in biblical type such as Goliath's armor bearer and in biblically prophesied foreshadowings of the False Prophet, most notably Rabbi Akiva pointing the way to Simon Bar Kochba.

A comprehensive understanding of the False Prophet will include the consideration of how the many false prophets of the Last Days foreshadow him. Also, we must understand that the stage will be confused by the fact that there will be ***many*** false prophets pointing to ***many*** antichrists. The key will be to understand the ultimate, unique one as something different than the various others who arise and foreshadow him. The Antichrist will engineer a betrayal, coming to power by a constellation of religious, political and economic means.

Chapter 12: The Contemporary Configuration Takes Shape

Already we see rumblings for this kind of scenario to take place. It is vital again to understand that the Antichrist and False Prophet will operate by spiritual seduction, intrigue, and betrayal. As we speak, the spirit of antichrist is preparing the apostate church for the coming of the Antichrist, just as the Holy Spirit is preparing the faithful Church for the return of Christ. The thrusts of the efforts of Antichrist to seduce and betray will as always be concentrated on Israel, the Jews, and the Church. For too long sincere Christians have focused only on one aspect of the seductive agenda designed in hell that will position the Antichrist where he must be in the ultimate satanic attempt to preempt the return of Jesus. The Church has focused on the seductions aimed at the world, but has understated the seductions aimed at the Church.

Christians observe the outwardly obvious trends alone, but deception and intrigue require that we understand the less obvious as well. Many of us can grasp that as the economy becomes checkless, it will soon become cashless with online purchases, bill payments, and cash transfers all being monitored by governments. The justification of this will be "national security" in order to counter terrorism and the financing of terror. In truth, this is nonsense.

For the sake of the international energy lobby, corrupt Western governments continue to openly allow Wahhabist Saudi Arabians and other sources of Muslim oil money to finance fundamentalist Islam and its institutions throughout the West, providing a fifth column for future jihad. Every western country that has ever allowed Islamic immigration has had social unrest and civil violence as a result. Yet godless politicians have allowed it to continue. Common sense actions such as security profiling Muslim airline passengers, and closing or restricting immigration from Muslim countries, are never undertaken by Western governments even though they know they are importing both a radical minority element and a majority Islamic element willing to go along with radical Islam. Think of it much the same as what happened in Nazi Germany. Most Germans were not

Nazis, but most Germans went along with the Nazis. Again, godless governments know this, and the western media and academic institutions ignore it. The war on terror is rather a device to defraud citizens of their rights and freedoms, and to give government license to infringe upon their lives in areas it otherwise could not have, including taxation and financial control. Hence government monitoring of Internet communications will facilitate the taxation of online banking and trading of every description.

This will prove to be an obvious prelude to no one being able to "buy or sell" without the mark of the Beast (Rev. 13:17). One by one, all of the necessary mechanisms and elements will be surreptitiously put into place in a manner that seems non-integrated, but which very quickly can and will be highly integrated. Again, such trends many Christians can see. What most fail to see, however, is that not only are there political and economic dimensions, but a religious dimension.

This will come in the name of "a theology of economic justice" with ideas that will come not from Scripture but from both Catholic and Protestant Liberation Theology alike. Be it Bonino and Sobrino from the Catholic side or Desmond Tutu and Jim Wallace on the Protestant side, the Gospel is being re-written based on a concept of reparation (a euphemism for forced wealth redistribution) instead of repentance, and a collective salvation based on an imagined social redemption instead of a personal one based on the atonement of Christ. Liberation Theology draws its hermeneutic from the subjective practice of consciousization, where one does not begin with what the Scripture says about social justice, but rather with one's political ideology, reading that into the text of Scripture as the beginning point.

On the political right, however, there was no need for consciousization. The political Protestantism of Northern Ireland has long had its false theological root in its Calvinism and Reconstructionism of Covenant Theology, and has been with us from Calvin's Geneva to Puritan England to Colonial Salem, Massachusetts.

Both the liberalism and Reconstructionism are unbiblical. ***Both*** are wrong, and ***both*** will be, and are being, used by the spirit of antichrist to seduce the Church into being the harbinger of the "*man of sin*" when the Church would rather be a harbinger of the return of Christ. This seduction is taking place within the Church on both the political left and the political right, with supposed Evangelicals on both sides of the equation.

Religious Motives Leverage Political Issues

Additionally, Christians have often looked closely at false peace treaties in the Middle East—such as the Oslo Accords which were quickly broken by the forces of Islam. The West ignores the Islamic doctrines of "*taqwid*" and "*hudna*." In *taqwid*, permissible lying to the infidel (non-Muslim) is not seen as lying but as mere military disinformation in the jihad. The doctrine of *hudna* means agreeing to a peace which the Muslim understands to be temporary until he can get a strategic advantage, but the infidel believes to be permanent. Yet in order to placate oil interests, western governments intentionally remain oblivious to such realities. And they pressure Israel to exchange land for peace when, in truth, that is theologically impossible both from the perspective of scriptural prophecy and from the perspective of jihadist Islamic dogma.

The administration of George H.W. Bush created a radical Islamic terrorist state in southern Lebanon operated by Hezbollah but controlled by Iran and Syria. Bush pressured Israel and handed Lebanon over to Syria on a silver platter in 1991. His son, George W. Bush, repeated the action of his father in Gaza, pressing for a unilateral Israeli withdrawal which resulted in a Hamas state, armed and controlled by Iran and Syria. The Bush family, closely aligned financially with the Wahhabist Saudi Arabian House of Saud through the Carlisle Group whose general counsel is anti-Israel former Secretary of State James Baker, implemented these accords with Islam in the name of "peace." This, even though it was inevitable that Hamas and Hezbollah would quickly take over and use the newly gained territory to continue the jihad against not only Israel but the West, as well as persecute Arab Christians. Indeed, the Bush family and many American politicians, including Barack Obama, are controlled by the spirit of antichrist with a *Quran* and Ramadan celebrations in the White House, and betrayals of both Israel and the persecuted Church.

Even many Christians do not understand how the outworking of international affairs in the political realm today is preparing for the Antichrist. But those who do will, at best, generally see it purely in terms of economic trends toward a one-world electronic currency, political trends toward a one-world government, and ecumenical trends toward a one-world religion. Far too few understand the seduction taking place ***within*** the Church, including what is supposedly the Evangelical Church. The political-religious environment we currently see has to a large degree already created the environment in which the False Prophet will point people toward Antichrist.

Antichrist Types and Their False Prophet Types

In the 1940s Billy Graham publically stated that the three biggest enemies to the Gospel of Christ are Marxism, Mohammedanism (Islam), and Romanism (Roman Catholicism). Billy Graham tragically changed his position. In his 1989 crusade in London, Billy Graham had a Roman Catholic Cardinal (later implicated in the protection of pedophile priests) on his platform at Earl's Court.

The front page of the Chicago newspapers disclosed a declassified secret White House recording of Billy Graham in conversation with Richard Nixon denouncing Jews and showing plainly that both men were vehement anti-Semites. Graham actually said if his Jewish friends only knew what he really thought of them, what would they think as Nixon and Graham discussed the need to stop the influence of the Jews in Hollywood, etc. (In fact, Hollywood has as many left-wing non-Jews as it does Jews as well from Michael Savage to David Horowitz to Bernie Goldberg to Dick Morrison to Ben Stein to Richard Pearl, to Michael Medved. A disproportionately large amount of America's conservative spokesmen are likewise Jewish.) Thus we see in Billy Graham's relationship with Nixon a religious leader who lent his public blessing for electoral purposes to a corrupt political leader who was vehemently opposed to Jews. The False Prophet and the Antichrist will do the same on a widely expanded scale. There has been no shortage of religious leaders following in the footsteps of Billy Graham.

On the political left Barack Obama has had as his pastor Jeremiah Wright, who preaches that Israel is a dirty word, and "God damn America," while spewing vitriolic, racially-charged epithets against white Americans. These actions are difficult to define as anything other than racist hatred. Obama's spiritual confidante, Jim Wallace, has stated that the redistribution of wealth is the gospel. Again, we have seen religious leaders pointing to a political figure like Obama. In one speech Obama belittled the Scriptures, and in another he stated that America is not a Christian nation while touting every anti-Judeo-Christian policy imaginable while being the first American president to distance himself from national Israel. The pattern is becoming more and more acute. Religious leaders in the name of Christianity are politically swaying Christian opinion in support of dubious politicians who somehow always manage to oppose Israel and the Jews no matter what the cost.

In 1982 the Reagan White House evacuated injured Marines to hospitals in Germany and Britain from Lebanon after the suicide bombings on the American embassy rather than to the nearby operating tables less than thirty minutes away in Northern Israel. This was done so as not to offend the Saudi Arabians, causing the Marines to instead arrive D.O.A. thousands of miles away. The unscrupulous actions of these politicians and the clergy who help get them elected are a mere hint of the relationship the False Prophet will have with the Antichrist, and the actions of betrayal that will result.

The Gospel & Politics

There is no biblical ground in the New Testament to align the Gospel message with a political party or ideology. Christians are rather taught in the Bible to be salt and light within their nations and societies, and to contend for biblical principles. The politically-related action outlined for Christians in the New Testament are chiefly limited to three essential things: praying for those in power, appealing to Caesar, and being good citizens as a witness and testimony while not bowing to man's laws when they directly contradict God's laws.

One evil that has resulted from this convergence of party politics and Christian belief on both the political left ***and*** right has been a compromise of the Gospel itself. In order to advance a socially redeeming moral agenda on issues such as abortion and freedom of religious speech, many Christians have compromised evangelism to groups like Roman Catholics and Mormons, seeking to have them as political allies. This is a seduction in itself. Any socially redeeming action undertaken by the Body of Christ must be subordinated to the scriptural Gospel and evangelism. It is spiritual seduction to think or do otherwise. We once again end up with a mere social gospel, remembering that the Antichrist is going to use a social gospel in large measure to seduce the masses and gain power. The same spirit outside of the Church operates inside the Church. While Christians can easily see the workings of the devil through the abortion and same-sex marriage agenda concerning these social issues, they are blind to the fact that they are likewise being duped into a social gospel.

This in essence is how the False Prophet will work: he will use a religious ideology capable of deceiving the Elect (up to a point) in order to lend credence to the *"man of lawlessness."* With the final Antichrist, however, it will be a greatly expanded agenda and have another feature not found with other political preachers, the capacity to do counterfeit miracles by satanic power.

It is not our suggestion that Billy Graham or the late Jerry Falwell were in any sense deliberate false prophets, but rather that they were seduced by the spirit of antichrist into behaving in the ***character*** of the False Prophet and in so doing claimed a role in preparing for the False Prophet. The ultimate False Prophet will go well beyond all other false prophets much the same as the ultimate *"man of lawlessness"* will go well beyond all other antichrists.

Chapter 13: Biblical & Historical Types of the False Prophet

In the New Testament we see high priests chosen from the Sanhedrin who functioned at the behest of Rome and the Herodians. These were largely Sadducees whose forefathers were righteous men known as the Zadokites or "Sons of Zadok" spoken of by Ezekiel the prophet (Eze. 40:4; 48:11). The Zadokites became corrupted during the later Hasmonean Period. They disintegrated into two evils that are in the Church today, and who will indeed play an important role in the activities of the False Prophet and his religious empowering of the "*man of lawlessness*." The Sadducees were interested in political and financial power. The purchase of the high priesthood was achieved by being in league with the hated Romans and their Herodian surrogates. We see high priests like Caiaphas and Annas who were opposed to Christ and feared losing their religious power to Him. Thus they were willing to bow the knee to the imperial power of pagan Rome as the price for retaining the privilege of their position. This is a tremendous foreshadowing of what will happen when the Antichrist arrives on the scene supported by religious leaders.

The primary religious leader, however, will not be a mere theocrat, but will have satanically induced power to perform supernatural signs and wonders. Thus we must understand how all of the false prophets in Scripture reveal some aspect of the final False Prophet. The nature of counterfeit miracles does not necessarily mean that the miracles are inauthentic, just as Pharaoh's magicians were by demonic power able to perform supernatural displays of power. The nature of the counterfeit rather lies in where the power comes from. The False Prophet will of course claim to be performing these signs in the name of the God of Scripture even though nothing can be further from the truth. Thus we have the warning of Jesus that a wicked and adulterous generation seeks a sign (Mt. 12:39). Jesus never allowed miraculous displays to be the focus of His message or His ministry, but rather "these signs follow" (Mk. 16:20) the preaching of the Gospel both in His ministry and in the ministry of the apostles He groomed.

We are moreover reminded that many believed the truth about Jesus through the preaching of John the Baptist although John performed no sign. This is of course in no way to deny or reject a biblical understanding or practice of charismatic gifts or miraculous displays of God's power today. It is simply to say that too much of what is practiced today in modern charismatic and Pentecostal circles of the Church is not scriptural, and the proponents of such deceptions often have a corrupted or false gospel. In some cases they have another Christ entirely, be it the Jesus who dies spiritually presented by E. W. Kenyon, Kenneth Hagin, Kenneth Copeland and their imitators, or miracles attributed to the Eucharistic Christ in mystical expressions of Roman Catholicism.

The Legacy & Pattern of False Prophets

Because Jesus iterated multiple times that there would be a proliferation of false prophets in the Last Days, we must understand the basic definition of a false prophet. In short, it is someone who speaks God's Word falsely, or who points people to another god which, when applied in the New Testament sense, can mean to another Christ. We see the basic definition in Deuteronomy:

> *"If a prophet or a dreamer of dreams arises among you and gives you a sign or a wonder, and the sign or the wonder comes true, concerning which he spoke to you, saying, 'Let us go after other gods (whom you have not known) and let us serve them,' you shall not listen to the words of that prophet or that dreamer of dreams; for the LORD your God is testing you to find out if you love the LORD your God with all your heart and with all your soul.* (Dt. 13:1-3)

A false prophet may indeed perform actual signs, yet he will point to another god. Likewise, in Deuteronomy 18:20-22 we are instructed that there are false prophets who make predictive prophecies specific as to time and events (as we later read in Jeremiah's conflict with Hananiah).

> *'But the prophet who speaks a word presumptuously in My name which I have not commanded him to speak, or which he speaks in the name of other gods, that prophet shall die.' "You may say in your heart, 'How will we know the word which the LORD has not spoken?' When a prophet speaks in the name of the LORD, if the thing does not come about or come true, that is the thing which the*

> *LORD has not spoken. The prophet has spoken it presumptuously; you shall not be afraid of him.* (Dt. 18:20-22)

Thus when we see those pointing to another god or another Christ, or who predict things in the name of the Lord that fail to happen when they are assigned a certain time, Christians are commanded to avoid them because they are demonstrably false irrespective of any signs they may perform.

The prophecies of Fatima with the claimed Mariophony and alleged solar phenomena are debunked as false because so many of these predictions such as the end of World War I on a specific date simply did not come true. The prophecies of Benny Hinn for the elimination of homosexuals likewise show him to be false and not of God.

The London 1990 false predictions of Mike Bickel and Paul Cain of the Kansas City (False) Prophets likewise warn Christians to avoid such deceivers.

In the same manner, the wild predictions of Cindy Jacobs that failed to transpire for Zimbabwe and elsewhere, and the outrageous predictions of Rick Joyner, Bob Jones, and Bill Johnson made over adulterer Todd Bentley, define these men as among those Jesus warned us to avoid in the Last Days.

A complete list of false prophets by scriptural definition operating in the Church today would be too exhaustive for any one book, yet the trend is clear: people are following those false prophets that Jesus warned us would one day come—those whom we are commanded by Jesus to avoid. If Christians are unable to see through those who by scriptural definition are ***obvious*** false prophets, there is no way they will be able to see ***the*** False Prophet who is to come as the precursor of the Antichrist.

The New Testament Definition

To understand the theology of a false prophet we must again understand it in light of the New Testament explanation by the apostle Peter.

> *But false prophets also arose among the people, just as there will also be false teachers among you, who will secretly introduce destructive heresies, even denying the Master who bought them, bringing swift destruction upon themselves. Many will follow their sensuality, and because of them the way of the truth will be maligned; and in their greed they will exploit you with false words;*

> *their judgment from long ago is not idle, and their destruction is not asleep.* (2 Pe. 2:1-3)

Peter gives us three clear characteristics of these deceivers:

- They will seek to seduce the church with "*pareisaxousin*" —"*destructive heresies*"—that place truth next to error;

- Peter uses the terms "false prophet" and "false teacher" as if they were synonymous and interchangeable. If someone's doctrines are wrong it becomes inevitable that their prophecies will be false. Thus we see the false prophetic predictions made by Kenneth Copeland, Benny Hinn, Cindy Jacobs and others hand-in-hand with the fact that their doctrines are fundamentally wrong;

- Peter tells us they are driven by a motive of personal gain. This is precisely what motivated the high priests at the time of the crucifixion of Jesus.

Once again, unless there is a genuine repentance and recognition of the error into which they have sold themselves or been seduced, there is no hope for the devotees of the money preaching televangelists and other false prophets of our day. As the Scriptures tell us, if people "*fall down in a land of peace, how will you do in the thicket of the Jordan?*" (Jer. 12:5). If people cannot see the obvious, how will they avoid the less obvious?

What should be no less obvious to Christians today is again the tripod that Satan will use to bring the Antichrist to power. That is, the combination of economic, political, and religious means. What should be particularly frightening to saved Christians today is that the three legs of this tripod are already being advocated by Rick Warren in his pursuit of an interfaith global peace plan that is devoid of the saving Gospel of Jesus.

Once more, a social gospel has never saved a single sole or kept one person out of hell. Charitable activities are the result of regeneration, but in and of themselves they do not, and cannot, regenerate. Because such antichrist notions cannot save a single member of society, neither can they save society. While people push social gospels, this Christless counterfeit will not prevent the utter mayhem and human social, political, economic, and strategic catastrophe such abject pursuits are formulated to avert. In fact, under the hand of Satan a social gospel will promulgate those ills and impede the possibility of doing anything about them, because the real Gospel has been lost.

The Quintessential Example of Caiaphas

The figure who is probably the quintessential New Testament type of the False Prophet is Caiaphas. The epistle to the Hebrews teaches us that the Aaronic High Priest who made atonement for the sin of the people is the ritual type of Christ as our High Priest. Hence we have someone who was anointed of God to foreshadow **THE** Anointed One of God. Corruption in the priesthood dated back to Hophni and Phinehas, the sons of Eli the priest mentioned in 1 Samuel 2. These were unbelievers driven by greed, yet who found themselves in a position of religious power that they simply misused for their own aggrandizement. And their father failed to correct them until it was too late.

Whenever nepotism and theocratic politics prevent godly clergy from defrocking ungodly ones, the outcome will always be doomed. We have seen this today repeatedly with the failure of honest preachers to confront money preaching televangelists and counterfeit revivalists. They would rather let destruction come at the expense of the people and to the dishonor of the Lord than act to remove such clergy. This will be one aspect of how the False Prophet will come to power.

We see in Caiaphas someone motivated with that same kind of greed for power and wealth. Caiaphas put himself ***in place of*** Christ as a judge of Christ. Had he judged on the basis of the Word of Christ (which is as much the Torah as it is the New Testament) he would have known who Christ was. In Matthew 26 we see his self-serving and auto-preserving antics and manipulations at the religious trial of Jesus. In the position which he occupied, he again had to operate in league with the dreaded Romans and the Herodians; by default he paid homage to Caesar as the pagan ensigns of the Fortress Antonio towered over the House of God on the Temple Mount.

In this, however, he was hardly unique. When Christ was born, Herod—a major type of the Antichrist—likewise operated with the participation of the chief priests (Matthew 2:4). What made Caiaphas unique, however, was that during his tenure he prophesied correctly (Jn. 11:49-52), just as backslidden King Saul had prophesied (1 Sam. 10:11). He was able to exercise spiritual authority and, although with wrong motives, even spoke truth, correctly elaborating on the Word of God. The False Prophet to come will in some way do the same. What we see in John 11 will be replayed in some way by the False Prophet. What is also important, however, is his denunciation of Jesus as a blasphemer for proclaiming Himself the Son of God. It is again antichrist, according to John's epistle—that which denies the Father-Son relationship specifically (1 Jn. 1:22). And this, Caiaphas does.

No less importantly, however, is that under his tenure as high priest the people were incited to say, "*We have no king but Caesar*" (Jn. 19:15). To this day, in Hebrew liturgy Yahweh is proclaimed as King of the Universe, and we know that Jesus was proclaimed even by Pilate to be the King of the Jews (Jn. 19:19), who as a direct descendant of King David He rightfully is. In using his religious position of leadership to persuade and inflame the populous to claim that not only is Caesar their king but that there is no other king, Caiaphas exhibited antichrist connotations even then, and showed what will happen in the future. Caesar was deified; emperors were worshiped. Thus the declaration, "*We have no king but Caesar*" was not only a rejection of the true Christ as King, but an embracing of a false one.

The False Prophet to come will likewise in some way operate with a charismata, but will use it and his position to both convince people to reject the biblical Jesus and proclaim their allegiance to a false one. It is absolutely imperative that Caiaphas be accurately understood as a type and a shadow.

Acting in the Character of the Dragon

The False Prophet in Revelation 13, although a religious leader, speaks as a dragon as did Caiaphas, as did Mohammed, and as did the medieval popes. As we see in the Book of Revelation, the two modes of attack used by Satan are the dragon (the aggressive persecutor) and the serpent (the spiritual seducer). With the fall of Adam the serpent first beguiled the woman Eve, a figure of Israel and a type of the Church. The serpent first came, however, as either a biped or a quadruped before being divinely judged to crawl as a snake. The dragon and serpent are both active from Genesis through Revelation, and both will be pivotal in the escapades of the Antichrist and False Prophet. Caiaphas and the Sanhedrin managed to seduce the people (hence the reference by Jesus of the backslidden clergy in Matthew 23:33 as being a generation of "serpents"), but they attacked Christ Himself in the character of the dragon.

This dragon-like nature of the False Prophet in Revelation 13 is prefigured by the violent nature of Caiaphas, witnessed in the arrest of Christ, complete with the bribery of Judas, a type of the "*man of sin.*" Thus in the final persecution of Christ we see active a type of both the Antichrist and the False Prophet. There are in the behavior of Caiaphas three additional features evident that are going to prove important in identifying the ultimate False Prophet:

1. He defiled God's Temple (the physical body of Jesus). 1 Peter 2:5, Ephesians 4, and multiple other passages of the New Testament show us that the physical body of Jesus was represented by the physical structure of the Temple. And Hebrews 9 directly connects the destruction of the Temple with the destruction of Christ's physical body. The same will prove true for the Church in the Last Days. The true Body of Christ will face an onslaught initiated not at first by the civil authorities, but by the religious authorities in collusion with them. The persecution by the Antichrist will commence with the actions of the False Prophet against the Body of Christ.

   It is typologically non-coincidental that at the religious trial of Jesus before Caiaphas, accusations were made against Him for saying He would raise the Temple up in three days (Mt. 26:61). Eschatologically, the same will in some sense prove true for the faithful Church (Hos. 6:2), although there are differing interpretations of what the "third day" means in that context;

2. Just as two false witnesses were brought by Caiaphas against Christ in Jerusalem, in Revelation 11 two true witnesses will bear witness for Christ, also in Jerusalem;

3. It was at the time of the arrest and trial of Jesus ordered by Caiaphas that Peter began to follow at a distance while most of the other Apostles fled. So, too, when the False Prophet acts directly against the Body of Christ, there will be a scattering and we will see Christians keen to save their own necks, publicly distancing themselves from Christ. As always, the future is in the past.

To understand this we must realize that what Jesus told the apostles and disciples when He sent them out in pairs in Matthew 10:15-22 did not happen to the followers of Jesus at that time, but did later happen to Jesus Himself and will happen to the faithful Church at the end of the age. This includes being brought before governors and kings, being betrayed even by parents and children, and being hated by all nations for the sake of Christ. The impetus for this persecution will come from the False Prophet.

Again, the urgency of understanding the importance of Caiaphas as ***the*** major type of the False Prophet cannot be overstated. He sets the template for what will happen to the faithful Church throughout most of its history, and paints the picture of what the False Prophet will do as a dragon at the end of the age.

The Dragon That Looks Like a Lamb

> *Then I saw another beast coming up out of the earth; and he had two horns like a lamb and he spoke as a dragon.* (Rev. 13:11)

In Revelation 13:11 we have the perfect picture of a deceiver who looks like a lamb but is in fact a dragon, of whom we have a picture in Caiaphas, and a picture that has been painted time and time again with each successive pope.

Even in the modern world Pope Pius XXII was in league with Benito Mussolini while Hitler made a concordat with the Roman Catholic bishops of Bavaria, and the Roman Catholic hierarchy directly participated in the genocidal extermination of the Serbs and Jews by the Ustashi Nazis in the former Yugoslavia at the behest of Archbishop Stepinac. (Stepinac was beatified as a candidate for possible sainthood by Pope John Paul II.) John Paul II, Pope John XXIII, and Pope Benedict XVI were all party to the *Criminales Solicitaciones* instruction protecting pedophile clergy at the expense of the children whom they violated. Such men all look like lambs but behave like dragons. This exemplifies the description of the False Prophet in Revelation 13, and is embodied in the character of Caiaphas. All of them are religious figures who look like lambs but behave like dragons.

Ahitophel as a Type

Another biblical type of the False Prophet is Ahitophel in 2 Samuel 15-17. Here we observe King David on the Mt. of Olives with his closest followers, realizing he was about to be betrayed. This of course prophetically foreshadows the weeping of Jesus the Son of David on the same location. It is here that Ahitophel, who had been offering sacrifices and acted as an advisor and confidante to David, is disclosed as a traitor who not only secretly collaborated with Absalom but advised Absalom to depose his father the rightful king.

Ahitophel had an outwardly good reputation as a royal counselor, knowing intimate details about David and his court, but was in league with David's opponents. Absalom would not have managed to gain the momentum he did without the assistance of Ahitophel. More importantly, however, it was Ahitophel who played the pivotal role in persuading the people from the northern tribes to forsake David and follow Absalom. The False Prophet will do the same with reference to the rise of the Antichrist and, like Ahitophel, he will be as much a religious figure as a political one.

We can understand Ahitophel as a kind of Old Testament version of French Cardinal Richelieu in the court of Louis XIV or Cardinal Woolsey in the House of Henry VIII. Although Woolsey did the political and religious beckoning of the king, he also betrayed him, acting in his own interests. Ahitophel's relationship to Absalom is akin to the False Prophet's relationship to the first Beast in that he again appeared like a lamb but behaved like a dragon. It was Ahitophel who urged violence against the House of David and against David himself.

For this relationship between Ahitophel and Absalom to make sense, however, we must understand Absalom as typifying the Antichrist. He wanted the place of David just as Antichrist will want the place of Jesus the Son of David. Absalom died accursed of God, hanging on a tree after arriving riding on a beast of burden in 2 Samuel 18. Again, this is an account of a wicked betrayer doing something that would imitate the later actions of Christ. As Absalom had his Ahitophel, the Antichrist will have his False Prophet. They will be of like character, motive, and modus operandi to a noticeable degree.

Rabshakeh

In our consideration of the king of Assyria, particularly Sennacherib, Rabshakeh typifies the False Prophet just as Sennacherib typifies the Antichrist in his mode as king of Assyria. In addition to Isaiah there are synoptic accounts of this in Chronicles and Kings (2 Ki. 18-19; 2 Chr. 32; Is. 36-37). Rabshakeh delivered a religious message in order to urge God's people under Hezekiah and Isaiah to follow the king of Assyria. Rabshakeh challenges the theological premise of Hezekiah and his deputies in trusting the God of Israel, pointing to the fact that Sennacherib conquered other kings, including Pharaoh. So, too, the False Prophet will champion the cause of Antichrist by using religious speech to paint him as invincible. He will then offer material incentives for them to change their theology. While it is beyond the scope of this book, we do warn readers of the Word-Faith message of televangelist money preachers who likewise attempt to induce and seduce Christians into aberrational theology by false offers and guarantees of material and financial blessing. This, too, is an activity of the spirit of antichrist.

More importantly, however, in Isaiah 36:10 we see that Rabshakeh falsely claims to be speaking for the God of Israel. So, too, in his character, the False Prophet will misrepresent himself as speaking for the authentic God of Christians and Jews. In verses 11-12 we see the leaders of God's people trying to shield the people from hearing the seductive words of Rabshakeh by asking him not to speak in Hebrew, but Rabshakeh, failing to persuade the leaders, rather takes his message directly to the people. So, too, the False Prophet will attempt to speak to the flock over the voices of any shepherds warning them not to listen.

In Isaiah 36:21 we see that God's people did not even reply to Rabshakeh. The False Prophet will not be someone to engage. In 37:3 we also see that the day of this conflict will be a day of distress that is related to the sin of God's people. But in 37:4 we see a kind of virtual ventriloquism where Rabshakeh speaks the words of the king of Assyria just as the False Prophet will speak the words of the Antichrist. And in this verse and in the verses that follow we once more see what Daniel would later describe as speaking blasphemies against the Most High (Dan. 7:25). This all provides us foreknowledge and insight into the manner in which the False Prophet will function and what he will attempt to do.

In our treatment of the king of Assyria as a type of the Antichrist, we looked at the relationship of Rabshakeh to Sennacherib as an indication of what kind of relationship the False Prophet will have with the Antichrist. Here, however, we more concentrate on Rabshakeh himself as an important type of the False Prophet.

John Hyricanus

When it comes to historical types of the False Prophet we are reminded that we do not look in any sense to extra-biblical sources for our doctrinal understanding, yet we must bear in mind, that the Antichrist will deceive the Jews (and also the Arabs to some degree). We must therefore comprehend the messianic expectation of the Jews no matter how biblically untenable those expectations may be. He will do as they expect.

In *The Dead Sea Scrolls* we read a *peshurim* on Psalm 37 which is connected with the Book of Habakkuk. In these documents we read of a figure called "*hacohen harasha,*" mentioned four times in 1QpHab and one time in 4QpPsa. This is a sobriquet on the wicked high priest. He has been variously identified as Jonathan of the Maccabees and John Hyricanus I—a high priest who wrongly proclaimed himself to be king—the brother of Hyricanus, Aristobulus I, and Alexander Jannaeus, circa 103 B.C., who had a military alliance with Cleopatra in Egypt and who killed the proto-Pharisees who at that time were righteous and doctrinally upright.

It is not unlikely that Hyricanus and Alexander Jannaeus both speak of this wicked high priest. The wicked high priest is said by some scholars to be the same as "the liar" who begins benevolently but ends badly by deceiving the people, although others say "the liar" and the wicked priest are two different individuals. The liar bears an acute resemblance to Simon Bar Kochba, who as we have already addressed, is a major type of the Antichrist with his clerical adjunct Rabbi Akiva—a foreshadow of the False Prophet. This liar is described in the Qumran literature thusly:

> The Liar
>
> Some scholars do not differentiate between the Wicked Priest and the Liar ("Man of the Lie"), another sobriquet used in 1QpHab. For example, the description of the liar building "his city of vanity with blood" (1QpHab 10.10) has been marshaled another clue to the identity of the Wicked Priest

The association of Alexander Jannaeus with Cleopatra, given the prophecy about Cleopatra in the Book of Daniel (Dan. 11:17-20), makes Alexander Jannaeus a curious figure, as does the quest by John Hyricanus to unite the high priestly and royal offices. Hyricanus also destroyed the Samaritan temple on Mt. Gerizim, thus centralizing Jewish worship on Mt. Zion to the sides of the north with whom the Antichrist will be associated. What is most important about the wicked high priest, however, is that he emerges as the opponent to one who is called "the teacher of righteousness." We read the description of him as follows from the Dead Sea Scrolls:

> "Moreover, the arrogant man seizes wealth without halting. He widens his gullet like Hell and like Death he has never enough. All the nations are gathered to him and all the people are assembled

> to him. Will they not all of them taunt him and jeer at him saying, 'Woe to him who amasses that which is not his! How long will he load himself up with pledges?
>
> Interpreted, this concerns the Wicked Priest who was called by the name of truth when he first arose. But when he ruled over Israel his heart became proud, and he forsook God and betrayed the precepts for the sake of riches. He robbed and amassed the riches of men of violence who rebelled against God, and he took the wealth of the peoples, heaping sinful iniquity upon himself. And he lived in the ways of abominations amidst every unclean defilement."
>
> —1QpHab, col. 8, lines 411

It is again important that we understand that Jewish mysticism assigns a future prophetic meaning to these things whether we do or not, and that the Antichrist will play upon this in his efforts to deceive the Jews. We can understand how the teacher of righteousness whom the wicked high priest opposes is Jesus the Messiah. Whoever this wicked high priest was is unclear. Indeed it may have been more than one individual as some scholars contend. What is clear, however, is that whoever this figure is, he prefigures the False Prophet to come.

Roman Catholic Parallels

We must further take note of the fact that in Roman Catholic eschatology a Roman emperor figure will be proclaimed as "hero" by the last and final pope. Again we do not draw our theology or eschatology from Roman Catholicism, but we must understand what they believe in order to understand in part what the False Prophet must do.

What is vital, however, is to keep in mind that the historical types of the False Prophet will always behave in the character of the biblical types. We likewise in Acts 5 see the high priest persecuting the apostles and charging them not to preach Christ, pronouncing it a breach of both religious and civil law to do so, their civil authority being accorded to them by their allegiance to Rome. So, too, inquisitional Roman Catholicism has behaved in the same manner. Both Beasts—the Antichrist and the "*man of lawlessness*"—are equally "antichrist," from the Greek carrying the meaning of both "in opposition to" and "in place of." We see this in Matthew:

> *"But do not be called Rabbi; for One is your Teacher, and you are all brothers. Do not call anyone on earth your father; for One is your Father, He who is in heaven. Do not be called leaders; for One is your Leader, that is, Christ."* (Mt. 23:8-10)

In verse 8 Jesus warns against calling a man "teacher" as a religious title. Here He uses the Hebraism, *"Rabbi,"* technically meaning "great or exalted one." Scripturally, One is our Teacher: the Holy Spirit who leads us into all truth. In verse 9 Jesus commands that as a religious title we call no one on earth our *"father,"* "for One is your Father in Heaven." And in verse 10 He outlaws calling a human our *"leader,"* for our one Leader is Christ. Thus by calling himself "infallible" when speaking *Ex Cathedra* as head of the papal Magesterium, claiming to be the final teacher on matters of doctrine, the pope puts himself in place of the Holy Spirit. In verse 9, by calling himself "The Holy Father," he puts himself in place of God the Father. And in verse 10, by calling himself "The Vicar of Christ" he puts himself in place of Christ. Thus the pope puts himself in place of Father, Son, and Holy Spirit, exalting himself by usurping the titles and authority reserved for God alone.

As the Holy Spirit is the true Vicar of Christ, and Christ communicates the Father's love to us, the False Prophet replaces the Holy Spirit in Roman Catholic theology which he seeks to extend to other faiths along the lines of the pontifical tradition of pagan Rome, as we have reviewed earlier. The papacy fundamentally remains an antichrist institution controlled by the spirit of antichrist. And the pope is by precise scriptural definition ***an*** antichrist.

His behavior, however, is again in accordance with the high priest Annas who persecuted the apostles, the high priest Caiaphas who arranged the murder of Christ by the Romans, and the court theocrats who persecuted Jeremiah, the Old Testament shadow of Christ. We must exercise caution, however, to note that these were the deeds of individuals who often acted in collusion with pagan non-Jews who were no better and not infrequently worse. There is no basis scripturally or historically to place any corporate guilt on Israel or the Jews, be it the Jews of that time or the Jews of today. Not all Jews were party to these outrages and many non-Jews certainly were.

Mormon Parallels

Another example would be the Mormon agenda as more Evangelicals seek common ground with the Church of Latter-day Saints. They do this despite the fact that in every aspect of its doctrine and history Mormonism is an antichrist belief system with an entirely different Jesus, racist orientations, and a false doctrine of atonement.

In the Mormon doctrine of atonement as taught by their false prophet Brigham Young, black people are "ugly, depraved, mischievous, and descendant from angels cast out of heaven" for refusing to side with the Mormon Jesus who is the spirit-brother of Satan, as opposed to the scriptural Jesus who is the only begotten of the Father (Jn. 1:14).

The basis of Mormon belief is the deification of man, which goes straight back to the Garden of Eden where Satan who attempted to deify himself seduces man into thinking he can do the same. Thus, as the true God wants man conformed to the image and likeness of His Son Jesus, Satan wants man conformed to the image and likeness of his fallen self. Mormonism teaches that as God was, man is and as God ***is***, man ***will become***. Brigham Young taught staunchly that any Mormon marrying a black person would have to be killed, and that this "doctrine of atonement" cannot be changed—although later generations of Mormons attempted to hide and ameliorate it. Thus we have a false Christ, a false doctrine of atonement, a false view of man that, while portraying itself as based on family values, has a theology and history of violence with its founding pioneers having carried out massacres.

Joseph Smith becomes a kind of incarnation of their idea of Christ while Brigham Young is his False Prophet. Yet it presents itself as having a salvific agenda. Mormon eschatology believes that Mormonism will rise to the occasion at a time of serious moral, social, economic, and political chaos and save the day. And already, professing Christians are swallowing the bait. Many Christians are emulating the Mormon emphasis on family values, ignoring the high divorce rate, the suicide rate, and the rate of clinical depression in Utah where 70% of the population are Mormon. Because many Christians are in ideological agreement with the political views espousing traditional American values of figures such as Senator Orin Hatch and news commentator Glenn Beck, they are oblivious to (or choose to ignore) the fact that such men subscribe to the Mormon false Christ, false atonement, and false idea of salvation.

Few Christians realize when Glenn Beck is inserting beliefs directly from the Book of Mormon into his television presentation and editorials. Such spiritual seduction must be seen from a religious viewpoint as utterly antichrist even though the principles which such men espouse are broadly Judeo- Christian.

Attacked Not For What They Say, But For Saying It

The character of the False Prophet as a religious leader will follow the same pattern as those court theocrats who persecuted the Hebrew prophets and rejected their Messiah. They will always have as the hallmark signature of their treachery the ad hominem approach. They will attack the people of God not for what they say, but rather for saying it. This was true of Jeremiah, it was true of John the Baptist who was murdered by Herod the Great (again, a type of the Antichrist), and it was true of the Sanhedrin in the Book of Acts. It was also true of the papal bull issued against Luther for writing the *95 Theses*. Although Luther ended as badly if not as murderously as any nefarious figure, he began right and his *95 Theses* were solidly true.

As the spirit of antichrist operates in the apostate church today, we witness the same effect. The apostate church and its leaders do not levy doctrinal arguments from Scripture, exegetically validated to substantiate their position. Rather, they embrace the political correctness of multiculturalism much as took place in the 1st century of the Roman Empire. True Christians upholding the truth are incriminated not for what they say, but for merely saying it.

However hypocritical the ad hominem approach is, it has existed from biblical times and throughout Church history, and it still blossoms in the post-Modern world. The False Prophet will play the same game expertly where scriptural truth will be ignored or mutilated beyond exegetical recognition for the sake of purely political considerations. The violence of the inquisitional pontiffs, the cruelty of Calvin's Geneva, and the Puritan witch hunters alike, forge this hybrid of twisted theology and political and religious hypocrisy.

The ultimate, however, is yet to come in the person of the False Prophet. He will wield this kind of power as no other ever has, and he will do so by the very hand of Satan himself—even though, like the Sanhedrin, the popes, and the ultra-Calvinists, he will falsely claim to do so in the name of the God of heaven.

Chapter 14: The Harbinger

The illumination of the Holy Spirit can never be replaced by mere methodology. Nonetheless this is not to say the Word of God is without method, and our understanding of it must likewise not be methodical. John Wesley was the first major figure to be identified with this precept found in Scripture, "Seek me not in a waste place (*tohoo)*" (Is. 45:19). (A better translation of *tohoo* than "a waste place" is "chaos" as found in the NASB, or "void of organized form and structure" as in the Creation narrative of Genesis.)

When we apply this principle to the quest for discovering the identity of the Antichrist and False Prophet, it is once more foundational that we recognize the modus operandi of a culprit as counterfeiter. Whatever God does in and through Christ, Satan will attempt to mimic. Thus we must understand how God operates in order to understand how Satan attempts to operate in mimicking the ways of the Lord.

Jesus had a harbinger in the person of John the Baptist who was by birth a member of the Aaronic clergy, yet who went against the corrupted Levitical establishment of the Sanhedrin. He did this, however, without deviating toward any rejection of what was ordained in Scripture. This would appear to distinguish John the Baptist from groups such as the Essenes. Satan must therefore have his harbinger in place for the Antichrist. This harbinger will be a clergyman and a dynamic figure to whom people would gravitate in a troubled time, much in the character of John the Baptist. In short, the False Prophet will be to the Antichrist what John the Baptist was to Christ as the one who prepares the way and points to his advent, and their ministries become concurrent and convergent as did the ministries of Jesus and John. The dragon-like nature of the False Prophet will imitate the anointed boldness of John. But we must grasp this in greater detail.

Harbingers are in essence precursors, and the False Prophet will counterfeit John the Baptist, the precursor of Christ. John the Baptist operated in the power of the Holy Spirit (Luke 1:15), so the False Prophet will operate in the power of the spirit of antichrist (1 John 4:3). This demonic precursor relationship is characteristic of antichrist cults such as in the relationship between Joseph Smith and Brigham Young in Mormonism, Charles Russell and Judge Rutherford in the Jehovah's Witnesses, and not least of all in the relationship between the Bab and Bahaullah in the Bahà'ì sect. The Bab (meaning "Gate") claimed to be the Mahdi or 12th Imam of Islam in Persia, circa 1868. The sect found its "holy land" in Acco where the Bab was imprisoned for 24 years. The Bab's remains are entombed in the Bahà'ì botanical gardens on the slopes of Mt. Carmel, site of Elijah's conflict with the priests of Baal. Bearing in mind that John the Baptist, the precursor of Jesus, operated in the spirit of Elijah, we note the historical importance of Bahà'ì in our attempt to discern and understand acute details of the False Prophet.

The Bahà'ì sect is totally eclectic and syncretistic, with a total of nine religious figures including Buddha, Mohammed, Jesus, Moses, etc. These figures are seen as the respective messengers of God for their respective eras, Bahaullah being the last and greatest of these, with the Bab as his precursor. Because Bahà'ì came from Islam with an Islamic messianic figure, yet found its holy land in geographical Israel, it considers itself at harmony with both Islam and Judaism, as it encompasses all of the world's major religions. This sect also seems so peaceable that it is looked upon as benign. All of these details, including the syncretism, the precursor, the willingness of Israel and the Jews to accommodate it, its translocation into Israel and specifically Galilee, its identification with the stomping ground of the prophet Elijah the Tishbite on Mt. Carmel, make it appear benign to most Jews, who do not know that all of these features are trails of Antichrist.

Bahà'ì's origins are in the East and Islam, but the largest percentage of its followers are in the West from the Judeo-Christian world. Its ability to appear lamb like (Revelation 13:11), and not least of all its precursor, all form a historical outline nearly approximating a future historical blueprint for much of what the Antichrist and False Prophet will attempt to do.

In the Character of John the Baptist & Elijah

Elijah, Elisha, and John the Baptist all have the same spirit. That is, the same anointing and character from the Holy Spirit to fulfill the same kind of ministry. Much as the prophet Samuel introduced the rule of David which foreshadows the rule of Christ, John did with Jesus his cousin. Samuel was the last of the judges, yet the first of the prophets (not including Moses and

Joshua, etc.). Samuel represented the last figure of the period of judges and the first figure of the period of prophets and kings, arriving on the scene before David just as John would arrive on the scene before Jesus.

John the Baptist was similarly the last figure of the Old Covenant and represented the highest standard of righteousness under the Law. He was a man not like other men. Apart from Christ Himself, he was the greatest man who ever lived, being more than a prophet and, once again, the last figure of the Old Covenant era and the first figure of the New Covenant era. When the apostles required a replacement for Judas, it was necessary to find one who had been around, not from the beginning of the ministry of Jesus, but rather from the ministry of John (Ac. 1:21-22). The False Prophet will in some way counterfeit this and succeed in doing so up to a limited point. He will seem to be a man not like other men. And although John did no signs and wonders, the False Prophet will attempt to compensate for his dissimilarities with the character and holiness of John by a fanfare generated by satanically empowered supernatural phenomena. As John was the most unique ***good*** man apart from Jesus, the False Prophet will be the most unique ***bad*** one of co-equal wickedness with the first Beast whom he heralds. We must understand the pattern.

In the ministry of Elijah, the wicked woman Jezebel—whom Jesus uses to personify the spirit of false religion and as a metaphor for the harlot church and bride of Satan (Rev. 2:20)—coveted Naboth's vineyard (1 Ki. 21). She used lies and treachery to get it for King Ahab whom she really did not honor, but used as a vehicle to honor herself. She stands as opposed to a faithful bride who will seek the honor of her husband and, in turn, be honored by him. This is the visible difference between a faithful Church and an apostate one. The harlot church is in pursuit of self-glorification and sees Christ as a mere means to achieve it. The harlot church, in league with the other false religions of the world following the model of the pontifical *Pax Romana*, will be the domain over which the False Prophet presides.

The actions of Jezebel in the days of Ahab foreshadow what will transpire in the Last Days with the Antichrist. The apostate church will in effect deify itself and pay tribute to the Antichrist in order to advance its own interests. This is what Jesus warned of in the Olivet Discourse, "*Whoever is in the field must not turn back to get his cloak*" (Mt. 24:18), meaning the mantle of authority. We have explained that false religions and cults are auto-deifying institutions where their imagined god is simply their meal ticket. Muslims do not worship Allah, but Islam; Roman Catholicism does not worship God, but "Holy Mother the Church"; Jehovah's Witnesses worship the Watchtower Society; Mormons worship the Church of Latter-day Saints; and Orthodox Jews worship Talmudic Judaism. Not least of all, Liberal Protestantism is hyper-humanism in Christian masquerade, worshiping fallen man.

All of these things will be orchestrated by the spirit of antichrist under the direction of the False Prophet, and any refusal to acquiesce will face eradication. Apostate Christendom motivated by self-serving interests will follow the False Prophet who will deliver their souls to the Antichrist. Thus the warning of Jesus not to return for the mantle of authority in a scenario where the work of the Lord has become more important than the Lord of the work, and the ministry and the Church have become idols.

Zedekiah & Ahab

As Jezebel coveted the vineyard of Naboth (1 Ki. 21), Satan in the person of Antichrist will covet the vineyard of the Lord—both national and geographical Israel, and the Church. Ahab the husband of Jezebel had multiple false prophets but there was one who was most vocal and influential—Zedekiah the son of Chenaanah (1 Ki. 2:23). He was a violent man who claimed to have the Holy Spirit speaking through him, and he despised Micaiah for his challenge. This false prophet Zedekiah, who stood out above the others in a time of intrigue, deception, and military conflict, is a picture of the False Prophet to come.

The Lord had put a lying spirit from Satan in his mouth in judgment against the house of Ahab (1 Ki. 22:23). The New Testament parallel of this concerning Antichrist is in 2 Thessalonians 2 where, with the deception of the Antichrist, the Lord Himself will in judgment again send a deluding influence to make those who do not love Him and His Word believe the lie of Satan. Those who choose false prophets will be given over to them. Likewise, the False Prophet will claim to be the final authoritative voice who speaks by the Holy Spirit, but in fact, as with the pope, the False Prophet will be the one who positions himself ***in place of*** the Holy Spirit and castigates all who would dare question his claimed authority.

It is interesting to note for instance that this pattern has always been at work. When the liberal Roman Catholic Jesuit theologian Hans Kung made heretical statements with a low Christology concerning the Person of Christ, there was no serious Vatican backlash. Yet when he questioned papal infallibility he was stripped of his credentials as a Roman Catholic theologian. The False Prophet will operate along the same line. Like Ahab, he will most probably have many false prophets in his service but there will be one unique one in the likeness of Zedekiah.

Thus Jezebel turned Ahab against Elijah and tried to kill him. So, too, John the Baptist, having the spirit of Elijah, experienced the same fate. Herodias turned the wicked king who she manipulated for her own ends once more, as it were, against Elijah in the person of John the Baptist who had his spirit. Both Ahab and Herod the tetrarch (not to be confused with Herod the Great) foreshadow the Antichrist just as Elijah and John foreshadow the Elijah who is to come. The false religious system personified by Jezebel and Herodias and her daughter Salome will turn the political authorities under the Antichrist against Elijah in this conflict to come.

The centrality of John the Baptist must be properly comprehended to understand in what way the ministry of Elijah prophesied by Jesus and Micah will come into play again prior to the return of Christ. But it is also essential to understand this in order to anticipate what the False Prophet will do in an attempted imitation of it that will gain formidable success among unbelievers, unbelieving Israel, and apostate Christendom. Only the faithful will be able to understand. The False Prophet will seek to counterfeit the Holy Spirit in the same way Zedekiah did in the epic of Ahab, and as Caiaphas did, actually prophesying correctly (Jn. 11:49-52).

As the first Beast of Revelation 13 counterfeits God the Son, the second Beast counterfeits the Holy Spirit by being a counterfeit of John the Baptist who was filled with the Holy Spirit from his mother's womb (Lk. 1:15).

Chapter 15: The Final False Prophet

> *Then I saw another beast coming up out of the earth; and he had two horns like a lamb and he spoke as a dragon. He exercises all the authority of the first beast in his presence. And he makes the earth and those who dwell in it to worship the first beast, whose fatal wound was healed. He performs great signs, so that he even makes fire come down out of heaven to the earth in the presence of men. And he deceives those who dwell on the earth because of the signs which it was given him to perform in the presence of the beast, telling those who dwell on the earth to make an image to the beast who had the wound of the sword and has come to life. And it was given to him to give breath to the image of the beast, so that the image of the beast would even speak and cause as many as do not worship the image of the beast to be killed.* (Rev. 13:11-15)

As a matter of some complication, we see that the False Prophet does not come from the sea like the first Beast, but from the earth (Rev. 13:11). While the sea has to do with the raging of the nations in the Last Days as in Psalm 2, the earth normally has to do with Israel and/or the Church. This may possibly suggest a Jewish ethnicity to the False Prophet, although there are alternative explanations and we cannot be definitive at the present time. It should be noted in this regard that the Vatican has consistently put itself forward as a proposed peace broker between the Islamic and western worlds, and has called for the internationalization of Jerusalem which is sacred to Judaism, Islam, and Christendom. We are told in Daniel that the Antichrist himself will *"enter the Beautiful Land"* (Dan. 11:41), and in Revelation 11 that there will be a Tribulational Temple. The reference to the earth as opposed to the sea may be able to be interpreted not so much as ethnic references but geographical ones which would accommodate the factor of the False Prophet emerging from the earth.

It is from Jerusalem that Christ will reign from the throne of David for a thousand years. And in the early phase of his tenure during the first 3-1/2 lunar years, the Antichrist and False Prophet will make some apparent headway toward a counterfeit of the Millennium. Thus the importance of Jerusalem in Revelation 11 and elsewhere.

Revelation 13:12 instructs us that the False Prophet will exercise the same authority of the first Beast, He will do so in his presence, using his religious position with his political influence to cause those who dwell on the earth to worship the first Beast who counterfeits the resurrection of Jesus after a seeming assassination. He is able to perform great signs to include causing fire to come from heaven. This will in some way be an attempted satanic counterfeit of the power of the two witnesses in Revelation 11. A possible eventuality of extraterrestrial phenomena cannot be discounted in regard to these astral signs.

In verse 15 the False Prophet is able to give breath to the image of the Beast. There are enough books speculating about the Beast being a bionic automaton or a genetic clone with an embedded super-computer. How these technologies will actually play out in any possible facilitation of these prophecies coming to pass are still matters of speculation and it is not at the present time to be conclusive. However, with the development of organic microchips, artificial intelligence, and the cloning of human tissue, it is obvious that the pace of science and technology push these possibilities beyond the realm of the fanciful and into the realm of the practically possible. If a cloned replica of a deceased political leader could be developed, the question again becomes, "From where does it obtain its immortal soul and from where does it get a spirit?" What is clear from Revelation 13:15 is that the False Prophet gives breath to the image of the Beast, causing it to become animated, and will decree capital execution of those refusing to worship it.

This is the satanic attempt at recreating man that has been Satan's ambition since the Garden of Eden in the Book of Genesis. God in the Person of Christ breathed on Adam, causing him to become a living soul. The Hebrew term "*nephesh*" derives from the word "breath." Yet as we read in Psalm 150, even animals have such a soul; only man, however, has a ***living*** soul. What we are organically, homogenously combined with what we are spiritually, constitutes our immortal souls. This transpired at the creation of man when God in the Person of Christ breathed on Adam. Now we see Satan through the person of the False Prophet breathing a mimicked immortal soul into the image of the first Beast. Satan the counterfeiter will go to the ultimate lengths of counterfeiting resurrection, second birth, and even new creation.

The action of the False Prophet breathing into the image would solve the potential question of, for instance, from where would a cloned human organism get its soul cum spirit? However, this is not the main point, although it is a potential factor to be considered. Rather, the main point is that, as God breathed on Adam before the fall of man, after the resurrection God once more in the Person of Christ breathed on regenerated man when the resurrected Christ breathed on His disciples saying to receive the Holy Spirit (John 20:22).

So the image of the Beast will receive the spirit of antichrist which is synonymous with the spirit of Satan. This is a diabolical parody of the creation and new creation we have in Jesus. False religion mimics true religion. This will be the apex achievement of the False Prophet. The first Beast cannot do as he shall unless the second Beast so empowers him. So, too, the Antichrist will achieve the full depth of his wicked power through false religion not only personified by, but incarnated in, the False Prophet.

Again, we must understand the shadow. The emperors of the Holy Roman Empire likewise were crowned by popes as were kings of Catholic France. Medieval European history, however, affords us nothing more than a dim glimpse of what lies ahead. Of all the antichrists there will be none like the first Beast whom the others hint at in comparison. Likewise, of all the false prophets there will be none like ***the*** False Prophet of Revelation 13 whom all of the others merely foreshadow. To understand this properly we must recognize that just as Joseph, Moses, Isaac, and Jeremiah among others are types of Christ, Satan has types of the Antichrist whose identity the Lord Jesus reveals to the faithful Church. The others, however, will not see or understand this until it is too late.

Part Six: The Final Antichrist

In an ideal world this final section would, on the basis of the material found in the previous sections, simply need to be tallied up into a sum of events that would give us two "Wanted" posters with the photos, identities, and aliases of the two arch-villains in all of human history. Unfortunately the world in which we live is not ideal but fallen.

Thus far I have attempted to address and redress the flawed approaches and oversimplified methodologies that too many others with noble intentions have pursued in the quest to identify the final Beast.

I have also wanted to affirm those approaches and conclusions reached by others at various points in Church history that are correct in what they said yet deficient in what they omitted. When these prophetic events have met their destiny and Christ returns in glory, this book and any others influenced by it will likewise be remembered for being correct in what it said but wanting in what it failed to say. The reason for this is simple: it is not intended to be an indictment of those brethren in Christ past and present who, while understanding certain important aspects of Antichrist, were unable to correctly fathom others. Just as no one knew who the "*son of perdition*" was until Jesus revealed him, neither shall we.

My best efforts thus far should, by the grace of God, serve one function: it is the next road sign on a correct road. It can correct the many mistaken detours that too many of us have been diverted onto in pursuit of knowing who this figure shall be. Of this I am sure: everything in this book and the approach it has taken is the correct mechanism, or at least as correct a mechanism as presently can exist, in our Holy Spirit guided endeavor. It may or may not be my last word on this subject. Indeed, while there is no progressive revelation of these mysterious truths, there is a progressive unmasking of these truths by the Holy Spirit—truths that are already contained in Scripture and which will be verified by history and, to some degree, already have been.

It is not possible to author a proper epilogue for this book as the book of necessity remains unfinished. The Holy Spirit may show me and hopefully others with increasing clarity what is to take place with reference to the one who comes before Christ. It is on this note that we must understand the theological and spiritual nature of the harbinger. This relates variously to the two witnesses of Revelation 11 and to the ministry of Elijah that must take place before the return of Jesus. The specifics of this reality lie beyond the parameters of this book. Nonetheless, as John the Baptist came in the spirit of Elijah, the spirit of Elijah must in some way be active prior to Christ's return. And as always, Satan will have his counterfeit. The False Prophet will counterfeit the ministry of Elijah preparing the way for the true Messiah in a diabolical attempt to prepare the way for the false messiah, the Antichrist whom Jewish believers in the Hebrew tongue call "*Zar HaMoshiach.*"

Whether his name will be "*Soter*" from the Hebrew Gematria of "6-6-6" (carrying the double connotation of false savior because of the Greek meaning of "Soter" being related to the Greek terms for salvation and life; e.g., *sozo*), I do not know.

We must be aware and remain vigilant of all contingencies carrying scriptural support lest we ourselves become detoured onto the road of speculation. We must confine ourselves to what can be known for sure. Not least of all, it is imperative that we avoid conspiracy theories about things such as Freemasonry and the Illuminati, although there is certainly an element of truth in the wicked nature of Masonic mystery that no Christian should be party to.

On a separate but related note, the mega importance of understanding Scriptures speaking of the Antichrist both directly and indirectly must be comprehended in the overall light of biblical eschatology. Again, the prophecies of Daniel, Ezekiel, Isaiah, Zechariah, and 1 and 2 Thessalonians particularly are vital, but for the sake of brevity lie outside the content of this book.

I would also strongly urge that we bear carefully in mind that the seven churches of Revelation 2-3 precede the proper revelation commencing in Revelation 4:1, and that to this end the material covered in the book I authored on the subject of the church of Laodicea (*The Dilemma of Laodicea*) be seen as co-requisite to this writing.

The prophetic significance of contemporary events in the reunification of Europe, events in the Islamic world, events in the Ecumenical and interfaith movements, and events revolving around Israel and the Jews, cannot be overstated in their relevance to the identification of the Antichrist.

In one sense this book is not only, or perhaps not even chiefly, concerned with the doctrinal theology of the Antichrist himself, but rather with providing God's people with the tools and instruments needed to prepare further to scripturally understand him when he eventually shows up on the world stage. While the types and shadows are absolutely vital in themselves, the hermeneutical approach by which we understand them is more important still. A pure mathematician will learn calculus for the sake of calculus, but a physicist will learn calculus in order to explain physics. If we fail to do the math right, we will not be able to explain the dynamics. So, too, the exegetical hermeneutics and midrashic and typological approach to biblical interpretation displayed in this book are in a sense just as important as the doctrinal conclusions arrived at by their employ.

In Britain and in various countries of Continental Europe we may still visit the castles and ancestral manor houses of royal and aristocratic families tracing a genetic lineage of nobility over a series of generations. Today we can trace the bloodline of a dynasty through mitochondrial DNA, but for centuries the only means of comparing resemblances were portraits and later photographs. We look for common facial and other features from father to son and son to grandson, often visible in a sequential series of pictures hung on the wall of a gallery, corridor, or stairwell in the family's primary abode. The castles of Britain and Europe abound with these, but with royal families the picture collections in the hermitage of St. Petersburg or the National Portrait Gallery of London are the most inclusive. The family look, stare, facial expression, or other anatomical feature is captured by the artist with the aim of reflecting the character of the family or dynasty, showing the relationship of the founders of the clan to the present time. In identifying the Antichrist, the same principle holds true. His types and shadows both biblical and historical help discern the features and character of the reprobate to come.

The Word of God is a picture book of prints of these paintings and photos. While the pictures in the gallery cannot definitively peg the final villain without being acutely familiar with his forebears, there will be very little if any prospect of pegging him. Having seen all the paintings and photos, bear in mind in while reading this final section that the one to come will resemble his forebears.

The ultimate Antichrist will seek with very considerable success to superficially but convincingly imitate the person and nature of Jesus as none other has ever done or will do again. In Revelation 17:8 we read that he will come from the abyss and go to destruction where the Greek word is "*apoleia*." In the context, however, this could be read as "gone to destruction or perdition, as going to destroy."

> *"The beast that you saw was, and is not, and is about to come up out of the abyss and go to destruction. And those who dwell on the earth, whose name has not been written in the book of life from the foundation of the world, will wonder when they see the beast, that he was and is not and will come.* (Rev. 17:8)

This is a devastating and frightful attempt to so counterfeit the Lord Jesus Christ that unprepared experts could be deceived because the preparation is not only intellectual but also spiritual.

This satanic parallel of who was, who is, and who is to come, is the ultimate counterfeit of the Antichrist. It reflects the ultimate ambition of Satan even in eternity. That is, the Lord Jesus is the God of Israel made flesh, and from the Old Testament into the New He is called "*ashar, hya, hovav-yavo*"—this is the meaning of the tetragrammaton, that is "*Yahweh*" Himself who Satan wants to replace

Having failed to do this in heaven, his temporal means to achieve it on earth will be through the Antichrist.

Chapter 16: The Number of the Beast

Working Out the Puzzle

Some people find fitting together a 1,000-piece jigsaw puzzle calming, others find it frustrating, but most people find elements of both when they endeavor to make the puzzle match the picture on the box. The problem in pursuing the Antichrist is we have a jigsaw puzzle, but the box has no photograph. Rather, it has a text of what the picture will be once all the pieces are assembled. As one works one's way through fitting pieces together, one quickly discovers there is no organized sequence of how the different fragments match each other. But the further one progresses slowly and steadily, it becomes more apparent as to how it all fits together.

Yet as one goes forward matching piece to piece, several pieces in one place of one color and several pieces in another place of a different color, it becomes more confusing and nebulous before it becomes clearer as to how it all works out. Assembling a puzzle is not a haphazard pursuit; it is not disorganized or chaotic. It rather brings order to that which is already haphazard and disorganized.

Some people turn the puzzle pieces face down on a table, looking only for geometric compatibility in the shapes to see which fits before they turn the pieces up to see how it looks. Another approach is to try to segregate various pieces according to color. However, the best way to piece together such puzzles is to combine both methods; it is not a chaotic or random approach. The Word of God is no different. The Scripture tells us that God's instruction to us is to "seek Me not in chaos" (Is. 45:19). No place do these principles apply more exegetically than in the area of eschatology inclusive of identification of the Antichrist. We are dealing with something that appears to be disorganized, with multiple pieces of information that do not seem to fit together but we know somehow do. And in the earlier stages one cluster of pieces that fit do not appear to go with another cluster. It is as if we are not doing one puzzle but several simultaneously until we progress far enough that the overall picture begins to take shape.

The subject of Antichrist is very much like this. In one place on a large table we piece together biblical types; in another, historical types based on principles rather than texts of Scripture. In one place we begin to assemble the pieces that tell us about the Antichrist's designs on destroying Israel and the Jews; in another place we begin to assemble those pieces concerning his designs on corrupting the Church. In one place we deal with overt New Testament teachings of the Antichrist found in the epistles; in another we piece together the bits dealing with the Old Testament typologies. Functionally, although we are doing ***a*** puzzle, in the process we are actually doing ***several*** puzzles simultaneously.

As we work our way through the project it just does not seem to make sense how it all integrates cohesively until we reach an advanced point. This is precisely what takes place in this book. There are several puzzles being pieced together at the same time, which, by the grace of God, at some advanced point will make comprehensive sense and present us with a unified and well-defined picture. What appears to be chaotic is not; what appears to be haphazard is systematic.

Those performing basic scientific research in physics, chemistry, and biomedical sciences know this pattern well. In a pursuit to find a cure for a disease some work is being done on contagions, others on protein structures and enzymes, others on anti-bodies, others on genetic structure, and still others on purely clinical research and statistical analysis on everything from family medical histories to percentage probability response to varying therapies. It is all part of the same cause with the same aim, but widely different things are taking place at the same time.

In a military invasion, terrestrial strategy, naval strategy, aerial strategy, amphibious strategy, and covert operations are all going on at the same time. And in the chaos of battle it may be difficult for commanders to coordinate all of what is happening at the same time, but coordinate it they must. It is no different in the objectives of this book. We are looking for a solution to a problem, and the faithful believers in Jesus are the vanguard of the coming invasion of Christ who will take back this fallen world. It will all ultimately make sense, even though it may not seem to when we deal with the objective in multiple facets that need to be coordinated, but often do not seem to relate until an advanced point in the project.

One example of this is dealing with the number of the Beast in all of its aspects including the personal possessive of "*his number*" and also "*the number of his name*" as well as its related component simply called "*his name.*" On one hand we are simply dealing with the number of the Beast and its multiples wherever it occurs in Scripture. This focuses simply on the number itself where we discover that "666" appears and reappears multiple times in differing ways with various figures, all of whom prefigure the Antichrist in some way. At the same time, at the opposite end of the table we are putting together other pieces concerning "666" that are specific to the elements of Gematria, alphanumerics, and the number of names in Greek, Hebrew and Aramaic, and in some cases possibly Latin, which can moreover involve translations from one language to another.

We are doing different things at the same time that have no obvious point of contact, yet we know they both have to do with "666" and both will ultimately fit together and complement and confirm each other. Before we embark on a 1,000-piece jigsaw puzzle, in order to succeed and not give up, we anticipate the process ahead of time and accept that we will be piecing together different fragments at the same time that will, in the earlier stages, seem to be incoherent in terms of their relationship to each other. Yet they are not incoherent, and in the end it all makes sense. So will this book and, much more importantly, will the Word of God. We are addressing one of the most complicated and mysterious subjects in divine revelation, and a difficult endeavor where human intellect alone can never answer the final questions.

Although we must apply ourselves with all diligence in the prayerful study of this matter, we must be mindful that it was Jesus alone who identified the "*son of perdition*" to His disciples. In the final analysis, it will be Jesus alone who once again with regard to the Antichrist does the same thing.

It is More Than a Math Problem

> *Here is wisdom. Let him who has understanding calculate the number of the beast, for the number is that of a man; and his number is six hundred and sixty-six.* (Rev. 13:18)

Without wishing to cast aspersions on pre-Tribulational Dispensationalists or others who misunderstand the issue of imminence in their clinging to a pre-Tribulation Rapture, it is important for us to understand that these brethren are, on this point, misguided. Many of these, however, must be fairly reckoned as faithful Christians, and as such are indwelt by the Holy Spirit. We also note that such brethren are much closer to the truth in this age of apostasy than those who deny the Rapture entirely, or who assume Preterist and Replacement positions. We may rest assured therefore that in some way and at some time the Lord will make known to such believers that their thinking on this point is erroneous. Indeed, many subscribing to it do so on the mere basis of it being what they were taught, without coming to their own Holy Spirit guided conclusions.

We again refer to proponents of this position such as John MacArthur and the late Dr. John Wolvoord of Dallas Theological Seminary. While John MacArthur indeed teaches many true things, and has commendably refuted many false doctrines, he believes that the place of the Rapture in Scripture is to be found not overtly in the text but between the lines.

The notion that the climax of pre-millennial history to be recognized in the *Parousia* of Christ in His Second Advent with the Rapture and Resurrection was omitted from Scripture by the Holy Spirit is unpalatable and less than logical. Although the specificity as to precise dates was not found concerning the First Coming of Christ in biblical prophecy, Daniel 9 does place it into a narrow time frame, and Scriptures such as Micah 5:2 and Isaiah 9:6 directly and overtly describe the Nativity in addressing His First Coming . To say that His Second Coming will be different is a position without any textual support from Holy Writ. The precise date of His First Coming was withheld, as was the precise date of His Second Coming, but the timing of it in the sequence of prophetic events is stated.

Malachi spoke of the harbinger coming in the spirit of Elijah, which, according to Jesus, had a fulfillment in the person of John the Baptist. But Jesus also made it clear that this has a double fulfillment. Thus if the Messiah could not come before the harbinger the first time, there is no basis to argue that He can come imminently tonight unless we can identify such a harbinger. There is, of course, no shortage of persons suffering from delusional psychosis visiting Jerusalem annually claiming to be such a person, but so far none of them have been authentic. In short, if someone in the spirit of Elijah had to come before the First Coming of Christ, and if someone in the spirit of Elijah must precede His Second Coming, the Second Coming cannot take place until that happens.

Indeed, imminence remains true that Jesus may come tonight for any of us individually (and we should live our lives accordingly), but it is doubtful that Christ will return to take the Church collectively until we know the harbinger. It is, moreover, only with eisegetical monkey tricks and *reductio ad absurdum* misinterpretations of 2 Thessalonians 2 that anyone can assert that the Antichrist does not need to be identified prior to the *episunagoge*—our gathering together to Jesus.

It is also inconsistent with the patterns and logic of Scripture that the culminating event of *heilsgeschichte* in the salvation history of the Church could be omitted from prophetic and apocalyptic literature primarily dedicated to preparing the Church for, and informing the Church about, the event. Once more, as John Wolvoord admitted, there is no passage to be found anywhere in Scripture directly teaching a pre-Tribulation Rapture. As the modern patriarch of pre-Tribulationism admits, it is just not in there because God did not put it there.

> *And he causes all, the small and the great, and the rich and the poor, and the free men and the slaves, to be given a mark on their right hand or on their forehead, and he provides that no one will be able to buy or to sell, except the one who has the mark, either the name of the beast or the number of his name. Here is wisdom. Let him who has understanding calculate the number of the beast, for the number is that of a man; and his number is six hundred and sixty-six.* (Rev. 13:16-18)

This final identification of the Antichrist that must precede the return of Jesus in Revelation 13:17 states that in order to engage in commerce one must have either his name or the number of his name. While we may speculate as to whether this will be some manner of alpha-numeric or digitized code, the following verse 18 indicates conclusively that those who not only have "*wisdom*" but "*understanding*" will calculate the number of the Beast.

Not Just "Wisdom" but "Understanding"

The Scriptures tell us that there is a difference between "*wisdom*" and "*understanding.*" Every man or woman of understanding, by definition indeed has wisdom. But not everyone who has wisdom has as yet attained understanding. Wisdom involves the quality, virtue, and illumination of the Holy Spirit for acquiring understanding, and grasps the reasons for doing so. In the final analysis, understanding is the goal and fruit of divinely imparted wisdom. In part we may say that having knowledge, even spiritual knowledge, is one thing; knowing what to do with it is another. We may also say that having knowledge is the ends but the wisdom with which, and by which, it is acquired is the means.

Not least of all, it is important to know that understanding is not simply intellectual; it is spiritually intuitive ***plus*** intellectual. That is to say, it is a matter of divine revelation. In other words, we ***know*** by the illumination of our spirit by the Holy Spirit, but we ***understand*** what we know with the Holy Spirit-sanctified mind.

The pursuit of study of end time prophecy will prove useless unless it is a prayerful study. Data can be acquired by the intellectual processes of the mind but proper interpretation and application of the data cannot be so acquired. This requires the work of the Holy Spirit and our spirit. The mechanics of this process are not difficult for a faithful Christian to comprehend, because with their salvation it already happened to a first step degree. A person may hear the Gospel and grasp its explanation intellectually, but until illumination by the Holy Spirit takes place and someone is convicted of sin, they cannot become regenerate, even though in intellectual terms they grasped what was presented to them evangelistically.

This process then kicks up to a second stage in the area of discipleship where an intellectual knowledge of Scripture that results from merely reading it or listening to it in a recorded format is interpreted on a higher spiritual plane to them by the work of the Holy Spirit who in turn empowers the believer to live this teaching out practically in their own lives. When we deal in the realm of end-times prophecy and eschatology, however, this process kicks up again, as it were, to a third level where the believer has gone from regeneration to discipleship and from discipleship to understanding. Hence in John's epistle where he speaks of Antichrist he links this to "loving not the world" (1 Jn. 2:15-17).

Just the same, as one cannot become a disciple if one has not yet become a convert or regenerate, so, too, one cannot become a man or woman of understanding unless one is first a disciple. What this means is that carnally minded Christians with strong attachments to the world already lack wisdom and are therefore incapable of attaining understanding. If those who already know the truth are not living it in divinely empowered sanctification, there is no basis for God to show them anything deeper because they fail to act on what they already have. Indeed, the mechanisms God has ordained to point them toward deeper things have been rendered dysfunctional by their worldly mindedness. Backsliders cannot understand the things of the Spirit any more than unsaved people except that they are haunted by the fact that they know the truth and the Holy Spirit is trying to draw them back to Jesus through repentance.

In noting that the natural man cannot understand the things of the Spirit (1 Co. 2:14-16), we are reminded that those who will be able to identify the Antichrist will be aware of the fact that they are supernatural men and women because they are absolved by the Spirit of Jesus. Unfortunately, in the present age of the Church the supernatural aspect of what we are to be has been distorted into something unnatural, and what should be the regenerate has devolved into the degenerate. Sadly this is in no place more true than among too many of my fellow charismatics and Pentecostals. If such Christians do not repent and heed the hortatory proclamations of the Book of Proverbs to obtain wisdom, understanding, and discernment, they will evaporate into the unattainable. Deception due to lack of discernment will become inevitable.

The Need for the Application of Biblical Wisdom

This is a general truth, but, again, as a "*kal v'homer*" principle, it is an eschatologically indispensable one. We have an allusion to the Antichrist in Proverbs 2:12. The preceding verses highlight the urgency for wisdom, understanding, and discernment which must be discovered as hidden treasure. In biblical typology silver speaks of the price of redemption (as in the half shekel of silver for the firstborn), yet the exhortation is to search for this deeper knowledge as one would search for the silver. The same as one would find salvation in Christ by becoming a believer, once one has become a believer the net goal must be the pursuit of such hidden treasure. The verses following verse 12 warn of backsliders who leave the path they were once on and return to walking in darkness. This continues through verse 16, where the next step becomes spiritual seduction by the adulteress—false religion figurative of both a corrupted Judaism and a corrupted Christianity.

> *My son, if you will receive my words*
> *And treasure my commandments within you,*
> *Make your ear attentive to wisdom,*
> *Incline your heart to understanding;*
> *For if you cry for discernment,*
> *Lift your voice for understanding;*
> *If you seek her as silver*
> *And search for her as for hidden treasures;*
> *Then you will discern the fear of the LORD*
> *And discover the knowledge of God.*

For the LORD gives wisdom;
From His mouth come knowledge and understanding.
He stores up sound wisdom for the upright;
He is a shield to those who walk in integrity,
Guarding the paths of justice,
And He preserves the way of His godly ones.
Then you will discern righteousness and justice
And equity and every good course.
For wisdom will enter your heart
And knowledge will be pleasant to your soul;
Discretion will guard you,
Understanding will watch over you,
To deliver you from the way of evil,
From the man who speaks perverse things*;*
From those who leave the paths of uprightness
To walk in the ways of darkness;
Who delight in doing evil
And rejoice in the perversity of evil;
Whose paths are crooked,
And who are devious in their ways;
To deliver you from the strange woman,
From the adulteress who flatters with her words; (Prov. 2:1-16)

As a ***general*** truth we may understand verse 12 as ***a*** man who speaks perverse things as in ***any*** of those who do so, but the text tells us, rather, that it is ***the*** man who speaks perverse things. As the Prophet Daniel relates, the Antichrist will speak blasphemously atrocious things against the Most High (Dan. 11:36). It is therefore not merely a situation where only those who have understanding will know the identity of the Antichrist; those who lack understanding (including Christians who lack it) will be taken in by Him. They will be seduced by false religion. This must be held strongly as a cardinal tenet in calculating the number of the Beast, which is the ultimate key to his identity. The occurrence of combinations of 6's and their multiples with various figures in Scripture is a marker identifying them as typifying the ultimate Antichrist, revealing something about him that must be understood in order to ultimately determine his identity.

Such recurring numerical combinations are likewise transponders telling us that we are navigationally on the correct course to identify him. But the final identification will not be based on the types, but on the number of his name. When the Holy Spirit reveals this we will see how he replays the actions of all of his types, first biblical, but also historical.

We again bear in mind, however, that there are those types named in Scripture whose further characteristics prefiguring those of the Antichrist are gleaned from the pages of extra-biblical history. There are those types who are purely scriptural; secondly there are those types who, in light of what Scripture says of Antichrist, do indeed typify him, but the record of their actions is found outside of Scripture.

Lastly we have a third category named in Scripture: some of whose actions are found in Scripture but others outside of it as well. All of these will come into play in the final identification of the Antichrist, but the ultimate deciding factor will be in the number of his name, which will require wisdom and God-given understanding to accurately calculate. It is, we are told, the number of a man (Rev. 13:18).

Yet Another Counterfeit

We again revert to the characteristic trait of counterfeiting Christ. When Jesus came it was, in retrospect, evident how the heroic figures of Old Testament Israel—ranging from the patriarchs to Moses and Joshua, the prophets like Jeremiah, kings like David, and the inspiring figure of Joseph from the Book of Genesis—all foreshadowed Him. Their own experiences were in different ways incorporated into His life and experience. These were shadows of Christ, but they were not the means by which he was finally identified as the Messiah. It was His having the name of God and His resurrection that proved who He was, further testified to by messianic miracles that only the Messiah could perform.

When the Antichrist embarks on his venture it will be equally obvious to those who understand how he likewise co-opts and replays the experience and actions of his shadows. And so, too, he will ultimately be identified by counterfeit messianic miracles, by a counterfeit resurrection, and by his name that will not be the name of God but rather the name of a man, who will try with some success to look fully human and fully divine, but unlike Jesus he will not be. There are many keys, but the main key to the main lock in revealing his identity will be in his name that will seek to eclipse the name that is indeed above all names. (Jn. 17:6)

The relationship between the name and the *"son of perdition"* is encompassed nowhere more concisely than in the high priestly prayer of Jesus in John 17:6 and 12:

> *"I have manifested Your name to the men whom You gave Me out of the world; they were Yours and You gave them to Me, and they have kept Your word...While I was with them, I was keeping them in Your name which You have given Me; and I guarded them and not one of them perished but the son of perdition, so that the Scripture would be fulfilled.* (Jn. 17:6, 12)

As we have noted, in John 17:6 the name of God is manifested in Christ; in verse 12 we see the contrast between those who are kept in the name of God by Christ, and the "*son of perdition*" being the title of Judas Iscariot, the single most important shadow of the Antichrist in Scripture and the title of the ultimate Antichrist whom Judas is a reflection of. Just as those in Christ who were not of the world were kept in a divine name at the time the "*son of perdition*" sprung his trap, once more it is the faithful believers who are kept by Jesus from the evil one while they are still in the world, who will escape the trap. The high priestly prayer for Jesus was indeed for his disciples at that time, but also his prayer for true believers of all time. The third and ultimate application, however, will be for those in the days of the "*son of perdition*" who once more understand the difference between the right name and the wrong one—that is, the name of God and the name of man.

How to Calculate

The number of the Beast occurs in a number of places in Scripture. The most oft-repeated mistake by many Christians is they commence by attempting to tabulate a numerical value in the name of some historical, political, or biblical figure. This is a flawed approach in terms of where to ***begin***; such attempts should not come into play until a ***later*** point. Only after the nature of Antichrist and the spirit of antichrist are understood, and then only after the multiple types foreshadowing him (first of all in Scripture and then in history) are comprehended, should any effort to decipher the number "666" be pursued. Once we do embark on the endeavor to understand "666," however, the beginning point should not be with names of figures, particularly not extra-biblical figures, but rather by asking the question, "Where else does '666' occur in the Word of God?"

Here it is important to remember that it is not simply the number of his name, but the number of the Beast. Distinct terms are used in varying contexts. The number of the Beast occurs in association with the Antichrist persona in addition to being specific to his name. Whenever we see the number "666" used in the Word of God either directly or by mathematical composite, the Holy Spirit is trying to show us something about the Antichrist to come and how he will be identified.

The number "666" occurs in Ezra 2:13 as "*the sons of Adonikam, 666*" and in Nehemiah 7:18 it reads "*667.*" We have an apparent discrepancy in the two accounts of the number of the sons of Adonikam, and in order to identify the Antichrist, both this discrepancy and another like it in some manuscripts of Revelations 13, where the number is "616" is found, must be addressed and resolved.

"*Adonikam*" means, "my Lord has risen." As Adonikam came from Babylon after the Captivity this suggests that the Antichrist might be a Jew who returns to Israel from the Diaspora. Indeed large numbers of Jews immigrated to the modern state of Israel from Turkey, Iran, or Iraq. If this were to be the case for the Antichrist it would provide a viable resolution to the problematic issue that there are prophetic texts in Scripture suggesting the Antichrist will come from the Arab or Islamic world while other texts support a Jewish identity, and others still a European identity.

In today's world as in the world of the Roman Empire individuals can carry multiple identities just as did Paul the apostle and the Herodian kings. They can be ***both*** occidental and oriental, ***both*** Jew and Roman. Today we have political figures such as Rahm Emanuel whose family is Israeli but who is an American, having at one time held dual nationality. It is not inconceivable that a political or religious figure could be born in the Arab world, immigrate to Israel, and from there immigrate to Europe. Indeed many thousands of Jews have done precisely that.

There is strong implication of one Beast coming from the earth and the other from the sea in Revelation 13. We must remember that ***both*** Beasts are ***equally*** Antichrist although we colloquially refer to one of these as being ***the*** Antichrist. As always, the sea is indicative of the nations and has a prophetic correlation in Psalm 2, while the earth has to do with Israel. The sons of Adonikam numbering "666," as it were, came from the sea to the earth having come from Babylon, and entered restored Israel. The two Beasts' earth-sea dualism at the very least strongly suggests the capacity of Satan working through Antichrist to deceive both the Jews and the Gentiles.

In the Character of Solomon

The most significant Old Testament figure with which "666" is repeatedly associated is King Solomon in his backslidden period where the number is recurrent. It is in fact used more with King Solomon than any other figure in the scriptural record. This begs the question as to what aspects of the Antichrist the Holy Spirit is highlighting to us by employing this number so repeatedly in the canon of Scripture in direct association with the backslidden King Solomon.

> *To understand a proverb and a figure,*
> *The words of the wise and their riddles* (Prov. 1:6)

Solomon, we are told in the books of Proverbs, Kings, and Chronicles, had a level of insight that was recognized by all, including the queen of Sheba. As we shall see, according to the prophecies of Daniel the same will be true of the Antichrist. The king of Tyre, a major type of the Antichrist, is called "*wiser than Daniel*" (Eze. 23:8), and is the only figure of which we have a biblical record apart from Christ who was wiser than Daniel. The Antichrist will by satanic power likewise be singularly unique. It will be a matter of God-given knowledge in the wrong hands. To understand this we must comprehend what "*the words of the wise and their riddles*" means.

The basic method by which the ancient Hebrews explained spiritual truths was by riddles known as the "*mashal/nimshal*." The *mashal* is a description of something in everyday life, while the *nimshal* is the spiritual truth or principle it illustrates. The Book of Proverbs that Solomon largely authored is known in the Hebrew text as *The Book of Mashals*. The parables as taught by Jesus were simply elongated mashals.

Jesus would pose a riddle as in Matthew 21 where He quoted from Proverbs 5 in the Parable of the Vineyard, teaching that the vineyard would be given to others. The New Testament record of this draws on the Septuagint translation of Proverbs 5, paraphrasing it, with Jesus explaining its meaning. The vineyard would be given to others because, knowing He was the true Son, the religious leaders incited the people to reject and kill him in order to preserve their own religious domain and the position of social privilege and financial interest that accompanied it. The Sanhedrin, like Herod (a type of the Antichrist), tried to kill the rightful heir so they could usurp His dominion for themselves. This is the spirit of antichrist working through religion to turn people against the Son.

One reason the Sanhedrin hated Christ was that He told them the "*hetayim*," that is, the solution to the riddles. The Sanhedrin understood the explanation of the parables about themselves. They detested Jesus because

He was taking what they saw as their secrets, which were the keys to their power and privilege, and explaining it freely to the *"am ha aretz,"*—that is the common people of the land. Jesus was feeding the masses with the hidden manna as the deeper truths of Scripture (Rev. 2:17).

The Pharisees should have been feeding the sheep but instead misused their knowledge to create a political and financial powerbase for themselves as a theocratic aristocracy which, among other things, exploited the poor. Jesus was taking their jewels that were the key to their position of power and wealth and presenting it freely to the poor. As well, He was warning that the keys to understanding the Scriptures, which were the keys to the kingdom given to the Sanhedrin, would be taken from them and given to others—the Church (Lk. 11:52). The church at Ephesus was also warned it would lose its light of understanding the Word of God if it would not repent; the lamp would be removed from the lampstand (Rev. 2:5).

This issue of understanding and insight is foundational to discerning the uniqueness of the Antichrist. He will be in the character of Solomon, exhibiting a remarkable understanding of among other things the theological and the philosophical, and he will be something of a master in his knowledge of the Scriptures. Having the character of Satan, he will know how to misquote it convincingly, as we witnessed in Genesis 3 and Matthew 4. To comprehend how this will transpire we must understand what happened when Solomon, having that insight, backslid.

Once again, according to Ezekiel 28:3, the king of Tyre (a metaphor for Satan and a type of the Antichrist) is *"wiser than Daniel."* Excluding Christ, this can only be found in one other figure—that is in Solomon. We see Solomon's capacity to function on this level in his dialog with the queen of Sheba. But it happens at this time when his heart turns from God that the number of the Beast strikingly appears and reappears in connection with him. This indicates that the Antichrist will be viewed, at least initially, as a positive insightful figure with the unique character and spiritual depth that will entail an incredible command of Scripture.

The turning of Solomon's heart was not immediately visible. After ingratiating himself with the masses and with the Jews, as well as much of the Church, the Antichrist will like Solomon become consumed with spiritual pride. But again, he will appear to be beyond reproach and untouchable, with no visible indication of the backsliding and deception that has taken control of his heart. However, what was visibly apparent with Solomon will also become visibly apparent with the Antichrist to come; that is, the number of the Beast, "666."

Again we remember it is not only the number of his name, but it is distinctly called *"the number of the Beast"* (Rev. 13:18) and is used throughout Scripture to mathematically describe not only his name but also his person. What is again crucial to note is that the remarks by the queen of Sheba lauding the ability of Solomon to respond to questions of hidden truth (2 Chr. 9:2) parallels the description of Satan in Ezekiel 28:3 where the one who is wiser than Daniel is told, *"There is no secret that is a match for you."*

Solomon and the Gentile Woman

Let us consider the Scriptures surrounding Solomon that foreshadow these events to come. The number of the Beast appears clearly in reference to Solomon in both Kings and Chronicles.

> *Now when the queen of Sheba heard about the fame of Solomon concerning the name of the Lord, she came to test him with difficult questions. So she came to Jerusalem with a very large retinue, with camels carrying spices and very much gold and precious stones. When she came to Solomon, she spoke with him about all that was in her heart. Solomon answered all her questions; nothing was hidden from the king which he did not explain to her.*

(He knew the "*hetayim,*" that is, "*the words of the wise and their riddles.*")

> *When the queen of Sheba perceived all the wisdom of Solomon, the house that he had built, the food of his table, the seating of his servants, the attendance of his waiters and their attire, his cupbearers, and his stairway by which he went up to the house LORD, there was no more spirit in the her.* (1 Ki. 10:1-5)

(The spirit went from the Gentile woman.)

> *King Solomon gave to the queen of Sheba all her desire which she requested, besides what he gave her according to his royal bounty. Then she turned and went to her own land together with her servants.*

(The weight of the gold which Solomon received is revealed just when she turned and went to her own land together with her servants.)

> *Now the weight of gold which came in to Solomon in one year was 666 talents of gold,* (1 Ki. 10:13-14)

2 Chronicles 9:13 states the same thing: "*the weight of gold...666.*" The Antichrist is strongly identified with wealth and gold.

Let us remember the "good girls/bad girls" illustration. Good women personify the faithful Church (and in some contexts a faithful Israel), while bad women represent the harlot church, false religion, backslidden Israel, etc. Jesus uses the queen of Sheba, a Gentile woman, as a metaphor for the Gentile Church.

> *"The Queen of the South...came from the ends of the earth to hear the wisdom of Solomon; and behold, something greater than Solomon is here.* (Mt. 12:42)

What we see here is that the Gentile woman came to hear the teaching of Solomon as the Gentile Church came to hear the teaching of Jesus. She was intrigued because Solomon knows the words of the wise and their riddles and no spirit is left in her.

The Working of the Holy Spirit

The Restrainer in 2 Thessalonians 2 is the Holy Spirit. It is chiefly here that the Pre-Wrath Rapture position fails, wrongly identifying the Restrainer as an angel. It is also here that the pre-Tribulation position fails by equating the removal of the Holy Spirit with the Rapture and removal of the Church. For one's eschatology to be correct, one's pneumatology must be correct.

Jesus breathed on the apostles after His resurrection, telling them to receive the Holy Spirit (Jn. 20:22). At that time they were born-again and the Holy Spirit indwelt their hearts as regenerate believers. But Jesus then instructed the apostles to go wait for the Holy Spirit for He had not yet been poured out on the Church, and would not be until the Hebrew Feast of Weeks known as *Hag Shav'uoth* which Christians call Pentecost. Hence there was a distinction between the Holy Spirit ***indwelling*** individual believers and the Holy Spirit being ***poured upon*** the Church under the headship of Christ. There was an intermittent period ***between*** the two events of the Ascension and Pentecost. There will once again be such a short period. Just as Jesus left and sent the Holy Spirit the Holy Spirit will leave and send Jesus.

During this period the Church was not united in power and existed only embryonically; it was not yet properly born, although it existed in an antenatal sense. When the Holy Spirit is removed as the Restrainer the Antichrist will once more take his place in the House of God, both in the Tribulational Temple and in the apostate church. The apostles and other disciples had the Holy Spirit in their hearts, but the Holy Spirit was not yet convicting the world of sin or infusing the Church with the authority and power to proclaim the Gospel.

When this period returns it is again something typologically compared to the night. In both Matthew 23 and the Song of Solomon the bridegroom comes in the night as well as Jesus coming like a thief in the night, and Isaiah's refrain, "how far is the night" (Is. 21:11)? We are thus told to work while we still have the light; the night will come when no man can work (Jn. 9:4). In order to understand this period we must be aware of the other time in biblical history when it happened—that is the period between the Ascension and Pentecost. In John 12:35-36 Jesus said the Light (being Himself the true Light) is among them, and they should walk in it lest darkness overtake them, but they would have it only a little while longer. Once He died, rose, and ascended the Light was no longer here until the Holy Spirit came.

The Church likewise has no light of its own but only reflects the light of Christ. So, too, the biblical passages that speak of cosmic phenomena have a spiritual meaning beyond the darkness of the cosmos. When the Antichrist is manifested the Church will no longer be able to reflect the Light of Christ. The sun will be darkened and the moon turned to blood (Joel 2:31; Ac. 2:20). Persecution of the Church and obscuring the light of Christ on the earth speak of this Tribulation period before the wrath of God is poured out on the kingdom of Antichrist. This we know as "the Day of the Lord" that will be inaugurated by the Rapture and Resurrection. The faithful Church will not experience the judgment of God, but will experience persecution by Antichrist. The Church will have become so corrupted that the persecution that God allows will in fact have become a necessary evil to ensure a spotless bride. A worldly church will compromise, backslide, and follow Antichrist.

We must understand that the Ascension of Jesus, as with His Resurrection, were prolific events. We see this in Hosea 6:2: as His death becomes our death when we pick up our crosses and trust Him for our salvation, so His life becomes our life, His Resurrection our Resurrection, and His Rapture our Rapture. In Hebrews 1:1 we are told we are already in the Last Days in the broad sense that the Resurrection and Rapture have already begun with the Resurrection and Ascension of Christ. There have already been ***many*** antichrists; what we are waiting for is ***the*** Antichrist, and our role in a Rapture or Resurrection that has already commenced.

The importance of this period between the Ascension and Pentecost cannot be overstated, although most of what the Pre-Wrath position affirms concerning the identity of the Antichrist and the timing of the Rapture and Resurrection (between the 6th and 7th seals of Revelation) is absolutely accurate (Rev. 7:9-17). The Restrainer preventing Antichrist from full ascension to power is the Holy Spirit, but the removal of the Holy Spirit is not the Rapture of the Church. The apostles already had the Holy Spirit in their hearts but the Church corporately did not have the Holy Spirit; only the individuals within it had the Holy Spirit.

This is the difference between the ***indwelling*** and ***outpouring***. They were two separate events when Jesus came the first time, and the removal of the Holy Spirit will be two separate events when He comes again. The first by removing the Holy Spirit from the Church as God's agency to deal with the world in terms of salvation, and the second the removal of the faithful Christians by Rapture. The Spirit was given in two stages and will be taken in two stages. It is this first stage that is pivotal in the exploits of the Antichrist, but the faithful believers will already by this time know who he is. They shall know it, and they alone, because the *"son of perdition's"* identity will have been revealed to them by the Lord just as Jesus disclosed the true identity of Judas as the *"son of perdition."*

With reference to "666", however, this is illustrated for us in Solomon's relationship with the queen of Sheba. First the spirit goes from her, then she whom Jesus uses as a type of the Gentile Church goes to her own land, leaving a backslidden Solomon with the Jews. The Holy Spirit will be taken at some point thereafter, and, as with the queen of Sheba, the Church will be taken. This will leave the Antichrist who, like both Solomon and Judas, had been counted among God's people along with the Jews, whom he will bring to the brink of utter destruction. He will be prevented only by the return of Christ with the victorious Church.

There is, however, warrant for expressing further caution lest there be any misunderstanding. The Holy Spirit will ***never*** be taken from the heart of God's people. Jesus said, "*I will never desert you, nor will I ever forsake you*" (Heb. 13:5). And it is the person of the Holy Spirit who communicates Christ to and through us. The Holy Spirit will, however, be taken from the world. God has said His Spirit "*will not strive with man forever*" (Gen. 6:3), just as took place in the days of Noah. The age of grace will come to a close, and in the Book of Revelation God will revert to dealing with rebellious man as He did in the Old Testament—on the basis of wrath, not mercy. And it is during this time that He will turn His primary focus, not to dealing with mankind as a whole, nor with the Church that no longer exists on earth, but rather on the judgment, repentance, rescue, and final salvation of His own people Israel.

As the queen of Sheba saw her spirit depart followed by her own departure simultaneous with the identification of Solomon with "666," so, too, it will happen to the predominantly Gentile Church.

Solomon and the Weight of Gold

> *Now the weight of gold which came in to Solomon in one year was 666 talents of gold,* (1 Ki 10:14)

> *Now the weight of gold which came to Solomon in one year was 666 talents of gold,* (2 Ch 9:13)

It is not without significance that the number of the Beast is ascribed to the weight of gold. As with Judas, Solomon was a man who came to a point where he venerated wealth above the higher virtues to which he previously seemed to subscribe.

In addition to the period between the Rapture of Jesus at the Ascension and the day of Pentecost, which will be replayed in reverse with the Spirit going, then the Body of Christ being Raptured, there are other periods in biblical history—particularly in the Old Testament—that foreshadow this period. Because this book has as its purpose instructing Christians how the Antichrist will be revealed, we are not focused on the ventures he will embark upon after he has been revealed and the faithful Church departs. There are major sections of Daniel and Revelation dealing with the Antichrist that lie outside the parameters of this book which concentrates on his identification. However, the ministries of Elijah, and of John the

Baptist who had his spirit, are further indicative of the gap in time between the Ascension and Pentecost that will reoccur as the gap between the removal of the Holy Spirit and the Rapture and Resurrection.

The Law and the Prophets were preached until John, but then the proclamation of grace and truth ensued with Jesus. John was the last figure of the Old Testament era under the Torah, but also the first figure of the New. This is why the apostles needed to select a candidate to replace Judas, the "*son of perdition*" who had been active not from the onset of the ministry of Jesus, but from the time of John. (Spurious teachings that the apostles acted wrongly in selecting Mathias and should have instead waited for Paul are erroneous.) The ministry of Jesus as presented in the Gospels is introduced with the ministry of John operating in the spirit of Elijah. Elijah's conflict with Ahab and Jezebel, with the sons of the prophets meeting in small groups of fifty, prefigures this coming period. So, too, does the conflict of John the Baptist with Herod, a type of the Antichrist.

These accounts, however, while important in understanding the overall eschatological paradigm and scenario, are less important in understanding the process and pattern by which the Antichrist will be identified. Although an understanding of these events reinforces our overall capacity to comprehend the broader concept, the central episode is with Solomon and the queen of Sheba where the number of the Beast, "666," centrally comes into play. It is in fact the last thing that happens before she and her servants are taken away.

We do not base doctrine on type or foreshadow. Type and foreshadow as always, however, ***illustrate*** and ***illuminate*** doctrine. We read these accounts of Solomon, the queen of Sheba, and "666" in light of 2 Thessalonians 2, and we read 2 Thessalonians 2 in light of the accounts of Solomon, "666," and the queen of Sheba. Solomon's identification with the number of the Beast in relation to the queen of Sheba whom Christ uses as a type of the Church graphically illustrates how the events of 2 Thessalonians 2 are going to transpire.

Solomon and His Court

While the number of the Beast is directly stated in both the Kings and Chronicles accounts in the queen of Sheba narrative of King Solomon's reign, the number begins to appear even earlier. In the celestial court of God in Revelation 1 the architectural features and furnishings occur in groupings of "7," but with Solomon they occur in groupings of "6." The inclusion of such detail in Scripture by the Holy Spirit is not inconsequential.

> *Moreover, the king made a great throne of ivory and overlaid it with refined gold. There were six steps to the throne and a round top to the throne at its rear, and arms on each side of the seat, and two lions standing beside the arms. Twelve lions were standing there on the six steps on the one side and on the other; nothing like it was made for any other kingdom.* (1 Ki 10:18-20)

> *Moreover, the king made a great throne of ivory and overlaid it with pure gold. There were six steps to the throne and a footstool in gold attached to the throne, and arms on each side of the seat, and two lions standing beside the arms. Twelve lions were standing there on the six steps on the one side and on the other; nothing like it was made for any other kingdom.* (2 Ch 9:17-19)

We read that there were six steps with six lions on either side leading to his throne. Thus we again see the number of the Beast leading to the throne of Solomon. The indications were already present. While we must exercise caution in finding parallels in every detail, there is no question that the kinds of musical instruments with which Solomon surrounded himself in 1 Kings 10:12 and 2 Chronicles, with the pomp, harps, etc., resemble that which surrounds the throne of Satan in Isaiah 14:11. They also resemble those that were played signaling the commencement of worship of Nebuchadnezzar's image (Daniel 3) whose dimensions also add up to "666," and which prefigures the image of the Beast in Revelation 13.

> *The king made of the almug trees supports for the house of the Lord and for the king's house, also lyres and harps for the singers; such almug trees have not come in again nor have they been seen to this day.* (1 Ki. 10:12)

> *'Your pomp and the music of your harps*
> *Have been brought down to Sheol;*
> *Maggots are spread out as your bed beneath you*
> *And worms are your covering.'* (Is. 14:11)

> *Therefore at that time, when all the peoples heard the sound of the horn, flute, lyre, trigon, psaltery, bagpipe and all kinds of music, all the peoples, nations and men of every language fell down and*

> *worshiped the golden image that Nebuchadnezzar the king had set up.* (Dan. 3:7)

Solomon and the Ships of Tarshish

> *For the king had ships which went to Tarshish with the servants of Huram; once every three years the ships of Tarshish came bringing gold and silver, ivory and apes and peacocks.* (2 Chr. 9:21)

The increase in trade in the ships of Tarshish narratives surrounding Solomon after he is identified with "666" also is indicative of how the Antichrist will control international trade and commerce. The ships of Tarshish motif in Scripture is always negative. Such ships are destroyed by God using the east wind as His instrument of destruction (Ps. 48:7). And the east wind called the Euraquilo destroyed the ship on which Paul travelled in Acts 27:14. The word "wind" ("*ruach*" in Hebrew and "*pneuma*" in Greek) equally means "spirit" in both languages—that is, a spirit of destruction. Although it may have been a different place called "Tarshish," it was a ship going to Tarshish on which Jonah travelled when he was tossed overboard to drown.

After the faithful Church is removed there will be a judgment on the economy and infrastructure of Antichrist's empire of a magnitude that is without any historical precedent. Those who are drawn to him by financial and commercial self-interest in the pursuit of wealth will be quickly disillusioned once the faithful Church is removed. Their gold will mean nothing as we read in the epistle of James (Ja. 5:3). We must understand that the Word-Faith preaching of contemporary televangelists is the sin of covetousness and the worship of mammon, and is not of the Spirit of God who tells us to store up treasure where neither moth nor rust will consume them (Mt. 6:19). Such greed is instead of the kingdom of Antichrist, financially seducing worldly-minded Christians to trust in this world.

The number of the Beast is once again applied not only to the name of the Beast, but to the Beast himself and his trappings, especially his wealth, money and commerce. Thus we see the relationship between the weight of Solomon's gold typologically and the number of his name in Revelation 13 being required to engage in commerce and financial transactions (Rev. 13:17). As backslidden Solomon prefigures the Antichrist, with "666" associated with money and commerce, so, too, in Revelation 13 "666" is associated with money and commerce.

Concerning commerce and the number of the Beast we would exercise caution about undue speculation which cannot be scripturally supported. One example of this is the emergence of a Christian version of pop culture where elements of modern life are quick to be assigned some spiritual meaning. For instance, the Hebrew letter equivalent to the number 6 is "*vav,*" and some have proposed that it means "www," as in "World Wide Web." The fact that the electronic economy is propelling the world toward an integrated global economic union is without dispute; however, the letter "*vav*" is not a "w" in Hebrew as there is no letter "w" in the Hebrew language. "*Vav*" is pronounced as the Latin "v" or sometimes as the letter "o" but not as a "w." We would note, however, that multiples of "666," such as the number "18," where found in Scripture do merit prayerful examination as they may reveal a combination of three sixes in the alphanumerics of the original languages.

Mark, Name, and Number

When we consider that there are many antichrists and diverse figures in Scripture with no "666" associated, we cannot dogmatically maintain that the recurrence of the number of the Beast and the names and titles of others is not typological of the ultimate Beast of Revelation 13. We must note for instance that in both Greek and Hebrew there is one "*onoma*" that gives us an accurate gematrial value both in Greek and Hebrew, this being "*Maitreya,*" the New Age Messiah expected as a redeeming figure by New Agers in the West and various mystical Buddhists in the East. Again we have "mem" = 40, "yod" = 10m "tav" = 400, "resh" = 200, "hey" = 5, "yod = 10, and "aleph" = 1, again totally "666." Translated into Greek, however, Maitreya becomes "*Maitreas,*" likewise amounting to "666."

Bearing in mind that the Antichrist will attempt to be "all things to all people" in a demonic parody of Paul the apostle in 1 Corinthians 9, ascribing "666" to multiple figures in name and or title may not simply be that all are typological of the final Antichrist. However, the Antichrist may be all of them, and "666" may fit both his name and title, but also more than one title. He will indeed be "in place of" the Son of God amounting to "666" from the Latin, but also Maitreya amounting to "666" in both Hebrew and Greek. We must think beyond the parameters of mutual exclusivity. Although we emphasize the importance of wisdom, the plainest meaning of this understanding in Revelation 13:18 ("*eko nun*" in Greek) is to have a mind which can "*paphisato*" or simply "add together."

There is a straightforward yet complex element to all this. Identification of the Antichrist will in one aspect be simple and straightforward, while at the same time being extremely complicated. The counting of the number of his name is designed both to hide an identity and to reveal it. Much of the focus of believers for centuries has concentrated on this pursuit from the viewpoint of connecting Rome with Babylon. We must among other things bear in mind that long before the Treaty of Rome that initially established the European Common Market which has evolved into the European Union, Charlemagne had the same ambition; but this would have required the blessings and assistance of the papacy. Thus we note that the number "666" in Greek also is the value of "*Lateinos*," that is, "King Latinus" or "the Latin king." Latinus as well as Titan and Evanthas are three names the early church father Irenaeus cited having to do with "666."

But again, as Irenaeus warned, even in the 2nd century we cannot be quick to assign the identity of the Antichrist to anyone based purely on the numerical value of their name. This for the simple reason that multiple people could have names amounting to the number of the Beast. The importance of Irenaeus is due to his association with Polycarp who had been a disciple of John. He constitutes an early source which may have come originally from John, the author of Revelation. An example of Irenaeus' importance is that he states that deviant spellings of the number of the Beast in some manuscripts are copyist errors, and that the number is indeed "666."

Other early sources, however, are more dubious, one of which is Clement of Alexandria whom Origen claimed as his mentor. Problematically, it is with these figures as well as others in Alexandria such as Basileus and Valentinus that Gnosticism first came into the Church, due in part to the early nascent influences of Philo. Clement and Lucian of Samosata, among others, propagated the idea of numerical triangulation in calculating the number of the Beast as in a triangle. For instance five became "fifteen" for the three "5s." 120 is the triangular of 15, and the triangular of the 8th is 36 times 36 equaling 666. This 8th was related to Revelation 17 where the 8th is one of the seven (Rev. 17:11). There was also an infatuation in Alexandria concerning the Antichrist's identity with 9 because the 9th day was a market day in ancient Rome and the gematria of ninth was "*telios*," meaning "the end." Piecing these things together led them to look for an antichrist figure; the closest of which they could agree on was, again, Nero.

Citing the prohibition of Jesus against basing doctrine on extra-biblical tradition, they also noted that the alphanumeric value of the Greek word for "tradition"—"*peridosis*"—was "666." In the 2nd-century document, *The Sibylline Oracles*, the Greek gematria of the name of Jesus—"*Iesous*"—in the segment "will name reveal" is "888," called "great God came clothed in flesh." Thus with a clear gematria for Christ as three "8s" it has been thought that Antichrist will be the same, a straightforward gematrial meaning.

We know for instance from the ruins of Pompeii there are inscriptions referring to people simply by the numerical equivalent of their names. Before Pompeii was destroyed in A.D. 70, one inscription reads, "I love her whose number is 545." And in a burial yard another commemorates, "Harmonia whose number was 45." Thus we have hard archeological evidence that the number of things was commonly known in the Greco-Roman culture of the 1st century. There can be little doubt that the number of the Beast, that is the number of his name, will be in some way consistent with this, bearing in mind once again that the term "*onoma*" may also mean "title."

We must also take great care in understanding that Satan has a vested interest in preventing Christians from the prayerful study and consideration of such problems. And to this end, as always, he has raised up deceivers within the Church to misguide it. It is urgent that faithful Christians avoid the radical extremes of Preterism which falsely claims that all prophecy surrounding the Antichrist, the Great Tribulation, and Babylon the Great were totally instead of partially fulfilled in the 1st century. It is likewise urgent that Christians who love the Lord and cling to the blessed hope of His return avoid both those who are rebuilding the Tower of Babel, such as Chuck Colson, Peter Kreeft, J. I. Packer, and Tony Campolo, as well as the Emergent and Purpose-Driven agendas of Rick Warren and Brian McLaren. Confronted with the direct contradiction between the explicit and unmitigated demand of Jesus to be on the alert and watchful in Matthew 24, and the overtly contradictory instructions of Rick Warren to avoid end-time prophecy, faithful Christians must understand that they cannot believe both Jesus Christ and Rick Warren. One of them is a deceiver, and the deceiver is not Christ.

Just as frightening is the false teaching coming out of Rick Warren's church by his deputy Richard Abanes who authored the book *End Time Visions*, where on page 117 he teaches that there is nothing in Scripture linguistically or otherwise that indicates that the mark of the Beast is in any sense literal. If one does not believe there is a literal mark of the Beast in spite of the fact that the Greek word "*charagma*" means a literal mark, without which one will not be able to engage in commerce, this is notoriously dangerous. We are forced to regard Abanes as an extremely dangerous figure who deceives others, and is demonically deceived himself. Wittingly or unwittingly such men are the true instruments of Satan who faithful Christians will see through and avoid as well as warning the brethren concerning their satanically inspired exploits.

We have two instances where the Book of Revelation uses the term "*mark of the Beast*" (Rev. 16:2; 19:20). We have three places where it is referred to as "his mark" (Rev. 14:9; 15:2; 20:4). We also have the term "*the mark of his name*" (Rev. 14:11). There is some probably minor controversy as to whether these terms are in fact synonymous and would depend in part on how we translate the word "*or*" in Revelation 13:17 as in "*the name of the Beast* ***or*** *the number of his name*." What is clear, however, is that there does not appear to be any scriptural or logical basis to determine anything else when we are speaking about a straightforward alphanumeric equivalency that is a gematrial value.

The Gematria of "Soter"

It has been speculated that the Antichrist's name will be "*Soter*" from the Hebrew Gematria of "6-6-6" (carrying the double connotation of false savior because of the Greek meaning of "Soter" being related to the Greek terms for salvation and life; i.e., *sozo*). This I do not know. What we do know is that this is essentially a transliteration of the name "Sethur" found in Numbers 13:13; this name of Sethur the son of Michael from the tribe of Asher is the one and only name in Scripture that is the perfect Hebrew gematria of "666." It is for sure that this obscure appearance of the name of this otherwise obscure individual is significant in determining the identity of the Antichrist in some way.

While the number "666" is widely used in connection with a number of nefarious figures in a number of ways, this is the one and only place it is used with the name of an individual. Speculatively it may indicate an at least partial Hebraic identity of one of the two Beasts, but perhaps a more important suggestion is that he will arise from relative obscurity. He is listed with a core of men who are heads or leaders and was a representative of a tribe among the spies dispatched by Moses (Num. 13). As with the disciples there were twelve in number, but because of the two sons of Joseph they total thirteen. Because of the second golden-calf rebellion under Jeroboam, Dan would be dropped and not included in the later listing of Revelation 7. The tribe of Asher, however, would be included among the final twelve.

So, too, there is a typological correspondence between the twelve tribes of Israel (and twelve sons of Jacob) and the twelve apostles who are their New Testament parallel and equivalent. Judas came out of the twelve. When Judas as the *"son of perdition"* was revealed at the Last Supper a total of thirteen were likewise present. There has been considerable speculation by some that the Antichrist would be from the tribe of Dan, which begs a number of other questions, such as how will tribal identity be verified? (This is a question outside the scope of the purpose of this book.)

Going back to the Middle Ages, the presence of Judas as the thirteenth led to a superstitious myth of "13" being a bad or unlucky number to the point where even in the modern world architects will use the 13th story of a building as a level not counted among the floors, perhaps used to facilitate air conditioning, heating, and ventilation systems. Many modern hotels and office buildings go from the 12th to the 14th floor. There have even been cities with numbered streets that go from 12th to 14th Street. Putting superstition and myth aside, however, there is some basis to associate 13 with the presence of a Judas even though it may not be the 13th in any particular order. Yet as one of the twelve was a deceiver, so, too, a man whose gematria is "666" is named among the leaders of the twelve tribes.

Reading the Gospels carefully, there was nothing except that which was viewed in retrospect that would have led any of the apostles to know that Judas was the *"son of perdition"* or was any different from the other Apostles; only Jesus knew. There is nothing concerning the representative spy from the tribe of Asher that would indicate that he is in any way different from any of the others except that the number of his name is "666."

This is again the only individual in Scripture the number of whose name is the same as the number of the Beast. We can only guess if there is any significance that his father's name was "*Michael*" meaning "like unto God." The Hebrew concept of sonship did not simply mean pedigree but also "in the character of" (such as "son of righteousness"). There may be a remote hint that the one whose number of his name is "666" may be in the character of one who appears to be "like unto God," making his disguise indiscernible apart from divine revelation. No matter how we observe Numbers 13, however, it is impossible to ignore not only the possibilities but the high degree of probability that there is only one figure in Scripture whose name without mitigation is "666" in the original text, and it is Antichrist.

In Summary

The proposed theories in the resolution of "666" date back to at least the 2nd century and have ranged from the plausible to the ridiculous, from the quantifiable to the speculative, and from the verifiable to the conjectured. In any contemplation of the final solution to this riddle it is important to understand that as with all of eschatology we are warned by the Prophet Daniel that none of the wicked will understand (Dan. 12:10). We are also told that what was sealed by Daniel (Dan. 12:4) is unsealed in the Book of Revelation (Rev. 22:10), and that as we draw closer to the return of Jesus the Holy Spirit will progressively illuminate the explanation of these mysteries just as these visions were explained to Daniel and to the apostle John.

We might say that the meaning is already uncovered, as it were, hidden in plain sight. But as Daniel told us, "*those who have insight*" will in the character of the Maccabees "*give understanding to the many*" (Dan. 11:33-35). And as Jesus told us, the good and faithful servant will give the proper food at the proper time with regard to the things of the end (Mt. 24:45). The faithful believers will understand these mysteries, including the number of the Beast, despite their complexity.

> *"They are all straightforward to him who understands,*
> *And right to those who find knowledge.* (Prov. 8:9)

We additionally take heart at the fact that, as the Book of Ecclesiastes tells us, it is the glory of God to conceal a matter but it is the glory of man to seek it out. Concerning the number of the Beast specifically, we may be sure of the following facts. While it is ultimately a number of man and a number of his name, and it is "666," this may apply to a title as much as to a personal name and may apply to the names and titles of those who typify him. It is important for us to keep in mind that nothing of verifiable substance is a mere coincidence, be it "the king of the Latins"—"*kum latineos*"—or the papal title *Vicarious Felii Dei*, or the numerical associations of the number of the Beast with Adonikam returning from Babylon where "666" had been used in pagan religion, or the "666" propositions of Irenaeus to the multiple other figures with whom the number of the Beast is associated—even to the architectural features and dimensions of Nebuchadnezzar's image, Goliath's armor, and Solomon's throne. None of this is coincidental, and each instance provides at least one piece of the puzzle that will all make sense to faithful believers who pursue the Lord and His wisdom, for He is our wisdom (1 Co. 1:30).

By far the most important key in correctly deciphering the number of the Beast and the number of his name is a personal faith in Christ. Those who are faithful want to understand, and, in the fullness of God's time, will understand. When all of the pieces fit into place it will make perfect sense. However, it is not only "666" that is the final confirmation of the identity of the Antichrist; it is moreover when he takes his place in the Temple of God. In other words, the Lord does not simply give us one litmus test but two.

If a radar system fails, an aircraft still has transponders in its instrument flight system. A plane is not navigated only by either radar or transponders, or just by visual recognition of landmarks, but all three modalities come into play no matter how advanced the avionics package, satellite navigation systems, transponder technology, or over-the-horizon and Doppler radar. Personal vigilance by the pilot remains paramount. He watches all of those indicators to arrive at the destination and land the plane safely. No amount of technology can compensate for human error beyond a certain point. A derelict, untrained, unqualified, or inebriated pilot is a dangerous man. So, too, are pastors and Christian leaders who are biblically unqualified or ignorant, caught up in spiritual drunkenness (Mt. 24:49; Job 1:5; 1 Th. 5:5-8), and who do not know how to use the instruments God has given them or how to discern the times and the climate.

The times are perilous, and by the time the identity of the Antichrist becomes unmistakably evident to all when he fulfills the prophecy of 2 Thessalonians 2:3-4, it will already be too late to know what to do. ***All*** of the indicators must be monitored before one arrives at the destination. In the Last Days faithfulness and understanding are always linked—one being a barometer of the other. Foolish virgins cannot see in the dark without oil in their lamps (Mt. 25:1-13) any more than a drunken pilot can see in a storm without being able to properly read his instruments. The goal must not be to wait for the Antichrist to break a treaty with Israel or to set up an abomination of desolation in the Temple and be worshiped in backslidden Christendom, but rather to already know who he is and what he will do ***before*** these things happen. The means to do this will be to understand "666" in light of, and on the basis of, the things aforementioned and explained to the most definitive degree that is presently possible.

Again, there is merit in being familiar with all plausible theories, but I have sought to be dogmatic and conclusive only about those things of which by the grace of the Lord I am absolutely certain. I do not at the present moment have "666" completely figured out; neither do I believe at the present does anyone apart from the Lord Himself. Moreover, I do not believe that at the present time of this publication it can be conclusively and absolutely known. The only conceivable conception could be that the Antichrist and/or False Prophet are already alive (a very distinct possibility) and they will know who they are before anyone else does. What I can be absolutely and conclusively dogmatic about at the present moment, however, is that when the Holy Spirit does reveal what "666" means to faithful believers, it will be in accordance with the indicators, features, caveats, and teachings contained in this book.

Chapter 17: Attributes of the Antichrist

Jewish Anti-Semitism

In order to understand the identity of the Antichrist, our priority must be to understand Jewish anti-Semitism, first of all from Scripture and from scriptural history, both with individuals such as Menelaus and the Herods, as well as corporate units such as the tribe of Dan. We must also understand Jewish anti-Semitism in light of both ancient and modern history.

Two of the major Jewish types of the Antichrist, Jacob Frank and Shabbatai Zvi, both converted to anti-Semitic religions. It is reported in serious media sources that Ahmadinejad, the Iranian madman and hater of Israel and the Jews, has a Persian-Jewish surname coming from the Persian word for a Jew who made *taliths*, or prayer shawls. There may have been elements of Persian Jewry in his paternal bloodline. (Similar claims have even been alleged about Adolph Hitler, but no one has been able to seriously prove the assertion with hard documentation.)

In High Gate Cemetery in London is the grave of Karl Marx, the radical Jewish philosopher who is the father of Communism. Marx was a professed atheist, the son of Jews who assimilated into, and at least nominally professed, a cultural Christianity. Some have suggested that at one point in his life Marx may have been involved in Satanism. Marx never denied, nor did he ever emulate, his Jewish ethnicity. On his grave is his epitaph, "The philosophers have only interpreted the world in various ways; the point is to change it."

Concerning history, the Book of Ecclesiastes tells us that there is actually "*nothing new under the sun*" (Ecc. 1:9). Concerning the Antichrist, however, the prophet Daniel tells us that he will seek to change the times and the law (Dan. 7:25). Karl Marx the Jew, in fact, merely echoed what Daniel said of the Antichrist.

As Christ has 3-1/2 years, so Satan will demand equal time. And he will receive it for two times, a time, and a half time (Dan. 7:25); within these restrictions and parameters, God allows for 3-1/2 lunar years at least, when Antichrist will exercise lordship over history and human events. Marx founded an atheistic, humanistic monster that promised justice and alleviation of suffering in the human condition, only to unleash a tyranny that killed more people than Hitler and, second only to Hitler, was the most anti-Jewish force in human history. Yet it came from a Jew. Few things exhibit not only the spirit but the character and the working of Antichrist more than what Marx initiated, yet he was a Jew.

Jewish "self-hatred" has been the subject of humor among Jewish comedians such as Woody Allen, and the subject of intellectual debate among Jewish academics reacting to anti-Zionist Jews such as Norman Finklestein. Hollywood script writers and crime-story authors chronicling the history of legendary American gangsters have often retold in print and on film how Meyer Lansky collaborated with Italian Mafia gangsters against his fellow Jewish gangsters such as Benny Seagal. These, however, may be little more than petty instances of individuals engaging in anti-Semitism; Marx and the diabolical anti-Semitic tide of blood of millions on four continents was not petty. As antichrist as Marxism is, it is only a shadow of what is on the horizon.

We must also understand that the *Quran* is in significant measure a bastardization of Judaic texts which oriental Jews were forced to edit and compile at the point of a sword. It has yielded an Islamic militancy that has become as bad as Hitler's in its disposition toward Jews. As Islam teaches, "The last day will not come until the tree says to a Muslim, 'There is a Jew hiding behind me; come and kill him'." We must recall that in the 18th century Jacob Frank, who was widely accepted among many Jews as the Messiah, converted to Islam.

Several of the kings of Israel perpetrated atrocities against their own people according to the scriptural records of the Books of Kings and Chronicles. Their persecutions were more cruel and prolific than what the people suffered at the hands of Pagans. Josephus records how in A.D. 70 the Zealots (*Sikkim*) butchered their own people with a blood-thirsty cruelty far more barbaric than anything undertaken against them by the Romans. Not least of all it was Jewish collaborators with the Seleucids in the days of the Maccabees who betrayed their own people most notoriously. This was just as the Herodians had done in the time of Jesus (bear in mind that both Antiochus and Herod the Great are major types of the Antichrist).

Although Jesus wept over Jerusalem (Mt. 23:37-39), and Paul the apostle was so grieved for his fellow Israelites that he wished if possible he could be lost if they would be saved, false Christians would later in a Hellenized Church redesign their version of Christianity as an anti-Jewish religion. This, even though it was begun by a Jew who loved His people to the point of willingly laying down His own life for their salvation, and forgiving their betrayal of Him to pagan Roman killers.

On the bases of Scripture and history, both ancient and modern, we can in no way suggest that Jewish identity and anti-Semitism are mutually exclusive. The tragic irony remains that Jews themselves are the authors of systems, entities, and philosophies that have either directly or indirectly resulted in the genocidal shedding of more Jewish blood than any other. Any notion that the anti-Semitism and Jew-hatred of the Antichrist of necessity excludes or precludes the possibility of at least one of those Beasts being of ethnic Jewish decent is not plausible; indeed a cogent argument can be made that the diametric opposite could be true. From Menelaus in the days of the Maccabees to Marx in the more modern day we see not only the recurrent phenomenon of Jewish anti-Semitism, but a record of notorious hatred of Jew against Jew no better than, for instance, the hatred we have seen and experienced in Northern Ireland of supposed Christian against Christian, or of Muslim against Muslim in the Iran-Iraq War. The history of Jewish anti-Semitism is a curious one, but it has too often been a major determining factor in biblical and Jewish history for it to be ignored. And we would be grossly unwise not to carefully bear this in mind when considering the subject of Antichrist.

Along this line we have already considered the individual aspect of Jews who go against their God, their heritage, and their people when we considered the character of Menelaus in the Hanukkah epic, and how his relationship to Antiochus IV shadows something that will transpire within international Jewry when the Antichrist is manifested. There is, however, another possible aspect that warrants at least cursory mention, and that is the tribal factor surrounding the tribe of Dan.

The Tribe of Dan

Because of the incident involving the second golden calf that took place in the region of Dan during the days of Jeroboam (2 Ki. 10:29), a tribal curse was invoked on the tribe of Dan. The prophetic destiny of Israel's tribes and the nation and people who come from them are all foretold in Genesis 49 and project forward to Revelation 7 and 14 from where the tribe of Dan is excluded. In order to keep the number 12, the tribe of Joseph is divided into two: Ephraim and Manasseh. Our point of origin in understanding the prophetic outcome of the tribe of Dan must, as with all of Israel's tribes, come from the revelation of the future concerning these tribes that God gave to Jacob their patriarch.

> *"Dan shall judge his people,*
> *As one of the tribes of Israel.*
> *Dan shall be a serpent in the way,*
> *A horned snake in the path,*
> *That bites the horse's heels,*
> *So that his rider falls backward.*
> *For Your salvation I wait, O LORD."* (Gen. 49:16-18)

Here we see the pronouncement of the patriarch of the tribe of Dan, whose name carries the meaning of judgment. *"Dan shall judge the people,"* we are told, but he shall *"be a serpent in the way"*—that is, *"a horned snake in the path."* The typology here is disturbing. As in Genesis 3, Dan is described as a *"nachash"* – a manifestation of Satan as a deceiver with the capacity to beguile the woman, with Eve as a figure of Israel and of the Church. He is, however, referred to as a *"horned snake."*

In the Book of Revelation where we read of the dragon and serpent both cast down, we have a robust enfleshment of Satan on the earth. This points to the Antichrist with the dragon describing persecution but the serpent describing spiritual seduction and deception. The term in Hebrew is *"shfeefone,"* meaning having an anatomical feature (probably some kind of horns) capable of bruising, breaking or overpowering. This has direct relationship to Satan in Revelation 20:2 and 12:9 as *"the serpent of old."* Revelation 12 is again pivotal in addressing both the identification of Antichrist and what his actions will be. The term here for *"horned"* in Genesis 49 is not the usual term *"keren,"* which typologically denotes some form of kingship; it is rather a term denoting an anatomical capacity to overwhelm and break. This is what will happen when Satan and his angelic beings are cast down and the devil enters into the Antichrist. The satanic power of deception will be matched only by the satanic power to overpower and overwhelm.

This direct connection between Antichrist and the tribe of Dan must not be ignored. The horned snake also forms some kind of impediment or obstacle in what is translated *"path,"* the term being *"arah,"* meaning a well-trotted road or caravan route. Spiritual seduction and violent opposition will obstruct the path of God's people.

We are told, however, that the serpent "*bites the horse's heels.*" Here we must rely not only on typology but on etymology. Horses were animals of war for use with chariots, etc.; they were not conventional beasts of burden or transport. The word for "hooks," however, appears also in the following verse in connection with the tribe of Gad, but in verse 17 the serpent Dan shall cause the riders of the horses to fall back through biting the heel. The conventional Hebrew word for "heel" is "*akov*" and it is from where we derive the Hebrew name "*Yakov.*" But it also comes into play in Genesis 3 where the prophecy that the seed of the woman, (the seed being a picture of the Messiah) shall crush the head of the serpent after the serpent bruises the heel (Gen. 3:15).

As we see in Genesis 49 and throughout the Old Testament, Jacob—that is "*Yakov*"—is a corporate solidarity who represents the ethnic Jewish nation and people. Thus although the seed of the woman will destroy Satan, Satan will only be able to damage the heel of the Messiah due to His resurrection. The midrashic implication of this is Satan will try to preempt the Messiah's destruction of him by destroying the Jews prior to both the First and Second Coming of the Messiah. The word used here for "heel" in Genesis 49:17-19, however, is an etymologically related word "*iqqbah,*" having the Hebrew root "*ayen-kofbeth,*" the same precise spelling as "*Yakov*" or "Jacob," a metaphor for national and ethnic Israel. The serpent in Genesis 49:17 is able to immobilize those traveling on the traditional path. As a result, in verse 18 we have Jacob's expression, "*For Your salvation I wait, O LORD.*"

No one will be able to stop the Antichrist except Christ. The word here for "wait" is "*qavah,*" meaning to collect or band together in order to expect. What is important here is that the term "heel" is used of the tribe of Dan, of the serpent in Genesis 3, and is used by Jesus of Judas, the most important type of the Antichrist in scripture in John 13: 18: "He who eats my bread has lifted up his heel against me." Here Jesus is quoting the prophecy of "*the son of perdition*" in Psalm 41:9. This lends further weight to the case that the Antichrist will infiltrate the Body of Christ to a very high degree, be counted among us, and will have eaten the same spiritual food (that is, he will know the depth of our doctrine); yet, as with Judas, something will be terribly wrong (1 John 2:19).

At the Forefront of Spirital Seduction

Most of what Scripture goes on to say concerning Dan is not complimentary. The wicked son of Leviticus 24:12 is from a Danite woman. Dan stood on the mount of curses when entering the Promised Land under Joshua (Dt. 27:13). But it is more than curious that a figure from the tribe of Dan was at the forefront of the construction of the holy Ark and Tabernacle in the Book of Exodus (Ex. 31:6). It is when we arrive in Jeremiah 8:16-17, however, that we again see Dan once more used in conjunction with the serpent.

> *From Dan is heard the snorting of his horses;*
> *At the sound of the neighing of his stallions*
> *The whole land quakes;*
> *For they come and devour the land and its fullness,*
> *The city and its inhabitants.*
> *"For behold, I am sending serpents against you,*
> *Adders, for which there is no charm,*
> *And they will bite you," declares the LORD.* (Jer. 8:16-17)

Representing the geographic north of the country, Dan is the source of the coming punitive invasion from the north. But we again see the serpents who bite; and the adders "*for which there is no charm*" are a picture that God will send spiritual seduction and judgment in direct connection with the Antichrist, as we see in 2 Thessalonians 2.

Dan was a tribe that left its first inheritance awarded by God in the days of Joshua (Josh. 19:40-47), and rather relocated itself in the north of the country above the other tribes (Judg. 18) where it would eventually lead the ten northern tribes into unspeakable idolatry and rebellion with the second golden-calf incident (1 Ki. 12:20). It is not our argument that the Antichrist will be a descendant from the tribe of Dan or from the region of Dan, but we must note that although Jesus was legally a descendant of David from the tribe of Judah through Joseph by provision of Levirate marriage, the Messiah could not be a descendant of Jeconiah. Thus the blood lineage of Jesus needed to come through His mother, whose Davidic genealogy we read in the Gospel of Luke. Even the Mishnah confirms, "*Miriam bat Heli*" (Sanhedrin 25c). So, too, the paternal lineage of Antichrist may need be a non-Jew of Arab or Assyrian Arab origin, like the later Edomites or the Idumeans, who may be a Jew by religion but who maternally may have

Jewish origins as we see in Leviticus 24:12 with the wicked son of the Danite woman.

Whether or not mitochondrial DNA will at some future point be able to determine with any certainty if someone is of a particular tribal origin (somewhat successful experiments have already taken place with the tribe of Aaron among Jews with Levitical names such as "Cohen," "Seagal," etc.), we cannot at this point say. But what we can say is that at least typologically and in figure the Antichrist will act in character with the fulfillment of Jacob's prophecy to the tribe of Dan. Moreover, Antichrist will, as always, need to counterfeit Christ by means of imitation. Christ was born in the south but migrated north because of the Herods, types of the Antichrist. So, too, the tribe of Dan came from the south and migrated north. Additionally, the Jewish bloodline of Jesus in the Gospel genealogies is traced through Mary, while the kingship line is traced through Joseph. There are other instances of matra-linear genealogies in the records of the Old Testament like in Ezra and with the daughters Zelophehad (Num. 27). The Antichrist may indeed mimic this, but we see such acute imitation nowhere more than with a maternal descendant of the tribe of Dan.

Talmudic Judaism

We must further recall that unlike the God-given Judaism of Moses and the Prophets, the corrupted Judaism denying the messiahship of Christ and the Father-Son relationship is, like Islam, an antichrist religion which we call "Talmudic Judaism." Talmudic Judaism, moreover, will be used by Satan and has been used by Satan to attempt the destruction of the Jewish people. The rebirth of the modern state of Israel as one example, prophesied by both the Hebrew Prophets and by Jesus, was championed by secular Jewish Zionists but opposed by the rabbis because, after rejecting its Messiah, Judaism mutated into Talmudic apostasy.

This apostate Judaism which corrupted scriptural Judaism with *Talmud* contains a body of Jewish law called "*Halacha*" which legislates that Jewish identity is matra-linear and not patra-linear. (This is not specifically taught in the Scriptures where there are also arguments for identity being paternal as in "the children of Abraham, Isaac, and Jacob" and not of "Sarah, Rebecca, and Rachel or Leah.") That Satan must deceive the Jews with a ploy to destroy them requires that he feigns some acceptance of an antichrist religion that has rejected its own Messiah and will culminate with the near destruction of their people and nation if Yeshua (Jesus) the true Messiah did not return to save them from themselves and from the Antichrist.

The Church of Christ vs. the Church of Antichrist

On multiple occasions we have pointed out a change that has taken place in what is popularly called "Evangelicalism" in recent years, but which began in the late 1970s, gaining momentum throughout the 1980s. It is a phenomenon that was foretold by a host of noteworthy figures, some dating back a hundred years, such as J. C. Ryle and Charles Spurgeon. In the 1950s, A. W. Tozer likewise warned what would become of mainstream Evangelicalism in the forthcoming decades. And in the 1960s Francis Schaeffer accurately forecasted what would happen to the Church at the end of the 20th and into the 21st century. All of these and others were proven right even though the things they were predicting seemed incredible at the time they first wrote of them.

When I witnessed the delinquent spectacle of counterfeit revivals championed by false prophets in Kansas City, Toronto, Pensacola, Lakeland, and elsewhere, with New Age mysticism being called "spirituality," and Kundalini Yoga being called "manifestations of the Holy Spirit," I and others were absolutely astounded how so many people calling themselves "Christian" could be so deluded.

Moderate Pentecostals and biblically-based charismatics such as I, and others like I, were shunned for explaining how such deceptions were not what took place during the great revivals of men like John Wesley and George Whitfield, and were neither of biblical Pentecostalism nor a genuine charismata. The world laughed at the Church, and so did the devil. In retrospect I came to realize that, in considering men such as Todd Bentley, John Arnott, and Rodney Howard-Browne, the prediction of Charles Spurgeon had come to pass just as he warned it would: "A time will come when instead of having shepherds feeding the sheep, the church will have clowns entertaining the goats."

We have observed how an older generation of Pentecostal preachers wept as televangelists made mainstream the imitators of heretics such as William Branham, E. W. Kenyon, and A. A. Allen, who the early Pentecostals rejected as deceivers. Again the world laughed as the money preachers discredited the Church, and Satan once more had a field day as hireling pastors refused to shield the sheep from the wolves.

It got to the point where not only the false doctrine and clinically undocumented healings attributed to a pathetic figure like Todd Bentley were not enough to keep him out of ministry, but neither was open adultery when he abandoned his wife and children and took off with another woman. Rather, he was "restored to ministry" by Rick Joyner. The alleged prophecies of Joyner, C. Peter Wagner, Che Ahn, Bill Johnson, Cindy Jacobs, and others regarding this immoral man all proved to be false predictions, yet people still tolerated them. The same was no less true of Mike Bickel's Kansas City (False) Prophets. Despite the sexual immorality of Bob Jones and the homosexuality and alcoholism of Paul Cain on top of their false prophecies such devious deceivers were allowed to stay in ministry, still winning the fervor of the naïve and undiscerning.

It has for many years been my contention that if people claiming to be saved Christians cannot see through obvious deceivers such as Benny Hinn, multiple divorcee Paula White, Kenneth Copeland, and Todd Bentley, what will happen when ***real*** deception comes when a satanically empowered Antichrist is able to perform acts that are truly supernatural?

Yet with the Emergent Church the state of affairs has degenerated even further into mysticism and the rejection of Scripture as propositional truth due to figures such as Brian McLaren. A long list of Inclusivists and Universalists claiming to be Christian, bearing the names of William Young (author of *The Shack*), Brennan Manning (author of *The Ragamuffin Gospel*), and Britain's Steve Chalke, openly deny that Christ died for sin, while Tony Campolo, Colin Chapman, and others no longer hold to salvation through professed faith in Christ alone.

In light of these trends we are once again confronted by the ugly reality that the apostate church is no longer simply Roman Catholicism, Liberal Protestantism, Eastern Orthodoxy, or pseudo-Christian cults such as the Mormons. It now includes much of what was accepted as "Evangelical." As Christ is building His Church, Satan is likewise building his. While the Holy Spirit prepares the Bride for the coming of the Bridegroom, the spirit of antichrist prepares the harlot for the coming of the Beast. And his harlot church will include many who are claiming to be "born-again."

The Temple

> *You also, as living stones, are being built up as a spiritual house for a holy priesthood, to offer up spiritual sacrifices acceptable to God through Jesus Christ.* (1 Pe. 2:5)

Believers are the stones being built into the heavenly temple. Paul said of Peter, James and John, they "*were reputed to be pillars*" (Gal. 2:9). And to the faithful church of Philadelphia in the letters to the churches in the Book of Revelation Jesus says, "*I will make him a pillar in the temple of My God*" (Rev. 3:12). Believers are the living stones of the temple.

Visitors to Jerusalem and the Temple Mount are met with huge stones in the Wailing Wall. They are bigger than the stones in the pyramids. It is to those stones the apostles are referring in Matthew 24. "Just look at these stones," they say; to which Jesus responds, "*Not one stone will be left upon another*" (Mt. 24:1-2).

Jesus entered Jerusalem on the back of a donkey while the people sang the *Hallel Rabbah* on Palm Sunday. This was taken from Psalms 113-118:

> *"Hoshana, hoshana ben David!" Hosanna to the son of David!*

> *"Baruch habba'beshem Adonai!" Blessed is he who comes in the name of the Lord!*

The religious establishment reacted in horror as they saw everybody going after Him. They rebuked Jesus: "Tell them to be quiet! Tell them to be quiet!" And Jesus responded: "*If these become silent, the stones will cry out*" (Lk. 19:39-40). In essence He was saying that if the Jews do not praise Him and recognize Him as the Messiah, the Gentile Church will.

Jews thought they were special because they were Abraham's children; in their minds they were the rightful leaders. When they came out to hear John preach, they boasted, "We are Abraham's children; we are special." And John the Baptist replied, "*From these stones God is able to raise up children to Abraham*" (Lk. 3:8). It is Midrash. It is not the Western way of thinking.

> *For we are God's fellow workers; you are God's field, God's building.* (1 Co. 3:9)

It says in Peter it is a place where sacrifices are offered (1 Pe. 2:5), and calls the Church *"God's building."* Believers are God's temple. Paul uses the same typology.

> *from whom the whole body, being fitted and held together by what every joint supplies, according to the proper working of each individual part...* (Eph. 4:16)

Different parts of the building have different functions. One of the purposes of the gifts of the Spirit is to build unity in the Church. And then he goes on to describe this further. In Ephesians it says that Jesus is the cornerstone (Eph. 2:16). The apostles and the prophets are the foundation and they are being built up as God's temple. Believers are the temple. There are seven places in the New Testament that say believers are the tabernacle, using different words in Greek: *oinos*, *naos*, etc., but the basic word is "tabernacles"—*mishkan* in Hebrew.

The physical structure of the Old Testament tabernacle teaches about the Church in the midrashic line of reasoning. Hosea describes a resurrection scene which reveals that what happened to Jesus will happen to believers.

> *"He will revive us after two days;*
> *He will raise us up on the third day,*
> *That we may live before Him.* (Hos. 6:2)

When Jesus said, *"Destroy this temple, and in three days I will raise it up"* (Jn. 2:19), they thought He was speaking of the physical Temple, but He was speaking of His body. The Church is the Body of Christ. It gets raised up. Paul said, "You are a temple of the Holy Spirit" (1 Co. 6:19).

God is a tri-unity and man is a tri-unity: body, mind, and spirit. The physical body is the outer court. The Holy Place in the Temple—the *Maqomah Qodesh*, the *haggio*—is the mind, the soul. The Holy of Holies is where God's Spirit dwells. *Eros* love corresponds in some way to the outer court, *phileo* love to the Holy Place, and *agape* love to the Holy of Holies. Love is expressed on those levels. Only the Holy Spirit of God can express *agape* love. Unsaved people are incapable of *agape* love. It is only when someone is born-again in God's Spirit that they can be capable of it.

Jesus is the Husband of the Church. The husband is the head of the wife as Christ is the head of the church (Eph. 5:23). Sex in a Christian marriage represents Jesus going inside of the Church, causing the Church to be fruitful. When someone goes inside their wife they are entering God's Temple. It is a holy thing. It does not mean it is not erotic, it does not mean there is no romance, it does not mean there is no pleasure in it, but it does mean it is a holy thing, reserved for those who have been sanctified by Jesus.

One of the reasons that sexual immorality and sex outside of marriage is so evil in the sight of God is that it is meant to reflect Christ's relationship with His bride for whom He gave His life. Christ expects a husband to be willing to give his life for his bride the way that He gave His life for His Bride. Generally, if a husband were really going to give himself and love his wife the way Christ loves the Church, he would not have a submission problem with his wife. Believers' bodies are temples, Jesus' body is a temple, but the Church is ***the*** temple. There are seven places in the New Testament that say the Church is the temple, the Body of Christ. It even gets resurrected in three days in some sense.

The Antichrist wants to sit in the Temple of God. That is what he is going to do. But what does that mean? Does that mean the physical Temple on Mt. Zion? This is not to say it does not, but it means something much, much, ***much more*** than that.

The Abomination of Desolation

Having laid a foundation for understanding the midrashic elements of the stones and the Temple, one can better understand the passages in Daniel and Revelation that use the same typologies for the Antichrist's prophetic agenda. This begins with what is called *ha shiqutz ha meshomem*. It is Aramaic, not Hebrew, better known as the "Abomination of Desolation." *Meshomem* is the modern Hebrew word for "boring." *Shiqutz* is a word that occurs in many places in the Bible. It is related to the derogatory Yiddish word for a Gentile woman, *shiksa*. It literally means "a slimy reptile." Joseph is a type of Jesus and he married a Gentile woman (Gen. 41:50). Moses was a prophet like Jesus and his family hated him because he took a Gentile woman (Num. 12:1). Those are types of Jesus, taking the Church as a Bride, establishing an alliance with the *goyim*.

Now the *sheqetz*, or *shiqutz*, occurs in many places in the *Tanak*, the Old Testament. It is usually translated "detestable things" and it is often applied to something called "Baal worship." The Hebrew word for "husband," "master," and "owner" is the same word: *ba'al*. The "owner of the house is *ba'al habayith*. The "owner" or the "proprietor" of a business is *haba'al*. The "husband" is *haba'al*.

Satan wants to take God's woman. He wants to be worshiped in Heaven and on earth in God's Temple. It does not happen in Heaven; he is cast down. So he tries to take God's woman on the earth. Adultery and idolatry are the same. Idolatry equals spiritual adultery. That is why Jesus said *porneia*—immorality, sexual immorality—is the only grounds for divorce. Like Hosea, the only way God would get rid of Israel was if she played the harlot. When Israel went into idolatry God called it adultery. "O daughter of Zion, you played the harlot; you have gone after other lovers" (Hos. 4). Satan wants to take God's woman and to be worshiped as God. That is what he wants and that is what he is going to get to a degree and up to a point. Satan wants to take the woman, so he devises a plan to do it. But ultimately, in Jesus there is triumph.

It is necessary to understand the nature of Baal worship against which Elijah contended and against which Elijah will contend again in some way, whatever the "spirit of Elijah" ultimately means. *Baal* is "husband" and this Canaanite God is called *Baal Hashamim*. The way he is worshiped even has a resurrection myth. He is resurrected every spring. Liberal scholars try to say that Christianity is just copied from Baal worship, but this ignores the fundamental differences. It is just the opposite. Nonetheless, Satan wants to take God's woman.

Satan has two modes of attack: the dragon and the serpent. The serpent is the *sheqetz*, the *shiqutz*—the slimy reptile representing deception. What the Abomination of Desolation involves, literally, is Satan using deception, coming as the serpent to beguile the woman, to deceive her so as to take her as his wife and make the House of God desolate.

Whenever the Temple Mount is being defiled it reveals something about this phenomenon. When the Roman General Pompeii entered the Holy of Holies, and when Antiochus Epiphanes set up the image of the beast in the Temple, they both foreshadowed the Antichrist.

The Third Temple

Most of the popular pondering among both saved Christians and religious Jewish nationalists is centered on the question of reconstruction of a third Temple. This would of necessity be the Tribulational Temple described in Revelation 11 and should not be confused with the millennial Temple of Ezekiel. We must also out of hand reject suggestions that the great synagogue of Jerusalem built two kilometers away could be considered in any sense a rebuilt third Temple.

We must also note that Samaritanism was and is an apostate Judaism from the Book of Nehemiah until John 4. It has always had an alternative holy mountain in Mt. Gerizim, rejection of the Hebrew prophets, alterations of the Torah, a separate priesthood, a hybrid people of mixed pagan-Assyrian and Jewish origin, and an alternative system of blood sacrifices that have never ended but persist to this day. Although John Hyricanus destroyed their temple, the Samaritans, presently existing as a small community residing on Mt. Gerizim and in Holon (a suburb of modern Tel Aviv), are legally recognized as Israeli Jews. Given the typology of Sanballat, the Samaritan leader who falsely claimed in the days of Ezra and Nehemiah to have the same God and sacrificial system as the Jews (Ez. 4:1-2; Neh. 2), we see a demonic element in the still existing Samaritan religion, although as we are told in Acts 8, in the 1st century many Samaritans believed in Jesus. In the Great Commission the apostles were instructed by Christ to go to them immediately after they went to the mainstream Jews. And Jesus personally revealed Himself to the Samaritan woman as the Messiah before He openly did so to any others, of which we have a Gospel record (Jn. 4). The Samaritan Judaism of Mt. Gerizim, however, likewise rejected the Messiah as did the mainstream Judaism of Mt. Zion.

What is important in considering the Samaritans, however, is that they were like the Idumean House of Herod, mongrelized Jews and, moreover, as much Assyrian as they were Hebrew both ethnically and in their allegiances (Ezra. 4:2). This has to be kept in mind when we consider those verses associated with the king of Assyria, or simply "*the Assyrian*" (Mic. 5:5); it casts some suggestion that the Antichrist will be of that nation. Thus once again, as with the Idumean House of Herod, the Samaritans present a scenario where the Antichrist can appear as both a Jew and a non-Jew, as both an Arab-Assyrian or an Assyrian-Arab (as the Assyrians would often be seen by modern identity), yet also somehow a Jew. In no case, however, can we present an argument that the Samaritan blood sacrifices or even a Samaritan temple on Mt. Gerizim could be the Tribulational Temple of the Antichrist. The questions of Temple reconstruction remain concentrated on Jerusalem.

Will it be rebuilt? Even today there is already an Abomination of Desolation on the Temple Mount: the Dome of the Rock, the Mosque of

Omar. Upon the mosque is this quote from the Quran, "God has no son." That is a partial fulfillment of prophecy.

Julian the Apostate, Constantine's nephew, tried to re-paganize the Roman Empire (not that Constantine truly Christianized it), and he tried to rebuild the Temple. And all these mysterious fires and things happened on the Temple Mount. ***Many*** Abominations of Desolations, but one ***ultimate*** one!

An Evangelical archeologist, Dr. James Fleming, found Herodian stones under the present *Sha'ar Ha Raqhamiim*, the "East Gate" of Jerusalem. If Dr. Asher Kaufman is right, from where the high priest had to stand on the cleft of the Mt. of Olives to see through the East Gate to the Holy of Holies on the Day of Atonement would mean it is not necessary to tear down the Dome of the Rock to rebuild the Temple; it was actually somewhat north of it. This is not to deny that the Temple or some "ecumenical center" can be rebuilt, but it means something much more than that: Satan wants God's woman.

When Jesus died, the veil of the Temple was torn from the ceiling to the ground (Mt. 27:51). The *mechisat* between Jew and Gentile was destroyed when the veil in front of the Holy of Holies was torn. An actual, physical event happened in the physical Temple, which was a sign in itself. But what was important was not that sign. What was most important is what that sign represented—that because of the blood of Jesus man was no longer separated from a holy God.

Even if the Temple is rebuilt and an image is set up (with some kind of robot or abomination in there)—even if that happens (and this is not to say it will not)—that is not what is going to be most important. What is going to be ***most*** important is what that represents: Satan being worshiped in the Tabernacle—in the Temple .

Look at what is happening in Canterbury Cathedral today: Hindu gods, Buddhist gods, African witchdoctors' gods being worshiped along with a homosexual clergy presiding. That was the whole pagan thing: cult prostitution and homosexual cult prostitution happening in Greece. They were powerless to go up against it. It was part of their religion. Today there is gay dancing in churches. "Oh, Jesus, you came to liberate the gay people." That is what is happening. The Abomination of Desolation is ***already*** happening; in many respects it is ***already*** here.

Christians should take note of, but not mainly focus on, the Temple being rebuilt. This is not to say it is not going to happen, but the Abomination, the *hashiqutz hameshomem*, is already happening incipiently.

The serpent is already beguiling the woman, trying to take God's Bride. It is already happening. But that is what they want, so that is what they are going to get.

Chapter 18: The Person of the Antichrist

As Jesus being God incarnate was the most unique man who ever lived, Antichrist will approximate an incarnation of Satan and convincingly attempt again with unprecedented success to present himself as a Christ-like figure initially. At the same time, we must realize that in the operations of Satan which will be expressed through the Antichrist and False Prophet there is a second diametrically opposing aspect. On one hand Satan comes as an angel of light and attempts to counterfeit by disguising his persona and camouflaging his agenda as a righteous cause. At the same time he will embody the personality of Satan himself and stand in 180 degree contrast to the character of God manifested in Jesus Christ. Jesus was a man of power who behaved as a man of peace; the Antichrist will present himself as a man of peace but show himself to be a man of treacherous power. Hence he will display features of both a lamb and a dragon in the person of Antichrist.

Satan is the most powerful being God created—of such power he vainly imagines he can usurp the place of God His Creator. So Antichrist will encompass this essence of Satan's nature, imagining he can usurp the position of Jesus. He will attempt to effect this by likewise presenting himself as a global savior figure and the hope of national ethnic Israel. To achieve these aims he must either by deception or obliteration silence the trumpet of the true Church. If possible, the Elect indeed will be deceived (Mt. 24:24).

Already we see tokens of what the Antichrist will do through the many antichrists foreshadowing him, as the spirit of antichrist opens the door for his arrival. As we have multiple times pointed out, the acclamation given to the papacy despite the grotesque antichrist doctrines of Roman Catholicism is but one example. Another of course would again be building bridges for Mormonism. Both of these things among others are creating an arena into which the Antichrist and False Prophet will enter. Much of the Church is already being predisposed to it.

Satanically Powered

The individual groomed by Satan will know who he is before other people will. And as we have said, he will not simply be demonically possessed, but satanically possessed, a diabolical uniqueness shared only by Judas and the False Prophet. He will know who he is before anyone else does. There will undoubtedly be Satanists and cultists involved with everything from heavy metal and mind-altering drugs to criminally insane psychopaths who will believe themselves to be this person. This will include practitioners of a wide range of activities from lycanthropy to black magic, and the stream of figures exhibiting traces of this character have become more frequent in the last century not only in their deranged madness, but their capacity to mesmerize others. Hitler, Stalin, and Charles Manson are hardly miniatures of the "*man of lawlessness*" although they do highlight certain things about him and what he will do. These wicked figures, however evil, reach their goals by means of ordinary demonic power, howbeit accentuated to a high degree. The person of Antichrist, however, will go well beyond this and do it with a power that is not only demonic but satanic.

In the incarnation of Jesus, a body was prepared for an eternally existing Christ. Satan, however, is a created being and can create nothing. But he will go further in the deification of self than anyone else ever has when he counterfeits the resurrection of Jesus. At that point when he comes back to life he will not simply be the same person he was, nor will he be simply satanically possessed to the uttermost, but he will be in effect Satan incarnate or something very closely approximating it. Again, the Antichrist, the False Prophet, and Satan are the satanic trinity. Jesus was fully human and fully divine. The Antichrist upon resurrection will be fully the man he had been and fully Satan.

To understand the resurrected Antichrist we must again understand the resurrected Christ. Jesus was the same person in the same body after His resurrection, yet He appeared and behaved differently than He had appeared and behaved prior to His crucifixion. This includes becoming invisible, the transportation of Himself to another location automatically, and the capacity to dematerialize and walk through walls. It is not unlikely that after his resurrection the Antichrist may attempt to copy the nature of the resurrected Christ. At that point he will become totally invincible to all except Christ Himself. This is a direct parody of Jesus who as a vulnerable man was killed but rose invulnerable, glorious and immortal. This will again be achieved through the agency of the False Prophet.

After the Removal

As we have discussed, there will be a gap in time between the removal of the Holy Spirit and the removal of the Church that corresponds to Jesus giving the Holy Spirit indwelling His apostles and the day of Pentecost when the Holy Spirit is outpoured. We understand that this period when the Holy Spirit is removed will be what Daniel called "*shattering the power of the holy people*" (Dan. 12:7). We also understand that the removal of the Holy Spirit will replay Genesis 6:3 when God's Spirit ceases to strive with rebellious man.

We note additionally that as Jesus had 3-1/2 years of public ministry the Antichrist will demand and receive equal time. The "*mystery of lawlessness*" functioning through the spirit of antichrist is already operational. The removal of the Holy Spirit (not to be confused with the removal of the faithful Church) is what is restraining Antichrist from assuming full power (2 Th. 2:6-7).

We again reiterate in regard to these things that apart from their wrong eschatology the Pre-Wrath people are closest to the correct position which although is indeed pre-wrath in that the faithful Church will not experience the wrath of God, it is better termed "Intra-Tribulational." There is indeed a distinction between the meaning of the Greek words "*philipsis*" ("tribulation") and "*paresmos*" ("wrath") which the pre-Tribulation advocates tend to confuse. In not understanding the removal of the Holy Spirit, however, Pre-Wrath Christians who are otherwise correct falter just as pre-Tribulation people correctly understanding the Restrainer to be the Holy Spirit likewise falter in equating His removal to the Rapture. While we would not divide with either our Pre-Wrath or pre-Tribulational brethren over these issues, in order for the Antichrist to be identified both errors must be corrected.

As we have already addressed, once the faithful Church is removed, most of the focus of God is re-concentrated on His dealing with Israel and the Jews and not the Church. The doctrine of "Tribulation saints" is amplified out of all reasonable proportion to anything Scripture says on the subject. Many of the erroneous beliefs associated with the Tribulation saints are not derived by exegesis but in the faulty hermeneutic of eisegesis; not by inductive conclusion but deductive opinion.

Once the faithful Church is removed, the "Day of the Lord" will be inaugurated and God will pour out His judgment on the kingdom of the Antichrist. Grace will come to an end and God goes back to dealing with Israel under the Law that Israel has broken. There will be a replay of the judgments and plagues on biblical Egypt being poured out on the planet. And the events of the fall of Jerusalem in both 585 B.C. and A.D. 70 happen again to the Jews on a much worse scale. Their existence will be preserved only by the victorious return of a triumphant Christ, His feet standing on the Mt. of Olives in Jerusalem.

In a final act of desperation the Antichrist will assemble his forces in the plain of Megiddo in northern Israel for the final assault on Jerusalem. Speculations that the Antichrist will have a direct major role in either the first battle of Gog and Magog in Ezekiel 38-39 or in the conflict with Iran in Daniel 10 are just that—speculations. Again, these events, or a Psalm 83 scenario, may indeed create strategic opportunities for his ascent through a situation so desperate that Jews and Gentiles alike will be consumed by a terrified obsession for peace, fearing what will become of the human race.

The Solomon Syndrome

It is not our purpose to engage in speculation that would take us beyond what Scripture states, although we do maintain an awareness that some Satanists claim backslidden Solomon as the author of *The Satanic Bible*, some Masonic literature claims Solomon in his Jerusalem quarries as the real founder of Freemasonry, and some ascribe him as the source of archaic Illuminism thousands of years before Felix Weisshaupt, etc.

It is also not without significance that the true understanding of what became of Solomon was known by the revelations given to Iddo (2 Chr. 9:29), the same figure the Book of Chronicles twice sets forward as the introducer of Midrash (2 Chr. 13:22; 24:27). When Solomon falls in 1 Kings 11, we see him turning to demonic idols in order to placate the women he wanted to seduce. Some of these, such as Chemosh and Amon, were worshiped opposite the Temple Mount in images set up by Solomon on the Mt. of Olives. As well, Ashtoreth, the female cult deity was worshiped (1 Ki. 11:5). The Antichrist, like Solomon, will be closely associated with the construction of the Temple. We must understand that to gather women to himself, Solomon absorbed their religions by placing a Pantheon on the Mt. of Olives (1 Ki. 11:7). The Antichrist will behave likewise.

Reverting to the typology of women both good and bad as figures of either the Bride of Christ or pictures of the harlot church or false religious systems, the Antichrist will accumulate all religions to himself pantheistically. This includes the recapitulated Ashtoreth under the guise of Roman Catholic mariophonies and Hindu goddesses, to idols worshiped by human sacrifice. To this end we must understand that as Molech and other gods were worshiped by human sacrifice, so, too, the only assurance of salvation in Islam is to be "*shahadi*"—that is, to die in a jihad against the infidel. Thus we see Muslim mothers in Iran and Gaza raising their children to be suicide bombers.

These things are simply the ancient demon religions of the Near East once again in conflict with the worship of the one true God. To further extend the reign of his political and economic power, the Antichrist will incorporate the false religions of the world generally, and of the Middle East particularly, even if Ashtoreth worship is falsely assigned to Mary and Molech worship is falsely assigned to Allah, the Nabataean moon god now confused with the God of Abraham by Muslims. The propensity of Solomon to get women by religious means typologically foreshadows how the Antichrist will operate by bringing all false religious systems into his realm.

The complexity surrounding Solomon as a type of the Antichrist derives from the dilemma that in the Song of Solomon and in the Gospels he also foreshadows Christ. This phenomenon in one sense renders Solomon as a perfect type of the Antichrist because the Antichrist will attempt to look like Christ. And with Solomon we have a figure who is a shadow of both.

We can of course conclude from his favorable mention in the New Testament in the Gospels (Mt. 12:42; Lk. 11:31) that Solomon quite likely at some later point repented personally, although his sin persisted among both Jeroboam and Rehoboam and beyond. This, however, is unrelated to how Solomon in his backslidden state typifies the Antichrist. This element of wisdom, moreover, displays the full character of Satan as Ezekiel 28:31 tells us that Satan has greater wisdom than Daniel. Apart from Christ Himself, the only person recorded in Scripture with wisdom greater than Daniel's is of course Solomon whose domain and wealth are calibrated in direct connection with him by name with the figure "666."

The positive acclamation and affirmation that Solomon received, only to later plunge the nation into what was at that time an as yet unprecedented level of idolatrous debauchery presents to us an outline of what the Antichrist will do. Indeed, to a degree it suggests something of how he will achieve it. We again return to the fact that everything visible about Solomon mitigates against any remote suggestion he had secretly become a nefarious figure with an agenda that will be replayed by the Antichrist. This remains so until such time as it was impossible to do anything about it unless one is removed from his domain, like the queen of Sheba and her followers. The shock and surprise that of all people Solomon could have so quickly reached the apex of treachery and wickedness tells us what to expect with the Antichrist. His identity simply could not be known except by "666." Only when it was too late did the others who did not evacuate with the queen of Sheba realize what had happened, what he had gotten them into, and what they had gotten themselves into.

Despotic political leaders from Nero to Napoleon to Shaka Zulu to Hitler and Mussolini to Barack Obama all arise as shining stars, only to become shooting stars that fall very quickly. These historical-political foreshadowings of the Antichrist, however, although of the same spirit, only vaguely indicate the magnitude of what he will do. To understand this, we must again come to his counterfeiting of Christ where we have the bright and morning star (2 Pe. 1:19; Rev. 2:28, 22:16) and star of the morning (Is. 14:12) passages in Scripture applied to both Christ and to Satan. Although the Hebrew vocabulary is not identical, it is almost identical; one looks very much like the other. This has provided some involved in Masonic deception to confuse God and the devil and it constitutes the theosophy of Satanists who say God and Satan are the same. This paradox will come into full play with the Antichrist. The closest person or thing we have seen for this in Scripture or in history is backslidden Solomon who foreshadows ***both*** Christ and Antichrist.

In the description of Satan, sometimes accurately translated into "Lucifer" in certain renderings of Isaiah 14:12, the Hebrew term is "*ben saachar*," meaning "the son of the morning." In Job 38:7, however, the term is "*boqer*," which can be translated as "dawn stars" as in coming out of the darkness. They are two different terms. It has its New Testament equivalent applied to Christ where, in order to distinguish Him from the other angelic beings, the Greek definite article "*ton*" appears. Here Jesus is called "*the bright and morning star*" (Rev. 22:16), employing the Greek word "*basporos*" for "bright," meaning "light" (a feature not inherent in *saachar*), and using the Greek term "*astera*." Thus while the angelic beings are "stars," Jesus is **THE** star or "*bright and morning star*" as we see in 2 Peter 1:19 where it can also be accurately translated, "a day star that arises in our hearts." While there is a distinction in the vocabulary in the original languages, any distinction is nebulous in the translations.

The distinction between Solomon as a type of Christ and Solomon as a type of Antichrist is likewise blurred at the early stages. The sun is of course astronomically the star that outshines other stars in the early hours of the day. Satan and the Antichrist will simply be the brightest of the stars at the precipice of dawn. We must remember that no other figure in the Old Testament foreshadows Christ throughout an entire book of Scripture except for Solomon in the Song of Solomon where his romance with Shulamite has its parody in God's romance with Israel and Christ's romance with the Church. Once more, apart from "666," there is nothing that would open the lid on the negative typology of Solomon and how it relates to the final identification of Antichrist.

In the Character of the Historical Types

We can be sure, however, that the person of Antichrist will be like his historical types. The situation of Weimar Germany created the atmosphere and conditions conducive to the rise of Hitler. The situation in Russia after the death of Lenin likewise created circumstances that lent themselves to the ascension of Josef Stalin. The mayhem of post-revolutionary France likewise supplied the constellation of events for the rise of Napoleon. In most such historical circumstances hyperinflation and economic turbulence resulting in political and social upheaval were factors. The same was true in Mao's China after the Second World War with the deposing of Chiang Kai-shek. Huge pictures and statues of Communist leaders such as Mao or Korea's Kim Jong Il show the propensity of fallen man to deify false saviors. The continual re-embalming of the corpse of Lenin for public veneration was not merely a profession of faith in political and economic Bolshevism; it assumed a religious ethos. Rejecting the true God, fallen man will worship himself. And rejecting the true Savior, he will always find another god no matter what he claims philosophically, even if he professes atheism. The Antichrist will understand this as no one else ever has.

Even in the dogmatically atheistic Sovietism, icons in Red Square portrayed Marx and Engels as the prophets of the savior who is to come; the savior was Lenin. For all of its power and evil, including its ultimate anti-Semitism and persecution of Christians, Sovietism was dead in 75 years. The Antichrist will multiply that effect exponentially. The wickedness and hatred of the Church and of the Jews will exponentially eclipse that of

Sovietism. Like Sovietism that turned against the Jews despite Marx and Trotsky being Jewish, so, too, will the kingdom of Antichrist. The longevity of his reign, however, will not be 70 years, but only 7 at most. It will be as if something more than ten times as wicked as anti-Semitic and anti-Christian Sovietism will be terminated in one-tenth of the time the Soviet empire was. Again, this is a vague analogy, but the macrocosm can only be understood by examining a microcosm.

In reaching outer space and conquering much of the world so quickly, in part by broken treaties at Yalta and Potsdam, the patriarchs of Sovietism sought to immortalize themselves, actually thinking that the dark empire they created would prevail. In touching the apple of God's eye, however, through their persecution of the Church and the Jews, the superior power of God's judgment collapsed their hopes to nothing. Likewise, through breaking his treaty with Israel and showing signs in the heavens that go well beyond Sputnik, the Antichrist will think himself capable of being immortalized. Ultimately he will seek to achieve this by direct satanic means, but most probably also by means of a satanic misuse of science that we will see in the image of the Beast. We again make reference to the increasing alignment of molecular biology, computer science, holistic medicine, particle physics, and the occult, as we have already explored. Satan is putting all of the preparations in motion.

In order to understand how Satan is engineering historical events to implement the kingdom of Antichrist, we again return to his copying the actions of God and Christ. Before Jesus was born the world experienced a *Pax Romana*. The Romans established coastal trade routes borrowed from the ancient Phoenicians, allowing an increase in transportation that allowed missionaries with Paul and Barnabas as their prototype to travel internationally with the Gospel. Greek was the *lingua franca,* and the Hebrew Scriptures were translated into Greek with the Septuagint. Throughout the Roman Empire there was a large Jewish Diaspora awaiting the Messiah and an increasing number of Gentile God-fearers drawn to monotheism. The Romans implemented and organized a postal system that allowed the epistles to be sent church-to-church. They also constructed a network of well-made roads and bridges, some of which still exist today and a few of which remain operational. Everything was in place for both the coming of Christ and the rapid proliferation of the Gospel because God is the God of history.

The same will be true as Satan prepares the world for the coming of the Antichrist. Economic, political, social, cultural, and technological trends juxtapose themselves to greet the one who is to come and rapidly carry his false idea of salvation to the ends of the earth. More serious still, is that the Antichrist will seek to "change the times and the laws," and for two times, a time, and half time (3-1/2 lunar years) these will be given into his hand (Dan. 7:25). Within this fixed parameter God will temporarily forfeit His lordship of history to Satan. This again relates to the removal of the Holy Spirit.

The Difficulty of Understanding

It is impossible for a seasoned world traveler to explain the world and its nations to a small child who cannot even grasp concepts such as time zones and continents. The only way for the world traveler to teach the small child is to hand him a globe. The globe cannot teach the child all there is about distant lands, but it can teach the child enough to be able to recognize that if he travels in a certain direction at a certain longitude and latitude, he will arrive at a certain location. Just by knowing what is on the globe, if he flew directly west from California he would know that it was Japan he was flying over when he could at last see land at the end of a long flight.

We must think of end-times prophecy in such terms where the Word of God is our globe. As the world turns, times and seasons change and it is easy to become confused unless we understand what is happening by looking at the globe. So, too, it will be all but impossible for even spiritually mature and biblically knowledgeable Christians to wholly understand where we are going and the meaning of the changes we are seeing unless we understand them in light of the Word of God.

There is a big difference between boarding a 747 in Los Angeles and flying trans-Pacific toward Tokyo, and sitting in one's bedroom holding a globe and drawing an imaginary line with one's finger from Los Angeles to Tokyo. However, the latter teaches enough about the former for us to know what to expect. The analogy fails, however, in that we must not only know the directions in which the Church, the Jews, and the world are going, but we must know the identity of the terrorist who is planning to hijack the plane. This becomes particularly complicated when there are many terrorists; we must identify the final, ultimate, specific one.

The Last Supper Replayed

Let us consider again when Jesus divulged the identity of the "*son of perdition*" in the person of Judas, bearing in mind the "*son of perdition*" is also in the person of Antichrist. No one among the apostles had any idea who the betrayer was, and they were flabbergasted when Jesus revealed him. Jesus handed Judas the Paschal sop, giving him a last chance to repent before telling him to do quickly what he was planning to do (Jn. 13:2). There will indeed be a Last Supper just as when the first "*son of perdition*" was identified. It is more than curious that when Judas took his life, the Scriptures describe him as having gone "*to his own place*" as if he were to reappear again in some fashion (Ac. 1:25). This is not to imply a reincarnation as we see Elijah, Elisha, and John were the same one in spirit but different people.

Again, in speaking of Elijah, Jesus identifies John as having been Elijah, although not the same person but in the same spirit and character. Yet in the same breath Jesus acknowledged that Elijah is to come again (Mt. 17:10-13). So, too, it will be with the "*son of perdition*." The last supper will not be a Lord's Supper, but a feeding of the faithful believers enabling them to know who the "*son of perdition*" is. Again, the good and faithful servant will give the proper food at the proper time (Lk. 12:42).

This, too, is disconcerting because there will be some who will be party to this knowledge and will misuse it as a means to acquire an ungodly exercising of power. They will begin to beat their fellow servants and eat and drink with the drunken—the drunken being those who are unprepared for the return of Christ. He is coming like a thief in the night (1 Th. 5:2), and as the New Testament tells us, a drunkard gets drunk at night and associates with those who are unprepared and unfaithful. We have seen a prelude to this already in such deceptions as the Toronto Blessing and a counterfeit false revival in Pensacola where so many pastors and leaders who at one time had been solid Bible expositors, turned to beating their fellow servants by venturing into heavy shepherding and jumping on board with the spiritually drunken.

Another aspect of this is, again, with the Maccabees who understood the nature of the deception. The experienced within their own ranks the betrayal and the sin of the Hebrew collaborators with Antiochus Epiphanes. Yet as Daniel 11 tells us, those in the character of the Maccabees having the insight will be targets of betrayal.

We see another picture of the Last Supper in Acts 20 when the young man, unable to stay awake, falls out the window in his sleep. It was Paul's final meal with the leaders of the church at Ephesus, a city with an unbelievable degree of demonic power due to the worship of Diana of Ephesus. We are told in Acts 20 that during this meal there were many lamps in the place. As Jesus said, the eye is the lamp of the body (Mt. 6:22), the Word of God of course being the lamp, and the teachers of His Word being the eyes. While we cannot base doctrine on type, the implication appears to be that one or more teachers will teach the others in much the same way Elijah fed the sons of the prophets during the siege of Jezebel and Ahab who likewise typify the reign of Antichrist (2 Ki. 4:38-41).

It will take place at a time when the Church will be tired and will drift into sleep at the hour it should be most crucially prepared. What happened to Christ at His arrest foreshadows what will happen to the Church. Just before Caïaphas sent his cohorts to arrest Jesus, the apostles slept. They had already been fed and knew who the "*son of perdition*" was. This will happen again.

Every detail surrounding the way the "*son of perdition*" was identified by Jesus and what both Judas and Caiaphas did are guides to show us what the Antichrist will do. As always, we can only understand the future by first understanding the past, and only understand the macrocosm by understanding the microcosm. Judas was good at hiding his agenda. Antiochus was good at hiding his agenda. Herod was good at hiding his agenda. Pompeii was good at hiding his agenda. But the Antichrist will be much better.

When Benito Mussolini made the Lateran Treaty with the pope, the alliance of Italian Fascism and Roman Catholicism was cemented. In a future reflection of the relationship between the Antichrist and False Prophet, Mussolini in concert with the pope built a church on the Mt. of Beatitudes in Galilee. Again, such a union in Europe between a false Christianity and a dictator who begins as a seemingly benevolent populist who wants a foot in the Holy Land is but a slight indication of what is to come. But it is again necessary for us to understand Italian Fascism and Sovietism in order to understand the coming history already taking shape on the horizon. The basis, however, must be the Word of God itself.

In the Character of Jezebel

Without doubt a future factor in the workings of the Antichrist to come will be a religious environment falsely uniting Scripture with paganism in the way Jezebel seduced Israel. In the Book of Revelation Jesus speaks of Jezebel seducing God's servants to eat food sacrificed to idols. The transubstantiated Eucharist is another Christ in place of the true one, and hence is utterly antichrist. As we have maintained already, corrupted Christendom will be the means of ascent to the Antichrist deception.

In 5th-century Ephesus the attributes of Diana were assigned to Mary at a church council where she was proclaimed to be "Mother of God" in a religious fanfare copied from the Babylonian Tammuz worship against which the Hebrew prophets contended. Today the Vatican proposes Mary as the unifying force between Christendom and Islam, while such false teachers as Tony Campolo teach Evangelicals that mysticism is the common ground between Christianity and Islam. It is obvious that Jeremiah's lamenting of the Jews sacrificing cakes to the queen of heaven will have an eschatological replay in the veneration of Mary (Jer. 7:18). But this again points to the unfaithful woman using her husband for her own glory. Of course we realize that the mischaracterization of Mary by both Roman Catholicism and Islam has nothing whatsoever to do with the actual Mary of Scripture who is blessed among women (Lk. 1:42) any more than the Eucharistic Christ of Roman Catholicism has anything to do with the real Jesus.

Jezebel died before Ahab, with dogs lapping up her blood from a puddle (2 Ki. 9:36). This death of Jezebel is a picture of the judgment of false religion described in the Book of Revelation. When Jezebel was dead Ahab continued the relentless pursuit of his own agenda without her. He had outlived his usefulness to her, and she had outlived her usefulness to him. So, too, we read in the Book of Revelation that once the Antichrist uses the false religious confederation represented by the great whore for his own purposes (Rev. 18), he will simply get rid of her and she will come into the judgment that Christ promised her in His message to the church of Thyatira (Rev. 2:2). For the Antichrist, false religion and corrupt politics alone are simply a means to an end. His highest ambition is to magnify himself above the Most High. All who he deceives, including his agents, will simply be his expendable stooges. He is not like Christ, but up to a convincing point he certainly will know how to look like Him.

Hints from Judas' Personality

The human personality of the Antichrist is revealed to us through the human personality of Judas Iscariot. His spiritual character is revealed to us through the character of the kings of Babylon and Tyre in Isaiah 14 and Ezekiel 26. Thus we have an understanding of his soul and his spirit. His physical appearance, however, is a more difficult matter. We should take into account that as Isaiah prophesied, Jesus had no form or comeliness that we should look upon Him (Is. 53:2). And in imitation of Christ, the Antichrist may follow suit. It will be more what he does and says that impresses and captivates people in an attempt to mimic Christ.

Like Judas, the Antichrist must initially surface inconspicuously as a figure unlikely to achieve so much power so quickly. This will be akin to yet transend far beyond obscure figures in the political or religious realms who "come out of no place" and seize power in an attempt to change everything. There is a reason we have already seen this happen with politicians promising change yet only delivering change for the worse and turning against Israel. Barack Obama is a case in point with black Islamic figures such as Louis Farrakhan calling Obama "Messiah." We have also witnessed the parallel phenomena of rising stars within the Church such as Rodney Howard-Browne or John Arnott driving Evangelicalism further into apostasy. They come from nowhere and seek not only to change the nature of the status quo, but to replace scriptural orthodoxy with doctrinal heterodoxy. Again, this is the spirit of antichrist already at work both in secular politics and Church politics.

It is probable that the Antichrist will first appear as an unlikely figure again, trying to copy Jesus who had no form or comeliness that people should look upon Him (Is. 53:2). We see this in Daniel 7:8 where the Antichrist first appears as a little horn, not a big one, yet upon ascending to power voiced great boasts. This is repeated in verse 20. Although beginning as a little horn, he is almost instantly in appearance greater than its associates. He instantly turns against the saints and overcomes them until Christ lays him low and (in verse 22) gives the kingdom to the saints. The Antichrist will first, however, seek to speak out against God and the true believers, once more with an aggressive agenda to make alterations in the times and the law. (verse 25). The possible connotation here is that he will seek to amend legal principles deriving from God's Law. Moreover, the spirit of antichrist continues working through the spirit of the age; we already see this happening where corrupt courts with evil judges deviate from the principles they were sworn to uphold. They do not interpret and apply the laws, but redefine and rewrite them. The theological counterpart to this, as we have already established, is the *pseudologon* evidenced in corrupting biblical translations.

The same effect is reiterated in Daniel 9 which paints Antichrist in the character of Antiochus Epiphanes. He emerges as a small horn in verse 9, but quickly grows up to challenge the Host of Heaven. He, causes the stars to fall to earth in a replay of the fallen angelic rebellion and in direct reference to what will happen just prior to the Rapture when the stars in the sky again fall to earth (Revelation 6:13). The Antichrist in his early stages will not be someone who will gain much attention or be perceived as having either the wicked agenda he is committed to, or the power base to achieve it.

Popular lithographs, Hollywood film actors, and cover designs of books generally portray the Antichrist as a tall, attractive male. We need to be aware of the fact that this may be a misconception that Satan will use to further impede the recognition of the Antichrist. We once more come back to the fact that the apostles had no idea who the "*son of perdition*" was from anything he looked like or visibly did. There is, however, one important clue: Judas managed the finances of Jesus and His apostles. The Antichrist will seek influence in the Church he intends to seduce and betray through the use of financial means, although in going out from among us, he was not really of us (1 Jn. 2:19). It is for certain that the Antichrist will be some kind of false brother in the faith.

The human personality of Judas again seemed to make him appear a charitable individual concerned with the poor, although he actually was not. In this he will be the ecclesiological equivalent of what in nomenclature we call "a limousine liberal," able to command more adulation from the naïve he manipulates and cons to advance his own interests with more skill than any Evita Peron or Barack Obama. Like a pope who blesses children while protecting the pedophiles who exploit and violate them, he will be able to completely misrepresent himself as the opposite of what he actually is. Like televangelists who outwardly profess Christ but preach and worship mammon, he, too, will have the power to seduce. Again, politicians, popes, and TV money preachers are the mere microcosms. Unless we can see through these there is not a chance to see through the macrocosmic deceiver of all time who may or may not already be alive.

It is important that we avoid obtaining our theology from novels which fictionalize eschatology. I do not wish to be critical of the authors of such books or their motives, particularly of Tim LaHaye at a time when interest in the Rapture and the return of Christ and the approach of the Antichrist are declining so rapidly. Such well-selling books as the *Left Behind* series if nothing else revitalize interest in eschatology and provide something of a counterbalance to such literary deceptions as *The Purpose Driven Life*, *The Shack*, *The Prayer of Jabez*, and *The God Chasers*. However, it is a globe that indicates the direction, not a soccer ball, even though both are round.

My fear is that too many sincere Christians are having their eschatology and understanding of the Antichrist framed and defined by fictitious works instead of by Scripture. Even though I acknowledge that parts of the plots in such books are in accordance with Scripture, and that some unsaved people may come to a saving faith in Jesus through them. What we can know about Antichrist as a person can only come through Scripture.

To summarize the person of Antichrist, however, we would again say that if one wants to know what kind of person God is as an individual, look at Jesus. So, too, if we want to know what kind of person the Antichrist will be, look at Judas. Judas is the human mirror reflecting the character of the Antichrist in much the same way Jesus reflects the character of God.

Satan's Angelic Powers

On a final note, however, we cannot proceed without taking one last factor into account. Satan not only has angelic power, but his angelic power is superior to that of other angels—possibly rivaled only by Michael and, speculatively, in the estimation of some, possibly Gabriel.

We know that before the fall Satan was the angel in Heaven overlooking the place of God of which the Ark of the Covenant according to the epistle of Hebrews is an earthly copy. There were two angels overlooking the Ark (for our purposes here we use the terms "angel" inclusively for "*cherubim*," "*seraphim*," etc.). Satan was as powerful a being God created without replicating Himself. He vainly imagines himself capable of usurping the rightful place of God. Jesus spoke of different fallen angels (demons) as varying in power. Some for instance could only be cast out by prayer and fasting (Mt. 17:21). Above all, there is Satan whose angelic powers exceed those of other angelic beings—at least those that have fallen.

"Michael," however, has the Hebrew meaning of "like unto God," and he may have been the second angel overlooking God's dwelling represented by the statue on the Ark and therefore of equal power with Satan. Thus we see his intervention in the warfare in Daniel 10 which was able to turn the tide. When Satan was displaced due to his sin he was obviously replaced. Thus, deductively, Gabriel (whose name means "the mighty one of God") may be the other angel. Both Michael and Gabriel are associated in both Testaments with God's salvific purposes for Israel and the Jews.

Holding to such angelic powers we again return to the question of incarnational theology. We have noted that the Scriptures show resurrection and incarnation, but not reincarnation. Once more, we define as "mysterious" but not necessarily scripturally inexplicable how Judas as the "*son of perdition*" can return, much the same as we can ask how the Two Olive Trees already active in Heaven in eternity can re-enter time and space in Revelation (Zech. 4:3, 11; Rev. 11:4). Here we again must take careful note of angelic powers and the capacity of Satan which exceeds conventional angelic power.

The Scriptures, particularly the New Testament, make clear that angels can come in human form in some manner of enfleshment. The author of Hebrews writes we can actually "entertain angels unaware" (Heb. 13:2). And in the resurrection narrative we see the angels announcing the resurrection of Christ manifested in human form (Lk. 24:4-5). The same, however, is true of the fallen angels we call demons. We have references in the New Testament (the Epistle of Jude), and in the Old Testament (the Book of Genesis), where we read of angelic beings who left their rightful abode even though by creation they were the sons of God. Their deeds were wicked and they are obviously fallen. We reject later notions that these were simply descendants of a purely human source based on a misunderstanding of the Hebrew term "*geborim*"—meaning "mighty ones," having the same Hebrew root as the name "Gabriel." These were in fact "*Nephilim*"—that is, "fallen ones."

Although not as a manner of doctrine or canon, we do accept the historical record from the book, *Jasher*, that these events transpired on Mt. Hermon in the days of Jerrod, and resulted in the procreation of demonoids. Thus it is entirely possible for Satan to appear as a human, inhabiting human-like flesh, since even his inferiors have that ability. There were later traditions proposing that these were rather descendants of the sons of Noah, but when we see the use of the term "*sons of God*" in Job 1:6 it is clear that these were angelic beings, which also dovetails with Jude 6. We cannot derive doctrine from so-called Deutro-canonical or Apocryphal sources, yet the historical and literary importance of such is undeniable. It is therefore curious that Jubilees 10:5 reports that Satan demanded a tenth part of the fallen angels to pursue his designs on mankind (while the others were confined and imprisoned) until the end of the age.

We also note that Scripture teaches a hybrid of demon and human. When we take these matters into consideration we have an easier avenue of explanation for satanic incarnation, although as we shall additionally consider, a kind of zombification that goes beyond the superstitions of voodoo can also come into play when Satan counterfeits the resurrection of Christ with the resurrection of Antichrist. The role of biogenetic engineering and bio-interactive digital technology, when considered in light of the reconvergence of science and the occult increasingly in vogue, provide a final dimension in our ability to resolve and understand how Satan will incarnate himself in the Antichrist.

Lastly, the Antichrist and False Prophet will show signs in the heavens. As Jesus is to return from the sky, we must leave the door open to the theoretical possibility that Antichrist will mimic this. Without doubt, fascinations with the extraterrestrial are largely occult and parapsychic in nature. The expanding interest in such activity is, without doubt, of prophetic significance eschatologically and will in some way relate to the Antichrist.

The types and shadows we have considered thus far may be compared to a stale cake. The supernatural phenomena facilitated by fallen angelic power and possibly augmented by demonic corruption of science and technology may be compared to the poison icing. Just as the world has never seen a person like Christ, neither will human history have witnessed a person like the Antichrist.

The Engines of Deception

This Antichrist will deceive Israel and the Jews by fulfilling the rabbinic expectations outlined by Rabbi Moses Maimonides concerning a great scholar and sage ushering in a promised period of tranquility and prosperity for the Jews, and by performing not only counterfeit signs and wonders (*"nissim v'niflaot"*) through the False Prophet, but in essence doing what they wanted Jesus/Yeshua to do at His First Coming.

Antichrist will deceive the nations not only by the counterfeit signs and wonders (which will include astral phenomena) but by bringing a false peace and harmony akin to what took place just prior to the advent of the

Babylonian Captivity (Jer. 6:14). The Antichrist will do this in a climate where people are terrified by the nuclear threat (with a willingness to forfeit personal freedom in exchange), by restoring to some degree a previously known prosperity, and a healing to the environment.

In essence, he will initially counterfeit the millennial reign of Jesus.

He will deceive the apostate church, however, by an intense spiritual seduction that will likewise include the counterfeit signs and wonders. (They are counterfeit because the powers behind them will be misrepresented as being from God, but in actuality will be demonic even though they will be a convincing counterfeit of the miracles of Christ.) The con-artist, money-preaching televangelists have already paved Satan's way for this. It will include a false peace based on the ecumenical/interfaith unity we are warned against—the very Christless kind currently promoted as a social gospel by Rick Warren uniting with other faiths and other gods (2 Th. 5:3). He will deceive the apostate church with an unprecedented false concern for the poor and disenfranchised, acting in the character of Judas with the costly vile of perfume. He will further deceive it, however, with a misguided insight into the Scriptures as Solomon displayed at the very precipice of his backsliding.

Finally, he will manage to delude and seduce the apostate church with his introduction of a counterfeit Millennium that will last no longer than 3-1/2 lunar years (if that) before it is exposed as a lie and a con. The way for this has already been prepared by the Dominion Theology of Reconstructionist and Deuteronomist Calvinists, "Kingdom Now" hyper-charismatics, and Latter Rain Pentecostal extremists. (These are not to be confused with Calvinist and charismatic moderates or scriptural Pentecostals.)

What is important to remember at the present time, however, is that the nations, unbelieving Israel, and the apostate church are already deceived. The further and greater deception by the Antichrist and False Prophet will therefore not be difficult.

What is also important to remember is that the apostate church is no longer simply Roman Catholicism, Eastern Orthodoxy, Liberal Protestantism and pseudo-Christian cults (the ecumenical deception of Chuck Colson; the Word-Faith money preachers such as Kenneth Copeland and Benny Hinn; the false revivals spanning from Kansas City and Toronto to Pensacola and Lakeland; the proven false prophecies of Mike Bickel, Pat Robertson, Cindy Jacobs, Paul Cain, Gerald Coates and Rick Joyner; the

Purpose Driven (Lie) of Rick Warren; the hyper-Preterism of Reconstructionists; the Emergent Church of Brian McLaren; the so-called New Apostolic Reformation of C. Peter Wagner; to the annihilationism and anti-Zionism of John Stott; the union of Christianity and Islam on the basis of mysticism taught by Tony Campolo; the pseudo-Christian Shamanism of Yongee Cho; the rank rejection of the substitutionary atonement of Jesus Christ for sin by Steve Chalke and author of *The Shack* William B. Young). The apostate church awaiting the Antichrist is much of what is today popularly regarded as Evangelicalism.

As with Mordecai and Esther with the advent of Haman (Est. 1:13), as with the Maccabees with the advent of Antiochus IV (Dan. 11:33-35), and as with the Sons of Issachar (1 Chr. 12:32), by the grace and wisdom of God there will once again be those who understand and take action.

Chapter 19: In Conclusion

The subject of the Antichrist is a very deep one, as the subject of how he will be identified is the most challenging aspect of eschatology. The repeated warning of Scripture and of this book is that only those truly desiring the return of Jesus, as new creations and holding fast to Him on the basis of His Word, will be able to understand when the time arrives. Those who will understand will have been groomed by the Holy Spirit already so that when the last pieces of the puzzle fit in, something which has been complicated and uncertain will be clear and settled. Among the faithful there will be no question as to the identity of the Antichrist, and the imminent return of Jesus once the Antichrist is identified.

As much as I respect and agree with the motives of the authors of such books, and while I do rejoice in the fact that people have been saved through such books, there is a need for caution in addressing the subject of Christian novels about the return of Jesus. Eschatology is real and should not be fictionalized for any doctrinal purpose. This book is not a fictionalized treatment (although some pre-Tribulationists as well as most radical Preterists will treat it that way).

To understand these things takes wisdom, a wisdom that God gave to the early Church—to a Jewish Church. And in the Last Days believers need that same kind of wisdom. But to get that wisdom they need that same kind of holiness, dedication and radicalism. Those who have wisdom will know what to do, it says in Daniel. Those who have wisdom will turn many to righteousness (Dan. 12:3).

If these things are going only into one's head, it is rather useless. In fact it is something worse than useless because believers are responsible for it. "The scroll is sweet in the mouth and bitter in the stomach" (Rev. 10:9).

Once someone attains knowledge they are responsible for it; it must go into the heart. If the Holy Spirit is speaking, it is going to have an impact on their life. It is going to cause people to stand up and want to be Christians. And more than that, the wise men—the same kind of wise men in Daniel—what did it make them do? Wise men deliver souls. It will result in a radical evangelism. Not something done in the flesh, but done in the Spirit—

something radical. "Let he who has wisdom"—this wisdom is not man's wisdom; it is God's wisdom. It is what the apostles had and it is what today's believers can have. There are two kinds of Christians: the ones who ***are*** deceived and the ones who are ***not***. And already we see how many Christians (born-again Christians) are being deceived. The serpent is already beguiling the woman. Other gods are being worshiped in so-called churches.

The Jews in the time of Jesus' incarnation did not recognize the obvious signs taking place before them. Many Christians do not recognize the obvious signs taking place today. The events in the Middle East are among those signs: the Jews returning to Israel, the Jews returning to Christ in numbers that have been unseen since the early Church. It is getting dark out, and it is going to get a lot darker yet, and even a lot darker after that. But the Light is going to get brighter and brighter and brighter for those who really love Jesus.

We are going to go one way or the other. The Temple is going to be destroyed again. Not one stone will be left standing upon another. The Holy Spirit restrains Satan. There are three things that restrain him: one is human government. But when the Antichrist comes, all political dominion is given into his hands. The second is the Gospel being preached. But a time will come when the Gospel as such will not be able to be preached. The Church will be persecuted. And the Holy Spirit is the third thing. He will not deal with the world any longer; He will only be for the hearts of God's people. The Church will not be held together as bricks; it will be thrown down. The Temple will be destroyed, but raised up again, just like Jesus' body.

That is what is going to happen. There is a time of darkness coming, but the time of darkness is already here. People do not want to know these things. They do not want to hear about it. And soon it will be too late. The wise virgins had oil in their lamps ahead of time. When the bridegroom was coming and it was so dark, the others came to the wise ones and said, "Give us some oil." They responded, "We do not have any time to give you the oil, you should have been getting that oil before now." Jesus wants believers to have the oil in their lamps, the illumination of the Holy Spirit, ahead of time (Mt. 25:1-13).

This is not to say that the ancient Jewish way of interpreting the Bible makes other people who do not follow it inferior. If the Jews were so smart, how come they did not recognize Jesus as their own Messiah when the

Gentiles did? God turned His grace from the Jews to the Gentiles back then, and in the Last Days He turns His grace back to the Jews. He begins by bringing them back into the Church, and with that comes the full Restoration. *"I will make a new covenant with the house of Israel and the house of Judah"* (Jer. 31:31; Hebrews 8:8).

With whom will the new covenant be made? With the Baptists? With the Pentecostals? With the Plymouth Brethren? With the Church of England? With the Restoration Movement? No, it is made with the house of Israel and the house of Judah.

Although still growing in certain quarters, and growing numerically in much of the Third World, Christianity is dying in the West. Moreover, it is dying a self-inflicted death, committing suicide morally and doctrinally, and, as a result, numerically. The instruments for taking its own life are Ecumenism, Emergence, Purpose Driven agendas, psychology, false doctrine, plus the love of money. And in the character of Laodicea, its lukewarmness keeps it blind to its true declining state. As always, Jesus wishes to restore it, even though at this period there is little to do except strengthen the things that remain (Rev. 3:2). However, despite the legalism, extremism, and doctrines of much if not most of the present Messianic Movement, He is restoring in a spiritual sense the Jewish character and root including the understanding of Scripture that was held by the 1st -century Church. Regarding the identity of the Antichrist and the process of his identification, it will be only those who have a heart for Jesus and a mind to understand what the Word of God is telling us that are going to be able to make that identification and not be deceived.

As with the secular world, the worldly churches, including those falsely called Evangelical, are deceived already, being seduced by the spirit of antichrist to succumb to the *"man of sin"* instead of being prepared by the Holy Spirit for the return of Christ. The wise virgins will see; the foolish will not (Mt. 13:1-25). The faithful will understand; the wicked cannot. At this very moment, every Christian who professes a personally saving knowledge of Jesus is being prepared by the Holy Spirit to either identify the Antichrist and prepare for the return of Christ, or be hoodwinked by the Antichrist into not being able to identify him until it is too late. As we read in Daniel, those who know their God will take action.

It is sad and unfortunate that often irrational and inconsistent argumentation is posed by so many well-intentioned believers who think that the identification of the Antichrist is only for the believers of the

Tribulation. Indeed, few doctrines are more overstated than the doctrine of "The Tribulation Saints." Most of what the Word of God tells us is that after the Rapture, during the "Day of the Lord," the purposes and intent of God will be concentrated on Israel and the Jews. As we have asserted, during this period the Church as we know it will no longer even exist on the planet. It is my certain expectation that the Holy Spirit will show more and more pre-Tribulational Christians the folly of their presuppositions and the deficiency of their hermeneutical arguments. Indeed no small number have already seen it, and are seeing it.

There is far less hope, however, for those who have gravitated into Rapture denial, extreme forms of Preterism, hyper-Calvinistic Reconstructionism, and its hyper-charismatic bedfellow Dominion/Kingdom Now Theology. There is far less hope still for those who have bought into the satanic lies of Ecumenism, Emergence, and the Word-Faith prosperity con game. It is not only the purely secular world that will not understand what is happening, but neither will much of the so-called Church.

As always, those who truly love the Lord and His Word, no matter how dark the horizon becomes, will not be left in the dark. They will identify the Antichrist before the coming of Christ. Others will sadly hold onto the bankrupt theology of cliché-based doctrine we hear in such hideous colloquialisms as "you are waiting for the Antichrist while we are waiting for Christ." This is akin to one expectant mother saying to another, "You are waiting for labor contractions; I am waiting for a baby." We all want the baby, but you cannot have one without the other. The contractions will, however, be cut short with the "*kolobo*"— the divine caesarean section known as the Rapture. But caesarean sections are performed to prevent labor pangs from being overly prolonged to the detriment of the mother. The Lord shall indeed intervene and cut short any suffering of the faithful Church which will escape the clutches of the Antichrist. In order to escape these clutches, however, it is imperative that the faithful Church knows who the Antichrist is before anyone else does.

The Parable of the Fig Tree & the Other Trees – The Epilogue

> *Then He told them a parable: "Behold the fig tree and all the trees; as soon as they put forth leaves, you see it and know for yourselves that summer is now near. So you also, when you see these things happening, recognize that the Kingdom of God is near. Truly I say to you, this generation will not pass away until all things take place. Heaven and earth will pass away, but My words will not pass away.* (Lk. 21:29-33)

Oversimplification is a dangerous thing. What makes it dangerous is that, although not being wrong in what it says, it nevertheless creates the delusion that a complex issue is fully comprehended and a complicated problem or puzzle solved. One may accurately identify and arrange the factors as the first step of an elongated polynomial or quadratic equation. What has been done as a first step may be entirely correct, but the equation is hardly solved. If one pretends that it is solved, even though there was no error in the first set, one is still left with what amounts to an error. It is moreover an error of the worst kind because one has no awareness of the fact that it could be wrong.

Those who have attempted to learn the Parable of the Fig Tree from the Olivet Discourse (Mt. 24:32-35; Mk. 13:28-32; Lk. 21:29-33) have rarely even identified the factors of the first step. Conventionally this has been interpreted as the national re-establishment of the state of Israel. Here lies the problem. While the state of Israel in its re-establishment is of certain prophetic significance eschatologically, it is not the ***only*** factor. Neither is it the full meaning of the fig tree. One would be hard pressed to inductively prove that the fig tree is a metaphor for national Israel on the basis of anything stated in Scripture. Although we would agree it relates ***to*** Israel, to find its meaning ***as*** Israel is a deductive opinion and not an inductive exegesis based on the internal evidence of Scripture itself. Moreover, in Judaism, both ancient and modern, the fig tree is more associated with the Tree of Life, while in the New Testament, the olive tree is more associated with Israel (Rom. 11). Thus the fig tree has not been properly identified in its meaning in any thorough sense.

Again, however, this is not to state that the fig tree does not symbolically relate to Israel, and it is certainly not to imply that the national restoration of the state of Israel is not of prophetic importance; it absolutely is. Thus even the first step of the equation is not correct if the first factor has not even been properly valued and identified.

Moreover, the conventional approach conspicuously fails to take into account other integers. If an equation calls for solving for "x" and "y" and "z," one cannot merely solve for "x" and pretend to have the solution, particularly if they have not properly understood the "x." The Parable of the Fig Tree that Jesus highlighted as so important for understanding the events heralding His return must be read synoptically. Jesus did not ***only*** say to learn the Parable of the Fig Tree. The Olivet Discourse must be studied and understood comprehensively and synoptically. When we examine Luke 21:29 Jesus instructed us to rather learn the Parable of the Fig Tree "***and all trees***." The full meaning of the fig tree lies beyond the scope of this book but demands an exhaustive examination of the term from the Old Testament all the way through Revelation 6:13.

There is only one other place in Scripture where we see the Parable of the Fig Tree and the other trees. This is in the Book of Judges 8-9, where the sons of Gideon or Jerubbaal are betrayed and murdered by a half-brother named Abimelech. The sole survivor of the plot was Jotham, who attempted to warn the others because he understood the nature of the betrayal which he related by a Parable of the Fig Tree and the other trees:

> *"Once the trees went forth to anoint a king over them, and they said to the olive tree, 'Reign over us!'*
>
> *"But the olive tree said to them, 'Shall I leave my fatness with which God and men are honored, and go to wave over the trees?'*
>
> *"Then the trees said to the fig tree, 'You come, reign over us!'*
>
> *"But the fig tree said to them, 'Shall I leave my sweetness and my good fruit, and go to wave over the trees?'*
>
> *"Then the trees said to the vine, 'You come, reign over us!'*

> *"But the vine said to them, 'Shall I leave my new wine, which cheers God and men, and go to wave over the trees?'*
>
> *"Finally all the trees said to the bramble, 'You come, reign over us!'*
>
> *"The bramble said to the trees, 'If in truth you are anointing me as king over you, come and take refuge in my shade; but if not, may fire come out from the bramble and consume the cedars of Lebanon.'*
>
> *"Now therefore, if you have dealt in truth and integrity in making Abimelech king, and if you have dealt well with Jerubbaal and his house, and have dealt with him as he deserved—* (Judg. 9:8-16)

The bramble, Abimelech (whose name means "my father the king"), reigned over the other trees. The ascension to power of the bramble was due to the self-serving reluctance of the olive tree, the fig tree, and the vine to assume responsibility. Thus by default the bramble was able to lure the others into accepting the bramble to reign over them (Judg. 9:1).

The refusal of the olive tree to compromise its own sleek plumpness, the fig tree to compromise its own sweetness, and the vine to compromise the cheer derived from its new wine opened the door for the bramble to position itself opportunistically and manipulate the others into its snare. It was Jotham who understood this parable, and, in the character of the good and faithful servant in the Olivet Discourse, attempted to warn others what was happening. This very much corresponds to the Maccabees and those who would in the Last Days come in the character of the Maccabees. Daniel 11:33-35 refers to the Maccabees who gave understanding to the many concerning Antiochus Epiphanes—that is, Antiochus IV, a quintessential type of the final Antichrist.

Israel was seduced by Antiochus. The sons of Gideon near Mt. Gerizim were seduced by Abimelech. Yehuda the Maccabee understood, and with his sons warned others. So did Jotham. The key to this parable is the unfaithfulness of God's people both in Israel and in the Church. We see the unripe figs not ready for Christ to come falling to the earth just before the Rapture between the 6th and 7th seals in Revelation 6:12-13. We must understand that as a representation of the Tree of Life not only looking back to the Garden, but looking forward to Revelation 22:2, "*the leaves of the tree were for the healing of the nations.*" The leaves are thus figures of good works. Jesus cursed the fig tree because it had leaves but no fruit. So Israel in His first coming had a work-based righteousness under the Law but not the fruit of the Spirit. Normally the leaves and fruit appear almost simultaneously, but not quite. When Jesus cursed the fig tree it was not yet the season for fruit *"for the Son of man is coming at an hour when you do not think He will"* (Mt. 24:44).

In the sunny climate of the Middle East the figs grow under the leaves which protect the fruit from solar scorching. Without the leaves the fruit is destroyed; as it says in the epistle of James, *"Faith, if it has no works, is dead"* (Ja. 2:17). The leaves are altogether necessary and important, but not edible. The leaves are not what Christ is looking for. For although one cannot have fruit without leaves, it is possible to have leaves without fruit; that is, the fruit of the Spirit, the divine nature of Christ manifested in and through us emanating from His eternal love. We do not therefore entirely reject the budding of the fig tree as the explanation of the parable being a picture of Israel again naturally blossoming, but there is plainly much more to it than this.

The *shemen zeit*—the "olive oil of anointing" and the new wine of the Holy Spirit manifested in worship—have become obsessions to the contemporary Evangelical church. Yet those in the modern Church who most speak of anointing and worship tend to understand it the least. Among Word-Faith deceivers material affluence has become the uniform of anointing. And the worship of "worship," reducing the worship of God to the level of entertainment, has been transformed into a Christian music industry that is not what the Word of God means by the word, "worship." As we read in Isaiah 24:7-8:

> *The new wine mourns,*
> *The vine decays, All the merry-hearted sigh.*
> *The gaiety of tambourines ceases,*
> *The noise of revelers stops,*
> *The gaiety of the harp ceases.*

The present party will be over like a drunk recovering from a hangover realizing he has wrecked his car, lost his wallet and credit cards, and run over his wife and children the night before while intoxicated. The carnal church will wake up too late and realize the party is over and what they thought was the "joy of the Lord" had been a drunken illusion. They will learn that the fund-raising television Praise-a-thon's and counterfeit revivals dating back to Toronto, Pensacola, Kansas City, Lakeland, Holy Trinity Brompton, Kensington Temple, and elsewhere were really no revivals at all. They were simply stupid, drunken fiascos with the spiritual equivalent of cheap booze served to the biblically ignorant and undiscerning by so-called "Holy Ghost bartenders" such as Rodney Howard-Browne and his ilk.

Carnality, false doctrine, psychological manipulation masquerading as the leading of the Holy Spirit, and New Age mysticism masquerading as New Testament spirituality will pave the way and set the stage for the colossal deception. More than this, however, the deception will not simply be the workings of Satan, but will be in the character of the false prophets of Ahab against whom Micaiah prophesied. The Lord will put lying spirits into the mouths of these deceivers, causing the heretical churches to believe them (2 Chr. 18:19-22). As we are again warned in 2 Thessalonians, the Lord will send a delusion upon them. (2 Th. 2:11-12) God will in fact give them over in judgment to a spirit of error.

The ecumenical movement of Chuck Colson, the false revivals of men like John Arnott, the money preaching of Kenneth Copeland, and the false prophecies of Rick Joyner, Mike Bickel, and the Kansas City (False) Prophets are not simply deceptions of Satan, but judgments from God. It was indeed Satan who inspired David to number the people in his effort to build the kingdom in his own strength and design, but the Lord ordered it in judgment (2 Sam. 24:1). Even the devil must ultimately do the will of God, although his works will be destroyed.

It was the unfaithfulness of God's own people that brought about the power of Antiochus IV and of the deified emperors in Israel. So, too, it will be the unfaithfulness of both Israel and the Church that will unlock the gate for the Antichrist to come in and take over. Yet the Lord will have His prophets like Micaiah who understand, His Maccabees who will give understanding to the many, His Jothams who will know the Parable of the Fig Tree and the other trees, and His good and faithful servant who will give the proper food at the proper time (Mt. 24:45).

Addendum

There are a number of other aspects and scriptural passages concerning the subject of the final Antichrist that this book has not explored. There are, for instance, dozens of many types of the Antichrist ranging from Absalom to Ziklag who typologically provide small pieces of the larger puzzle. As we get closer to the return of Jesus the Holy Spirit will reveal a progressively clearer understanding to faithful believers. However, what is more important than anything stated in this book about the Antichrist, is that even as we get closer to the Lord revealing him the focus of our hearts must remain fixed on our blessed hope, the return of Jesus, and not on His diabolical impersonator.

It is not my suggestion that I or anyone associated with our ministry are unique in understanding the things we have attempted to set forth in this book. More importantly, neither is it my assertion that there are not others who will also by the Spirit of God receive revelation into the Scriptures concerning these and related matters as we anticipate the *Parousia*. It is my prayer that the Lord will indeed so illuminate others. Jacob Prasch and Moriel Ministries do not claim any monopoly on the light of understanding. The name "*Moriel*" in Hebrew means "God is my Teacher." To you, the reader, remember God is your Teacher also. One is our Teacher who is in Heaven, and it is not Jacob Prasch or any other mortal man, even when by the unmerited grace and mercies of God the Lord in His sovereign wisdom would see fit to make use of such unworthy and undeserving vessels as I.

It is also my prayer that the unlearned or the egotistical would not attempt to base doctrine on type, allegory, or metaphor, which would not only be a fundamental misunderstanding and misuse of scriptural Midrash (2 Chr. 13:22) but a Gnostic counterfeit of it. My hope in authoring this book is that it helps lay to rest at least some of the fruitless speculations of the well-intentioned ignorant in regard to these matters, and not compound what is already a sizable and growing mess.

Finally, this book should not be viewed as a definitive guide on how to identify the Antichrist. With the help of the Lord and my friends at Moriel such as Danny Isom, David Lister and others I have tried to the best of my ability to direct the people of God, both Jew and Gentile in Christ, to the correct road of understanding on how to pursue this vital quest.

I can in no sense guarantee that those who have understood this book in its entirety will be able in the final analysis to identify the ultimate two Beasts of Revelation 13, assuming that they or we are still here when the time for them to be revealed has come upon us. What I ***can*** guarantee, however, is that those who have ***not*** understood it, or who flatly reject it, or even deny the need for it, such as those subscribing to the lies of Satan being propagated in the Church, will most certainly ***not*** be in a position to identify the Beast from the earth and the Beast from the sea.

I ***can also*** guarantee that those who love the Lord Jesus, who seek His kingdom and His righteousness, and are led by His Spirit on the basis of His Word, will certainly know what to do and how to do it. They will know everything they need to at that hour.

Come quickly, Lord Jesus! *Maranatha*!

James Jacob Prasch

Index